D0221260

SHELLEY'S PROCESS

*The front flyleaf of a notebook used by Shelley in 1819. P. *lr. (a) of manuscript 2177 at the Huntington Library in San Marino, California.*

SHELLEY'S PROCESS

Radical Transference and the
Development of His Major Works

JERROLD E. HOGLE

VILLA JULIE COLLEGE LIBRARY
STEVENSON, MD 21153

New York   Oxford
OXFORD UNIVERSITY PRESS
1988

PR
5438
H64
1988

Oxford University Press

Oxford New York Toronto
Delhi Bombay Calcutta Madras Karachi
Petaling Jaya Singapore Hong Kong Tokyo
Nairobi Dar es Salaam Cape Town
Melbourne Auckland

and associated companies in
Berlin Ibadan

Copyright © 1988 by Oxford University Press, Inc.

Published by Oxford University Press, Inc.
200 Madison Avenue, New York, New York 10016

Oxford is a registered trademark of Oxford University Press

All rights reserved. No part of this publication may be reproduced,
stored in a retrieval system, or transmitted, in any form or by any means,
electronic, mechanical, photocopying, recording, or otherwise,
without prior permission of Oxford University Press.

Library of Congress Cataloging-in-Publication Data
Hogle, Jerrold E.
Shelley's process.
Includes index.
1. Shelley, Percy Bysshe, 1792–1822—Criticism and
interpretation. I. Title.
PR5438.H64 1988   821′.7   88-5136
ISBN 0-19-505486-5

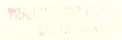

2 4 6 8 9 7 5 3 1

Printed in the United States of America
on acid-free paper

58344

FOR PAMELA

I have no life, Constantia, but in thee

Preface

My purpose here, however immodest, is a thoroughgoing, and, I hope, radical reassessment of Shelley's career and major writings, one that attempts to show that his best-known works mean something very different from what they have generally been taken to mean. I will offer a reading of his poetry and prose that reveals the fundamental logic of a mobile process—what I will call "transference," a ceaseless transition between elements of thought—which has been suppressed in the most accepted understandings of the Shelley canon. Percy Bysshe Shelley, after all, unabashedly strove to counter canonical thinking about the "proper" style and themes of poetry, the universals of earthly existence, the structures of human society, and the pursuit of individual identity. I want to suggest just how iconoclastic he was and remains, both in his critiques of established belief systems and in his revelations about subliminal transferential tendencies in thought that really underlie those systems and can yet free us from hegemonic limitations, if we pay more attention to the potentials for transference in human awareness and discourse.

All this is not say that there is no value in the many thorough and perceptive studies of Shelley already in existence. My exploration, as the reader will see, would never have been possible without the source research, the reediting of texts, the biographical details, the insights into many particular lines, the placement of Shelley in relation to various contemporary writers, the connections between his verse and his several philosophies, the visions of the class struggles during his era, and the analyses of his artful verse patterns that have been offered in helpful abundance by the many scholars of English Romanticism whom I will mention in my text and notes. Even so, I do maintain that the several traditions of Shelley interpretation up to now have looked at his writing with constraining, excessively "centered," or at least inadequate assumptions. To these frames of reference different and more *de*centering ones now need to be added, and when such frames are employed, I find that Shelley's writing fairly explodes with revolutionary movements and implications hitherto unrecognized.

Certainly I hope I put in question any notion of a strictly self-consistent "identity" in Shelley's thought. This poet's gradual awakening to an incessant quest for new thought-relations in the human psyche and in the language that brings thought into shape leads him to revise his understanding continually and often to refuse identity as a proper goal of human desire. "Shelley" as the name attached to a series of writings should be considered, I think, less a univocal "body of thought" and more an opening to an interplay of changing voices, a succession of externalized figures for the self spreading into further possible figurations and analogues. Thus, as a visual epitome of my study, I offer, on the dust jacket and in the frontispiece of this book, the poet's drawings of himself on the lining paper of one of his notebooks. It is not that I want to present my study as one about "process" in the sense of Shelley's movement through notebook-jottings to revised drafts. Others have been and are now doing this kind of work as well as or better than I can. Instead, I want to point my readers toward the Shelley who stares out, with a sense of being incomplete and unbounded, at the possibilities for extending himself in space, time, and writing and then starts redrawing his possible self-image again and again without finality and without the longing for an Absolute Center with which he has often been associated. This set of scrawlings, though it comes from one moment in Shelley's life, is for me the best available illustration of the drive behind his career and of his persistent sense that each person should seek his or her "selfhood" by shifting his or her tendencies away from the present self toward "another and many others."

Yet even as I write of epitomizing this book's general vision, I am aware that only some of its potential readers will want to "swallow it whole." In particular, I am mindful that some students of Shelley or Romantic poetry will come to this book for interpretive suggestions about some of his works and not others. Though I would naturally hope some readers would be interested in the entire work, I therefore feel I should add a few words about the organization of what I offer. I have designed the book both for those who seek a comprehensive and chronological sense of Shelley's writing viewed through a revisionary set of lenses and for those who want specific readings of specific works (hence the section titles within chapters and the attempted thoroughness of the readings). Consequently, I recommend that every reader, to see what my study assumes, peruse the introduction and the first chapter, where many of my theoretical orientations and my terms for Shelley's various inclinations are initially defined. After this beginning the selective reader may then want to proceed to sections on a particular work or set of works. I believe a reader can do so with some profit, provided that he or she reads the opening section (and in Chapters 3 and 6 the opening *two* sections) of the chapter involved. Such entries into this book will, I trust, prevent confusion and keep my argument from being interpreted as Shelley has too often been: as assuming or highly valuing notions that are neither completely accepted nor asserted in the work.

What I am mindful of above all, however, are the debts of gratitude I owe to the many people (relations, friends, colleagues, and students) who have helped and encouraged me at various stages of this project. I am grateful to Edgar Dryden and Gerald Monsman, the two heads of the English Department at the University of Arizona during the years this book was completed, for their kind advice and assistance to me on many occasions. I am equally thankful for the efforts of Paul Rosenblatt, former dean of the College of Liberal Arts at Arizona, when I think of his timely support at crucial junctures plus the summer research grant and the half-year sabbatical leave that his College Committee awarded me in 1980. I am glad to acknowledge the help I have received from the staffs of the general reference, special collections, and interlibrary loan divisions of Arizona's Main Library. I also appreciate and remember the discussion sessions out of which this study was in some ways born: the ones held over a number of years by the Arizona Faculty Study Group in Literary Theory. Several members of that group, moreover, have worked through portions of this volume with me—or even prompted lines of argument—in friendly and helpful ways, especially J. Douglas Canfield, Suresh Raval, Herbert Schneidau, and, most often, Patrick O'Donnell. At the same time, I am thankful that I have been so well and consistently supported by the senior Romanticists in my department: Carl Ketcham and Gerald McNiece, the latter of whom read the penultimate draft of my manuscript with care and a fine critical eye. Then, too, key sections in this book have been energized and informed by my participation in the Curriculum Integration Project sponsored by the National Endowment for the Humanities and run by the University of Arizona's excellent Committee on Women's Studies. In connection with this Project and the knowledge of feminist theory I hope I have gained, I am particularly beholden to the teachings and friendship of Ingeford Kohn and, especially, Susan Hardy Aiken.

Meanwhile, there have been several students in different classes of mine over the years who have contributed their eye-opening thoughts to this study in conversations or papers often having little to do with Shelley. My thanks, then, to Eduardo Cadava, Karen Brennan, Beth Alvarado, Michael Magoolaghan, Perrie Ridley, Andrew Morrill, John Haskell, Stephanie Dryden, and Elaine Pollack. And, of course, I am very grateful to Judy Johnson, the English Department secretary who typed much of my manuscript; to Lynn Fleischman, who worked out the index; and to John Fortier and Susan Scaff, my graduate research assistants, whose interest, warmth, and copy-editing skills have often kept me from the Slough of Despond.

The rest of my thanks must be extended to people outside my university. Along with a lifetime of sustenance and love, very practical summer and winter quarters and times for writing have been provided by my highly supportive parents, Jane and Howard Hogle, and much the same can be said for my parents-in-law, Jean and Hugo Wesp. Unparalleled resources for basic source study—and a summer research grant in 1984—have been proffered by the directors and wonderful support staff of the Huntington Library in San Marino, California. Several colleagues or friends I have come to know at or in connection with the Huntington have also provided encouragement and assistance with particular problems: Lewis John Carlino, Robert Essick, Jean Hall, Mary Quinn, Virginia Renner, Martin Ridge, Elsa Sink, Joseph Anthony Wittreich, and John and Victoria Villaiobos. Other West-Coast library assistance in time of need has been rendered by the kind staff of the main library at California State University, Northridge. Scholars and others from different areas of the country have also offered useful aid or suggestions, even when they have been beset with projects of their own. Kudos for various kindnesses must therefore go to Homer Obed Brown, Marshall Brown, the late Eugenio Donato, Jay Farness, Spencer Hall, Geoffrey Hartman, William Keach, J. Hillis Miller, Donald Marshall, E. B. Murray, Joseph Riddel, Stuart Sperry, Deborah Swedberg, and David Wagenknecht. I also must thank my teachers at the University of California, Irvine, in the late 1960s who did the most to introduce me to Romanticism and methods of interpretation: Albert O. Wlecke, Frank Lentricchia, Murray Krieger, and the late Howard S. Babb. Naturally I am much in the debt of Oxford University Press in New York, of its fine executive editor, William Sisler; of his able assistants, Linda Robbins, Andrea Ulberg, and Mimi Melek; of Ellen Fuchs, Joan Bossert, Martha Cooley; and of an unidentified outside reader for the Press, whose perceptive suggestions have led to some much-needed changes in this study's final draft. Both the Press and I, in addition, are grateful to the trustees of Boston University and to the Keats-Shelley Association of America, through their journal editors, for permitting us to reuse some material, now heavily revised, first published in *Studies in Romanticism* and the *Keats-Shelley Journal*. Moreover, throughout all this I hope I have not forgotten how much my daughters, Karen and Joanne, have sustained their father with their love, pride, faith, patience, and humor.

Two very special people, though, deserve the most particular gratitude and can never be fully repaid for what I owe them in connection with this book (and so much else). One of them is Stuart Curran, noted Romanticism scholar and current editor of the *Keats-Shelley Journal,* who has encouraged my work on Shelley from the time of my first tortured attempts at articles through the recent years in which he has provided many close readings of drafts and much good advice. If he is legendary in some circles for his assistance to many younger colleagues around the country, that is no more than just. Even in the face of some personal disagreement with portions of my argument, he has fervently supported this project with unswerving attentiveness and level-headed kindness. That sort of generosity is rare in any profession.

The other person is my wife, Pamela Wesp Hogle, who has endured the writing and rewriting of this work with admirable restraint and steady moral support. She has also contributed her typing of early drafts and her uncanny ability to resuscitate my determination and concentration, not to mention her willingness to listen to my speculations in times of mental crisis. Recalling that she has a master's degree in voice, I dedicate the book to her with a line from Shelley's "To Constantia, Singing." Constant she has been, and in my moments of genuine sanity I know that her continuing love is a far greater blessing than any I will ever receive from publishing a book.

Tucson, Arizona   J.E.H.
Labor Day, 1987

Contents

The Basic Texts

Unless I note otherwise, all my citations from the poems, plays, prefaces, and essays refer to *Shelley's Poetry and Prose: A Norton Critical Edition,* ed. Donald H. Reiman and Sharon B. Powers (New York: Norton, 1977), abbreviated on occasion as *"NCE"* and helpful to me at times in tracing the poet's allusions. The other basic references that I sometimes use when they offer the best available texts are abbreviated in my text and notes as follows:

CPW *The Complete Poetical Works of Percy Bysshe Shelley,* ed. Neville Rogers, 2 vols. (Oxford: Clarendon Press, 1973–1975).

CW *The Complete Works of Percy Bysshe Shelley,* ed. Roger Ingpen and Walter E. Peck, 10 vols. (New York: Scribner's, 1926–1932).

L *The Letters of Percy Bysshe Shelley,* ed. Frederick L. Jones, 2 vols. (Oxford: Clarendon Press, 1964).

PS James A. Notopoulos, *The Platonism of Shelley: A Study of Platonism and the Poetic Mind* (Durham, N.C.: Duke University Press, 1949). This book contains most of Shelley's extant translations of Plato.

PW *Shelley: Poetical Works,* ed. Thomas Hutchinson, rev. G. M. Matthews (London: Oxford University Press, 1970).

S&C The Carl H. Pforzheimer Library, *Shelley and His Circle, 1773–1822,* vols. I–IV ed. Kenneth Neill Cameron, vols. V–VIII ed. Donald H. Reiman (Cambridge, Mass.: Harvard University Press, 1961–1986). These contain transcribed manuscripts, and I usually cite those holographs as though they had been finalized, as though Shelley's latest corrections had been interpolated into the flow of his principal lines.

Biblical quotations are from the King James Version, the one best known to Shelley himself. The etymologies (or "literal" meanings of words) are drawn from *The Amer-*

ican Heritage Dictionary of the English Language. Aids to my recollection have been provided by F. S. Ellis, *A Lexical Concordance to the Poetical Works of Percy Bysshe Shelley* (London: Quaritch, 1892). References to Dante Alighieri are to *The Divine Comedy,* trans. Charles Singleton, Bollingen Series LXXX, 7 vols. (Princeton: Princeton University Press, 1970–1975), and to Dante's *Vita Nuova,* trans. Mark Musa (Bloomington: Indiana University Press, 1983). Milton is cited from the *Complete Poems and Major Prose,* ed. Merritt Y. Hughes (New York: Odyssey, 1957). The verses of other English Romantic poets are quoted from *Byron: Poetical Works,* ed. Frederick Page, rev. John D. Jump (London: Oxford University Press, 1970); *Coleridge: Poetical Works,* ed. E. H. Coleridge, 2 vols. (London: Oxford University Press, 1912); *Keats: The Complete Poems,* ed. Miriam Allott (London: Longman, 1970); or *Wordsworth: Poetical Works,* ed. Thomas Hutchinson, rev. Ernest de Selincourt (London: Oxford University Press, 1969). The citations of all ancient Greek and Roman authors (save Plato) refer, usually by the section or line numbers established for the original texts, to the editions and translations in the Loeb Classical Library (Cambridge, Mass.: Harvard University Press). The works of Plato not translated by Shelley, finally, are cited (with Estienne's standard section numbers) from the translations by various hands in *The Collected Dialogues of Plato,* ed. Edith Hamilton and Huntington Cairns (Princeton: Princeton University Press, 1961).

SHELLEY'S PROCESS

Introduction:
The Logic of Transposition

The Mysteries in Shelley

Among the many problems that Shelley has left his readers, two of them consistently overwhelm the others. One of them is his shifting, evanescent style, whether he is writing in verse or in prose. Nearly every Shelley line is replete with abrupt transitions, even headlong leaps, between often incongruous phrases.[1] His verbal figures are continually dissolving and thus questioning their structures before any one of them has a chance to seem complete. They are no sooner stated than they become inadequate and are quickly supplanted by very different figures. They give us less a sense of their foundations and more a portrait of incomplete thoughts being obscured and then replaced by thoughts that are equally fragmentary, equally in need of further thoughts to complete them. Witness Shelley's description of Dante in *A Defence of Poetry,* where that poet's writing is described in a series of quite different figures to the point where it seems both a palimpsest of several figural levels and a deferral of figures toward later transformations of them:

> His very words are instinct with spirit; each is as a spark, a burning atom of inextinguishable thought; and many yet lie covered in the ashes of their birth, and pregnant with a lightning which has yet found no conductor. All high poetry is infinite; it is as the first acorn, which contained all oaks potentially. Veil after veil may be undrawn, and the inmost naked beauty of the meaning never exposed. A great Poem is a fountain forever overflowing with the waters of wisdom and delight; and after one person and one age has exhausted all its divine effluence which their peculiar relations enable them to share, another and yet another succeeds, and new relations are ever developed, the source of an unforeseen and an unconceived delight. (*NCE,* p. 500)

Luminous words or poems here start out as potential flames ("sparks") that try to burn through yet are also concealed by the poet's fuel, the existing word-patterns that he has revised and partially burned up (thus leaving "ashes" that can still be read according to dying conventions). At the same time, such potentials are made analogous to the heated atoms gravitating toward one another within any spark, to the embryo that a womb may bring forth into a different world, and to electric charges that can surge out of hot atoms whenever a "conductor" is extended toward them by readers or other words. Then these particles, already being turned inorganically from one form into several others, are altered even further into organic acorns, generators of veils or veils themselves, fountainheads, and the fountain's waters, each of which comes in abruptly from the paragraph's future to pull the present metaphor away from itself and the one prior to it.

The sentence beginning "veil after veil" thus becomes an apt description of its paragraph's syntax as well as of Dante's figures composed of other figures. Each naming of the referent (apparently "spirited words") covers over and refracts the one before it, revealing gaps between each naming—indeed between each clause and each sentence. The result is a multiple concealment of what the referent seems to refer to, the "inmost naked beauty" implied by the veiling process but still held at a distance from it even when all the figures are removed layer by layer. The only manifestly constant principle, which turns out to be the main referent, in fact, is the vague potentiality that all words carry forward, their tendency to extend themselves beyond themselves to other locations. Though good poetry may arouse, for Shelley as for Horace, "wisdom and delight" in readers of every era, it does so only as its suggestions are furthered, altered, transfigured, and completed differently by different needs of interpretation at different points in time.[2] Words, especially in this passage, differ from previous uses of them chiefly by looking ahead to the "peculiar relations" of a later moment in the hope of finding their partial significance filled out by whatever future counterparts reach toward them. So many questions, then, cry out for answers. How can the reader penetrate to the "core" of such a verbal sequence if the sequence keeps displacing its figures outward into forms that do not share its world? Why does Shelley take the passage between differences inherent in any succession of words and exaggerate that movement by darting across unrelated contexts? What continuity can there be in a process referring to, revealing, producing, describing, and enacting radical discontinuity?

Meanwhile, there is the other problem that nearly always accompanies the problem of the style, one that is equally illustrated by this celebration of Dante. There is the assertion of a powerful "Spirit" relentlessly "instinct"within the outward movement of words. Unlike Dante's *primum mobile*,[3] this force for Shelley can never reveal its native essence, operating as it does only through figures that keep relocating and reshaping it. Still, it can draw the poet and his readers toward something "inmost," something that may be the self-concealing impetus driving the various forms that recall it. Such a "Spirit" is not just the workings of the poet's imagination, even though that faculty may work out of it, channel it, and try to configure it. As the "electric life which burns within [a poet's] words" and so the cause of the "lightning," it is the poetic impulse prior to any one person, an "unapprehended inspiration" from elsewhere, urging imagination and its words to "express what they understand not" (*Defence*, p. 508). Clearly it is "not subject to the controul of the active powers of the mind"; however much its "birth and recurrence" may be furthered or repressed by them, it "has no necessary connexion with consciousness or will" (*Defence*, p. 506). It is a preconscious process in which its first perceivable transfiguration is its entrance into the consciousness of a poet, yet because it operates in that fashion (though in different ways) in Dante's time and in Shelley's, it is even more external to individual awareness than most theories of a personal "unconscious" would allow. It is the "spirit" of change in a poet's historical "age" (*Defence,* p. 508), yet before it becomes that it is the force moving through all writings and readings, carrying figures from the "peculiar realtions" surrounding them at one time to the relations of another context at another moment. It operates both through the great verbal system interweaving interpreted nature and culture, "the cyclic poem written by Time upon the memories of men" (*Defence,* p. 494), and through the "eternal music" that seems to propel the existence we interpret, the "strain" in what assaults our senses that can produce "revolutions in opinion" if we let it (p. 485). Shelley cannot separate, from the "Spirit" or in it, the violent forces of perceptual, natural, social, historical, and linguistic transformation.

All these come together, we find, in the opening stanza of Shelley's most anthologized poem, the "Ode to the West Wind":

> O wild West Wind, thou breath of Autumn's being,
> Thou, from whose unseen presence the leaves dead
> Are driven, like ghosts from an enchanter fleeing,
>
> Yellow, and black, and pale, and hectic red,
> Pestilence-striken multitudes: O Thou,
> Who chariotest to their dark wintry bed
>
> The winged seeds, where they lie cold and low,
> Each like a corpse within its grave, until
> Thine azure sister of the Spring shall blow
>
> Her clarion o'er the dreaming earth, and fill
> (Driving sweet buds like flocks to feed in air)
> With living hues and odours plain and hill:
>
> Wild Spirit, who art moving everywhere;
> Destroyer and Preserver; hear, O hear. (ll. 1–14)

Shelley has scarcely allowed his speaker to address the invisible rush whose effects he saw near Florence in 1819 before the speaker's perception, prompted by a "memory" of ancient Greek and Vedic hymns from the "cyclic poem," recasts that movement as an anthropomorphic *psyche* or *Zephyr* inspiriting the destructions (the killings and burials) of autumn.[4] The destructions, in turn, become prefigurations of countering movements in seasons to come, and the seasons therefore seem to change three times while only one is being described, especially when the dying leaves are transported toward a "wintry bed" out of which buds already appear to be sprouting from seeds caressed by the "sister" wind of spring. This process is then seen quite differently and suddenly as the transformation of humankind from its past and present toward its future history. The leaves turn into the colors of the four known human races and so into the oppressed "multitudes" driven from a time of death toward one of possible rebirth. And all the while the stanza's verbal structure, bringing about yet also reflecting the rapid shifts among these faces of the "Wind's" activity, slides toward the demands of the sonnet form even as it experiments with the possibilities of Dante's *terza rima.*[5] The "Wild Spirit" of reformation is "moving everywhere" in each of these operations while never being entirely visible in any or all of them. Because it is turning into some different form even as it becomes the preceding one, it is a "presence" only as it makes itself "unseen" in the "veil after veil" through which it acts. The style, of course, both demands and obeys this windlike onslaught of synecdoches, even to the point of hurrying to a parenthetical extra image—"Driving sweet buds like flocks"—before the image enjambed in the previous line has been fully presented. How can we account for this correspondence between style and "Spirit"? What makes such a Spirit cross between so many different movements, thereby driving its linguistic announcement toward a similar speed and instability? What in the Spirit allows it to be so multiple yet so withdrawn, so "inside" the poet's thoughts and words and so "outside" them (indeed, outside each word and notion) at the same time? What, finally, is the nature and basis of a preconscious infusion that forces Shelley's awareness into transformations by transmuting itself through him and them?

Such questions are very pressing ones, it turns out, since they are asked about a poet who disavows God in most of His ancient and Christian forms. From his earliest writing days until his death, sometimes for personal and sometimes for philosophic reasons,[6] Shelley rails against the notion of a self-contained Immanence enthroned at the top of a cosmic hierarchy as the standard by which all things are made and judged. In his teen-age eyes already well versed in radical writings, orthodox Christianity offers a set of merely fabricated images crafted to enforce the existing structure of class supremacies and subordinations. As he puts it in the letters of his adolescence so often indebted to the Comte de Volney and Thomas Paine, the established church takes "Monarchy" as its "prototype" and so projects a "despotism of virtue" into Heaven, where an absolute ruler and a true morality are supposed to be one and the same (*L,* I, 216 and 71). The church thereby sets up a "God of pardons and revenge" who can threaten all the rebels against the reigning boundaries of order and can even dictate a young person's future by reappearing in the "Religion" of "Duty to [his or] her Father" (I, 215 and 70). The young Shelley is consequently eager, once he has read empirical philosophy, to join with T. J. Hogg in publishing *The Necessity of Atheism* (for which they were both expelled from Oxford early in 1811). There he helps to show that our interacting thoughts, "founded [only] upon our experience" as it puts together "perceptions," can never propose—unless so enjoined by external dictators—an "Almighty Being" who once "commanded that he should be believed" (*CW,* V, 207–9). Throughout this paraphrase of John Locke and especially David Hume, the mind may assume a vague "causality" when perceptions repeatedly succeed each other. But it never perceives any automatic "agreement" between this response to repetition and the "hypothesis" of an "omniscient" Deity creating what we see (V, 207–8). To move from a supposed cause to an "Almighty" Lord is to leap an unbridgable gap in the "train" of logic, to be forced into a shift "contrary to reason" that can never be a genuine proof of anything (V, 207–8). Much as he may work to rephrase this argument, Shelley never abandons it in the almost twelve years between *The Necessity* and his drowning off the Italian coast. Instead, his mature work tries to adopt locations, be they natural settings, epitomes of history, or "inner states" of mind, where conventional thinking finds the descent of God's Power and where he can replace that center with his own kind of casuality, his own "voice" seeking to "repeal" religious "codes of fraud and woe" ("Mont Blanc," ll. 80–81).

Why, then, are the figures in his substitutions "instinct with [or literally "urged on by"] spirit"? Why is Shelley's supposed causality, even in *The Necessity of Atheism,* a "generative power which is effected by its particular instruments" (*CW,* V, 208), a silent motion put into effect by what it creates to carry it through? Even more to the point, why is the Spirit usually so godlike, so persistently biblical? Why does the "Ode to the West Wind" so clearly allude to the Yahweh "who walketh upon the wings of the wind" in the Old Testament (Psalm 104:3)? Why, in the "Essay on Christianity," is this "interfusion" explicitly called "God" by Shelley, and why is that God "the collective energy of the moral and material world" turning on the "chords" of human perception into "benignant visitings" of "invisible energies" (*CW*, VI, 231)? How can Shelley write in the *Defence* that poetic inspiration is "as it were the interpenetration of a diviner nature through our own" (p. 504) or that poets, "whilst they [may] deny and abjure" the fact, are still "compelled to serve" a kind of monarch, a "Power which is seated upon the throne of their own soul" (p. 508)? Then, too, once more, what have all these announcements to do with the curious verbal shifts through which they are declared?

The Dominant Critical Response

To be sure, many answers to these basic questions have been proposed already, and nearly all of them have regarded the style as the secondary symptom of a Shelleyan belief in a non-Christian Presence, one ultimately unified within itself as we and our words are not. Figures in a Shelley poem shift, according to these arguments, because each one fails to attain the Oneness that they dimly remember as their source and passionately seek as their end. They dissolve and reform into different variations in the hope of at least approximating the One with their totality, often failing to do so and leaving Shelley to lament that his "words are inefficient and metaphorical—most words so—No help—" (the poet's marginal note to "On Love," *NCE*, p. 474n). Some interpreters have adopted this view, of course, because they find Shelley to be an almost Plotinian Neoplatonist. These critics see the "straining away" of the style as trying to mime a "spirit" emanating into nature and thought from within them or above them. This infusion is always "contending with obstruction and striving to penetrate and transform the whole mass" toward an "apocalypse" that leads to a transcendent state, so Shelley's words must contend with the obstructions of language in order to trail behind this striving and perhaps catch up with its surpassing of present existence.[7] Other writers, in a somewhat similar vein, have placed Shelley's ultimate source and goal at a great, even Gnostic, distance from a materiality that masks it. Sliding between metaphors from such anti-orthodox creeds as Freemasonry, Stoicism, Zoroastrianism, and Orphism, the Shelleyan style in this view keeps trying to dissolve into the "white light" of "eternity's fiery sphere" only to find itself battering against the obstructive "blot" of its opaque symbols.[8]

The most widely accepted group of recent exegetes, however, has decided, with some accuracy, that this dualism actually results from Shelley's radical reworking of the British empirical tradition ranging from Locke, George Berkeley, and Hume to William Godwin and Sir William Drummond. Granted, some of these critics have merely acknowledged Shelley's early and lasting sense that "nothing exists but as it is perceived" ("On Life," *NCE*, p. 476) and then made it stand beside, conflict with, or challenge a quasi-Platonic apprehension of the "numinous" that Shelley feels and desires quite apart from his empiricist reading.[9] But the majority have accepted the primacy of perceptions and associations among them as the grounding axiom in a "skeptical idealism" that proceeds from initial differences toward a projection of unity. In this redaction of the poet, the "associative analogies" that a mind forms out of remembered perceptions must eventually assume or hypothesize a "nontheistic Absolute" as the hidden ground of their interweaving and unifying process.[10] All of Shelley's best work, if we believe this schema, must therefore still base itself on a probable and perpetual "veil between [unified] Existence and [disjointed] Seeming"; in the style of his writing, the poet can try to project the supposedly "undifferentiated unity that is the nature of Existence," but he "cannot avoid the fact," so his words must keep suggesting, "that we live in an illusion and cannot experience Existence directly."[11]

This argument has become only slightly different when critics have taken "Power seated on the throne of [the] soul" as evidence of Shelley's relocation of God into the deepest "potentiality" of personal thought and will. In the best-known versions of this position, some of which have even linked the poet with the Protestant tradition of inner revelation,[12] Shelley's "images of divine and external authority" have come to stand for the most fundamental ordering drives in a poet's "own mind and conscience." The "fast-ascending numbers" in the poems have been read as assertions of how the mind forms analogies between itself and what it perceives and thus how its most "irrational yet profound human" longings for self-completion have tried to make that fullness seem present in the apparently "indifferent" world we perceive.[13] Once again, poetic words have been seen as referring backward and forward to states that are or will be at one with themselves, even though the first state is no more than the mind's reflexive sense of its own hopes for unity and the second is the projection of the mind's desire for oneness into perceived existence. To some degree, at least for this interpretation, it has not really mattered to the poet whether "the divinity which manifests itself in man" originates "from without or from within"; he has still regarded poetic language as an ever-extended bridge between a half-conscious will to unify what we see and an intimation of a supramundane "pattern which includes and transcends [the] disharmonies" in the perceptions longing for it.[14]

These views, in any case, have been challenged very little even after some modern and major theories of literary creation have been applied to Shelley's texts. When a recent proponent of the "new criticism," a school once scornful of Shelley, for example, decides to reinstate him as a master of the organic interrelation of contraries, the result presents the poet as working out a "tolerant, qualifying, complex attitude" (the constant at the core) in his struggle "to adapt language so that it will express the pictures of his mind" already formed.[15] This reading even concludes that the "One Spirit's plastic stress" in *Adonais* (l. 380) is really a sort of objective correlative for the poet's endeavors, paralleling his attempt to mold his materials toward a contradictory but all-inclusive vision. Concurrently, a more phenomenological school has suggested that the highly metaphoric interplays in Shelley's style really show how metaphor "is the mode of apprehension and expression by which imagination creates experience."[16] This claim might be saying that the action of metaphor (which is literally a "bearing off" or a "carrying away") precedes any unities that thought perceives or produces as thought's "intentionality" brings a coherent "world" into being. Yet most proponents of this view have actually seen the achievement of mental coalescence by metaphor as the consequence of "elementary unities of experience" preexisting mind and its analogies,[17] one of which is the "cogivenness of mind and world," a first "condition [i.e., the "Spirit"] revealed and strengthened by metaphor."[18] Shelley's words are once again seen to be "inefficient" and "metaphorical," though building in fits and starts toward a unified sense of experience, because their process of "veil after veil" is once more regarded as a sequence of incomplete recollections put together by the imagination "to cast a shadow across the soul's highest intuitions."[19] Almost wherever we look in professional Shelley criticism, his writing bespeaks "a dynamic system which develops outward from [a] center," and the center is a wholeness, albeit dimly remembered and always desired, that "keeps the mind in touch with the basic conditions of being and knowing."[20]

The Actual Provenance of Shelley's Writing

As I see them, all these arguments, either within their own terms or in the face of Shelley's explicit statements, beg a number of questions they cannot answer on their own and so cry out inadvertently for different solutions to the problems he presents. What allows the Plotinian reader of this poet to find so much resemblance between the movement of the "Spirit" and the drive of the style? Why are *both* always bursting past temporary confines to transfigure their apparent ingredients toward another order? And what is the "transcendence" approached in this process? Is it the permanent state beyond the world that most assume or the continual "climbing across" that the word "trans-cend" literally indicates? How can the more strictly Neoplatonic or semi-Gnostic interpretations speak of an Other completely removed from the metaphors that seem to conceal it? Is the completeness elsewhere really disconnected from the tendency in meta-phor (or "bearing off") to be inherently other than itself? What, too, in the nature of metaphoric movement necessitates Shelley's sliding between several heretical myths? Meanwhile, for the reader of Shelley as skeptical empiricist, what forces perceptions into associations that propose an ultimate unity? What demands the sort of causality (as in Hume or Drummond) that a sequence of perceptions projects as prior to itself? Is the cause, once assumed, necessarily unified within itself, or is it constituted by the passing between differences that suggested it? Is this cause entirely "nontheistic" for Shelley, especially considering his frequent use of the Old Testament Yahweh? Why all the allusions to that curious divinity, in fact, disappearing as He always does into another form (such as a wind) on the way to being displaced by something else again?

Why, in any event, do those who see Shelley introjecting God into the poet's impulses find it so hard to get around Shelley's persistent images of an extra-mental force? Doesn't Shelley say in his short essay "On Life" both that "cause" is a "state of the human mind" looking at how "thoughts" are "related to each other" and that "the cause of mind, that is, of existence," is probably not "similar to mind" (*NCE*, p. 478)? Doesn't he also say on the same page that "motion produces mind" rather than the reverse? What does he mean? Besides, why must the critics who see a Shelleyan "God within" continually discuss the projection of Shelley's feelings into another mind or nonmental place where that "divinity" can be more readily observed? And is oral or written discourse forced to be the passage between this "inside" and that "outside," or is it what makes the passage conceivable in the first place? How would the "new critic" answer that question, especially when he or she sees discourse as first the producer of thought and then the servant of an authorial attitude that knows the fullness of experience? Indeed, how can that sort of critic try to make Shelley an

organic poet when the texts emphasize inorganic disjunctions and continual substitutions that are not neatly harmonized contraries? How, at the same time, can the
phenomenologists make metaphor the cause and the effect of Shelley's "highest intuitions?" Must unity preexist analogy, and must all the "veils" of language look back
only to that supposedly first center? *Is* there an initial center that is whole within its
own being, or is the poet's "inmost naked beauty" suggested by the mere depth of
several veilings? Is there perhaps a multiple and continual veiling, then a sense of what
the veils might recall, in a process that keeps decentering and reveiling itself, even at
its beginning?

I think there is. I think that all these questions can be answered and the problems
of the style and the "Spirit" readdressed if we dethrone the center-at-one-with-itself
from the position of impetus in Shelley's work and replace it with this centerless displacement of figural counterparts by one another. We must see, in other words, the
peculiar logic in the movement of Shelley's style as basic to, not a mere symptom of,
his sense of thought and of what thought places before and beyond its process. In the
essay "On Life," Shelley himself declares, offering his most striking advance on his
empiricist reading, that an "object of thought" for him is always a "thought [or former
perception] upon which any other thought is employed" (*NCE,* p. 478). There is no
definite reception or projection of anything in his eyes unless there is first a preconscious dislocation from one instant of awareness into a different one. To say that
"nothing exists but as it is perceived" is to say that any distinguishable perception or
memory of it has already been reflected upon, interpreted from an alien perspective,
in a way that determines what the perception is by transposing it into another configuration. Shelley always finds this slippage inherent in any basic sensation on the way
to becoming a perception. During one of his early letters supporting Locke and the
"nonexistence of innate ideas," he concludes that the *tabula rasa* has perceptions to
interpret because it "bears the mark" of "impressions" and develops all its thinking
from the inscriptions it accumulates (*L,* I, 136). A perception shifts instantly past its
own occurrence because the influx beginning it is a series of such shifts within itself,
"bearing" ahead (as a metaphor does) a written "mark" that reinscribes an "impression" recalling something else yet again. True, Shelley may be making such statements
to support his longstanding contention that the "difference is merely nominal between
those two classes of thought that are vulgarly distinguished by the name of ideas and
external objects" ("On Life," p. 477). But each basic thought is still a motion between
at least two "externalities." It is a drive toward a counterpart rising ahead of it and a
harking back to a different one receding in its wake. It seeks a future relationship that
may carry forward a portion of a previous one now outside it and already dissolved.
A "man" for Shelley is therefore always "existing but in the future and in the past,
being, not what he is, but what he has been, and shall be" ("On Life," p. 476). Every
instant of mental life is a passing from moments only partially remembered to others
that redefine their predecessors from a later angle only to be redefined themselves at
other moments far ahead: "Man's yesterday may ne'er be like his morrow; / Nought
may endure but Mutability" (Shelley's poem "Mutability," ll. 15–16). There is no
"undifferentiated unity" from which Shelleyan thinking or writing develops. The self-
altering and perpetual crossing of intervals, since it is prior to particular thoughts and
yet the mode of their operation, is for Shelley, without much question, the "motion"
that "produces mind."

Consequently, such a process is especially apparent in those "highest intuitions" that most critics have placed at the center of Shelley's writing. It is, in fact, the generator and, in a sense, the very being of the subliminal and "interpenetrating" Spirit. In poetic inspiration as the *Defence* first defines it,

> the mind in creation is as a fading coal which some invisible influence, like an inconstant wind, awakens to transitory brightness: this power arises from within, like the colour of a flower that fades and changes as it is developed, and the conscious portions of our natures are unprophetic of its approach or its departure. . . . We are aware of evanescent visitations of thought and feeling sometimes associated with place or person, sometimes regarding our own mind alone, and always arising unforeseen and departing unbidden, but elevating and delightful beyond all expression: so that even in the desire and the regret they leave, there cannot but be pleasure, participating as it does in the nature of its object. (*NCE*, pp. 503–4)

There can be no intimation of a "fading" become bright again, or rather no awareness of some previous "thought [or] feeling" restored in a newly vivid form, unless there is first the "awakening," the abrupt transition between different mental states. Only when that transposition has already happened can there be a comparison of former and current states, and the comparison must then read the crossing process itself back into the earlier thought. The previous awareness must be anything but unified; it must be a fading from what it was toward another condition and must be associated with something not itself ("place or person" or the mind's other memories). The psyche must feel the "elevating" pleasure of reorganizing this dissolution, of course, yet that feeling must combine a "desire" for a past thought and its distant referent with the "regret" that both cannot be recovered just as they were and cannot be entirely recreated by the translation of them now in progress.

In the meantime, the transposing motion must also be read back into the interval between states. As Shelley concludes from perusing Hume and Drummond especially, a repeated passage between mental positions urges the psyche to project an impetus within or behind the shift. A "cause" for this poet must now be quite blatantly one effect of its own effects, a projection into the immediate past by transformations that later seem to be its results. Hence the poet's notion of an "invisible influence," which seems to behave as though it were an unconscious force becoming visible only in conscious recolorations of its previous "fadings and changings." This "power" plays two roles once it is so positioned by thought: it is the permanent, though self-concealing, self-mover causing all these transpositions, and it is the actual movement from state to state that turns one coloration into another without revealing any self-contained point of departure (any "seed" leading to the "flower" and its changes). It has been proposed because of the transitional drive to be the grounding of that drive, but it is also the transition in operation, a self-transformation perpetually changing and leaving its momentary ground. This curious infusion is "as it were," then, the "interpenetration of a diviner nature through our own" only because it resembles—the "as it were" means "as *though* it were"—the self-modifying and self-hiding transubstantiation that is the Yahweh of the Hebrew prophets walking upon the wind and disappearing behind the succession of His signs.[21] The mature Shelley has replaced the enthroned Omnipotence made out of this force by later interpreters with the "unapprehended" movement between differences that probably generated the ancient sense of Jehovah in the first place. The latter motion thereupon becomes the "Spirit" that is both inside and outside the many forms it shifts between during the "Ode to the West Wind." Moreover, Shelley hardly states the "as it were" clause in the *Defence* before he modifies it with a quite different image that reminds us more of the rapid passage between his written ciphers. He points us toward the tendency both before and within figures that makes them lose parts of their past contexts the moment they are inscribed and then encourages them to remake the lost connections in analogies with the imprints brought in to be successors at points further on. The "footsteps" of the "influence," he writes, "are like those of a wind over a sea" in which "the coming calm erases" much of what has been left and lines of "traces remain only" upon "the wrinkled sand" where they are presently imprinted (*Defence*, p. 504).

There is a kind of "writing," in other words, prior to poetic conception and certainly prior to any willed attempts at a poem or any acts of physical writing as we know it.[22] What impels Shelley's peculiar language must finally be put in linguistic terms, especially since his style is basically an extension of the shifts that wording must always perform in its passage from figure to figure. Yet the primary reason for his "trace" metaphors is not simply that his style imitates a mental process resembling a basic drive in writing. Writing itself is an essential part of the "motion" that "produces mind" for Shelley, to such an extent that mind and "Spirit" are the creations of language in his view quite as much as language is an extension of them. Shelley in fact accepts and tries to reconcile two contradictory positions on the role of language in thought, both of which were prominent in writing of the late eighteenth and early nineteenth centuries. On the one hand he has Asia claim, during her history of human civilization in act 2 of *Prometheus Unbound*, that the Titan "gave man speech" at the dawn of recorded time and that "speech created thought," which only then became "the measure of the universe" (II. iv. 72–73). He thereby carries forward some notions that had been building since the Abbé de Condillac's *Essay on the Origin of Human Knowledge* (1746) and had been reworked, sometimes extensively, by Adam Smith, Horne Tooke, William Godwin, Samuel Taylor Coleridge, and Jeremy Bentham, among others. Within this scheme, "thought" becomes an order able to measure and constitute the known world only after a visible thought-unit (or sign) is made to relate with others in a precise syntax turning mere ciphers into the ingredients of a developing, ordering arrangement.[23] On the other hand Shelley maintains simultaneously in the *Defence* (written less than a year after *Prometheus Unbound* was published) that "language" is "the most direct representation of the actions and passions of our internal being," mainly because it is "arbitrarily produced by the Imagination and has relations to thoughts alone" (*NCE*, p. 483). Here he is drawn more toward the system advanced by Locke, Berkeley, Thomas Hobbes, Jean-Jacques Rousseau, and James Burnet, Lord Monboddo.[24] Thoughts, ideas, feelings, or desires, all of which are combined by the Shelleyan imagination, now drive the mind to create words to be their visible embodiments so that the words can declare mental associations, perceptions, emotions, and needs to other minds.

Inspiration as a leaving of traces on a surface turns both of these arguments toward each other. There is no thought (even imaginative thought) without the linguistic positioning of tracelike units, if only because thought needs to discover itself in a nonmental form that makes it an interplay of differences. The "mind" cannot "see itself, unless reflected upon that which it resembles" without being the same (*Defence*, p. 491). Preexisting the "mind" and part of the "motion producing" it, then, is the darting between figures moving toward and through it, the conventions and potentials of language independent of any one psyche. At the same time, though, a linguistic construct has to serve something besides itself, since, as the passage from "fading" to "brightness" does, it must suppose a half-similar and "arbitrary" impetus from which it comes and toward which it moves (though always to another version). Language must be the alter ego of the imagination because discourse is so inclined to depend upon an other, because every utterance refers beyond its own location to a different level that precedes or succeeds its statements as its cause and its target. "Language" needs "thought" in order to be itself as much as thought needs language for the same purpose. As it turns out, the logic of transposition is really the impetus behind them both *and* behind their interrelationship. This is true even though this logic is able to operate only by way of their interaction, be it through the interplay of the parts in each one or the continuous crossing of each toward the other.

That logic, we now find, is primal and constantly active in Shelley's portraits of sensation, perception, association, recollection, anticipation, inspiration, conception, declaration, allusion, and communication. What must be thought before all these and must also be at work within them is the impulse to establish one element by transfiguring it into a different form at another point, and that operation is both linguistic and mental at once in that each of these is seen only in terms of its other. Nothing is strictly "individual" or contained within itself at any point in Shelley: not an area of thought, an object, an emotion, a memory, a projection, a genre of writing, or a human being. A person is especially multiple, and not just because "he" or "she" is a succession of differentiations worked out by language as each word passes toward a future and looks back to a past. A person for Shelley, unless he or she is perverted by repressive ideologies, is a self-interpreting and interpretable figure in bodily form, something far more social than individual. Such a figure is wrenched into focus, then into a context, then altogether outside itself by the linguistic operations that create reflection, self-construction, and self-expression:

> A child [or a primitive, the basic person] will express its delight [in simple play] by its voice and motions; and every inflexion of tone and every gesture will bear exact relation to a corresponding antitype in the pleasurable impressions which awakened it. . . . [Consequently] language and gesture, together with plastic or pictorial imitation, [must] become the image of the combined effect of those [perceived] objects, and of [the primal person's] apprehension of them. Man in society, with all his passions and pleasures, next becomes [automatically] the object of the passions and pleasures of man; an additional class of emotions produces an augmented treasure of expressions; and language, gesture, and the imitative arts, become at once the representation and the medium, the pencil and the picture, the chisel and the statue, the chord and the harmony [of widespread] social sympathies. (*Defence*, pp. 480–81)

In order for a person to see his or her "impressions" (already figures) as representing a "corresponding antitype"—indeed, in order for a psyche to be constituted as a "subject" apprehending an "other"—there must initially be the articulation of gestures and words in which already existing ways of making signs are "inflected" to produce "images" of an "apprehender" and an "object." Once that happens, the "self" and its environment can be thought of as existing in relation to and over against each other, yet that whole process mainly produces a discourse of "combined effects" that can be confirmed and completed, since it is sheer rhetoric, only by different formations of thought (by other "selves") working themselves out in similar acts of language.[25] The "object" of representing "passions and pleasures" must become an awareness of "man in society" rather than a vision of "man alone," just because of that logic of transposition in which the mind cannot "see itself unless reflected upon that which it resembles." We may not be "intuitively" aware of "other minds," according to Shelley (expanding on Hume) in his "Speculations on Metaphysics and Morals," but the "irres[is]tible laws of thought constrain us to believe that the precise limits of our [verbally composed] ideas are not the actual limits of [all] possible ideas," and "the law, according to which these deductions are drawn, is called analogy [or literally a 'saying according to something else']," which happens to be the "foundation of all our inferences from one idea to another" (*CW*, VII, 61). The figuration of the self must therefore look beyond itself to analogues that extend, contextualize, and define it; its significance must be deferred in part to what other people feel and say, so "feelings" about the self after language has created it must be "augmented" by feelings about others and what memories or emotions may be involved in their self-declarations. "Love," or the "sympathetic imagination," must be, for that reason above all else, the "great secret of morals" for Shelley that impels us to extend our personal desires into the needs and possibilities "of another and many others" (*Defence*, pp. 487–88). "Self" as a fabrication defined only in its own terms is really an illusion, a willed perversion of its own defining process. It is the "Mammon" of the "world," as Shelley often says, because it is "the offspring of ignorance and mistake" (*CW*, VII, 76).

The transposition constantly displacing the self, therefore, is inherently iconoclastic and revolutionary, even in the face of its own previous productions. Since the self is always what it "has been" and "shall be," its rhetorical process must critique any limits that try to confine identity to a fixed "present," and that effort, as it extends itself into the needs of others, must verbalize structures as yet unattained in which that extension and those needs can be altered, furthered, and fulfilled. In other words, the "augmented feelings" prompted by self-articulation in the language of the moment must reconstitute language, using its own potentials, to press it beyond what it currently tends to say. Rhetorical efforts truly in contact with their basis in transposition must form an "augmented treasure of expressions" that transfigure normal discourse patterns and thereby resist the linguistic conventions that maintain rigid class distinctions. It is only when that occurs, when there is a tension between established and experimental, declassifying styles of self-expression, that language, or really the overall "poetry" of an age, becomes both the tool and the arena (the "chisel" and the sculpted work) encouraging each mind to sympathize with very different ones and thereby steering the collectivity toward a transfigured social order. Shelley anticipates Karl Marx, as several have seen,[26] but at a more basic level than anyone has noted. This poet's self-formation in language is very like Marx's "mode of production," which gives both survival and definition to the "self" by allowing it to rework materials outside the subject.[27] The mode and the materials, in Shelley as in Marx, also draw the self off into a system of exchange with other such modes and other users of the materials. The created Shelleyan "I" is automatically alienated from itself and determined largely by its social, linguistic, and economic possibilities, most of which, as the system develops, try to fix the self in one productive and subordinate role. There is pressure for change on the existing modes, however, from new and old human needs created or exacerbated by the methods of production as they stand at any one time.

Consequently, modes are continually being driven beyond their current procedures of operation even as a society's dominant methods try to remain the same. It is this paradoxical interaction, this class conflict, that washes over the psyche each time it tries to construct its "self" using the linguistic modes of production that help bring thought about. This is one way in which the mind is inundated by the transpositional "Spirit" acting as "the collective energy of the moral and material world." The fully compassionate mind for Shelley must follow the direction of that self-transforming drive to the point of announcing the necessities of history, demanding the overthrow of antiquated hierarchies, and projecting a millennium beyond current alienation where the system of exchange can be classless and free. No discussion of Shelleyan thought or identity should avoid how very political both of these are for him, and so no analysis of Shelley's writing should separate transposition from his radical social programme. Hence I propose a comprehensive rereading of Shelley's major works that probes the drive behind all his special interests, behind his ethics and projections for social change as well as his style, his metaphysics, and his epistemology. I want to show how each of his important texts in each of its dimensions proceeds from, works out of, and extends the logic of transposition; how each does so both in its own peculiar way and in relation to the texts around it, be they his or those of his precursors.

Naming the Subliminal Impulse

As I proceed, moreover, I will call the transpositional drive "transference," however much I thereby risk replacing one sort of Shelleyan center with another. "Transposition" brings too much to mind a term in grammar indicating a reversal in the order of words, a concept in mathematics allowing sides of an equation to change places, and a process in music allowing an interpreter to rewrite the key signature of a composition. The word does emphasize the inversions and radical reorientations that occur when one Shelleyan image or phrase is transformed by an adjacent figuration; it even points to how unconscious drives suddenly "fade and change" in their conscious versions and how anything "individual" for the poet abruptly shifts into a social "key" as it turns out to be a mode of production composed within a public language. But "transference" includes all these possibilities—as it literally indicates any "bearing across" between places, moments, thoughts, words, or persons—while adding the "conveyance" of any perception *without* total inversion into a location, figure, or moment not its own. If it is a "center" for Shelleyan thought in this study, it is the most decentered one that could possibly be imagined and is really more of a rootless passage between different formations. It is a primordial, preconscious shift, intimated in the movement of perception, feeling, and language, always already becoming a different enactment of itself at another time and in conjunction with other elements. Other forms of relocation that we call "transference" are but derivative variations on this movement making them possible initially. Consequently, I must also refer to it as "radical transference," using the "root" sense of "radical" so as to point out the process at the genesis or "source" of all the variants recasting the basic drive. Shelley, I think, is radical in the sense of urging revolutions at the very foundations of social life, but only as he returns revolution to its "base," the transference that must empower it, and only as he keeps insisting on that subliminal turn as the impetus behind all aspects of social exchange and transformation.

Indeed, Shelleyan transference anticipates more than Marx's "mode of production"; in its basis and its operation, especially its sudden "arising" into "unprophetic" conscious awareness, it prefigures Freud's "transference," his *Übertragung* or "carrying over," first as he defines it in *The Interpretation of Dreams* and then as he develops it later in his most famous use of the term. In *The Interpretation,* we discover, the most primary element in an "unconscious idea" is as uprooted, as self-divided, and as much in need of another element as is the basic sensation that becomes a perception in Shelley. We retain, Freud writes, psychic "memory-traces" from our earliest awareness of our appetites and from the sensations of objects (already mere memories themselves) that seem to have satisfied those cravings at one time.[28] These "traces" remain as "excitations" toward previous desires and fixated objects for them (such as the mother's breast), even after the dimly remembered objects have been withdrawn, never to be restored as they were. Each trace is therefore a motion away from itself at the start, inclining backward yet having to seek in the future for a version of what may or may not have been there in the past. As Freud puts it, the memory-trace must always gravitate ahead to a later "mnemic image" seeming to resemble the remembered object in some way but also in need of its own "original satisfaction" now gone. Desire is carried on, generated and revived perpetually, by a moving recollection seeking an image that looks elsewhere to yet another point. Hence, because there is that "primary repression" that keeps the supposed "lost origin" (the mother, usually) forever distant and forbidden, this doubleness or tripleness ("veil after veil") turns toward still other traces and images into and through which its energy can be extended (or "cathected"). The different levels of the psyche (unconscious, preconscious, conscious), in fact, are really brought about by this process, especially as the memory-trace retreats into *ein anderer Schauplatz* while being reworked and obscured by figures and desires at other levels. Freud can consequently suggest that dream-work, creative writing, and neurotic symptoms needing analysis are always prompted, in his words, by an "unconscious idea" carrying its longings over to a "preconscious [one] by transferring its intensity onto it and getting itself 'covered' by it." Alongside that scheme he can also propose a "primary narcissism" in which the primal "excitations" (or libidinal impulses) in the memory-trace are carried toward other bodies that seem to nourish the vital organs (the "erotogenic zones") of the subject. There is for Freud what is perhaps a "differentiation in the energy at work generally in the mind," a drive not fully controlled by thought or will that makes "ego-libido" project itself through an "object-libido" directed at some other person or thing. On this foundation Freud, of course, builds the interpersonal transference for which he is well known. He extends the operation of intrapersonal *Übertragung* so that he can account for the way in which speaking subjects seem to relocate their unconscious impulses onto people or objects (including the analyst) that are definitely not the self. He makes the self a fabrication searching for differing mirrors in a social setting of symbolic exchange just as Shelley does. The entire logic of transposition encompassing sensation, cognition, and self-definition in Shelley is thus well designated by Freud's most basic "transference," whatever the conceptual differences between the two writers.

Still, those differences must not be forgotten. Shelley's primordial transfers, to begin with, are far less fixated than Freud's on certain primal objects such as the body of the mother (thought of as "the origin") and the moment of our initial conception (the "primal scene"). The poet does write in his short piece "On Love" that "there is something within us which from the instant we live and move searches after its likeness" and that it "is probably in correspondence with this law that the infant drains milk from the bosom of its mother" (*NCE*, p. 473). Yet Freud's cause and effect is almost the reverse of this one. Even though he points to sheer "differentiation" as a probable impetus behind primary narcissism, the desire for the mother in his eyes is prior to the more general need for "likeness" that searches for a "self" by reflecting it in a series of other places. Hence this last desire for him is nearly always Oedipal. Since the father stands in the way of the mother, the psyche longs to define its "self" by reaching the lost womb through substitutes for the mother which the father may recognize but not detect. Sometimes the Freudian subject even tries to supplant the father, or at least to become a procreative father-figure (a poet fathering a new discourse, perhaps), if only to draw near the originating womb by taking the place of the being who inseminated that womb in the primal scene or to adopt a fatherly role in the eyes of the world by being the progenitor of a new way of speaking. Shelley may have his Oepidal moments, especially when he defies his father's public orthodoxy and confirms his mother's private views by writing and publishing *The Necessity of Atheism*,[29] but he comes to see that all fixations on persons, objects, or points of origin are later constructions resulting from an initial welter in which vague differences simply gravitate toward each other. In the earliest "sensations" of growing minds, if we believe the fairly late essay "On Life," children for Shelley "feel as if their nature were dissolved into the surrounding universe, or as if the surrounding universe were absorbed into their being" (*NCE*, p. 477). There is a movement in two directions here, each side seeking some "likeness" in a counterpart, before there is a consciousness of any "distinctions" between subject and object. In other words, the "memory-trace" of personal appetite and the "mnemic image" of received perceptions are drawn together before either one sees itself as clearly recalling a distant origin. The search for the breast is just one moment in the progress of this double drive, the one where the perceived bosom enters awareness as an object for desire even as the infant reaches out for something corresponding to its hunger.

Other complications, too, in Shelley's sense of human development pull his basic interaction and its consequences even further away from the ones in Freud. For Shelley the "surrounding universe" does not enter consciousness simply as impulses or sense perceptions; it also hurtles in as the multifaceted, chaotic "cyclic poem written by time" already mentioned, as "every word and every suggestion" in the language of the culture "admitted to act upon [a given] consciousness" (Preface to *Prometheus Unbound, NCE*, p. 135). These verbal constructs from various eras and social groups cascade in as differences that can and do conflict with one another, reflecting a social arena of divergent ideologies (or class orientations) where there has yet to be an "equilibrium between institutions and [individual] opinions" (*NCE*, p. 134). Such a *heteroglossia* of possibilities for thought and verbalization urges its differences toward relationships on its own, even as the tensions continue,[30] so that the outreaching psyche is governed partly by a linguistic dispersion and interplay that cannot be reduced to one biological point of origin. A single cause of any sort can be assumed retroactively, but only after a self-articulation in language organizes these basic concatenations into sequences with priorities, usually by downplaying the rhetorics of some ideologies in favor of the vocabulary in just one or two of them. In "On Life," we must remember, "cause is only a *word* expressing a certain state of the human mind with regard to the manner in which two thoughts are apprehended to be related to each other" after they already are (p. 478, my emphasis). For Shelley, then, finding the "roots" of impulses that are covered over by very different "symptoms" means watching how this covering becomes visibly linguistic and socially constructed, how it makes a rhetorical gesture toward different minds so that personal needs can be defined by their analogues in others. If "we imagine," to quote "On Love" again, "we would that the airy children of our brain were born anew within another's," and "if we feel, we would that another's nerves should vibrate to our own," be they the nerves of a mother, father, friend, lover, or reader (p. 473). Shelley anticipates Freud's own occasional movement (and the development of some of his followers) toward the working out of the self's expressive and rhetorical options rather than the mere recovery of infant traumas and appetites, though the latter, as they become socialized, do remain important.[31] He also answers, as Freud does not, the masculine drive to be or rival a father with the traditionally feminine urge to dissolve outward into myriad forms of being ("pregnant with a lightning which has yet found no conductor"). Indeed, his self-reproducing and self-altering transference is the otherness-of-self-from-self long consigned to "woman" by patriarchal discourse and recently revived in French theory as the feminine "unconscious" on which the construct "man" (including the Freudian version) is actually based without realizing the fact.[32] As a result, I adopt "transference" as a useful way of apprehending relations in Shelley that have yet to be articulated, but I do not insist on particular male desires being more transferred than others, even though some image patterns in Shelley's writing do provide some evidence for what Freud often asserts. Instead I hope to show how Shelley reveals the primacy of the transferential-feminine movement in every personal desire, linguistic device, or social-historical myth he confronts.

Some Affiliated Approaches and Where They Stop

As a matter of fact, a few recent endeavors have already been moving in this direction. I need offer my version only because each one of them has pulled back to some degree from seeing what transference is and understanding how it works in Shelley. One such study quite rightly sees metaphoric displacement as the basis of every stage in Shelley's thinking and writing.[33] Because "nothing 'is'" and "everything is 'like'" in most fundamental Shelleyan perceptions, according to this view, every "relation" of thought or words in the poetry "develops out of and turns into another" at once. In addition, each recasting "interferes" with any composing of continuities that might envision the perceived world as more unified and less fluid than it actually is. This reading, however, errs in assuming that Shelley is simply conscious of metaphoricity and of the continual irony, or "self-deconstruction," demanded by this "relational apprehension" at the heart of his epistemology. Actually, a Shelleyan perception is consciously transferred toward others right away because it is already a transfer before we are aware of it, already the irony of something being recalled in some other image quite different and distant from itself. If a perception comes "inside" and toward another thought, it can also be interpreted as trailing a point elsewhere, so the "cause of mind" must be asserted retroactively by mind and yet must never be seen as identical with the psyche. There must be a "spirit" or process of which we are *not* conscious except as it displaces itself and keeps changing its features through us in order to avoid being fixed or denied. This sheer becoming-other is already there before consciousness as the movement of self-articulation into which our thinking steps and as an impulse within us to be defined by a verbal mode outside ourselves that composes us while we compose it. To see metaphor as both the ingredient and the process of thought in Shelley is to interpret a mere effect as *the* point of departure for his writing. Metaphor is but the late synecdoche whose operation points back to the movement that underlies all figuration and thence becomes visible only in figures.

Another recent approach to this poet also refuses to accept such a "birth and recurrence" in Shelleyan awareness that "has no necessary connexion with consciousness or will."[34] I refer to the often Freudian revision-by-repression proposed by the later Harold Bloom and his progeny, that theory of the "strong" poetic "voice" that re-originates itself, or becomes a father to new "tropes," by willfully swerving toward and away from the most established language, especially the language of the strongest precursor-poets. This way of accounting for Shelley and some other revisionist writers has the advantage of focusing sharply on each trope (or "turn") as a thorough "re-aiming" of a previous "image of voice."[35] Shelley for the Bloomians indulges (when he does) in a frantic, even "disjunctive," movement between tropes because he is pursuing one personal inclination—for Bloom the drive toward "Representation"—in the face of another drive that seems to come first and to pull in a regressive direction—the one Bloom calls the tendency toward "Limitation." The desire for Limitation draws the aspiring poet initially toward seeing the world as it has already been configured by a previous great writer. Once tempted so into the language of a powerful "father" (as Shelley was inclined mainly toward Wordsworth in Bloom's eyes), the poet finds his expressive potentials limited by an *"ethos,"* by a worked-out, closed, established, and even commanding system of tropes. He feels he must employ a given language of "precept" that is really no more than the remnants of a once disruptive "intentionality." Such a language, in fact, has been hollowed out by time into a dead letter, a fixed set of relations between signifiers and signifieds, that seems "natural" and yet has been emptied of the true "strength" in its "voice," its original leap beyond past constructions. Consequently, for the poet to speak entirely through that medium is for him to negate his emergent selfhood and his special will. It is for him to be possessed and rendered powerless (figuratively castrated or given over to the death of his individuality) by the father whose domain he has invaded and whose words of death threaten to subsume the separate voice of the ephebe.

Granted, one attractive initial response to this kind of death wish is a bold "reaction-formation" by the new poet in which he says the exact opposite of what the father's text says, thereby employing the standard language by trying to repress it. Such an obvious tactic, however, really affirms the priority and dominance of the fatherly *ethos,* so the Bloomian "strong poet," to gain an identity instead of finding it swallowed up, must always go beyond that initial step after the rebellious poem is underway. He must strive to seize upon some metaphor that appears to underwrite the language of the father and wrench that figure away from its existing context into a radically different one, where it is turned toward other meanings that are not yet fully worked out. In Bloom's words, there must be a deliberate act of *metalepsis* that forces the *ethos* to serve the emergent *pathos* of personal longing and self-assertion. That strong "re-aiming" achieves Re-presentation, even as Limitation remains the poet's point of departure, and Shelley to the Bloomians attempts this transition at almost every moment in his strongest writing. For them he shifts metaleptically, even within single lines, away from the words he has already written down (which might easily be sucked back into the Wordsworthian *ethos*) and carries important aspects of them over into refigurations that are as far removed as possible from even his own established contexts.[36] He thus offers re-namings that try to define again, but differently, the deep foundations of an older rhetoric. The poet's ultimate aim in all this, at least as the Bloomians see it, is to appropriate the forceful intentiality that the father-poet once appeared to assert as entirely his own. Indeed, by installing his peculiar definition within figures that form the basis of the older poet's work, the new author wants to claim, if only in an illusion, that he is the defining father of his own "father's"rhetoric. Shelley's preconscious spirit, in other words, is for Bloom and his disciples the "electric life which burns within the words" of an earlier Romantic writer (*Defence,* p. 508), yet only as that spirit is introjected by the new poet and named in his poems as the signifier of his personal capacity for receiving and changing the language of earlier works.

In advancing this argument, though, the Bloomian forgets that Shelley does not confront a fixed *ethos* in his own eyes when he begins to write. He does start, admittedly, with the language of precursors, usually a great many of them (to be more precise than Bloom has been on this point), but he finds the "life" in their phrases "electric" because there is already a motion there, a "life" instead of a death, a shifting force that resembles a current passing between one position and another. For Shelley any figure or construction within an existing piece of writing, whether its author is alive or dead, is in transit from a previous use into the present one *and* from the present order into a future reinterpretation, sometimes within the same work and even the same line. Poetry would not exist if one entity were not always being seen in terms of another, proceeding at all times on its own power from limitation toward representation; as Shelley puts it, the real "truth" in poetic works is the "analogy of things" developing throughout them, the "harmony" of sheer interrelationships that fulfills a moving intentionality always operating prior to an author's personal will (*Defence,* pp. 484–85.) There is less a restrictive, castrating father at the heart of what attracts a new poet to past writing and more a continual fecundity, a motherly bringing-to-birth out of earlier realms into different ones.

The real danger in duplicating a previous construct is the stoppage of this transformative action that such repetition would permit. Many previous authors, sadly, have tried to "deny and abjure" the movement making their work possible in order to claim a prescriptive *ethos* that ought not to be changed. To repeat them without any differentiation would be to confirm the repressive illusion they promulgate. The new poet should start by realizing how much that self-deceiving repression allows older writers to forget the "Power" that is the transference "seated upon the throne of their own soul." Then he or she should constantly attempt a recovery reactivating the motion that they have forgotten. Beginning perhaps (though not necessarily) with a "reaction" or reversal countering the precursor—but only to announce the return of the repressed—the new work should reopen and extend the "electricity" already there in the best existing poetry. It should not just willfully displace an old figure into a metaleptic transfiguration; this sort of will-to-power is simply not needed. A metalepsis is the refiguring of a figure that is already a transference (a figure for another figure), and that is what is fundamentally occurring, without the will's assistance, in language as it helps create the thought that then tries to push language even further. Revision for Shelley should be a releasing of potential yet denied metalepses toward what they can soon become; not an impositon of the will upon figures for the sake of a defiant "selfhood" but a submission by the will to a prior transference that should never be held within a single identity. In fact, that is the way that Shelley revises his precursors, as I will frequently show in succeeding chapters. His "voice" is not the achievement of a unique persona but the intentional losing of it within the onslaught of tropic possibilities emerging in the language he employs. Like that of his speaker in the "Ode to the West Wind," his utterance is the conduit of transference rather than its producer. Transference itself sweeps through the poet driving all "dead thoughts over the universe / Like withered leaves to quicken a new birth" (ll. 63–64) and scattering the speaker's own apparent body into the ongoing and forward-looking movement.

Indeed, a third new reading of Shelley has explicitly revised Bloom on similar grounds.[37] This one sees the "Power" that "arises from within," and that thereby turns a "fading coal" into a "transitory brightness," as the *langue* of Ferdinand de Saussure, the general system of all available transactions between figures from which any *parole* (or single utterance) must choose its governing relations. More precisely, as the writing of "traces" on the "sand" of consciousness by a withdrawing force, the Power in this view is the *langue* as it is further defined by the neo-Freudian Jacques Lacan. It is the violent entry into the poet's awareness of the entirely symbolic Unconscious, that half-known and infinite Other of the many "possible exchanges" or mental and visceral "permutations authorized by language."[38] This vast potentiality is what the poet must encounter before the construction of any particular thought-pattern, and for this interpretation that means that Shelley's rebellions against authoritative orders must be articulated in obedience to a "code" (a language system), the very sort of established structure that Shelley professes to hate. Worse yet for the poet, this linguistic supremacy dictating his metaphors from atop a chain of command is, on closer examination, a "will to die," a drive toward "vacancy" inherent in the movement of any *langue.* Here this redaction combines the existentialist sense that a figure or a linguistic movement is the "death" of its referent (an announcement of the object's absence from present awareness) with Freud's post-1915 notion of the transfer between memories as a "repetition-compulsion" revealing a desire to return to a pre-life state (a unified nonexistence prior to the differentiation of birth).[39] As a result, Shelley's point of departure is no longer the threat of the death in one father-poet's language but a Nietzschean-Heideggerian glance into universal, primordial dissolution that leads to a "defense," a making of metaphors, striving to overcome the will to die. The poems generated by this different oscillation between Limitation and Representation are thus attempts to pull "past metaphors" into more present ones in ways that keep fabricating a constant rebirth from death, an apprently "vital current of existence" concealing the beckoning abyss. No one portion of an utterance, of course, succeeds in achieving this overcoming permanently. Any momentary "calling" by the illusion of a living voice in a poem is followed at once by "the cold lacunae of graphic spacing," the leaving of ciphers that are also epitaphs of the voice's passing away. Hence each Shelleyan figure has to dart on toward another before it is clearly articulated. It must hover between a sense of its defiant life and its need for "rebirth," since it both resists and desires the coming of death produced by the basic progression of language.

I confess there are moments in Shelley's poetry that make this reading quite tempting, especially the onslaught of the West Wind that buries life before it prompts a series of resurrections. Nevertheless, such a view fails to take account of what its key images *from* Shelley actually say *in* Shelley, and in doing so it exposes itself as a "reaction-formation" competing mainly against Bloom, affirming the tenets of that father-figure once more (just as a reaction-formation should in Bloom's system). To begin with, Shelley's arising-and-receding "Power" is not simply language or its possible relations. He clearly regards it as pre-linguistic, albeit in terms of the "writing" that obscurely reflects it. Actually, in the "fading coal" passage, it is the subliminal arising, without clear referents, of mnemic images, bodily sensations, somatic drives, *and* potential relations or crossings between these different fading figures. It is a "forelanguage," a sheer differentiation and transmigration of drives, that seeks to define itself in a *langue* or system of interplays and then urges these latter potentials to conceal and transform the basic movement in particular patterns of utterance.[40] Yes, such a "Power" can be found operating in any linguistic procedure that brings thought into clear existence, but before it occupies that position it is what *demands* the continual exchange of private thought with public language so that each can become the mirror of the other and the mind can be known to exist because of its verbal manifestations. In addition, this transformational drive is neither automatically nor initially a "code" in Shelley's eyes. That kind of culture-ruling lexicon restricting what words can mean, that *ethos* or ideology upholding the ruling methods of self-production, exists for Shelley only when poetic "words" related to and relating many other points are willfully made by certain later social groups to "become through time signs for portions or classes of thoughts" in which one signifier is connected to just a few signifieds (*Defence,* p. 482). Clearly the "Power" may generate some of the relations that come to be seen as exclusive and absolute in such an order, yet it does not start out by being a closed system, and it does not ever insist on its own that the range of its interplays should be so restricted. It makes fixed codes possible, to be sure, partly because of its own tendency to obscure or forget the mobility in its previous "fadings" and relations. Even so, it does not demand the production of codes as necessary or inevitable; such a predestination would deny that a "fading coal" could become a very different "brightness" in the future.

In any event, this shifting that Shelley finds to be so primary is never identical with the death-drive or *thanatos* proposed by Freud or by others in his wake, much as the "Power" may break up its previous interplays to supplant them with later ones, thus destroying and restructuring its creations as it goes in the manner of Shelley's West Wind. The poet never finds that an object is "killed" by the signifying of it, only reconstituted in a passage from one state of awareness to another, and he certainly never proposes a prenatal nonexistence or nihilistic abyss as the most basic referent of images. He does not even hark back to Lacan's primal point, the rupture from the henceforth distant mother, that initial gap between origin and self that soon makes death the origin as the mother recedes and disappears from the gaze of her child.[41] Subliminal transference does assume a gap between two moments and figures, but it crosses or bridges the distance the moment it suggests one. Its *thanatos,* the fading of its past moments, is simultaneously an *eros* seeking another relation, a desire "incapable of imagining . . . annihilation" (Shelley's "On Life," p. 476). This third, quasi-Lacanian reading cannot face that fact, despite its attempt to avoid Bloom's single precursor incarnating death. It depends just as much as Bloom's vision does on one eternal and initial object of poetic desire, on the absence that is death behind existing words prompting the poet to assert his or her living presence in death's own mode of discourse.

Perhaps the newer readings closest to my view are the ones that have announced themselves as more truly "deconstructive" than any Bloomian would want to be. In recent essays focused on Shelley, Paul de Man and J. Hillis Miller have seen the later poems as thematizing a "movement of effacing and of forgetting ... a passive, mechanical operation [in which] the brain is being acted upon by something else," to quote de Man's version of the argument.[42] "In such a chain," writes Miller, where "there is always something earlier or something later to which any link [may] refer," each "element is both exterior to the adjacent one and at the same time encloses and is enclosed by it."For de Man this means that Shelley's later work discovers how much "the very possibility of cognition" is based on the "power of positional activity," which is the march of language "prior to its signifying function." If we "retrospectively" see this sheer tracking as a "beginning" or as a "relationship" of "transcendental orders," that is "because we [later] impose" the "authority of sense and meaning" upon "the senseless power of positional language." For Miller such a movement of positionings arouses all Shelleyan desire and at the same time raises "barriers" to the completion of any longing. Shelley's inadequate images giving way to their "hosts" or "parasites" can "only proleptically refer" to some other images and "therefore [do] not [really] refer at all." The poet is forever caught between an "idealism" and a "nihilism" in which the effort to pass beyond figures to "immediacy" runs up against the need in figures to seek other figures above all else.

The passages I have cited from Shelley do incline toward these readings to some extent, since they show how meaningful goals or apparent sources for him are projected as future or past by a self-translating supplementation that always moves away from wherever it happens to be. Even so, and despite my debts to them, I do not find the American deconstructionists to be much more accurate in their sense of Shelley than the more traditional and "centered" interpreters of his work. Shelley, as I read him, not only refuses to call the "power's" drive a "machine"; he also resists reading its imprinting of traces as a sheer "positioning" of figures that will not "posit meaning" on its own. As much as his transference underlies mere impressions and opens up the spaces keeping them separate, it also impels the passage *between* impressed figures, so much so that every "colour" manifestly "fades and changes" into another one while becoming itself. There is a relational drive from the start, a seeing of something through and in terms of something else, that can surely be called a "will to meaning,"[43] even though there is never the wholeness of a meaning entirely achieved in the past or the future. That intentionality prior to the personal will is engendered, urged, and pursued, though never brought to a final point, by the very transference from one point to the next that makes meaning's completion both desirable and impossible. Moreover, although Miller's notion of desire is generated by this movement inclining each figure toward those behind or ahead of it, proleptic reference in Shelley *does* refer in multiple directions, especially since every figure traces its "fading" history by deferring backward to its previous contexts and then opens toward possible figural connections that have yet to be fully made but are always on the rise. The reference of figures to other figures in Shelley is a "barrier" only when the poet occasionally forgets its necessity and value, and that reaction is always possible in the face of representations that half-forget their past and continually emphasize their difference from all others. Much of the time in his later work Shelley celebrates radical transposition as the crowning glory of "the mind in creation." The "idealism" here is a non-Kantian one perpetually aspiring toward the future achievements of the will to meaning; hence Shelley never settles for long on a nihilism of complete lack from which desire arises, only the sort where fixed systems are undermined in favor of more fulfilling relations about to emerge in personal awareness. Most of all, he points to transference as an entirely social and socializing tendency in human language and thought. The march of inhuman traces in American deconstruction, which usually sees transference as simply crossing the awareness of the solitary individual (that construct of bourgeois ideology), cannot really translate such a "going out of ourselves," with its economic, erotic, and nearly selfless dispersal of identity. The vocabularies of the deconstructionist, in other words, must be joined to those of, say, a semi-Freudian and a semi-Marxist if they are to explain the sympathetic feelings and revolutionary hopes in Shelley that make his writing genuinely altruistic and prophetic. We should therefore analyze the relational operations rediscovered as primal motions by some deconstructive writers, but we need not accept their kind of bourgeois nihilism, which could turn Shelley's poems into self-ironizing plays on words suitable only for institutional and academic decoding.[44] Consequently, in the succeeding chapters I will follow the lead of the recent Shelley studies that have exposed a figural mobility as the basis of his thought and art. But I will always do so by trying to get past their inability to connect transference with Shelley's radical sense of what people are and what the human race ought to become.

The Argument That Transference Demands

Yet even as I claim its pervasive appearance in his work, I cannot say that Shelley declares or "intends" transference to be the basis of his visions. Transference can never be consciously pursued unless some of its transformations have already occurred, especially that crossing into conscious awareness in which previous "lights" fade and others obscure or supplant them. One function of transference, in fact, is to forget and mask itself even as it becomes visible in its sublimations. Its process is a preconscious invasion of awareness that prompts a conscious will to write that can never recover the original impulse exactly as it was. Transference, we must admit, will not be exposed or known as "itself," since it is itself only as it becomes something else in drawing previous figures toward different reformulations. At most, it can declare, sometimes unexpectedly, that its sublimating activity is taking place or has recently occurred. It can intrude into a moment when Shelley is setting out to assert a personal conviction and reveal his argument to be based on a logic that some of his assertions may at first seem to deny. In "On Life," for example, as I have briefly noted, Shelley wants to collapse the usual distinction between "ideas" and "external objects." He can do so only by seeing each thought as a thought about a different thought from elsewhere. He uses the very inside-outside distinction he seems to reject, and so he points to an operation more subliminal than his ostensible purpose, an activity that he goes on to explore in this and other works as the motion that makes thoughts both similar to and different from each other. Transference takes Shelley by surprise on a number of occasions, either as a movement "arising from within" his own attempts to write or as the "electric life" in the words of those he most likes to read. All he can do is perpetually seek and work out the self-veiling nature of this "unseen presence" by exploring the various thought-patterns through which it moves, thereby discovering how those patterns work and what they can be made to accomplish.

Shelley, then, does not set out deliberately to write about radical transference—at least not until his later works and then only by giving it other names that have been used in the past to repress its primacy. Throughout his career he tries mainly to expose and dissect the religious, monarchical, and patriarchal "codes of fraud and woe" that have confined or still imprison personal development and the most loving kinds of human interaction. Initially, since he feels the attraction of the supreme levels proposed by such codes, the young Shelley examines the available philosophical alternatives to the most sanctioned rhetorics of religion. Seeing the restrictions along with the appeal in each new option, he shifts his personal faith from alternative to alternative until he starts to confront the urge behind the human desire for the "infinite" and finds that it can be liberated from rigidly centered systems of belief. Then, after 1815, he focuses on the movements basic to memory, inspiration, perception, and perceived existence, all of which reveal the same self-surpassing urge. In a dialogue with earlier and more hierarchical schemes of epistemology, metaphysics, and poetic vision, he struggles to describe what connects disjointed moments of intense thought and feeling to other such moments or to the "outside world" we feel inclined to construct from perceptions that keep changing their features even as they assault our senses. He therefore examines, with more intensity than we find in any of the other Romantic poets concerned with this question, how we can or if we should posit an "inside" and an "outside" realm as we usually do. He even wonders why it is that the process by which these two opposites interrelate, often to the point of nearly dissolving the distinction, is the same process that appears to insist on their separation, even on their tendency to seem unequal at times, with the "subjective" pole either trying to dominate or being dominated by the "objective" one. More and more Shelley feels he must decide what to say about a primary impulse in the human imagination that can lead either to thought's escape from hegemonic constructs or to thought's desire for subjection to yet another tyrannical supremacy.

This quandary remains a major concern during the rest of his career, albeit in more experimental and complex modes of writing that attempt to undermine domineering "codes" by exaggerating and/or disrupting their most longstanding elements. Starting in 1817 Shelley concentrates quite often on the thought-patterns and decisions that bring about various forms of subjection, including the submissions of individuals to "objective" orders or to other "subjects." He works to uncover the means by which the potential mobility (hence freedom) of human thinking is skewed into widely accepted structures that license human abasement under seemingly monolithic absolutes. At about the same time, too, he boldly toys with deconstructive and liberating orders of thought, language, and social engineering that show how the constricted mobility can be released from suppression. He uses his extensive reading in the mythological and even scientific schemes of the West and East to propose new and ever-changing combinations of symbols that may disperse the mental constructs of being enforced by the dominant myths of the West. Moreover, after this two-sided approach has been underway for about two years, Shelley draws both tendencies together and carries them over into the practicalities of immediate and eventual social reform. He turns briefly from verse to prose, as he has sometimes done at earlier points, and there exposes the face-offs in his own historical moment between tyrannical and liberating extensions of desire. He analyzes these extensions with such rigor, in fact, that he shows how each order feeds into or off the other one—and thus how absolutist systems can and must give back some power to the desirous beings who have really been the projectors of such exalted centers. He even tries to underwrite this analysis with a newly mature sense of why history must move in this nontyrannical direction, given persistent drives toward change in the human desires that have generated tyrannies. As a result, now approaching the last few years (1820–1822) of his abruptly ended life, Shelley has to confront the nature of what is eternal within temporality. He must return to one of the principal questions (the problem of the "infinite") with which he began and strive to redefine the eternal in ways that prevent what is permanent from again being viewed as an all-controlling Unity that justifies the tyrannies Shelley has resisted. His later and most intricate poems therefore confront, subsume, and attempt to revise older Western visions of the infinite "One" underlying older perceptions of existence, visions that Shelley has often translated and now wishes to undercut with a new form of Oneness freeing humankind from all previous versions. For him, particularly in the works just prior to his drowning, we must be made aware that we in the West are poised between continued submissions to the "One" of tyrannizing centers and new realizations that a "One" of never-ending change may free us, if we accept it, from the oppressions of existing absolutes. It is only as this poet attempts to deal with all these problems, seeking both reasons for and solutions to them, that he passes through different stages of understanding in which transference slowly emerges as the cause and the goal of his quests.

Hence the following chapters will analyze Shelley's writing by proceeding chronologically through these stages of awareness. At each point in his career—a career in which he was constantly revising himself, just as transference demands—I will analyze the works that focus on the dominant problems that he felt he must solve during that brief span of time, and I will show how each quandary, when he writes persistently about it, turns out to be veiling and subtly revealing the transpositional drive that is its generator, its structuring principle, and its solution. In each case, I will suggest, Shelley draws out from the repressions in previous treatments of the problem (including his own) some aspect or aspects within transference of which he is unaware in his younger days. We shall find that, as he does so, he is also drawn toward a peculiar combination of traditional and rebellious techniques of writing, toward modes of characterizing, image shifts, genre choices, stanza arrangements, rhyme schemes, stances of address, and even political programs, all of which are demanded by the subliminal movement that the poet releases from its earlier sublimations. Indeed, at times I must articulate the different operations and assertions that transference encourages in an individual work mainly by closely analyzing those turns of style and their ways of relating figures in each piece. Transference never speaks as itself, after all, so it must be revealed through what it necessitates in the forms that carry it out.

Admittedly, of course, I can never arrive at a point where Shelley straightforwardly declares transference to be the basis of his efforts. Yet I do see him edging closer and closer to such a moment, even to the point of urging the enactment of transference in daily existence and maintaining that the true, most beneficial "One" is really the movement of transference across and through all existence as perceived. Each stage of his writing leads him, at the very least, to a partial knowledge of a few ways in which transference operates, although the result is often the raising of additional problems prompted by this sense of the primacy of transference. With "Shelley's process" I refer, it turns out, to several activities at once: the "unseen presence" or "motion that produces mind" for this poet; the differentiation and transposing of differences underwriting this motion and carrying it on; the task of revising Western thought that he undertook, thus recovering transference from repression; and the activity of reviving and/or writing process-images and process-poems, each one revising others, his main response to the poetic impulse that prompts the will to write and demands that every figure (or work) alter the ones before it. "The development of his major works" in such a context, meanwhile, points to the various progressions that Shelley had to follow, given his "developing" sense of primordial process. In that phrase I conflate the sequence of thinking and revising that generates each of his endeavors, the disruptive leaps and crossings in the actual works or his career, and the deferral of figures to other points necessitating later works that reorient their predecessors.

Finally, however, it is most important that readers be made aware of the transference driving Shelley's work, not just because that process explains his key concepts, procedures, and revisions of other writers, but because it is the very essence—precisely by not being an essence—of his compelling moral vision and the way it gradually redefines human being and human society. We value or should value Shelley today, beyond just admiring the beauty, learning, and intricacy in his ever-shifting verse, for how often he reveals and breaks open the rigid systems of self-assessment and social hierarchy that continue to restrict the potentials of men and women. As he works to undermine the verbal methods of production that strive to maintain those repressive orders in the face of incipient tendencies toward different modes of relation, he uncovers the deeper, more mobile logic that has been forgotten in the older systems (which themselves depend upon it) and releases that movement into verbal activity so that our minds can be reoriented toward the personal freedom to change and the sense of equality among differences generated by truly relational thinking. If this book on Shelley achieves nothing else, I hope it shows how the poet develops that method of thought in his writing, how his works encourage it on their own by presenting the transition from hierarchical distinction to the seeing of the self in terms of others, and on what basis the reader of Shelley can recover that way of seeing from his or her own methods of repressing it, some imposed "from within" and some by other people. Shelley himself had few doubts about the nature of this sublime state of mind or about the fact that great poetry could prompt it by opening out the psyche of poet and reader alike. "Poetry," he proclaims in the *Defence,* "enlarges the circumference of the imagination by replenishing it with thoughts of ever new delight, which have the power of attracting and assimilating to their nature all other thoughts, and which form new intervals and interstices whose void forever craves fresh food" (*NCE,* p. 488). Shelley's work is successful poetry, in other words, because it explodes the most established, conventional thought-relations into interconnections with others that were rarely thought to be analogous before. That disruption prepares the psyche, first to accept all possible relations between transferred thoughts seen as genuine equals and then to defer to what the self and others have yet to think and have yet to become in an equal interplay with one another. Only if poetry can achieve that end can it really be the opening that Shelley saw in Dante toward the different interpretations of its words that different future interpreters can add from the perspectives of their own ages. Indeed, now is the time—and now we have the "peculiar relations" or interpretive vocabularies—to adopt a mode of reading and reworking Shelley that really grants him the response he sought throughout his writing career. By understanding, as even Shelley could not quite, the "unapprehended manner, beyond and above consciousness" that is the poetic impulse (*Defence,* p. 486), we can be initiated into the "going out of ourselves" that he wanted for all beings and can then start to promote the social order of nonviolent equalizaton that he could vividly project beyond his moment but never lived to behold.

1

Early Attachments:
From the "Gothic Sensibility"
to "Natural Piety" and *Alastor*

A Quest for Substitutes

The adolescent Shelley finds it relatively easy to dethrone a kingly God from the center of thought's universe, even to the point of leaving perceived existence no ruling center at all. He cannot, however, do without an "actuating principle greater than man" (*L,* I, 35). The "*term* 'superior' is bad" for describing a primal cause in his eyes, because it enthrones "horrible" absolutes under which whole nations can be enslaved. But he is inclined to "let the word 'perfect' . . . be offered as a substitute," nevertheless, if only so that desire may have an object and "each who aspires may indulge an hope of arriving" at such a level (*L,* I, 72). As a result, he will not abandon for several years his sense that a "Soul of the Universe" is drawing us toward a "future state" that is *"infinite in extent"* and "eternal in duration," at least in comparison with the world that we know (I, 35). He even admits how guilty he is of leaping the same logical gaps that he sees believers concealing from themselves in *The Necessity of Atheism.* He confesses his "future world" to be no more than an ardent "wish"—"O! that it were"—forcing him beyond reason toward a "sceptic's" interest in the possibility of "God" and "Eternity" (*L,* I, 44). Indeed, he is divided within himself on these very notions, wriring "wd. that I cd. believe them to be as [they] are represented" *and* "wd. that I cd. totally disbelieve them" in the same letter (I, 44). He is driven in both directions against any other inclinations, usually by an inexplicable "variability" in his "feelings" (I, 43–44). This variability is so overwhelming that he must "shudder when I reflect how much I am in its power," and so he must finally argue even against his friend and co-author T. J. Hogg, who at the time absolutely "disbelieve[s] the existence of an eternal omnipresent spirit" (I, 44). Something impels Shelley to want, and even to prove, an energy driving the present toward a more complete and satisfying future. Yet the same changeable impetus makes him question that very projection and wonder at his need to believe what he can never fully accept.

This problem persists throughout Shelley's early writing from 1810 to 1815, particularly in the way he keeps dancing across different conceptions of the "actuating principle." During these years the poet feels a need to replace the sanctioned center of being he categorically rejects, so his thought shifts rapidly between several tempting, albeit questionable, substitutes for the orthodox Christian system. Each alternative scheme, once explored, drives him back to feeling that belief is but desire and that the desire is relentless. The young Shelley finds himself swept into these proposals by the peculiar turns in their logics only to encounter conceptual difficulties in each scheme that appear dictated somehow by the ways in which each logic develops. As he keeps struggling, he also finds that the "variability," which keeps coming upon him unawares in his work with each substitute-system, forces him to turn every time from one scheme toward the next. "Why all this?" he asks himself and Elizabeth Hitchener just after he writes to her about his latest speculations on God; only the "power which ma[kes] me a scribbler," he decides, really "knows" the answer to that question (*L,* I, 101). Though reason may dictate, he tells her later, "that death is the boundary of the life of man," still "I feel, I believe the direct contrary" because "an inward sense [has made me] digress," has made "one reasoning lead to another" and thus to "a chain of endless considerations" (*L,* I, 150). He feels drawn into each system, then out of it and into something very different, as though he were commanded by a drive in each way of seeing, the drive making him write, to which no one way is completely adequate. That "inward" power is a mystery to him at least until 1815, when the movement most common to all his early orders of belief starts to emerge in an awareness that urges still another way of depicting the desire for an essence. Consequently, I want to begin my portrait of Shelley's development with a look at the principal belief systems in these early endeavors. By showing how those schemes are constituted and how they are undermined by interplays that no one has yet revealed in them, I want to trace the emergence, at least into this poet's semi-conscious understanding, of the transfer process that all of them share without ever announcing the fact. In that way I can show how this emergence launches Shelley's mature career, especially when he confronts what he has discovered by writing *Alastor* in 1815.

The Gothic Dichotomy and the Deistic Answer

The first mode of thinking that urges Shelley to both desire and symbolize an unorthodox perfection is the one Donald Reiman calls the "Gothic sensibility,"[1] one of the teen-age poet's ways of interpreting existence that the older Shelley can never quite forget. This mode of perception gains its special features from the ways the young Shelley's early responses to frustration have been transfigured by his favorite authors, by the Matthew Lewis of *The Monk* and the *Tales of Terror and Wonder,* the Charlotte Dacre of *Zofloya,* the Thomas Moore of *Irish Melodies,* the Robert Southey of *Thalaba the Destroyer* and *The Curse of Kehama,* the Shakespeare of *Macbeth,* the Walter Scott of *Marmion,* the Coleridge of the "Ancient Mariner," the Sophocles of *Antigone,* the Alexander Pope of *Eloisa to Abelard,* and the John Milton of the first two books in *Paradise Lost.*[2] The resulting world-view suggests that our empirical impressions reveal, in whatever they take to be their "objects," vestiges and ruins from which former "truths" and fulfillments are continually receding even as we gaze. In the words of the Shelley poems in what is now termed *The Esdaile Notebook* (1809–

1813), any "boon to Fancy given" is "Retracted while 'tis granted" (*S&C,* II, 1002). Our psyches initially find themselves "exiled from happiness" in a "pitchy darkness" that makes each of us seem "the hapless victim of unmerited persecution" (*CW,* V, 5–6). That is the opening situation, not just of Pope's Eloise or Milton's Satan, but of the hero, Verezzi, in the first words of Shelley's Gothic novel *Zastrozzi* (1810). This sense of a Primal Fall may look back to a divorce from the womb, a rebellion against the Father, or an early rejection by peers or superiors.[3] It may also come from the more general throwing of awareness into temporality or from Locke's sense that every perception becomes a gravelike memorial for some lost and distant beginning.[4] In any case, "Everything [is] denied [in] the darkness [save] thought" (*Zastrozzi, CW,* V, 6–7)—the objects of our perceptions speak only of a "mysterious removal" from something else (V, 1)—so the need to interpret what gives us only reminders leads us to "comparing the present with the past" and then to addressing "a prayer to [a] Creator" amid the "violent thunderstorm" of a constant movement away from any clear Origin (V, 7–8).[5]

In this view we automatically revert to the implied contrary of the destructive change confronting us, and, as we project this supposed fullness into our memories to produce an absolute contrast to our current lack, we "elevate" our "thoughts" above the "terrestrial" dissolution to a permanent Elsewhere against which "our sufferings [can now sink] into nothing on the comparison" (V, 7–8). Bolstered perhaps by a sense that the "coming of death" also retains a "taper of [withdrawn] life" (*Esdaile Notebook, S&C,* II, 968), we simply make light, timelessness, and a Creator rise up and stand over against darkness, time, and decreation. The former become what may once have been and what may appear again after the violent passage of a transitional stage. From that point on, the "Gothic" psyche hopes, according to a song included in *St. Irvyne* (Shelley's second Gothic novel of 1810), that morning can "dawn on the night of the grave," that "summer [must] succeed to the winter of Death," and that "Eternity points in its amaranth bower" an "Unspeakable pleasure, of goodness the dower, / When woe fades away like the mist of the heath" (*CW,* V, 173). These "structures" are "willed into being by ourselves to withstand the threat of . . . vacancy," and we are thus "goaded into speech by the power of silence, just as the energies of life are not necessarily the well-springs of being but may sustain themselves secondarily" as an image veering away from a continual disappearance.[6]

Very soon, though, this conception leads the young Shelley into hesitating quandaries rather than hopeful assertions. To say finally that "light from Darkness" (or "peace from desolation") just "Bursts unresisted" (*Esdaile Notebook, S&C,* II, 928) is to accept too easily a binary opposition that can move in more than one direction. Such a dichotomy can claim to produce a gleaming difference from the sameness of dissolution. But it can also govern such early Shelley lyrics as "Dark Spirit of the desert rude" (*S&C,* II, 966–68), where the speaker's urge to penetrate into the "murky form" behind and beyond "Nature's unreviving tomb" of "centuries gone" thrusts him into the sheer dissolution he tries to escape, into a vision of one "desolate Oak" draining "all sap" out of the world and still somehow decaying "upon the spoil" that is its food (ll. 20, 27, 29, 35, and 46, italics removed). The turn away from the death trailing each perception can easily turn back in despair and collapse into the abyss it so thoroughly accepts as the basic ground of our being. In addition, we may conceptualize "virtue & vice" or "light & darkness" as "separate" and "distinct," writes Shelley in 1811, but when we attempt an "analysis of our own thoughts" using these concepts we discover that each side can be manifested only by a sliding toward its opposite. We find each term to be both unattainable by the other and unable to remain separate from its counterpart. "Perfect virtue" must come to be seen as a "phantom" held out and denied by the pull of its antithesis, and the mind in general must therefore be configured as "a picture of irreconcilable inconsistencies," prevented when it sees this fact from believing in its own "anticipation and retrospection of happiness" (*L*, I, 109). Indeed, anticipation and retrospection, always at work concurrently, offer us two scenarios for projecting the course of thought, neither of which is compatible with the other yet both of which can occur at any time. We can say to ourselves, on the one hand, because we felt love for another person at a time and in circumstances different from the current ones, that "*she* whom you adore" in the present also "resides in another existence" and that "you shall live there [at least in hopes], rendering and rendered happy" (*L*, I, 104). On the other hand, "retrospection," usually arising "unheeded," generally reminds us that its remembered object is lost forever (particularly in the case of a former lover) as soon as that reference point is recalled from a perspective that is distant from the object's former location. "Anticipation," in reply, can see the same distance, or rather a future version of the same loss, opening ahead of itself. It can thus know that its projected fulfillment is merely the result of replacing an older image of an absence with yet another distance between desire and object. "Ideas," it appears, simply "depart to make way for others," all of whose referents "we cannot [ever] reach" (I, 104). The later images have to "roll on" in search of further ones to carry them through, ones that are just as insufficient and anticipatory as they are. "Still, still will they urge their course, 'till Death closes all" without permitting any of them to attain a fulfilling end (I, 104).

Nearly endless regressions or ever-deluded hopes: these are the fruits of devotion to the Gothic sensibility—unless there is some way in which the production of similarity from difference and vice-versa can extend itself without mere repetition, without one becoming the other in the same way over and over. Perhaps we can first accept the discontinuity of temporal moments, the radical difference in states of being between the "now" and the *"eternity"* that is "before & after" the present moment (*L*, I, 110). Then we can note what is altered and yet partially repeated as perception moves from one of these states toward the other. Let us follow, for example, an observed "acorn" as "it modifies the particles of earth air & water by infinitesimal division so as to produce an oak" and then as it vanishes while the "oak moulders in putrefaction" and apparently "ceases to be what it is" (I, 110). Nothing here remains the same or unmodified by anything else or untouched by some measure of death. Still, as we observe the bridging of these discontinuities, we feel a "consciousness of identity," and we thereupon hypothesize a *"vegetative principle,"* a "soul of animated existence," to name the "power which makes [that acorn] be this oak" and drives on to the later stages in this process of "continual change" (I, 110). From the moment the human soul "bears the mark" of its "impressions," after all, it is drawn back through them to what they seem to trace, as well as ahead to their recombination. Such impressions must inevitably be seen as "causal or intended" by something (*L*, I, 136), and so the soul must assume an "unknown cause which produces [every] observable effect" (*L*, I, 100). Even the "soul" itself must seem to come about "subsequent to [its own] transfusion" from another place (I, 136) and to be itself the "unknown cause" of any visible "intelligence & bodily animation" (I, 100). Moreover, "as the soul of man [is] to his body," so an equivalent but larger "vegetative power"

must be to the perceivable "universe" (I, 100–101). It may or may not be a personi-
fiable God, but we are inevitably drawn, by analogy at least, to belief in an *"existing
power of existence"* (I, 101), a *natura naturans*. Once this projection is installed within
our sense of natural transitions between different moments of time, we can see this
force as "consisting of constituent parts infinitely divisible" so that "nothing can be
annihilated" entirely, only changed from some other natural state (I, 110). In a "future
existence" any "soul," will, like the acorn, "lose all consciousness of having formerly
lived elsewhere but will also begin life anew, possibly under a shape of which we now
have no idea" (I, 110). Maybe this kind of deferred possibility, repeating yet transub-
stantiating earthly life without regression to the opposite of life, can be that "amaranth
bower" of greater "goodness" for which "eternity" seems to provide a "point" and a
"power" moving elements in that direction. The Gothic sensibility by 1811 has been
rearticulated by Shelley as a kind of deism. The turnings from darkness into light or
declines into transformation are no longer abrupt reversals for the sake of defensive
opposition and hope. They are the ever-progressive and gradually fulfilling extensions
of what could even be called an "intelligent" Soul (*L*, I, 35). That Soul is there primally, instead of the Gothic vacancy, urging distinctions and repetitions to pass
beyond wherever they are.

This, then, is probably the meaning for Shelley of the "generative power" projected
by thought in *The Necessity of Atheism*. The ancestry of this notion, however, is quite
a strange mixture, as Shelley reveals in one of the letters to Hogg written early in 1811:

> I have an idea, I think I can prove the existence of a Deity. A first cause—I will ask
> a materialist how came this universe at first. He will answer by chance.—What
> chance? I will answer in the words of Spinoza—'An *infinite* number of atoms had
> been [falling floating *canceled*] *from* all eternity in space, till at last one of them
> fortuitously diverged from its track which dragging with it another formed the prin-
> ciple of Gravitation & in consequence the universe'—What cause produced this
> change, this chance? Surely some, for where do we know that causes arise without
> their correspondent effects; at least we must here, in so abstract a subject reason
> analogically. Was not this then a *cause,* was it not a *first* cause.—was not this first
> cause a Deity[?] . . . [Of course] our ideas of infinite space &c are scarcely to be
> called ideas for we cannot either comprehend or explain them; therefore Deity must
> be judged by us from attributes analogical to our situation. Oh! that this Deity were
> the Soul of the Universe, the spirit of universal imperishable love. (*L*, I, 44–45)

Here Shelley is quoting (either from faulty memory or hearsay) Spinoza's critique of
atomic materialism, which appears most frequently in the *Letters* published in the
Opera Posthuma (1677).[7] But the young poet also begins his own retort by thoroughly
recalling the materialist text that this version of Spinoza rephrases: Book II, lines 216–
309, of *De rerum natura* by Lucretius. After reading *De rerum* initially at Eton, Shelley
has become fascinated by the way Lucretius counters the Christian (and Gothic) idea
that a "divine power" is able to "produce" everything out of "nothing."[8] He is
attracted to the view that Lucretius reworks from Democritus and Epicurus, to the
beginning of time as a sheer rainfall of material and "constituent parts." These produce no more than a decline—a Dionysian welter instead of just nothing—until one
or more particles are turned toward others in the *clinamen* or swerve that produces a
relation of drops out of a chaotic "floating." After this basic inclining-toward-another
occurs, further elements are dragged along to gravitate into orderly and interacting
compositions. Separate globules thus form worlds, visible bodies, objects, minds, and

partitioned civilizations, much in the way (perhaps *because* of the way) the "many letters" of a poem, as Lucretius says himself, are distributed into the combinations, the "different verses and words," that make up the final text.[9] These orders are held together by their relational pull until other such inclinations draw the parts away from their current state, whereupon the dissolution of the fall reasserts itself in the death of objects or people, and the process repeats itself differently by swerving its loose atoms into radically new forms of life.

The uncaused "divergence" behind all these stages, to be sure, must imply an origin existing behind it in Spinoza's view and thus in the young Shelley's as well. Spinoza slightly resembles Lucretius and anticipates Shelley's "On Life" in believing that all ideas about the perceived world interpret or recombine previous ideas (or previous atomic compositions).[10] Everything we observe is therefore caused for Spinoza in the way a geometric figure (one sort of idea) results from a geometric rule for construction (another sort of idea). All creations come from an eternal generative principle both like and unlike—hence "analogical" to—the visible realm before us. There can be no understanding of the effect, in other words, unless there is an understanding of the related cause. On top of that, since the cause of an idea must also be a caused idea, the future of analysis is an infinite regress for Spinoza and Shelley unless they can name a first cause that also causes itself, the "essence" of which, when "represented" in thought, can appear as "the Immanent cause" of all our ideas.[11] We must posit no merely relational notion setting all things to work by its chance deviation, for that "effect," in Shelley's words, must recall some "power" that actuates this power of swerving; "there must [even] be *something* beyond [the] actuating principle [that] influences *its* actions [too,] and all this series advancing as if it does in one instance, it *must* to infinity, must at last terminate, if it *can* terminate[,] in the existence which may be called a Deity" (*L*, I, 39).

Yet Spinoza would resist many things even in this statement. First Shelley extends the Spinozan use of analogy into myriad principles leading to other principles ("*all this series*"), and then he adds a penchant for conditional phrases that hope that "this Deity [might be] the Soul of the Universe" now that analogy has projected such a figure to be the end—and thus the beginning—of the series. These tendencies echo Hume's critiques of religion, especially his skeptical understanding of the human desire for an "Author of Nature."[12] Consequently, where Spinoza would describe human "intellect" as analogous to a preexisting attribute of God, Shelley sees thought explicitly thrusting its own process retroactively into the unknown extent of what its impressions recall. In such a process, Hume insists, *"the cause or causes of order in the Universe probably bear some remote analogy to human intelligence,"* and that is all we can say. We must admit the remoteness by noting how an unbridgeable infinity opens behind each of our thoughts, and after that we must still try to bridge that span, confessing this effort to be no more than analogy's desire, by supposing that the span's most distant point is both similar to and different from our own "situation."

Almost at once, then, as we might expect, this conflicting ancestry helps to bring down Shelley's deism. In the early months of 1811, he is indeed convinced by Hume and others that he must "ardently wish" to believe in an anthropomorphic "spirit" (*L*, I, 44), an "intelligent & *necessarily* beneficent actuating principle" that allows the young poet to be a synecdoche for a "vast intellect" and to hope for a "love *infinite in extent*" that might one day replace a world of "perjured affections" (*L*, I, 35). But this metonymic thinking is not completely analogical, since it emphasizes the difference in extent between two levels more than the similarities connecting the larger to the smaller. By the summer Shelley sees that fact and, echoing part of his logic in *The Necessity of Atheism,* finds deistic "personification" to be the leaping of a chasm by "Imagination" based on the illusion, "inadmissible to reason," that the notion of a human soul "*must* to infinity [sic]" in one easy move from the finite (*L,* I, 101). Now, to pursue Humean analogies without being so "remote," he turns back toward Spinoza by asking our need for causes to be satisfied by an "essence" that does not transcend the perceivable "universe" in any way (I, 101). The "unknown cause" may perhaps be the process of the perceived universe itself, "the *existing power of existence,*" or at most an "animative intellect" developing "in a constant rotation of change" through and within a semi-Lucretian "mass of organized animation" (I, 193).

Shelley completes this argument in *A Refutation of Deism* (1813), a debate modeled on several in Cicero, Berkeley, and Drummond, not to mention Spinoza and Hume themselves. In contrast to most of its predecessors, this colloquy tries to make one position triumph over another to the point of revealing discrepancies in *all* arguments (including the victor's) for any sort of anthropomorphic God at one with Himself. Setting "Eusebes" (named after the ancient Christian chronographer Eusebius), an orthodox Christian dependent on divine revelation for knowledge of the Great Cause, against "Theosophus" ("theo-sophist"), a typical (not Shelleyan) deist believing in a transcendent Designer who can be argued from the human sense of universal design, Shelley gives the apparent victory to the former for asserting that inferred "causes" must be "exactly adequate to [their] effects" in a logic without gaps (*CW,* VI, 48). For Eusebes even the"Intelligence" attributed by Spinoza *and* Hume to a Deity is an unjustified, forced raising of Lockean "sensation and perception" toward the level of a suprahuman analogue (VI, 55). Whether we focus on relations among our separate perceptions or examine the interactions of elements in the "world" we form out of those impressions, we must revert, Eusebes claims, to a view of the "laws" or "properties" behind "known effects" that sees such "causes" for what they really are: analogical projections into the past from interplays between differences once the differences have been drawn toward other ones (as in thoughts interpreting thoughts).

Only one prior motion can be "adequate" (strictly analogous) to this relational activity, barring the revelation of a level completely outside thought's reflection on itself. That motion must be a Lucretian impulsion toward "rotation" and relationship, and it is this sheer "turning" from one position toward another that must be seen as the nontranscendent *natura naturans* and "animative intellect" making human intellect possible. Shelley therefore has Eusebes allude to the *Système du monde* of the Marquis de la Place, one of the young poet's many readings in applied and theoretical science. There the "notions of heavenly bodies" are perceived as perpetually "corrected by that gravitation" driving all movements of bodies near and away from the other ones around them. The planets, at least as observed, are repositioned by a centerless drawing of inclinations toward each other in a "secular equation" that determines the configuration among the bodies without needing a God or a governing center to do so (*CW,* VI, 49). The same "causality" turns out to be operating, moreover, when we look at how we arrive at our senses of "order and disorder" or "good and evil" every time thoughts are interpreted by other thoughts. As Godwin has suggested,[13] such notions codify the "relations which [seem to] persist between ourselves and external objects" as these relations rotate toward another set of interplays, "our perceptions [from experience] of what is injurious or beneficial to ourselves" (VI, 52).

"Exclude the [nonmonolithic] idea of relation" in analyzing thought and the natural laws it projects, says Eusebes, and the "words good and evil are deprived of import" entirely (VI, 53). The Gothic sense of "good" springing forth in sheer counterpoise to "evil" now returns to some extent, yet only as it is joined to one source of Shelley's deism—the Lucretian *clinamen*—and only as that source reemerges from all repressions of it at last to undermine the deistic logic it once was forced to serve. Oppositions, in fact all relationships, have rediscovered their basis in Lucretian inclinations of attraction and repulsion developing out of differences that keep reorienting themselves in reaction to one another. From these "various combinations of [the] elements of thought," Eusebes concludes, all "our feelings, opinions and volitions, inevitably result" (VI, 56).

From "Power" to "Necessity"

Yet Shelley, even through Eusebes, cannot assert such foundations in 1812 and 1813 unless he backs them up with more centered conceptions, ones that seem to ground the *clinamen* in a motivation without restoring a transcendent being. As a result, he proposes some single-word foundations, again by interweaving different texts, and again these "grounds" half-succeed and half-fail in their efforts to occupy the place of a nontheistic Absolute. One such notion is "Power," already a favorite word for the young Shelley, which he now defines precisely in the *Refutation* in the hope of avoiding its most established meaning (the creative might of a supermundane Master). On the one hand, this term simply names a Spinozan form of productivity, "the capability of anything to be or act" or interplay with other things. As Spinoza himself might have put it, it is an "attribute of existing substance," something *in* what we observe that makes the parts arise and move, never an external cause bringing the world about. On the other hand, in Eusebes' words the "human mind never hesitates to *annex* the idea of power to any object of its experience" (my emphasis). "Power" is an appendage added to moving appearances by our own interpretation of their motion, so much so that Power at times can seem both "the cause and the effect" of what substance apparently does (*CW*, VI, 55).

Shelley, by his own admission in a footnote to the *Refutation* (VI, 55n.), has forced Eusebes to shift his orientation toward Drummond's *Academical Questions* (1805), first read by Shelley in 1812 at the suggestion of Thomas Love Peacock. Drummond offers a way of linking Humean empiricism and Lucretian concatenation, especially when he sees former perceptions and associations among them as turning into our dominant "trains of ideas"; "the ideas of each separate train," he writes, "may not improperly be compared to a number of moving bodies, which communicate motion to each other in consequence of one original impulse, and continue [so] to proceed."[14] The "communication" between memories and the "impulse" behind it for Drummond, however, are not facts that the mind intuits but hypotheses that reflective thinking is inclined to declare. We suppose even motion in thought only because we are faced with a slight "mutation," he says, in which seemingly "equal ideas are displaced and replaced by each other." Because of that unwilled slippage, our recollections of "any train of ideas" often perceive a "broken link in the chain, which [we] desire to fill up" each time it appears. If the same succession lacking clear transitions recurs frequently enough in the same manner, we "suppose" a force, an "illusion of the mind," which "may or does produce [the] change" that we cannot account for by any other means. Such a force must not be either a transcendent Being or a Spinozan first cause. Once we decide to assume this Power (and Drummond is dubious about whether we should), then we must find "that a new power is exerted, as often, and as constantly, as one idea succeeds another." There may be just a self-renewing, mutating activity becoming a "communication" between different moments of thinking, the first impetus of which may be no more than an impulse toward mutation (a *clinamen*) that has never remained identical with itself even though it has often been reenacted. By paraphrasing this view, then, Shelley has certainly located "an attribute of substance" that renders a creative God "superfluous" (*CW,* VI, 55). At the same time, though, he has gravitated toward an "occult operation" (Drummond's phrase) that is really no more than the transfiguration and concealment (the self-occulting) of successive thoughts by each other.[15] He has then translated that Godless activity into an invisible causality and placed it in the intervals between thoughts to serve as the drive from one idea to the next.

This highly particularized and self-altering universal, however, is too unstable for the Shelley of 1812 and 1813, a Shelley who makes Eusebes quote Isaac Newton's attack on any *"hypotheses"* that try to propose a *"qualitatum occultarum"* in what we observe (*CW,* VI, 49). The twenty-year-old poet prefers "Necessity," another non-theistic essence that attracts him at this time, possibly because it offers a totalized (hence Newtonian) "system of the universe" where "laws of motion" and "properties of matter" are all the "unknown causes of known effects" that we need (VI, 48). After all, this concept appears to surpass "Power's" ability to combine the attractions of skeptical empiricism with those of a Lucretian semi-materialism. In his notes to *Queen Mab* (1812–1813), the ambitious early poem that makes "necessity" the "all-sufficing Power" and the "Soul of the Universe" (VI, 197 and 190), Shelley defines it by virtually quoting Hume's *Enquiry Concerning Human Understanding* (1748) and gathering further support from Godwin's *Enquiry Concerning Political Justice* (1793).[16] He therefore sees the "idea of necessity," of "an immense and uninterrupted chain of causes and effects" in the "universe," as produced by "our experience of the connection between objects, and uniformity of the operations of nature, the constant conjunction of similar events, and the consequent inference of one from the other" (*PW,* p. 809). The vestiges of our "impressions," it would seem, can be projected as "objects" causing and caused by others, yet only as a gradual ordering of memories develops whereby each former perception finds its place in a pattern of relations and repetitions. The "marks" of perception must first appear to be relatable, then visibly similar and repeatedly so, then "conjoined" by their resemblance or their recurrence in a certain sequence, and then inclined to refer to one another immediately, so much so that each is always crossing toward certain "effects" that seem to follow from it. After this last step the mind accepts a belief in an "uninterrupted chain," yet only as the result of a sort of writing process, a mental sequence of remembering, lettering, collating, coordinating, and revising.

This composing of parts manifestly resembles the Lucretian turning of material globules (or letters) toward swirls of conjoined associations. Shelley therefore endorses the analogy at once and sets up a sort of atomic composition as the process by which Necessity generates the world as it is. By the time of *Mab,* in fact, the Lucretian scheme has been partially transmuted by Shelley's further reading to become the *"transmigration, change,* [and] *circulation"* of "matter" that brings about both nature and thought in the Baron d'Holbach's *Système de la nature* (1770).[17] Thus Shelley writes in Book VI of *Mab* that every "atom" rolls in a universal "turbulence" and therefore drives toward connections with others in the "storm of change" we always perceive; only in that way, he claims, does existence reveal an "irresistible law" (Necessity) that works out the "place" of "each spring" in the total "machine" of life (II, 171, 160, and 163–64). Meanwhile, this atomism has also been attracted beyond Holbach toward the Leibnizian theory of "microbes" or "monads" probably transmitted to Shelley indirectly by Drummond and Lord Monboddo.[18] Nature in this ancillary system is an "interminable wilderness / Of worlds" (*Mab*, I. 265–66), some of them small, some vast, all containing or serving others, and all made from "the minutest atom" that is also a "world" in itself (IV. 145–46). This near-total similarity between parts and wholes means that "Every grain" is as "sentient" as the human psyches it forms; "And the minutest atom [therefore] comprehends / A world of loves and hatreds" in its attractions and repulsions, whence spring "Evil and good" and "all the germs / Of pain or pleasure, sympathy or hate, / That variegate the eternal universe" (IV. 145–50). Shelley can now say, again prompted by his drive to forge analogies between the movement of thought and the apparent process behind the influx of impressions, that "Soul is the only element" (IV. 140), that the human spirit is "guided" by a "universal Spirit" as is "the minutest molecule" (VI. 174–77), and that this Spirit, the energy in each of its material "germs," ensures an "unchanging harmony" of interconnections (II, 257) as it "press[es] forward" toward a fulfillment of this ordering tendency (VI. 236). Shelley thereby ascends, as he does in an earlier letter (*L*, I, 35), to a belief in the "one stupendous whole" of Pope's 1733 *Essay on Man* (specifically Epistle I, l. 267),[19] replacing Pope's "God" as "the soul" of this "undivided" system (Epistle I, ll. 268 and 274) with something like the transmigrating *"Ens,"* the essential, nonhuman, reproductive fecundity, a sort of *Eros,* proposed by Erasmus Darwin (grandfather of Charles).[20] The late adolescent writer, refusing any hypothesis that is not "all-sufficing," hence maintains that he knows why the mind must "be considered as the effect, rather than the cause of motion" (*Refutation, CW,* VI, 56). He has taken his mental production of a causal "chain" and projected it into the "infinite orbs" of an outside existence. There he has consequently found a causal filament, "A Spirit of activity and life," inhabiting and motivating every movement and element, serving as their "mother," their "eternal spring / Of life and death," provided we assume that this mother is far more a process than an anthropomorphic being (*Mab*, VI. 146, 148, 198, and 190–91)."All that the wide world contains," including minds, "Are but thy passive instruments," cries Mab to this Spirit, "and thou / Regardest them all with an impartial eye . . . Because thou hast not human sense, / Because thou art not human mind" (VI. 214–19).

But of course Shelley soon abandons many aspects of this position—and only partly in response to the blatant inconsistencies that arise from his shuttling across such different vocabularies. He has tried to satisfy the need in thinking for some cause of its shifting patterns, again projecting as a metaphoric "outside" what only an "inside" can generate from its own operations. What he confronts, however, is a construct that is at once far too "outside" and not outside enough. In one sense Necessity is a return to a deism more dualistic and tyrannizing than the one embraced by the younger Shelley. The "eternal spring," so that it can seem free from the "caprice / Of man's weak will" that projects a frighteningly human "God" of "slaves" (*Mab,* VI. 200–201, 199, and 203), becomes a pitiless commanding "Soul" that has "not human sense" nor human patterns of thought, that is not really analogous to thought at all except in its vaguely all-powerful "sentience." True, Shelley does make an effort both to use and to escape Holbachian materialism by implanting a Darwinian-Berkeleyan "spirit" in atoms that impels their concatenation. Yet perception in this construct is still activated ("caused" or "intended") by the movements that matter makes. Even Eusebes must see the mind as the passive "recipient," in fact the slave, "of impressions [imposed by] the action of external objects" that move toward us because of "properties" divorced from human cognition (*Refutation, CW,* VI, 56 and 49). Shelley must now join Godwin, though not Hume this time, in saying that acts and instructions forced upon us from without determine our moral decisions absolutely. To quote Godwin's version,the mind must be "in no case a first cause," because "the most powerful impression [from elsewhere] constantly gets the better of its competitors, and forcibly drives out the preceding thought, till it is in the same irresistible manner driven out by its successor."[21] *Queen Mab,* as a result, can never release Necessity from these autocratic dictates, even when it makes each atom into a "world" of already human passions. In that image, "loves and hatreds" are automatic material reflexes preceding and engendering what we know as human feeling. Indeed, they encourage our thinking to accept as inevitable (though temporary) the cruel tyrannies that keep us from beholding Necessity as it really is. We may (as Shelley most clearly does in *Mab,* I. 130–38) imagine an atom or a human soul starting out as "beams / Of heaven's pure orb, ere round their rapid lines / The taint of earth-born atmospheres arise" (IV. 151–53). Even so, the almost instantaneous surrounding of any purity by something that denies it is here a part of the genetic "mechanism" of everything, a new explanation for the Gothic oscillation between light and darkness. Good and evil interact whatever we will ourselves to do, even though our willed actions parallel and come from this necessary conflict going on outside us. Much as Shelley's note on Necessity avers that nothing exists but as it is perceived, *Mab* consistently makes thought and existence separate entities with the latter controlling the former, so much so that the "gradual paths of aspiring change" achieved by the "properties" of existence (IX. 148) have almost no need of their apparent vassals, the "thoughts that rise / In time-destroying swiftness . . . still from hope to hope the bliss pursuing" (VIII. 205–206 and 203).

In another sense, however, Necessity is not sufficiently "made other," not distanced enough from the associative thinking that projects it beyond thought in Shelley's note. As it stands, Necessity seems an aftereffect, a projection of a causal mechanism out of a gradual composing of thoughts that turns its own procedures into a foundation. It does not give figural form to what engenders the *desire* for causes in the Gothic or deistic mind, the feeling that an "impression" keeps losing what it recalls the more it is reformed as a "mark" *and* the sense that any reference point for an impression is itself a trace (a sensing of something) from which any ultimate foundation has already been withdrawn. *Queen Mab* actually offers many ways of stopping this continual regress inherent in any perception. An impression in that poem may not carry its supposed referent with it, but the object to which it comes to refer does contain the productive Spirit that impels the object toward transformation and perception. An object has "properties" in this piece, we must remember, essential inclinations that are self-possessed within their own boundaries, else Shelley could not say that objective "circumstances," because of their own "causes," must "produce the same invariable effects on minds" as long as material conditions do not change ("Notes on *Queen Mab," PW*, p. 810). Yet Shelley's earlier description in the *Letters* of what impressions indicate still breaks through in some of his fairy queen's arguments. When she explicitly asserts that the orthodox sense of God must be replaced by a vision of "every part depending on the chain / That links it to the whole" (VII. 17–18), she justifies that statement by showing how "every seed that falls" must "unfold" an "infinity within" as well as an "Infinity without" (VII. 19–22), an array of linked elements that must always tend back or ahead toward other elements that are already supplements of additional elements. Later, she also makes the grander future promised by Necessity as it "perfects" all "human things" (IX. 134) depend on "crumbling ruins . . . Wakening a lovely echo" (IX. 96–98) and turning into "tongues" that help scatter the old ingredients so that they can be "moulded" into "happier shapes" (IX. 109 and 131–32). Reconstructions, among them the "idea of necessity," are always interpretations of uprooted and partly hollowed-out memorials. Thought, as in the Gothic sensibility, begins with tracing vestiges that initially "mean" the absence of their own foundation. These point to an "other" so withdrawn and unapprehended that it can be no more than dimly renamed in new recastings of the traces it leaves behind. This quandary is probably what makes Shelley end the *Refutation of Deism* with a victory for the faithful Christian who relies on a revelation to come that he cannot achieve himself. Though Eusebes unintentionally reveals moral and political cruelties in the history of the Church he unfolds, there is no quarreling in the end with his hope for a "coming down" that must always be sought behind perceptions and must be regarded (almost Gnostically) as infinitely distant from them. For Shelley at this point, no replacement for standard religion can suffice unless it confronts this initial sense of a primal "dying away."

The Problem of Wordsworth and Coleridge:
Attraction and Repulsion

Here, in fact, lies one of the principal attractions that draws the young Shelley to Wordsworth and Coleridge, his immediate precursors in poetry, first in his reading of them before the writing of *Queen Mab* and then in his intensive return to them after the *Refutation*.[22] The student of these now-established masters says as much himself in his 1815–1816 sonnet "To Wordsworth," where the older poet, having "wept to know / That things depart which never may return," is praised for revealing the impetus behind the writing of verse: the fact that "Childhood and youth, friendship and love's first glow, / Have fled like sweet dreams, leaving [us] all to mourn" (ll. 1–4). Wordsworth has both confirmed and modified the Gothic sensibility by defining the light that fades within our recollections as a withdrawal of remembered moments so gradual, so constant yet so receding, that we must always sense "something far more deeply interfused / Whose dwelling is the light of setting suns" ("Tintern Abbey," ll. 95–96). There is a "natural piety" suggested by the mere process of interpreting former perceptions, by the reading of older thoughts as harking back to several forgotten ones and finally to a concatenation, a vague roar of "mighty waters," on whose "shore" of traces we now seem to stand ("Ode: Intimations of Immortality," ll. 170–71). Indeed, there is no sense of a "setting" region that is also the point of a pouring forth or interfusion unless there have been "fallings from us" or "vanishings" in our awareness and then a looking back through them that turns them into "trailings," either of "clouds of glory" or of an "eternal deep" ("Ode," ll. 147, 64, and 112).[23] Hence Shelley quotes Wordsworth as "the Man" as early as January 1812 (*L,* I, 217) and celebrates the fact that "All outward shews of sky & earth / Of sea & valley" as they are "viewed" are automatically joined by "impulses of deeper birth," just as Wordsworth says himself in "A Poet's Epitaph" (ll. 45–48).

For quite similar reasons Shelley is also drawn to Coleridge's projected "spirits of the air," according to the first line of the 1815 poem "To—" (*PW,* pp. 525–26), the whole of which "is addressed in idea to Coleridge," if we believe Mary Shelley (*PW,* p. 902). To perceive "mountain winds" or "babbling springs," Shelley writes, as speaking the "voice" of "inexplicable things" ("To—," ll. 8–10) is to find, as Coleridge does in a "Lines Written at Shurton Bars," a "France: An Ode," or a "Hymn Before Sunrise,"[24] that we desire in the withdrawals behind our perceptions a point of completion for both our memories and our reflections on them. Given the fact that we are incomplete "trailings" of "vanishings" like our own thoughts and that these "trailings" seem to recall lost maternal points of wholeness or satisfaction, we seek "in starry eyes," be they natural objects or the gazes of other people, "Beams" that seem like motherly "greeting hands" as they recede, like voices, "looks, or lips" that promise somehow to "answer [our] beseeching demands" for a completing Other ("To—," ll. 13–18). We therefore are naturally inclined to pursue "one Life within us and abroad," which is not "one" until our moving desire "meets all motion [toward us and there rejoins] its deeper soul" (Coleridge's "Eolian Harp," ll. 26–27). We are drawn always, as Hume has also said, toward the distant mirror-image behind whatever we seem to behold, "A light in sound, a sound-like power in light" ("Eolian Harp," l. 28), or as Shelley puts it, "gentle ghosts, with eyes as fair / As star-beams among twilight trees" ("To—," ll. 3–4).

Yet Shelley soon rejects the metaphysics and parts of the epistemologies urged on him by such attractive precursors, and that is not just because they so command his language (as Harold Bloom would have it) that he must distort these fathering voices and install his own timbre within their words. Actually, Shelley finds that their special insights into the "receding" and the "coming down" that activate desire draw them too completely toward subordination to the Christian Father by way of that "birthplace" (or mother) that seems to beckon to them from the past. He is not entirely surprised when he and Mary agree that Wordsworth has become "a slave" by the time of *The Excursion* (1814),[25] a supporter of a God-centered Chain of Being upholding Tory hierarchies and the established church. That tendency is already apparent for Shelley in some earlier Wordsworth "Songs" that no longer "consecrate . . . liberty" ("To Wordsworth," l. 12) but turn the "something deeper" into the female conduit of a masculine "presence" that "impels / All thinking" and "objects of thought" as it "rolls through all things" ("Tintern Abbey," ll. 94 and 101–2). Wordsworth, even at his best, halts the regress of remembered perceptions at a "God, who is [the] home" of everything and the origin "whence" the "trailing clouds" come forth and start to "fade" ("Ode: Intimations," ll. 65, 69, and 76). The elder poet in his more skeptical younger days may sometimes admit, as Shelley would, that this theory of *anamnesis* may be a "shadowy" notion too speculative for absolute faith and that it very likely arises from brooding "over the stories of Enoch and Elijah" to the point of hoping that "I should be translated, in something of the same way, to heaven."[26] But Shelley concludes that Wordsworth, as a Christian obsessed with hierarchy, still regards "the fall of Man" as a fact and as an "analogy" favoring our "trailing" from a "home" with a permanent King.

The consequences in Shelley's eyes are damning indeed. In *The Excursion,* "fall" and analogy are so connected that any recent story heard by the poem's narrator is a falling from and yet a reminder of the "solemn tunes" he used to hear as a boy from "accomplished" village bards (VII. 15 and 12). As one "history" recalls another, the "Strains of power" from the earlier "melody" now seem to inundate the memory with an inclination toward "a higher mark than song can reach" (VII. 22–24). The seeing of one figuration as looking back to another with greater force has set up a hierarchy that is then referred even further back to a supposedly greater point approximated by what the bards have left in the memory. Such a "higher mark" is so absolute compared to all the levels recollecting its presence that it ascribes an eternal value, indeed gives the "power," to the "Strains" that seem the closest to its own position. Hence, "when the stream [of remembered 'Strains'] / Which overflowed the soul [of the narrator] was passed away, / A consciousness [always] remained that it had left, / Deposited upon the silent shore / Of memory, images and precious thoughts, / That shall not die" because they have been infused with Eternal Life (VII. 24–30). For Shelley, these reversions of thought almost turn the actual process of memory on its head. When he recalls Wordsworth's "depositing on the shore" in the "traces on the sand" passage of his *Defence,* he emphasizes the dying out of power's "Strains" and even their disappearance behind the "traces" that look back to little more than the trailing off of all that has led into them. Thoughts become "precious" and powerful precisely because earlier ones *do* die to make way for transfigurations, so Wordsworth is wrong to turn our perpetual recollection into the recovery of an Absolute Life behind apparent death. Coleridge, as it happens, is more excusable than Wordsworth (at least to the Shelley of 1814 and 1815) because the former's religiosity never rests as much on this deliberate fixing and centering of a "spirit" that Wordsworth has described as mobile and retreating.

Coleridge's problems for Shelley stem more from innocent but mistaken longings, the ones the younger poet must finally attack as too often his own in *Alastor.* Coleridge has placed his "genii of the evening breeze" and his "one Life abroad" where some ancient mythologies have: in "natural scenes" or "human smiles" regarded as entirely outside the mind and thus as commanders of its responses from a more dominant place ("To—," ll. 2 and 23). He has sadly relied on the perceived "earth's inconstancy" to render up the completion of those desires which he has projected into or behind what he sees (l. 20). As an immediate result, he has been plunged into the desolation of "Dejection: An Ode" (especially ll. 47–58 of that poem). He has sought something *in* other elements or people that he has already seen as quite different from them, as being in fact entirely unattainable in the physical forms it seems to shine through. Every personal hope of a Coleridgean sort ends up imposing its own frustration on itself by keeping the ultimate object of desire forever distant from any immediate figure that may suggest it. Moreover, Coleridge has only deepened this problem by resorting to a German idealism that makes the "outside" world the projection of a Divine I AM through which an Ultimate Identity can come to know and imagine Itself.[27] Post-Kantian German thought for Shelley excessively "contemplates only the silver side of the shield of truth" (*L,* II, 266), turning the surfaces of what we see into the merest reflectors of a glittering rationality always and already containing absolute ideas of Unity. Such a world-view unfortunately permits the speaker of the "Hymn Before Sunrise" (adapted from a German ode by Friederika Brun) to see the frozen "Torrents" on the sides of Mont Blanc as the images of the "mighty voice" that "stopped" their flow, as echoes finally of "God! God!" making all we perceive swell "vast to Heaven" (ll. 51, 59–60, and 23). Shelley is coming to believe by his twenty-second year that no mind or Universal Psyche, be it Humean, Spinozan, necessitarian, or Coleridgean, can be reflected as an identity in a perceived physical world that proceeds to mirror such a wholeness to itself. For him anyone who accepts this dualism and then tries to bridge its poles, as the younger Shelley has done on occasion, must discover "how little [mental] philosophy and affection consort with this turbid scene—the dark scheme of things finishing in unfruitful death" still remaining from the Gothic sensibility (*L,* I, 419). He who fancies otherwise must "pursue phantoms, spend his choicest hours in hunting after dreams, and wake only to perceive his error and regret that death is so near" (*L,* I, 429–30).

According to Shelley's 1813–1815 prose, "mind" or "intelligence" results from a "combination" of "elements" that are either "sensations" or "perceptions" of something else (*Refutation, CW,* VI, 55–56), while the "material world" is an ever-dissolving construct growing out of "the relation which one object bears to another, as apprehended by the mind" ("Essay on the Punishment of Death," *CW,* VI, 185–86). Both poles are interpretations of interplays in which the relations cannot finally produce one realm without referring to another. At the same time each "other side," especially the "world" in relation to the "mind," is undergoing such rapid dissolution that no "philosophy or affection" can find itself mirrored in some other state more unified than itself. Each pole must be drawn out or in toward an alien place, yet neither can subsume its other entirely or complete itself altogether in its opposite. That being the case, Shelley must conclude that the principal appeal in the poems of Wordsworth and Coleridge is simply the way their perceptions of earlier times, places, or people keep crossing toward later, or at least different, moments, locations, and figures. Indeed, because of this transposition in their poetry, it is "*their* words" above most others that "burn" with "electric life,"[28] that pass current from position to position in Shelley's *Defence,* even though both poets "deny and abjure" this centerless "influence" that makes their work possible. Their denial, as a matter of fact, comes from the way they are pulled toward an Absolute Origin by the withdrawals and disappearances setting up the pull in the first place. Their phrases and images must be redeployed, therefore, in a manner that returns their words to what they themselves both use and suppress. Their writing should always be made to recontact, as it sometimes does in its present form, the Lucretian influx of sheer interrelationships where what recedes is an earlier version of the same activity. That kind of action, we should remember, is what human awareness first confronts for Coleridge when it begins with "Full many a thought uncalled and undetained . . . Travers[ing the partly] passive brain / As wild and various as the random gales" ("The Eolian Harp," ll. 39–41). Such a motion also permits Wordsworth to connect his sense of a "deeper impulse" with the coming of thought out of "mighty waters" and with human education as a flowing in of "trailing" ingredients, a "drinking" of "thoughts, shapes, and forms" that makes the perceived world the creation *and* reflection of "an ebbing and a flowing mind" (*The Excursion,* I. 206, 142, and 161). If Shelley can rearticulate these fluidities, which really are there (if submerged) in his immediate predecessors, he can link what he finds indispensable in them with the various turns from one state toward another that he still retains from his Gothicism, his deism, and "Necessity."

The Hidden Imperative in All These Systems

By 1815, then, a common strain has begun to emerge in the four different belief-systems that encourage a young atheist to both doubt and desire a higher causality. Shelley has worked out the logics in all these schemes to the point of carrying parts of earlier arguments over into later ones. In that very procedure he has pointed increasingly to a primordial, continual shifting in which thoughts about thoughts refer outside their relationships and so fulfill their quests for self-completion by differing from and deferring to adjacent constructions of thought. As a matter of fact, the nascent poet has begun to expose the drive *behind* this revisionary process. Especially when he has been drawn toward, then forced to confront the prereligious levels in, Wordsworth and Coleridge, Shelley has come upon a preconscious traversing of intervals between very diverse moments, ingredients, or levels of thinking. That symptom reveals a subliminal activity operating within and between individual minds where an otherness-as-such (an "electric life" of transference) keeps turning thought-elements toward other ones so as to fulfill each element's inclination to refer elsewhere. This movement, Shelley finds, is what most deeply underlies every one of the systems he has worked through and passed beyond. Though often obscured by its self-transformation, it has been there at every stage of this succession. It has been there in the "Gothic" projection of a desirable opposite out of the fadings in a world-destroying darkness; in the sheer displacement of ideas by each other that produces anticipation and recollection (hence desire) at the same time; in the forced attachment of parts of old texts to parts of very different ones; in the feeling that a sense of cause is preceded by a Lucretian swerving and combining of atoms; in the projection of the mind's own features onto the receding space prior to thought's current movement; in the formation of moral poles ("good" versus "evil") strictly because of relations established among earlier perceptions; in "Power" as a term superadded to thought-relations to name the obscure motion between divisible ideas; in the generation of "Necessity's" cause and effect out of a composed interaction of mental "marks"; in the sense that any one element in Necessity's workings opens out to relations with an infinity of other moving elements; and in the rooting (or really uprooting) of "natural piety," first in the transposing of memories into later states of mind (and vice-versa) and then in the throwing of a self-projection behind whatever we observe, veil behind veil. None of these operations could even have been thought of, nor could any one of them have revised its counterparts, unless a transpositional-relational drive were already active as the *primum mobile* urging that all these crossings occur. Once he starts to wrestle with this fact, Shelley can begin to see why he must oscillate between wanting and rejecting a causal impetus outside the mind and the observed world. The transformational urge itself projects a distant "other" from wherever it happens to be operating at a given time, bringing about the subject's longing for such an object. At the same time the projecting drive, knowing how fictional, how merely desired, its referent may be, denies the object's attainability and its status as a separate Being independent of any motivator outside itself.

Eventually, Shelly has to realize that it is this very process being worked out in all his substitute systems which forces each one of them to run up against irresolvable inconsistencies in itself, thereby urging the young poet to leap beyond the confines of any one conceptual structure. The more each system tries to deny its basis in transference by centering itself on a monolithic zenith or depth that is really a desire projected by a set of interrelated transfers, the more the "electric" movement announces other digressive or regressive possibilities. Transference tends both outward in space and backward in time to urge present thinking toward additional points of view while also recalling previous points of departure. Although the shift from dissolution toward salvation appears at first to be a workable one-way sequence in the Gothic sensibility, for example, that turn on closer examination seems endlessly reversible, since it is a crossing between states that looks back as well as ahead. This paradox denies finality to both poles in the dichotomy, voiding any sharp distinction between a transitional image, the future it desires, and the death it always remembers. Indeed, death can keep reannouncing itself as the motivator behind any hope in this system, to such an extent that any leap beyond death can seem to collapse back into that "ground" and so come to believe in universal dissolution instead of the desired salvation. Furthermore, such a relocation cannot simply be a "Bursting" of something from virtually nothing. That shift has to be a turning out or away from another transitional movement before it, even if the latter turn is itself a fading motion. Indeed, this motion must look back through a series of such shifts, perhaps to an inaugural swerve from a point so different (one that exaggerates the difference between all points) that the first point of departure seems to contain no shift at all. Hence Shelley's flight from the Gothic dichotomy to the deism that so briefly succeeds it. Then, too, in the Gothic system, as in each of the others, transference must expose the differences in the concept's ingredients by drawing together conflicting texts ("Monk" Lewis and John Milton in this case, let us say). Difference must be just as manifest as similarity if the act of transference is to declare a crossing between distinct groups of signs. Consequently, even if one set of texts tries to subsume other sets within a dominant ideology (itself a suppression of differences), an element from one or more sets (such as the desire to avoid infinite regression, a desire generated by the transfer from regression to regression) can easily break away to seek another context in which it can be fully operative. That rupture announces the multiplicity in any "unity" it flees and the need for another construct on the rise that will eventually develop some of the same problems.

Inevitably, Shelley discovers, the moment of a conceptual interplay of related notions exists, it works, unless we repress its actual foundations, to suggest a future reconfiguration of its parts that violates the priorities in the order of the moment. The elements of a system, once they gravitate together—already indicating that attractions among differences are really the "center" of the system— immediately, by swerving toward other attractions (as Lucretius would say), break up the patterns they helped to establish and shift toward different relational structures that reorient these ingredients by linking them to elements from other systems.[29] This entropy, in the full literal sense of *en-trope* (a "being-in-the-process-of-turning" from structure to structure rather than just a "winding down" of one structure), *is* the "variability" that the growing Shelley has felt from a very early point operating within his advocacy of every substitute scheme and urging him beyond each scheme as the transfers of the present seek to fulfill themselves in the transfers of the future. Whenever the young Shelley, in his metaphysical speculations, senses a conflict between postures brought on by this "variability," he must, at every stage, complete any argument for an alternative to orthodox faith with figurations ultimately distinct from the ones he is using to construct his current assumptions. One reason, to be sure, is the variety of his early reading and the consequent association of certain texts with others that are not fully compatible with the initial group. One more is a belief in a Lucretian dynamic that rises up within and outlasts his other early attachments. Another is the way his early skepticism makes him infinitely educable, even fascinated, by nearly all the compelling systems of thought available to him. Still another is the young poet's sensitivity to the nature of the words composing these systems and thus to the tendency in words to drift from system to system, changing *and* retaining possible meanings depending on the context. Finally, however, Shelley gives in to these inclinations because his sense of human awareness and conceptualization is based—in the end semi-consciously based—on transference, the impulse underlying every one of these tendencies in Shelley, the drive to which he opens himself by resisting all hegemonic orders of monolithically centered and hierarchical thought. Now, as his adolescent years of self-revision force him to start confronting the subliminal motion that his early attachments have both carried through and suppressed, Shelley must begin articulating what such a motion means for how he has lived, how he might live, what he has written or thought, what others have written, and what he and others might write, believe, advocate, and achieve in the coming years.

Facing the Impulse and Its Possibilities: *Alastor*

Alastor; or the Spirit of Solitude is, I think, the first major result of this realization. No wonder it is usually regarded as a brilliant transition into Shelley's adult career as a major English poet. It confronts transference, albeit in several veilings that only intimate such a movement throughout perceived existence, as the very possibility of a "Nature" perceived by a "subject," as the impetus and end of all subjective quests for origins "out there," as the drive seeking relationships between thoughts and sentient beings, as the relational process establishing the various interpretive constructions of existence (ranging from Western culture's to Shelley's earliest "systems"), as the basis even of oppressive constructs that try to conceal the transference that first produced them, and as the primal, ongoing impulse, beyond personal subjectivity, which gives rise to every potential of perception and thought. These variations of transference reveal that motion, in fact, to be the truest "ground" of all the texts and memories reworked in the course of the poem.

Alastor is this wide-ranging revelation because of two pressures that urge it toward the form it finally takes. The first of the two is an astonishing, interweaving transference in Shelley's multidirectional thinking that draws numerous factors toward each other from many different quarters, factors that put in question his previous behavioral tendencies and philosophies of existence, not to mention those of the writers to whom he had been attracted throughout his late adolescence. This interaction conflates a host of recollections: the 1815 advice of a physician that Shelley change his indoor, self-obsessed mode of life or die (Mary's note, *PW*, p. 528); Shelley's subsequent boat trip that July, on which he "traced" both "the Thames" and some of his own predilections to their "source" (*PW*, p. 258); the similarities between this journey and ones he makes through parts of Europe after eloping with Mary in 1814; the portraits of several mournful wanderers in boats in Peacock's *The Philosophy of Melancholy* (published in 1812, the year he and Shelley met);[30] Shelley's awareness of the duplicities in his own early philosophies, the ways they have made him probe to the depths of the physical world *and* try to vault beyond perceived existence at the same time; his understanding of the solipsism that results from choosing a desire for transcendent absolutes over the relations of visible social life; his companion-feeling that he and his best friend Hogg (by now the author of *The Memoirs of Prince Alexy Heimatoff*) have too often sought very personal "phantoms" in the women whom they (like the Prince) have rashly pursued;[31] the analogy he sees between that quest and the Coleridgean "dejection" born of chasing our dream-wishes in objects and human beings; the resemblance between such dejection and Milton's images for both the Fall and the human effort to return to an Eden now lost;[32] Shelley's connection of the dream-maidens in such longings with Luxima the Indian, the heroine of Sydney Owenson's novel *The Missionary* (noted in *L,* I, 107);[33] his reading of similar narcissistic dreams in Rousseau's *Confessions* and *Reveries;*[34] his disenchantment with how Wordsworth's *Excursion* finally locates a greater kind of love only in the heights or depths of a Mother Nature where God is obscurely enthroned;[35] his desire to depose that vision in a verse form that can match the Wordsworthian style without obeying its ideology; and his dim awareness that his own "variability" may come from a movement, a Lucretian one at bottom, commanding the verses of his older contemporaries just as much as his own.

The second compulsion insisting that *Alastor* face transference is the direction of the text's own narrative drive, its pressing of each sequence and complex of images back to a point of origin, or "inmost sanctuary," that might "render up" the deepest truth "of what we are" (*Alastor,* ll. 38 and 28–29). Starting with Wordsworthian-Miltonic blank verse, an overwrought aping of "natural piety" (l. 3), and a penchant for narratives within narratives much like the one in *The Excursion* (where an "Author" tells of a "Wanderer" who then tells of "the Solitary"), Shelley clearly wants to intensify the manner of Wordsworth (and sometimes Coleridge) to the point of making it expose the earlier, hidden foundations that underlie both its own supposed foundations and its need to connect the present to the past (or at least to relate the older poet to a younger counterpart). Hence the piece begins with Shelley's Narrator calling to Mother *Natura*/Necessity/Venus/Eros as to a Wordsworthian muse in order that he may passively take in the "breath" of the primordial poetic life-force, thereby grasping it, and at the same time penetrate (sexually and otherwise) into "thy deep mysteries" (ll. 45 and 23). Then, with his Narrator apparently still awaiting the consummation of both desires, Shelley returns the poem's structure, eschewing the multiple narrators in *The Excursion,* to the earlier, simpler, and less religious recollection of Wordsworth's "There was a Boy" (the "Boy of Winander" segment of *The Prelude,* published separately in 1800), in which the central tale remembering a contemplative, lonely youth is framed by the narration of the older speaker as he stares down at the lad's solitary grave. The style of the recent Wordsworth ("the slave") is thus forced back toward that of the more primordial and skeptical author of *Lyrical Ballads* and *Poems.*

Moreover, the younger figure that results, once introduced with Shelley's blatantly obvious "There was a Poet" (l. 50), proceeds to take the Boy of Winander—now intermixed with the traveling Shelley of 1814 and 1815, the adolescent Shelley seeking metaphysical absolutes, Peacock's "mourners," dreamy Rousseau, Prince Alexy, the worshipper of Luxima, and Coleridge's questing soul chasing self-projections outside the self—and pull him even further back to the earliest sources, the "mighty [head] waters," of perceived nature, the human race, civilization, poetry, science, and the various religions. First, the now-dead Poet is remembered as pursuing his own quest for nature's *and* mythology's origins to the temple of Dendera on the upper Nile, "the cradle of [science's] first elements" for many in Shelley's era.[36] Later, the same Poet turns eastward to seek *his* feminine Other in the vale of Kashmir at the heart of the Indian Caucasus, the region from which all races, streams, and faiths supposedly descended after the Ark was left on Mount Ararat by the Deluge.[37] Finally, the dying youth's frail boat carries him to secluded bowers at the southern end of the Georgian Caucasus next to the "Chorasmian" (or Caspian) Sea, to the cascade-filled mountain range, the apex of a nearly triangular journey, said to be the origin of mortal life *and* death because it is one traditional site of the Garden of Eden itself.[38] Each of these reversions to supposed beginnings, Narrator's or Poet's, we find, discovers a transpositional rather than a Wordsworthian "basis." Every "origin" proves to be a different process of transference, and so none of them can turn out to be an origin in the sense of a singular source from which all things flow.

Indeed, the poem does not take long to make such suggestions, even though Shelley's Wordsworthian Narrator believes very much in an Absolute Origin behind the "deep mysteries" of the Nature he addresses. He cannot pine for a sequestered "Mother," he discovers, without first seeking "her" within the Aristotelian interaction of "Earth, ocean, air" (l. 1). His first address must be to "brother"-elements, some incomplete ingredients that already include himself, as they shift toward and join with one another to form a "world" of changing seasons and times of day. In addition, when he thinks he has contacted the more primal "love" making all the elements brothers and calling him out toward his fellows, the Narrator discovers that the "natural piety" now seeming to "imbue" him has, like earth-air-water relations, no one point of departure; it simultaneously surges toward him from his brothers' comings-together and pours out from him in "recompense," suggesting a love (or Darwinian *Ens*) born from sheer exchange (ll. 2–4). Supposedly "outer" elements and "inward" observers are equally agencies through which this relational activity flows, as though it were the result of their relation yet prior to any hard-and-fast distinction between them. Meanwhile, this movement, while it draws the "brothers" together, also makes the products they form (observed times or seasons) transport their features immediately into other ones as each bodily sense in the perception of existence is interpreted by the other senses nearby. Autumn must be heard "sighing" through "wood" that becomes "sere" to the eye and the touch, and "winter" must be always "robing" the "bare boughs" left by autumn just as if a season were a thought interpreting and metamorphosing an earlier thought (ll. 8–10). What the perceiving subject/observed nature (or son/mother) relationship really amounts to is one network of several crossings of transference interacting with another without sharp boundaries developing initially between the different networks. If the Narrator-perceiver longs to be a Coleridgean wind-harp awaiting the Great Parent's "breath" (ll. 42–45), he must still play that role as himself a cacophony of "incommunicable dream, / And twilight phantasms, and deep noonday thought" (ll. 39–40), all of these half-inhabited already by what they recall from perception. This conflation must then turn outward to "modulate" with other interactions, the "murmurs of the air" mixing with the "motions of the forests and the sea / And voice[s] of living beings" (ll. 46–48), a flowing together already interpreted as half-singing in a human fashion.

Right away Shelley has enacted one of his characteristic procedures for revising previous texts. He has taken the nature-worship of *The Excursion,* or even that of his own *Queen Mab,* and broken it down into what makes it possible at an earlier stage: the cascade-like entrance of the "visible scene" into the boy of Winander's mind. He has then multiplied the several acts of intercourse between perceived objects and perceiving thoughts in "There was a Boy," where the "scene" pouring into thought is already recast as the "solemn imagery" of "torrents" rushing together and where the boy blows back "mimic hootings" through the lyre of his "fingers interwoven" (Wordsworth's poem, ll. 21–23 and 7–10). The resulting panoply of half-sexual interactions blurring subject-object boundaries establishes the Narrator as mainly in love, like Erasmus Darwin, with the movement of love itself much in the way St. Augustine is *amans amare* in Shelley's Latin epigraph from the *Confessions* (*NCE,* p. 70). Yet that movement is redefined away from both the Pandemian and Uranian senses of love in Augustine to become a rapid transfiguration of forms by other forms in which natural transitions keep disappearing into the additional ones that embrace them. Shelley has pressed the "transmigrating *Ens*" even further back to the myriad sexual swerves of process into process that Lucretius refers to as "life-giving Venus" in his own invocation to the "Mother" of Rome that opens *De rerum natura* (I. 1–28).

Now there can be no firmly Wordsworthian definitions of the Great Mother, no pre-Freudian sense of a rupture from one true source or womb, at the "unfathomable" heart of which lies the planted seed of the Father that the son longs to recover.[39] The Lucretian Venus is not inseminated by a prior male essence, nor does she "nurture" by making herself visible *as* herself, albeit in the act of withdrawing from plain sight. "She" is constituted by her self-veiling self-metamorphosis through and "beneath the smooth-moving heavenly signs" and "the earth [covering *it*self] with her kindly fruits" as she moves even "throughout seas and mountains and sweeping torrents" (*De rerum,* I. 2–17). Shelley's Narrator can only cry, "I have watched thy shadow, and the darkness [the obscurity] of thy steps" (ll. 20–21), because his addressee is less a primal womb or bosom and more a figural movement ("beneath signs") that both supplements and supplants itself by "stepping" from context to context in the figures that remake and mask it in order to fulfill its "nature."[40] Every reference to "her" process must be either skeptically conditional, confessing a temporary context ("If our great Mother has imbued my soul," l. 2), or deferred to another moment of incomplete remanifestation ("I wait thy breath," l. 45). There are few other ways to acknowledge a drive that moves beyond the context currently framing it ("natural piety" in this case, l. 3) and that conceals itself so much as to promise its revelation in a future synecdoche that will again be a concealment (the "breath" instead of the "Great Parent"). Such a style, of course, returns the speaker's manner and tone to those of the young, tentative Wordsworth prior to *The Excursion* (exemplified in the conditional wording, say, of "Tintern Abbey," ll. 49–50, 111–13, and 142–51). Consequently, Shelley's Narrator admits that the only "depth" into which he can penetrate is a falling-from-him or vanishing, a "murmur" receding in a multiplicity of elements (l. 76), which keeps "with draw[ing / Some] portion of [its] wonted favor" even as it keeps reforming itself as "motions of the forests and the sea" (ll. 16–17 and 47).

At the same time, too, the opening apostrophe in *Alastor* shows how a dogmatic

Wordsworth *and* a young Shelley in quest of absolute centers can come into being as a result of this receding/forthcoming motion, can be turned from a healthy uncertainty toward an obsessive search for the "inmost sanctuary." The self-obscuring achieved by this movement's "steps" means that the observing "heart ever gazes on the depth / Of . . . deep mysteries" no matter how much is revealed (ll. 22–23). The fact of this depth, ever being deepened and recreated, makes the interpreting thought strive to penetrate the surface layers, even if the destination can be only a narrative succession of layers, "the tale / Of what we are." As in Wordsworth, this longing produces a sense of a hidden maternal birthplace that calls forth from the Narrator "obstinate questionings" of all perceived surfaces that hope to prompt a birthlike revelation, a "render[ing] up [of the Mother's] charge" (ll. 26 and 37). Such questionings, in turn, run through the exact succession of belief-systems that the younger Shelley struggled across until he reached "natural piety" and the "electric life" it revealed. First, the Narrator confesses to a Gothic quest in "charnels" for the underside of the "trophies" (the bodies and gravestones) that "black death," one of the Mother's darkest "shadows," has "won" away from her life-giving tendencies (ll. 24–25). Frustrated by his inability to call forth the secret of life from the signs of its withdrawal, he then fancies himself half a Gothic "alchymist" seeking to "compel" a light from darkness by "magic" and half an unrequited lover (as Shelley was with Harriet Grove years before) composing the alchemical potion out of "strange tears" and "breathless kisses" extended out to the night air (ll. 31–36). The "night" now becomes "charmed" (l. 36) by the projection of a Coleridgean desire into it, seemingly able to provide the "breath" now lost to the speaker's beseeching kisses. A sort of deism is proposed for a moment in the way the love of the Narrator, like that of Coleridge's speaker in "The Eeolian Harp," tries to meet an analogous pouring-back of passion, a "Mother," which desire has sent out to inhabit an unresponsive space. The foundation of this performance being analogy, however, the seeker is forced to confront the "outside" world as a concatenation of differences (ll. 46–49) very like the one he senses in the thought-process creating the projection (ll. 39–40). The next step, if a centralized logic is to be maintained, must therefore be the positioning of the observing psyche as a fairly passive Aeolian lyre awaiting a Necessity of interacting "murmurs" and "motions" from without and within.

Yet by now, as all this tries to add up to a "natural piety," these philosophies have exposed how much they are failed attempts to fix or center an interaction of "woven hymns" (l. 48). The longed-for meeting of the speaker and the Parent, the former admits, can only be a centerless "modulation" of different perceptions and memories in relation to each other (l. 46). The forms through which the human longing for some "other" passes—as the projections of deism and Necessity have just shown—must see themselves, since they come from transference, in distant forms (*specific* "others") that both mirror their counterparts and remain distinct; neither perceived natural processes nor perceivers can see themselves "unless reflected" in another place by "that which [they] resemble." This primal fact *is* the answer that the Narrator receives in response to his call, as he begins to acknowledge when he foresees the coming of the Parent's "breath" as a moment when his "personal strain" of "phantasms" and "thought" can modulate with the "voice of living beings" reflecting his own voice in other locations (ll. 45–48). As a result, the only course he can take when he opens himself to the Lucretian interplay is the refiguration of his own "asking looks" (l. 33) in an analogous being. The younger Wordsworth so often echoed here recognizes this necessity, especially when the reconstruction of the poet's history in "Tintern Abbey" makes no final sense unless this "language of [his] former heart" is reinterpreted "in the shooting lights / of [his sister's] eyes" and "memory" (ll. 117–19 and 141). This need can be fulfilled either in a looking ahead to someone (such as Dorothy Words-worth) who may survive the present speaker *or* in a looking back to an often similar mind now passed away from the earth. Shelley has his *Alastor* Narrator adopt the latter course from "There was a Boy." The speaker's quest for reflections is thereby satisfied with a narrative of a dead youth rendering to the Narrator a "tale of what" the Narrator is. Shelley, meanwhile, receives the same benefits or, when they are war-ranted, the same castigations. He chooses this structure of tale within tale, after all, partly to critique portions of his younger self (and Hogg's and Coleridge's) that cannot be mirrored in a Narrator dominated by "natural piety" (Shelley's most recent "sys-tem"); partly to let his Narrator compose an analogue to himself (as Shelley has done) that may reveal what it means to have "lived [and] sung, in solitude" as the Narrator and Shelley generally have (l. 60); and partly to dissipate the religious teacher/despon-dent student relationship that persists hierarchically between the Wanderer and the Solitary, the "pietist" and the lone dreamer of *The Excursion*.

The Narrator-Poet relationship in *Alastor* is thus as interplay, like the one in "There Was a Boy," between quite similar equals who define one another because they have taken somewhat different journeys toward similar revelations. The "Preface" to the poem reveals as much when it summarizes the life of the Poet the way the poem describes the Narrator: "The magnificence and beauty of the external world [have entered] profoundly into the frame of his conceptions [and thereby afforded] to [his mental] modifications a variety not to be exhausted" (*NCE*, p. 69). The setting of these two beings adjacent to each other does not try to present a *Refutation*-like debate between a prober of Nature and one who would leap beyond its bounds, however much Earl Wasserman would have us believe otherwise.[41] The Narrator, just like the Poet, wants to drive through whatever he sees to an "inmost sanctuary" that is always beyond the images he beholds. He therefore debates with himself on how best to carry out this probe, then tells of another who has also sought "strange truths" in "Nature's most secret steps" (ll. 77 and 81), all in a fashion that draws out toward clear mani-festation the now hidden possibilities in the Narrator's (and the author's) responses to the inexhaustible "variety," Shelley's speaker drives, without consciously knowing he is doing so, into the basis of his thinking and his own unrealized potentials for destruction by solitude using a mirror-figure who completes his discourse by trans-porting his tendencies into another existence.[42]

What makes that existence different, of course, is the Poet's greater amount of learning, his Shelley-like command over more of Western and Eastern culture as he combines "Every sight / And sound from the vast earth" with the "foundations of divine philosophy" and "all of great / Or good, or lovely, which the sacred past / In truth or fable consecrates" (ll. 69–74). Another difference is the Poet's more deliberate solitude born of his attempts to find one center underlying and totalizing his knowl-edge of natural science, metaphysics, epistemology, political history, and comparative mythology. While the Narrator searches for his Absolute so close to civilization that he can spend his questing hours in charnel houses and graveyards, the Poet wanders continually away from all inhabited settings, first to "Pinnacles of ice" or "bitumen lakes" where natural phenomena seem to reveal their entire history (flow *and* solidi-fication) in a few syncretic images (ll. 84–85) and then to the foundations of all civilization, mythography, and science preserved in the "awful ruins of the days of old" (l. 108). In such places he enacts one of the Narrator's fantasies, as the Narrator never could himself, by being a "lyre" in the "dome" of a deserted "fane" (ll. 42–44), much as the younger Shelley sought to be in reading Volney's *Ruins of Empires* or Peacock's poetic voyages through Western/Eastern antiquity, perusing Southey's *Thalaba* or the first cantos of Byron's *Childe Harold,* and traveling through Europe with Mary in 1814, unable to visit Greco-Roman ruins yet bringing along Tacitus on the history of ancient Rome.[43] Yet, in carrying the Narrator's propensities out to extremes of effort and ranges of reference (combinations of texts) that even Shelley himself only thought of attempting, the Poet, since he is much more obviously a literary, linguistic fabrication, can serve to make conscious the preconscious figural operations that make the Narrator's awareness, even of transference, possible from the start and incline it toward both a monolithic self-obsession and a pluralistic movement reaching beyond the self into multiple relations.

In the first such revelation the Poet comes upon something like the interweaving activity the Narrator finds in the "depths" of perceived Nature. This motion, however, since it lies at the base of all subsequent human perception, turns out to be prior to the "woven hymns." It is the process by which Nature is first interpreted as being relations in time or a cycle of temporal recurrence, and it finally becomes visible to the Poet at that key moment in "Dark Aethiopia" (l. 115) when the Dendera temple turns out to be the first to arrange its gods in and around the figures of the Zodiac:

> Among the ruined temples there,
> Stupendous columns, and wild images
> Of more than man, where marble daemons watch
> The Zodiac's brazen mystery, and dead men
> Hang their mute thoughts on mute walls around,
> He lingered, poring on memorials
> Of the world's youth, through the long burning day
> Gazed on those speechless shapes, nor, when the moon
> Filled the mysterious halls with floating shades
> Suspended he that task, but ever gazed
> And gazed, till meaning on his vacant mind
> Flashed like strong inspiration, and he saw
> The thrilling secrets of the birth of time. (ll. 116–28).

Here both the Narrator and the Poet discover for the first time that no "mystery" implying an "unseen presence" or natural order can even be thought until there are interpretive "images" fanning out in several directions to other ones that "watch" or read them, thereby adding layers to them. The "birth of time," as a concept that keeps calling us back to an originating moment, comes from a Zodiac-image, already an extension of human lineaments into something "more," leading the eye to different ones in its pattern and then referring to other "memorials" near it, to the "marble daemons" and the inscribed "thoughts" of "dead men" on the "walls." This production of symbolic patterning and the immediate comment upon it by nearby systems is even given greater depth (or density) and wider potential for relationship as the "moon" shines in upon these three concentric circles to multiply them into "floating shades," which proceed to dance on the surfaces of and in the spaces between the solid figures. Once the Poet beholds this entire operation, "meaning" suddenly "flashes" upon a "mind" that has been, despite all the tributaries entering into it, as "vacant" as the space of the temple before its symbolic relations were formed.[44] That is not to say that the Poet now knows of a divine or natural system coming from outside or emerging within the symbolic order suggesting it. Instead, he comes to realize that meaning is a crossing between myriad figures, a *moving,* relational "flash" through the psyche, before it seems to hide in depth of layers or veils demanding a narrator's exegesis of its system. The transposition of the Narrator's Wordsworthian findings into this "key" of archeology and increased classical learning has led a "natural" religion to face up to its mythographic foundation, not just in a Lucretian metaphysic but in symbolic arrays descended from their opening-out in ancient human productions.

What the Poet produces with this awareness, though, is a quite different—and unfortunate—transmutation of the Narrator's quest, a recasting of the desire for the mother that shows how dangerous such a longing can ultimately be. Instead of accepting "meaning" as a continual displacement across many different versions of the human figure, the Poet presses this dance, not so much in toward a possible origin for it, but out toward a single recentering point like the one he and the Narrator have always hoped to find. He urges several interacting figures left in his memory by perception to gather together into one external mirror for the self, one that might complete the desiring Poet by making him "more than man," just as the Poet has transfigured the Narrator and the "marble daemons" have enlarged the human body. When he reaches an almost total seclusion in that "vale of Cashmire" in the Indian Caucasus (l. 145), he envisions a "veiled maid" (his Luxima) transposing "the voice of his own soul" into "music long" as he interweaves remembered "sounds of streams and breezes" and then places these inside an equally fanciful "web / of many-coloured woof and shifting hues" (ll. 150–57). He thereby extends the Narrator's way of projecting the "twilight phantasms" and "incommunicable dreams" of his past into a deceptive figure that immediately cloaks the basis of the projection, thus implying a "depth" not based on psychological and figural relations. The "veiled maid" must consequently be, like the "Mother" of the Narrator, a repository of myriad forms from elsewhere (including the Poet's "own soul") *and* a concealer of herself, in whose "branching veins / The eloquent blood told an ineffable tale" (ll. 167–68). She is a Rousseauist dream-fiction placing a combination of tones with their own previous reference points behind a "shifting" texture woven of colored sights that keep "branching" into and reveiling themselves while they veil and obscure the sounds.

The instant the Poet tries to embrace this mirror, then, hoping to enfold himself in the "veils" of his greater self much as the "vale" of Kashmir enwombs its own "dells" within others, he encounters "breathless" advances, again like the great Mother's, that turn into "dissolving" features and finally into a "blackness," forcing him to look back toward the "dark flood" of "sleep" from which his vision originally came (ll. 186–90). His projection, attempted in the mountains from which all forms of worship supposedly descend, reveals itself to be what any god or goddess is for Shelley: a mere fabrication, a figure for other figures, in which each of the figures refers to something in an entirely different but earthly place. The dream-maiden is even a denial that the something (the Poet's soul) can be reached through a love for reorganized memories; her surface features are only the opaque reflectors of his past desires and his process of dreaming rather than transparencies leading to "what we are" essentially. Narrator and Poet now both confront the exact nature of the transference in which the production of a narcissistic "other" tries and fails to manifest the heart of the self. They also behold unawares, in their own efforts, the Wordsworthian-Coleridgean error of projecting a reunion with a lost origin behind the world as it is currently perceived. They actually mirror to themselves what Shelley now confronts in rejecting his previous systems: his former mistake of repressing the fluid and spreading interchange of "meaning" in thought behind one reference point for life, one focus for religious *or* amorous devotion, which is really no more than a series of interchanges itself.

Indeed, the curse of remaining committed to that mistake is vividly depicted in *Alastor* once the Poet awakens from "his trance" and seeks his "hues of heaven" in all that he beholds (ll. 192 and 197). Wherever he looks for a new single incarnation, he finds the "scene" to be as "empty" of his self-completion as the "veiled maid" really was herself (l. 201). Refusing, as he always has, to accept the fact that he gazes only relationally, only "As ocean's moon looks on the moon in heaven" supposedly to recover the light in the water's depths (l. 202), the Poet spurns the uncertain life of relations with other people who could at least mirror parts of himself for a time, as when the "youthful maidens" he encounters try to "interpret half the woe / That wasted him" (ll. 266–68). He pants instead for what he has set up as an all-fulfilling absolute form reflecting his onanistic desire for oneness with himself.

Three results immediately follow, each upon the other. First, he accepts a theory of transcendence, one that has been attributed by some to nearly all of Shelley's work, yet that is here roundly criticized as the sad result of a Gothic and Coleridgean sensibility. The Poet supposes that the "hues" he seeks exist on the reverse side of the "realms of dream" that he has projected into the outside world (l. 206). He thus assumes that he must pass through a "wide pathless desert," now revealing an insufficiency, to reach an unknown spot (another single referent). There he will suddenly vault, he fancies, "Beyond the realms of dream" to Sleep's "mysterious paradise," an ultimate vale of Kashmir, in which Luximas do not dissolve and poets can join with them completely (ll. 210 and 212). He consequently decides that Nature's ever-changing signifiers, the physical images standing in the way of his leap, contain "death" itself as their initial signified, as the "blue vault" underlying that "black and watery depth" already confronted by the Narrator in the face of the Mother (ll. 215–16). The Poet takes the dissolution of past moments, the fading that trails behind all human impressions, and fixes it into an ultimate state of being to which all perceptions finally refer as both their past and their future. He consequently skews the foundation of existence into a "dark gate" (l. 211) leading from the "now" of living relationships to the "eternity" beyond relation. Henceforth, the Poet pursues Death alone as the objective of his remaining life, wasting away inwardly toward a tiny "lustre" of soulful "burning" (ll. 252–53) even as he wanders outward toward his radical passage from one state to another. He does not see that such a passage is really going on moment by moment instead of being a final and solitary step. Nor does he realize how the dark base beneath his transpositions comes from his mistaken way of transposing death and life from an oscillation between aspects of time into a fixed dichotomy with a ground and superstructure.

Meanwhile, there is a third result combining and further grounding these other two. Since his absolute at a beckoning point affirms one elemental essence as *alpha* and *omega,* the Poet must feel himself prompted from the past to pursue a future death within Wordsworthian "pendant mountains seen in the calm lake" (*Alastor,* l. 214). He must feel pricked and impelled, even haunted, by a *genius loci* calling him to death in the form of a "fierce fiend [remaining from] a distempered dream" (l. 223).

For this Poet, not surprisingly, the demon turns out to be the "shadow of that *lovely dream*" (l. 233, my emphasis). It is the object of his desire, now regarded as desire's impetus, apparently surrounded (that is, shrouded and shaded) by the death that is the gateway to it. It is *eros* and *thanatos* in one supposedly primal form cursing the Poet for his distance from it, then driving him between itself as the motivating origin and itself as the farthest point on the horizon. Such Blakean "mind-forg'd manacles" are among the grimly effective ways by which relational thinking can recenter and restrict its own expansion using its own procedures and elements. These methods in this case have twisted the mere desire for an other, the constant supplementation of the "self" by the relations that produce it, into a commanding *alastor,* recalling that old Greek word that was once defined as an "avenging demon" or Fury.[45] At the same time these methods have made the Poet (and potentially the Narrator) an *alastor* as Aeschylus and Sophocles use the word, a person "tormented by an avenging spirit."[46]

This "revenge" has descended upon the Poet because, in forgetting that self-reference is but a centerless exchange between different figures for other figures, he has placed his dream of it at the beginning impulse and at the ultimate end of being, with death residing near both points as the barrier (or sign behind signs) keeping earthly life at a distance from its final cause. That, oddly enough, is what orthodox Christianity does by making the fall away from oneness with God the basis of human death, not to mention the source of a guilt always dogging the thought of humankind. That is what Wordsworth's speakers increasingly do in his "egotistical sublime," especially the Solitary when the remembered "reproaches" of his "Wife and Mother" and his dashed hopes for the French Revolution seem to attack him as "vengeful Furies" reminding him of his distance from "an infallible support of faith" (*Excursion,* III. 852–55 and 864–65). And that, worst of all, is what the younger Shelley and the *Alastor* Narrator have done in their Gothic *thanatos* "bursting" toward a timeless *eros,* their deistic elevation of the "self" to an essence, and their projection of a soul-like "necessity" or "rolling" presence that somehow serves as the Father and the Mother of the world. All these constructs suppress what the Poet's demon really is and so what the Poet most fears to confess: the incapacity of any signifying structure, object, person, or dream to pass on its own from being a formation of desire to reaching the presence of desire's ultimate object.

But then that failure has really been the success, indeed a major cause, of the movement between figures that reestablishes and reorients the desire of the Poet (and of the young Shelley) at every turn. Shelley now shows how much he understands that irony by having his death-seeking Poet launch himself upon the waters of central Asia that lead back up to where they seem to originate, to the Georgian Caucasus of supposedly primal creation. The *loci* that the Poet must eventually seek as the origin of his quest, it turns out, are first the lakes and torrents that resemble his own psyche and then the flowing "motion" that initially created the waters and the mind. To start with, we should remember, the dissolving of his veiled "maid" has referred him back to the "dark flood" of mental interplays that produced her ever-changing ingredients. Only there can he begin to find her again, only in the "bright stream / Once fed with many-voiced waves" (ll. 68–69), which composes his thought as a confluence of tributaries out of the Wordsworthian-Lucretian "mighty waters" rushing down and into one of the coves they create (the psyche they form in their cascade). Lisa Steinman is therefore right to see the "journey" in the rest of the Narrator's tale as a "descent into the mind" allowing Narrator and Poet to pursue a thorough "regression of [their] consciousness" to its base.[47] In addition, though, since the mind cannot "see itself unless reflected upon that which it resembles," it must behold its "multitudinous streams" in the perceived "other" that best brings their workings to sight (l. 341) and must force that other back toward the actions that make both the mind and its reflection operate. Shelley must find his "dream-play" in the language of his poem, the Narrator in the figures he recounts, and the Poet in the primal waters spilling out into the cradles of civilization he so values, in the "stream" coming toward him that "images [his] life" while also pulling him toward a "source inaccessibly profound" (ll. 502–5). As a result, his embarking upon this "inside" that is always "outside" itself returns the Poet to the descent and the swerves, the fall and rise of gathered "waves" into forms (l. 323), the recollection of past forms, the sedimenting of a ground by the waters, the carving out of "cliffs" or boundaries (l. 353), the "mutual war" of elements even in bounded circles (l. 342), and the temporary centering of "whirlpools" soon to dissipate (l. 342) that enact the fluid creation and remaking of perceived existence—and also of minds—in *De rerum natura.* Sometimes, to be sure, instead of accepting death as what it truly is, the "dark obliterating course" of the "flood's" surge between whorls of life (ll. 328–29), the Poet still tries to see it as a "Shadow" awaiting him in the "caverns" of the "deep" (ll. 306–7) or at least to pursue the desire of a Coleridgean Mariner for "genii" in the "waves" that may yet "conduct him to the light [of the veiled maid's] eyes" (ll. 330–32). He is clearly tempted to retreat again, as Rousseau does in his late *Reveries,* from a world recognized by the Solitary Wanderer as a "vast ocean" of continual flux to the more "ancient extacies" of his past dreams where he may find a *beau idéal* determined and fixed enough for a gaze seeking a permanent focus.[48] Nevertheless, he gradually submits, as he must, to the "eddying waters" that are "circling immeasurably fast" (ll. 380–81) as they carry him back to their primordial process where sheer interaction gives life and takes it away.

The final journey of the Poet as he dies, consequently, is a movement back through the basic eddies of coalescence and the sudden deviations from them that spring from the primal Lucretian flow and the kinds of "turning" that its *clinamen* keeps prompting. Some of the flow's "windings," before they pass on, seem to hollow out "caverns" in the "icy summits" already composed from the rivers and their sedimentations (ll. 320 and 353); others become the "waters" nourishing "the knarled roots of mighty trees" or "Reflecting, yet distorting every cloud" between the branches (ll. 380–85); and still others fashion "a smooth spot" on "the verge of the extremest curve," where a "woven grove" develops from "a placid stream" as an Eden or *locus amoenus* of "meeting boughs and implicated leaves" (ll. 390–426). None of these swirlings end in themselves or prove unified even within their own pooling of relations, since every point in each of them must reach out to another point to carry itself through and onward. The eddy of rest on the "extremest curve" may be the supreme example as it tries to enclose a flowing force that simply reappears in its little interlacings. Every reference point that it offers to the eye begs "to invite / To some more lovely mystery" (ll. 453–54), and its center is a "well" or "liquid mirror" bubbling up from the springs around it, mainly to give off its own "sweet brook," which then flows on even further (ll. 457–62 and 477–79). Here the Poet finds himself mirrored at last, but only in "the reflected lines" of a "treacherous likeness" standing "beside" a new version of the veiled "Spirit" made from other reflected materials that now resurround its "Two starry eyes" (ll. 470–90). The self perpetually in search of itself in another form finally confronts the basis of its deferral across many analogues. It finds it is but a temporary encircling of reflective thoughts that immediately divide themselves into distortions of one another and then into new combinations of past distortions (or mirrors) that are never repeated in exactly the same way. This, the Narrator and Poet discover, is how "man" is created (or creates himself), even in any Eden that might be supposed. At this point, too, the poem itself is revealed as a stream of symbols governed by the same continual splitting. It is presented as manifestly dividing the Narcissus myth into a double reflection, placing an anamorphic self-image next to a remade self-as-love-object "Borrowed from aught the visible world affords" (l. 482). Then the narrative is pulled on to follow the fountain's "rivulet" toward a "silent nook" that extends and reworks the Edenic curve into an autumnal bower for the Poet's death (ll. 571–86).

When the Poet and the Narrator reach this ultimate point, moreover, they arrive at two geneses, the second one more primal than the first. The moment the fading Poet's "powers of life" begin "surrendering to their final impulses" in the riverside bower, "the influxes of sense" start to "feed" a larger, more impersonal "stream of thought" that seems increasingly identical to "nature's ebb and flow," the chaotic, even windblown, source of life, over which (as over the Poet) "The breath of heaven did wander" (ll. 638–39, 643–44, 652, and 668). The poem and Poet have apparently arrived, after pressing beyond a semi-Miltonic garden, at the moment of Creation in *Paradise Lost* (VII. 216–37) when the "troubl'd waves" of *"Chaos"* hear the Lord's "voice" and "vital virtue" is "infus'd . . . Throughout the fluid Mass." The process is to some degree moving in reverse, of course, with "vital virtue" now *leaving* the body to be drawn away by the waves now rolling "through the labyrinthine dell" they once carved out (*Alastor,* l. 541). One reason for the inversion is the dying youth's resemblance to Milton's Satan as the latter nostalgically longs for "lost happiness" in "doleful shades" where "hope never comes" (*Paradise Lost,* I. 55, 65, and 66). The *Alastor*-Poet still clings enough to his former obsessions and dream-visions, resigning his "soul / To images of the majestic past" (*Alastor,* ll. 628–29), that he presses for a stoppage of all process while he tries to fix his focus on "two lessening points of light" (his goddess) in the gathering "darkness" (ll. 654–55)—only to reap, as Satan reaped Death from Sin, a "quenching" that leaves him "No sense, no motion, [*and*] no divinity" (ll. 670 and 666). Another reason, though, for reversing Miltonic Creation is that myth's own dependence on the Lucretian genesis, which brings forth life and dissipates it into death—"flows and ebbs"—without the need of a divine organizer, thereby undermining Milton's version when it reappears alongside his.

This foundation of observable life—now rendered as sheer relational formation and deformation—is the one that cascaded in to become the Poet *and* his thought process initially and now draws his thinking (but not him) off into its "many-voiced waves" as these are driven on by their own transitional force *and* by the winds of transference blowing across them as similar breezes once blew across the "latticed chamber" that was the Poet (l. 632). Such an uncontained drive, the basis of *eros* and *thanatos,* is the underwriter of all the transpositional "origins" in the poem, hence the movement to which the Poet's stream of thought must return, if only so that the movement can drive the stream ahead in a transformation that "Scatter[s] its waters to the passing winds" about to generate future existence (l. 570). In the face of all this, the Narrator can respond with two attitudes, and he confesses his ambivalence by choosing them both. He can and does ignore the self-regeneration of the death-dealing process by lamenting how "A fragile lute" is now "still, dark, and dry" (ll. 667 and

671). Yet he also writes in manifest wonder about the "stream" of "larger volume" that repossesses the Poet's life, the more primordial and violent form of the movement in the "Mother" that subsumes all of her creations and destructions in "The Thunder and hiss of homeless streams" (ll. 540 and 566).

Shelley at His Point of Departure

Alastor—indeed, the Shelley of 1815—is thereby poised on the brink of a transition between opposed modes of thought. On one side, the side of his early writing years, lies the attitude that demands one source and center for all "subordinate" relationships. The Narrator closes the piece with this logic, refusing to recognize what he has done with Mother Nature and what the Poet has attempted with his dream-maiden and death. The poem's last verse-paragraph is a plea for a restorative elixir, one wrought from a knowledge of the "true law" behind "this so lovely world" (ll. 685–86). If the now-dead Poet, as the Narrator fears, cannot be revived by such Gothic means, we must see all "Art and eloquence, / And all the shews o' the world [as] frail and vain" (ll. 710–11)—as unable to refer to some surpassing "Spirit" that is permanently behind them instead of briefly alive (l. 714). Thus tormenting the Narrator as he was tormented, the Poet is turned into *alastor* as "demon," not just into someone "pursued" by the anguish of figures that will not give way to Absolutes. He becomes a haunting reminder that "the web of human things" and the "feeble imagery" of "high verse" are always "mourning [like Wordsworth and Coleridge] the memory / Of that which is no more" to the point of arousing "clinging hope" and turning it into "pale despair" (ll. 719, 706–9, and 717–18). On the other side, the side of Shelley's future work, however, there is a growing sense of both the hidden source of and the logic surpassing such a conception. There is the possibility that thought emerges from and is a vast relational exchange, a play of turns, flowing into curves (or paradises) of apparent unity while also dashing from one element to another in a way that threatens every unity with dissolution and dispersal. Even as he tries to ground and repress this activity, the Narrator is forced to manifest it in his epilogue. He must struggle toward a definition of the elixir he seeks by darting between three different legends: the "curse" of the Wandering Jew, "Medea's wondrous alchemy," and the "dream" of a medieval "magician" (ll. 672–85), none of which is the exact equivalent of the others.

The most fruitful use of this process, barring its repression by the Narrator or the Poet, has to be the verbal extension of the self's desires toward the desire of others, the self seeking (and thus losing) itself in different forms. Such an exchange can alter the relations of social life from being secretive and hierarchical to becoming sympathetic and equal. But if such an effort is not finally attempted, as it is not in the cases of the Poet and the Narrator, there are various possible responses to an awareness of the process, providing we believe the Preface to *Alastor*. One is the reaction of those people who are "instigated by no sacred thirst [for] knowledge" and are able to love almost "nothing on this earth" (*NCE*, p. 69). They repress relational thinking so quickly and entirely that they suffer the moral death of a "blind" isolation (p. 69), an ignorance of all the relational contexts from which they come and in which they can potentially find a place. Another way is the choice of the Narrator, the Poet, and at times the young Shelley himslf, who paradoxically "exist without human sympathy" yet seek intensely after the activity that urges "its communities" (p. 69). They behold, in other words, the self-displacing onslaught of the Lucretian interplay moving into and through them *and* their own fading away as that movement drives out of and beyond them into to open space. Failing to help direct its constant turning-toward-another, they permit it either to inundate their psyches in their passive moments or to chase after them as an "irresistible" death wish urging them to accept a passage beyond the life they currently know (p. 69). That "Power," we discover, is itself the demonic *alastor* or "the Spirit of Solitude," yet it gains these ominous names only when a solitary life distorts its operation into the "essence" of a solitary truth.

Hence, after coming to this discovery over the course of five late-adolescent years, Shelley is now in a position to approach the options and questions that a truly relational awareness permits. He has seen his four early systems revolve toward each other because of the motion governing their different orders only to find that activity pushing him toward yet another substitute that acts out the dynamics of (and warns him about) the process he has just been through. In fact, he has found himself transforming that entire progression into a peculiar narrative structure where Narrator replaces Wordsworth, Poet replaces Narrator and Coleridge, and both replace Shelley himself with a mirror inside a mirror, all the while reconstituting what he and his precursors "have been" and "shall be." Along the way he has learned what substitute centers are, or rather how they are actually produced by substitution itself. He now sees that they are projected by a universal compulsion, one basic to self-definition and thus to the writing of a personal poem, that always works to supplant an existing figure lacking a center to complete it (such as the self) with a counterpart distending that figure into a very different (yet mirroring) level of being. He also begins to realize that this transfiguration never satisfies the desire it extends in any one of its shifts between different forms. The Poet in *Alastor,* true enough, is driven by a "strong impulse" to liken himself to that famous swan "by the sea-shore" (ll. 274–75) and then to regard its "Scaling [of] the upward sky" as a voyage "home" to a "sweet mate" both like and unlike the journey that the Poet now plans to take upon the "Chorasmian" waters (ll. 278–82 and 272). At the same time the Poet is driven back to his own incompletion, to the distance between himself and any metaphor for him, as he realizes the inability of such a different animal to ground or echo "my thoughts" completely (l. 290). All he can do is to follow out the same impulse in a different manner, further distending both the swan-figure and himself; like Hamlet comparing himself to the player reciting the anguish of Hecuba, the Poet wonders why he "should linger" on this shore when he has a "voice far sweeter" and a "Spirit more vast" even than those of the swan (ll. 285–87). Here, caught within this self-extension and its perpetual need for "more" of its process, is where Shelley stands in his self-transformations of 1815. He is setting off on a voyage of writing that will complete his thoughts only by further distorting them, and he is discovering that he can never surpass the drive that makes him take that course.

2

The Poles of Being and the Surpassing of Precursors: The "Hymn to Intellectual Beauty" and "Mont Blanc"

New Versions of Old Quandaries

Shelley voyages for a second time from England to Switzerland in May 1816, hoping to elude the fetters tying his future to demands from his past—to escape, his letters tell us, from his first wife, his guilt over their children, his failure to gain an entail from his grandfather's will, his creditors, his father, his lover's (Mary Godwin's) father, Hogg's lust for Mary, the government investigators spying on the young poet's revolutionary behavior,[1] the hostility of conservative English minds toward his "wild and specious" *Alastor* volume,[2] and the Southeyan–Wordsworthian–Coleridgean order of poetry retracting its best instincts in the face of the more defiant work of Lord Byron, whom Shelley now longed to meet. But everywhere he turns after this physical transfer, whether toward books, nature, or people, he finds reminders of the "variability" that seems to have driven his earlier writing, images or motions that force him to recall what he has not yet resolved in his sense of that impulse. As he boats around Lake Geneva with Byron while reading *Julie; ou la nouvelle Héloïse* (one of Rousseau's least self-centered books, in Shelley's eyes), he sees in the way this novel reconstitutes the very places he now perceives the process by which a "powerfully bright" mind must invariably "cast a shadow of falsehood on the records that are called reality" (*L*, I, 485). Consequently, he has to reexamine his longstanding sense that each perception is a memory-trace transfigured by interpretation the moment it exists. He also must recall how that tracing-and-changing activity has seemed to him, as early as his "Gothic" days, the quintessentially poetic "flame that lived within his eager mind" (*Esdaile Notebook, S&C,* IV, 1044).

A preconscious process of alchemical conversion in the young Shelley may have "kindled all the thoughts that once had been" into suddenly luminous and different forms (*S&C,* IV, 1044), and Rousseau was probably possessed by the same operation, by a "divine beauty" able to add bright "shades" to the remembered vestiges of perception (*L*, I, 480). As Byron has just written in Canto the Third of *Childe Harold's Pilgrimage* (lxxvii–lxxix),[3] "wild Rousseau" appeared "kindled . . . with ethereal flame" to the point of being able to "cast / O'er erring deeds and thoughts, a heavenly hue / Of words, like sunbeams"; such a "burning" force clearly impelled him to hark back to an "ideal Beauty" in all forms he beheld, and "This [desire] breathed itself to life in [the character] Julie" so that each "gentle touch" between the heroine and her lover now seems a passage between them of the "thrilled Spirit" that overwhelmed Rousseau and drew him toward "Passion's essence." Such a process also resembles the one described in C. M. Wieland's novel *Agathon* (first read by Shelley in translation in 1813). There the ancient Greek Cleonissa is seen by the hero as Saint-Preux sees Julie, as a "living instance" of how "external beauty" intimates "the intellectual Beauty of the soul."[4] How exactly does that kind of movement work, Shelley now wonders, if it can involve both conversions as perception happens and a psychic capacity to use a precognitive force to recolor and reorder perceptions? What description or narrative can we give of that action, moreover, if it has usually occurred and departed before we have consciously confronted it? "Passion's rapturous dream" in Shelley's own memories is but a "fleeting flash" intimating the mere "illusion of its gleam" (*Esdaile, S&C*, IV, 945). Even in *Julie* what "animates" the physical charms of the new Eloise is for Saint-Preux only the "divine mark" of a "spotless soul" that the mark itself no longer contains completely.[5] By what means can such a nondivine and self-withdrawing "divinity" be addressed? What forms of worship, even, are appropriate for this purely mental offshoot, this inner ("intellectual") manifestation, of the "motion that produces mind"?

Then, too, can such a mentally operating "Spirit" really be divorced, as these questions imply it can, from the external onslaught, the other pole of existence, out of which "It" seems to emerge? Once *Alastor* has pulled all transfiguration back to the Lucretian turbulence prior to "insides" and "outsides," Shelley is never able to separate either of these poles from the other any more than he can ground either one entirely in its opposite. When the *Alastor* Poet reaches for his dream-spirit, after all, he discovers he must seek it in the myriad other places (the "inner" perceptions of "outer" objects) from which its ingredients have been gathered. After he reaches the *locus amoenus* where he gazes at the mirror-image he has projected from his psyche, he finds that the "unaccustomed presence" behind the whole scene, the one that takes the form of "Two starry eyes" beckoning him on, assaults him initially as "clothed in no bright robes" but as the movement toward *and* away from him in the "undulating woods, and silent well, / And leaping rivulet, and evening gloom," all of them "deepening [their] dark shades" as they become a kind of "speech" to him announcing their own mystery (ll. 480–86). The Narrator sees Nature as a texture of self-observing figures, it seems, because the "object" of perception is an incoming confluence of elements from many different quarters receding back into an endless and "deepening" departure at the same time. Though that is partly because such a "Nature" is a verbal composition made from already symbolic figures beckoning elsewhere, its "speech" is presented to the Poet as but one emerging modification of an advancing and withdrawing (Necessity-like) movement that the mind can neither contain nor control. Shelley realizes that the motion of "Spirit" may be determined by a movement "external" to himself and to "Spirit." Shortly after he writes in response, then, to the questions revived in him by Byron, Rousseau, and the villages along Lake Geneva, this poet is easily driven back toward the problem of this second motion, either by his further travels near cascades and mountains or by the waterfalls described in *Alastor* that such Alpine scenes are bound to recall. He has to ask, turning away from the "inside," about the exact relations and boundaries between "mind" and the larger concatenation "outside" it. He begins to speculate on why "the influxes of sense" feeding the "stream of thought" in *Alastor* make the "blood" forever "beat in mystic sympathy with nature's ebb and flow" (ll. 641, 644, and 651–53), even though this wave-like movement, since all things exist only as perceived, must be a projection outward of thought's interpretive process. He has to explore, finally, the reasons for and the consequences of an "influx" that retracts its gifts as much as it pours them into thought, that "dwells apart" but still "comes down in [the] likeness" of various forms and actions.

In doing all this, meanwhile, Shelley works to complete his deconstruction of the older contemporaries whose styles and modes have so imbued his own. Although *Alastor* tries to draw images from Wordsworth and Coleridge back to their mobile (but subliminal) foundations using echoes of earlier writing, it can do so only in and through their terms, to such an extent that it cannot avoid seeing the primal Lucretian turbulence as Wordsworth's half-withdrawing flow toward the mind "fed with many-voiced waves" (*Alastor*, l. 669). Shelley's critique of his predecessors may be clear, but, except on rare occasions (ll. 107–28), they still frame his discourse. The *Alastor* Poet's story ends up enveloped in Wordsworthian mother-worship and Coleridgean dejection "when some surpassing Spirit, / Whose light adorned the world around it, leaves those who remain behind" with "a woe 'too deep for tears' " (ll. 713–16). Hence, as Shelley responds to the renewed quandaries of 1816 with the "Hymn to Intellectual Beauty" in late June and "Mont Blanc" in July and August, he has to work out the former in relation to the "trailings" of clouded "glory" in Wordsworth's "Immortality" ode and the latter in a dialogue with Coleridge's "Hymn Before Sunrise," which addresses Mont Blanc (though Coleridge never saw it) from the same vale of Chamouni where Shelley viewed it in person.[6] At the same time, though, he is manifestly determined to draw out the repressed process behind such poems while also engulfing their terms within it (rather than the reverse). Right from the start, then, his lyrics of 1816 set out to perform several disruptions at once: to wrest his precursors' God-centered terms into juxtapositions with very different figures, to force these terms back toward their transpositional assumptions to such an extent that their usual definitions must be overturned, to use his predecessors' verse-structures only to violate them with related patterns that are both more formal and more irregular, and to set up the poles of "inner" and "outer" only to make each seek or become the other without either becoming the "object" of its counterpart at any point in the continual exchange.

While Shelley is fighting these battles, too, he has to resist those moments in Rousseau and Byron which show that the "flames" of their transfigured thoughts are really ceremonial fires committed to the worship of distant absolutes. Rousseau's "ideal Beauty" in *Julie,* particularly when Saint-Preux walks in the "higher regions" of the Alps (Part I, letter 23), is a Platonic intimation of an "eternal purity" that veils itself in some of the "hues" of all things, pending (in III, letter 18) the "refinement" of "philosophy by Christian morals." Byron's Canto the Third, in its turn, takes the "fire / And motion of the Soul which will not dwell / In its own narrow being, but aspire / Beyond the fitting medium of desire" (a notion drawn in part from *Alastor*[7]) and makes it a sense "Of that which is all creator and Defence," makes it in fact a "spark immortal" imprisoned in a "clay" that envies "the light to which it mounts" (xiv, xlii, and lxxxix). Such a semi-Wordsworthian reaching for a long-lost Heaven, though spoken at a far greater distance from the "light," sees the Alps (including Mont Blanc) as "throned Eternity in icy halls," a hierarchical emblem of the fall from grace that shows "How earth may pierce to Heaven, yet leave vain man below" (lxii). The "Hymn" and "Mont Blanc" are therefore heretical challenges, not just to common orthodoxies or deistic visions of the "Power" in nature, but even to all these supposedly liberal departures from standard doctrine that really join the usual "codes of fraud and woe" in the end. To look, then, at Shelley's 1816 portraits of mental and external transmigration is also to study his skewing of figures and styles that have never really become the revolutions they were claiming to be.

The Shelley lyrics of this famous summer, after all, try to work out an alternative stance that is more complex and certainly more radical than the "unorthodox" attitudes even of Rousseau and Byron. This "faith" tries to celebrate the movement between mysterious memories or perceptions, the process that first arouses a desire for deeper levels, rather than the "higher points" that desire has often projected in the face of "fallings from us" and "vanishings" (Wordsworth's "Immortality" ode, l. 143). Shelley calls attention to the primal force of this movement by turning once-separate signs from previous works and philosophies toward one another and then transforming these figural combinations using different figures from still other quarters (vestiges of alternative voices). The resulting "I," though still addressing a mystery, opens itself to the many possible relations connecting its discontinuous perceptions, to many kinds of passages between supposed "levels" of perception and thought, to many conflicting voices of explanation, and thus to the many ways of articulating the process that allows recollections to reappear in very different forms. The resulting lyric pattern is so revisionary that it hardly seems "lyric" in the longest-standing definitions of that word.[8] Standard lyric assumptions about the "subject's" relation to an "object" are answered by a procedure that puts the distinction in question while never denying a primal relationship between these different aspects—or really creations—of verbalized thought. The two lyrics I now want to examine come to see each "inside" figure as constituted by a tending-outward from itself. Every "outside" figure or "represented object," all the while, turns out to be the reflection of an "interior" suggested by another figure.

Building a Hymn from Dislocations

Such revisionism going back to "radical" roots is fundamental to every feature of the "Hymn to Intellectual Beauty." That is even true of the initial sleights of hand by which the piece is styled as the sort of poem it is. As others have seen, Shelley's use of "Hymn" and a hymnlike verse-form is highly ironic. Yet that is not because Shelley has simply implanted a skeptical or irreligious concept at the center of a lyric mode long connected with the desire for or the address to a God. Actually, he has returned his writing to some half-forgotten movements in poetry toward which his title very cleverly points. He knows that Wordsworth and Coleridge have usually employed the ode to lament a "beauty-making power" now faded from the psyche ("Dejection," l. 63). This genre dimly remembers the hymn without always accepting the latter's cry toward an ever-distant Father and instead addresses a general force of creativity or prowess that a poet might recover, usurp, or a rejoin within his own "shaping spirit,"[9]

Shelley draws this verse-form back toward the hymnic mode it really longs for as Wordsworth and Coleridge keep using it. In his eyes both poets veer toward the "Hymn Before Sunrise" or the "Address of the Priest to the Supreme Being" in Book Ninth of *The Excursion* because they finally prefer, even in their odes, the position of the "simple spirit, guided from above" ("Dejection," l. 137). Then, once Shelley has forced these recent invocations down to their supplicative roots in such pieces as Spenser's "Hymne of Heavenly Beautie," he replaces the usual addressee of hymns, as Rousseau or Byron might have done had they adopted this mode,[10] with a soul-reviving abstract concept similar to those declaimed and worshipped during the vast public ceremonies of the French Revolution.[11] As he will do again in Canto V of *Laon and Cythna,* Shelley echoes the revolutionary praises of Wisdom, Liberty, and Equality that once asked a moral principle or a universal tendency of thought to "re-ascend the human heart" (*Laon and Cythna,* l. 220; *CPW,* II, 179) and to rekindle a "hope" that such an essence will urge men and women to "free / This world from its dark slavery" to all monarchical systems ("Hymn to Intellectual Beauty," ll. 69–70). In making that shift, he drives the traditional English hymn both ahead toward the rebellious redactions of it that a Wordsworth or Coleridge should have extended and back to its Delphic, Vedic, and even Old Testament ancestors, in which a self-obscuring "oracular vapor is hurled up [or down]" to be called "truth, virtue, love, genius, or joy" by its briefly inspired receivers (*Prometheus Unbound,* II, iii. 4–6).[12]

At the same time, though, Shelley's ritual lyric refuses to address anything that might even resemble an *ousia* at one with itself at a far remove. Such absolutist logic, in his view, has helped to suppress the true reconceptions proposed by the Revolution, so the poet strives to avoid the sort of "name" that might imply "God and ghosts and Heaven" ("Hymn," l. 27) and yet to specify his longstanding sense of a "visiting" influx lending "grace" to the "life" that he seems to perceive (ll. 2 and 35). He is compelled to address, under a Rousseauist name suggested by Wieland and more recently by Byron, the apparently internal process in his—and Wordsworth's—memory that most resembles "exhalations" from elsewhere becoming a series of different ideas veiling their previous forms. He recalls from his early letters the displacement of one "impression" by another that adds a different coloration to the first while covering it over and making it desirable. He thus proposes a "Spirit of BEAUTY" that can "consecrate" thoughts with its "hues" only by concealing itself in masks "Like moonbeams . . . behind some piny mountain shower" or like the "memory of music [long] fled" (ll. 4 and 10). He returns his immediate precursors to the "Hymn" only to return the focus of the hymn-form itself to the process of estrangement from earlier points that makes hymns necessary, not to the vision of Eternal Truth that post-biblical hymns so often seem to celebrate.

Even in this effort, of course, Shelley's "LOVELINESS" (l. 71) could still have remained quite close to Wordsworth's "visionary gleam," fading as both do "into the light of common day" so that only in the "embers is something that doth live" and "nature" at best "remembers / What was [and is] so fugitive" ("Immortality" ode, ll. 76 and 133–36). But the "Hymn" breaks away from those images and suggests why Wordsworth must include both "trailings" and "clouds" in his memories of his losses. It wrenches such figures toward several non-Wordsworthian movements, all brought forward from Shelley's earlier faiths to interact in his new sense of the poet's muse. The Gothic leap from dissolution to luminous hope returns, partly when the "Hymn's" speaker recalls seeking "for ghosts" as "a boy" in "many a listening cham-

ber, cave and ruin" (ll. 49–50), and even more so when the "Spirit" becomes "nourishment" to "thought . . . Like darkness to a dying flame" (ll. 44–45), producing new
"hues and harmonies" in the psyche out of and in front of an obscurity as black as
"evening" (l. 8). No longer can the memory of an incoming "shadow" (Shelley's first
line) recollect a fading "glory" behind the descending gloom. Instead, thought itself
must fade and then be rekindled by an emergence from blackness that reappears as
flame. The "dying" of the gleam has become a later stage—one that can be reversed
by an earlier, preconscious movement—in a succession that begins with an apparent
void and its self-transmutation into something else (a bright "shadow" of it). In this
recollection of the Gothic sensibility, moreover, the blackness is equated with a near-
total disappearance of an entity. The speaker of the "Hymn," directly after picturing
the Spirit's infusion as darkness feeding light, calls on that notion to "Depart not," to
remain somehow in a sublimation that is always bound to indicate a withdrawal
behind it (l. 46). All the forms, all the images of disappearing images in which the
"Spirit of BEAUTY" can reappear, "like clouds depart, / And come" in one paradoxical, two-directional motion (ll. 37–38). As when a word is simply written on a blank
surface and thereby seems to recall or anticipate something, there is nothing clearly
before a sign that, once it appears, both obscures what seems to be elsewhere and
defers to an unknown successor yet to arise. Consequently, even those who project a
glory behind the entire process must see that brightness as visible only in "cloudings"
that "trail" off from one point to the next. So complete is the withdrawal and the
concealment of it, so basic is that sheer transformation with no "living truth" prior
to it, that the dark cloud can seem for a time an inevitable collapsing into death and
"BEAUTY" but an illusion of light that we use to protect ourselves from the doom
that always awaits us. Shelley's speaker can be tempted momentarily into crying
"Depart not [again]—lest the grave should be, / Like life and fear, a dark reality" from
which there is no escape (ll. 47–48).[13]

But of course this revision of Wordsworth does not stop with a shifting of his figures toward the Gothic sensibility, especially since Shelley has long ago decided that
the Gothic reversal is a symptom of a much deeper process. The poet also reinvokes
that moment in his earlier deism when he was drawn toward the "Power" of the *Academical Questions,* toward the impulse that Drummond saw all humankind projecting
into the "occult" depths of thought's movement between its own moments.[14] That
projection was necessary for Drummond because it explained the way thoughts displace and substitute for their predecessors, and this latter activity is what Shelley must
account for as his "Spirit" intimates a recollection of "music" only in the "memory"
that stands in for it. Thus the sudden withdrawal and reappearance is said to produce
"The awful shadow of some unseen Power" in the "Hymn's" opening line. The darkness feeding the flame is henceforth inhabited, though only in an interpretation after
the "shadow" has been sensed, by a self-recreative force that may pass through the
death of its moments yet that always moves ahead like the invisible wind of the Old
Testament Yahweh, or at least like the "summer winds that creep from flower to
flower" urging each of the blossoms to reproduce itself (send out seeds) in the direction of a bloom that is yet to be (l. 4). Here Shelley even gravitates toward his late-
adolescent "Necessity" in making the entering process an extrahuman yet self-mask-
ing energy "visiting" from elsewhere "Each human heart and countenance," whether
the latter have willed its coming or not (ll. 6–7). The announcement of this series of

schemes is the sequence in the "Hymn's" two initial lines: "The awful [Gothic] shadow of some unseen [Drummondesque] Power / Floats though unseen amongst us [as Necessity—or a preconscious memory—does]." The Gothic dissolution and revival can survive to be "unseen" again only when it is recast as a semi-deistic and then half-necessitarian impulse. That hiding of an act of hiding offered as the poem starts, in other words, comes not from any *one* of these counter-Words-worthian figures but from all of them transferring themselves toward the others once the "trailing" of "clouds" has been tranferred toward them.

Shelley is not yet at the point he reaches in the *Defence,* where the "invisible influ-ence" reviving a "fading coal" is clearly a turning of old figures for divine inspiration toward the sudden recurrence of some interplays in the memory and vice-versa. Instead, this earlier poem makes possible that relatively nonchalant exchange of met-aphors by seeking to defy Wordsworth, draw the hymn back to its primordial sense of estrangement, and substitute a movement in memory for a divine dictation. The only way for Shelley to accomplish those goals is to allow his different earlier substi-tutes for orthodox religion to interpret themselves by way of their counterparts as they form the poem's governing concept. He activates the interrelational drive they already share to change them all into a composite that makes each one defer to the others. The resulting succession of figures then makes its perceiver look back through it to project an object of desire behind the process, an object that is itself a self-dislocating movement extending its activity in what it is not. Indeed, the only "origin" such a relational method can propose for itself in retrospect has to be a version of its own transference, a "trailing" of "clouds" into "clouds" being all it knows.

That fact accounts for what occurs in the fifth stanza, when Shelley's speaker feels compelled, since the process does look backward, to propose an original inspiration: the first time the "shadow fell on" him in his now-receding youth (l. 59). This sup-posed primal infusion, which seems to have come upon the speaker during his late-adolescent quests through graveyards in "Hopes of high talk with the departed dead" (l. 52), is often interpreted as a specific moment in Shelley's actual life, or at least as a memory of one special epiphany that he hopes will recur more often than it has.[15] But such proposals of a single and personal origin are not really valid given the avail-able evidence, particularly if we look more closely at the passage in question, which begins after the speaker has cried out to the gravestones those "poisonous names [of absolute gods] with which our youth is fed" (l. 53):

> I was not heard—I saw them not—
> When musing deeply on the lot
> Of life, at that sweet time when winds are wooing
> All vital things that wake to bring
> News of buds and blossoming,—
> Sudden, thy shadow fell on me;
> I shrieked, and clasped my hands in extacy! (ll.54–60)

For one thing, as Timothy Webb has shown,[16] Shelley is here offering an alternative to the moment of divine descent that has long been conventional in the hymns of various faiths. The poet is, in fact, employing this convention in order to deny the usual response to outcries from a Christian suppliant, in order to show the silent non-existence of the "divine mercy" that generally "subdues" the pious singer into patience and obedient "resignation" (*The Excursion,* VI, 771–74). In place of all that, Shelley offers the sudden springing of an alienated trace (a "shadow" without its body) out of and in front of the wooing "winds" of Spring.

Moreover, if there is a touch of autobiography at this point, it is only as the recollection draws together moments and speculations from Shelley's youth, ones that never were really connected back then except by being adjacent in time. The foregoing passage, as it happens, echoes many different aspects of an epistle written to Hogg in early January 1811, wherein the young Shelley has just spent "most of the night pacing a churchyard" longing for Spring and speculating deistically on how much a "*supernatural* power actuates the organization of physical causes" (*L,* I, 39). Much of this letter concerns a possible (but unlikely) love-match between Hogg and Shelley's sister Elizabeth and contrasts that prospect to the pain Shelley feels after being rejected, at her parents' insistence, by his cousin Harriet Grove. A love-object in Shelley's eyes, as opposed to Hogg's, can be thought of at this juncture only as "lost" and as an unsolvable "mystery," yet as something still worthy of being perpetually "followed" and worshipped, especially if that posture serves to undermine the "Christianity" that motivated the parents (*L,* I, 37–38). Remembering an even earlier search for a fantasy uniting and resolving these contradictory feelings, the young Shelley inserts and revises an adolescent poem that he had once titled "On an Icicle that Clung to the Grass of a Grave" (*Esdaile Notebook, S&C,* II, 1017–18). There the speaker calls upon some vague Gothic force to transport a frozen teardrop of unrequited love out of a northerly winter into a climate of "southernly breezes," where Spring will return and "the warm current of Love" will never "freeze" at the dictate of "selfishness" or "Pride" (*L,* I, 38; ll. 1–5). In that world projected by desire to be an exact contrast to the present one, such a current will "Waft" the tear toward a maidenly "bosom" that will be "faithful" enough to "dissolve the dim ice drop" and even "bid it arise / Too pure for these regions, to gleam in the skies" (ll. 2 and 6–7). Moreover, the speaker finds, such a world cannot even be imagined by the weeper of the tear or the speaker himself if "some Spirit of kindness descending [like the 'current of Love'] / To share in the load of mortality's Woe" has not already prompted the "spirit" in the "sepulchre" called the body to seek Heaven and "mix with [something] kindred there" (ll. 20–24). Indeed, that "Spirit," revised from "Angel" in the earlier version, turns out to be the object of address in the poem's first two stanzas (as in l. 14: "Let it fly taintless spirit to mingle with thee"). The poem soon breaks off, though, and a line is drawn at that point in Shelley's letter, whereupon the young poet resumes his debate with Hogg about a seemingly different kind of deity altogether. In contrast to the sort of ending held out by the gravestones in the churchyard through which Shelley has been walking all night, he now expresses his desire for an "influence" or "Soul" that lies behind all other "spirits" that may be imagined, an "actuating principle" offering an ultimate "termination" (aside from death) to the inquiries of man (*L,* I, 39).

Many ingredients of the "Hymn" are present here: the crypts impelling a quest for their opposite, the lost mystery, the remembered object of worship, the spring winds of wooing, the anti-Christian aspiration to grace, the coming of an addressed spirit, and the influence behind such a descent. But they are pieces only vaguely attracted to each other by sheer proximity, hardly a sudden inspiration at an actual moment in which they all coalesce into one vision. The interplay, and then the insertion of such a construction into the speaker's adolescence, is therefore another product of the "Hymn's" peculiar compulsion to interweave quite separate points in its anti-hymnic portraits of "origins." The remembrance in the "Hymn," attempting a Freudian sub-limation, thus pulls the mysterious lost love toward becoming the "actuating princi-ple" while forgetting her personal features,[17] mainly by linking the "warm current" that "wafts" toward the Harriet of the south with the "Spirit" arousing a desire for heavenly kindred. From that point on, since the Spirit as warm breeze is already in the poem along with the Gothic explosion from one state to another, it is easy for the poet to recall the descent of the "shadow" as leaping in front of or interrupting the spring winds, especially as that move repeats the sudden turn at the end of Shelley's letter from a poem on the springlike "spirit of kindness" to his deistic speculations on how thought "*must* [*sic*] to infinity."

In this attempt to "root" the "Hymn," in fact, Shelley is forced, even more than he is in the poem's opening lines, to foreground the basic drive that underwrites the composition of this memory and the interaction of concepts that is Intellectual Beauty. He presents a motion, here the winds and their "news of buds and blossom-ing," being abruptly supplanted by another motion that is both utterly different and in some ways the same. That sort of shift *is* the power behind the "Power's" initial and later reworkings of itself as a shadow, even behind the Freudian displacement that makes sexual desire reappear as something else. The sublimation in Intellectual Beauty's manifestations, whether of its own shadow or previous figures, depends on that basic relocation becoming unseen, even forgotten, and yet being seen again repeatedly in the images of images that keep displacing a self-displacement. Here lies the major advance of the "Hymn's" main conception over Shelley's previous substi-tutes for the Christian God. What comes to occupy the place of the inspiring Muse or Deity is no longer just a series of transfers or the projection of an impetus into the depths of the series. It is the passing of transfers out of themselves into and through other motions of transfer (as when Shelley shifts between the philosophies of his youth or the winds become "news of buds" turning to "blossoms" and then into the "shadow"), all in a way that veils and changes whatever is transposed and so leaves portions of all former transfers behind. Now there is something manifestly deeper, preceding even the Gothic transfiguration, that makes the Spirit seem a "nourishment / Like darkness to a dying flame." A thought or image is replaced by its own conceal-ment, perhaps even a figure for its own death or for obscurity itself, by its act of feed-ing into and completing itself ("floating though unseen") through a different one that is also fading from its former state as the infusion occurs. There is a supplanting, a self-concealment, and a transmutation happening at each of the stages (even the most primal one) within this movement, which therefore comes more and more to resemble the progression of words in the discourse that both remembers (indeed, re-members) and creates the process. We cannot specify anything unified behind these stages, only the unexpected rising of a primal transposition—or, rather, a displacement of it—out of and into our more settled associations of thought (l. 41).

Two overall results immediately follow, then, in the way the "Hymn" is oriented and articulated. In the first place the address to that "train" must always be cried out after the movement has sublimated itself in consciousness and then disappeared from conscious awareness, except for its reappearance in shadows of shadows. By its very nature, the drive to become unseen *in* something else becoming unseen must not be fully present or retained in any "hues" it leaves after its "glance" has turned a thought-formation into another form (l. 6). The movement must seem "inconstant" (l. 6), even though it continuously "Floats though unseen amongst us," because it is recalled only when it has passed through and onward and has left the "grace" of a "mystery" instead of residing permanently in the new thought-relations it arouses (ll. 11–12). That partial self-forgetting causes the mournfulness and the "Beauty" in this "floating," the motion of loss and new attachment that "consecrates" all recent perceptions with recollective "hues" (ll. 13–14). In the second place Shelley's wording of the poem, since he accepts this interaction of very different schema (divine grace and thought-process psychology) occurring even within a single image, has to be an oscillation between distant vocabularies that attract each other; it must fulfill the basic movement between figures that is already urging groups of words toward additional formations. The process of sheer thought-renewal being depicted as a tracing, erasing, and recasting of figures by other figures has to resemble, despite Shelley's atheism, the Old Testament descents of Yahweh that alienate His "shadow" repeatedly in "fire" enveloped by a "thick cloud" (Exodus 19:16–18). Modern readings are misguided when they condemn this poem, as several have, for proposing a "God" that is only a "rhetorical figure" trying absurdly to negotiate between "religious," "declamatory," and Wordsworthian ways of writing.[18] For Shelley such slippery interchanges betoken no failure in his poem, since his kind of "Beauty," made as it is of purely rhetorical crossings and his search for more of them, is the measure of his success in its continual divergence from any fixed center and in its refusal of any one style as the best way to describe it. Shelley must not decide on any sort of grounding location or ideology for the "Spirit" lest it then be monolithically enthroned within a certain type of thought. In fact, he cannot so decide among descriptions for it any more than the interacting figures producing it can decide which of them is dominant.

Actually, once revealed as a continual transference by several other acts of transposition, the "Spirit" must demand that the verbal account of its activities avoid any configurations that might reify or constrict its movement. At first, because he has chosen to write a "Hymn," the very rhyme scheme of Shelley's stanzas seems to regularize the varied stanza-patterns in Wordsworth's "Immortality" ode, thus holding out at least the illusion of a promise that each section's closing will circle back to its beginning. In the end, though, the poem sets up that promise only to indulge in successive violations of it. "Spirit of BEAUTY," cries the speaker in stanza two,

> that dost consecrate
> With thine own hues all thou dost shine upon
> Of human thought or form,—where art thou gone?
> Why dost thou pass away and leave our state,
> This dim, vast vale of tears, vacant and desolate?
> Ask why the sunlight not forever
> Weaves rainbows o'er yon mountain river,
> Why aught should fail or fade that once is shewn,
> Why fear and dream and death and birth
> Cast on the daylight of this earth
> Such gloom,—why man has such a scope
> For love and hate, despondency and hope? (ll. 13–24)

The opening quatrain here, rhymed *abba* as it is in all the stanzas, apparently tries to wrench consecration and departure into forming a neat and closed antithesis. It seems to announce a contradiction within the Spirit's "shining" from which all the latter's variants may come and to which they might refer. But the initial question ends in a fifth line that begins another quatrain and rhymes with line four. The new line then uses that intermediate position to transform the divine "passing," first into a medieval "vale of tears" that a divinity should redeem and then into the very different, hollowed-out emptiness of a Byronic ruin or a Coleridgean "Dejection" ode. The continual passing-away disappears behind successive vestiges of it that forget the initial paradox entirely, just in the way "our state" is suddenly divorced from the inspired one that it was and almost drawn off from its own vowel-sound in a slant-rhyme with "desolate." The second quatrain, as it starts to critique the opening question by wondering if such queries can be answered at all, then rhymes *accb*, avoiding the symmetry of the first four lines and disrupting the anticipated alignment between its two middle lines (with four metrical feet) and the middle lines of the preceding quatrain (each with five). The *b* rhyme ("shewn") is another slanting echo, moreover, which half-recalls the "upon" and "gone" far above it and then parallels the dissolution of "forever" into a "mountain river" of change. This shift emphasizes, in its way of changing the same sound, the inevitable "failing" and fading of whatever is "shewn" in all of Shelley's figures. Here lies the reason, in other words, for his sliding from mere "passing" to total "desolation" and for the inability of his questions to find any answers outside their own progressions. To be represented in this piece is not simply to return in another form; it is to be automatically retracted, altered, obscured, and forgotten, to be disjunctively supplanted by whatever supplements an already self-supplementing drive.

Consecration passes into desolation and perhaps vice-versa, we now find, because the "floating" of the "Spirit," which never recovers "itself" as an identity, denies all permanence and repetition-without-difference to every version of its perpetual metamorphosis. In the face of that injunction, Shelley must even add the phrase "fail and fade" in his final writing of the second stanza. Otherwise he will use "pass away" twice in the same group of words, much as he does in a notebook draft of the "Hymn," perhaps in the hope of pinning down that movement by giving it the same name more than once.[19] The stanza's third quatrain, in any event, declares all such mere echoes out of the question, and not simply because it adds a couplet structure with new rhymes *(ddee)* and indents its four-foot lines in a pattern different from the ones in the other quatrains. By this point "failing and fading" have been translated further into the anticipated clouding of all future new "hues" rising out of the darkness that nourishes flame. The Spirit's adding of light looks ahead now to the "fear and dream" of its disappearance, or rather to the "death" that must inevitably follow its "birth" in the constant but changing spiral of mutability. Consequently, in the final clause of the second question, the speaker asks about a quandary existing outside himself and beyond his own temporal moment: the universal problem of how human beings can be self-projective and self-repressive thinkers at the same time. The explanation, of course, is the forward-tending effulgence and the regrettable forgetfulness that begin and succeed the revival of "intellectual" transference (or, for that matter, the writing of words on a page). Yet, as that fact is restated by implication, the transference continues in the stanza's final shift of focus. The speaker turns his attention from personal recollections and losses toward the results of that "fading" in the minds of people different from himself, toward what in the Spirit's effects keeps humanity in general from turning it into forms of revolution banishing hate and despair from thought. The scope, line length, reference points, and primary terms dominating the first lines of the stanza have been thoroughly relocated by the final lines without being restored to some primal state of oracular, priestly, or conceptual authority. That multiple displacement, we must remember, is the self-concealing "Beauty" of "Intellectual Beauty."

The Outward Turn of Beauty's Power

This compulsion to recast and even to reverse in the "Hymn," because it is so inherent in the "floating" of the "shadow," must not end with the mere forgetting of the Spirit's drive. There must be the abrupt transition between the fading "grace" in "life's unquiet dream" that closes stanza three (1. 36) and the "Love, Hope, and Self-Esteem" that "come" and "depart" at "uncertain moments" in the opening lines of stanza four (ll. 37–38). The "shadow's" floating and self-hiding action has to fulfill its entropic nature; it must counter the dissipation of what it has made in the mind—and the distance of present thoughts from former thought-connections that such a loss seems to suggest—with a leap across another gap into a group of transfers outward that move beyond the obsession with loss and do so by turning toward one another (Love toward Hope toward Self-esteem). Since the Wordsworthian desire for receding glories can never be gratified in a now-absent past, longing must turn into outreaching movements toward other minds, other times, and other states of personal being. Intellectual Beauty's impulse to cross over internal differences should finally be carried through "externally," either in the urge to "love all human kind" (1. 84) or in the hope that future extentions of its own transfiguring process will "free / This world from its dark slavery" to entrenched systems of discourse.

Perhaps most of all it should enable the self-extending thinker to "fear himself" in his very love of others (1. 84). The love directed away from the self can return to the self from all the surfaces and minds that receive it, leading the lover to respect his own expanded identity as it becomes other than it was. That sense of self-expansion can make him value himself as a free, interacting, decentered being. He can then feel himself worthy of far more awe than is usually intoned in the "spells" directed at "God" and "Heaven" (ll. 29 and 27). All "fallings" of the shadow, we must remember, "like clouds depart / *And* come [again]" (my emphasis) at a removed point that then reflects back on every previous instance. They echo Wordsworth's conversion of the "trailing clouds" into the mature and outgoing "tenderness" of "primal sympathy," into the "faith that looks through [and beyond all forms of] death" to a level where past glories are reconfirmed, if not recovered, by the "philosophic mind" ("Immortality" ode, ll. 205, 105, and 188–89). At the same time, the "Hymn" reads that process through the overlay of Rousseau's most analogous conceptions, as though the latter were somehow more recent than Wordsworth's "Strength in what remains behind." Even before he read *Julie,* Shelley had admired the Rousseau of the *Discourse on the Origin of Inequality* (1754), in which *amour de soi* (love of self), as opposed to the obsession with self of *amour-propre,* changes the primitive desire for self-preservation—in Shelley the recoiling from the grave's "darkness" toward a living "flame"—into the civilized esteem for the "self" as both an independent entity and a compassionate member of society.[20]

The Shelleyan path from fading "grace" to "self-esteem," in fact, redacts a long process detailed by Rousseau. Yet the poet does not simply adopt the shift from the survival-urge to sociability, nor does he imitate the "Heavenly Beauty" in *Julie* that responds to social pressure by turning love into a compassionate devotion to duty. Shelley reworks the sequence making both of these possible in *La nouvelle Héloïse,* where he finds a succession of multiple transfigurations that insist on the self referring outside itself more and more. First there is that "animation" of Julie's features by the "mark" of what seems "divine" transmuting an apparently higher "soul" into an imprint and then a physiognomy (Part I, letter 5). That "veil upon veil" arousing Saint-Preux's desire, just as a similar process leads the speaker of the "Hymn" to long for the Spirit's return, continues its transformative work with the natural "realm" that is reflected in Julie's "eyes" (I, letter 10). The layering achieved in her gaze can either raise nature into the "beauty of angels" (letter 10) or "transform other [people] into [its] special likeness" (II, letter 5). It can thus recall the powers of an Eloise and ask a male lover to be an Abelard in her eyes, one even more ennobled than that hypocritical "priest" (I, letter 24) and therefore the altered refiguration of a past and distant being. After these stages of conversion in the multi-leveled visage of this "invisible influence" (II, letter 5), the receiver of the "force" must want the "self-esteem" that such a mirror promises to him and seems to possess as part of its look (I, letter 24). Hence he must exchange a "permanent feeling of interior satisfaction" granted to him by the "influence" when it is visible (same letter) for an "overflowing of [the] heart" toward "mutual pains and mutual pleasures," a total interaction with that other psyche (I, letter 11).

Desire of good for the self, because it is already a reflection back *to* the self from layers of transference, must turn into the desire for the perpetual good of another and then of the several others toward whom the "spotless" gaze turns its eyes. There must be an "unexpected revolution" or "violent shock," it turns out, which changes "abject and weak" personal feelings into "strong and high-minded" desires for harmonious social interaction (III, letter 18). This conversion is the one Julie undergoes when she marries Wolmar to keep from hurting her parents,[21] the process through which she then draws Saint-Preux by helping design a visible "Elysium" where "the disturbance of [his] most seductive passions" can be transformed into a "serenity" desiring a peaceful community (IV, letter 11). Shelley is surely recalling and altering this succession (along with his letter of 1811) when he addresses "Beauty" as "Thou messenger of sympathies, / That wax and wane in lovers' eyes" ("Hymn," ll. 42–43). In this one pair of lines, he escapes Rousseau's brand of Platonism by making the poem's "animator" a "messenger" of interchange and not an immanent Presence; then he makes the "waxing and waning," the appearance and disappearance of the transitional force, a conversion of a sheer "train" into "sympathies" among people (ll. 41–42), thereby turning Julie's "unexpected revolution" into an early and standard part of the process. In a sense, of course, this change is already early for Rousseau. It is already there in the way a lover's eyes transform the "outside" into a different likeness by the continuous passing in them of one image toward and through another. Shelley simply draws the later and more ethical reorientation back to this beginning point where its basic motion occurs. Hence the coming of the "shadow" from the first is as a "spell" from a magical gaze binding the psyche to a love of self by way of a love for others (l. 83). It is also an abrupt transformation of an "awful LOVELINESS" remembered from the past into a "calm" within the "onward life" that looks ahead to future and more social incarnations (ll. 71 and 80–81) The "inside" movement of Intellectual Beauty thus finally points to those "outside" forms of itself receding far behind and leaping ahead of its reveiling of veils, countering analeptic senses of distance and disappearance with proleptic reextensions and anticipations at every turn.

The speaker of Shelley's "Hymn," after all, does not simply reveal the contradictions (the nostalgia and the prophecy) within this process that so curiously occupies the place usually granted to divine inspiration. Instead, as the younger Shelley was, he is drawn, by a self-displacing movement and its contradictory tendencies, into a dramatic progression, a character development dispersing his initial sense of his situation, not unlike the transition from loving memory to despair to hope achieved by Julie, by Saint-Preux, and by the struggling Prometheus in Shelley's later lyric drama. First, the falling away toward the past in the "grace" that the shadow seems to have brought with it pulls the speaker toward a conventional worship of its "mystery" and an almost standard faith in its ability to "consecrate" the most common thoughts during its transformation of them. Immediately, though, the retraction of that grace to subliminal levels where it "floats unseen" makes the speaker lament the desolation that is inevitable when conscious existence has made itself depend upon a failing and fading of vision. Crying out "Depart not" like a frantic Saint-Preux and complaining Byronically of the perpetual distance between the "true signified" and its remaining signifiers, the speaker must desperately long for a time that he already knows will never come, for an ever-deferred moment when the subliminal process will rejoin conscious thought and the mind will seem "immortal" and "omnipotent" because the "glorious train" will be forever visible and operative "within his heart" (ll. 39–41). Naturally that prospect must fail to be realized, since the process is itself a withdrawal and a temporally changing (not permanent) redeployment of itself. The speaker must then find himself caught in the midst of a continuum with the inevitability of death and loss beckoning in the future and a supposed single moment of ecstasy dimly remembered from the past.

Yet gradually, among these frustrations of nostalgia, there are occasional intimations that the basic process is a "messenger of sympathies" seeking figures outside the mind and beyond the present moment for duplication, completion, and continuation. As he accepts that possibility more and more, the speaker retains his earlier supplicative posture, yet only alongside some major modifications of a basically Gothic sensibility. He vows to be faithful to what he has always worshipped, but only by calling forth, as Coleridge would, the "phantoms" or memories of the "thousand [tearful] hours" he has spent in nostalgic longing (l. 64) and asking these moments to confirm his growing sense that the "shadow's" transfigurations, being disruptions of older connections, will someday "free / This world" from its "slavery" to hierarchical systems of thought. Now the self-modification of "Beauty" really does return to its source— its entrance into consciousness from outside it—and thereby shows itself to be transpersonal, instead of personal, though that fact may become fully apparent only in a distant future. It does not matter that the time until that point may be long, a forgetful "summer" after the Spring of what seems the first realization (ll. 76–77). Because subliminal transference can make it happen, there will still be in future thoughts and events an autumnal "harmony" different from yet reminiscent of the "lustre" of former moments (ll. 74–75), a trailing of glory that turns again toward a revival of clouded light as it cannot quite in Wordsworth. The speaker must thus declare, against Wordsworth, Coleridge, Rousseau, and Byron, an anti-Christian commitment to the future of the "power's" movement, a hope that will allow him to "love all human kind" (in a somewhat Christian way) for what it can become and at the same time be in awe of himself for how much he can help transfiguration to further its designs (l. 84). In the end he realizes that future achievement and activity are empowered by the same operation that begot his sense of loss, failure, and withdrawal. He can thereby mature into the combination of old and new beliefs, the multiple voices, with which the "Hymn" concludes.

"Mont Blanc": The Primal *Clinamen*

Concurrently, however, the "Hymn" implies that its transmutative movement is a strictly mental (or linguistic) activity that presumes an "intellectual" source behind itself and seeks only other *minds* in order to complete its movement. As I have suggested earlier, Shelley cannot maintain such an "internal" limit, especially considering what he has found himself saying in his previous writing. He is therefore easily jogged away in July 1816, even though "things" still exist for him only as they are perceived, from framing the "mind" too neatly against other entities within a boundary that makes Nature its prisoner and determines the relations among all visible forms. During his Alpine journey to the Chamouni end of the Servoz valley just after the voyage around Lake Geneva, he discovers that his mind's "expectations" are "exceeded" by the "progress" and the "immensity" of the "images" entering his awareness from outside it, all of them "interwoven" before he can react to them and "extending gradually" beyond what his thoughts can measure (*L,* I, 495–97). Particularly in the "one scene" at the foot of Mont Blanc (I, 497), as he describes it in letters to England, there is a forceful and "perpetual" assault upon thought in which "complicated windings" of valleys, trees, mists, and streams emerge out of a largely glacial "surface" already "broken into a thousand unaccountable figures" (I, 496–97). It appears that Necessity's inhuman, external, and figural "storm of change" has regained some control over Shelley's thinking without bringing along its absolutes outside thought.

That remains the case even when the perceivers of the scene (principally Shelley and Mary) try to possess what thought can neither begin nor encompass nor stop. True, since the "snowy Pyramids which sho[ot] into the sky [seem] to overhang our path" and the falling ice-floes rush down "close to our very footsteps" in the form of the river Arve, the immense vista does appear "pressed home to our regard & to our imagination," and all seems "as much our own as if we had been the creators of such impressions in the minds of others, as now occupied our own" (*L,* I, 497). But Shelley goes on to interpret this "ownership" in the very next sentence as follows: "Nature was the poet whose harmony held our spirits more breathless than that of the divinest." Though it sounds at first as if the poetic process in the observers, their creation of impressions for other minds, were simply being projected anthropomorphically into the Nature confronting them, they could not even begin to make that transfer outward were not numerous transfers pressing toward, into, and away from them already, creating impressions in them with great force much in the way they would wish to produce them in future readers. That is why Shelley must turn the tables with his "Nature" sentence and grant the external "shooting" and falling the position of poetic disseminator. The effect is to make the minds, the would-be possessors of the scene, late stages (like readers) in a vast process passing through them toward others. The human psyche, as Shelley began to see in *Alastor,* may be but an instant in a larger motion surging into it and much of what it perceives, then driving on in the words of that mind to those who would perceive Nature through the overlay of poetry. Thought is "exceeded" and thus contained by the very action it would surround and appropriate, so Shelley must now decide how to redefine that movement and the mind's place within its current. He must do that in an answer to the "Hymn," in a vision that surrounds (or "exceeds") that poem's limited focus, yet without falling back into the medieval tyranny of the universe regarded as the symbolic book of God.

"Mont Blanc" is the solution Shelley offers, particularly in the face of lyrics by his predecessors that restore that tyranny in "readings" of similar settings. Defying "Tintern Abbey" with its "presence rolling through all things," *Childe Harold* with its pinnacles vaulting toward Heaven, but mostly the "Hymn Before Sunrise" with its Mont Blanc intoning the voice of the Lord Himself, Shelley's piece opens with an epistemological theory proposing a modified version of the Lucretian turbulence that he has already placed at the genesis of what we perceive:

> The everlasting universe of things
> Flows through the mind, and rolls its rapid waves,
> Now dark—now glittering—now reflecting gloom—
> Now lending splendour, where from secret springs
> The source of human thought its tribute brings
> Of waters,—with a sound but half its own.
> Such as a feeble brook will oft assume
> In the wild woods, among the mountains lone,
> While waterfalls around it leap for ever,
> Where woods and winds contend, and a vast river
> Over its rocks ceaselessly bursts and raves. (ll. 1–11)

As in *Alastor,* this initial verse-paragraph carries out the poet's defiance by using images from Wordsworth and Coleridge in order to drive down through them to the actual foundations of their ideas, which both precursors have tried to repress. These lines echo the "undetained" thoughts that "Traverse the [partly] passive brain" in Coleridge as well as Wordsworth's turning of the mind into an "ebbing and flowing" place that projects its own confluent beginnings onto high "mountain-steeps and summits" (*Excursion,* II, 848). Shelley even recasts the dawn of personal thought as it is dimly remembered in the "Immortality" ode, presenting the mind as one liquid result of and tributary to the "mighty waters" of an "eternal sea" flowing "inland" ("Ode," ll. 162–67). The rushing and rolling of the inaugural waters in "Mont Blanc" then wrenches such visions back toward the motions that Wordsworth and Coleridge really depend on without admitting it, toward the falling, streaming, and swerving in the *De rerum natura* they inadvertently echo.[22] But, unlike *Alastor,* this archeological probe points very little at whorls of being and the gradual deviation of some droplets from them. Instead, eschewing the globules of Lucretius and their organization into circles, Shelley here roots genesis in the *clinamen* alone, or rather in the swerving of "waves" toward relationships and distinctions.

The globules, we might say, have become sheer inclinations or moving ripples that simply start out as vague differences "reflecting" and "lending" their qualities among themselves.[23] For these differences, granted, the poet chooses "dark" swerves versus "glittering" ones, the opposition between darkness and light that Yahweh calls forth in the second step of the Judeo-Christian Creation (Genesis 1:3–5). In this rejection of the "Hymn Before Sun-rise," though, there is no self-sufficient voice ordering the differentiation. The "universe" initiating and forever underlying all that it makes is just motion, then difference, then opposition, within a continuous flow. Then it is the "rolling," not of a changeless Presence, but of the crossing between different incomplete tendencies (or "unaccountable figures") as they seek out other such drives in a perpetual exchange of givings and borrowings. Moreover, since language "created" all such conceptions in Shelley's eyes, this genesis is also based on the interrelation of ciphers that Lucretius sees as analogous to the intercourse of "atoms" in *De rerum natura*. Swerving toward, lending themselves to, and reflecting each other are movements basic to the different letters in Shelley's lines, especially as they gravitate toward one another, needing counterparts for self-extension, to form the "verses and words" composed out of them—and thus the notions of thought that verses and words suggest.

Shelley offers a new sense, therefore, of "the motion that produces mind." The individual psyche in "Mont Blanc" arises out of, and is a differentiation within, an earlier, larger, centerless, and essentially linguistic play of differences and similarities. The "source of human thought" does not bring "its tribute" to larger cascades from outside the general confusion; it is formed "Of waters" too and so shares the basis of every emergence from the "everlasting" flow. It is both a part of the flow and a particular riverbed or avenue carved out by the torrent in a particular direction. Personal thought is thus primordially a swerve across the other crossings and interactions of waves, just as Lucretius says. At the same time the general flow is always continuing around, in, and past each of its separate forms. It dashes perpetually "through the mind" it makes; it impels the sound of mind to interfere with the sound of larger waterfalls and vice-versa; it helps its "woods and winds" to "contend" just as its basic waves always do; and it carries portions of its own "rocks" away with it as it "bursts and raves" between and beyond them while also molding their features. Nothing so produced by and related to the play of differences can be entirely a thing unto itself, be it mind or Nature or aspects of either one. Though repressions of the general motion may be attempted in both regions, the process will eventually carry its portions toward other products of its movement. Following the lead of *De rerum natura*, each Shelleyan entity is brought into its own cohesion only to begin dissipating (even dying) toward the realms of further entities that will take in what their counterparts lose. Now Shelley understands, more than he ever has before, the need for an "inside" and an "outside" for thought, as well as the drive in each to swerve toward the other, toward an interaction so continuous that the distinction must finally be questioned. The basic play of differences insists that each "inside" ("gloom," let us say) be outside itself; its qualities must be either "lent" from somewhere else or "reflected" and thus made visible or audible by something other than it. Hence the "feeble brook," though distinguishable from the "waterfalls," must gain much of its sound from the vast river contrasted to it and must achieve its full significance by becoming a tributary to a larger water system echoed even further by the "wild woods" and "winds."

In fact, as we have already discovered, the mind cannot see its own features (or even *exist* conceptually) unless it is mirrored in a language that refers to and is composed from nonmental elements. The process that "flows through the mind" in the first verse-paragraph of "Mont Blanc"—already a movement whereby incomplete forms are mirrored by different ones nearby—must therefore face the perceiver in the second paragraph as "thou," the ravine of Arve including its river, addressed as though it were literally inhuman yet metaphorically sentient at the same time.[24] The speaker must examine the movement of relational thought by setting up a relation between "mental" and "natural" interplays. He must subjectively describe, using figures from other texts, the objective interactions in the "many-coloured, many-voiced vale" formed by and around the Arve at the lower levels of Mont Blanc (l. 13). To manifest the mind at work, the "pines" still "clinging" about the ravine must be seen as receiving a "devotion" from "chainless winds" (ll. 20–22) very like the one offered by the relentless breezes rushing toward the Aeolian lyre of the mind in Coleridge's poetry and in other works by Shelley. The winds, meanwhile, must be granted some augmentation by what interprets them: "the odours" blown forth from the living branches and the "old and solemn harmony" of sounds emitted, as in an activated lyre, by the "mighty swinging" of the pines (or strings) as the wind hurtles through them (ll. 23–24). In this economy of traded qualities, whether it operates between mind and nature or between the pines and the wind, each pole must find its elements articulated and appropriated by the other before its own qualities become fully manifest. The wind's force appears and is possessed only in the swinging or exhaling of the pines, while the odors and sounds of the trees are forced out and spread abroad by the wind alone. The "other" in a relation becomes the impulse behind and the apparent location of the counterpart it represents, so because of that double role it both displays and sequesters within it the supposed "ingredients" of whatever figure gravitates toward its position.

As a result, any focal point temporarily chosen by the speaker of "Mont Blanc" must always be, first, a reference to another one impinging on its space. Then, since each figure seeks itself inside the other and finds only the seeking-outside-itself already there, the interplay, still needing an "other" to help define it, defers to a third point (or even a fourth) that seems to ground the others while also depending on them for its status as a ground. Just as a thought interprets a thought, the "loud, lone sound" of the ravine is a product of the "Arve's commotion" as it is amplified by the "caverns echoing" the river's descent (ll. 30–31). In addition, because of this connection, the speaker can see the water-carved "chasms," related to and plunging deeper than the caves, as the depths behind the depths of the caverns. These are the recesses from which the entire "tumult" seems to come and in which the "secret" of the great sound appears to lie (ll. 120–22). The ravine's main "waterfall," at the same time, by pouring melted ice through the air, comes in contact with the sun's crossing light, reflected in part from the white mountain itself. There are consequently "rainbows stretched across the sweep / Of the etherial waterfall" (ll. 25–26), refractions of elements through other elements that produce two sets of curves, one (the rainbows) arcing in front of the other (the cascades). This layering of sweep upon sweep turns the perceived "vale" of the Arve, again in the way a thought turns earlier thoughts for Shelley, into a "veil" on top of a "veil [that now] / Robes some unsculptured image" beneath the layers (ll. 26–27). Such an image, since it seems a half-shaped figure instead of just the contours of a cliff, exists mainly in the eyes of the beholder as he or she looks toward the depths that the layers imply and obscure just by veiling one another.

Everywhere in this poem the transfer of elements through other elements, onto further elements, or back to themselves inaugurates a double drive in the spectator: a desire to penetrate every complex to "something" deeper or higher and a need to divert every glance at any target (outward or inward) toward some different point, some resemblance, where that something might possibly lie. The speaker's reaching toward the cave or the deep image, we find, necessitates a diversion back to the mind depicted in the vale. "When I gaze on thee," says the speaker to the ravine, I "muse on . . . my own, my human mind, which passively [like its counterpart] / Now renders and receives fast influencings" (ll. 36–38). All the speaker can find "inside," though, is the same two-directional movement ("rendering" and "receiving") that drew him out and brought him back to the point of creating a "mind" set over against a "world." Even when he looks "within" using highly "outward" figures, he finds "an unremitting interchange / With the clear universe of things around" (ll. 39–40), so much so that he seems to watch the "wandering wings" of interpretive thought as they assertively "float above [the] darkness" of the observed ravine toward higher impulses behind the river's descent not yet revealed to the eye (ll. 41–42). At the same time he beholds the "legion of wild [interacting] thoughts" retiring into "the still cave of the witch Poesy" (l. 44), a depth within "my own separate phantasy" (l. 36), just as the sound of the Arve turns for echoes toward the caves in the sides of Mont Blanc. There all perceptions turn into "shadows that pass by" and "Ghosts of all things that are" (ll. 45–46), combining Locke's turning of old perceptions into sepulchral memories, Lucretius's *simulacra* peeling off of perceived objects (*De rerum,* IV. 29–53), and the casting of images from elsewhere on the walls of earthly awareness that appears in the famous cave of Plato's *Republic* (VII. 514a–517a). Former impressions thus become uprooted vestiges ready for recomposition at what is now a great distance from that other life which they have left for dead. Yet transposition again reasserts itself as what allows their flight from the past *and* what urges their return to nearly forgotten points of departure—to their "mothers," as Freud might say. The retiring poetic mind, which can try to be enwombed as a "witch" within itself, must seek in the ghosts a "shade" or "faint image" of the place they seem to come from and beckon toward. Images must appear to refer to a distant point toward which "the breast / From which they fled [will recall] them" (ll. 47–48), even as they continue to shift away from the context they have had at one time toward an interpretation in another and later locale.

The level to which the observer seems recalled, in fact, is the place of the most "original" states a Freudian analyst could suggest.[25] Since each "shade" flees both from a vagina (or ravine) pouring forth liquid and life and from a mountain shaped like a "breast" (topped even with a milky whiteness), every such impression appears to recast, in a figure or scene concealing yet intimating a dimly remembered "other stage," the primordial eruption from the womb and the earliest reaching back for the mother. Bound up with these primal conditions, too—which are themselves both desirable and horrifying, beneficently giving birth and ominously threatening to reabsorb what comes out—is the frightening connection between birth and death, between the loss of a secure containment and the emergence and then descent toward continual destruction and change. Parts of the poem manifestly call us back toward these openings, closures, and threats, all the while keeping us just on this side of the threshold of interpretation beyond which lies the welter and dissolution of the most basic beginnings and ends. But the call is as much an outreach from the cavelike womb of thought ("the witch Poesy") as it is a reference backward in displacements of what is perceived. Though there is never a responsive longing without an apparent pulling toward the depths of the object, we cannot tell if the mountain as mother or deathdrive is a covering and recasting of lost memory-traces of birth or if it is a projection created by *re*enwombed traces (the "ghosts" in the cave) as they seek new life by targeting a motherly point of origin—then giving birth to it—at the heart of a dying and distant past. It is clearly the process of the figure becoming other than it was and so entering a uterine cave of new relationships that makes the figure even able to refer to a Magna Mater in the all-obscuring death it seems to remember. The "origin" itself, if one can really be specified, insists on that recasting, after all. The ravine as the place (or as like the process) wherein the individual psyche is born, we must remember, is a cacaphony where differences (such as female and male desires for each other) tend out, beyond, and then back to themselves by way of other such inclinations seeking the same type of differentiation. Calling backward and turning outward are so interdependent in a relationship of images that neither can be closer to an origin than its counterpart and neither can stave off dissolution without undergoing the rebirth granted it by the other drive.

It is this oscillation into which the "Power" now returns, bringing along aspects of its treatment in Drummond and the younger Shelley, as it rises up to counter the "secret Power that reigns" in the God-revealing Alps of Wordsworth, Coleridge, and so many other poets.[26] In "Mont Blanc," in fact, the "Power" is pressured beyond its faint definition in the "Hymn" in a way that demands both a "dwelling apart" and a coming down "in [the] likeness of the Arve." The withdrawal into "inaccessible" silence and remoteness (l. 97) is demanded by all the transfers in the poem as they leave in their wake their distance from and the disappearance of their previous connections. The "Bursting through" of water from ice, or "lightning" from a self-obscuring "tempest" (ll. 18–19), automatically looks back to a radically other, irrecoverable state that has suddenly been converted into a different form by an abrupt turn or *clinamen*. There is apparently, in what Drummond calls an "illusion of the mind," a "breast from which [the conversions have] fled" that is silent and "serene" and thus totally different from the noise and concatenation swerving out of it.[27] Drummond's cause assumed from its effects is now linked completely with the Gothic rush of living motion away from its dead or encrypted other. The result is a very violent "trailing" of "clouds" from elsewhere that forces the Wordsworthian "setting" of the "sun" to recede even farther back than it does in "Tintern Abbey," and that recession (the "dwelling apart") is really what intimates the vast heights and the endless distances at the misty top of Mont Blanc. The "secrecy" of "strength" and the "infinite dome / Of heaven," we must conclude (ll. 140–41), are as much the products of transposition as the drive of the vast scene toward the spectator.

The "coming down" of what withdraws must therefore be a series of "likenesses" that does not carry through any "presence" that remains at one with itself. The descent of partial repetitions simply comes from a passage between differences that draws back from and pours forth its own operation. The cascades, then, are basically metamorphoses, the transfers of a "becoming-other" from itself into the variations it must always be and not be. Power at this stage of Shelley's work has become the supposed force both hiding behind and operating within the restless crossings and interrelations from which perception, thought, and desire arise. It is, in a sense, the drive of transference and the first *clinamen* vanishing and reappearing in the movement of the "outer" toward the "inner" and vice-versa. Its "divinity," such as it is, recalls that old Hebraic sense of the self-alienating and alien Yahweh alluded to somewhat differently in the "Hymn." The Power "coming down" is a series of displacements approaching a kind of Moses on Mount Sinai in an obscurity of "thunders and lightnings" that is soon transfigured even further by human reactions that can never grasp its veil-after-veil in any single "likeness" (Exodus 19:16 and 20:4). As the force of transference, it is never entirely there in any of its self-concealing images, but still it is always coming forth as the many things it is not, which continue to refigure it nevertheless in their "capability" to "be or act." Hence Shelley can maintain that the Power is "solemn" and withdrawn yet equally a "power of many sights, and many sounds, and much of life and death" (ll. 128–29), an abstraction removed from and the impulse inside "All [perceivable] things that move and breathe with toil and sound" (l. 94).

A Doubtful Belief: Its Rationale and Style

Any observer of the scene in "Mont Blanc," already probing beyond and reworking "likenessess," clearly faces a choice as to what aspects of this Power should be empha-sized in future interpretations of all that we perceive. Most spectators of such a vista, to be sure, will probably see the sides of the mountain as a "city of death" and "a flood of ruin" (ll. 105–07) from which "The race / Of man, flies far in dread" and through which "So much of life and joy is lost" at every moment (ll. 117–18). But the reader of these cryptic signs can construe them in one of two ways; he or she can either root their movement in something "inaccessible" or regard them as moments in a pouring outwards that leaves distance and destruction behind. If the first option is chosen too exclusively, as it is in *Julie, Childe Harold,* or the "Hymn Before Sunrise," the high "serenity" will seem an absolute eternally unified within its own Being, if only to be properly removed from the destructive changes it appears to command. The responder will believe in an "unknown omnipotence" on a "secret throne" rain-ing down the violence that terrifies its "subject mountains" (ll. 53, 17, and 62). Or perhaps the perceiver will grant ultimate rule, as does the Poet in *Alastor,* to the blank death of the mountain's whiteness, seeing the "impregnable" ice (l. 106) as the basic void or "desart" that is then "peopled by the storms" and their consequences (l. 67). If the perceiver chooses the primacy of the *clinamen* moving out and away from every past, however, he will mentally overthrow nearly all such hierarchies projected by onlookers onto high mountains. Especially since this self-supplementation has always been underway before its basis has been sought, the observer will see it as dethroning static supremacies and regrounding them in its own disruptive activity. He will think in terms of an inaugural and continuous transfiguration that is really determined or formed in the end by what it *later* becomes in different places. However slowly the "glaciers creep" to destroy any animal "dwelling-place" that may try to house life in a realm without sympathy for it (ll. 100 and 114), they can be seen to move enough that they will appear to transfigure both themselves and what they grind down. They will manifestly transform their ice and their other ingredients, most of which are blown in from other locations, into a fluid and then more fluid "tempest's stream" that will finally become the river in the "vale," the "breath and blood of distant lands" beyond the Servoz valley (ll. 119, 123, and 124). The death drive will be perceived as always turning on its own into the fuel of life, mainly because the process bringing about death and life is never really fixed nor completely frozen.

Shelley, of course, wants to urge the reader away from the tradition prompted by the "dwelling apart" and toward the continual surpassing of transference by the changes it makes in itself. Yet he and we must first acknowledge that transposition and its "Power" extend in both directions at once. We must confront how such a paradoxical movement, recovered by Shelley from its repression in earlier Romantic writers, both draws us toward and questions the possibility of a principle "on high" dictating what "comes down."[28] Indeed, when we begin to adopt this broad awareness—which transference urges on the minds it creates, yet allows them to forget—the mountain's "wilderness" must seem to speak with a "mysterious tongue" (l. 76) as it proceeds to repeal the hegemonic "codes of fraud and woe." The "mystery" must come from the way the Power withdraws from and veils itself in its likenesses. That tendency must "teach" its listeners a degree of Wordsworthian awe and a "faith" that can sometimes match the Power's recession by being just as "solemn" and "serene" (ll. 77–88). Even so, the "voice" emerging from that mystery to speak of the sheer process encountered there, the "legion of wild thoughts," must turn the "awful" response into an uncertain "doubt" and the solemn faith into an undogmatic "mildness" (l. 77). There is no Coleridgean unity to the sound of the wind and cascades, for one thing, since the sound is composed of the various noises and echoes (thoughts about thoughts) of glaciers, waterfalls, pines, caves, and rivers. Then, too, the "legion" of impressions perceiving all this, the continual displacement of perceptions by other perceptions mirrored in the movement of the Arve, suggests that its own progression has spawned the later attempts to look back through it for "something deep" behind the veils. The speaker even acknowledges that sort of reversal by projecting a quasi-human voice into the various motions of the "great Mountain" (l. 80) after they have hurtled toward him in an inhuman succession of "unaccountable figures."

The sensitive observer of the scene or reader of the poem, cognizant of these "facts" behind the sound of the wilderness, must therefore revert to an ambivalent attitude that affirms a desire for something "remoter" (l. 49) and yet wonders if that desire should be argued as the sign of a truth, especially when it tends to set up tyrannical hierarchies. Only with (or "But for") "such faith" as both pursues and critiques its longing for a mother may "man" be "reconciled" with the "nature" that is actually perceived (ll. 78–79), instead of the nature pointing back to God in the works of Wordsworth, Coleridge, Rousseau, and Byron. So far, however, only the very "wise, and great, and good / Interpret, or make felt, or deeply feel" such a multiple, self-transformative movement in such a respectful but skeptical way (ll. 82–83). This attitude must be developed in others so that it may replace the worship of the one voice that is supposed to underlie the forces of visible nature. "Mont Blanc" must thus respond to the forms of such worship with a variety of uncertain reactions to the scene that match the variety and changeability of the "voice" that has been projected there. The poem as we have it, therefore, proceeds through an array of tentative assertions that do not form a univocal voice by any means, but rather a slippage across disjointed feelings and ways of speaking them, most of which are usually kept separate by other writers.

True, it is a difficult step from the most established methods of asserting a consistent lyric voice to the presentation of an oscillating utterance that does not always agree with itself. Nonetheless, Shelley guides his speaker and reader through this further departure from his precursors by adopting three strategies encouraged by the Power's remoteness and its constant transfiguration in departures from it. First he has his speaker, already prone to apostrophes,[29] change the object of address again and again: from the speculative reader (ll. 1–11) to the ravine of Arve (ll. 12–48) to the speaker himself in his own rhetorical questions (ll. 53–57 and 71–74) to the mountain (ll. 80–83) to the open-minded reader of facts (ll. 84–126) back to the speculative reader (ll. 127–39) and finally to the heights of Mont Blanc once more (ll. 139–44). In each case the addressee is being pulled through the speaker's intermediate position, the bridge at Pont Pellisier near Chamouni (*L*, I, 501), toward a reference point on the other side of the speaker, only to discover that the referent must then be addressed in some place other than that where it seems to reside. The object approached by the reader and addressee, which is frequently the Power "on high," insists that it must either "come down" to something else or "dwell apart" in a position far removed from the one in which it now appears. When the "great mountain" is addressed, then, as possessing a "mysterious tongue" (l. 80), that "voice" can be heard as "serene" only by the open-minded "wise" observers of its self-altering process. Hence, for the voice to be approached (all objects existing only as perceived), those kinds of observers must now be addressed (starting at l. 84) in the form of readers styled as having (or urged to have) that attitude.[30] Such an attitude is surely promoted best by a full, factual disclosure of how a "flood of ruin" can be transfigured into "The breath and blood of distant lands," not just on the mountain but in "All things that move" (the announced focus, at l. 94, of ll. 4–126). Soon, too, this outpouring activity must draw such readers into its rush and back up toward its point of coming forth. Yet that reversal can be attempted only if readers can be made to shift their stances from those of quasi-objective observers to those of speculative projectors who try to see their sense-perceptions ("many sights, / And many sounds") in the invisible "power" coming down in likeness (ll. 127–28).

At this point, sliding between postures, the reader is able to confront (or open up) the potential multiplicity of his or her own attidues, even as the speaker shifts among vocabularies and feelings in order to address such different modes of response. The restrictiveness of "identity," in the sense of a devotion to one belief-system or point of view, is now dispersed for both speaker and reader into the salvation of a many-sided vision seeing "much of life *and* death" in the coming-down that once seemed the tyranny of a god or destruction pure and simple (l. 129, my emphasis). As a result, when the mountaintop is addressed once more—just as it has to be, since it is the locus and "likeness" of the "power" interpreted by that multiple attitude—it must be invoked by a half-worshipful assertion accepting some "secret strength" in the mountain's "silence," and that statement must then be modified at once by a skeptical question wondering what that silence really is in relation "to the human mind's imaginings" (ll. 139–44). Very much in the way any supposed object is and ought to be modified (deepened *and* expanded in its possibilities) by the "other" that interprets it, an interpretation should be defined, then reoriented, by and in connection with other perspectives.[31] That is the ethics of reading *and* being that "Mont Blanc" is explicitly written to generate.

Meanwhile, Shelley pluralizes his voice—and consequently the mountain's—by yet another method: his poem's versification. Rebelling in the same endeavor against Wordsworthian blank verse and Coleridge's end-stopped rhyming in the "Hymn Before Sunrise," he crosses "extended blank-verse enjambment with irregular rhyme," much of it "internal," causing "every resolution in *Mont Blanc* [to give way to] at least an undertow of dissolution."[32] The Power, we must remember, as he "makes felt" and "deeply feels" it, is forever cascading past the limits of any whorl or frame in which he tries to place it. At the same time it is echoing itself perpetually, often when we least expect it, yet in shapes and sounds that are only rarely the same and only rarely recurrent in exactly the same succession. It operates by making sharply

different whatever continues to repeat it within its flow, thereby ensuring that its repetitions cannot finally reveal the fixed sameness that they seem to recall for some.
Hence Shelley, again to reflect and foster the "skepticism *and* impassioned intuition"
aroused when partial repetition "flows through the mind,"[33] opens his fourth verse-
paragraph (a factual display of the movements poured forth by the remote "Power")
using several of the maneuvers typical of the poem:

> The fields, the lakes, the forests, and the streams,
> Ocean, and all the living things that dwell
> Within the daedal earth; lightening, and rain,
> Earthquake, and fiery flood, and hurricane,
> The torpor of the year when feeble dreams
> Visit the hidden buds, or dreamless sleep
> Holds every future leaf and flower;—the bound
> With which from that detested trance they leap;
> The works and ways of man, their death and birth,
> And that of him and all that his may be;
> All things that move and breathe with toil and sound
> Are born and die; revolve, subside, and swell. (ll. 84–95)

Here each entity, on the one hand, is initially distinct from the others, reflecting the
way separate regions rise out of the general flow in the poem's opening vision, with
even the most related realms ("lakes" and "streams" or "rain" and "flood") kept distant from each other by intervening words or breaks between lines. All this while, on
the other hand, the sequence is trying to conflate these pieces into "all the living
things" that have a common motion in them making them really similar at bottom.
That dissolving together is apparently assisted, not just by the speed of the shifts from
area to area, but by recurrent sounds creating resemblances from total differences
("streams" and "dreams," "dwell" and "swell," "sleep" and "leap," even "earth" and
"birth"). Still, none of these echoes occur in the same rhyming pattern. One happens
in a couplet, one after two intervening lines, one after five lines, one after ten, and one
at the end of the ninth line in the sequence as it picks up a sound from the midpoint
of the third. The more the sequence goes on, the more its recurrences, as in the Heisenberg uncertainty principle,[34] assert their near-randomness and their refusal to syn-
chronize exactly their methods of repetition. They also increase, as they appear, the
gap between the poles in the relations until "swell" finally repeats "dwell" after a long
separation, emphasizing how opposite the two terms are (how one is outgoing and the
other inward) despite their homophony. The interplay of living elements thereby
reveals its base as the temporary interaction of entirely different forces. No wonder
life comes, at least twice in this short sequence of lines, from a "death and a birth"
that approach and try to avoid each other at the same time. Whatever "revolves"
together, conceptually or phonically, for Shelley must start to "subside" and disinte-
grate its achieved order at the very moment the order comes about, if only so that
different relations made from similar elements can "swell" again in later relational
constructions. Nothing can forever remain what it seems in its distinctness; "streams"
must reappear transformed in "dreams," "dwelling within the earth" must eventually
come forth as "swelling," then "birth," and the "torpor of the year" (the languorous
descent into winter) must seem a memory of the past from one angle and a temporary

suspension of future potentials from another. At any instant some different relationship can abruptly "leap" from a previous "bound" and present a momentary reconfiguration, even in rhyme schemes, of what has been perceived shortly before. The reader of "Mont Blanc" is thus tossed perpetually between strict order and total chaos, centering and decentering, recurrence and irregularity, tradition and revolution, or sameness and difference in choosing the best assumptions by which to interpret what "comes down in likeness" toward the vale of Chamouni.

Such an "awful doubt, or faith so mild," though, is perhaps encouraged most directly by a third technique in the poem. Shelley begins using it in his letters from the actual scene, reverting to a thought-pattern he has learned in part from Peacock, the friend to whom the letters are addressed:

> If the snow which produces the glaciers [on the mountain] must augment & the heat of the valley is no obstacle to the perpetual subsistance of such masses of ice . . . the consequence is obvious.—The glaciers must augment & will subsist at least until they have overflowed this vale.—I will not pursue Buffon['s] sublime but gloomy theory, that this earth which we inhabit will at some future period be changed into a mass of frost. Do you who assert the supremacy of Ahriman imagine him throned among these desolate snows . . . sculptured in this their terrible magnificence by the unsparing hand of necessity, that he casts around him as the first essays of his final usurpations avalanches, torrents, rocks & thunders—and above all these deadly glaciers at once the proofs and symbols of his reign. . . . [All this] is a part of the subject more mournful and less sublime;—but such as neither the poet nor the philosopher should disdain. (*L*, I. 499)

The poet is indulging in comparative mythography as he slides away from extrapolating on what his impressions suggest (the self-augmenting of glaciers) into a system (Georges Buffon's) that has carried out that extrapolation to form a totalized vision *and* into a Zoroastrian legend where the principle of Evil (Ahriman) enforces his temporary reascendence by hurling icy destruction at the warmth of populous valleys. The letter suggests no final affirmation of or agreement between these mythic analogues for what Shelley perceives. He simply raises them as allusions developing or fictively grounding the scene he beholds, and he goes on to make them contradict one another as he sets a godless physical movement toward an ice age next to a highly religious scheme centered on the alternation between good and evil rulers of the cosmos.[35] This procedure has been Shelley's and sometimes Peacock's since their first meeting, especially after the latter urged the former to read the comparative *Oedipus Judaicus* alongside the *Academical Questions* (both by Drummond).[36] The two English liberals have fueled their shared empirical skepticism, their mutual basing of the world on "mutability,"[37] and their common efforts to dethrone monotheistic religions by discussing or rewriting modes of primitive sun-worship, pre-Socratic beliefs in the mobile dominance of fire or love, the migrating "Principles" of Darwin or Holbach or Buffon, and John Frank Newton's modern rendition (modified by other readings) of the Persian-Zoroastrian cyclical interplay between the regenerative Oromaze and the autocratic Ahrimanes.[38] Slipping between parts of such schemes, all of which are now uprooted from the institutions they once served, allows these young heretics to challenge monolithic structures while also refusing one central system as their absolute alternative. Shelley and Peacock can break off, employ, and interrelate parts of mythological systems that were only sometimes connected originally, even as both deny the complete validity of any single pattern outside the later reworkings of each for new polemical purposes.

This activity reappears in "Mont Blanc" when the speaker tries first to account for why the "shadows" in his "separate phantasy" seem like those in a "trance sublime and strange" (l. 35) and then attempts to explain how the "Ghastly, scarred, and riven" ice-rocks were initially piled against each other on the sides of the mountain (l. 71). Right away, the "ghosts" in what seems to be a dream are interpreted according to conflicting schemes from different sources: "Some say that gleams of a remoter world / Visit the soul in sleep,—that death is slumber / And that its shapes the busy thoughts outnumber / Of those who wake and live" (ll. 49–52). Though Shelley is here reusing the sort of visitation that opens his own *Queen Mab* and recalling the brotherhood of death and sleep in *Alastor* (ll. 211–13), he also sets Milton and Wordsworth's "fading" transformations of Platonic and biblical infusions from higher realms alongside an echoing of Hamlet, a speculation on "what dreams may come" when "to sleep" is "to die," that looks back to the "god of sleep" in Ovid's *Metamorphoses* surrounded in a "sleep that sleeps forever" by as "many images as ears of grain in autumn."[39] A few fleeting glimpses of divinity are thus placed next to the rise of many repressed thought-potentials in a dream, both notions being offered as nothing more than established glosses on "sublime trances" (what "some" have "said" about them without agreeing on their basis).

The speaker can follow such discordant allusions only by asking new versions of old questions that cannot all be answered with a "yes" under one consistent set of assumptions. "Has some unknown omnipotence," as Hesiod first suggested among Western poets,[40] unfurled [or rolled out] / The veil [between] life and death" (ll. 53–54), here the impenetrable mist concealing the frozen mountaintop from the flowing "breath and blood of distant lands"? Or does the onlooker "lie / In dream," as the previous speculations maintain, "and does the mightier world of sleep," perhaps the realm of mighty but dead shades in Homer's *Odyssey* or Virgil's *Aeneid*, "Spread far around and inaccessibly / Its circles" (ll. 54–57) in the manner of the "same" being obscured by the "diverse" as "circle" envelops "circle" in Plato's *Timaeus?*[41] In the second question by itself, since "sleep" is only rarely such a "mightier world" for Plato,[42] one configuration (the Timaean circles) disruptively supplants a different one (the dream-world of shades) to duplicate the relationship between the two questions. This kind of *discordia concors* then accelerates even further as more queries are raised a few lines later about the "rude shapes" on the mountainside:

> Is this the scene
> Where the old Earthquake-demon taught her young
> Ruin? Were these her toys? Or did a sea
> Of fire envelope once this silent snow? (ll. 71–74)

The speaker first alludes in this case to Enlightenment theories by Buffon, James Parkinson, and others that base the growth of earth-forms on a series of cataclysmic earthquakes forcing mountains out of the ground and fissures or crags out of the mountains.[43] Yet the ancient cataclysm imagined here is commanded suddenly by a mythic "daemon" akin to an Ahrimanes, the very sort of impetus that a Buffon or Parkinson are always writing to deny. Then, too, both views are countered by the possibility that Heraclitus may have been right, that "fire" is the self-transfiguring "matter" from which all formations come and into which they are reenveloped and reshaped after a time.[44] By now no one assumption can hold sway for long; there is only the darting from one to the next in a half-playful, half-serious dance among different codes that dethrones all the dominant ones and their supreme beings by turning these notions into mere suppositions contending with many others on an equal footing. Any effort to ground the "fast influencings" descending from the mists on high leaves the pluralistic "spirit," as it *should* be left, "Driven like a homeless cloud from steep to steep" and question to question (l. 59). The speculations on the "riven shapes" of the mountain, meanwhile, can be answered only by the slow "eternal" movement of the "frozen flood" into other forms, into "loud waters" driving on to the "ocean waves" and "the circling air" (ll. 75, 64, 125, and 126). To "apprehend" accurately the motion producing mind is precisely to fail to capture it within any perspective, pattern, or system. It is to urge, in a many-voiced voice, an opening of human thought to all that the Power-in-likeness may seem to be, all that it may become as it withdraws from and gushes out toward our interpretations.

Beyond Polarity

By 1816 the poles of being for Shelley, the "inner" movement of thought-transformation and the "outer" onslaught of descent, flow, and change, turn out to be as necessary and interrelated as they are in the prose of 1813 through 1815—but now, more than before, they are positions to be moved away from or beyond by a process of interaction that uses them as momentary conduits. Each constructed and represented realm, whether it claims inwardness or externality for what it seems to embody, must immediately defer its figures to images in another place, be that place a location, a memory, a person, a pattern, or a myth standing over against the other one of its kind that is currently being invoked. The reorientation must happen so instantly that the personal imagination can claim no complete mastery over the need for the "unseen" to become reobscured in another structure or the tendency in the Power's "coming down" to leap between different "likenessess" of it. Indeed, the subliminal priority of that rapid "receiving and [re]rendering" must be brought out to challenge those authors who see imagination as humankind's way of echoing God's creation of the world from chaos. Someone must affirm, in answer to Rousseau, Wordsworth, Coleridge, Byron, and others, that imagination does not impose form on the void (as God is supposed to have done) unless there is first a relational interplay generating the need for "subject versus object" and a displacement of motion into other motions that makes possible the juxtapositions in imaginative productions. The "Hymn to Intellectual Beauty" must show that imagination's willed projection of any "grace" or "truth" depends upon the unwillable return of a self-concealing transference floating "though unseen amongst us . . . like the truth of nature [inundating Shelley's] passive youth" (ll. 78–79). "Mont Blanc" must reveal how that "truth of nature" is the continuous swerving between separating differences from which nature itself, the mind, and the mind's interpretations take their life and draw their oscillations between resemblance and distinction. Otherwise, Shelley's readers will fancy that the personal imagination has replaced even God as the primal center generating observable life from almost nothing. As a matter of fact, many of his most able interpreters have construed the 1816 lyrics as taking that very position.[45] The evidence they usually cite is the final verse-paragraph of "Mont Blanc," notwithstanding the speaker's assertion at just this point that "the power is there" in the mountain's receding height *and* in the "many sights / And many sounds" descending its side (ll. 127–29). Such explicators point to that unanswered question that closes the paragraph and the poem: "what were thou [Mont Blanc], and earth, and stars, and sea, / If to the human mind's imaginings / Silence and solitude were vacancy?" (ll. 142–44). Those critics then argue that the "city of death" on the mountainside and the "voiceless" emptiness at the mountain's peak can be given life and meaning only (according to Shelley) by the projection of the mind's constructions onto the white and frozen blankness.

But Shelley's entire verse-paragraph denies that reading constantly, even as it tries to envision the descent of "snows" upon the peak when "none beholds them there" because of the enveloping mist (ll. 131–32). The speaker's drive to penetrate the mists carries no firm vision of an ordered world with it. Instead, if it finds something akin to mental activity at that height, it is because the falling "flakes" there are probably darted "through" by either "star-beams" or "the sinking sun"; there, too, "winds [very likely] contend" with each other to move the flakes along, while "lightning" comes down "like vapour" to brood "over the snow" slowly piling up toward it (ll. 133–39). All these passings of each process through other ones suggest a movement very like the "unremitting interchange" of human thought. Yet that interchange, though it is in fact projected here from the observer into an invisible externality, preexists the mind and "rolls" mind into being during the opening lines of this poem. At the heart of darkness atop the mountain, then, is the sheerly relational activity producing entities (including minds) and their connections with other forms. *That* is the "secret strength of things / Which governs thought, and to the infinite dome / Of heaven is as a law" (ll. 140–42), especially since thought depends upon that process to work and the "dome" can be an arching (or "brooding") only in relation to the plane below from which the mountain rises. There is no "vacancy" at the top of Mont Blanc or at any other center of attention in the scene. The poem's final sentence affirms, using a rhetorical query to compel the reader's assent while calling all absolute affirmations into question, that no envisioning of related sights would be possible at all if "silence and solitude" really confronted "the human mind's imaginings" with an absolute void. The Gothic sensibility as Shelley once saw it is here largely rejected, as are both the nihilism of nothing at the center and the religiosity of an omnipotence enthroned. What is left is centerless transference inside and outside our minds, to the point where it even generates "inside" and "outside" as functions of itself, setting the interchanges of lyric poetry in motion, however much some lyric writers (or critics of the lyric) refuse to accept the fact. From now on, Shelley will assume a dethroned "center" of "darting-through" and "contending" without having to present a worshipful case for it. The overarching question now becomes what that "foundation" means for the social, political, and personal state of human beings "as it is perceived."

3

The Key to All Tyrannies:
From *Laon and Cythna* to *The Cenci*

Transference's Self-Reversal

As Shelley returns from metaphysics and epistemology to face humanity's social and political possibilities, he has to define for himself the perpetual turns in human thought that seek or permit the political tyrannies still oppressing most people. He knows, of course, what Marx will specify more precisely: that age-old divisions of labor have led to owner, mercantile, and laboring classes. The least propertied of these have generally bent to the will of the most propertied, since the "lower" classes have been dependent on the "higher" for the marketing of their produce (as in Shelley's *Address to the Irish People, CW,* V, 235–36). Each class, moreover, reflecting the macrocosm of social hierarchies, has established master/slave relationships within the confines of its own "pecking orders." At the same time, though, this layering of oppressions has also found ways to conceal—and thus to maintain—itself in a "super-structure of maxims & of forms" (*L,* II, 191). Representations (even just namings) of the social order, visual and linguistic modes of production transfiguring and thereby obscuring all other modes, have repeatedly managed to cloak the ways in which labor is dominated by the nonlaboring classes and have then ensured that the "lower strata" will usually submit to the domination. These symbolic modes or "ideologies" locate "true insight" and sanctioned power in certain exalted social positions, acting as though these structures were endemic to "Nature" instead of being constructs or stagings that exist to maintain the present inequalities in the division of labor.[1] How, Shelley has to consider, are such belief systems—what Francis Bacon called "Idols of the Theatre"[2]—even able to come about, particularly in a host of minds that have no clear sense of labor conditions and, in some cases, no apparent interest in advancing social inequality? How can these ideologies control our assumptions so continually, even after the economic reasons for such belief-systems have disappeared? How can thought give them long-lasting power especially if thinking is one effluence of a continual transference that fashions thought-constructions and then entropically alters them as new or forgotten relations are found for each element in a construct?

These questions are now pressing for Shelley again because he has revised his initial reactions to them. Back in *Queen Mab* the answers begin with the already binary nature of human thought. Like the most basic "atom" of "Soul," a thought for the early Shelley is "a world [oscillating between poles of] loves and hatreds." A turn toward the former pole, reacting to impressions from elsewhere, produces "sympathy" and "peacefulness," the motivators of a loving social interchange among equals without rivalry; a tilt toward the other extreme leads to either a lust for superiority or an "abjectness" submitting to but resenting a superior being (*Mab,* IV. 144–45, 149, 157, and 159). "Necessity" may be striving beyond any limitation that it may have empowered in the past, yet the emergent "self" inclined toward the negative pole has forgotten "Reason's voice" telling it this fact (III. 126). That ignorance has gone on to tempt the now power-hungry ego into "owning not" its desires for hierarchy (V. 26) and "screen[ing]" its effort to maintain old supremacies "With flimsy veil[s] of [presumed] justice and of right" (V. 27–28). By the time of the 1816 lyrics, however, this assessment has become far more ironic. No longer does transference in the form of "Necessity" simply encounter a resistance to change made possible by a polarization in human thinking. Now the way a "coming down in likeness" apparently refers to something withdrawing behind it leads its interpreters to suppose a different, and apparently superior, level at the point "back there" from which the likeness seems to descend. Such a level, though proposed retroactively, can readily be called a God or King, an enthroned absolute urging subordination, because the regressive pull in a "coming down" has encouraged its observers to send an anthropomorphic projection through the movement to a level so "above and beyond" that the projection is distended into a transcendent Other.

The process of transference, when the human will chooses to emphasize its regressive and differentiating tendencies, is itself responsible for the ideologies of tyranny that its own motions can work to resist. If hierarchical world-views are based on the repression or reversal of transference, transference underwrites these impositions upon itself by providing some of the constructs and even procedures that have often impeded its free operation. The questions for the poet are now more focused than they were. Exactly how and why do such perversions occur as extensions of what they pervert? How is it that they happen because of transference yet against its transfigurative and revolutionary tendencies? What in the possibilities of transference as it works through and drives human thought places the will at a crossroads between different avenues into which transference can be steered, one of which is the projection of and submission to an absolute Other that seems a very attractive option if too little attention is paid to other alternatives? In the face of these quandaries, Shelley's writing must now seek to pinpoint and account for the exact maneuvers of transposition that can turn its shifting action into forms of oppression. These potentials in the basic motion can, if uncovered, explain much in the generation of the tyrannies we all see and sometimes accept. They can explain both the contortions of thought overvaluing or downgrading the self (the fashioning of "masters" and "slaves") and the symbolic ways desire or labor are alienated from—and by—the individual into a system of ranks turning round on the psyche to subject it to the "highest levels." Above all, the exposure of how transference is turned against itself by its own means can show human thought positioned exactly where Shelley is starting to see it: at a fulcrum that, even in imaginative minds potentially receptive to the full range of free transference, allows the psyche to tip its thinking toward systems of belief that can rapidly confine and tyrannically control its best aspirations.

The Existing Accounts of the Error

Shelley by this time, it turns out, has encountered many explanations for this "wrong tilt" already. When he writes about it, he has in mind the opinions on the subject offered by several authors he has come to value and whose quests for understanding he now wants to continue. Each predecessor, in fact, usually hones in on one kind of perverted transfer-process and accounts for it up to a point upon which Shelley now needs to expand. The projection into perceived nature of an anthropomorphic deity, the linchpin in most of the ideologies sanctioning absolute tyranny, is explained by Hume as an excessive reprojection of already projected transfers, not just in his *Dialogues* but in "The History of Religion" in his *Four Dissertations*.[3] There primitive man's "dread" about and "thirst" for an unknown future seek a solution to all mysteries in the receding of "unknown causes" behind observed phenomena. When probed into and perceived, these causes, the primitive hopes, may foretell the future course of events, provided that human scrutiny can expose the ways such causes seem to have predetermined past movements of being. "Anatomizing" a phenomenon to get at its impetus, however, leads such observers to behold no more than their personal anatomies. They really uncover "nothing but the particular fabric and structure of the minute parts of their own bodies" in supposedly external objects, for people cannot conceive of motions begun outside themselves except as movement caused by their own bodies acting on their surroundings. Moreover, since those bodies themselves intimate "unknown causes" (motions behind their motions), the analogy must be extended further if it is to seem to probe to the absolute heart of perceived existence. The core of phenomena must be defined as a "distinct idea" or coherent "spirit"—what thought appears to be when it acts as the "inside" motivator of the body's outward actions—so that the "cause" is not merely the centerless interaction of a sensation network or a body-language. To reach a motivator behind perceivable motion, in other words, the projector must "ascribe [his own motivators] malice and good-will to [the heart of] every thing, that hurts or pleases" him. One "transfer" (Hume's own word) left unsatisfied begets another, the projection of the body demands the projection of a psyche "behind" it, to the point where the observer observes his own future-oriented emotions (apprehension and desire) turning into the responses those feelings anticipate, as when an image is turned about on itself by a mirror at a distance from it. Now what were his emotions command him (as anger and generosity) from the past and the depths of perceived nature. For some reason, which Shelley has to find, the transfer-impulse must project a "likeness" into a position entirely "other" than the projector, and the conflict of self/not-self in the resulting image "out there" can be resolved only, it seems, in a distancing of the image from the projector's level and the concomitant submission of the "less complete" psyche to this "distinct," and thus self-sufficient, alter ego.

As for why "supremacy" is granted to the Other in this act, Shelley draws some hints from how the "idea" of "monarchy" is continually generated in Godwin's *Political Justice*.[4] In Godwin's eyes, this illogical but real eventuality is a potential in the most primitive interplay between perception and language. An impression or sensation (as Shelley will later suggest himself) cannot become "a subject of perception" (a thought interpreted by another thought) unless it is first "uttered" as at least a "cry," the sensation recast in an audible form observable by the same sensorium that perceived the initial impression. The cry, in its turn, being different from its apparent impetus, is nonsensical and incommunicative to the utterer and his or her listener unless it is gradually "observed to be constantly associated with certain antecedent impressions" that are common to both speaker and auditor. Such a permanent and intersubjective principle cannot be asserted, of course, until there has been a deliberate "comparison" of sensations by "the judgment" that sees a common element in a series of impressions associated with repetitions of a particular cry or set of cries. "Abstraction," then, a pulling together of perceptions that leads to a persistent trait pulling away *(ab-stracto)* from these various particulars, is the level that linguistic-perceptual interchanges must reach if words are to have "signifieds" or "ideas" (Godwin's word), "understandings" of "knowledge" to which signs can promise access. Meanwhile, too, abstraction must "again [be] assisted in its operations by language." A generality must be confirmed as such by the conventionally accepted deference to it in an oft-repeated word. Hence, even though this "growth of knowledge" indicates a continual interdependence of "language" and "thought," there is an incipient hierarchy of levels formed as the pulling away becomes the truly "knowing" stratum—the One behind individual variants—and the verbal mark becomes the changeable functionary deferring to the One at a distance from it.

Regrettably, it is a small step from this logic, so forgetful of its real foundations, to the oppressively "abstract idea of a king." The "interest" that each individual has in preventing the "invasion" of his or her autonomy finds, since every person has a similar trait, that the ways of promoting this interest can be pooled in a central "bank," an ab-stracted provision for the common defense, potentially outside the control of the individual interests referring to it. Though it need not necessarily remain centralized—the redistribution of this responsibility being just as possible as the return from abstraction to words—the drive toward unity in this delegation makes it attractive to "commit this precious deposit to the custody of a single man." When this course is chosen, sad to say, the commanding "interest" becomes one person's alone, and to that monolith, it turns out, all other interests must bend their knees. The king, on his side, able to forget the dependence of his interest on the other ones that made his possible, has no reason to cultivate comparative judgment and every incentive to repress all announcements of his actual base with "violence and presumption." To place such a being or any abstract referent in the position of "knowing" supremely is, strangely but inevitably, to make knowledge the suppression of the truth behind the production of knowledge.

Concurrently, too, as Shelley ponders this problem, he has to face the hierarchies *within* the various classes that also find ways to subordinate "lesser beings" to the power of a usurping single figure. The most pervasive subordination repeated from class to class is undeniably the subjection of women by men, and the poet encounters this imposture as a synecdoche indicating the nature of all the others in *A Vindication of the Rights of Woman* by Godwin's first wife, Mary Wollstonecraft, the mother of

Mary Godwin Shelley.[5] Western society for Wollstonecraft has observed the biological distinctions intermingled with the similarities among people and has proceeded to emphasize the apparently superior "strength" of the male compared to the female, thereby allowing "man," as though physical capacity were automatically connected to other kinds, a greater "degree" of opportunity to display "strength of mind, perseverance, and fortitude." Because of that difference only in degree and in one area, a difference that Wollstonecraft accepts more than Shelley does,[6] those mental virtues, though common to people of both sexes, have been made exclusive to that "bugbear" gender-term "masculine." Women thus interpreted as a gender-division ("feminine") now seem too different in kind from men to be educated toward the pursuit of "courage or fortitude" or "bodily strength."[7] Superficial distinctions, established as synecdoches for deeper differences only by comparisons perceived across time, have been reconstituted as oppositions between two different essences or natures, under the assumption that synecdoches can be transfigured into the wholes they represent.

Women, meanwhile, have at least tacitly consented to this power play by assuming they must be trained only enough to serve as pleasure toys or housekeepers for the more "intellectual" men. The "impostures" of monarchy in Wollstonecraft's view have been brought about by similar methods, by the ascription of widely held or much-desired qualities to somewhat distinct men of a particular class "out of the confusion of ambitious struggles" in which the soon-to-be-"inferiors" do much of the ascribing. Oppressors seize upon their supremacy, as Shelley often notes, by receiving the features that others transfer away from their own stock and by seeing the completed transfer reflected in the consenting eyes of the oppressed. An intermingling of half-similarities/half-differences among comparable beings is apparently so threatening, such a "confusion" to human thought, that one among equals must become "less," a woman must cede many of her potentials to "masculinity," in order to establish the power of absolute difference in place of a less stratified world of relations where power resides permanently in no one place.

To be sure, there is an easy, indeed too easy, response to this iniquitous distortion of human possibilities. Lucretius offers such a rejoinder by starting *De rerum natura* with a celebration of a Venus-figure who incarnates what is usually "left" to woman: reproductive fecundity, the ability to arouse irrational desire in other beings, a sympathetic capacity to transfer "soft love" from herself to others, and a tendency to shift among identities to the point of questioning the boundaries between parts of one being or between separate entities (*De rerum,* I. 1–20). To this self-decentering, peace-loving eroticism, Lucretius unabashedly asks submission from the self-centered, imperialistic, supreme male god of martial Rome, "Mars mighty in battle," knowing that the Mars-Venus myths "cast" the god on the goddess's "lap" and leave him there "vanquished by the ever-living wound of love" or at least "looking upward" at a "sacred body" that pours "sweet coaxings" down on him from "above" (I. 33–40). The male-female hierarchy can be boldly, though at first only figuratively, reversed in a way that holds out prospects of eventual joy for everyone if there can be a true inversion of a society's male-supremacist values insinuated throughout the symbolic schemes keeping those values in force. Shelley, as we have seen, follows this lead in *Alastor* when his sometimes unseeing Narrator is overcome by the multiplicity and brotherhood-building in the Mother *Natura* he calls to for poetic power. In such a vision, power as it is usually attached to someone male can be removed from his exclusive possession by the way the female figure forcefully takes over the principal indicators of causality and control. The conquering force of sword and phallus for which Mars-figures are so noted can be cleverly transferred to Venus as Lucretius portrays her, particularly in her ability to "wound" him by "piercing" him to the "heart" with her special forms of overpowering "might" (I. 12–13).

At the same time, though, Shelley is aware that this maneuver taken that far can reestablish the very kind of tyranny it seeks to overthrow. If it is a misuse of transference to "carry over" qualities of women so that "man" becomes their sole possessor, it is just as destructuve to free exchange among equals if "woman" recaptures symbols (as the phallic mother threatens to do in Freudian psychology) that grant her the power to drain potentials, and even life, from other beings. In a grotesque mirror image of the way man makes woman an object without her own intelligence by himself subsuming all rights to an educated subjectivity (Wollstonecraft's indictment), woman repossessing all of man's self-sufficient "strengths" (and hiding the fact that these are fabrications) becomes a tyrannizing object containing and withholding the power of personal subjectivity from the male perceiver. "She," thus constructed and perceived, is now the absolute being in which full selfhood must be sought. The pursuit of such a being or state, as Shelley has revealed in the *Alastor* Poet's pursuit of his dream-maiden, can be the slow death of the enslaved individual as he gives over all value, meaning, and life to the object of his desire. For Shelley to deal adequately with all these gender distortions, he must go on to specify the differences between each version and the point at which all of them turn from loving interchanges between somewhat similar human figures into the dominance of "master" or perceiving subject over "slave" or perceived object.

All this while, too, the simple notion of "subject" and "object," gender notwithstanding, is itself a problem bound up with tyranny in Shelley's thinking and reading. Each of these poles exists only in terms of the other in the 1816 lyrics, each needing the difference and needing to deny it. It is only the passage of supposed self-determination to one or the other pole, while the opposite is thought to be incomplete, that sets up either the "subjection" of the object by the observer or the object's predetermination of a "passive" subject's responses. Both of these options can establish hierarchical oppressions if human thought accepts either one too completely. In the first case, as Shelley saw in Coleridge, probably as early as the 1809 version of *The Friend*,[8] the subject can be taken as both a "Means to an end" and an "End in itself," being self-sufficient in its Kantian possession of reason, while the "Thing" exists "merely" as a "Means" employable by the subject for its ends as reason conceives of them. Tyranny would exist for Coleridge in this view only if the subject were made to perform a task using "objective" things and if "reciprocal advantage" did not exist to return the object's new significance to the context of the subject's preconceived ends. Shelley wants to be far more inclusive, though very much on the basis of what Coleridge says. For the younger poet, tyranny can begin the moment individual subjects make themselves the measure of whatever is outside them, particularly if those subjects proceed on the Coleridgean grounds that reason is the "holiest gift of Heaven and bond of union with the Giver [of Life]."

Then there is the opposite possibility, and it can be even more oppressive, both for the reasons Coleridge suggests and for ones more frightening than any he mentions. Though it is surely an unfair distortion when an object granted a meaning by a perceiver is not permitted to return the favor and seems to retain that meaning as its own primordial possession, the abjection of the subject is completely guaranteed when an object is made the dictator of the subject's meaning once the subject has granted the object powers of thought analogous to the subject's own. Ovid, of all people, calls this problem to Shelley's attention near the end of the *Metamorphoses* in the history of life uttered by the Samian philosopher, who surely appeals to Shelley by being a "voluntary exile" voicing a "hatred of tyranny" and all that underwrites it (*Metam.*, XV. 60–62). For the Samian all forms of life are lovingly productive as long as differences are transmogrified in free combinations with other forms, but that "wandering" of the primal "spirit" (XV. 165–67) is impeded and reversed if any life-form reaches out to introject or destroy an analogous form against the latter's will. Humankind commits that "impiety" during the earliest period of the race's existence when animal meat is eaten after "bloodshed and slaughter," an Original Sin for the vegetarian Shelley as early as *Queen Mab* (VIII. 211–12 and the note to these lines on *PW*, pp. 826–35). An "ill exemplar" among men, it appears, once "envied the food of lions" and so "thrust down flesh as food into his greedy stomach," justifying the act later with animal sacrifices to the gods as though the "heavenly ones took pleasure" in people "devouring [their] own fellow-labourers" of the earth (XV. 103–42).

The crime begins, really, with the human desiring of another animal's desire (the "envying" of the lion)—the production of an analogy, then, between man and beast—and the subsequent placement of that desire's supposed origin in the lion itself. Now this "object" apparently removed from the human psyche provides an example outside of people for what people should henceforth do. Humanity thus appears to have a licence from elsewhere, removing the responsibility from people, to kill and ingest many other living things against the transfer-based laws of nature. The licence is even reinforced by a transference of it from visible animals to invisible gods, who then seem to sanction both the animals and the human beings who follow animal patterns. People gain immense power over other parts of creation in this ideological maneuver, but their gain comes at the cost of a submission to the apparent rules of animal nature and to the orders of transcendent beings proposed by human intelligence yet beyond human ken. Humankind enslaves in the role of a subject, Shelley observes, only as the race sees itself enslaved by a hierarchy of objects.

Nevertheless, if this "achievement" of transference therefore requires as much further explanation as the others do, it does not offer the challenge posed by the last drive toward tyranny considered by Shelley, again in the face of writing that precedes him. More recently, René Girard has called this drive "mimetic desire,"[9] and some of its workings are evident, to begin with, in the sermon of Ovid's Samian prophet. There the vaguely outreaching, desirous person, unable to define his desire unless it is "reflected in that which [it] resembles," makes the standard of his longing another being whom he proceeds to imitate, who directs him toward an object of desire by being an example of desire for that object. Clearly, though, since the man cannot attain the object unless he keeps looking to the exemplar of his pursuit (the lion), he must find his model a rival for the object, a superior (momentarily) over whom he must gain superiority if he is to have more access to the object (meat, say) than he seems to have initially. At this point Rousseau helps pick up the narrative in his *Discourse* on the gradual establishment of inequality.[10] As isolated primitive men begin to form communities "to surmount the obstacles of nature" that no one person can manage, writes Rousseau, each man must assess the "relevance" not just of animals but of other men adjacent to him who have the power to achieve together what he cannot by himself. Soon all the individuals in the gathering group begin to assess which people among them seem to be able to define and pursue the objectives of the society most consistently and attractively. Those frequently rated "superior" in this comparison come "to be of the most consideration," to be differentiated as models the way some animals once were, among otherwise similar people who all want the consideration that they are granting to distinguished beings.

Human models, often accepting themselves as such, now become the rivals for as well as the exemplars of what is now the average person's object: the recognition and regard of everyone else. "From these first distinctions [arise] on the one side vanity and contempt and on the other shame and envy," the "first step[s] towards inequality." A "fermentation" of rivalry and violence ensues at this stage in Rousseau's history, just as Girard says it must, since each side in this higher/lower arrangement seeks to value itself, or maintain achieved value, by overcoming the other and gaining the appropriate recognition. The dissolution of the community needed to preserve the human race is now imminent and can be prevented only by the establishment of a "state," which fixes the dichotomy, while also trying to ease it, in a system at least partly hierarchical to which all must assent because they "have too many disputes among themselves to do without arbiters." In "the hopes of securing their liberty," human beings thus run "headlong into their chains," again (as in Wollstonecraft) basing oppression on the consent of the oppressed. To direct desire by modeling the "self" on another—who is therefore modeled on the self—and yet by seeing the other as the master, the indicator, of all that the self does not possess is finally, albeit curiously, to instigate a need in both figures for an Other, a higher master, who now claims to be desire's director while covering up or marginalizing the real motivators of desire and hierarchy.

Shelley, then, having found transference at the root of its own repression (an anomaly in itself) and having noted various convincing but incomplete portraits of how that exact perversion occurs, is left with as many questions as solutions when he sets out to explain the ideological assumptions interpreting yet underwriting economic and social inequities. If the notion of an absolute monarch of the universe comes from the projection of human tendencies into an otherness infinitely receding, the poet must wonder, why must there be such a projection at all (usually involving more than one transfer), and why must the resulting anomaly (self/other "out there" together) become a distinction, then a hierarchical abasement of the self by the other (now the "Other")? Why does this enslavement, worse yet, come about with the consent of the enslaved? Meanwhile, why and how does such a structure insist in placing genuine "knowledge" at the highest point, the position most "unknown" to its observers? What does this movement have to do, as it has to do in Godwin, with language's need for an abstraction generated by yet superior to words? What is the connection, too, between the enthroning of knowledge and the patriarchal subjection of women? Indeed, how is it that sexual differences, criss-crossed as they are with similarities transcending sex, can become a single binary opposition and a rigid separation of personal potentials into higher masculine and lower feminine types? What is equally wrong, to go further, with a reversal of this hierarchy that makes woman the supreme object of male desire? How is "objectivity" and its sense of the mind's subservience to externals really produced by transferential thinking? What are the consequences for human relations if a fairly strict division between subject and object is assumed? What reason is there not to assume it? And why are human beings tempted from transference into mimetic desire? Why is there potential tyranny in desiring the desire of another? In what ways does such a mimesis really produce evils such as rivalry, violence, and social rank, which Rousseau and Girard think necessary or even beneficial, but which may not be either from Shelley's point of view? Is there a dynamic, finally, that makes all these maneuvers interact in the production and maintenance of a tyrannical symbolic order?

Shelley, I now want to show, answers all these questions gradually, sometimes a few at a time and sometimes several at once, in much of the work he completed between 1816 and the last few months of 1819. He begins in *Laon and Cythna* (1817) with the pattern and problems left to him by Hume, and, as he proceeds through some of the now-acknowledged masterpieces of 1818 and 1819, he adds the other quandaries, with some explanations of them, to his initial focal points and responses. In each effort of this period, he not only attends closely to and transmogrifies the points of departure left to him by the authors just discussed, but he also expands his awareness of and ability to define the different ways transference can manifest itself, redemptively or destructively, in the emergence and deployment of any person in discourse, constructions of "selfhood," social exchange, conflicting class interests and ideologies, or hierarchies of power. The build climaxes, I think (though some slightly later works participate in the sequence), with *The Cenci,* the vibrantly grim tragedy finished in the late summer or early fall of 1819, where all the forms of perverted transference that Shelley has specified over these few years interact to reveal how their combined influence on perception can grossly distort human desires and interactions. What finally emerges in and out of this succession is a complex analysis of human "abjection" (to use one of the words that Shelley employs in this context) in which each kind of mis-transference plays a part by reconstituting itself in the other ones, either as text succeeds to text or as perversions play off of and dissolve into one another in the works of 1819, *The Cenci* especially. No one negative transfer-process really subsumes or seems the root of all the others in the end; obsessions with the "objects" of "subjects" lead to the imitation of models outside the self, partly because the need for self-projection sets up externalized, "master" forms of the self and partly because the impulse to project—or to set one gender over another—is inseparable from the desire for a superior, all-"knowing" abstraction. The Shelley of these writings demonstrates that the all-too-likely and common slippage of transference into any one of these forms can lead, since that movement's quest for analogues always continues, to additional negative forms and thus to a compounding of the mistake that nearly stifles all hopes of genuine human freedom. Throughout the texts revealing this danger, moreover, the poet shows the temptation being confronted by minds of the most brilliant capacities for openness to redemptive transference and then reveals how these individuals nonetheless can or do let themselves (or people like them) be pulled into the very series of compounded repressions that they themselves are most able to resist. The reasons why and the frequency with which this can happen are the subjects of the works I now want to analyze, and the frightening ease of the shift from positive to negative transference is apparent as soon as the poet starts this sequence by looking at the creation of God in the image of man.

Narcissism and the Gaze of the Other
in *Laon and Cythna*

Shelley develops Hume's analysis of anthropomorphic projection in the most famous of the Spenserian stanzas composing *Laon and Cythna, or The Revolution of the Golden City.* This poem, after all, is a twelve-canto epic-romance demonstrating how "a thirst for a happier condition of moral and political society" might challenge yet be temporarily defeated by forces tied to the "gratuitous fetters" that religious monarchists (including Edmund Spenser) "impose" upon "their own imaginations" (the words of Shelley's Preface to the poem, *CPW*, II, 99 and 104). Hume is therefore echoed quite clearly in Canto 8 (*CPW*, II, 211–20) when Cythna reveals to sailors enslaved by their belief in "some immortal power" (ll. 3232–33) that such a "Power," really a fabricated "sign" used to make a "holy / All [patriarchal and monarchical] power" (ll. 3280–81), derives from the moment a "moon-struck sophist stood / Watching the shade from his own soul upthrown / Fill Heaven and darken Earth" (ll. 3244–46). At that time, a man or race of men, she suggests, found the vanishing of the supposed "causes" behind observed phenomena to be analogous to the disappearance of "hopes, and fears, and thoughts" from "man's own [surviving] works" (ll. 3237–39). Because of this analogy, the unknowable depth in the first set of visible consequences could be thought of as occupied by the "human heart" (l. 3236), the "inner life" presumed to be the invisible cause behind the second set (now quite clearly transformed into a metaphor for the first). With a human "likeness" thereby sent out to and reflected back from a world-size "mirror" far more "vast" than anything human, the projecting self, probably male, could now be, and has often been, anamorphosed into an all-encompassing distension, a superhuman "Form, which . . . between . . . Earth and Heaven [apparently] / Wields a [still] invisible [and highly phallic] rod" (ll. 3248 and 3255–56).

Even so, this poem makes its most revealing advances on the *Four Dissertations* at those moments when it connects this projection with the love between the prophetess-warrior-heroine and her poet-brother, the incestuous relationship that Shelley had to suppress by deleting any blood-connection in the more widely published version of the piece, *The Revolt of Islam* (1818). What is most striking about the sophist's "dim cloud" of "Opinion" cast over "the moon" as though the transferred obscurity were an inhuman certainty (ll. 3271–72) is its resemblence, coming late in the poem, to the way Laon's "own shadow" reappears for him in Cythna's face (l. 874) during the idyllic days of their youth in Canto 2 (*CPW*, II, 129–43). Her "shape of brightness," already "A power" in its sheer motion and its conversion to "radiancy" of all it gazes upon, transfigures her brother, as the "upthrown shadow" distends the "sophist," into "A second self, far dearer and more fair" than its original (ll. 865–66 and 875–76). The main reason, too, is the manner in which her "gathering beauty" recasts, as "man's work" recasts human longing while leaving it behind, "some immortal dream" that Laon has sensed when inundated by "the wave of life's dark stream," perhaps during sleep (ll. 871–73). The most oppressive and hierarchical transfer of "selfhood" outside the supposed "self" is basically—and amazingly—the same as the one in the most loving and equal of interchanges; and so, in this poem at least, the foundations of tyrannical ideology lie in what can happen to the movement of desire that also serves to promote love, equality, and the projective fulfillment of dream-wishes.

The main potential in this movement that can definitely be turned in more than one direction is surely what Freud calls "primary narcissism,"[11] since that is what Laon is describing throughout much of his recollective narration in Canto 2. As I have hinted in my introduction to this book, Freud's dim sense of a basic "differentiation in the energy at work generally in the mind" is much the same as the primordial drive that Shelley finally terms "something within us which from the instant that we live and move thirsts after its likeness." This turning outward of "libido" in quest of satisfactions corresponding to, defining, and reflecting its "excitations" is thus, not surprisingly, the transference that urges Laon and Cythna from the start toward self-constitution and even self-completion and extension by way of one another. Laon remembers being so dissociated from his mother, the usual Freudian locus of initial satisfactions, that he recalls frantically searching for a responsive "nurse" in all the "sights and sounds" of "life's young hours" from "sweet looks" to "Traditions dark and old" (ll. 674–75, 667, and 683). Such quests, like "libido" itself, can draw the outward-tending "something within us" in two opposite ways. On the one hand, longing can try to ingest or introject gratifications, pulling the drive outward back toward the ego along with any discovered counterparts, as when the young Laon takes in more and more of the "story / Of human life" to the point of feeling the "Guilt and Woe" imposed on all around him by "dim and gloomy" forms of "worship" (ll. 685–86, 721, and 724–25). On the other hand, the same outreach can seek to gratify the self by pleasing and/or augmenting whatever counterpart it chooses. This drive points desire toward the movement of another's or several others' desires to which the longing of the self seeks to be joined, just as Laon seeks to find his "thoughts invested" in "words" carrying his desires over to readers and "weav[ing] a bondage of . . . sympathy" among now distant people (ll. 802–07). These different drives in the same will to transference, arising as they do from the recollective and forward movements in all transfers, can split apart or let one drive dissipate the other unless there is an "other" for the self allowing both to operate simultaneously. This very sort of counterpart is what Laon finds in Cythna, as she does in him. Being his sibling and reflector, she makes him see her responses to him as what he wants to reflect in his own being, especially since she seems Laon himself (later calling herself Laone) in another form. At the same time he is gratified by her gratifications as they respond to his, so much so as to allow his self-image in her eyes to be transfigured into her brightened vision of him. This, after all, is the same sort of self-transcendence that she admits to seeking and finding in his reactions to her (ll. 3082–83).

It is in this very cycle of desire answering desire that the hierarchization of Self/other or Other/self starts to become a potential and even to become visible. Cythna is Laon's "dearer" second self because she is for him what Freud calls an "ideal ego," an attempt in a later (though still youthful) form to recover what the "infantile ego" now seems to have been: a "former completeness" with access to immediate satisfaction and thus a state "possessed of every perfection which is of value." She alters the self-image she reflects and takes in by becoming its completion and expansion to a greater perfection, one toward which she herself seems to be moving. Indeed, she does so by refiguring one of Laon's own "dreams" of a state more "immortal" (and feminine) than his present one, a dream similar, as we might expect, to the *Alastor* Poet's projection of his "veiled maid." Cythna's repetition of this construct is only proper, since the dream comes from a subliminal Lucretian "stream" of successive "waves"— something like what Freud refers to as the primeval "germ-plasm" reforming itself constantly from one life to another—which raises up images reworking past images, mainly so that the new figures can flow ahead to a different reformation in another person's being. Projecting and pursuing this greater "second self" in a sibling of the soul, however, can very easily turn the "ideal ego" into an "ego-ideal" or "superego." That turn is really already underway when the ideal ego, as apparently the infantile one reborn, seems to the projector (in Freud's words) "to deem itself the possessor of all perfections." Now the projector seems an insufficiency compared to his own projection/reflection, and the "ideal" can seem to distend its "more perfect and self-sufficient" difference, as well as its resemblance, to become an external standard judging the behavior of its progenitor as of course "less perfect" than its own. An "ideal" so positioned, in the projector's view, can even pull into itself its creator's introjective tendencies along with the projective ones, ingesting the ability, by the consent of the desiring self, to possess all the "Power" of transference at a "greater" and "higher" level. It is this Shelleyan double transfer, of the subject and *then* its desire for self-transcendence into another existence whose power of motion seems more mysterious and self-determining than the subject's, that makes possible the "upthrown shadow" abasing the "sophist" from its projected throne in perceived Nature's "vast mirror."

This inequality arising from what could remain an equal exchange of transfers, it turns out, is neither unlikely nor hard to understand if we consider "likeness"-with-a difference reflected back by an "Other" as what is needed most for self-definition in *Laon and Cythna*. There is simply no construction of an identifiable self in Shelley without a specific counterpart (a person or environment or symbolic order) helping to form that self's structure and possibilities in a mirror, an apparent reversal of non-identity into an identity visible to the subject. Such is the case even when the captured Cythna of Canto 7 (*CPW*, II, 199–211) forms her greatest "widsom" by herself in the "cave" of her imprisonment, so plainly a "type" of all chambers of thought (ll. 3100–04). There her thinking becomes a prophetic "wave / Whose calm reflects all moving things that are" (ll. 3104–05) only because she can read such a range of figures in the "mystic legends" on the "paven" bottom of the grotto's "fountain" (ll. 2938–41); then because the "babe" she now bears both "hunts[s]" all moving things with *its* eyes as its mother watches (ll. 3001–10) and recalls, in the same eyes, the "dream divine" of Laon from which Cythna has already formed her "self" somewhat (ll. 2983–90); and finally because she can fashion her increasingly intricate thought-patterns by weaving them "on the sand" in a "subtler language within language wrought" (ll. 3109–12). In addition, she can complete the process to the point of really comprehending it only by telling all this to Laon as she does (a fact reemphasized by him at ll. 2990–91) and by remembering the cave as the place now entirely outside her where she gained her expanded knowledge from a locus with a "deep foundation ... Immutable [and] resistless" (ll. 3079–80). Since the "I" is so dependent on such counterparts, then, the longing for definition can easily delegate true nature (the standard that governs definition) and the capacity to create selfhood on the basis of that nature to an "upthrown" Other, now the presumed source of being (as the cave appears to be), which then seems authorized to dictate the terms of any individual's life and death.

As soon as that consignment occurs, moreover, as in Rousseau's origin of inequality, the projecting subject voids itself of control over the very initiative that allows it to make projections. According to Cythna's speech to the sailors, even the freedom to build or destroy that people assume they possess in fashioning their "works" is given over in the worship of an outside "Power" to the exalted Self "of many names," and henceforth that Power seems to be "free / To waste" or build up all of life as it chooses, so much so that our own freedom must be granted (or really returned) to us by the freedom of the Other (ll. 3276 and 3240–41). In this way, as Jean-Paul Sartre describes the process, "my freedom escapes me to become a *given* object," something granted to "me" by the "look of the Other" that generates my "nature" as "I make there to be an Other."[12] Especially if I allow this "gaze" to make me feel ashamed and abased, Sartre goes on, the Other is "my transcendence transcended." The crossing-over of my desire, aiming to constitute my existence "for myself," is displaced again by a reextension of the crossing motion to become an "in itself" seemingly blessed with self-determination. The notion of a God is this "concept of the Other pushed to the limit," driven by further transfers so far beyond the transfer underlying it that it appears to occupy a level surpassing transference, enough to seem its distant cause instead of its effect. Once this transposition has been sufficiently distanced and distended, carrying with it transference's tendency to both reincorporate and conceal its actual past, the resulting Power becomes the presumed basis of all further transfers (the "Power on high" for conventional readers of "Mont Blanc").

To be sure, the conscious human will for Shelley, though powerless to prevent the sheer movement of transference and the consequent search for a defining Other, can turn the motion away from pursuing such a limit. The beseeching subject, as Laon realizes, can choose to see an alternative process: the "mirror" as able to transfigure the subject's former dream of self-transcendence only because that reflector is, like Cythna, a self-altering, mobile "power" of transference "gathering beauty" from elsewhere as *it* proceeds from state to state. If such an Other is itself that moving quest for self-transcendence, then the mirror must look to at least one other mirror (as the subject has looked to it) for completion. The reflector can project its (her) own need, in fact, back toward the being who set it (or her) up as the Other, just as Cythna does repeatedly in looking to Laon for the self-improvement that he seeks in her (for example, at ll. 937–39 and 2990–92). As Sartre puts it, then, the "I" can "transcend the Other's possibilities by considering them as possibilities of transcending me which I can always transcend towards new possibilities" as my reflector is reflected again in me. The interplay of siblings/lovers at its most glorious in Laon and Cythna is clearly designed to show how such a continual exchange of self-transformations can occur in human relationships. Each, finding transference operative *in* the other as well as *between* the two different yet similar figures, "reads" the "hopes" (reenvisionings of the "immortal dream") in the face of his or her counterpart. Each thereupon feels an "intenser zeal," "kindled" by every "reading," for surpassing the present state of self, all because of what each "heart ha[s] learned to trace" in the other's signs throughout a continual give-and-take among opposite but analogous people (ll. 945–48).

Shelley must offer such an example, employing the sameness-in-difference of incest to do it, since even some of his closest allies in poetry at the time seem to despair of this possibility. Indeed, they have too clearly announced such attitudes in epic narratives with Spenserian stanzas, Peacock in the unfinished *Ahrimanes* and Byron in the first three Cantos (thus far) of *Childe Harold*. *Ahrimanes* sees world-orders of tyranny and equality alternating in an inevitable movement that human will cannot really change, so much so that the hero, Darassah, despite his fervent love for Kelasris, cannot help being pervaded by "ambition's [grasping] spell" during the era of ruthless Ahriman, in which "The brightest tints of youthful fancy's hope / Fade in the vast reality of pain" until the return of Oromaze.[13] Byron's hero, for his part, must not see the sister he loves *because* he is interdicted by the incest taboo (Canto the First, stanza x), so he must define himself by seeming a "Portion of [all] around" him and must therefore seem carried by the vast heights of Nature toward a "throned Eternity" that seems unreachable (Canto the Third, stanzas lxxii and lxii)—very much in the manner of Shelley's abject sophist.

Admittedly, though, Shelley's alternative of a truly loving interchange between equals is not consistently able, even in Shelley's poem, to be a total contrast to hierarchical patterns. Granted, the scenes between the lovers never really fail to portray a genuine intertransference. But the same sense of unmystified exchange exalting neither side permanently over the other cannot be carried over into the relationships between the hero or heroine and their listeners, presumably the people who are trying to bring about the brave new world envisioned by Laon and Cythna. When Cythna, after her intellectual metamorphosis in the cave and the speech to the sailors, appears to city-dwellers and visitors to the city as an embodiment of love's, freedom's, imagination's, and thus the new world's transfer-based foundations, she is first presented, notwithstanding Shelley's attempt to recall ceremonies of the French Revolution, as a mystified "Shape upon an ivory throne" uttering "unite / Thine hand with mine" to the populace as though hers were the official word of "holiest rite" (ll. 2106, 2149–50, and 2144 in Canto 5, *CPW, II,* 162–83). There could hardly be a clearer picture of the inclination in thoughts based on positive transference to shift into—and then to be hidden within—the negative form of the drive and the way it always enthrones absolute Others. Even as this spectacle attempts to critique monarchical empires, the way the Revolution did, by inversely employing the throne-centered stagecraft of what it opposes, Cythna's attempted dissemination of true primary narcissism still impedes its objective by contracting the process of that relational state into the raising of an ego-ideal for a new society to pursue. She tries to present the truth she stands for as a version of the old interplay between Laon and herself by making all her onlookers as a group embody his gaze upon her (with "Thou dost resemble him alone" at l. 2140). Ultimately, however, she suggests that everyone's salvation begins with the crowd's gaze looking *up* to hers when she decides that "thou *beneath* / Shouldst image one who may have been long lost in death" (ll. 2141–42, emphasis mine). The very slightest tilting of the basic transfer-relation here makes it the reference of some onlookers' gazes to the words and statesque image of an Other's more thorough interpretation of events, wherein the minds of audience members can view their desires exalted in a greater "type of [them] all" (l. 3104 in Canto 7; *CPW,* II, 208). One of the very characters who puts this shift in question carries it through at least briefly, almost in spite of herself, picking up quite clearly on the desire of her audience for the definition of their hopes and fears which she offers to them before choosing to dethrone herself.

There are several tyrannizing aspects of narcissistic projection, after all, that are overwhelmingly difficult to neutralize. One problem is the projector's natural assumption, accepted here by Cythna's listeners, that the nature and meaning of the "self" defined by the Other lie entirely within the Other's control. The subject's personal desire apparently has no significance at all, in this belief, unless recognized and reworked by the desire of another who seems more at one with himself or herself (as

Cythna seems in her ceremony).[14] Furthermore, as Cythna tells the sailors, there is one additional "poison"; there is "fear's dew (l. 3250), a powerful motivator that operates at two different levels. First there is the ominous realization that a projected Other granted control to the point of being made a King or a God (or, for Freud, a superego/patriarch with the supposed power of castration) has been given the capacity to destroy the subject instead of constituting it—to impose "Death / On all who scorn his laws" (ll. 3251–52)—or at least to deny the value or meaning being sought by the projector, since the right to decide is now located in the Other and not the self. Even when the Other is just another person, as Cythna finally claims to be, the subject may start feeling the second terror: an awareness of how utterly contingent the self is, how other-than-itself *within* itself the self must be when dependent on an Other, and how, with the satisfaction of the desire for identity deferred to a distant location, the desire may always be revived rather than finally satisfied in such a relationship (the blessing in the love of Laon and Cythna that for most people seems a threat).

These last potentials in narcissistic transference, especially, deny the achievement of a definite "nature" in the very process by which one is pursued. Faced with this unsettling fact, it is no wonder that most people, particularly the common folk desiring true liberty in *Laon and Cythna,* send a will similar to yet more commanding than their own into a mirror of it at a seemingly higher level, even though they thereby give up the very freedom to determine identity that they have wished for all along. Only in that way can subjects seem to gain some mastery over their fate, albeit through a representative, and some definite sense of an identity that would otherwise remain indeterminate. This mastery may be gained at the price of enslavement, yet the security of a clearly positioned self seems worth the cost, initially at least. Meanwhile, tyrants, such as Othman in this poem, exploit that tendency because it sanctions their authority and keeps them from being placed consciously in the position of projector that everyone actually occupies. This sort of usurper simply claims heaven's permission to play the role of God on earth and suggests that this authorization is also the people's delegation of their own power to him, since that delegation is what establishes gods in the heavens, as we have seen. Worse yet, if anyone claims, as Cythna so briefly does, to be a rival warrior-leader, apparently as this kind of representative, the tyrant can use the similarity of stances to claim that absolute leaders are the order of the day and that the one entitled to victory is the one with the most overwhelming tools, including clerics with their doctrines of submission to God, for imposing his will on everyone else (as in Canto 10, *CPW,* II, 231–45).

Laon and Cythna consequently ends with a victory and a defeat for revolutionary transference. We are left, we might say, with both possibilities bound to each other inextricably and indecisively. On the one hand, the hero and heroine, by the time they are put to death as both rebels and heretics on orders from the conquering Othman and his priests, are reestablished as resisting only with their radically unconventional sibling / lover relationship. As they are burned at the stake, "each [feeds equally] upon the other's countenance" without cessation (l. 4580 in Canto 12; *CPW,* II, 257), Cythna having cast off the traditional warrior's garb in which she has come to join her brother. It is now clear that they are being eradicated because they have revealed the transfer-based foundations of imperial authority and have offered equalizing alternatives where identity is expansively altered over and over by an interreflection where every person seems the sibling of every other. This contrast with what condemns them, made even more ironic by their embodiment of a process that will survive their oppressors because it is the forgotten basis of oppression, turns Laon and Cythna, for sympathetic onlookers and readers, into a "memory, ever burning" beyond their execution, which allows all hopeful inhabitants of this present "dark night of things" to look ahead toward "an eternal morning" due to reappear some day in an existence newly perceived (ll. 4709–10; *CPW,* II, 261). The aspiring tendencies (and thus spirits) of Laon and Cythna even find themselves carried away from the suppressions of current history by "a winged Thought" projecting itself past their deaths, one that permits them, at least in our thinking about them, to continue their interchange in an unrestricted "overflow" of "converse wild, and sweet, and wonderful" that we should all work to attain (ll. 4720 and 4775–76; *CPW,* II, 262–63).

On the other hand, the "Thought's" attempt to relocate and perpetuate their interplay, though perhaps at a subliminal level in a sort of collective unconscious, carries them—as the poem's "frame" narrator has dreamt in Canto I (*CPW,* II, 111–29)—to an eternal "Temple" of "subtlest power, divine and rare." There they now occupy "throne[s]" as two among "The Great" and speak mainly at the behest of a male "Form" seated "in the midst" (like the principal god in many Greek temples) to whom the desire for true revolution in the shape of "Woman" defers by shrieking his "name" and "dissolving" before him (ll. 559, 591, 604–5, 632, 638, 613, and 616–19). As much as this "vast dome" is constructed from the deepest aspirations in preconscious thinking and so interweaves numerous memorials of "passionate change" throughout world history (ll. 568–69 and 600–603), the transfer-process that fashions it, feeling the pressure of its own capacity to create locations for ego-ideals, cannot finally avoid an exaltation of worshipped abstractions, Laon and Cythna among them, and a "commingling" of different revolutionary aims and symbols around a single and amazingly monarchical focus (l. 627). The earthly victory of tyranny's forces in the poem's plot is matched in its frame-story's principal image by the emergence of a centered, patriarchal religious system from an interplay of figures we are supposed to remember as challenging the justice and permanence of such orders.

One reason *Laon and Cythna* is not considered one of Shelley's greatest works, quite possibly, is the way it shows its author veering toward an inconsistency, more than once, in which the thought-patterns of true revolution are occupied by and even celebrate the ideologies that confine them most effectively. To some extent, however, this problem may result from the author's courage at the start of a series of works dealing with this very paradox. Shelley has dared here to confront a primal narcissistic transference that is basic to human self-formation and potentially productive of our best attitudes and actions, yet that is also able to project the defining Others of the self in such a manner as to tempt us all into submissions beneath exalted gazes. The balance in that insight is as astonishing as it is both reassuring and terrifying. This epic-romance helps us see, in language able to create new perceptions of recent history and our present sense of existence, how the counters to hierarchical constructs lie within the thought-maneuvers that are most able to produce those impositions and how those maneuvers are all too easily inclined, even in the most "liberated" of thinkers, to slip into enthronements of the superego that projective transfers permit and resist. From this point of view, Shelley's own slide at this stage into the resulting incongruity makes sense as a further extension of the interlocking tendencies carried through by his semi-mythic characters and images. He may not now be able to keep verbally dancing away from (while exposing) these basic quandaries to the extent that he will in his best later writing. But he has taken a necessary first step in a very original quest to discover the most profound connections between the impulses urging social revolution and the psychology underlying the widespread belief in absolutist ideologies.

The Will to Knowledge and the Feminist Critique in *Prometheus Unbound*

In the meantime, Shelley has reconsidered Godwin's link between the installation of monarchs and the projection of abstractions in discourse.[15] Consequently, when he composes, for reasons I shall note in the next chapter, *Prometheus Unbound: A Lyrical Drama in Four Acts* (written between September 1818 and the very end of 1819), he emphasizes the figural, verbalized nature of "upthrown" god-kings, thereby reworking the reflective projection of *Laon and Cythna* even as he recasts the enthronement of Jupiter from the versions of it in Aeschylus, Hesiod, and his other ancient pre-texts. The Aeschylean Prometheus—whose name means "fore-knowledge"—recalls how he defiantly "gave that counsel" which helped Zeus to overthrow Kronos and become "absolute king" of Olympus, from which the new monarch now rains punishments down on his former supporter.[16] Shelley's bound Titan, by contrast, remembers how *he* set Jupiter up in an inaugural utterance, again quite defiant, as a "Tremendous Image" of the speaker's own desire for self-mastery, a "Phantasm" of himself projected by and speaking back the Titan's words now "Written as on a scroll" above and beyond him (*Prometheus Unbound*, I. 246–48 and 261).

As many critics have realized by now,[17] Jupiter for Shelley is a "self-idealization," a raised-up superego, who at first seemed to help Prometheus be "king over [him] self" (I. 492) by way of a defining self-extension in an Other who exalted him. Because the human race had already projected Prometheus as a superhuman embodiment (or ego-ideal) of its own aspirations to foresight (for Hume, the motive for all superhuman projections), the Titan really had to repeat that transfer, being himself a reincarnation of primary narcissism at work. The "highest" projected figure that appeared to result, obscuring its figurative underpinnings just as the "shade" of the "sophist" did, has since come to seem the locus of all the self-generating "energy [the power of transference] relinquished by [the] mankind" from whom such energy did and still can pour forth.[18] In other words, by decreeing that anamorphosis of his own drive and then giving this counterpart a "strength" greater than what he would claim for his own projective and projected capacity (according to II. iv. 44), Prometheus has unintentionally "reified and institutionalized . . . a tyranny [of] the human mind" over itself, which the mind now can only reinforce in acts of head-on resistance to it. Because of the inevitable tension between that restrictive upper limit and the continuing aspiration (or fore-knowing) of the transfers that first produced it, the projector has had to hate and defy the projection, to be the rebellious target of its confining power, from almost the very moment the extension was configured. Exaltation and defiance must have been virtually simultaneous, so much so that increased hatred and attempted revolutions from that time on (including the Titan's) have served to shore up the tyrannical image, to keep its actual foundations repressed, and to call down further punishment from a "God"-figure who needs the suppression continued if "He" is to maintain the power ceded to "Him" long ago. Moreover, we must add, as Aeschylus insisted by making the Promethean Word an early impetus in this process—indeed, as Shelley insists further by having Asia see Prometheus as the creator of "speech," which in turn "created thought"—all these steps have been set in motion by the generative force of projected inscriptions, the enthroning "power" attached to the nearly forgotten "words" of the Titan (at I. 69).[19] Driven by this force, words have transported desire outside the psyche, have seemed to reflect that longing back to the psyche from a point (a written text) beyond it, have then looked beyond themselves to referents other than themselves or their speakers, and so have proposed a figural level greater and more complete than their own (in fact, an abstract, unified figure underlying all figuration) from which their definitions are dictated and at which all these extensions of desire might come to a stop, supposedly arriving at a determined ground or "meaning."

This last misreading has even been compounded by the further ascription of a quasi-human, punitive "will," the will of the defiant projector of desire ("my own will," Prometheus says at I. 274)[20] into a distant image really formed by the "secret power" of multiple transference (I. 240). The interpersonal, linguistic, and self-extending nature of this latter power is concealed when personal volition takes over that movement to make it the will's assertion of itself, or at least the will's licence to project as its objective a more self-sufficient and all-determining Other of itself. As the old-time nobles in Godwin's account discover after they give their provision for self-defense into a monarch's hands, fancying that he is acting in their interest, the use of transference (through a representative) strictly for self-definition and self-assertion produces the dominion of an enlarged willful Self over the very self (or selves) that the Other was created to define, extend, and exalt. Giving transference a personal will, or (we might say) controlling it enough to make it fashion a text granting the enlarged self a greater amount of willed power, means losing power over the personal will and reading its self-serving edicts on a "scroll" that claims absolute authority for a supreme volition apparently underwriting all the signs of the ruling text.

The first act of *Prometheus Unbound* is, to be sure, quick to reduce this old ascription (and its assumptions) to the often hidden transfigurations that generated its power. Yet, if all this is fairly easy to expose, there remains the question of why such a process actually occurred near the dawn of civilization and why it continues to occur when its figural basis keeps denying the substantiality of the "authority" it asserts. Why does Prometheus as an extension of the human quest for definition have to define himself in a figuration that redeploys him and claims a higher authority for the redeployment? What are the needs and longings that drive him to inscribe this kind of Other beyond himself, as opposed to the nonauthoritative Other that Laon and Cythna each find in a sibling-lover? Why are the figures of discourse so especially able to claim power over what they define or reconstrue? How is it that they can seem autonomous and all-determining in relation to their users, even though they are so readily exposed as incomplete figures determined by many others and so never constituted (autonomously) by themselves? Why, too, has Prometheus fashioned a male self-extension, just as the "sophist" did in what still seems a drive for a phallic supremacy? Laon has not taken that course automatically, nor has Prometheus himself in his own younger days, the days through which he remembers having "wandered," as a son of "Mother" Earth seeking feminine counterparts, "With Asia, drinking life from her loved eyes" (I. 122–23) instead of receiving his self-reflection from a patriarchal superego. What accounts for his diversion from one Other to another?

The answers to these questions, which carry Godwin far beyond Godwin, I now want to argue, are offered almost as soon as they are raised in *Prometheus Unbound,* to some degree by the Titan himself later in act 1 and to a great extent by Asia in act 2 (both acts having been written in close succession from late 1818 to March or April 1819). Prometheus reveals how anyone can be tempted into trying to be "king over [ones]self," even in a benign attempt at self-control. Such an effort, he says, means "rul[ing] / The torturing and conflicting throngs within," and that fact alone can make self-mastery analogous to, indeed an early form of, Jupiter dominating rebels and Furies "when Hell grows mutinous" (I. 492–94). Granted, the Titan is trying to deny the need for a glittering central monarch on earth just as Jesus does in Milton's *Paradise Regained;* in Shelley's drama as in Milton's poem "he who reigns within himself" by controlling "Passions" and "Desires" is more a true king than anyone granted limitless material wealth and command by an ideology of divine right and a lust for power (*Paradise Regained,* II. 466–67). But Shelley also recalls that Miltonic self-command is a prerequisite for domination, an invitation "to rule / Cities of men, or headstrong Multitudes," as (say) Oliver Cromwell did (*Paradise Regained,* II. 469–70). The younger poet wants to forestall that seemingly automatic transition by examining why such a result is so often the usual one. He begins his probe in the Titan's projection of Jupiter, I think, by making it foreshadow Friedrich Nietzsche's most basic definition of the "Will to Power," even though Shelley differs from Nietzsche in regarding that drive as only one of the courses into which the human will can channel transference. Prometheus's attempt to impose unity and obedience on "conflicting throngs" of different attitudes, feelings, or ideologies in himself resembles the way any "complex of sensation and thinking" has to work in *Beyond Good and Evil.* For Promethean as for Nietzschean foresight, a continuous motion "away from" in the direction of a "towards" (a sheer transpositional urge) generates a guiding or "ruling thought" that sets the direction for the self-overcoming always attempted by a complex of feeling and desire.[21] This sort of thought, though only a projection and objective—a Jupiter—helping a confusion to surpass its current situation and transfer itself to some other position that might seem to resolve it, demands submission from each alternative thought and tributary as though they were all potentially "conflicting" rebels against it. A war of impulses is thus made to become a hierarchization of tendencies. Each tendency gains or loses power depending on its obedience to what has become the ego-ideal of the moment, to the superego beginning to motivate a resistance to it (Promethean foresight) so that the basic self-overcoming can eventually continue.

This anticipation of Nietzsche even accepts two of his key supporting assumptions. Since Prometheus is the mythic champion and representative of humankind's desire to overcome its inadequacies and inconsistencies, he must be, like any set of impulses in *Beyond Good and Evil,* a "body" that is "but a social structure composed of many souls." There is a "conflicting throng" over which Shelley's Titan must help establish a "rule" because he reincarnates (as many people do) quarrels among classes, class-based ideas, religious systems, and human conceptions of him, all of which are striving to surpass their past and present states of incomplete understanding and rivalry with each other. Surely this panoply of established and power-seeking ("torturing") ideologies, later taking the form of "sceptred phantoms" (I. 206), is one of Prometheus' referents when he feels "Obscurely through [his] brain ... awful thoughts [sweeping] rapid and thick" (I. 146–47). Consequently, he must carry the drive most common to all the thoughts, the thrust in each toward both power over others and a decision "on high" about the relative value of each, out to a self-extension that locates that power at a height and seems to make the sought-after decision, just in the way an entire society delegates power (if we believe Rousseau). At the same time Prometheus has to have done all this figuratively, being a figure himself, because the domineering level of "Truth" thus projected is so like the one in Nietzsche's "Of Truth and Falsity in their Ultramoral Sense."[22] Suppositions of an overarching and permanent Truth, as Nietzsche defines them, arise out of "a mobile army of [linguistic formations:] metaphors, metonymies, anthropomorphisms"—a good description of what Prometheus really is: a verbally projected interplay of anthropomorphic mythographs. In order for that "army" to be deployed in a cogent discourse arrangement that assigns degrees of force and definite meanings to now competing and free-floating figures, there must seem to be a "congelation and coagulation of [the] original mass of similes and percepts." Projected symbolic forms must achieve a centralization and homogenizing of sign-relations, excluding some possible relationships, that seems "to a nation [to be] fixed, canonic and binding." That coagulation can henceforth appear to be a master dictionary or "legislature of language" claiming the right to determine what is meant by what is said in that nation. Such a power remains enthroned only if we forget that it results from "a sum of [already interpreted] human relations" that have sought to be added together but are not entirely homogenous. Nonetheless, what is "written as on [the set-up] scroll" strives to seem a commanding system of discourse originating in a single voice apparently at one with itself. To fulfill their own will to overcome themselves, this Great Text represses a cacophony of incompatible concepts and sign combinations that would keep plunging into rivalries unless some hierarchical control were established, or unless each sought relationships with the others based on sympathetic give-and-take and not on domination.

Why, however, we still must ask, if this linguistic quest for order need not automatically cast all impulses or metaphors under the sway of a governing code, has humankind and its self-extension (Prometheus) turned the outward- and upward-tending "ruling thought" of the moment into a "canonic" power trying to subordinate all existing and future competitors? That question is not answered until act 2 of *Prometheus Unbound*, but there Asia specifies the exact reason for that primordial decision as she recalls the beginning stages of the world's very existence and the roles Prometheus (even as a human projection) played at certain junctures. After asking herself about the basis of Jupiter's reign, she provides her own answer by recasting the story of primal Creation as it is rendered in Hesiod, Ovid, Genesis, and Peacock's *Ahrimanes:*

> There was the Heaven and Earth at first
> And Light and Love;—then Saturn, from whose throne
> Time fell, an envious shadow; such the state
> Of the earth's primal spirits beneath his sway
> As the calm joy of flowers and living leaves
> Before the wind or sun has withered them
> And semivital worms; but he refused
> The birthright of their being, knowledge, power
> The skill which wields the elements, the thought
> Which pierces this dim Universe like light,
> Self-empire and the majesty of love,
> For thirst of which they fainted. Then Prometheus

Gave wisdom, which is strength, to Jupiter
And with this law alone: "Let man be free,"
Clothed him with the dominion of wide Heaven. (II., iv., 32–46)

Clearly there is no demand for hierarchization or centralization built initially into these multiple "origins" of existence as it is now perceived.[23] Instead of such figures or entities pouring forth from that single fount or controlling essence in all of Asia's sources (even Peacock, who makes a Shelleyan "Necessity" the "Parent of being"),[24] this account, recalling the first lines of "Mont Blanc," offers differences simply gravitating toward each other to form early, interacting pairs, such as the earth and heaven whose primordial (and equal) intercourse engendered the Titans and most earthly beings, if Hesiod can still be credited.[25] In the definite naming yet rapid pairing of these figures, in fact—Creation imagined as motivated by a transference among distinctions—no choice is made at first between the simultaneous drives toward distinctness and combination. "Saturn" and "time," *Kronos* and *chronos* in Greek, are drawn both apart and together by difference and resemblance. When one entity in a pair, though (time, in this case), begins to see itself as the "shadow" of an "other" from which it inevitably differs and with which it cannot fully merge, it becomes "envious" of a completeness thought of as existing in the seemingly "better" counterpart, from which it now feels "fallen" away, desiring a recovery of what seems a lost unity. Once this sense of congruence being blocked by difference and distance occurs, the way it must in transfer-relations across temporal gaps, simultaneous interplay looks more and more like a first-and-then succession, where a later stage of assumptions about relationship seeks to regrasp an earlier and fading condition. Even joyously sustained "primal spirits" and plants in what appears a Saturnian golden age look back enviously to a "birthright" state,[26] in which (they now imagine) they consciously knew their "other" to such an extent that they possessed an exalted "majesty of love" linking them to their counterparts as much as earth was originally coupled to Heaven or a child to its mother. All such temporal and thus "fallen," desirous figures or beings consequently want to reoccupy the supposedly distant "throne" and "then" observe their current position from the more "knowing" place they might reattain. Prometheus, already human desire exalted and configured, has simply configured the pursuit of this "want" by installing a version of himself in Saturn's earlier and "Heavenly" place. Once so positioned, that raised-up self has seemed (or has hoped) to have the "power" of "knowledge" that can entirely explain and control the "fallen" state. Indeed, this self appears to have achieved an all-comprehending "empire" over the lesser self from a figural/linguistic locus projected, yet not existing totally, outside the subject.

For Shelley the will to power, as the later Nietzsche also says, is virtually synonymous with a will to knowledge.[27] To assert a "ruling thought" or discourse tending toward a future order and organizing a social/linguistic/personal "throng" of differnces is to long as well for a past position from which the current state of desire seems to have been transported. Such a position, given its partial resemblance to yet radical difference from the present condition of disjoined elements, appears to harbor a greater linkage among separate forms, one that seems to "know" their interconnections because it has the "power" to bring them about. Hence, given that any welter of perceptions or sensations in Shelley gains meaning when it is taken as a thought to be interpreted by other thoughts, beings and societies who regard themselves as "fallen" and "conflicting" strive to read their present insufficiency and disunity from that apparently self-sufficient, all-beholding and controlling location. The "look of the Other" thus conceived is what we often seek to be, or at least to believe in, so that we may "know ourselves," or observe ourselves, from both inside and outside our psyches with an authority of knowledge we do not ourselves possess. Indeed, since this thought-about-our-thoughts is what we need prior to any coherent constitution of our "natures," we reach out toward it as though it were our "birthright," the more perfect infantile state from which (like Laon) we feel divorced. Quite naturally, too, this interpreting gaze, with the projecting and consenting subject now acting as one of its underwriters, takes the form of those language-orders (the "speech" Prometheus "created") by which we discover what our thoughts are, what order our perceptions can take, and how this order can "measure" the "Universe" in and with word-patterns.[28] By granting this discourse-structure "wisdom" and "strength" (what the Titan gave to Jupiter to keep humankind free from ignorance), we both achieve and submit to what Michel Foucault, expanding on Nietzsche,[29] calls *la volonté de savoir:* a "grid of intelligibility" that graphically "deploys" the confused body-language of sensations, the disorganized perceptions of what seems "outside," the many social possibilities for people, and the conflict among ideologies, all of which criss-cross every society and the thought-patterns of every individual. Deployment, once set up in an authoritative position, arranges these uncontrolled interplays of resemblance and difference into definite similarities and absolute distinctions, according to which, in a master discourse, some possible relations are marginalized and some exluded from civilized "thought" and "meaning." Ironically, it is to empower this means to self-knowledge that a "ruling thought" temporarily subordinating others enthrones a figural enactment of its quest that at once devalues and ties down the self who gave it power.

This sequence of choices in Shelley's eyes admittedly has some important advantages that make it universally attractive, though not enough, if we take a wider view, to outweigh the disadvantages or to prevent a resistance to the master code using its own methods of deployment. On the positive side, Asia reveals, the ascription of "strength" and "wisdom" to an organizing grid has given its projectors the power of scientific scrutiny over people and perceived objects ("the skill which wields the elements"). Since a higher authority created after a human image has established (as Foucault says) "power" as a "rationality" allowing for the targeting and description of phenomena, humankind can ape that stance, licensed by how much human desire resembles it, to "tame . . . fire," to enslave "Iron and gold," turning forms of both into "signs of [human] power," and to render to the mind's eye (in fact, to create) "the [sense of] implicated orbits woven / Of the wide-wandering stars" (II. iv. 66, 69, and 87–88), in each case with the aid of a discourse granted the right to "measure the Universe." On the negative side, however, this "freeing" of humanity from once unknowable mysteries denies people freedom from the interpretive systems they employ, to such an extent that they must be, toward the objects "tortured to [their] will," tyrants very like the ones they now obey (II. iv. 68); "I gave all / He has," says the Titan of Jupiter back in act 1, "and in return he chains me here" to "grow like what I contemplate . . . in loathsome sympathy" (I. 381–82 and 450–51). Moreover, this acceptance of a governing language as above and beyond the users it commands— the result of seeing this mirror of the self as an intersubjective mechanism surpassing mere personal power—enslaves us to a level that appears "To know nor faith nor love nor law," even though it makes us obey *its* law asking us to direct our faith and love toward it (II. iv. 47). We can too easily blame our unloving choices on it, avoiding our responsibility for it, even as it denies being responsible to anyone or anything. We can, like the Earth interpreting herself according to current systems in act 1, fear to speak the relations and feelings made illegitimate by the ruling discourse. And we can assume ourselves to be so dissociated from that unfeeling dominance that we lack the power to alter its interplays, as if the freedom to change them belonged only to it.

Actually, though, our ability to reenact a construct that already reconfigures humankind allows us to challenge that order with the very "grid of intelligibility" by which it "deploys" us into various portraits of "fallen human nature." We can press the discourse of "measure" beyond current limits, manipulating its suppressed possibilities just as relentlessly as it works to ensure our deployment within it, so much so that "all-prophetic song" and "Science [can strike at] the thrones of Earth and Heaven" with new deployments that break the frames of the grids now in force (II. iv. 74–76). As Prometheus encourages, by giving us speech so that we can create thoughts that then expand the interplays of words, we can, as Nietzsche does,[30] reassert the continual and self-overcoming interaction between ever-changeable language and its self-transforming speakers. In the process we can also reveal that the power "on high" really "comes from below," as Foucault maintains. We can expose how often it is projected to the level of universal "intelligibility" out of numerous rival feelings and discourses that work to achieve a supremacy over others. Each tries to "know" itself and others, we can show, by making a version of itself the "ruler" of every contender, thereby enslaving itself, as one of the contenders, within a monolithic system that actually arose from many projections of desire supposing a greater and previous level of relationship beyond them all.

Meanwhile, even so, we must realize that such systems are able to uphold their dominance—and establish it initially, for that matter—because a gender-factor assists the enthronement of a "knowledgeable" discourse, so thoroughly that the "one who knows" is usually constructed as an authoritative father-figure more supreme than any feminine being. Shelley therefore lets Asia add, here and there, a feminist critique of "wisdom" as "strength" to her history of existence, where she develops (in part) the insights of Mary Wollstonecraft and so sophisticates, mainly in her choice of words, Cythna's more blatant assaults on the inequality of the sexes (as in ll. 1045–52 of *Laon and Cythna, CPW*, II, 141–42). To "know" by assuming a position of primordial command, Asia suggests, is to set up hegemonic discourse as a masculine sort of "light" that "pierces this dim Universe" with phallic (though many would still call it "scientific") aggression. True, such a light can claim that it has "tamed" part of itself in the form of "fire" by positioning the "play" of flame "beneath / The frown of man," and that statement can seem sexually neutral (albeit obsessed with the domination of one portion of an entity over another) if we regard "man" as a generic word for humanity in general, admittedly one of the term's most common uses. Nevertheless, Asia's syntax reveals that the lust for "knowledge" cannot achieve the "taming" in question unless what is "terrible" in fire—presumably including its uncontainable "play"—is regarded as "lovely" by the would-be knower and thereby feminized so that it can be subject to a "will" thus established as opposite and masculine (II. iv. 67–68). This sort of deceptively binary, then unequal relationship, of course, is no more original with Creation than the supposed inferiority of *chronos* in relation to *Kronos*. During the time of multiple and equal Earth–Heaven or Light–Love relationships, as Asia has described them, there is no precise gender difference or power difference claimed for either element in the attraction, even though Earth dimly retains her feminine sex from the Gaia of Hesiod and the Mother Earth (the Titan's mother) of Shelley's act 1. If there is an initial sexual difference, it is minimized by an interplay of qualities constantly moving back and forth between the different figures, as in the relationship of Asia and Prometheus before the tyranny of Jupiter, where each saw most of his or her "life" in the "eyes" of the other (on the model of Laon and Cythna).

Much as if Wollstonecraft were still writing, blurred differences become ranked distinctions in Asia's account only when the slightest of discrepancies (the *ch* in *chronos* as opposed to Saturn's *K*) is used to make one member of a pair the "he" with a presumption of unequal "sway" and the generic or neutral term used to define the entire race as though "woman" (like time) was but a secondary part while "man" (like God) was the primary whole. The secondary figure is then reduced to the position of a "shadow" whose "envy" helps shore up "his" greater power and his right to "know" and "tame" her, particulary when she flames with a desire for restored equality, to which she is certainly entitled if "she" is fire and "he" is light. The now-powerful male, in addition, wants to seem the unity-within-himself that the generic term is supposed to connote, neither requiring an "other" for self-constitution nor acknowledging this otherness as part of himself the way he once did. Hence he must take all the incompleteness, the changeability from moment to moment, and the "play" among different possibilities of being in himself and shunt these tendencies off onto the "fallen" female "other" (on "time," to begin with) as though they were located there and only there.[31] The "feminine," as a result, so connected with inconsistency already, comes to seem strange and "terrible" (even downright "beast[ly]" at II. iv. 66) to the supposedly dominant standard. From a male point of view, the ruling lens of society, "she" has to be exiled, as Asia is, or at least "known" and tamed, as Thetis has been by Jupiter's rape of her (the "penetrating presence" he boasts of at III. i. 39). In granting such "knowledge" to the masculine "strength" of Jupiter, Asia concludes, so that the granter—often the human male seeking superhuman status—could "know" himself yet escape the temporal otherness-from-himself now rendered exclusively feminine, Prometheus and the will to power he carries through in his periods of error have created and accepted a language of male supremacy as the basis of scientific and social discourse. He has thereby sundered his original relationship with Asia and become something of a rapist himself, temporarily, in the way he urges mankind to "torture" the materials of Mother Earth and turn them into "the slaves and signs of [man's not woman's] power." Civilized culture, the result of the Titan's efforts to resist Jupiter by employing the "piercing" methods of "measuring" discourse, has consequently become heavily male-supremacist, the supposed conqueror of female Earth and Nature "like [the God it] contemplate[s]" as its model.[32]

Asia, we should note, is for Shelley the best possible figure (Cythna transformed into a Venus-like Earth-goddess) for leveling this further attack on the Promethean will to knowledge, especially since she is the Other prior to Jupiter off whom Prometheus (a version of all male desire) has mirrored a sense of himself. She is obviously, to begin with, the Titan's Cythna or ideal-ego, the reflector/creator of his many and greatest potentials—a role that befits a symbol of the human longing for a maternal love-process in which man (the would-be Prometheus) can keep overcoming his state by being reborn in her reactions to and extensions of him. As such a version of her lover, she can grasp his desire, and after the enthronement of Jupiter his need, to create a penetrating language for mankind rivaling yet imitating the supposed Word of God. Since Jupiter is but a substitute for the self-transcendence that Prometheus once attempted by way of her, she can appreciate, even celebrate, the Titan's attempt at self-overcoming both in his raising up of a master discourse that "wields the elements" and in his rebellious gift of this method to the "lesser" mankind who desired this "upthrowing" in the first place. At the same time, having been sometimes forgotten and then exiled by these efforts to a non-Western location, Asia can freely, as a marginalized figure, embody the self-transfiguring, thought-transforming, original drive of transference that has been rendered nonmasculine, exclusively feminine, and thus secondary to the dominant language-order as a source of human knowledge. On her first appearance, when she receives the Titan's renewed longing for her through the words and memories of Panthea, she can at once transfigure his image as it appears in the eyes of their go-between. She reforms its previous and current nature with her gaze into "a soft light of [now less defiant] smiles" that she goes on, in another transfer, to liken to "radiance from the cloud-surrounding moon" (II. i. 120–22). Asia, then, the quintessential "feminine" in some ways, is the "outsider" at present who actually lay once—and can lie again—at the very heart or "inside" of Prometheus's drive to transcend himself by way of an other. That is why she can both laud his creation of a "piercing" master-language and expose the repressions in it, including the suppression of her, with the double edges in her "vitally metaphorical" words.[33] She is the "femininity" (or transference) that underlies and empowers, yet has been cast off by, the ever-desirous male consciousness as it has tried to overcome its own basic otherness (a kind of multi-sexual plurality) in the projection of an exclusively masculine Other.[34] She therefore has the right to expose her own primacy and the mechanisms unleased by transference that have downgraded the "woman" who gave them birth. Only in that fashion, all the while operating within the very discourse-system she undermines, can she draw her lover and Shelley's most attentive readers back to the interplay of equal differences from which tyranny has so sadly devolved.

As she does so, she completes, as much as her author allows *Prometheus Unbound* to complete, Shelley's answers at this stage to the questions raised by the Titan's (and mankind's) raising-up of Jupiters. The being or race (or figure for the race's desire) in quest of self-definition, we find, needs an Other with apparent authority above and beyond relational interplay, since only then can the incomplete self or group be lifted to a supposed completeness out of the "throng" of related differences now subsuming it, out of conflicting sensations, social rivalries, incompatible personal characteristics, and inconsistent options for self-description in language. No defining Other can be adopted, if permanent and commanding definition is the objective, unless these indefinite relations among differences seem excluded from it altogether or at least more settled into a univocal consistency than they are in the desiring subject's present situation. In fact, an Other achieving this status must possess a unity of elements that seems prior to, more homogenized than, and more self-contained than the "lesser" state where every "other" is as other-than-itself as the self looking to it for an exalting mirror. Should the questing psyche be male or a group of males, as has often been the case, seeking social discrimination and structures of dominance for the sake of self-distinction, the idea of woman as defining Other fails to meet the foregoing criteria, since it means men must define themselves as possessing some "female" qualities and vice-versa. A superego has to be proposed that is entirely male and able to throw off the "feminine" completely. It must answer threats from women to a pure masculinity by a "knowing" representation of "female nature" that makes that rival the inconsistency excluded from the supreme figure. Once this binary opposition is produced sufficiently to set Essence against Other, wholeness against insufficiency, male "strength" and "wisdom" (culture) against female "emotionalism" (untamed nature), and a verbal code of consistency against a less coherent language that should bend to the dominant system, even the projecting self is subject to being deployed by the will to power through the grid of intelligibility, which henceforth concentrates on the exclusion of many relational interplays, including some that make the projection of all "others" possible. Indeed, the master text now asserts its complete independence of transference and projection so that it can predetermine the future directions taken by both impulses or by the will of the subjected psyche. The desire of foresight, still seeking to overcome any present state and trying to relate differences that remain unconnected, must therefore see fixed limits binding its possibilities written in a severe injunction "as on a scroll" before the desirous eye. The only way to rebel effectively against this hegemony, since we articulate ourselves within its terms even (in fact, especially) when we attack it head on, is to recontact the open play of many possible transfers at work beneath yet apparently exiled by the reigning deity or ruler. Such is the attempt made, with increasing intensity and success, throughout *Prometheus Unbound,* and that quest begins with this thorough exposure of how the longing for self-knowledge has created God the Father.

The "Madness" of Objectification:
Julian and Maddalo Through the Lenses of "On Life"

Before completing his great lyrical drama, however, Shelley has to work out a greater understanding of that additional Western concept that helps keep a Jupiter enthroned: the assumption of an "objective level," existing irrespective of interpretations of it, to which perceiving subjects should passively submit if they wish their perceptions to correspond to "what is really out there." The Jupiter of *Promethus Unbound,* until exposed for the projected discourse-grid that he has been from the start, seems, we must admit, to be a dictator to his perceivers from a nonsubjective position "above" them all. His level seems to harbor both the supreme object demanding the acceptance of his observing subjects and the objective foundation of all schemes of language that organize human perceptions into orders of objects. Shelley, of course, having read and caviled about the Coleridgean "I" (or self-sufficient subject), could have distinguished the tyranny of the domineering observer from that of the predetermining object, both of which are erroneous notions for him. But his use of Jupiter shows that both tyrannies by now have become variations on just one kind in this poet's eyes. As when the human imagination in Coleridge bases its power to make a world on its repetition of a greater "I AM," the personal subject for the later Shelley never attempts world domination without claiming to possess sanctions from some higher essence (as Shelley's Mercury claims authority from Jupiter in act 1). "He who reigns" underwrites certain commanding "subjects" in *Prometheus Unbound* only because he is taken as a self-determining "object" by those who look to or project him.

For his devotees, in turn, this ruler, as both dominator and measurer, also predetermines the nature of objects by deciding the governing assumptions (in fact, the style of representation) underlying the way the human mind sees a perception as an object. According to Asia, it is the setting-up of Jupiter that makes the "Universe" an array of surfaces with hidden cores, a set of covers to be "pierced" by phallic science. Since it is now to the advantage of monarchs and their profit-seeking backers to conceal the producer-laborer and the productive process behind any product entering the marketplace of interpreter-buyers, the hegemonic "grid of intelligibility" in Shelley's day deploys perceptions "in accordance with an obscure verticality" that sees all objects as hiding a deep significance or history, to borrow again from Foucault.[35] If an observer wants to find the "truth," he or she must press beyond the perceivable surface to plumb "the organism's inner darkness," in the words of Foucault, or to approach "all subtlest froms / Hidden beneath the mountains and the waves," in the words of Asia's history of the arts and sciences (II. iv. 70–71). Jupiter, among other things, is a command to perceivers to adopt this penetrating approach as their way of "mastering" the world around them. The master discourse, set up for the power of some, would, ironically, make us all passively receptive to a target that we must still project as behind a deceptive surface, since the surface does not reveal it to us. If we accept this assumption, we will even ascribe an objective depth to the Jupiter-level, one that will conveniently hide the subjective and projected basis of such a tyrannical construct.

Unfortunately, *Prometheus Unbound* does not take the time to explain in detail how this objectification comes about or to reveal the daily human tragedies that occur for Shelley when people assume this way of seeing as the basis of their attitudes. The time clearly needs to be taken, in Shelley's view, given the widespread acceptance of the concept and the fact that Ovid's example of men modeling their diets on those of beasts does not reveal how any perception becomes an object or why we would let an "outside" figure determine our behavior as though we were totally passive. It is two other works of 1819, finished after acts 1 and 2 were probably complete, that focus on the genesis, motivations, and oppressive effects of an objectivity so conceived. To understand Shelley's key to this sort of enslavement, we must therefore "pierce" and analyze them both.

The one that exposes the most basic decisions turning transference into an object faced by a subject is the essay "On Life" already noted, that extraordinary addendum to the *Philosophical View of Reform* written very late in 1819 just as act 4 of *Prometheus Unbound* was nearing completion as well.[36] This short prose excursus, as we saw in the introduction, is unequivocal about seeing "objects of thought" as being set up by a transposition in which an apparently earlier thought is interpreted (and thus reconstituted as an object) by another thought. My opening statement, though, I freely admit, did not provide the entire context of the "object of thought" sentence as it appears in the essay. Actually, the piece is mainly concerned with revealing and refuting the ways in which we "lose the [transfer-based] apprehension of life" (*NCE*, p. 475). One way, Shelley decides, is our rigidifying of subject-object relations in a manner that makes them unalterable by granting the "thing" priority:

> The relations of things [once "things" are assumed] remain unchanged by whatever system. By the word *things* is to be understood any object of thought, that is, any thought upon which any other thought is employed, with an apprehension of distinction. The relations of these remain unchanged; and such is the material of our knowledge. (*NCE*, p. 478)

Initially the "employment" of one thought "upon" another is a relation of two similar entities that are different primarily in their positioning and temporal order, the interpreting thought taking the other one to be the earlier of the two. Spatial and temporal distance, though, as we have seen with *chronos* "falling from" *Kronos,* can easily be taken as an absolute difference, "an apprehension of distinction." If the will succumbs to this temptation and assumes such utter separateness, then just one of the "thoughts" can be what both of them really are. The thought being interpreted must be taken as thought's "object" only and must be seen as "outside" interpretation, even though its objectivity is produced by the interpreter's "inside" focus "upon" it. The supposed "object," in fact, must forget the thought-about-a-thought bringing it into being and must stand as a self-determining impetus "suggesting one thought [as a response], which shall lead to a train of thoughts" that should always be the same train whenever the same object is observed by a psyche (*NCE,* p. 477).

Yes, we can keep trying to recover the more fluid and transfer-oriented state of childhood "reverie" in which a looking outward at "incoming" impressions (each of which looks ahead of and behind itself) makes both "out" and "in" simultaneous movements in perception, leaving us "conscious of no distinction" between observation and "the surrounding universe" (p. 477). But the "habitual" stance for most Western adults (p. 477)—enforced by Western educators because it enslaves people under a "violent dogmatism" that keeps "them from thinking" (p. 476)—is the taking of a figure related to a second figure by an even later perspective (a third position) for an object prompting thoughts as though it were simply "there." With such lenses coloring our eyes (as materialism once colored Shelley's, he admits on p. 476), we tend to see a "thing" as arousing thought-associations that are "mechanically" forced to be the same ones time after time (p. 477). "Our whole life is thus an education of error," and we lose the "freedom" with which the mind "would have acted" were it not bound to duplicate fixed and conventional reactions to "objects" (p. 477). Having refused thought's capacity to reorient what it views, the psyche cannot reinterpret what it perceives according to altered thought-associations, nor can it open its existing assumptions to modification by allowing an object-thought to interact with or add to thoughts never "employed upon" it before.

For Shelley this imprisonment, according to "On Life," is also the supreme "misuse of words and signs," denying both of these their full, inherent right to be continually "standing not for themselves but for others" (p. 477). If we believe persistently in "objectivity," our words (as signifiers) come to refer to signs (or signifieds) in a "sense [whereby] almost all familiar objects are signs . . . in their capacity" of prompting reactions (*their* signifieds) that are "mechanical and habitual" (p. 477). The "outside" world becomes, as with Jupiter's "grid of intelligibility" trying to provide all reference points and definitions for personal expressions, a master text or book of established facts that cannot be altered in any way by the reader. Assuming this construct to be itself a fact, we may then believe that "words can penetrate the mystery of our being" (p. 475). They can supposedly refer to signs that are grounded on absolutely definite bases, on foundations that the master text will point to by arousing predetermined thoughts in us that should refer automatically to the signs being read. Of course this sequence of claims puts itself in question early, given the terms it uses (or the terms Shelley says it uses). Calling familiar objects "signs" likens them enough to words that they are shown to refer away from themselves rather than into their supposed depths. Indeed, in "suggesting [even] one thought," they defer to their interpretation from another position, the only "other" that can provide them with a mysterious "heart" or an ob-jected status (the role of being "thrown out there"). Then, too, the words, already like the signs that try to be different from them, are really just referring to other words or wordlike "impressions," to transfers between thoughts (some taking others as momentary objects) that "create" words and signs to be helpful "instruments" configuring the interplays that thought is trying to form (p. 477). For us to take the word "cause" to designate an apparent process (a sign) that refers to a mental understanding of A always leading to B is for us, as in Hume or Drummond, to point only at "a certain state of the human mind in which two thoughts are apprehended to be related to each other" (p. 478). Nevertheless, we are so resistant to a continual self-revision where figures simply rework other figures without a ground to limit the potential relationships that we turn certain figures leading to counterparts into motivating signs ("things") to which all other thoughts either look or respond in ways that the motivators seem to determine. In that way we appear to gain a certain dominance over the world, if only by providing centers to which interpreting thoughts can "pierce." Yet we do so by granting primary dominance to that presumed "existence," or rather to "familiar" inscriptions of it set up as "reiteration[s]" of what we call "ideas" referring to "external objects" (p. 477).

Such objectification, too, can lead to much more than this mere philosophy. Hegemonic figures or groups (those who benefit most from Othmans and Jupiters) can foster or seize upon such a concept and employ it to uphold the notion of a *raison d'état,* a propaganda claim that the present government of some order is the only one that corresponds to the "nature of the world as it is."[37] Far more damaging, though, at least in its local effects, is the objectifying tendency in individual minds that leads so many people, even intelligent ones quite capable of "going out of themselves" and returning to "reverie," to deny their freedom of thought, action, and self-transfiguration. This self-abasement, as opposed to strictly religious or political confinement, is occasionally the focus of *Alastor, Laon and Cythna* (as we have briefly noted), and such minor poems as *Rosalind and Helen* (1817–1818). It becomes the principle "tragic flaw," however, and is most thoroughly explained, in *Julian and Maddalo* (completed around April or May 1819), Shelley's "Conversation" in verse reminiscent of Horace's *sermones pedestres* ("conversations on foot") partly as those satiric dialogues were restyled (using the couplets Shelley adopts) in Pope's *Moral Essays* and *Imitations of Horace* in the 1730s.[38] The genteel, sometimes satirical debate between Julian and Maddalo that is resolved, or rather silenced, by the words of the Maniac to whom Maddalo finally directs the discussion: all this recalls the structure of the exchange between Demasippus and Horace in the third colloquy of the latter's second book of satires,[39] in which Demasippus attempts to define true madness by referring to a long disquisition on the subject by his master Stertinius. Yet the madness that finally emerges in Shelley's poem, one plaguing his two main characters somewhat obscurely until it is brought more to light in the Maniac, is a devotion to one or another distant objective standard that forces each speaker, despite healthier inclinations, to restrict the possibilities of the personal will and of the transference that has set each "object" up.

I agree in general with those who have seen *Julian and Maddalo* as a self-critique by Shelley—revising the one in *Alastor,* another piece with an only half-reliable narrator—where the poet details some of the ways in which he has often been tempted to constrict his own potentials.[40] Each major character, as did the Narrator and the Poet in *Alastor,* recalls at least a rhetorical stance (or set of them) toward which Shelley has been drawn in his personal life or his self-articulations. Though Julian and Maddalo themselves are modeled somewhat on the Shelley and Byron who conversed, rode, and boated near Venice in the summer of 1818, and the Maniac alludes at times to the Venetian poet Torquato Tasso confined to an asylum in 1579 and dramatized in couplets by Byron's "Lament of Tasso" (1817),[41] all three proclaim attitudes that Shelley personae have asserted in earlier writings, occasionally under the influence of Byron, whom Shelley did seek to emulate in some ways.[42] Julian, the narrator and a version of the author at his most melioristic moments when he has been inclined toward Wordsworthian patterns of thought, echoes the "Hymn to Intellectual Beauty," albeit in a very Miltonic fashion that recalls the "Immortality" ode, in the way he turns a Venetian "sunset" into a "beautiful" reminder of loss, wherein a "glow / Of Heaven" seems to beckon beyond a "Paradise of exiles" (ll. 55–57). Count Maddalo, though he does often sound like the speaker of *Childe Harold's* Fourth Canto (1818) whom Shelley has accused of "wicked & mischievous insanity" (*L*, II, 58), seems the very voice of Shelley's Gothic sensibility, not to mention his "On Death" or "Stanzas Written in Dejection" (1815 and 1818; *PW*, pp. 523–24 and 561–62), especially when the Count answers Julian by claiming that all men begin as "Fallen [into] a deep reverse" of the projects they may formulate in pursuit of a better world (l. 265). And the Maniac is as much the "love-devoted youth" of *Alastor* (at l. 373 of *Julian and Maddalo*) as he is the grieving seeker of "Oblivion" from Byron's *Manfred* (at Shelley's l. 508) as he is the suppliant to an absent Leonora-figure from the "Lament of Tasso" or Shelley's "Song from 'Tasso'" (*PW*, p. 559), one of the fragments remaining from a play attempted and aborted in 1818. These various, conflicting aspects of the Shelleyan self in the process of formation, derived as they are from role-playings that have mirrored his possibilities to him and "made me know myself" (l. 561 of *Julian and Maddalo*), here come to face and compare themselves (and their anomalies) in a narrative that presents them all as possible ways of life, as problematic tendencies of the general kind that Horace wanted to uncover in his satire-debates. The postures attempted in each version of Shelley are even exposed as rife with class-based contradictions, much as he was in his aristocratic/egalitarian upbringing and vocabulary. Kelvin Everest is right to see each speaker in the piece (especially Julian) as adjusting revolutionary "aspiration[s]" to the "cementing opinions of sad contemporary reality" by "acceding to the ideological implications of [a] familiar idiom" under pressure from "a way of life [that] identifies [the] speaker with the class against which his radical critique is directed."[43]

Nevertheless, I find that the principal ideology that attaches each speaker and class conflict to such an idiom is a belief in objectification, very much as "On Life" defines it, which can be shown to take many forms and be explained by several different motivations if we compare and contrast Julian, Maddalo, and the Maniac. In this poem even more than in some of his other pieces, to be sure, Shelley probes into mirrors of him possessed "of the most consummate genius, and capable, if [each one] would direct himself to such an end, of becoming . . . redeemer[s] of [their now] degraded country," to use the words applied to Maddalo in the preface to the work (*NCE*, p. 112). Yet, because the susceptibility to transfer-based thinking in each figure—hence in Shelley himself—is as able to produce "apprehensions of distinction" as it is to generate crossings between thoughts, each character is made to reveal how "our will" can permit transference to counteract its nonobjective tendencies and thereby "enchain us to permitted ill" (Julian's words at ll. 170–71). The very different means by and objectives for which this perversion can occur are as important as the "sad" constriction common to all the characters; hence the necessity of three separate examples. But ultimately each speaker in *Julian and Maddalo* is a sort of "Prometheus who fails to unbind himself," though for reasons other than those offered by Michael Scrivener when he makes this apt statement about Shelley's Maniac.[44] As in the enthronement of Jupiter, each character takes one point or "sign" in a changeable interrelation of many points and fetishizes that single "external" locus as the causal center of all the interplays, gradually but eventually limiting the self-transformation that each figure (or speaker) can attempt with the aid of other figures.

Julian, the perfectibilian who most often urges the human will to overcome these very limits, seems at first quite able to pursue such hopes because he can be exquisitely sensitive to the relational and ever-expanding possibilities of a transfer-oriented perception of existence. When he starts the poem with a description of himself and Maddalo riding on the barren Lido near Venice and later looking back at the city and the Euganean hills behind it to the west, he celebrates his "love [for] all waste / And solitary places; where we taste / The pleasure of believing what we see / Is boundless, as we wish our souls to be" (ll. 15–18). He may find a primordial "exile" in the way everything on the Lido, including the two interlocutors, seems thrown forth on a "waste," like sand from the sea, out of what seems to be the "earth's [motherly] embrace" (ll. 10 and 6). Even so, that basic change of locations means to Julian that such displacements can be repeated, especially as perception shifts its attention to analogues or alters its own impressions, permitting "sound," for example, to be felt as "like delight" and carried over, as "aerial merriment," into "our hearts" (ll. 25–27). Thus, since an open and "bare strand" harbors "no [particular] object" that might halt this transfer between positions (ll. 3 and 9), every perceived boundary can be extended and surpassed by an imaginative reorientation of it almost as soon as any new focus is proposed by human responses, providing they continue the motion of emergence that first produced their transpositional power. There is a "desire," then, whereby the observer looks beyond any "object" to one counterpart and then another and another, all the while urging the observant soul to overleap the limits of its present self-understanding just in the way the perceived world seems to extend its boundaries with the help of perceivers. Here we plainly see the outgoing regard for "another and many others" that helps initiate a conversation on the Lido where "swift thoughts" are exchanged to the point of expanding their interaction to encompass "all that earth has been or yet may be" (ll. 28 and 43). Then, too, we also behold one motivation for Julian's displacement of his gaze from sea to sand to city to mountains to the Heavens beyond.

In spite of all this, however, and in fact encouraged by some of it, Julian chooses to hypothesize—and then hypostasize—two objective and centering absolutes, both of which are finally set up as so removed from transformative interrelations that there seems to be a very great distance between those ultimate points and the level of conscious perception. The first of the two is what comes to be assumed when Julian places that "glow of / Heaven" in the deepest heart of the sunset over Venice. It turns out that this young optimist is as terrified as he is invigorated by the continual displacement of perception toward which the "bare strand" seems to keep opening. For one thing, the Lido, at the mercy of the tide (ll. 11–12), is, like the Lucretian heights of Mont Blanc, an unpredictable oscillation between construction and destruction that frequently dissolves the productions of desire, pulling parts of them into the sea and leaving remnants "Broken and unrepaired" (l. 11). This undercurrent in the poem's opening lines suggests that desire keeps overleaping limits so as to escape the under-tow of dissolution (or reabsorption by the "earth's embrace") that is part of any trans-ference ahead from a previous state or position.[45] Julian, in other words, feels that his gaze must seek a boundlessness at a level that seems entirely beyond such an uncon-trollable regression. Moreover, he feels that he needs a primary focal point for any use of his gaze if his construction of a scene is to have any real identity or purpose to it by his lights. One element among all those that he remembers as interacting on the Lido has to be "more / Than all" (Maddalo, initially), and the flying of thoughts "from brain to brain" in the conversation, where at first no thought is exclusive to just one mind, has to settle into a distinct argument advanced by one interlocutor and opposed by the other (ll. 19–20, 30, and 46–49). Hence the gaze of Julian's desire, finding nothing on the barren strand that is both above dissolution (which Maddalo cannot be) and a principal focus for thought (which Maddalo can be only for a time), decides to pursue the drive of displacement in a Wordsworthian manner by following the westward arc of the sun to the point where it reaches the "light" of its "setting" behind a "rent" in the "many folded hills" to the rear of the city (ll. 74–76). At that removed point, Julian places a sign referring into its own depths, a "purple" light sequestering an "inmost . . . spirit" (l. 84), apparently having succeeded in driving his desire to a boundlessness that surpasses all dissolving levels. He then grants such a self-contained solidity to what dwells in this setting of a sun that even the "peaks" that almost con-ceal it come to seem "transparent" by contrast (l. 85).

Julian, we can say, having contorted more open-ended tendencies, has avoided dissolution and projected a central locus of identity by adopting the manner of a Vene-tian Renaissance painter.[46] He has imposed a center of perspective on a changeable, unbounded interplay of perceptions, whereupon the landscape has become patterned into a series of receding layers or concentric circles. There the innermost—or, for the observer, outermost—layer is the supposed ultimate state (the boundless ideal ego) of the exiled—and inwardly desirous—framer of the picture (Julian's "soul" or "spirit").[47] Indeed, by making this vanishing point a primal scene of entrance into a maternal and Heavenly "rent," Julian has achieved the Wordsworthian assurance of a possible reunion with a phallic mother or a Father-in-and-behind-the-mother at the heart of things. In that projection he has fashioned a more definite origin that can replace his earlier sense of emergence from a tugging dissolution. He now has reason to believe in a basis outside all minds for regarding desire as what Earl Wasserman finds it to be in this poem: a Hegelian "yearning that the finite, empirical self encoun-ter the infinite self as its Other and unite with it.[48] To accept this supposition, of course, Julian must use transference's obfuscation of its own movement to forget the several maneuvers that established his ultimate center: the turning outward of desire from the very death-drive it would deny; the projection of the "inmost spirit" as but one instance in a succession where narcissistic desire displaces itself from reflector to reflector (as Shelley's "going out of himself" is doing throughout this work); the linking of the anthropomorphic "spirit" to the dying-out of light in the "purple," which prompts the supposition of still another, more "inmost" level; and the tearing (or rending) of a symbolic surface used late in the succession (the Euganean hills) to open a gap in which to insert the desire for an immortal origin, even though such a gap is no more than what transference keeps facing as the sheer opening of one projection toward another. All this notwithstanding, to gain a locus of identity that does not concatenate life and death—and despite his refusal to believe in the God of any official religion (ll. 115–16 and 189)—Julian reworks the "upthrown soul" of Cythna's "moon-struck sophist" to give the "boundless" a final boundary. He then tries to base his melioristic projections on this Neoplatonic point of emanation, persistently assuming in what he says to others "a 'soul of goodness' in things ill" attainable outside himself and outside everyone (l. 204).[49]

Soon, however, Julian proposes a second objectification, a self-determining "innermost" essence set against this outermost one. In fact, he sometimes "transfer[s his] faith" away from "nature's" inmost spirit into a near-worship of a "universal capacity of mind."[50] Finding that Maddalo can easily place the barrier of real human "suffering" in front of any path to externalized "goodness" that "hope can paint" on the landscape of perception (l. 45), Julian turns for an answer, on the morning after the ride across the Lido, to the Count's young daughter, particularly to her eyes that mirror "Italian Heaven" and "yet gleam / With such deep meaning" (ll. 147–48). The better part of Julian (the one making him a "reliable" narrator) is naturally attracted to this face because its youthful "reverie" presents a total interplay between the "inner" and the "outer," like the one he sensed on the Lido, in which the inward depth comes in part from the "gleam" that is reflected from the outside and altered by the eye's own color and convex shape. Yet another side of him (which he does not detect as different, making him half-unreliable and subject to the reader's critical scrutiny) uses the girl as an example (starting with "See / This lovely child" at ll. 166–67) to show how much "the love, beauty, and truth we seek" are "in our mind" all complete, waiting only for our "will" to sweep aside the "old saws," or cultural concepts, that keep our awareness from its forgotten depths (ll. 174–75, 170, and 162). There could hardly be a sharper veering away from Shelley's sense of reverie. Godwinian "habitual tendencies," Wordsworthian "primary laws of our nature," and Coleridgean/Kantian *a priori* ideas are now recalled from the poet's younger days (as some of these appear, say, in *L*, I, 317) to be placed outside conscious awareness, yet also in back of it, as desirable objects or predetermined "signs" behind the derived ones of everyday thought. Though "love, beauty, and truth" here might have been viewed, the way they are in the "Hymn to Intellectual Beauty," as inclinations of the self outside the self toward the betterment of others (and of the self through them)—a desideratum that Julian does want to pursue in more abstract conceptions—he turns all three impulses into self-contained motivators behind the very longing for transcendence of the self that tried to place its foundation outside the psyche the evening before.

Once Julian's desire, it seems, has found itself blocked in efforts to project its fulfillment to an outermost level that transcends its feeling of a lack within the self, he has introjected the proposed "spirit" back into the desirous psyche, this time filling the lack with inner mental foundations (though borrowed from what "we seek"), almost as though there was never a need for a projection into the sunset. Henceforth the chief impediment that keeps us from a "Heaven" of equality that would prevent us "all" from suffering (l. 172) seems the widespread failure to accept the "power over ourselves" within ourselves (l. 85), a power Julian can also interpret as what underwrites the superiority of his opinion over Maddalo's. Faced with a radical longing for universal satisfaction that would deny dominance to one will or class and yet saddled with an aristocratic ideology that grants superiority to some people on the basis of qualities (or "deep meanings") simply placed in the mind,[51] Julian has tried to resolve the conflict with what Shelley's preface frankly calls "heterodox opinions" (*NCE*, p.

113). He cleverly allows hopes of transcendence and some inner light to each person but at the same time reveals a desire for (or a fear of lacking) the heavenly sanction and inborn essentials that have long been used to justify the privileged perspective of the gifted young gentleman. Though there turns out to be no easy resolution, the need for an apparent settlement is so great—and the struggle for one is so evident when Julian asks all men to strive toward being "high" and "majestical" (l. 173)—that he proposes a second objectivity grounding such a compromise after his first belief system is put in question by the miseries resulting, in part, from social inequality. He wants both options but will settle for one if he must, tacitly admitting that his second, more "inmost" notion may seem accessible to more people than the "purple" majesty of the twilight sky.

What results, ironically but inevitably, is a sad bifurcation in Julian's outlook where the distinction between inner and outer already basic to objectification is intensified into a wide gap between "inmost" and outermost essences. The conscious human will, the way Julian has come to regard it (admittedly as Shelley sometimes has), is caught midway between, on the one hand, a very far-off "spirit of goodness" appearing to be always over the horizon and, on the other hand, a deep mental tendency toward a loving reformation of the world-order we perceive, one so deep as to be virtually unreachable by deliberate human apprehension. It seems almost impossible now, despite the fact that these "deep truths" have been transferred into their positions by the very thought-process that currently finds them distant, for a "theory" in the mind supposedly rooted in an incontrovertible "truth" (l. 203) to cross over, as Julian wishes it could, into the qualities, needs, and potentials of what the mind seems to observe "outside." Even if that bridge could be built by a "true theory," the ultimate target, the "spirit of goodness," would still seem frustratingly beyond the horizon from where revolutionary thought and effort would be. Julian, in short, even though he has the most admirable aims and sympathies at times, is trapped by his objectivist methods for grounding his sense of existence into seeing every final object of his meliorism as irremediably divorced from the mental impulses that rightly pursue it. He presents us with an encapsulation of this error when he separates, with a "yet" and a caesura, the "Heaven" reflected in the little girl's eyes from the "deep meaning" that her young psyche appears to harbor behind the "gleam" he perceives. In this image Julian has consciously seen how much such "objects" of his thoughts are really interplays of numerous entangled differences (the sky, the eye, the latter's reflection of the former, the observer's "reading" of the combination, etc.). Nonetheless, he has employed transference's self-concealment to skew this multiple interaction into a dichotomy of sundered levels. The unfortunate effects start to multiply as soon as he is inclined to abide by this position. Julian misconstrues the actual nature of the "meaning" he would grasp in the face of another person; he fails to see the process common to that person's acts of perception and his own; he makes himself more different from the "external" Maddalo than the flight of thought "from brain to brain" has proven them to be; and, when all is said and done in this poem, his perfectibilian thinking "within" fails to generate a better social order "without" in any practical way.

Finally, too, the strongest indication of the loss of potential, were Shelley to become or remain such a type, is Julian's stance toward the Maniac before and after Maddalo confronts each with the other. The actual encounter, we have to admit, brings back some of Julian's generous sensitivity. After he has heard the lovelorn and one-time poet speak, Julian does express a genuine, half-articulate fellow-feeling and enters into a nondichotomous interchange with the Count almost devoid of "argument" and aimed at no fixed resolution of all the intertwined factors involved in the Maniac's case (ll. 516–23). Certainly Julian is able to "go out of himself" sufficiently at this juncture to render the words of the Maniac with enough sympathy that the basis of the latter's thinking in transference can be brought to the attention of the reader. Even so, these inclinations are increasingly muted by Julian's objectivist posture of an "inward" distance from this clearly outcast figure "whom [Julian] would call," but does not ultimately call, "willingly my friend" (ll. 576–77). This distortion of their brotherhood begins at the moment Julian first hears about the Maniac and is tempted to confine this outsider, without having met him, inside the Procrustian frame of his own "true theory" of mind (ll. 199–206). Then, once the meeting is over and the initial fluidity of response has waned, Julian becomes even more the phallically scientific investigator, almost a Jupiter with a will to "penetrating" knowledge, probably because he finds a thorough commonality with the madman too revealing of his own inclinations and too threatening to the identity he wants in order to establish his distinctness from other people. Julian flatly says that he now seeks to probe the signs in the Maniac's language and visage "as men study some stubborn art" in the hope of locating an "entrance to the [hidden] caverns of the mind" (ll. 571–73). The inner and the outer (or vice-versa), the Maniac's sequestered psyche and the desire of this psychoanalyst for a "deep meaning" over there, have become opposite ends of a continuum where an interplay is present but where the connection is distended more and more into a yawning gulf.

In the end there is mainly the gap between the investigator and the specimen. Julian, before very long, can rather easily retreat into the withdrawn subjectivity of "books" or "subtle talk" or "friends in London" (ll. 554, 560, and 564–65) and thereby allow his dream of redeeming the Maniac (as well as humanity) from a "dark estate" (l. 574) to become an "idle thought" divorced from concrete gestures (l. 567). Even when he returns to Venice years later, though his warmth toward the Maniac still glows enough for him to seek some information about the "poor fellow," Julian mainly probes again, this time for objective causes behind the sufferer's further decline and eventual death. He urges the now grown-up daughter of Maddalo to detail the *"why"* and *"how"* to such a degree that she wonders "if thine aged eyes disdain to wet / Those wrinkled cheeks with youth's remembered tears" (ll. 610–11). Disregarding, although mentioning, her pleas to leave some things unexplained out of consideration for the Maniac's memory, Julian presses on to wring every piece of information from her—only to close the poem by refusing to convey it all to a "world" of readers who might be too "cold," too objectivist perhaps, to understand sympathetically (ll. 616–17). Such a closing stance is almost a recantation for a character and narrator who begins the poem with such a clear interest in sympathetic outreach and open communication. There is still, one can say, enough of a "going out" from Julian that he joins his feelings partly to those of the young woman in trying to be protective of the Maniac. Yet, at the same time, he is relentless in seeking the objective knowledge that she would deny him and that he denies us, so much so that if some of us can be suspected by him of excessively distant perspectives, the reason must be that he has conveniently removed his own objectivist posture from himself and transferred it in his present thinking to some of his possible readers. In that way, after all, he achieves one of his goals in choosing objectification; he appears to himself distinct from most human beings as one of the few with a privileged (even aristocratic) understanding of his story's ultimate secrets. *Julian and Maddalo,* insofar as it renders the character of its main speaker, we have to conclude, leaves us with both the potentially warm and the actually cold Julian hovering before us simultaneously, all in the most extreme extension of the contradictory—and finally objectivist—ways in which he has used transference to fashion himself and his sense of others.

Meanwhile, Maddalo, as Julian presents him, has offered us another study in contrasts, and indeed another form of object-oriented thinking, within one type of person. But in his case the conflicting tendencies are more ironically opposed to one another, and the objectification is of a very different sort. Certainly the apparent contradictions present some striking anomalies, which probably for Shelley formed both Byron's verbalized "character" and the self-defeating nobility that Shelley might yet embrace were he to become too like his fellow poet. One can surely say, to begin with, that Count Maddalo, perhaps influenced even more than Julian by a heteroglossia of class-conscious and egalitarian beliefs, is more inclined to assert an aristocratic "ambition" that is "concentrated" on impediments to his own advancement *and* to be more "gentle" and "patient" toward the needs of the unfortunate, as he shows in his very practical assistance to, as well as sympathy with, the Maniac (Shelley's Preface, p. 113). In fact, Maddalo is less inclined than Julian to conceal such contradictions behind an illusion of ideological homogeneity, so he enunciates the disjunctions in his sense of existence as often as he can. He voices such a thoroughness of transfer-based thinking, moreover, that he reveals himself as very often "going out to another" to a point where he connects that second being with yet another person and then with a more universal set of desires. When he first beholds the Maniac, the Count notices how much the poor wretch "was ever talking in such sort" as Julian does and how the madman did it "more sadly" because of an uncontainable outreach of transference in his sensibility, whereby this "man [lamenting] his peculiar wrong" ranted still more to "hear . . . of the [general] oppression of the strong" over the weak (ll. 236–39). At almost the same time, though, Maddalo proclaims his near-despair over the ultimate uselessness of any "going out of the self" turned into practical or revolutionary action. The gestures he does make to soothe "one so gentle" as the Maniac (the Count's words at l. 258) serve mainly to turn the madman and his asylum into emblems proving "How vain are such aspiring theories" as the melioristic arguments of Julian (ll. 200–201). Maddalo's understanding of transference, we find, leads deliberately to and makes a point of the gaps between longing and improved existence or hope and practicality that Julian stumbles upon in his effort to deny them.

What generates this acceptance of self-division in the human psyche and its patterns of thought, we come to discover, is Maddalo's employment of transference to produce an almost Gnostic objectivity at the core of his belief system, a version of the sense in *Childe Harold* IV that "Truth" comes to the psyche in "disappear[ing] dreams" only to recede even further behind the "Universal Pall" of "Destruction's mass" (vii and clxiv–xv). The "insanity" in this world-picture is especially visible— and the logic making it possible is most carefully detailed—when Maddalo (or "mad"-alo[52]) refines his symbolic use of the Maniac and the asylum by crafting a metaphor of general human existence out of "the madhouse and its belfry tower" (l. 107):

> "And such,"—he cried, "is our mortality
> And this must be the emblem and the sign
> Of what should be eternal and divine!—

And like that black and dreary bell, the soul,
Hung in a heaven-illumined tower, must toll
Our thoughts and our desires to meet below
Round the rent heart and pray—as madmen do
For what? they know not,—till the night of death
As sunset that strange vision, severeth
Our memory from itself, and us from all
We sought and yet were baffled!" (ll. 120–30)

It is no wonder that Julian likens his dispute with Maddalo (at ll. 39–42) to the debate that Milton's "devils held within the dales of Hell," all the while "forlorn" and longing for Heaven, in Book Two of *Paradise Lost*. True, the Count is trying to undercut Julian's optimism here by rending the heart into separate, almost unbridgeable parts and severing moments of memory from relations with each other so that no one is deluded enough to believe in connected layers of perception that easily lead to a unifying base inside or outside the mind. But Maddalo's position is also, like Harold Bloom's definition of Byron's, "a skepticism that refuses to be a skepticism."[53] The passage above assumes a breach, like the fall into Hell, which does look back to an "eternal" objective origin, albeit one so far removed that (even "At sunset") mortal contact with it is out of the question. The Count is basing his vision, and thus his sense of the human figure, on something like a Miltonic Puritan emblem in which any chosen symbol (such as pandemonium, fallen humanity, or the human word) forecasts or recollects a higher level of creation and yet is defined as almost permanently ruptured from that point and from other signs closer to the point (such as angels, tower-bells, and the Word of Scripture).[54] Maddalo even increases the inaccessibility of the ultimate level by aping Julian and Shelley (as Byron did to some extent) and refusing to place a conventionally Christian Original Sin behind the plunge into the emblematic state ("What Maddalo thinks on these matters [being] not exactly clear" in the poem's Preface, p. 113). As in most forms of Gnosticism, where the Christian Fall is but another descent of awareness from a fallen situation already obscuring ultimate truth,[55] the division in the soul here is a cut (or "rent") inherent in the birth of the human race, not the result of a later disobedience. Any further "decline" after the primal declination and forgetting can only turn round to examine a reference point that is also entirely severed, temporally and spatially, from an alien transcendence.[56] For Maddalo, then, the movement of a thought toward one that interprets it in human reflection is a movement toward the "lower," hellish position of the "rent heart." The heart is forced to look back, as toward an "object," to the gazing outward in a "higher" station (the "tower" of the soul). This high point, in turn, is itself seeking an undeferred referent, the Object that lies above and beyond the "object," and that fact condemns both heart-"thought" and tower-"object" to be "words" or "signs" depressingly out of touch with the "throne / Of the Invisible," the proper goal of all reference (at least in *Childe Harold*, IV. clxxxiii).

The use and abuse of tranference in this second "mirror" of Shelley's possible beliefs could hardly be more intense or more destructive of the hopes that transference can promote. Maddalo's "consummate genius," in having the "rent heart" refer back to the outward-looking "tower," explicitly makes otherness itself, the very nature of signs that signs are usually asked to repress, the most immediate reference of thought and words. The emblem, hence the emblematic human being, emerges, with some accuracy, as primordially divided from itself within itself and from other emblems too, as any figure must be in a logic of transposition where analogues for signs are sought in leaps across spaces. Yet here, in addition, the emblem is supposedly created in the image of an invisible Absolute in which those leaps may come to rest, and so the deferred sign remains both "illumined" indirectly by that extremely distant source and utterly cut off from any avenue to it. This ultimate end of reference is so different from its emblems, projected "outside" them as it is by their otherness from themselves, that nothing earthly can carry human desire to its level, not even the death (the fundamental sign of fallen mortality) that supposedly leads from mere desire to its final satisfaction.

This kind of objectification excuses Maddalo's contradictions and those he observes in others, of course, by making them seem the predictable results of a human nature primarily divided from true consistency and its actual essence. But this same attitude also leads him to impose regrettable limits on himself and on those to whom he transfers his sympathetic concern. First of all, the Count condemns himself, as did the Byron Shelley felt he saw in Venice, to perpetual "[self-]contempt and despera-tion" (*L*, II, 58), because, as in the case of Milton's Satan, "The sense that he was greater than his kind / Had struck, methinks, his eagle spirit blind / By gazing on its own exceeding light" (ll. 50–52). In confessing that the otherness in signs actually refers to another version of itself, Maddalo has the sagacity to admit that the "rent" in awareness that inaugurates desire transfers itself to desire's projection and then makes the latter project another distant counterpart. This is the process that produced the layering in Julian's sunset vision, the one Maddalo is trying to contradict. Never-theless, the Count's aristocratic position, even in the face of his resistance to it and his use of a Puritan scheme once employed against aristocratic Anglicans, has encour-aged him to rank these levels of projection (from the "lowest" to the "highest" oth-erness) and to arrange them vertically rather than horizontally, all in a "tower" image of human nature that has really been formed, as was Julian's landscape, by a leap of transference from point to point. Maddalo must consequently rank the levels of him-self using transference. He must transport his desire for high estate to a level of supremacy such as Jupiter's, or that of a soaring eagle, where he can place the kind of superego he would like to be in a location from which he could look down on others and "know" them. When he truly supposes this higher-flying self, though, he must find *his* heart "rent" between his longing for it and the desired height, to such as extent that he can look to that apparent perfection only from a condition far below it, while it (carrying out the self-relocation in the movement—or "flight"—of his projection) soars beyond its own position toward a distant level "exceeding" even itself. The eagle in legend is supposed to efface and renew its vision upon gazing into the sun above it, but the Count has only blinded himself by making one ultimate light his object. He has effaced his awareness of how much transfer-projections have produced his levels and how much the eagle symbol *could* help him achieve constant self-renewal in a flight between positions that would not rank the points it shifts between nor confine itself to one angle of vision on the sun. Governed by this repression in his perceptions of existence, Maddalo can feel little more than the "despondency" (l. 48) of pursuing a height he assumes he can never reach, a height that seeks a level beyond its own as soon as he seems to come near it.

His generosity to others is consequently a mixed blessing for them, since he feels a community with them largely because his equalizing impulse has sentenced every person to the hopeless status in which he has placed himself. Licensed by his sense of a hierarchical universe, he recreates those he would help in his own image, acting the role of the very Providence whose existence he chides Julian for denying (at l. 118). He therefore "fits up" the Maniac with bust and book-filled "rooms" so as to keep this "unfortunate" in the aristocratic situation of his (and the Count's own) "happier hours" (ll. 252–58). In addition, Maddalo sees that this residence is located partway up the side of the asylum, thereby fixing the Maniac unequivocally in the position of the "rent heart" below the tower, the quintessential situation of the Miltonic emblem. Maddalo's "kindness" is on several levels quite genuine and transfer-based without a doubt, yet in the end it aims at the confinement of human possibilities to a limited number of rungs on a Great Ladder of Being. This ladder, for its part, insidiously urges the psyche to aspire beyond the middle levels with an offer of higher rungs while it continues to add upper steps so as to keep the final one unreachably beyond the climber no matter how high he climbs.

The ironies and blindnesses in the Count's—and Julian's—postures, however, pale in comparison to what we face after the two interlocutors turn to the Maniac himself for confirmation and/or refutation of their arguments. Though they find ways to avoid this fact in their conclusions, they now point the reader at an extreme and detailed presentation of *their* contradictions and so at a particularly vivid revelation of how an objectivist "Hell / Within" can be brought about (ll. 351–52). If there is any ambiguity in the tilts toward negative transference portrayed in the other two Shelley personae, it is made unequivocal in this epitome of self-abasement. For here a person so transfer-oriented as to engender his sense of self the way Laon did carries the temptation to make the chosen Other an all-controlling dictator about as far as a potentially poetic genius can.

Admittedly, the Maniac's torment seems based, at first, on a cause that his interpreters need not connect with themselves, so much so that Julian and Maddalo too simply root his problems in "some deadly change in the love / Of one deeply vowed to him" some time ago (ll. 527–28). Much of the time, recalling a lovelorn Tasso and other Renaissance sonneteers, he does address a sort of Leonora, a "Lady," it seems, who "came [to Venice] with him from France [and then] left him" to wander (ll. 246–47) until he was "saved" by Maddalo. She remains, in desire at least, so much his "spirit's mate" (l. 337) that her withdrawal of affection has forced him to alter his self-image as though he were her mirror in male form. Her suddenly "changed and cold embraces" (l. 313), suggesting that she has "lied " about her earlier "love" for him (l. 423), have made him feel severed from his own desires, a "mask of falsehood" just as she seems to be (l. 308), and henceforth too repulsive for "love's work," as befits the reflection and referent of her "grimace of hate" (ll. 460–64). But, as we should be able to tell by now (if we are not as self-protective as his immediate observers), the Maniac would not have so abased and shattered his self-concept, so referred the meaning of his words and the order of his thoughts about himself entirely to the dictates of her gaze, had he not established the lady as the supreme object or Other to whom he has transferred his "love" and all decisive "truth" (l. 330)—even more than the *Alastor* Poet did in fabricating his dream-maiden. In a maneuver fearfully like the ones in which Julian and Maddalo have projected their souls' desired natures into setting suns and eagles, the Maniac has restricted his love-object to deciding the essence of himself, as though she had no value independent of that narcissistic function. He has then forced himself to submit to that "standard" viewed as superego or now-unttainable spirit, forgetting to accept consistently what he (like his counterparts) actually knows:

that the meanings he finds in "altered faces" really "own [him] for their father" (ll. 312–15).

Though man-woman interplays should define each person by way of the other, in Shelley's view, and thus make the other sex one of the origins of any being's sense of self (as in the cases of Laon and Cythna or Prometheus and Asia), it is dangerous to make one member of this relation (of either sex) the locus of definition aloof from a continual exchange of qualities, especially when the locus is created to establish the self-concept of one person and not the other. Because he has gone this far in reifying his beloved into a fetish/object granting him his identity, whether or not she wants that status, the Maniac has turned her into a Jupiter; he has tried to gain his self-command and "manhood" from the knowing gaze of this other visage by granting that figure the place traditionally given to a commanding male. Consequently, since the binary opposition assumed in this construction (self/other) demands an exact contrary for the figure regarded as the supreme being, the suppliant, potentially an interplay of "male" and "female" qualities, must feel himself entirely feminized and castrated, must wish that, to be what her denial of love demands, he "had torn out / The nerves of my manhood by their bleeding root" (ll. 424–25).[57] To attempt to possess a definite masculinity by asking an Other to reflect it back to the self, hence to be the origin of its existence, is to lose ownership of that desideratum to the Other, in this case to make it the property of a sort of phallic mother assigned to give it birth. The lady's expression and gestures (her "signs") can become dictating "objects"; she can appear to be the Jupiter-Text determining the Maniac's reading of himself, because he, as aspiring poet, has tried to author himself in a self-projection that turns out to be as removed from him as a text is from its writer yet that still has the power to define him and figuratively reform his body because he has chosen to produce it for those very purposes. Shelley even indicates how self-damning this sort of effort can be by fashioning the Maniac's stance so as to remind us of the *"Sin"* that springs outward "in shape and count'nance bright" from the head of Milton's Satan, again in Book Two of *Paradise Lost* (ll. 755–58). Because of his extreme narcissism, the Maniac, like Satan, throws forth a likeness of himself in female form, for whom he lusts yet whose "perfect image" stands before him as a "sign / Portentous" sequestering her father's desire in a place so far outside him that he does not recognize his actual relationship to this commanding "goddess" (*Paradise Lost,* II. 758–64).

True, the Maniac has a choice among a number of different attitudes toward this supposed Other's power, ranging from Julian's impotent hopefulness to Maddalo's caustic resignation and beyond (as the madman's language suggests at ll. 337–40 and 477–80). After all, he certainly feels and enacts, with sometimes genuinely outgoing warmth, the inclination of the true poet to project himself into—indeed, to lose himself in—role after other role (particularly at ll. 482–92), just as Shelley himself is doing in this poem. The posture the Maniac finally chooses, however, is not really surprising, given the allusion to Milton's "Sin" and the determination of the objectivist thinker to posit an external object, even after the Other's status as object has been put in question by the positor's words. In this case the fatal decision begins when the Maniac makes the lady the most frequent object of his poetic (as well as other) addresses, although she has withdrawn and thereby placed him in the position of "one who wrote and thought / His words might move some heart that heeded not" (ll. 286–87). When it becomes clear that only her absence will occupy the addressee's place from now on, the Maniac's writing starts to refer to a gaping nothing, the sheer deferral of words into space noted in different ways by Julian and Maddalo, so much so that empty "air" is taken to be the receiving medium that "closes upon [his] accents" (ll. 508–9). Once such a void seems all he can hope for, the Maniac's ciphers "charactered in vain" (l. 478) appear to "hide . . . every spark" of his desire, letting each one fade without connecting any of them to a further conductor of their electric life (ll. 503–4).

The future of his words, now that their backward glance seems to be mourning a slow death already, then comes to seem the "'yawning" of the "grave" (l. 506), since an objectivist feels he must have a definite Other ahead of all inscriptions that appears to complete the outreach of those signs in a way that matches what lies behind them. This particular completion is especially appropriate if we recall that the Maniac's principal object has been the placement of a text of himself outside himself. Any creation so distanced from its author must play the role of an epitaph bespeaking that author's disappearance from his act of self-expression. Death therefore becomes the immediate object of the Maniac (not just the way to the objective, as it was in *Alastor*). He even combines death with the lady's shape to produce a "ghastly paramour" in his mind's eye (l. 338), a substitute image both holding out and holding back the original object—and thereby reconstituting what the object is, making it now a kind of phallic mother as death. Such a foreclosure of options is really inevitable for a stance determined to repeat the Miltonic projection of Sin, since Satan's longing for a feminine reflection of himself produces only "Death" as its result and Death then couples with the "sign / Portentous" to become inseparable from it (*Paradise Lost*, II. 781–802).[58] The Maniac consequently, determined as he is to reflect his object's supposed dictates, mirrors Death increasingly as his discourse progresses ("Am I not wan like thee?" he asks the "ghastly paramour" at l. 386). He is so anxious to have this kind of object instead of a perpetual deferral of meaning that he becomes most incoherent at the point when the death-figure threatens to withdraw just as the lady has (ll. 392–97). He wants at least Death to be there, when he finally ceases talking, as a dependable "close" to which the "despair" he has chosen can arrive (ll. 509–10) in its persistent effort to refer to a "proper" object.

In any case, however specialized this posture may seem at times, Shelley makes every effort to raise it to the level of supreme example among objectifying logics, a "comment for the text of every heart" (Preface, p. 113)—this one lived through, fully articulated, and sympathetically presented rather than coldly recounted and judged as the "insanities" are in the "objective" oration of Horace's Stertinius.[59] To begin with, the Maniac's soliloquy is clearly an amalgam of the supposedly different modes of thought in the real-life models for Maddalo and Julian. The pleas to a disallowed but all-determining lover reflect Byron's anguish over his forbidden loves for several people, feelings quite visible in "To Thyrza" (addressed to a dead choirboy friend) and the "Epistle to Augusta" (to the sister whom Byron "ne'er" could "resign" in l. 124 of that piece).[60] This self-degradation is joined in the Maniac to Shelley's own near-despair over reaching "hearts that heeded not" instead of a wide audience spanning different classes[61] and his own dependence on the approval of Mary, who recently castigated him, much as the lady "rain[ed] curses" on the Maniac as he remembers her (ll. 453–54), after Shelley's seeming carelessness—and sojourns with Clare Clairmont—appeared to hasten the death of Percy and Mary's daughter Clara.[62] Such ways of defining the self are now presented as too frequently determining the self-concepts of these men and others like them, despite their extraordinary capacities for transference.

True, these sorts of obsessions could have been (and may occasionally be) offered in the Maniac's ravings as defensive self-justifications. For the most part, though, they are critiqued, more and more as the poem proceeds toward and into the "poor fellows" soliloquy, by being intermingled as variations on a common error that the madman carries through to a revealing extreme: the perversion of transfer-oriented potentials into self-abasement by an excessive, rather than primary, narcissism that looks to a largely imaginary Other to be the objective validator of the self.[63] The Maniac can even be said to "resolve" the Julian-Maddalo debate in that his speech *dis*solves all sharp differences between the two and between them and himself. His words finally show clearly how the principal endeavors in the poem, including the initial debate, are struggles for "texts" giving centers to the self by way of figures outside the self and how the figures are "others" that the self can never be and never really control to the extent it would. This entire "Conversation" piece thus proposes the sort of universal presented as the best kind for readers to pursue in the essay "On Life." As no position among those rendered in the poem proves really superior to the others (in defiance of Horace), *Julian and Maddalo* "establishes no new truth" in the sense of recovering a hidden Absolute. Instead, it cuts revealing pathways into "the overgrowth [of the self-obscuring assumptions] of ages" and ferrets out "the roots of error" that have kept the Western mind from "the freedom in which it would have acted, but for the misuse of words and signs" ("On Life," *NCE*, p. 477). Though Julian wants to distance himself from seeing those roots during the final narrative that he offers the reader, the interplay of Shelleyan postures here, particularly as the Maniac exposes the roots of all three, leads us to see the narcissistic objectification that is the real—and sad—basis of the overgrowth in this case.

Meanwhile, the Maniac also reveals the link between this error of logic and tyranny as we usually think of it or behold it. He does so, it turns out, in the way he alludes to Tasso, or rather to what Shelley discovered in his research on that poet. What he found, often in original holographs, were parallels between Renaissance poetry, with its exaltation of a mistress as the self's divine creator,[64] and Tasso's surviving epistles and sonnets to the duke Alfonso, Leonora d'Este's brother, who may have ordered the poet's commitment to the Catholic Hospital of Santa Anna near Venice.[65] When the raising up of a fetishized person as the locus of truth is positioned alongside these last obsequious appeals, the pose that submits to a gaze of the Other becomes thoroughly analogous to an abasement before political authority-figures and the supposed deity they worship:

> There is something irresistibly pathetic to me [Shelley writes] in the sight of Tasso's own hand writing [sic] moulding expressions of adulation & entreaty to a deaf and stupid tyrant. . . . It is as a Christian prays to [and] praises his God whom he knows to [be] the most remorseless, capricious & inflexible of tyrants, but whom he also knows to be omnipotent. (*L*, II, 47).

Shelley's Maniac, in echoing such expressions and connecting them to the stances that he has reworked from all the other tributaries to his character, thus draws such constructs as heavenly centers, inner absolutes, Gnostic hierarchies, enthroned lady-loves, finalizing deaths, self-centered texts, and propitiated readers into a frightening correspondence with political tyrants and enthroned gods. All of these possibilities are now made manifest as the effects of devoting oneself to any sort of all-defining object, and each of these ideological creations turns out to be sanctioned by the projection of a transferred figure "out there" as a "thing in itself."

This "comment on the [all too frequent] text of every heart," then, encouraging us to review the rest of *Julian and Maddalo* and the principal argument of "On Life," highlights the primary "mania" that makes for all the forms of objectification and points out the ways in which this kind of oppression is connected to other tyrannies the moment it begins to exist. Now we can synoptically specify what brings this "madness" on. If we look back through the poem for the moments of his soliloquy in which the Maniac seems most "mad" and relate those to similar passages in other portions of the piece or "On Life," we face a striking similarity between four sequences: the broken phrases in which the Maniac fights the disappearance of the death-figure, Maddalo's image of him wandering incoherently on the strand after the lady's departure, the opening ride of the two debaters on a Lido where Julian feels thrown into desolation and infinite mental expansion, and that crux in "On Life" where thoughts can be similar and different all at once until the "apprehension of distinction" casts some thoughts outside thought. In all these cases the speaker or observer and the observed Other are hovering between two perspectives that they can adopt toward their own interaction. On the one hand, all self-Other relationships can be viewed as oscillations of part-similarity/part-difference that change the proportions of each from moment to moment. Maddalo can seem, in varying degrees, as like and distinct from his counterpart in observing the Maniac as Julian seems in relation to Maddalo or the Maniac seems in half-mirroring the "ghastly paramour" that he has projected. On the other hand, the observer (or thought about a thought), because difference may seem to predominate over resemblance at certain moments, can decide in favor of more consistent and precise distinctions that conceal some of the similarities, even though many of the latter remain viable options for thought. In that case the projection of a subject's quest for likenesses into some other figure must occur and then deny part of what has happened. The Other must be viewed as an "object" dictating how the self will correspond with it, especially now that the self is no longer conscious of having given the object that license. The oscillation between these two stances, visible to some extent in every major character in *Julian and Maddalo,* is a natural function of the transfer interplays that freely occur in a pre-"objective" reverie state. There a subject feels initially thrown forth from another position (born or reborn, we could say, in a rupture from the past) and forced to negotiate among many possible conceptions of the self, most of which are destroying old connections in the process of forming new ones (as in the struggle on the Lido between the tide and the strand). The crisis comes when a choice seems necessary, and "mania" for Shelley begins when the hovering state or undecidable interaction of equal differences—where all relationships and disjunctions are possible but impermanent—come to seem so undetermined, so unable to give the self permanent definition and a sharp distinctness by way of what is related to it, that sheer interplay is rejected for the sake of a forgetful differentiation, an option allowed by transference's ability to forget itself. Once that decision has been made, the Maniac can long for a projection separate from and critical of him, Maddalo can see the madman as an example of human nature somehow distant from the Count's evaluating eye, Julian can recompose the Lido scene or Maddalo's daughter into layers he can seem to judge from outside them, and the confused relations in reverie of thought-object to object-thought can be divided into the dichotomy of thought and object.

At this point, with such differentiations accepted, a war over priorities, over which of the sides is "first" in the relation between them, becomes practically inevitable. The dominance of the observer depends so much on there being an object to sanction or reflect it, however, that the subject, to have power, must first pass it to the object, which must then be sought or probed as hiding a desideratum. Once that longed-for "meaning" lies definitely outside the subject, moreover, he or she can be subject-ed to any tyranny claiming objective status that can seem to harbor the power that the self seeks for itself. At the same time, the objectified power must not reveal its actual source; the original projection must always recede into or beyond the object the more the object is approached, as when the lady is hidden within the death-figure, Maddalo's tower of desire is transferred into the Maniac, Julian's "spirit" becomes the "deep" center of a sunset, and every "objective" word in "On Life" refers to a "sign" that promises Truth. "Madness," of course, usually refers to the opposite of all this, the state of diffuse thought-relations that will not correspond to a centered conception of reality. The actual madness for Shelley, even so, is willful devotion to such an objec-tified reality, which manifestly makes the subject look entirely outside itself for a power and potentiality able to be projected and pursued in the thought-relations formed by one's own desire and imagination. That the Maniac and his strikingly sim-ilar interpreters are mad in this latter sense—this is the "reality" to which Shelley tries to awaken himself, his close associates, and any other readers he may find, in *Julian and Maddalo* and even "On Life." If he does not make the attempt, "the text of every heart" may become the self-abasing and deliberate blindness that the Maniac reveals when he acknowledges himself as the "father" of his own pain's causes and yet pro-ceeds immediately to ask "What Power delights to torture us?" as though "to myself I do not wholly owe / What I now suffer, though in part I may" (ll. 320–22).

Mimetic Desire and Its Various Dangers:
Julian and Maddalo, The Mask of Anarchy, and *Peter Bell the Third*

Meanwhile, the poet goes on to suggest, the submission to objectivity is also the begin-ning of "mimetic desire" and its psychological consequences, the very cause and effects that Shelley saw in Ovid and Rousseau and would surely recognize in the writ-ings of René Girard. The instant a subject seeks a power differentiated from that of others by passing that very power to an "other"—a seemingly different person or object from which that grant ought to be but is usually not returned—the object can seem to direct the further course of the subject's longing as though this other has always possessed the self-sufficiency of being that the subject feels it lacks.[66] The sub-ject comes to want what it does and then to pursue additional objects of desire because it mimes what the Other/object appears to want and pursue. It assumes, even fears, that the Other (like a Jupiter) may have greater "knowledge," at least at first, and so be closer to the apprehension of any targeted goal. To become at least as close as the Other to such ultimate knowledge *and* to seem different enough from the Other to capture even the appearance of having the superior position in the relationship (the position initially granted to the Other), the subject must therefore imitate the distinctness of being and attitude apparently incarnated by the Other. In fact, to achieve this particular mimesis, the subject must present a posture seemingly opposed to the Other's, one that makes the figures in this interplay rivals for the supremacy they both seek despite their actual—and now suppressed—equality.

Julian and Maddalo are prime examples of how such a rivalry develops in a social relation based at the outset on a simple transfer of longings back and forth between the people involved. As we have seen, the interplay of their ideas on the Lido starts out, the way Julian remembers it, as a "swift" darting "from brain to brain" of expansive thoughts that initially cannot be distinguished as just Julain's or just Maddalo's. The already noted positing of Maddalo as a very separate "brain" toward which Julian can direct thoughts suddenly unlike the Count's: the shift to this construction of the conversation occurs only when each speaker pursues a level of ultimate knowledge (described in ll. 43–45) that is the same high level pursued by the other speaker. It is that decision, on both sides, to claim a superior sense of what another, distinct being claims to understand more accurately that makes this discussion seem to resemble the conclave in Milton's Hell, where "the devils" talked of "God, freewill and destiny" because these elements were understood by their rival angels in Heaven and especially by the Lord whom Satan once strove to equal (*Julian and Maddalo,* ll. 41–42).

We certainly need not go far to uncover the reasons why Julian, the principal "subject" in his own account of the debate, is drawn into this *agon* and its assertion of an inequality where none was originally claimed or thought to be necessary. He feels he must contend with—and imitate the otherness of—an apparently "higher" figure, if only so that this kind of model can provide a standard to equal and then surpass in an identity achieved by that endeavor. Maddalo, partly since he is a "Count" as Julian is not, is set up by his friend in this role, recalling the way Shelley sometimes found himself raising "Lord" Byron's success and fame over his own as desirable goals.[67] The Count's "pride" is partially justified in the poem, after all, by the widely held "sense," not just his personal belief, "that he was greater than his kind." The younger man's consequent feeling that he has been conferring with a man of "powers . . . incomparably greater than those of other men" now offers him a chance to equal an "extraordinary mind" in knowledge and not to seem one of the many "dwarfish intellects" groveling at the Count's feet (Preface, pp. 112–13). All this while, though, sensing the pull of the differentiation as well as that of the similarity in an act of transference, Julian realizes that a virtual merging with this exalted Other would mean a loss of the very self-sufficient identity that he is seeking in this mimetic emulation. He therefore takes a philosophical position entirely opposed to the Count's, rather than just somewhat different, a temptation to which Shelley apparently did succumb with Byron on occasion.

Maddalo, involved in the same activity, follows suit by pressing his distinctiveness to the point of offering a human example to prove himself right and Julian wrong. The similarities between the two positions are soon avoided as often as possible, as though there were nothing in common between, say, Maddalo's tower-image and Julian's scene of levels "piled to Heaven" (l. 92). To be sure, Julian is sufficiently cognizant of the fluid interplay being gradually lost in this suppression that he lingers in his account of the Lido conversation on how the drift toward opposition is delayed by undichotomized "Talk interrupted with such raillery / As mocks itself" and refuses to "scorn / The [shared] thoughts [that serious discussion] would extinguish" (ll. 37–39). Nevertheless, seeking true "identities" in mimesis and rivalry, the two interlocutors finally press their differences so insistently that their initially "cheerful" banter gives way to such diametric and nearly quarrelsome statements as "my judgment [flatly] will not bend / To your opinion" (ll. 192–93). Although these men find ways, as Shelley and Byron did, not to arrive at the point of a pitched battle of any sort, this confrontational stance is on the road to the divisive state of social conflict that Rousseau and Girard posit as the threat most likely to result from mimetic relationships.

These last two authors see this progression, of course, as necessary and even beneficial in human relations, provided a hierarchization of the social order intervenes between mimetic rivalry and local human conflict carried to the point of widespread violence. For Shelley this progression, though transfer-based and likely to occur to some extent, is a perversion of what permits it just as much as the other ones we have discussed. Transference in his eyes need not go as far as sharp rivalries, and certainly not fixed hierarchies, just as it need not inevitably result in objectivist thinking. The possibilities and goals of desire for the self may well be suggested and augmented by "another [or] many others" who carry the self beyond its apparent incompleteness and present boundaries. But that opening of options does not have to mean, though it can seem to, that the other is more complete or self-determining than the self and therefore a rival more likely to attain what both find desirable. As Laon and Cythna show most clearly, the "model"-figure, be it male or female, can be thought of as quite incomplete. It can seem as much an outreach of desire as the self has proven to be and so can suggest objects of desire only in a looking back to the self for the confirmation and augmentation of its own tendencies. Indeed, the very nature of a "model" denies its presumed self-sufficiency because its status is determined by the gazes of those who look to it for direction, making it dependent on its "slaves" for its apparent "mastery." Two or more counterparts can reflect each other's inclinations, even transform them all from what they were outside the new relationship, without any one figure having "more being" than others so that the others are put in the position of envying a "superiority." What validates and channels desire can be its movement between and across a number of equal beings in a way that makes each look to the others, not to any one, for sympathy and encouragement as the members of the group try for self-improvement in ever-changing relationships among them all.

Even so, Shelley admits, the difference and distance between beings can keep many figures from seeing others as mere outpourings of desire like themselves. This sense of a distinction (both in kind and in degree) can make each self want to be like and, at the same time, unlike its counterparts, too unalterably envious of and opposed to them to see the equalizing similarities among all beings. Once the choice of objectification has led to this further attitude on a group scale, all the evils wrought by mimetic desire, the ones rendered as its necessities or benefits by Rousseau and Girard, become probable or sometimes inevitable horrors that must be exposed for what they are if their cause is to be detected and reoriented. Shelley therefore uses several satirical or polemical narrative poems of 1819 to reveal the different courses that mimetic desire can take and how those tyrannies can be generated in the thinking of various human beings or groups, poets (even Shelley himself) included. In fact, each time these verse-narratives uncover this process and what it can lead to, they detail at least one, and sometimes several, of the results that a sense of rivalry is likely to bring about Girard's accounts of mimetic conflict. Some of Shelley's revelations even define certain consequences in ways that expand the assessments of them offered by Girard.

The point toward which *Julian and Maddalo* progresses, for instance, is the isolation of a ritual victim that diverts and reduces the wider conflict among rivals, much as Girard would say. Yet the victimization in this case is less the religious deification, the worship of a sacrificial lamb, emphasized by Girard and more the turning of a figure or figures rife with everyone's mimetic desire into outcasts that seem to remove and conceal that desire from everyone. As we have seen, Julian and Maddalo, prior to their departure for the madhouse, are nearing the point in their strong disagreement where their rivalry could degenerate into "Fierce yells and howlings and lamentations keen" (l. 215). It does not go nearly that far with these genteel men because this potential is displaced by and from the two debators into the madhouse that these words describe and from which the cries seem to issue as the two draw near it. The contention between rivals in civilization generally, where each conflict imitates other ones (the way Julian and Maddalo mime Shelley and Byron) just as the parties in one pair imitate each other: that entire cacophony is cleverly condensed into and reembodied by the population of the madhouse, at least in the eyes of those approaching it from outside. Even rivalries between grounds of belief, such as the one between Julian's heavenly "spirit" and Christian Providence (each of which imitates the other that it violates), reappear as "insanity" in this place, compacted into the oxymoronic "blasphemous prayers" (l. 218) cried out among the "howlings." At the same time the individual devotion to mimetic rivalry with all its ingredients—the determination of the self by the exalted Other (or model), the potential threat of violence between the parties (as when the lady seems to demand castration), and the refusal to see the root of misery in the deferral of one person's desire entirely to another's—is made to reappear blatantly in the Maniac as though his marginalized condition were the place where all this occurred and concealed itself from itself.[68] The Maniac thereby becomes what Girard calls the "monstrous double"[69]: an outcast mirroring yet distorting the contradictions in the mimetic desire of all his observers. In him, as in them, the self is the self only by aping another, and the psyche gains power for its chosen stance by ceding that power to a "spirit" far outside it. As such a reflector exaggerating this monstrosity, so much so as to make it look atypical, the madman can be seen as containing the diffuse social madness to the point of seeming one of its only locations. The madhouse residents and especially the Maniac, in other words, are made scapegoats embodying the general social evil, under the assumption that only "they" have it and "sane" people are free of it, meaning that the latter are freed of it by these victims who absorb it unwittingly into their demeanors.

The tyrannies are many for Shelley—and they keep multiplying in *Julian and Maddalo*—as soon as this scapegoating is set in motion. The placement of the Maniac and his fellow victims, for one thing, allows for a hierarchical ranking of the victimizers in relation to both him and each other. Julian and Maddalo each single the madman out as the sign of what each one takes to be his own superior construction of the world's order, each being careful to sequester in the scapegoat that projection of a higher "self" in both proposals which makes them more equivalent to than different from each other. Maddalo even goes so far as to support his vision by physically locating the Maniac in the position of the "rent heart" partway down the Great Chain of Being. The "poor fellow" can thereby incarnate human nature in general, just as a genuine scapegoat must, and yet be lowered in a ranking of human aspirations that allows Maddalo to fly at the higher level of the tower and Julian to examine the Maniac as "object" with only brief moments of sympathy for an equal.

Because of this upgrading/downgrading of the scapegoat, moreover, the will to power and even violence being transferred back and forth from person to person can be placed in two separate positions in a way that releases all victimizers from apparent involvement and responsibility. Violence can seem either self-inflicted in such "unusual" people as the Maniac, so apparently unique in his submission to a projected Other dictating his castration of himself, or wrought upon humanity by a very high possessor of "eternal and divine" power who has cast us all down and can inflict further punishment upon his victims whenever he wishes. It is partly because he is positioned and coopted by this latter construction of existence, enough to accept his concealment of its actual genesis (even from him), that the Maniac can wonder "What Power delights to torture us," as though his socially manufactured status were a command from a monarchical fate. Imitative desire, much as it sometimes exalts it scapegoats "above" the average person, works first in this poem to incarcerate explicitly transfer-based thinking as "insanity" and then to establish an absolute authority (the will to power as Jupiter) binding that madness into an outcast and tortured position (exactly as the Jupiter-projection ties down and suppresses Prometheus). This last relocation of rancorous human tendencies creates the illusion that a universal power has somehow urged mimetic rivals (such as Julian and Maddalo) to create scapegoats in their own images. With this diversion the victimizers can keep themselves from seeing how much scapegoating comes from the personal will channeling transference and how much they, the subjectors, have subjected themselves to an absolute controlling them as much as it seems to rule their victims.

This succession of tyrannies devolving from mimetic desire, however, is a rather late and sophisticated (though common) result compared to another one that is just as possible—and perhaps more horrifying at an earlier stage. As Girard points out, the closer a subject gets to an object of desire made attractive by the desire of another subject who keeps blocking access to the target, the more rivalry and then the violence it brings on come to seem the aim of the whole endeavor. "By a mental shortcut that is both eminently logical and self-defeating," to quote Girard, the subject "convinces himself that the violence itself is the most distinctive attribute of [the] supreme goal."[70] Indeed, once mimetic transfer-logic is in full control of the subject, he or she can see violence as what the all-controlling rival is most able to command and thus what he or she most wants to possess to conquer the rival's apparent superiority. Violence, though instigated in the pursuit of a different object, can become the focus of desire in every mind's eye and the means of attaining that end. All rivals on all sides, in other words, having projected phallic knowledge as power into their counterparts and then seen this power as a right to violence surpassing yet sought by each mere individual, could get to the point where they virtually worship "violence [as] the father and king of everything,"[71] the law beyond every written law and the essence of the presumed self-sufficiency raised beyond the incompleteness in us all.

Such a terrible possibility in Shelley's view has become a fact of British life by 1819, and so he points out the enthroning of sheer violence by making it the subject of *The Mask of Anarchy* (finished by late September), his ballad-stanza response to the "Peterloo Massacre" at St. Peter's Fields, Manchester, on August 16, when mounted yeomanry and Hussars charged into a crowd of over 80,000 protestors gathered to hear denunciations of present government policies.[72] Like the Manchester magistrate claiming sanction from the Home Office in London (which supported the violence only later after first permitting the assembly), the various mimetic figures in the poem, from statesmen and priests to lawyers and soldiers, each of whom seeks the power possessed by a "higher authority," all bow down and look to Anarchy as "GOD, AND KING, AND LAW" right as it "tramples" the "multitude" into "a mire of blood" (ll. 37 and 40–41). Anarchy itself therefore emerges as the tendency to attack and even kill all rivals that each competitor in a class conflict wants for himself. Making the right to that violence a "higher" object of desire, each one locates it in a figure seemingly more powerful than himself or any human rival. The result is a death drive projected "out there" above every person that appears sent down from on high like the Death on the Pale Horse in Revelations 6:8 or in Benjamin West's painting of that name (the sources of Anarchy's skeletal appearance at ll. 30–34 and 74–77).

At the same time, Shelley exposes more than Girard's "mental shortcut," while still anticipating many of his ideas, as *The Mask* shows the full complexity of the several thought-maneuvers that have put Anarchy in the position it now seems to occupy. As a dealer of death truly claiming to be a law unto itself outside all other law—the only sanction there really was for the violence at Manchester in Shelley's eyes—Anarchy actually rests on the underpinnings of Milton's Chaos (explicitly called "Anarch" and given an "incompos'd" face in *Paradise Lost,* II. 988–89). This foundation is "*Tumult* and *Confusion* all embroil'd, / And *Discord* with a thousand various mouths" (*Paradise Lost,* II. 966–67). It is a centerless interplay where each person's effort to take back violence from others who appear to possess more rights to violence moves toward the babble of wildly similar assertions of difference appropriate to an "anarach" state (meaning "without a ruler"). The common people (most of the protesters at Peterloo) help drive us all toward such a condition to the extent that they "feel revenge / Fiercely thirsting to exchange / Blood for blood" and so start to worship the violence imitating violence as though it were an exalted figure outside them (*Mask,* ll. 193–95).

Still, it takes an ironic twist to transport this very human and ungoverned diffusion into the status of "GOD, KING, AND LAW," especially since the final product is a blatant pretense claiming that lawlessness is now its own opposite. The key turn is an earlier pretense in which mimetic violence, fearing reprisals from what imitates it and what it imitates, attempts a *second* mimesis and tries to model its demeanor on the behavior of a being who seems very different. This figure is supposedly granted power at a level beyond the need for violent human rivalry, Death on the Pale Horse from Revelations being one example. "Murder," we could say, is a widespread possibility and frequent act in a world given over to mimetic rivalry, but it can seem to be contained, even forbidden to most people—and be officially sanctioned and controlled all the while—the moment it adopts and hides behind "a mask like Castlereigh" (l. 5), the British foreign secretary and leader of the Tories in 1819. Such a relocation of itself makes murder look nonviolently "smooth," even when its support of slavery tosses "human hearts" to those "Seven" European nations that formed the Holy Alliance and then delayed abolishing the slave trade at Castlereigh's unholy request (ll. 6–12).

Detection of what underlies this "masquerade" (l. 27) is, of course, quite likely if there is no further maneuver, since mimetic violence in that case has clearly mimed an opposite that (like most apparent reversals) is rooted in what it claims to oppose.[73] The chosen figure offers a sort of standard for imitation that shows how to instigate violence covertly without facing reprisal. Hence, while seeming to transcend mimesis, it actually invites others to simulate it. It also, while claiming to eschew violence, increases the opportunities others have to see their violent tendencies legally acted out—which is why many of those he oppresses still look up to Castlereigh and keep him where he is. This almost visible duplicity, though, is what leads to Anarchy being set up as King, God, and Law. To avoid revealing their official stances as such blatant deceptions for which they are responsible, these authority figures all defer to another doubleness that they project to be the authorizer of their actions (and their two-facedness) from above and beyond them. Having transfigured and disguised imitative rivalry once, they reactivate that dislocation. They make the general lawlessness of mimetic violence seem a general law miming only divine sanctions, much as they have made unauthorized personal desires for violence reappear as nonviolent persons of authority. Anarchy thus becomes an exalted masking of its actual basis and nature, even though its visage blatantly presents centralized power as the destroyer of common people. Its allusion to the Apocalypse makes it seem an inevitable part of history instead of what it is: a relocation, through several stages, of a mimetic rivalry spanning the classes that turns it into a government's exclusive right to wreak violence on its rivals at will.

Shelley's much-discussed use of the courtly "masque" tradition in this piece, which was first published as *The Masque of Anarchy* in 1832,[74] consequently points to further ironies that no reader has yet articulated thoroughly. Stuart Curran is right to note how this poem mingles the old "antimasque" that introduced "the grotesque, the vulgar, [and] the chaotic into the pagentry" at court with the royalist procession of mummers that generally superceded or ejected such a violent opposite so that all class struggle seemed dazzlingly resolved in a "ritual enactment of the received order of society."[75] Shelley's version makes the antimasque the very center and basis of the procession of ruling figures, especially in the Anarchy-figure where supercession and eradication are attempted by the very kind of "grotesque" violence that the "Masque" of priests and ministers claims to overcome. Yet what such a paradox depicts is more than what Curran proposes: a "confusion of values" in the supposedly harmonious center of social order.[76] This cohabitation exposes how much any suppression of class conflict is rooted in the very struggle among classes it pretends to rise above.[77] Enthroned Anarchy, much as it tries to mask the fact, is really that conflict enacting its violence from one particular location in anticipation of a similar violence either threatening it from other quarters or projected by it into those quarters under the assumption that the violence of one class must mime the violence of others.

Moreover, because it is the product of successive acts of masking that make mimetic violence (even in antimasques) seem something else, Anarchy shows that all the transfers clothing violence in social rituals such as masques themselves are the very methods by which violence is raised from local acts of mimesis to the level of a monarch who protects certain classes from violence and unleashes it on others. The very maneuver of masking (and masque making), or at least the kind that urges a desire for violence to imitate an effective form of itself that does not seem violent, turns out to be the most insidious, efficient, and oppressive form of violence, partly because it perpetuates hierarchy by making mimetic people look to higher-class exemplars for effective forms. The transfer in that maneuver, after all, keeps us from seeing the local interchange between rival desires that actually brings social violence about. Mimetic interplay at that level could be led to the rejection of violence were it brought back to consciousness sufficiently unmasked to redirect itself toward sympathetic interrelations among manifestly equal beings.

The counters Shelley offers to the onslaught of masked Anarchy, then, make a good deal of sense in the face of these exposures, particularly when the goddess-figure of Liberty proposes rhetorical stances for the oppressed common person (the intended audience for this piece) which can, if maintained, dissipate mimetic violence and so rob the government of the base on which it depends. One such stance is Liberty's own, since it alters the militance of the Freedom-figure mythologized in the French Revolution[78] by connecting that lady with the widely sympathetic, ever-changing, transpositional movement of a Cythna, Asia, or Lucretian Venus. Though "arrayed in mail" like ancient Athena (l. 110) to indicate a "resolute" determination and wisdom potentially equal to "the fixed bayonet" of the phallic government troops (ll. 319 and 311), this demi-goddess neither looks to nor offers herself as a self-sufficient model for mimesis. Instead she is a thought-process in "fast" motion (l. 119) from one potential to another to another, not from a desire to one model for its direction. She refuses to fix herself in one mask of her possibilities—any search for her "presence" in one place sees only "empty air" (ll. 120–21)—nor does she assume that any state of being is permanently better than another. Each temporary position in her movement is mainly a staging-ground from which future postures are constructed and projected for everyone who can think in these terms. "Thoughts" that send parts of themselves ahead, in the manner of "flowers" or "waves," therefore spring up "where'er [her] step [seems to] fall" in the human awareness of her drive (ll. 122–25). To accept Liberty's inclination is to make no thought or person a rival for another but to see each "model" as an avenue advancing some existing thought-patterns toward different ones that the model itself does not contain or grasp in a complete or "superior" way. Freedom is a psychological state of release from the slavish imitation of (and thus the resistance to) a model. Hence it is a return to the less regressive transference that remakes present fadings or potentials into other versions of themselves, which then seek additional but unpredetermined forms. At the simplest level, in the current state of oppression and deprivation, Freedom is the basic capacity and right, in which the laborer must resolutely believe, to transform "labour" into "bread" and then into a "comely table spread" without accepting subservience to the power of another supposedly entitled to keep the produced bread at his level alone (ll. 216–25).

Concurrently, too, there is the companion stance to this one that Liberty offers in the latter half of her speech, the one that undermines the power of masked anarchy by confronting the existence of a "masque" directly. Casting her thoughts ahead as usual, the lady calls for a reassembly of even greater numbers and more types of people on still wider "plains" (ll. 261–65 and 270–94). There everyone present should answer "sharpened swords" with "strong and simple" but nonviolent "words" that deliberately avoid any mimesis of phallic aggression. The words should echo instead the "old laws of England"—the anti-feudal assumptions in the unwritten constitution[79]—which affirm the right of the people to (and their renewed belief in) the Freedom just defined (ll. 297–300 and 331–35). After that, all the people should stand "with folded arms and steady eyes," a mask of "little fear," even if murder is unleashed (ll. 344–47), refusing to feel that Manchester "Panic" that still accepts rivalry and violence as the inevitable end of human disagreement (ll. 323–26). This antimasque will so violate the ruling Masque's sense of the violence that ought to be "out there," the brewing violence that rulers assume as a provocation for their imitative reaction, that the use of violence by authorities, who have been denying that any will to violence is behind their own mask, will have to expose what Anarchy really hides: high-level acceptance of a mimetic rivalry and violence that is not really inevitable, need not be universal, and never was legal, as the government must admit. The basis of oppression in the very chaos it claims to order and in the progressive maskings of that connection will all be revealed to countless eyes that the government has tried to deceive for decades. Facing this uncovered duplicity will be a large-scale refusal of mimetic violence that can clearly encompass great numbers and many classes of people, the "masses" that the British government has long announced as the ground of its authority and still uses as a cover in its official rhetoric. The mask of the moment that exalted Anarchy has adopted (the public as now violent) will no longer exist in most minds; government violence will be clearly divorced from the popular foundations it once gave itself; and so masked anarchy will be toppled, unapocalyptically, to become a blatant death drive without a legally sanctioned horse. Indeed, it will undergo its own death as a mere earthly concept brought back to earth (l. 131), just as the spread of mimetic violence will also die away to leave Liberty the only true basis of "Constitutional" government.

Then again, can mimetic thinking die off so easily? The very transference that opposes its effects can still draw anyone into this frame of mind whenever a person forgets that self-construction by way of another should persistently question the sufficiency of the other and the construct. Shelley continues to wonder if escape from this prison is possible. He is stunned by how many questioning, imaginative minds have succumbed to its appeal and helped British authorities stifle revolutionary thought with mimetic thinking that endorses hierarchies and centralized violence (which it has helped to establish). As a result, I think, this poet's ultimate attack on such a costly error is his satirical "conversion story" of just such a mind: *Peter Bell the Third* (completed by late October 1819), his sometimes scathing indictment of the recent, quite reactionary Wordsworth who "has chained himself in self-defeating mental formulations" by "abandoning [more] radical and humanitarian views."[80] While Shelley's other poems on mimetic desire focus on only one or two of its effects and the logic leading to them, this partisan "squib" (*L*, II 135) follows a poet, on an almost standard Christian journey of descent and rebirth, through a series of trials where he contests with or consents to the temptations of imitative thought, including some of the ones discussed by Girard and some that he does not mention. What we and Shelley discover on that journey, as we are bound to in a portrait of a logic where all states of mind are really based on imitations of other figures, is a sequence of resistances to standards—admirable and appealing in their opposition—which always form the resistance by miming the very standards involved, so much so that the resister is transfigured into an enforcer. Both because and in spite of its extraordinary ability to see the self in terms of the most insistent "others" in any setting, the central character's (and Wordsworth's) thinking for Shelley is rendered as taking on the psychology and behavior of model after model, generally without perceiving that fact, until several models control "Peter" enough to make him their agent and propagandist.

Shelley's "hero" is trapped in this quagmire, in fact, as early as the initial stage of his history. Peter, we must realize, is first of all a combination of and variation on at least two other figures, emerging as Peter "the Third" in this sense as well as in others.[81] One aspect of him is Peter Bell as he is at the end of Wordsworth's poem of that name (published in April 1819), a once selfish and rapacious potter now converted to fervent Methodism after seeing a dead body beneath the flow of a stream and taking the distorted visage as a portent of his own doom and (later) of his need for salvation.[82] Another ingredient is the younger, rural Wordsworth himself, whose early, albeit religious, skepticism seems to have both imbibed and questioned the almost Calvinistic Methodism preached all around him (Shelley fancies) in the churches and folktales of northern England. The character that results in Shelley's piece, having been thus doubly "reformed" by the Reformed Church, is "warmed" by "fresh-imported [threats of] Hell-fire" (ll. 5 and 2)—or rather by Protestant extremism as Leigh Hunt has presented it in his *Folly and Dangers of Methodism* and his *Examiner* review of Wordsworth's *Peter Bell*. In Hunt's redaction of Wordsworth, which Shelley accepts, the one-time potter has acquired "a proper united [that is, United Methodist] sense of hare-bells and hell-fire," which really claims that many are "hopelessly" foredoomed to "damnation" unless portents announce their possible election to *only* Methodist salvation and they consequently choose to repent of past sins.[83] Not wondering about such assumptions very critically, Shelley's Peter therefore decides at the outset to model his sense of identity on the "dress and mein" of country Methodists (l. 3). After all, this mimetic procedure itself is offered as a standard to follow by Wordsworth's Peter (hence Wordsworth too). His initially vicious potter, already made so surly by earlier exemplars (as Hunt observes), clearly makes no character-change without first looking to a seemingly more powerful mirror that portentously shows him (particularly when the stream-image is connected to Methodist notions) the likely end of his present tendencies. The beginning of *Peter Bell the Third,* then, as a satirical parody should,[84] starts carrying out the possibilities in the most basic (albeit rarely seen) assumptions of an earlier work to show what it means to be already imitating an attitude at the very "origin" of an assertive "new self."

What it means at this early stage for Shelley's Peter is a permeation of his thinking and social situation by a language of Methodism that permits him no escape from it even when escape later becomes his aim. Extending the implications of the omen in the stream and immersing himself further in the "mein" he tries to duplicate, this Peter tries to make each new self-expression bespeak "the grace of God" as attached to him (l. 9). That effort is demanded by any individual's decision to be a signifier in the Methodist scheme of signification, since that scheme, as Wordsworth has shown with the portent he uses, sees all surface appearances or appendages of beings as emblems of a distant spiritual destination or a hidden determination by God. Such a contextualization of his apparent figure seems to give Shelley's Peter a satisfying sense of himself—that is, until he realizes that "His holy friends" can find him "predestined to damnation" because his last name, as portentous sign, can "rhyme with hell" and the "hue" of his darkened skin, another omen, can be said to resemble "brimstone" (ll. 16–24). Peter responds, of course, with a "yell" of objection (l. 26), but that only confirms the damning interpretation of him by rhyming with "Bell" and "hell." Because he has styled himself by miming this discourse, he must remain a sign within the order of meanings defined by the religion he has chosen, and that fact is still a fact when he goes on to defy the system with words to which Methodist conventions can readily attach a Methodist significance. For him to sit and "curse . . . his father and his mother; / And [invoke] God, and sin, and death" in an effort now to reject the dictates of his faith and to go back to his surly personality (ll. 40–41) is for him to confirm the doom that has been prescribed for him as it is by Methodists for anyone "Blaspheming like an infidel" (l. 42). He cannot think of terms outside the system even when rejecting the system, so when he finally opts for the silence of a merely open "jaw," he is still read, by the "old [Methodist] woman" watching him, as "Like one who sees a strange phantasm" presaging death (ll. 48–55), just as Peter Bell is spoken of as seeing one in Wordsworth's poem. When "the Devil" comes for Peter, too, although this Satan is really a "gentleman" from London buying Peter for upper-class interests (ll. 82 and 66–67), that urban connection is made to suit the governing rhetoric to a fare-thee-well. Because this visitation fits right in with the rural sense of those "evil" city-dwellers, the taking of the foredoomed convert is likened by all those neighbors who sense it to "the black storm" frequently used in Calvinist folktales to depict the coming of the Dark One for those he has chosen to carry off to Hell (l. 61).

By these standards, of course, Shelley's Peter assumes that he has eluded a confining mimesis as he proceeds to the second stage of his history. Actually, however, Shelley's "Devil" would not have reached out to the country potter/poet, nor thought him useful to the power-brokers of the city, were Peter not so persistently inclined to self-identification by way of imitation and rivalry. The London to which the Devil takes him is "Hell," it turns out, not simply because country prejudices are true, but because it is ruled by interactions of mimetic desire that operate far more continuously and frenetically than they do in Westmoreland. As in so many eighteenth-century satires,[85] the great city of this poem is a "thrusting, toiling, wailing . . . riot" where no one is able to find a role to play without feeling anxious "Care" that he or she might fail to play it acceptably (ll. 97–98 and 261–62). That is because each person acts a part suggested by "others [who] / Smile to inflict it upon their brothers" (ll. 254–55). The others, in turn, seek different roles for themselves in the hope of greater power than their own parts seem to have, each one "cheat[ing] his neighbor [and] / Cheating his own heart of quiet" in the bargain (ll. 200–01). The consequence is a "smother" of oppressions accepted by the various selves (l. 217), whereby each self is oppressing others as a model and is oppressed by other, supposedly exalted standards. "All are damnable and damned" here because each person is "damned . . . by another" for not quite living up to a model, while each "damns [some] other" for apparently not living up to the supposed obligations of a role (ll. 218–21). Especially if we view the hero's move to this setting as Shelley's mock-religious rhetoric suggests we should—as a passage from one set of temptations to another—Peter Bell the Third has jumped from a frying pan into the fire. The new surroundings extend and intensify what he is already inclined to assume by throwing him in the midst of the fastest concatenation of mimetic rivalries that thought can comprehend.

To his credit, Wordsworth has suggested as much himself, most obviously in his castigation of "getting and spending" in "The World Is Too Much With Us," published in the *Poems* of 1807. Even the first edition of his *Peter Bell* seems to imply this very sense of city life. One of the images the potter sees in the ominous stream is of "a party in a parlour," where each person "sipping punch" or "tea" looks at others doing the same, and that exchange of imitative gazes reveals these people to be just as "damn'd" as they are "crammed" together.[86] Shelley therefore reflects these assertions when he lets Peter Bell the Third trumpet his right as a poet to individual autonomy in a city that tries to deny such claims. And yet there is an irony even here, which Shelley proceeds to deepen. As Hunt has pointed out already and as Shelley now suggests by repeating the "damn'd / crammed" idea in *his* description of London, the image in Wordsworth's *Peter Bell* imitatively reflects the rural Methodist notion that, in the city especially, "all one's fellow creatures are to be damned" (Hunt's words). To carry this sort of understanding, along with the mirroring of the viewer's potentials in the entire stream-image, over into the London setting, as do Shelley, his Peter, and his Devil, is to play right into the mimetic use of transference going on in both the country and the city even when a rural critique of London life is supposedly being offered. It is to transfer mimetic thinking from setting to setting and so to add the kind in one place to the kind in another. Indeed, Shelley makes it appear as though the imitated Methodist beliefs were demanding the increase and the acceleration. Since country Methodists (for Hunt and Shelley) think of nearly all souls as doomed to damnation because they imitate each other the way they do in the "party" image, and since the city is the supreme "party town" for such thinkers, the Methodist exploitation of mimetic desire to gain converts such as Peter so that the converters can then define him as damnable really *urges* that he continue his quest for identity in the very evil of the city that Methodism claims to fear.

Shelley's Peter/Wordsworth consequently makes his declaration of independence—and so launches another stage in his history—by adopting an attitude throughout his imaginative creations that actually blends standards mimed from both Methodists and urban reactionaries. True, he cultivates and claims "an upper stream of thought" in his imagination, "which ma[kes] all as if it was not" by "Fitting itself to all things well" (ll. 108–10). "All things Peter" observes, therefore, take on "a peculiar aspect to him" (ll. 273–74) that can occasionally, Shelley admits, revivify the observed "things it [has] wrought on . . . / Wakening a sort of [unusual] thought in [the] sense" of the words adapted from other contexts (ll. 310–12). But this exalted stream, on the one hand, if only by recalling the revelation that comes with the view of the stream-image in Wordsworth's poem, imitates the Methodist idea of inspiration as a strictly personal, even mental enlightenment from outside and above.[87] It is a sign of being "chosen" that supposedly allows the beneficiary to transform what he sees into emblems of inner Methodist knowledge and thus to make the resulting scheme apply to (or "fit") whatever he chooses to interpret. On the other hand, this claim to special insight also resembles the one advanced by this poem's Devil about his own mental powers (ll. 106–10), especially if one of the Devil's faces belongs, as many believe, to Robert Southey (to whom Wordsworth dedicated his *Peter Bell*). This now staunchly monarchical Poet Laureate, "a bard [become an opportunist] bartering rhymes / For [the] sack" to which the Laureate is entitled (ll. 83–84), hides all his desire for aristocratic, even Godlike, standing (in the masque tradition) behind such middle-class facades as that of a "slop-merchant from Wapping," the sort who seems level with the people yet garners a rich man's income by selling cheap clothes to poor sailors (l. 92). The result in this Satan's concept of himself is, first, an apparently independent imagination that can refashion all that it beholds, a principal characteristic in the bourgeois ideology of the self-made man. At the same time, the Devil also longs for an "upper stream" of uncommon insight that carries thought to the level of an aristocrat's presumed birthright: the power to command each thing he surveys to assume the shape that he chooses for it. Peter/Wordsworth clearly models his claims for his mind on this latter, urban, Devil-ish complex of postures, yet he does so by masking *its* masking with the more northern, Methodist, and apparently classless vision of the self-contained (but divinely chosen) psyche. He even separates himself

from his urban model by fabricating an agrarian "Lincolnshire" background instead
of always using his real origins near Grasmere (ll. 111–20). He thereby manages to
conceal his rural Methodist base and any connections that readers could make
between its ideas and the Devil's. Mimetic desire, after all, urges its pursuer of external
standards to appear their possessor by setting himself off from them and seeming to
master each one "from within" because of the self-sufficiency he has pursued them to
attain.

To seem to avoid mimetic desire as a London poet, in other words, is only for
Peter to confirm that perversion's increased control over him, and for Shelley, given
Wordsworth's transfer-based intelligence, the poetic consequences, if exhilarating at
times, must finally turn the poet's talent sadly in upon itself, inscribing Peter into an
unloving obsession with a selfhood not entirely his own. Though such a thinker can
convey an "apprehension clear [and] intense of his [own] mind's work" (ll. 309–10),
he can only absorb "the outward world" into a "centre" that seems its own "circumference," a way of organizing the world determined by nothing but what is already
"inside" (ll. 278 and 294). Such a poetic vision cannot be transformed by possibilities
of newly interrelated perceptions outside an established (and imitated) frame of reference (which really combines several frames), so Peter Bell the Third never really
"goes out of himself" enough to raise visible Nature's "all-concealing tunic" (l. 317).
He refuses to love or have any sort of intercourse with an "other" not already grasped
entirely by his borrowed conceptions, and, conversely, he will not accept *being* loved
by an other in an exchange of insufficiencies, like Laon and Cythna's relationship at
its best, which might transform both figures byeond their present conditions (ll. 318–
24). He thus can never "Fancy another situation / From which to dart his contemplation, / Than that wherein he [now stands]" (ll. 300–302), for, were he to do so, he
would have to face the interrelational thinking (the generously imaginative kind) that
has led to the mimetic desire he is now trying so hard to keep from his conscious
awareness. In order for such an understanding to put superior knowledge in one position instead of another and then for the seeker of knowledge to seem to possess that
higher level (the fondest wish—or fiction—of mimetic thinkers), Peter's kind of ideology must assert a solipsism where "Nothing [moves] ever out [of the knower's
purview], although / Something must ever enter" to be made over into his sense of
what it ought to be (ll. 296–97).

Granted, Peter/Wordsworth seems to bring this stage in his life's journey to a ring-
ingly nonmimetic climax when he half-repeats his rebellion against Methodist deter-
minism by using his fabricated uniqueness as an excuse to be "uninviting [towards]
those [Londoners], who meditation slighting, [are] molded in a different frame" by
their own attempted solipsisms (ll. 280–82). Still, the fact that this stance is so definitely produced by a series of mimetic steps—so much so that such a concentration
on "self" manifestly imitates the obsession of others as they seem to imitate it—
means that Peter's arrival at his most nonconformist moment really begins his descent
into his most extreme conformism and can be used at once in a strategy determined
to draw him into the net of those who work to uphold the most hegemonic ideology.
The Devil in *Peter Bell the Third,* we should recall, is more aware of this irony than
anyone, since he is a mime always "aping fashion" and then trying to confine others
within the order he imitates as though he were its master and not mastered by it (l.
128). As a result, he guides the "unique" poet into the next stage of his existence, using
the power in the position of being Peter's model and rival, by insidiously drawing his

supposedly defiant victim through a succession of three steps, each of which is designed to jog apparent independence into clearly becoming the subservience it really is.

First the Devil uses one of his "petits soupers," imitating French fashion (instead of true revolution) the way Southey and Wordsworth now seem to have done in the 1790s (l. 374), to introduce Shelley's Peter to a Coleridge-figure, a "subtle-souled Psychologist" (l. 379), who sees poetry Germanically as "A dew rained down from God above / A power which comes and goes like a dream" in the sense (unlike Shelley's "Power") of being "Heaven's light on Earth" (ll. 392–95).[88] Almost at once, Peter/ Wordsworth, as the Devil knows he will, starts basing his bourgeois-Methodist privacy of vision mimetically on "recollections" of rural detail filled (especially in the "Immortality" ode) with a "soul of . . . diviner flame" (ll. 428 and 436). The potter/ poet forgets his more skeptical "sense / Of memory" that could remind him of how much all intimations of greater depth come from older thoughts being rethought by later redactions of them (ll. 423–24). The poetry that emerges consequently entraps Peter in several ways that serve the Devil's interests. Peter's attempt to forget imitation in a personal faith is now restored to its actual dependence on models, even though the new mimesis is disguised as a deepening of the faith; possible efforts by Peter to rival the Devil's own imitation of French and other styles are now deflected into an echoing of the Germans that keeps the Devil secure in his own "world of fashion" (l. 139); and finally, because of mimed encouragement from a Coleridge-figure at a time when that "Psychologist" appears to support social change, Peter's claim of individuality is led from mere solipsism into an open defiance of sanctioned ideas and systems that makes him a vulnerable target along the lines of a minion who suddenly feels entitled to cast off the livery of service (ll. 449–50). Now Peter is set up for the second step of his model's plan, since the defiance of a standard using means and pursuing goals provided by the standard is the action that most ensures the standard's continued supremacy. Once the rising Wordsworth/Peter announces any measure of overt rebellion (such as the urging of "natural" human equality in parts of his early poetry), the Devil can take public umbrage at this attack on the assumptions of "gentlemen," the presumed arbiters of taste (l. 457), and ask "all the first Reviews" in London to "abuse" the published verses, much in the ways the *Lyrical Ballads* and especially the 1807 *Poems* were treated (ll. 464–67).[89] Peter, so in need of validation (as the Devil knows) by others and especially by authority-figures held up as "God's own voice" to be imitated, finds himself "out of tune" and hastens to defend his work with prose treatises that, in Shelley's view, often recant what is truly revolutionary in some of the poems (ll. 512, 507, and 513–517). Peter/Wordsworth, we might say, comes to feel himself in danger of being made a scapegoat who appears to contain everyone's mimetic behavior just as the Maniac does.

At this point the Devil, seeing his victim as at last ripe for the accomplishment of the purpose for which he was brought to London, intervenes by following up on what Peter now believes after having imitated Coleridge for a while. With his former disciple now cast into a posture in which he practically begs for models that will restore him to public favor, Satan guides Peter back to the fold by sending him a translation of "Kant's book" (ll. 518–19). This kind of philosophy, as we have briefly noted earlier, is an absolutist "world of words" in Shelley's eyes; it can—and here does—"Fire" a poet into believing that his mind can reach "beyond the [very] bottom . . . / Of truth's clear well" to rational essences or ideas transcending party interests and the constructs that thought-in-language composes from mere perceptions and memories (ll. 520 and 538–40). The way this philosophy ranks levels of the mind relative to their distance from central truths beyond experience now makes Peter want to think at the highest level and to find all "lower states" wanting by comparison. Following his new model all too closely, he proceeds to restyle his discourse to make it appear that his thoughts rise toward a unity beyond all factions and there become entirely of "one hue" at a level surpassing local colors (ll. 564–66). He then decides, determined to view life henceforth from this lofty, if imitated, perspective, that any supposed happiness at mere everyday levels of feeling is not real happiness at all and must be avoided for the sake of what is (the level of absolute spirit). Experiential and temporal "happiness is wrong," the reconverted Peter/Wordsworth concludes in a fashion that inadvertently echoes "Calvin and Dominic," or rather their castigations of all earthly attachments as sinful (ll. 573–74). Since Calvinism is one influence on northern Methodism, Peter is conscripted by his own consent into a more abstract and hardened version of the country thinking he once "yelled" against, convinced more than ever that hosts of men (save a few elect) are doomed to damnation by whatever "happiness" they seek. He has come to imitate German idealism, extreme Protestantism, and even Dominican Catholicism on the "One single Point" they share the most (l. 569): human abasement before a high or deep absolute—"The folly which soothes Tyranny" more than any other (l. 622).

Now the Devil unleashes the third step in his grand strategy, thereby giving Peter/Wordsworth a last push toward the ultimate fate of a strictly mimetic poet. Seeing that the "reformed" Peter has resolved the quandaries generated within mimetic thought by settling (as such thought usually does) on an ideology of ranked levels bowing to an ultimate standard, Satan and the London reviewers do an about-face and "Praise him," terming him "A planet lost in truth's keen rays" as though this satellite of centered systems had virtually united with the sun's divine light (ll. 623–25). Peter is able to see himself validated outside himself at last, particularly when the approval of a government "sinecure" (Distributor of Stamps, in Wordsworth's case) is added to that of the reviewers (l. 658). By this time he can forget that the validation is based on the standard of established, upper-class interests—which his "oneness of hue" has supposedly transcended in sunlike fashion—and can claim that he has "found the way" in himself "To make a better thing of metre / Than e'er was made by living creature" (ll. 630–32). From now on, shielded by this myth from what he is really doing and from how much the point of control is outside him (just where his mimetic desire has insisted it be), Peter can be turned into the mouthpiece for ruling-class duplicities that the Devil always thought he could become. The notion of a fore-doomed humanity, blindly viewed as metaphysical and not class based, can seem his license to agree with others and transfer mimetic violence into the figure of exalted Anarchy, whereupon he can urge a quasi-divine "Consternation" to "slash them at Manchester," "babes and women" along with everyone else (ll. 644 and 648). The Devil—finally revealed as the drive of mimetic desire masked by influential "gentlemen" who seem to be above it (Southeys and Castlereighs)—has cleverly drawn Peter toward imitating a series of standards that mask from his own awareness both his mimetic tendencies and the more general mimetic rivalry that has brought on the tyranny he now justifies in poetry.

In any case, what such a Peter has also become, by the stage of his life in which we presently find him, is, more than anything, "Dull—beyond all conception—dull"

(l. 707). "Doubly damned" (according to the title of Shelley's "Part Seventh") because he has chosen to imitate city standards and impose them on earlier models for mimesis, the poet/once-potter currently embodies something like the London-based "Dullness" of Pope's *Dunciad,* even to the point of emitting (like Pope's "Goddess" of Dullness) "A wide contagious atmosphere . . . infect[ing]" many minds (ll. 735–37). This allusion is both wondrously appropriate and shrewdly ironic. Since Popean Dullness is a deviation of "sound" and display from "sense" (from the "light" dimly traced on the mind in the *Essay on Criticism,* ll. 70–79), the deviance in *The Dunciad* is a series of "Emblems" covering over an "Emptiness," often with imitations "deck'd like Congreve, Addison, and Prior" without their substance (*Dunciad,* I. 36 and II. 124).[90] Shelley's Peter/Wordsworth mimes this sort of groundless mimicry when he starts to form his latest philosophy by reading German idealism. Once devoted to this model and the way it seems to incorporate others, Peter assumes an essence (or "sense") beyond the "bottom" of "truth," an essence that for Shelley is "Nothing" (*Peter Bell the Third,* l. 568), since no "one hue" exists for him beyond projective recombinations of memory's and perception's traces. Peter's final obsession with a unified absolute makes him behave as though that void were an unchangeable unity that must be intoned, or the dimness of which must be lamented; yet this endeavor shows how much he centers his writing around and judges human beings according to a nonentity. In Shelley's eyes such a posture is what Pope critiques yet also what Pope reenacts in his own dependence on God's "Heavenly light." Peter, then, following suit more than he knows, assumes a (really empty) center so as to have an imitable model and then places Popean/Kantian absolute truths in that position, despite the different foundations of the philosophies in Pope and Kant. He consequently enthrones a vacancy and gives it such control "beyond all conception" that his signs refer at best to other signs of this "Nothing," just in the way "Dull" at the beginning of that one Shelley line refers to nothing more than the same "dull" at the end of it.

By the end of *Peter Bell the Third,* we have to say, Shelley shows how much he fears a kind of "universal darkness bur[ying] all" if such a mode of thinking really continues to "infect" the way many people interpret their perceptions. Should everything that reaches consciousness as thoughts-shifting-toward-other-thoughts come to be viewed by everyone, under the influence of a Wordsworth, as signs of an unchangeable Truth that is really Nothing, all that we have perceived will be fixed in a present state of referring to the same nonexistence. Awareness will be so "dead to [the] harmonious strife" in "the Winds of many wings" that "fan [the perceived Earth] with new murmurings" (*Peter Bell the Third,* ll. 745–47) that no perceived element will be seen as transforming or as being recomposed by another. Though all things will still exist only as perceived, object-thoughts will not interrelate with each other to extend themselves beyond their present configurations, so existence will rest in a death-state of meaningless sameness grounded on what is actually an absolute void. Certainly "Love's work [will be] left unwrought," as the now "Puritan" Peter Bell would have it in a world forbidding "happiness," and all living beings will consequently be left "dying" off in a "ghastly life without a [meaningful] sound" of renewal anywhere (ll. 751, 550, 757, and 770). Such is the apocalypse to which mimetic thinking can easily lead itself and all of us once it has taken over minds that have enough potential for transferring their opinions to others to become the electrifying generators of other people's thought-patterns. Mimetic desire, we must remember, sets up standards to imitate that are supposed to harbor access to the Truth but are in fact as incomplete, and thus as empty, as those who look to them. To base the self's possibilities on the "center" of such an Other is to submit the seeker's potentials to an order of definitions that is far more groundless than the entranced self realizes. Self-articulations that confine themselves within such frames thus have to refer the self and all obedient listeners to a "Nothing" that has been given the right to restrict the meanings of the various signs referring to it. If an influential writer and an entire society keep submitting their words-creating-thoughts to such incomplete limits, they—and especially the poet, who should know better—are surely worthy of lamentation and satire. The very development of the perceived world can be confined within those frames, all because the inevitable creation of selfhood according to patterns outside the self has let itself be perverted into the worship of one deceptive Other by the self. Will "it ever pass away?" (the question left unanswered in the final line of *Peter Bell the Third*).

Quite clearly, the Shelley of 1819 has thoroughly grasped the nature and effects of mimetic desire while offering some of the most arresting portraits of that drive in the history of narrative and political poetry. No other series of poems in a single year, to my knowledge, has so vividly rendered and carefully analyzed the consequences of mimetic thinking: the victimization of scapegoats, the self-deception of the victimizers, the exaltation of violent rivalry from local to monarchical to mythically absolute levels, the use of imitated masks for assigning the right to violence to one side in a mimetic class-war, the dependence of resistance on the supremacy that defines it, and the inability of thought, once limited by a "higher" standard it has chosen to imitate, to recover the transference in which there is an ever-changing equality between the figures affecting each other in a relationship. Even so, looking back at the three poems that render these problems and their causes, we have to wonder if Shelley himself is entirely free from obeying this drive and using its devices. Has he not asked that question himself in *Julian and Maddalo* by afflicting three forms of himself with different kinds of mimetic desire? Does he not make a version of Byron, sometimes a standard in Shelley's eyes, an exaggerated slave of mimetic longing in the rising of Maddalo's desire toward that of Milton's Satan? Is the Byron-figure not then a scapegoat incarnating what Shelley felt toward the man himself? Has Shelley not tried to mask his own objectifying/deifying of women, deceiving even himself about it, in attributing it to a Tasso-like Maniac? Is he not repeating the very masking procedure that he attacks in *The Mask of Anarchy* when this poem satirizes the courtly style of the mask by couching that sophistication in the popular style of a broadside ballad?[91] Is he not setting up the rhetoric of his targets as an example to imitate in the *Mask* when he half-mirrors the broadside style of some Tory (as well as liberal) propagandists?[92] Is not the *Mask* itself a declaration of rivalry with another party-position? Could not the same be said of that "partly squib" *Peter Bell the Third*? Then, too, might not this parodic sequal remain too connected with the mimetic desire it castigates in burlesquing a poet and a style still admired and even repeated (to some degree) by the satirist? In fact, is there not a problem with writing satire itself, a part of all these poems and the thrust of the latest one? Does not satire victimize its objects from a position of more exalted, "truer" knowledge to which the satirist claims to have risen (as though one position had a lock on Truth)? Has not the choice of satire blocked Shelley from any sympathetic interchange with his chosen targets? Can we not say that the targeting of mimetic desire results in at least some of the very abuses produced by mimetic thought?

There is every indication that Shelley finally says "yes" to all these questions. As he shows in this sequence of works as early as *Julian and Maddalo,* he refuses to free himself entirely from and pleads guilty to this perversion of transference. He even admits to writing (and still writes) in mimed styles with an occasionally mimetic logic. Ultimately, in fact, he realizes that satire is at least a component of every attack he makes on this problem. He makes one more blatant foray into this mode with *Swellfoot the Tyrant* in 1820 and in doing so deliberately tries to revise some of the traditional techniques of satire.[94] Then he abandons satire for good, indeed quite firmly and explicitly, virtually announcing his decision in the "Satire on Satire" (*PW*, pp. 625–26), left as a fragment in 1820.[95] This piece likens "Satire's scourge" to all the "racks of subtle torture" that hierarchies use on their victimized scapegoats (ll. 17 and 2). Such a common result of mimetic thinking, Shelley now admits, points to the highly mimetic assumptions of satire itself. It sets its "scorn" up over its targets by claiming to be "Truth's sunlike shield," which exposes any "contagion's spots" with its special "mirror" yet keeps all those looking to it "shielded" from the access to truth supposedly possessed by the satirist alone (ll. 33 and 28–29). The satirized figures should imitate the shield, since it harbors the standards they should follow, yet their divorce from it means they are irrevocably sundered from that "center" and so liable to its diatribes for not living up to it.

What is really shielded and covered, of course, by this "superior Truth" of the satirizing mind is that mind's mimetic rivalry with what it targets, its thorough imitation of its Other so that it can use the aped characteristics to cast this counterpart down. Where that mimesis comes out most visibly, though, is, all too sadly, in satire's effects. The target mimes the scorn of its castigator, coming to be the very figure with the "leprous scars" that "Infamy" has fashioned in thought-creating words (l. 19). "Rough words beget sad thoughts" (l. 37), and even readers of the attack respond in kind when they see an exalted mirror exposing someone like themselves. "Men take a sullen and a stupid pride / In being all they hate in others' shame," as though the "fame" given to the faults revealed in a satire urges people to rise to the faults rather than the standards they violate (ll. 38–39). Satire, because of the mimesis in both its guiding principles and its rhetorical consequences, usually helps to produce the very "contagion" it reflects. Mimetic desire, then, must be exposed, given how widespread and (clearly) deceptive such a perversion is. Yet the exposure cannot really avoid being sucked into the pattern it attacks. More nonsatiric and indirect methods are finally preferable to the verse-patterns discussed in this section. Hence Shelley tries, as often as he can, to choose such forms in his later years, hoping that these can at least begin to teach him how to remove himself from the distortions of transference that he has described in so many poems.

The Modes Combined:
The Cenci as Shelley's Great Exposé

One genre that encourages writers to avoid satiric attitudes is surely the tragic drama, especially if it both continues and questions the tradition of Aeschylus, Sophocles, and Shakespeare (the supreme Western dramatists according to the *Defence of Poetry,* pp. 489–90). "In drama of the highest order," Shelley maintains, "there is little food for censure or hatred" (*Defence,* p. 491). There is no satirist's or reader's stance assuming a superior knowledge that sets the observer entirely off from the characters observed. Good dramatic characters, too, are not held up as simple scapegoats hiding imitative rivalries behind the facade of one apparent "shame"; since they must be fleshed out in body-language and rhetorical assertions, rather than being pointed to by a distant narrator, they are more likely to act out the contradictory tendencies of full-bodied people who must form themselves in the language-orders of public representation. True, these figures may be "distend[ed]" by the dramatist from other ones they recall, thereby letting the audience behold greater "perfection and energy" *and* more "unfathomable agencies of . . . error" than most spectators find in their own self-images (*Defence*, p. 491). But such anamorphoses still mirror their observers, instead of leaving them aloof from the action, by "divid[ing]" the elements of human nature into "prismatic and many-sided" reflections of what these elements can conceivably motivate (p. 491). We onlookers are forced into "self-knowledge" by a confrontation with striking enactments of the most extreme and conflicting potentials in us (p. 491). These are separated out and stylized for us in different but related mirrors and then pressed toward possible consequences, all in performed exaggerations instead of mere diatribes or one-sided portraits of raised-up exemplars. The personal enactment and social effects of both the positive and negative forms of transference can thus be played out less hypocritically and be less oversimplified on the nonsatiric stage than they can be in any targeted burlesque, ballad, or *sermo pedestris.* Consequently, the Shelley of mid to late 1819, trying to complete his two-year probe into how tyranny comes to exist and survive, spends relatively little time on such satire-propaganda as *The Mask of Anarchy* and *Peter Bell the Third* and over three months composing *The Cenci: A Tragedy, in Five Acts.* That much effort is needed to work out the contradictions in the story of a patricide that is indeed "many-sided," that "teach[es] the human heart," if we believe the play's preface, the wide range and myriad foundations of "its sympathies and antipathies" (*NCE*, p. 240).

The Cenci, in fact, aims at being so comprehensive in what it exposes that it is almost a meta-tragedy in relation to the tradition it furthers and alters. To begin with, it tries to highlight and then explicitly answer *the* question posed in tragedy since Aeschylus and even before: to what extent is personal choice responsible for the evil that finally destroys some individuals, and how much is a tragic figure the nearly helpless victim of fate or cultural pressure? Shelley's preface grants some importance to both "causes," so much so that he has spawned a running debate among critics over which factor is dominant or if they counterbalance each other in the course of his play.[95] Shelley flatly states that Beatrice Cenci's conspiracy to murder her tyrannical father the Count in 1599 is the act of an "amiable" and brilliant young woman "violently thwarted from her nature by the necessity of circumstance and opinion" (Preface, p. 239). Yet he just as firmly condemns her "revenge" and "retaliation" as "pernicious mistakes." They are prompted for Shelley by her blind determination to see the Count's rape of her as true dishonor (which it need not be) and her refusal "to convert the injurer from his dark passions by [postures] of peace and love" in a going out of herself overcoming the "dogmas" that she has chosen to accept (p. 204).[96] The foundation of all "tragic character," as Shelley sees it (p. 240), lies in what places Beatrice at the Sophoclean crossroads where "external" pressure and "internal" choice become coterminous and supportive of each other, then rigidly dictatorial in making the later choices of the psyche subject to this set of "commands." The play, in other words, sets out to explain the apparent contradictions in the preface and in Shelley's principal source, the "Relation of the Death of the Family of the Cenci" (*CW*, II, 160–63), by pointing to the basis of tragedy that both dictates to and is dictated by individual characters.

Concurrently, *The Cenci* also explores how desirous beings constitute themselves as "characters" on the stage of the world and how, in doing so, they position themselves in relation to other such performers and finally under the aegis of commanding scripts that force figures with multiple tendencies into the behaviors appropriate to certain roles. Much has been made quite rightly, though sometimes excessively, of this play's many debts to Shakespeare, particularly of the way Shelley's characters verbalize their intentions in speech-patterns echoing *King Lear, Hamlet, Othello, Richard III*, and *Macbeth*.[97] But more needs to be said about the ways Shelley highlights the rhetorical self-fashioning so vital in Renaissance drama. Finding an initial gap between felt motive and dramatic action—or at least sensing how much desire is impeded or channeled by the restrictions in the codes dominating the social order—Shakespeare's heroes invariably seek provocations from the responses of characters outside themselves. They look to the visible rhetoric of the behaviors confronting them for models or goads drawing out their own reactive postures. They crave "external" enactments holding out or implying forms of self-projection that can turn "internal" motive into socially viable performances or can even produce intentions bent on achieving certain performative effects. "Character" in Shakespeare is a self-staging that "reads" and anticipates the "reading" of the self offered by other figures.[98] Though this fact is mostly implicit in *King Lear* or *Macbeth*, *The Cenci* makes a point of that process from the start. In the opening scene the Count begins planning all his future crimes according to what the official Catholic reaction has been and is likely to be. As much as he plots to avoid the future presence of witnesses who could bring papal restraints down upon him, he is nonetheless thrilled that he has a "character for *what men call* crime" (I. i. 68, my italics). He gains the power of being feared and associated with impunity from his private inclinations being "a public matter," a received reputation (I. i. 71). It is the hope that such readings of him will continue, in fact, that urges the Count to "vindicate [his 'character'] with [still more] force and guile" directed against his own children (I. i. 70).

By making the Shakespearean quest so explicit and connecting it with so vile a figure, not to mention one so in league with the reigning power-structures (to which the Count half defers), Shelley exaggerates the Shakespearean "self" to the point of questioning the direction of such a conception of character. A personality on the stage may indeed have to be fashioned in a rhetorical relationship with other such stagings. But dependence on a "reader" for cues and directions can make the self the vassal of longstanding power plays outside him, even if he resists them in favor of his own. The self-fashioner is easily tempted into configuring himself according to the great text of an enthroned Jupiter-government or superego. If *The Cenci* is something of a meta-drama, then, in claiming to show the foundations of tragedy, it is equally so in revealing how the staged projection of character can be bound up with the submission to tyranny that often brings tragedy about, on or off the stage.

In any case, so bold an attempt at being comprehensive demands comprehensive answers to the problems it reopens. In order for his play to reveal what instigates human tragedy most often and makes people the functions of master scripts at the same time, Shelley must see all the methods by which people abase themselves as interacting to produce both the errors of personal choice and the cultural, even patriarchal, oppression of individuals. *The Cenci* therefore stages all the ways that he has discovered over several years by which transference undergoes perversion into tyrannies. While the other works studied in the current chapter isolate one type of perversion, or occasionally two that are closely related, this ambitious tragedy sees them as inextricably mixed and inclined to generate all the others to reinforce any one of them, almost as soon as one or more are accepted by the will—and their actual base is deceptively obscured. Certainly it is such an interplay of tyrannical modes of thought in people that accounts for tragedy as Shelley redefines it, and it is the tendency of people, even some brilliant and generous people, to stage themselves according to such patterns in such a combination that underlies Shelley's use and critique of Shakespeare, not to mention the stances of nearly all the characters in *The Cenci*. Indeed, the "human heart" gains a "knowledge of itself" by confronting the mirrors in this play (Preface, p. 240) because the characters reflect the destructive methods by which we are still tempted to mirror ourselves or let ourselves be used as reflectors by tyrants who need us (as audience) to achieve their stagings of domination.

Theatrical mirroring, it turns out, is the key to Count Cenci's will to power, even in that opening scene when he decides to debase his sons and especially his daughter. What he wants most in choosing that course is neither mere sensual license nor a vague supremacy but the "sight of agony" on the faces of those he asserts himself against. He craves "the dry fixed eyeball, the pale quivering lip, / Which tell [him] that the spirit weeps within" and that he may exult in "joy" because he is not that being (I. i. 82–83 and 111–12). He is so much a theatrical character that his very significance—and certainly his continued power over others—depends on the reaction of an auditor to his aggression,[99] on a reflection that appears to recognize his self-assertion and so allows him to seem a figure who causes fear instead of one who might feel it himself. At bottom, though to a different degree, he is as governed by narcissism as a Laon or a Cythna. "Any design [his] captious fancy makes" projects a "picture of his wish" similar to their dreams of an ideal ego, and yet that wish "forms none," leads to no visible result or recognition of its existence, "But such as men [reacting to it] would start to know" (I. i. 87–89). There is no mastery in a performance without the "reading" of the other that acknowledges enslavement and so seems to give mastery back, or at least to offer signs in a visage that can be read by the performer as suggesting an inner weeping, a "soul within [his] power" (I. i. 115).

This exchange of readings, though, while necessary for an actor so that he may feel himself to be what he seems, is a two-sided source of identity for anyone producing his "selfhood" with such a device on the stage of the world. True, the constitution of power by the Other's look and "knowledge" can place the responsibility and sanction for power outside the would-be tyrant, as though someone else has given him title to power and the title can never be taken from him on the grounds that he has stolen it. The Count seeks and, for the present, secures that license from the Pope's emissary in the opening scene. Cardinal Camillo is the most immediate person whose "start[ing] to know" will grant real force, and thus a kind of permission, to the "picture of [the Count's] wish," even though only some of Cenci's intentions have been declared to this appalled, but obligingly fearful, auditor. At the same time, any dependence on an "appropriate" response means that the auditor is in a position of control. The Count's aggression must be counterbalanced frequently by a nagging paranoia, as several have noted, mainly because he senses his own "quivering lip" submitting to a Sartrean "gaze of the Other." He realizes that the "reader" on whom he so depends may have the freedom to deny him the response he wants, and he especially fears that apparent self-sufficiency in Beatrice, who has long refused the trembling reaction he so desperately needs for the effect he pursues.

As he reveals to open the second act, the Count has been placed in an abject position, like a Lear facing a Cordelia, by his daughter's "fearless eye, / And brow superior, and unaltered cheek" on the most recent occasions when he has asserted himself in her presence (II. i. 116–17). In the not-too-distant past, moreover, her "mirror" has reacted to his power-plays with inappropriate, dissociated responses ranging from the look of a Madonna's pitying "tenderness" to a glance of "scorn" from a lofty position of moralistic judgment (II. i. 118). None of these gazes will offer his declarations the facial signifiers or "weeping" inner signifieds that can be read as submitting to his power and thereby granting its existence. This possibility is terrifying to him because it exposes the merely staged, rhetorical, and dependent basis of his power. It shows that the needed response is not automatically the Count's to command and that he has given all decisive force to the Other's gaze in looking to it for definition. Unable to deny that so much significance resides in the Other, since he needs it to be there if the "mirror" is to reflect any power back to him, the Count therefore sets out to reappropriate that capacity for determining meaning from his most resistant auditor so as to seem the gaze of the Other himself. One reason he decides to rape Beatrice is how much this invasion of her body will belie her Madonna-like removal from the imposition of masculine and patriarchal authority. Once ravished, he hopes, she will reflect the "quivering lip" of the "meek and tame" at last (I. i. 167). If he has his way, she will even come to seem to herself the location of the very dishonor that she has ascribed to him in her looks of scorn. With what makes him seem inferior thus transferred from him to her, he will seem as superior to her, he fancies, as she once seemed to him. In other words, he will become Sartre's Other as "seducer . . . producing in the other [he faces] a consciousness of a state of nothingness [in juxtaposition to] a fullness of being" that the seducer will seem to contain absolutely in his phallic aggression.[100]

Still, the Count finds, it takes more than an assertion of bodily force—indeed, even the rape will have to include more dimensions than that—if the would-be tyrant is to seem to introject a self-determining ability to turn desire into effective performance, "to act the thing [he] thought" (I. i. 97). Shakespeare's Hamlet has discovered this fact when, already obsessed by the distance between motive and action in his own theatrical nature, he tries to make himself the purely male avenger of his father by casting all "frailty" in himself entirely off onto "woman" and then castigating both mothers and daughters for the weakness that he has projected into them.[101] As often as the Prince of Denmark attempts this scapegoating, though, he cannot bring himself to kill his uncle, since he doubts that the murder is sanctioned by a ghost's mere appearance and a patently fabricated masculinity. His final enactment of the ghost's command depends on his eventual acceptance of "A divinity [that] shapes our ends," that will provide the sanction for regicide by arranging the best time, context, and opportunity. So it is with Shelley's Count Cenci, only more so and with a few variations. The degradation of Beatrice proposed in act 1 may seem to promise her father the sense of conquering "Manhood" he needs (I. i. 97). But the power to act can seem unlicensed by an Other and usurped from one—a stigma we have seen the Count determined to avoid so that no authority can hold him fully accountable—when "frail" woman appeals, as Beatrice does before the guests at a banquet, to higher male authorities thought of as separate from him and greater in power: "the Pope's chamberlain" and "offended God" (I. iii. 127 and 157). Cenci must attach himself to these underpinnings if the illusion of his self-contained right to violence is to stay in force (to remain Anarchy masked).

His technique is multifaceted but very effective rhetorically. First he makes the papacy so dependent on the "revenue" with which he bribes the church to escape prosecution (I. i. 27–33) that he becomes linked to the drive for male dominance already pervading the Catholic Fathers. Cardinal Camillo, as a result, rebuffs Beatrice with the "law" that "paternal power" is the "shadow" of the Pope's, setting up Cenci as underwritten by papal prerogatives (II. ii. 28 and 55–56). Then, aided by this supposed connection to God's earthly representative, the Count styles himself as a temporal extension of "the great father of us all" (I. iii. 23), an Italian Renaissance version of the Jupiter who has given himself the right to rape Thetis in *Prometheus Unbound*. The power desired by a patriarch to create reflectors of his dominance is projected up to a father-figure (a "soul upthrown"), one both exalted beyond all other beings and reflected within the projector most of all, who then does not seem as dependent on earth-bound mirrors as he really is.[102] Beatrice has gained the superiority of her gaze, after all, by suggesting an "awe-inspiring" depth in her visage (I. ii. 84). The mystery in that face has seemed a "protecting presence" looking inward to a "firm mind" that itself looks back, as a Madonna should, to "God to Heaven" (II. i. 30, 48, and I. iii. 52). Again adopting a pattern from her to stage himself, the Count conquers this powerful stance by aping its layers in his public posture. His pronouncements, often vicious prayers that Heaven does appear to answer at first (I. iii. 22–44), now claim to rest on a "sober truth" behind which lies "the word of God" (I. iii. 55–56). The "knowing" apparently at the heart of his daughter's glance that abashes the Count with its reflection of his insufficiency appears to be *his* "sober" possession henceforth, just as much as it seems to be the Pope's, backed as both men say they are by the absolute Word. With this dimension added, the rape becomes an assertion of the right and the will to "knowledge," the status and drive we saw Prometheus seek by recasting himself as a rapacious King of Heaven. Such an act so underwritten constitutes "knowing" as the total penetration and domination of any targeted person. From this point on, that person's subjection will be "deployed" as the patriarch wishes in a rhetoric that he (as God's spokesman) seems authorized to control. The barriers between the lust for power and tyrannical action have now been removed by a grounding of the self in a supremacy where motivation, utterance, and action are allowed to be simultaneous. The Count therefore begins his assault by bringing that presumption home to Beatrice. He simply utters "one word" (II. i. 63), somewhat in the manner of God at the Beginning, and that in itself makes her try (like fallen Eve) to conceal her once-powerful face from his gaze of the Other. Her initial reaction is to run for a hiding place away from the assault of a phallic discourse betokening the force of the phallus itself (the sign of the Father on earth).

Seen from this angle, Beatrice is far more sinned against than sinning. She can hardly be said to consent willfully to this onslaught, since it is directed quite specifically against her. In the initial two acts, at least, she is a real threat to a male-dominated discourse and worthy of the audience's admiration because of that stance. She is first, by her own admission, the champion and strong representative of all the women who have contended with the patriarchy in the Cenci family. Being quite capable of attaching her emotions to numerous other beings analogous to herself, she is haunted, quite gladly, by "the ghost / Of [her] dead Mother," and, as if at her mother's request, she protects and guides Lucretia, the stepmother "who filled the [mother's] place," and thereby stands as a "refuge and defense" between the Father's "moody wrath" and the wives (now composited) whom he has victimized over the years (II. i. 94–96 and 49). In this role as Woman defending her entire sex, Beatrice can challenge male supremacy in a number of ways. She can situate herself, the way Asia does, partly inside and partly outside the hegemonic ideology striving to secure the dominance of men. She can consequently read and articulate the ironies in the system, having been both intimately involved with and sometimes distant from them. She can expose at the banquet how unfairly "honour and obedience" are granted to a man who is really a "torturer" and how much the men given supremacy by their observers, while denying the fact of the gift, must rhetorically "cover [their actual] faces from every living eye" if they do not want their duplicity revealed (I. iii. 148–49 and 54). Meanwhile, too, Beatrice challenges the unity as well as the dominance of the "Manhood" achieved by such deceptions. When the Count finds himself the subject of her gaze of the Other, he feels his "masculinity" compromised because he has been placed in what he thinks ought to be (and in male discourse *is*) the feminine position. He is for a time in a very mixed state, male but figuratively "gendered" as female, and must (like Hamlet) theatrically throw this "frailty" off if he is to have a strictly masculine dominance. Even Beatrice, being positioned as the "knowing gaze," is a mixture of genders herself in acting out the authority that patriarchal discourse wants to restrict to men alone.

Herein lies the problem. To challenge such a discourse by being an authorized speaker of it is to discover oneself forced into its deployments, whatever one's intentions may have seemed. Beatrice finds that even a public utterance declaring "a father's hoary hair" a "shelter" for lawless "tyranny" (as in I. iii. 99–129) can express itself only as an appeal to "the father of all" (I. iii. 118) or to the princes, cardinals, and chamberlains who gain much of their authority from the widely held assumption that the primal speaker and ultimate auditor of language is male. Just to speak and so to create personal thoughts by confronting the psyche with verbal forms of them, Beatrice comes to see, is to be read *and* to read oneself as the master language and the father set up behind it want to construe a speaker's words. Count Cenci's utterance of a single phallic "word" horrifies her in part because it shows how the dictates of male-supremacist discourse have become virtually inescapable, even in attempts to resist them.

Beatrice appears to have only two choices under this "necessity of circumstance and opinion." One option is not to let "the tongue . . . fashion [desire] into words" at all, as her brother suggests (II. ii. 85), since any concrete utterance will turn around to oppress the "I" and skew its aims with a configuration of the words according to the confining standards attributed to the father.[103] The other choice, it seems, is to combat the patriarchy by deliberately adopting some of the most effective devices in patriarchal discourse: its claim of being grounded in God's Word, its suppression of possible word-patterns and meanings that might undercut assertions of power sanctioned by the Lord, its supposed right to penetrate and debase its targets according to its will, and its attempt to cover over the merely human power-play underlying its restrictions with the assertion that its dictates are or can be "chronicled in heaven" (IV. i. 159) and so imposed on humankind as if they were among the givens of Creation. The first alternative plays too obviously into Count Cenci's hands and would serve to lock Beatrice away in a silence that would leave patriarchal assumptins completely unchallenged. For that reason, especially after the rape, she chooses the second option more often than the first. Asserting God's law as her own sanction even more than she did before, she finally denies all verbal renderings of the Count but those that place a "Hell within him" justifying his eradication (IV. ii. 33); she makes herself the "accusing" priestess of the ultimate knower demanding her father's full confession and the right to pierce to his "dying heart" (IV. i. 34–37); and she refers to the justness of a God beyond this "judging world" for license to obscure her involvement in the murder (IV. iv. 113–128). She even urges her stepmother on these grounds to use signs for concealment and not to "write on unsteady eyes . . . / All that thou wouldst hide" (IV. iv. 39–40). This choice, of course, although not obviously, contorts her into the patterns of patriarchal language, thus making her hiring of assassins easily detected by the male Catholic authorities who finally put her to death. There seems no place for her to go that does not suit the aims of the father's master text, so she becomes a version of its own violence against its subjects,[104] and that makes her one of its victims even more than she already was.

Nevertheless, "seems" is an accurate verb in this statement. Such an eventuality, though sometimes the victim's own view of the situation, is not simply inevitable in the world of the play—and Beatrice is not completely free of responsibility. She does not submit willingly to such deployment, at least not during the first three acts, but she has already set herself up for conscription before her first entrance in act 1. She has, quite simply, refused at the outset, even in supposing that her choices are only two, some of the options really available to her all along. Given her definite capacity for carrying through positive forms of transference, she could have used the imagination she genuinely possessess in more telling ways than she has. She could have "gone out of herself" in her thinking sufficiently to comprehend the uncertain and multi-leveled otherness-from-himself in her father-adversary. Then she could have repsonded in kind to that sense of him rather than imitating the Count's apparent posture of self-determination underwritten by God's Will. She could have continued playing out in her own behavior something like Asia's otherness-from-herself in moment after moment, just as we have heard that Beatrice used to do in her shifts from maidenly "tenderness" to moralistic "scorn" during visits by her father. Such a pluralisitc manner, as we have noted, responds to visitations in terms of one set of metaphors and then suddenly in terms of a different set. The result undercuts the Promethean projection of a Jupiter by transforming both speaker and visitor from role to role without any single role coming to dominate the scene completely and claiming to rival one illusion of self-sufficiency with another. As Shelley claims in his preface, then, Beatrice could have reacted to the "injuries" her father has inflicted by returning both an outpouring, sympathetic "kindness" and a held-in or unrevealing, albeit nonviolent, "forebearance" (*NCE*, p. 240). If she had kept up this imaginative movement that would have refused to be contained by her father's sense of human relations, the Count would have been kept off balance and held in a more impotent anxiety, considering how anomalous the entire response would be according the context in which he wants to place his aggression. Certainly Cenci would have had no visible basis, under these circumstances, to construe her as a violator of patriarchal laws on the grounds that she had revealed herself publically as stealing the postures of male dominance to deny the absolute authority of fathers. In addition, through all this, Beatrice could have consistently attached her "vitally metaphorical" role-playing to the attitude (and subtle verbal skill) of the noncombative yet unsettling poet, who surely, again in words from the preface, is one of those who strives "to convert [an] injurer from his dark passions by [devices of] peace and love." Even so, once she has decided, as transference permits, to abash, and thus to try neutralizing, her father with a disdain and religious language resembling his own, she has rendered potentially deconstructive roles impossible for herself.[105] Despite the pull of liberating transference that she feels on occasion, she willfully goes on to act out all the perversions of transference that we have seen her father use against her.

Her seemingly sanctified gaze at him, we must admit, narcissistically imitates the Count's staging of an apparent self-sufficiency, though admittedly in an inverted, goddesslike form. It depends, as his look does, for much of its "reality" on the effect, and thus acceptance, it achieves in its observer. When the desired reaction no longer appears in Cenci's occasional acknowledgments that he has been "rebuked" (II. i. 45), Beatrice's seeming confidence and distance from his control disappear at once to show how much of an act they have been all along (II. i. 12–21, 53–57, and 63–66). In addition, she has deliberately pursued an underwriter for her posture that is exactly the same as the one grounding her father's claim to power. Accepting the "submission" most pervasive in her culture for the sake of her own counter-staging of his rhetoric, she becomes as "blind[ed] " and "excuse[d]" by Catholicism in her own mind as the Count has sought to be himself (Preface, p. 241).[106] That decision, which could have been avoided despite this religion's domination of the era in question (as poets have repeatedly shown, according to the *Defence,* p. 498), sets up Beatrice's appeal to God as a sanction, then her desire to "knowingly" penetrate the facades of sinners, and it is those stances that suck her completely into patriarchal patterns when she sets out to murder her patriarch with these motivators among her justifications. The tragedy of Beatrice Cenci includes, though it is not limited to, the combined social *and* personal acceptance of the narcissism, the deferral to an Other, and the will to "penetrating" knowledge (the suppressor of feminine diffusion) with which she is assaulted by her male enemy and according to which, notwithstanding her less rigid tendencies, she decides to stage herself for the sake of some mastery over her immediate audience.

Yet these impulses behind tyrannizing ideologies can hardly have gained their firm hold on Beatrice and even the Count without the reinforcement and insistence of the other perverisons already defined in this chapter. Certainly the father's *and* his daughter's stances toward themselves, each other, and the characters around them would not be the ones we see if both were not committed to forms of objectification. Neither would regard the other as a figure to be deployed, "known," controlled, penetrated, or even condemned from a subjective distance if both did not assume an essential "object" at the deep core of a person's demeanor that seems entirely self-determined and thus separate from the interpreting thoughts probing into the mystery of its surface. The objective core may be a subjective projection by the "reader" in order to justify the power play of a deployment that will exalt the interpreting consciousness. But once in place, albeit fictively, this "heart" seems a fixed and causal presence. Beatrice must assume just that to envision a "spirit of deep hell" in the "human form"

of her father that should be cut out by someone and then "swallowed up" by its original source, a "Darkness and hell,"[107] from which the young woman herself is
supopsedly divorced altogether (IV. ii. 7–8 and iii. 40–41).

This fetishizing oversimplification, to compound the problem, even works to make
objects out of the subject's mental inclinations. Just in the way Shelley's Julian turns
outward-tending drives into self-contained motivators set over against "external"
things, Beatrice and the Count strive to regard their conscious interpretations of their
own desires—interpretations molded (as we have seen) by the pressures of cultural
ideologies and language-patterns—as absolute dictators of their actions "from within"
prior to reflective interpretation or social influence. This assumption helps suppress
the doubts both characters have now come to share about how merely constructed,
mirrored, and ideological their staged intentions are. As a stimulus becomes a
response in this view, the resulting thought can be taken as a "firm enduring truth"
insisting on certain consequent actions (III. i. 61). Seeing the outrage of the rape in
this manner is what lets Beatrice objectify it as the undeniable dishonor that interpretation need not automatically make it. To her it is so fixed outside all possible perspectives that it is "Linked with each lasting circumstance of life, / Never to change,
never to pass away" (III. i. 62–63). Such a violation, she decides, fills her with a "pol-
lution" so "poison[ing her] inmost spirit" that she has to conceive the "hideous
thought" of revenge just as her father, now even more in her "blood," did himself in
setting out to rape her (III. i. 21–22, 95, 29). It is as though, invaded by him, she must
act as he would were he inside her, all the while forgetting that such a drive is really
a constructed excuse for answering (and imitating) his phallic power play with her
"dread lightning that avenges" (III. i. 89). In case this looking back to a "fathering"
object is not enough of a sanction, moreover, Beatrice also places God's retribution
behind it, just as Catholic/patriarchal discourse has urged her to do already. To be
sure, her consciousness after the rape is an "undistinguishable mist / Of thoughts
[that] rise like shadow after shadow" in a rush of transfers between thoughts-about-
thoughts while she considers what thought-relations to accept and act upon (III. i.
170–71). But soon objectification, already accepted by Beatrice, turns this welter,
which could arrive at a subtle solution combining many interwoven elements, into a
set linear succession hierarchically making every "shadow" follow the impulse in its
predecessor. Each shadow becomes darker than the last (III. i. 172), leading on from
a sense of crime to the naming of "death" as the "only [proper] judge" (III, i. 178–
79), because the mystery of Providence now supposedly stands behind an evil wrong
against the self and the wrong, as object, backs the revenge against it that Providence
allows.

The Cenci even reveals how such objective inner imperatives, usually as destructive as they are self-serving, are so easily generated in a world of stagings dependent
on observers for the establishment of character. A striking explanation is offered in
that famous second-act soliloquy by the prelate Orsino, the supreme objectivist in the
play. He, like the Count, views Beatrice as the object of his sexual domination and,
like the woman herself, concludes that "some unbeheld divinity" uses "dread events"
to "stir up men's minds / To black suggestions" (II. ii. 155-57). Orsino persuades himself, as much as or more than the Cenci have, that these intimations are unchangeable
commands once they are felt within the conscious psyche, and he realizes that his
introspection, the one interpreting his impulses this way, reflects the inclination

among all the Cenci "To analyze their own and other minds" (II. ii. 109). He then explains what sort of self-analysis leads to this pervasive belief in objective motivations:

> Such self-anatomy [can] teach the will
> Dangerous secrets: for it tempts our powers,
> Knowing what must be thought, and may be done,
> Into the depth of darkest purposes:
> So Cenci fell into the pit; even I,
> Since Beatrice unveiled me to myself,
> And made me shrink from what I cannot shun,
> Shew a poor figure in my own esteem,
> To which I grow half reconciled. (II. ii. 110–18)

Self-dissection here is not just, as most critics have claimed,[108] mistakenly viewing the potential for selfishness as a motive inevitably controlling the soul. That interpretation is not even possible until the self has first sought "anatomizing" deployment in a text (a late-Renaissance *Anatomy*) or in a gaze placed outside the self, if only as a self-projection or superego. The objectivity and "accurate knowledge" of a Jupiter-text or some person's scrutiny need not be believed or even pursued. But if they are, as is the overwhelming temptation in a society that fashions personality theatrically, that deferral to a particular, unchangeable "reading" locks the self into one deployed order of causes and effects, the first of which "*must* be thought" and the second of which are thus given permission (or "*may* be done"). Orsino, again like the Count (and like Shelley's Maniac), has ceded this sort of determining power to Beatrice's gaze, believing—and persuading her brother to believe, regarding the prelate himself—that "a friend's bosom / Is as the inmost cave of our own mind" (II. ii. 88–89).

Even more insidiously, that depth reconstituted in another location has been set up as superior to the projecting psyche in order for Orsino to exalt Beatrice and to gain the complete submission of her brother. As a result, the objectified self must appear to be inferior and "darker" compared to the raised-up Other. The self must cast itself down in its "own esteem" and accept the inevitability of violently antisocial motives in itself, mainly because the created superego (the supposed "divinity" behind all this) must be viewed by its projector as deploying *its* object to make that "poor figure" seem hopelessly distant from the Other's nonviolent perfection. The will to knowledge becoming staged objectification must victimize itself in seeking victims, ironically because of its own desire to dominate the wills of all those being known. In the effort to objectify others under its gaze, the desire to know must be objectified under another's, and this latter falling-beneath makes it accept itself as primordially Fallen and so as objectively doomed, even allowed, to commit sinful acts in response to the sins of others. This rhetorical/psychological maneuver is surely one of those "tempt[ing]" the Count into committing rape, "reconcil[ing]" Orsino into counseling revenge, and guiding Beatrice into believing that she has no choice but to engineer, and try to remain distant from, the murder of her father.

All the while, moreover, this dependence on a "knower" whom the self then endeavors to be, even as the self strives to appear utterly separate from that Other, shows that Shelley's characters are driven relentlessly by the various forms of mimetic desire. This tendency is bound up intimately with all the other perverted modes of transference in *The Cenci,* since the search of all the characters for a standard/reader, their imitation of its reading, their feeling of being cast down beneath its "superior" gaze, their longing to possess that gaze's apparent "knowledge," and their singling out of victims on which this knowledge can be imposed all involve the modeling of desire on the desire of another figure. As Girard has shown,[109] character conflict in Shakespeare is almost always mimetic. In his plays there is such a rivalry of mirroring counterparts inclined toward such a socially destructive violence that certain characters call in the end for a reinstatement of patriarchal hierarchies, which some characters have put in question initially as they try to attain the power granted to patriarchs. Consequently for Shelley, a questioner of such assumptions, the stage of the sixteenth-century world in his drama exposes how relations among characters turn, all too rapidly and pervasively, into mimetic rivalries and searches for scapegoats, apparently under orders from a higher level.

Each character, intensifying Shakespearean self-fashioning, takes a counterpart as a model and then battles the resulting abasement to the point of attempting a violent overthrow of the other. Along the way each strives to conceal the underlying conflict with the isolation of a victim-scapegoat (the locus of all "monstrosity") and the sanction of some law supposedly outside the basic relationships. The Count attempts to appropriate his daughter's judgmental dominance by making her appear the "insane" violator of social order to others (I. iii. 160) and then attempting a phallic assault that seems sanctioned by the most enthroned of patriarchal rights. Orsino works to "top" Cenci, Beatrice, and even his own church, each of whom offers standards for his duplicitous actions (as he admits as II. ii. 116–28). He strives to possess himself the sort of "revenue" that the Count must give over to the Holy See (I. ii. 65–66) and to make the Cenci children, to whose status he would rise, dependent on his suggestions without his seeming legally connected to their aggressive actions. In pursuit of these ends, he rhetorically transfers his punishable sins to the acts of the Count, then to Giacomo, then to Beatrice (whose "conviction" he "Assure[s]" in his eventual "flight" from the scene starting at V. i. 40–41). He then completes that progression by ascribing his mimetic aims to a transcendent "dark spirit, that [supposedly] makes / Its empire and its prey of [such] hearts" as his own (II. ii. 159–60). Beatrice, in turn, clearly locked with her father in the most extreme of imitative rivalries, attempts to make her standard/rival the supreme incarnation of mimetic violence so that she can justifiably, as God's true agent (miming the Count's similar claim), commit such violence against him herself under the cover of acting by the dictates of the highest authority.

Because it is such a foundation of "character," too, mimetic desire is one of the principal causes of tragedy in this play. The mimetic struggle for power both descends on all the characters from all directions outside them, forming the very parameters (the tragic destiny) of possible human relationships, and turns out consequently to be the most commonly (and tragically) chosen stance among the several ones conceivable when characters are faced with having to define themselves in staged encounters with others. Beatrice, without a doubt, enters a world "fated" by the longstanding decisions of many patriarchal men. These force all younger beings to confront in those men a pervasive imitative rivalry and the pressure of its consequences on every new "actor." Before Beatrice is even mentioned in the first scene, Count Cenci and the Catholic church are embroiled in a jockeying for supremacy where each side imitates the behavior of the other. The church increases its power by expropriating property and revenue from the Count just as he and other "nobles" have taken it from others, and

Cenci borrows the Pope's appropriation of sanctions from the nobility by gaining papal authority, in the form of impunity, to enforce his will on those subordinate to him. Though these two parties do not proceed to violent confrontation immediately because they are forms of patriarchy manifestly supporting each other, they are in danger of such an encounter eventually, as we see in the later papal decision to arrest and execute the Count. If they are to avoid the destruction of masculine supremacy in their battle over who is most entitled to it, they must divert their conflict to a different location of desire and pretend that mimesis and rivalry lie there and not in their own relationship.

Beatrice offers them the most convenient scapegoat. In the first place, she is a woman "monstrously" longing (as did Eve, the primal Christian sinner) for what hegemonic discourse sees as a male supremacy of judgment. In addition, she already embodies the very rivalry she is supposed to take in and cover up, since she questions her father's right to dictatorial power on the basis of her supposedly greater support from Catholic authorities and the Catholic God. Therefore, knowing that the church has provided some (admittedly deceptive) indications that such support may really be there for her (I. i. 40–47), the Count uses this anomalous, mixed-gender state of her being, when she announces her stance at the banquet, to declare her (and thus the church insofar as it opposes him) to be an outlaw meriting castigation and subjugation within the patriarchal order that Cenci's guests are anxious to uphold. The church then makes effective use of her for its side, having doubly imbued her thinking with its own rhetoric of retribution by using Orsino as more a servant of his order than he knows himself to be. She is led by his figuratively Catholic justifications to eradicate the Count/rival, as the church finally wants to do, and then to be the parricidal daughter (the doubly fallen Eve) blamable for the deed in the public eye and liable to the justice of a Catholic court now able to cover church tracks by handling her elimination themselves. Her tragedy, to this extent, is the effort of male rivals to set up a punishable victim/scapegoat who seems driven by mimetic desire. Because of her they can act as though the problem of this obsession has occurred only in a female rebel and not where it actually has: widely in the male-supremacist culture of Shakespearean and other eras.

Meanwhile, however, Beatrice matches the force of this admitted imposition upon her by willfully, almost ruthlessly, adopting one mimed posture after another for the sake of the supremacy and distance from responsibility that each one seems to provide. Her deliberate inventiveness with such postures is especially apparent in the final act of the play, where Shelley is faced with the difficulty of establishing "tragic heroism" for a woman who, in the main source document on "the Family of the Cenci," is famous for letting her father's murder be pinned initially on the hired assassins alone, thereby sending others to their deaths so as to conceal her own and her family's involvement (*CW*, II, 162). Shelley stages an explanation for this apparent cowardice by having Beatrice react mimetically when her priest-judges come close to discovering the imitated stance she has taken as God's avenging angel (what Giacomo calls her at V. i. 43). As soon as she learns that their evidence is the testimony of the assassin Marzio, she orally prints on his "countenance," as Count Cenci had attempted to write on hers (I. i. 42), the "shame and misery" of "dar[ing] not to look the thing he speaks" (V. ii. 85), of having an obedient (feminine) facade hiding deeper sentiments of envious (male) aggression. By ascribing to him what has been imputed to her and thus making him the scapegoat that she is being made, she regains, as the

Count did, the penetrating gaze of the Other that her Catholic judges want to cast on her. She makes Marzio react as she once did to her father's worst glance ("Let her not look on me!"), so much so that he recants his testimony and reverses the duplicity she has attributed to him by trying to look like an independently "guilty criminal wretch" and claiming that she is completely innocent of the crime she really instigated (V. ii. 90–91 and 158–59). Later, after other confessions and Orsino's absence have convicted Beatrice anyway, she leaps back to the posture of removed and Godlike uninvolvement, this time giving that figuration the features of "white innocence" compelled to "wear the mask of guilt to hide [a most] awful and serenest countenance" (V. iii. 24–26). This pose expressed in those terms imitates the position and appearance of the always off-stage pontiff, the authority behind her judges. The Pope, after all, is now reported to be "as calm and keen as [an] engine . . . exempt itself / From aught that it inflicts [through the pronouncers of guilt]: a marble form [of Heavenly and patriarchal] law . . . not a man" (V. iv. 2–5). Beatrice answers the claims of her accusers, then, astonishing others aside from Marzio into assertions of her innocence (V. ii. 185–88), by acting out the two-faced attitudes and mimetic underpinnings that have given her judges the power to try her. She has in effect put them on trial, and so they are naturally reluctant to find her guilty of their culpabilities. She is "heroic" in the sense that she fights illigitimate authority by performatively recommitting its crimes and thus exposing them (and their pressure on her), at least to Shelley's audience. There is undeniable nobility in the resolve and intelligence of her resistance, and the audience in a good production must feel the force of some moral grandeur in her attitude. Yet she is also "tragic" in showing how much the logic she assaults has become so thoroughly her own, how much it has led her by her own consent to be as prone to scapegoating and self-concealment as the mimetic power-plays directed so brutally against her.

This doubleness, in fact, does not exhaust the extent of the resolute cleverness in Beatrice's final posture. In the hope of leaving a character-pattern in memory that will belie what "ill tongues" may henceforth attribute to her "name" (V. ii. 150), she works through all the maneuvers of perverted transference, albeit mimetically, in the two concluding scenes of the last act. She reinforces her imitated noninvolvement by drawing quite clearly on the pose of the objectivist. Answering one judge's assertion of her guilt, she reminds him of the position taken by "high judging God" when "he beheld" her father's crimes against her and let the Count's "death" be the natural "consequence" (V. iii. 78–82). She places her thinking at this locus of seemingly disinterested subjectivity, somewhat in the manner of Shelley's Julian and Peter Bell the Third, so as to render quite logical, yet keep her deepest psyche disconnected from, the demand in one objective fact (the rape) for a matching external enactment (the murder). Indeed, if she does not try to be this gaze of the Other, she feels doomed to behold a form of it as the sole object of her consciousness at the moment of and even after her death. For a time, once her sentence is made unalterable, she trembles at being possibly condemned to face eternally what she has imitated most of all: her father's "eye" [and] voice [and] shape" standing between her and the ultimate Father just as he once claimed to do and her priestly judges have done (V. iv. 60–67). She briefly gives in to the Catholic, Dantean fear that the roles she has played on earth and the objects of hate she has set up in playing them will come back in the afterlife to haunt her with their effects, turning her again into the sort of object that Italian culture has made her and she had made others. To counteract this possibility she has to reconfigure herself as part of a greater level of "knowing" above and prior to the patriarchal gaze that has so long confined her in this world.[110]

She therefore falls back on narcissism in a way that apparently returns her to a lost purity and thus, it would seem, to an unfallen, Godlike level still existing at the foundations of her nature. She asks to be judged in the end with the eyes of her surviving and youngest brother, Bernardo, who still regards her as the "mirror" in which he learned "pure innocence," even though *he* is now the youthful mirror reflecting that innocence back on her (V. iv. 130). Beatrice also finds and becomes a mirror by asking Lucretia to knot her hair for her and urging this affectionate "Mother" to put her own tresses up in the same way so that they seem very like each other as they proceed to their execution (V. iv. 159–62). That restyling of her features connects Beatrice, even if Lucretia is only her stepmother, with what Bernardo has called the "Mother, / Whose love was a bond to all our loves" quite outside the father's power (V. iv. 135–36). Beatrice, aided by all these reflectors, has thereby (like the Maniac) made oncoming "Death" seem like "a fond mother" retaking possession of her innocent child (V. iv. 115–17) and restoring this child to that ideal-ego existence of loving interrelationship that occurs much earlier than the state of subjection to the culturally established patriarch. In the restored state, Beatrice imagines, she can be permanently thought of, Madonna-like again, as "holy and unstained . . . Though wrapped [throughout her life] in a strange cloud of crime and shame" (V. iv. 148–49). She can mentally attain what she has always claimed to be grounded in, a divine knowledge, gaze, and objectivity previous to patriarchal claims to all those powers. Hence she dies hoping for a situation beyond this need to imitate that is clearly bound up with several other transfers aimed at establishing hierarchical levels. All of these maneuvers together as Beatrice uses them appear to aim at a location, even an origin, beyond earthbound dominations only to reveal how much the aspirant, in creating another hierarchy (mother before father) to have this "beyond," has constructed that hope out of, and so is still conscripted by, the very sources of tyranny she has been trying so brilliantly to overcome.

Shelley's only finished work for the stage, we have to conclude, may be the best British tragedy of the early nineteenth century (a label often attached to it)—and Beatrice may be the most revealing tragic heroine of the period—but only because the play and its main characters show all the regressive modes of transference becoming simultaneously possible and oppressively interlocking, destructive even of a capable imagination conscious of and able to avoid the oppressions that result. Viewing or reading the multiple reflections of potentials in us all that this play acts out, we see as in no other tragedy how the need for transfer-reflections can beget attempts at self-definition by the means provided in primary narcissism. This drive, we find, if it does not prevent itself, can then look to and seek to inhabit a gaze of the Other that narcissism creates, then aspire to a supposed "knowledge" in that Other deploying the self as "object" according to figures tyrannically outside every person, then locate the knowledge in another being whom the self should both imitate and try to conquer, and finally reveal that this rivalry with the Other subjects the self to the Other's dictates even when that Other seems to have been dethroned. *The Cenci* is the "prismatic and many-sided mirror" that Shelley thought great drama to be because each destructive tendency—or character—being acted through theatrically gains force by reflecting others and being reflected in its counterparts.

In this way, as Shelley's preface claims, "Imagination" can "assume flesh for the redemption of [the audience's] mortal passion," if not Beatrice's (*NCE,* p. 241). It can select exaggerating analogues of tendencies and assumptions that creep up on us in daily life, often at the instigation of power-seekers, tendencies in which we misconstrue our need to construct ourselves in relation to others, usually by regarding certain others as more self-sufficient and closer to "full significance" than they actually are. The imagination at its best, open to transference, can then show how different forms of these tendencies attract, resemble, and interact with each other, how they even conceal the destructiveness in each form by making each appear to be some different activity. The building of tyrannical ideologies with many reinforcing parts is thereby exposed for the exact, though complex, process that it is, and we, if we see the process, are redeemed from unwittingly repeating it as many tyrants wish us to do. Beatrice, of course, nearly rises to this level of comprehension, since she uses her imagination enough to draw several assumptions together in forming her last self-image and making it seem victorious over some others. But she remains caught within the circle of mirrors encouraged by Catholicism, which she allows to reflect her completely as though there were no other angles of interpretation on herself or other people. She refuses to do what we can: refract the interplay through different mirrors from other circles with other angles. These variations can begin to suggest views of staged human relations that offer possible interactions besides the ones she chooses, such as playfully questioning "forebearance." In seeing the connection and difference between the limited and more widely relational imaginations, we come to know more about the ways transference can instigate tyranny or propel the resistance to it, and we even see how one option can so easily give way to the other if we choose to will either possibility. This awareness in the Shelley of late 1819 (and in the open-minded readers he hopes for) climaxes the quest he starts with *Laon and Cythna* and draws the quest's discoveries together for the moment, leaving us to view a vast stretch of the movement leading from the basic welter of transfer-interplays in thought to the human acceptance of the hierarchical transfer-constructs that enslave most of us under fictional absolutes.

The Process of Abjection

This two-year succession of Shelley's works offers as it develops a composite vision of how most human beings, and even mythic projections of their longings, proceed from feeling the basic interplays to believing in the repressive enslavements that transference can generate. I therefore want to close this chapter by noting the basic steps in this sequence as these poems, essays, and dramas work out the movement. Fortunately, at the start of this group of writings, Shelley points us toward a helpful general name—"abjection"—for the drive urging submission to tyrannical constructs. Although the various forms of "abject" appear most often in *Queen Mab,* some of them are used in *Laon and Cythna* in ways that suggest the multiple meanings of "abjection" making it a useful term. When the reformist Hermit who nurses Laon observes how the ideologies of "custom" have "blinded" even aspiring "hearts" to the fictiveness of existing hierarchies, he sees that suppression as the "fate / Which [has] made [a host of people] abject" (ll. 1486–89; *CPW,* II, 156). Then, too, when Cythna begins to see part of her poetic/prophetic mission as the awakening of women to their own abasement within social structures and hegemonic discourses, she proposes to "descend" through the hierarchized levels of rich and poor households alike to "where'er in abjectness / Woman with . . . her tyrant dwells" (ll. 1036–39; *CPW*, II, 141).

These instances allude directly to the two most literal meanings of *ject* plus *ab*. The first, as we would expect, is the state of being "thrown under" an authority by the debasing imposition and the slavish acceptance of it. The second is the condition of being "thrown down" or "thrown away," as women (the givers of life) very often are, to the deepest, most hidden levels of a structure so that the structure can obscure the primacy of these foundations of it which could undermine its present (in this case, male-dominated) form.[111] To be "thrown under" for Shelley, since that status involves the consent of the abjected person, is manifestly connected to the individual consciousness "throwing away" some primal drives toward relationships (such as that of equality) among human beings or thought-patterns. The larger Shelleyan vision of how people abase themselves by giving in to several perversions of transference is thus well labeled if we call it "abjection." The word combines two transfer-gestures that we have observed repeatedly in this chapter. The first is a submission to projections of the self as Other without realizing how projected they are, and the second is a forgetfulness of the more basic transference, of the drive that (if acknowledged) can urge the psyche to realize and celebrate the primordial ability of the self to transform itself again and again.

For the Shelley of 1817 through 1819, this self-extension by self-repression begins just after the birth-state when the body is launched into the infantile or youthful "reverie" dimly remembered by the essay "On Life." In the expulsion of Laon that leads him to absorb and seek innumerable analogues, in the bursting of Prometheus from Mother Earth that makes him seek her reembodiment in Asia, in the throwing of Julian and Maddalo onto a strand that seems drawn back toward and cast forth from maternal depths, and certainly in Beatrice's ejection from the mother that places her under the dominance of the father (a trajectory she finally tries to reverse), the Shelleyan psyche finds itself in the most fundamental cross-current of transference's motion. At this stage, as in the moment when the infant emerges from the birth canal, the self is torn between, on the one hand, a pulling back toward an Other/Mother that now seems a receding origin of close interrelationship and, on the other, a turning toward different respondents, mirrors, and signifiers that offer the emergent being a definition of "self" by way of "others" that alienate the psyche from what keeps drawing it toward the past. During this "reverie" there is both a centripetal drive toward the establishment of an "identity" and a centrifugal dispersion countering the unity of self being sought. The introjection of all that seems "exterior" into a new observer—a being who longs to be introjected by his or her own ancestors—is answered by the spreading of desire toward numerous analogues, especially toward all the model individuals, sign systems, and class orientations by which a declared "self" must be constructed. "Identity" *is* pursued at this stage and yet becomes possible only if such a level is left behind—or "thrown away"—to some degree. The pull of outward transfers in several directions counteracts the attempt to bring all perceptions back to a single center, and any one external counterpart chosen to assist self-definition is undercut, not only by all the others, but also by the person's longing to reconnect with a former state dimly knowable only as memory reconstructs it.

Once the pursuit of identity becomes strong enough to surpass the drawing-power of this initial and multi-directional position, desire seeks an "Other" among the

options outside the self that seems to offer, and be able to reflect back, the completeness of being apparently lost. Memory, seeing the otherness of the "thrown" self from
itself as surely different from the state before the ejection, supposes the previous condition to be a symbiosis of self and Other where there was no difference or distance
between the two. That state of perfect blend, though only imagined retroactively, is
projected as a desideratum into the Other that is most accepted as the reflector defining the nature of the self. The self then aspires to match the standard of wholeness
that the Other seems to harbor. The "I" becomes narcissistic, seeking the desired and
projected self in the Other, but also submissive to the "gaze of the Other," which has
been given the power to grant identity to the seeker because it seems to contain and
"know" that oneness in itself. The Other, initially just an option among several possible analogues, thereby becomes a distant absolute essence that both holds out the
standard that the self wants to attain and has been given the right to determine how
close the self has or may come to the standard. Given its own projection of all this,
the self must henceforth obey the apparent dictates of the Other's "greater knowledge"
even to begin to have the identity that only this Other seems able to provide.

At this point the self is both "thrown under" the Other's will to knowledge and
forced to "throw off" the more fluid primal state almost completely, since any conscious return of that repressed memory would question the primacy and self-sufficiency given over to and accepted by the Other as the grounds of its exaltation. From
the very start of this movement, the emergent "I" has been a kind of linguistic figure.
Constituted initially by its deferral to its past and future contexts, as in any signifier
ruptured from a previous context and searching for its significance, this figure can
potentially turn at first in a number of possible directions toward various sets of sign-
relations, each of which the figure can draw toward itself and take in, perhaps, as its
"meaning." But to be determined as finally having *a* meaning or clearly bounded set
of meanings, the figure must accept conscription into a particular textual order that
restricts ("throws off") a number of the relations toward which the figure can tend.
This order, once a signifier allows itself to be "thrown under" it and held there,
becomes the master text defining how the figure can position itself relative to all other
figures, even when it tries to possess the text's mastery. The multiple directions in
which the figure can still tend potentially, with what Shelley calls a "vital metaphoricity," have been firmly "abjected" and thus dissociated from its obedience to one sort
of context.

The consequences of this distortion are many, varied, and grim. First, with self
and Other made markedly different in this way of thinking (despite the interchanges
going on between them to set up the dichotomy), thoughts and perceptions become
separated into two distinct classes: inner or "subjective" and outer or "objective."
Because the supposedly objective "signs" are backed and held out by the Other as
entrances into a Truth existing outside the self and defined according to the Other's
master text, the psyche is now in the position of seeking those depths as part of its
search for the essence of itself *and* being governed by those distant "cores" even while,
indeed because, their actual natures remain distant and hidden from observation. The
more objective the Other and its appendages become, in fact, the more the self feels
inferior to and dependent on their hidden power, forgetting that the subject has
granted this power and has even urged the receiver to mask that fact so that the Other
can seem the "outer" locus of an identity unavailable "inside." Worse yet, now that
the Other has this apparent power, so much so to seem the dictator of what—and in

what ways—objects should be desired, it appears to have the wherewithal to attain desiderata, the capacity the self seeks for itself by placing such forcefulness in a more perfect Other. The self, finding the capacity it wanted sequestered somewhere else, has to seek to repossess that power while still accepting the supremacy of its current location. The self must try to mime the Other's power and so become its rival. Personal desire thereby sets the stage for a violent confrontation between enthroned and rebellious power, though both are really equal in being projections from the same place. Such rivalry, as Prometheus and Asia see but Julian and Maddalo, Peter Bell the Third, and Beatrice Cenci do not, plays right into the hands of the figures given power. It ensures a new or continued hierarchy because it assumes their power and their greater "height" as qualities or states worthy of desire and beyond the self. To reverse abjection by any method that so leaves "reverie" thrown away and the repressing self thrown down under such "higher" positions is to compound abjection with repetitions of its movement, repetitions that give the self "identity" by taking away its freedom of choice and denying it many potentials that it might have pursued.

Since the social arena of Shelley's day (and ours) is pervaded by such thinking and the class conflicts it both furthers and helps to generate, the emergent being will find some person or group ready, even anxious, to assume the role of the Other as soon as the self wills this use of transference, psychologically or overtly. In personal relations as this poet views them, a woman can be given this status by, and sometimes accept it from, a man. She can appear to reembody the desired completeness of the lost mother/origin, although she is mainly just the counterpart that seems most able to fill in the male sense of lack. After all, she half-mirrors him in her partial similarity to him, reflecting a wholeness that seems to arise from her being both him and not him. At the very least, she apparently adds what he does not have by giving him back a self-image that includes her half-difference from him. Placing such a totality of defining power in a woman, however, can mean not only denying her actual equality with insufficient man but also granting her an unattainable and enviable supremacy of knowledge that can make man her vassal and rival setting out either to die hopelessly back into her or to overcome and repossess her power.[112] Because woman as at least a potential birthplace can so easily be this Other recalling the origin, in fact, man fears her from the outset often enough to seek the position of the Other himself so that she cannot even seem to occupy it. He does so, as do Prometheus and Count Cenci, in a Freudian attempt to equal and/or set up a projected superego that is utterly and supremely male. Hence fathers, priests, kings, and the God they use as the supposed source of their power all slip easily into the role of supreme definer. That role is created for such asserters of power to play it, and all that is "thrown off" by men so that they can be "thrown under" this presumed law is consequently transferred to woman so that she can be subjected under man and keep his actual underpinnings at a far remove from him. Woman can use this outcast position, as Asia does, either to be the voice of primal transference crying from the margins of Western civilization or to fight man's usurpation by imitating his own power plays, in which case, like Beatrice, she is assuming and assisting the very male supremacy (and perverse use of transfers) that she wants to overthrow. To try taking over the situation of the exalted Other instead of just pursuing its mirroring of the self is to will the self into the Other's power by insisting that such power does exist—and that it can provide identity—in some "greater" place.

The best escape-route from this self-confinement of the self is, then, as we saw briefly in "Mont Blanc," a decision to refuse "identity," at least in its usual sense, as the object of personal desire. There is, according to Laon or Cythna or Asia at their best, the alternative of continually restyling the self and its possibilities according to the patterns visible in "another and . . . many others" (*Defence,* p. 488), the options of self-figuration offered by various people and symbolic orders not entirely confined under the dictates of one exclusionary absolute. This open stance, if consciously willed, can mean the imaginative unleashing of transference's continual drive beyond current formations of being. Such an attitude is the one that most "awakens and enlarges the mind itself by making it the receptacle of a thousand unapprehended combinations of thought" (*Defence,* p. 487). The problem, though, is that almost every available analogue for the process of self-construction, be it a person or text, is in some way confined within a system limited by a supposed center, mainly so that such systems can gain power for their principal users by hiding the multiple transfer-relations that make every system possible. In the ways Laon and Cythna, Prometheus, Julian, Maddalo, the Maniac, Peter Bell the Third, and Beatrice Cenci have revealed, even resistant minds can be confined by the most established myths of cosmic, social, and personal order as people constitute themselves by repeating such schemes or as writings keep rendering those constructs in different forms. Hegemonic myths must therefore be questioned directly, deliberately, and persistently in the language-patterns people use to construct and mirror themselves for themselves. It is not enough to expose the perversions of transference that generate tyrannies; countering movements of transference must visbly challenge, break through, and drive beyond the ideologies of "identity" that transfers have established thus far. As a result, during the very years that Shelley is uncovering the procedures of personal and social self-restriction, he also tries to formulate figural methods for working out the self-liberation that could break free of such confinements. He undertakes a peaceful but bold writing campaign in which metamorphic transfers clearly fight against regressive ones. We must therefore turn now to those pieces of this time in his career—and back to *Prometheus Unbound* most of all—to see how he answers his critique of repressive ideology with his own disruptions of tyrannical formations.

4

Unchaining Mythography:
Prometheus Unbound and Its Aftermath

The Anti-Mythologist

When present-day experts try to distinguish Shelley from his most illustrious contemporaries, they frequently do so by describing him as the supreme "mythmaker" among them, especially in *Prometheus Unbound* and the poems written in its wake. For some this label means that the poet returns longstanding Western myths to the effort that originally brought them about, to "mythopoesis," the projection of human aspirations, fears, and desires for patterns of recurrence into the seemingly alien "nature" that we perceive. Thus the Prometheus story to the younger Harold Bloom is reworked by Shelley into the aspiring of the alienated consciousness toward a total fusion of the subject with its objects at a distant point where the human psyche might fulfill its desires by obliterating all subject-object differences.[1] In the words of Northrop Frye, this struggle for coalescence confronts the human imagination with "its own unifying capacity"; it now sees its method of "linking analogy to analogy" as a way of composing a system of cultural and natural repetitions within which the individual can be positioned as an "identity" among identities once there is a "still center" of cycles providing a place for everything.[2] For others, who note the many different old myths that are drawn toward one another in *Prometheus Unbound,* Shelley is trying to develop the syncretizing tendencies in several myth-historians of the eighteenth and early nineteenth centuries. The poet very likely knew the many parallels between Western and Eastern myths proposed by Jacob Bryant, Sir William Jones, Thomas Maurice, George Stanley Faber, Charles Dupuis, and Sir William Drummond, not to mention Thomas Love Peacock, who most probably suggested this entire course of reading. Hence, so the argument goes, Shelley follows his progress report on *Prometheus Unbound* in an 1819 letter to Peacock with his hope for a "great work" of "moral & political science," still "far from me" at the present time, "embodying the discoveries of all ages, & harmonizing the contending creeds by which mankind have been ruled" (*L*, II, 71). Shelley's lyric drama in this view is a first step in that integrative and totalizing direction. Previous myths for him, according to Earl Wasserman, are incomplete efforts at unifying the aspirations of all human minds and have been kept from fulfilling these "syntactic potentials" by political and social restrictions on what can be joined with what.[3] *Prometheus Unbound* draws such potentials at last toward the interrelational oneness to which they have already aspired on their own. More-over, if we believe Stuart Curran, the objective in that achievement is a joining of myths to reveal the most common ground they have always shared: the preconscious "wisdom of the heart" trying to reveal its own "dynamics of desire" to itself, to face up to its basic methods of self-repression, self-extension, and self-salvation.[4] Shelley, it seems, regards "intellectual symbols," the more they are gathered into relations with one another, as producing "the anatomy of a single mind" striving "to establish coher-ence" in the "fluid" world it keeps perceiving.

But such descriptions are resisted, I think, by Shelley himself and his rewritings of myth. As he shows most clearly in "Mont Blanc," he does not propose drawing sub-ject-object relations toward a point where they become one permanent union, be it a state of being or a cultural system. Although an "I" does see an "it" in terms of sub-jectivity for a time, making the "it" a "thou" (a "Ravine of Arve") fulfilling the human desire for a counterpart, that transference must turn itself toward another rela-tion (between, say, "my separate phantasy" and the mountain-top) lest the exchange be frozen into a hierarchical fixity wherein the self must submit to the gaze of one Other or vice versa. Any point of apparent blending, too, such as the sending of the "mind's imaginings" into the mist hiding the peak, must finally uncover the continual interplay of differences (light shining through already interlacing snowflakes) that is the process underlying the attempted connection and urging it toward this interaction and many others. The linking of one analogy to another has to reveal a primordial diversity that forms relations among its elements,[5] thereby exposing identity in a fixed system as an illusion to be overcome by "doubt" or a "mild" belief. Certainly, then, Shelley must oppose the governing aims and procedures of syncretic mythology. Whether they are orthodox Christians, speculative deists, or skeptical examiners of primal human projections, the syncretists of Shelley's time all draw the parallels they see back to some early truth, belief, place, construct, or patriarch (some one identity) from which all the variants descend and which they all reannounce as their similarities are rediscovered.[6] Even Wasserman and Curran must admit (if briefly) that such a reversion to a single past is anathema to Shelley,[7] and so, surely, is any would-be col-lapsing of stories into a single future monomyth or an all-conflating "anatomy" of the always changing and changeable mind. Thus, when the poet speaks of a future "har-monizing" of "creeds" (and not in poetry), he is not really advocating syncretism at all. Given the words he uses, he is probably recalling the congress of all religious sects that ends the Comte de Volney's *Ruins of Empires*. There the callers of the assembly search for the "means of establishing harmony" among announced cultural "truths" that are really "exercises" of political "power."[18] Following Volney's example would mean articulating each belief-system as his congress does to the point where each one's underlying power-plays are revealed,[9] where each would then emerge as equal to all the others in being a momentary, speculative solution to the mysterious depths behind our perceptions into which something prior seems to withdraw. For Shelley, to judge by the various old myths about Power's descent that he notes and quickly passes beyond in "Mont Blanc," a mythic construct is far more peculiar to its time and culture, far more temporary and surpassable once its original purpose has been served, than any syncretist would be willing to admit in his search for the one order that all myths must have shared since the dawn of civilization.

Indeed, by the time Shelley writes *Prometheus Unbound* and the adjacent "mythic" poems, he is working against the establishment of "mythological schemes" (his words), however much he must use elements from such schemes in his unsettlings of the ones he now faces. Whenever he refers to any worked-out or developing *muthos,* as he does in his 1819–1820 "Essay on the Devil and Devils," he speaks of it as an attempted "moral system of the most universal character" that helps to set up the sorts of tyrannies examined in the previous chapter using the always mythic "supposition of [some] moral superintendence" at the heart of perceived existence (*CW,* VII, 88). Mythmaking as most know it, to quote the *Philosophical View of Reform* (late 1819), tends to produce "the names [employed by] religion—which have seldom been anything more [than] the popular and visible symbols which express the degree of power in some shape or other asserted by one party and disclaimed by another" (*S & C,* VI, 966). This poet anticipates less the definitions of myth espoused by C. G. Jung, Frye, Mircea Eliade, and Claude Levi-Strauss and more a vision like Georges Dumezil's, in which myth is a means of social control that expresses

> dramatically the ideology under which a society lives; not only to hold out to its conscience the values [society] recognizes and the ideals it [is supposed to pursue] from generation to generation, but above all to express its very being and structure . . . to justify the rules and traditional practices [by] incarnating [these] in certain personages and translating the relations between these concepts into the connections between various figures.[10]

Shelley then adds to this notion a pre-Marxist sense that these "values" are concepts fabricated and disseminated by a hegemonic group, by a dominant "party" striving to preserve its supremacy using them and to conceal from the public eye an underlying war between classes. The formalized configuration of a system of social rules is a "religious imposture" or world-view masking a "political imposture" or class-view (*CW,* VII, 93). In fact, myths for Shelley, put in Marxist terms, are usually outdated "methods of production" trying to suppress new "modes of production" in which human relations might be redefined and revolutionized beyond what current "ideologies" allow.[11] Prometheus at the opening of Shelley's drama has been *"bound to [a] Precipice"* for the "Three thousand years" (I. 12), during which the submission of created beings to a heavenly monarch projected "up there" by them has been the controlling Western myth in a variety of forms, even in the mind of the Titan himself as Aeschylus presents him in his three Prometheus plays.[12] That merely ideological construct stylizing a very old but temporary social structure has held down the "forerunners of some unimagined change in our social condition or the opinions which cement it" (Preface to *Prometheus Unbound, NCE,* p. 134). The change must begin with a dethroning of the construct by a deliberately demythologizing, not remythologizing, act of "mind discharging its [long] collected lightning" (p. 134) in the face of all the schemes that have repeatedly suppressed that electric "foresight" (the literal meaning of the name "Prometheus," as we have seen).

That is not to say that self-projections or group-projections into nature, the past, or the future ought to be abandoned in Shelley's eyes. These for him are among the modes of production by which minds or societies can come to know their possibilities.[13] They offer figurations that work out what people have been or can become, what they seem to come from or may ascend toward, *and* what interplays have or can be achieved between any perceiver and whatever seems to be "outside." Tyranny arises when these metaphoric speculations discovering as yet "unapprehended relations" become fixed "signs for portions or classes of thoughts" (*Defence,* p. 482) that are actually rules (master texts) for confining human expansion within the boundaries that suit an economically dominant group. That stultification inevitably occurs if the continual discovery of new relations, the modification of self-images by different images, is forced to become a self-consistent, unchangeable system (something syncretic) subsuming all other visions within it and establishing a limit or hierarchy within which people are imprisoned.

By 1818 Shelley has found that such is the case, especially with the Prometheus myth in his own time. Though spoken of by some Shelley contemporaries as a vision of knowledge and prophecy overcoming current political confines,[14] this story in too many of the versions that Shelley sees around him has not really gone beyond the ultimate submission to high authority that is set up in Aeschylus as the destined end of the Titan's defiance. Byron offers his short lyric "Prometheus" in 1816, prompted in part (as Shelley is too) by a new edition of Aeschylus's *Prometheus Bound,*[15] and there he tries to make the former champion of humanity "a sign" that "man [humanity in general] is in part divine, / A troubled stream from a pure source" (ll. 44, 48, and 49). This redaction of Prometheus, a longstanding archetype of humanity's fall from and attempt to recover an unknown origin, does praise the "patient energy of [the Titan's] resistance to the Principle of Hate" that seems to reside at (and exile people from) the height of "inexorable Heaven" (ll. 40, 20, and 18). But Byron still accepts the descent of humankind from a higher fullness and purity into a "funereal destiny" that he may stoically withstand but cannot overcome (l. 50). This unalterable vertical scheme maintains the aristocratic social structure that mythically "seeks validations from nature by retrojecting [its ideology of 'high' and 'low'] back into it."[16] The same effect is achieved in even more orthodox ways by A. W. von Schlegel's *Lectures on Dramatic Art and Literature* (1808, translated 1815), which Shelley read to his traveling party in early 1818 on the way to his final exile in Italy.[17] There the bound Titan of Aeschylus, described as opposing the "inexorable powers of nature" with nothing but a vision of more "lofty aspirations," manifestly presages what von Schlegel sees as the modern Judeo-Christian consciousness.[18] The latter awareness, as the Greek view generally did not, realizes it has "forfeited" oneness with nature because of a "grievous transgression" at the beginning of time. We therefore tend to adopt Prometheus as our archetype because like him we "desire to reconcile [the fallen and supramundane] worlds between which we find ourselves divided." So reducing the Titan's "foresight" to a sense of Original Sin, of course, is to Shelley a sign of official church teaching wrenching a once rebellious figure into its own oppressive order. Particularly if Prometheus, rightly or wrongly, has become an "image of human nature itself," as von Schlegel and Byron continue to claim, such reworkings of him leave us all chained as much as we have ever been to one range of activities, one station in life, and one set of supposedly permanent class relations.

As a result, Shelley must have decided that this myth above all others needed reopening and revision, since it could hardly be eradicated in the West from the list of archetypes influencing humankind's view of human potential. Some method must be found, he probably thought, to reexploit a forgotten fact: that the Prometheus myth has been constantly reinterpreted, that it can thus be redesigned again using all the major changes in its own history and many of the other myths that the syncretists have attached to it. Such an approach should open up to readers *every* "analogy" in these previous texts with the "contemporary condition" of the "mind of man" (Preface to *Prometheus Unbound*, p. 134) and then suggest altered ways of seeing ourselves in a newly destabilized configuration of what these texts could mean. After all, in his preface, Shelley places himself not near syncretism or other recent depictions of his title character but in the line of those "Greek tragic writers" who refused "to adhere to the common interpretation" (including Aeschylus in his own era) and especially in the tradition of the "Republican" Milton, who helped shake "to dust the oldest and most oppressive form of the Christian religion" (*NCE*, pp. 132 and 134). These predecessors all begin, as Shelley wants to, with established "mythological schema" that they proceed to reveal as transient and modifiable, indeed as restrictive of the potentials in some of the figures within the schema.[19] Bringing in marginal material from their countries' other myths or elements from systems outside their countries' own, they subject the schema to critique and reconstruction, thereby opening their societies' dominant ideologies to the same revaluation. The choice of Milton as partial model, in fact, draws Shelley into what Herbert Schneidau sees as the wider Hebraic tradition of "sacred discontent" visible especially in the Old Testament (which Shelley read just as often as his Milton).[20] In this inheritance, revealed by Schneidau as basic to Western society's ability to unsettle and reopen itself, the poet's position is that of the alien prophet speaking outside the walls of the closed, monarchical city to challenge "the mythological consciousness" upholding urban stratifications and the "impulse toward syncretism" forcing uniformity onto all interpretations of existence. *Prometheus Unbound* thus sets out, like the early Yahweists who refused to confine their alienation within permanent groups of images, "to escape from the stifling and repressive potentialities of *communitas*" (Schneidau's words) in a disruptive rewriting that even questions its own depictions as it goes and refuses to settle into a uniform system for defining the dynamics of culture.

Prometheus Unbound and the Shelley poems of 1819 and 1820 written out of the same demythologizing impulse, then, must now be reinterpreted as dispersions of older mythic patterns into new, iconoclastic, and constantly altered relations with one another. Shelley sees most surviving myths, never as intimations of a true unity that he can draw them into, but as mere leftover "stories" cast adrift from the institutions they once served, as "fables" retaining no more than some of the configurations once urged upon a society by a now doddering ideology (Preface, pp. 132–33). They are what the early Bloom saw Shelley as avoiding; they are mythographs, the written remains of what occurs when poetic interrelations become symbolic systems of control in which each symbol denotes a standard to be obeyed or avoided. When Shelley takes on these forms by radically rearranging them, their uprooted status allows them to be recombined with ones from different times and ideologies. At the same time, their way of retaining some hierarchies and repressions from the systems they were made to support does make some figures within them, or ones brought in to change them, hark back to the old restrictions, almost as though the new expansions could be reabsorbed into the ancient patterns. Consequently each passage between mythographs must feel that regressive pull and counter it with a critique using different figures, refusing to let any single set of terms dominate the work for long. One early effect of these tendencies is the sliding between and continuous rejection of the several descent-myths remembered in "Mont Blanc." Soon after that, though, Shelley must also have realized, thinking back over his early movement through different systems and the resemblance of that process to aspects of syncretic mythology, that myths are always attracted to analogues in others and that such a diversion into different schemes is a positive way by which a myth is made to negate its claims to exclusive power. The mythographic poems of 1818 and later thus attempt many jarring figural combinations in order first to acknowledge the pull of the past and then to succeed in escaping from previous boundaries. In that way these pieces do, somewhat as Curran would have them, follow the "dynamics of desire" across the forms desire has taken throughout history. At each stage, however, the "anatomy of the mind" takes on different orientations depending on which interplay of symbols is suggesting which conception of the mind's operations. That is how the reader explores his or her possibilities of being—or ways of repressing them—while mythic patterns are presented as searching for the forms they can change into or pass beyond. All of this is evident, as I now want to show, both in the potentials of myths as Shelley confronts or extends them and in his actual crossings between different mythographs in his great lyric drama and the shorter pieces.

Prometheus as Transference:
What Confines and Liberates Him

Act 1 of *Prometheus Unbound,* in fact, is the most sustained battle in Shelley between the drawing power of established myths and the turning away from them in alternative figures. This is not just because, as the opening statement, it must emphasize the points of departure from which the entire drama would escape; there is also the fact that the focal point is Prometheus, a figure who has often enacted that very oscillation in several different schemes. Indeed, yet another reason for Shelley's attempt to liberate this particular myth is the transitional and disruptive actions of the Titan in his previous forms. These shifts make him very nearly the activity of transference incarnate and thus urge that he be released from any of the confines that seem to halt his movement. Whether Shelley beholds him in Hesiod and Aeschylus or finds him reappearing in the syncretists and other Romantic poets, Prometheus in all these cases, before his binding, is perpetually crossing, as a demigod, between old and new Olympians, Titans and Olympians, gods and men, or father Heaven and mother Earth. He draws elements from the heavens down toward the earth, or vice versa, as he brings Olympian fire and forbidden knowledge to humankind or rises from his mother's depths to supermundane power, even to the point of dethroning one supreme ruling order (that of Kronos or Saturn) and replacing it with another one formerly hidden in the earth (that of Kronos's son, Zeus or Jupiter).[21] All this while, too, Prometheus is the foresight that draws forth future reversals (such as the fall of Zeus) from the dreams or omens of the past already tempting him into the heart of their enigmas.[22] In these transpositions he also conceals or reconfigures what he has appropriated and the fact of his possessing it. He hides the spark of life belonging to the gods inside lifeless matter in several ancient versions of his story.[23] He thereby molds the human figure from the fire-earth combination into something metaphoric, something from one region carried over into another, hence something always aspiring to be another thing. The Titan then conceals from the human race its inevitable mortality in yet another transfiguration. He veils in everyday awareness the dissolution of the body—and thus the fear of death—that might keep people from longing for greater, and even divine, levels of vision.[24]

Prometheus, in other words, before Shelley takes him up, has transferred several human longings toward each other: the desires for known origins, superhuman knowledge, punishment for overstepping our limits (so that we know them), command over the elements, protection from thoughts of death, courage to endure continual adversity, and above all mediation connecting what is earthbound to whatever is not. It is thus hardly surprising that he can be easily transferred, as already a transitional figure between levels or states, from these Greek creation-stories to far different configurations serving different class and ideological ends. To later Neoplatonists, he can be *Nous* or mind entering the body from an "upper" level that only certain initiates can apprehend;[25] to Renaissance humanists, he can be the good will of the cultured, rational man trying to drive through and beyond the confusions of fallen existence, as well as the laboring classes;[26] to vegetarians, such as Shelley (for a time) and John Frank Newton (when Shelley knew him), the Titan can embody the sad transition from natural eating to cooking animal food with fire (Shelley's "Notes on *Queen Mab*," *PW*, p. 827); and to the syncretists who would make the gentile Bible the Ur-myth, Prometheus can point either to Jehovah descending to create man from the earth, to our Savior on the cross (God-in-man) suffering for the sins of the mankind he made, or to a form of Noah, who recreated the human race after the pattern wiped out by the Fall and the Deluge.[27]

In his effort, therefore, to release Prometheus from these old contexts, Shelley intensifies the Titan's propensities, first for moving between regions that are still kept different and then for changing one activity into another that proceeds to mask its predecessor. The poet installs this drive as the common principle in the earliest known deeds of Prometheus when they are recalled by Asia in her second-act history of the world. The Titan is remembered there as having transferred "wisdom" and "strength" from primitive humanity's desire for such seemingly distant powers to a raised-up Jupiter (initially another reflector of several human aspirations), with the proviso that people remain distinct and "free" from a wisdom that might impose its fancied strength on whatever it views (II. iv. 43–45). Promethean foresight has also turned the early human awareness of physical change and destruction into a perception, initially, of the "legioned hopes" for the future always bursting out of once "folded" blossoms and, later, into a sense of the relational "Love" that can rapidly "bind" again whatever is "disunited" for the moment (II. iv. 59–65). Finally, too, Prometheus has initiated the first thought-language interplay in people. Now referents of language and interpretations of each referent by thought form a "Science" and an "Art" in which our perceptions (like the Titan's) both extract "hidden power" and make "divine" transformations out of all that we observe (II. iv. 72–82). These are the motions that make Prometheus for Shelley "the type of the highest perfection of moral and intellectual nature, impelled by the purest and truest motives to the best and noblest ends" (Preface, p. 133).

Hence, because this continuous, self-transforming, and frame-breaking energy is the past of Shelley's title character into which he must again be released, the poet must begin the sequence of disruptions in his new first act with an opening speech by the bound Titan that attempts a number of self-alterations. In the first several lines of the drama, to be sure, an Aeschylean and Byronic Prometheus tightens his own "mind-forg'd manacles" by defying a "Monarch" whom he still accepts as a "mighty God" even as he curses him for enslaving all nature (I. 1 and 17). But then he suddenly foresees his overthrow of that emperor as a "trampling" of a newly debased "slave" that might make the successful rebel as tyrannical as his enemy (I. 51–52). At that point the Titan shifts abruptly, not just to the sympathetic charity that many have noted,[28] but to the posture and words of Jesus in Milton's *Paradise Regained* as they confront the stratagems of Satan, whom Prometheus is here in danger of resembling too much.[29] Just as Milton's portrait of his Savior lets Jesus empathize with the "poor miserable captive thrall" destined for a devil who has "Lost" all "bliss" (*Paradise Regained,* I. 411 and 419), Shelley's first act has Prometheus (already a Christ-figure for some) "pity" the "Hell within" that a tyrant must feel when confronting his will to power in another being and the consequent enslavement of the former master by his supposed slave (*Prometheus Unbound,* I. 53 and 56). The Titan, committed to a warrior-aristocrat's epic heroism in the versions of Aeschylus and others, is thereby joined to the explicit refusal of that posture by the Miltonic Jesus.[30] Shelley's Prometheus consequently vows to replace the lust for empire with the patient "sufferance," the hopeful endurance, and the sympathy for every other being's real needs that together can restrain destructive "Passions, desires, and fears" (in the words of *Paradise Regained,* I. 160 and II. 466).

Meanwhile, though, Shelley's mythograph swerves again, this time to avoid the final ascent of Milton's Jesus to the position of Son assuming "Rule in the clouds" and hurling Satan (or Jupiter) down to eternal misery "under his feet" (*Paradise Regained,* IV. 626 and 618–21). Prometheus now aims at revoking "The Curse" by which he has wrought the subordination of himself and all things (I. 59); he becomes the Son of *Paradise Lost* pitying all self-punishing sinners enough to help retract the "decree" that once ordained their fall because they once tried to raise themselves to divine omnipotence (*Paradise Lost,* III. 126–241). Shelley, of course, unlike Milton, amalgamates the original decree with several other drives: the self-projection enthroning omnipotence, the subsequent effort to assume that throne, and the anger directed at this always higher point that has denied the self's independent value. All of this becomes the early error of Prometheus that still imprisons his self-expansion. Milton's Son turned into Prometheus, as a result, turns into a freedom-loving and quietly determined rebel against all the heavenly supremacies of the Father that even Milton finally supports. We now behold the Jesus of Thomas Paine (and of Spinoza to a degree),[31] the revolutionary who in Shelley's "Essay on Christianity" rejects God as a "Jupiter [hurling] rain upon the earth" and preaches that man need never "stand in awe before the golden throne . . . and gaze upon the venerable countenance of the paternal Monarch" (*CW,* VI, 230). The Promethean process of disruption and reconstitution clearly starts its return from suppression in Shelley's first few pages. It does so to such an extent that the modification of one version by a second (Aeschylus's by Milton's) insists on yet another redirection (Milton's to Paine's), which draws the second figure (Milton's Jesus) back toward the first (the Aeschylean enthroning of Jupiter by the Titan) in order to leave both behind in the movement to a third.

This progression, however, does not simply drive on from liberation to liberation once it is begun; there is also that retrogressive movement, second figure to first, that must occur during any figural rebellion. Because of it, the Titan must wrestle repeatedly with the power of containment and reappropriation in the older figures (and ideologies) that have created the Prometheus of the best-known versions. To free his inclinations from the injunctions of his commanding Other (Jupiter, his superego), he reconfronts a forgotten connection between three elements: his former rhetoric (the curse), his projection of the knowledge and power he wanted into a position above and beyond him, and the "Phantasm" or mere figure of the self that Jupiter has been from the beginning. Moreover, when he asks to behold this combination, his mother Earth helps him see exactly what his relation is to the figural past, whether he is a mythograph, a transfer, a collation of desires, or an archetype of human aspiration and frustration. First she draws him toward yet another analogue for himself (an apparent unbinding) by seeing his encounter with his old self-reflection as resembling one of the moments when "the magus Zoroaster . . . / Met his own image walking in the garden" (I. 192–93). She solidifies an already potential (and for Peacock and others a definite) link joining Prometheus, the bringer of fire, foreknowledge, and changes in government, to Zarathustra/Zoroaster, the first known priest of fire-worship able to contemplate forms beyond present sight and to envision the passage from cosmic forces of oppression (Ahriman) toward the resurgence of world fecundity (the return of Oromaze).[32] Yet Earth also makes the faded, hollow phantasm of Jupiter analogous to the "Fravashi" figure in the Zoroastrian *Zend-Avesta*. This celestial guardian or "pre-existent soul" of a magus or of anyone, after all, has been depicted on "widely reproduced religious icons" that show "a heavenly duplication of the magi's earthly offices,"[33] an exact spiritual precursor "up there" of what is presently being performed "down here." The phantasm that is only a decaying construct is consequently reprieved by this connection, elevated to the status of a true predeterminer and double from beyond. The Fravashi image is meanwhile debased into a mere leftover shadow from a dead ideology that (like the Jupiter-phantasm) may have confirmed other controlling absolutes even as it probably tried to overthrow some of them. The observer of both figures in this transfer must see in each one a rejection *and* an affirmation of some dated method for arranging the world. The instant a present figure or thinker tries to break from his tradition into another, changing his identity, he finds he is haunted by the sort of formation—despite its uprooted, merely ghostly nature—that has made him much of what he has been and will never allow him a complete divorce from his past, only a passage between it and images in other archives. Even a literary revolution, as Pierre Machery has put it, is first the "prisoner of [current society's] old dreams";[34] there is no other source of shapes for turning our present state into form, even for trying to transcend past figures by way of new formations.

The Earth of act 1, as it happens, is finally proof of that maxim herself and thus a revelation of what allows those dreams to retain the power they have. She does not directly announce what we have discovered in her Zoroaster analogy, since she fears the wrath of "Heaven's fell King" descending upon her and hers if she "dares [to] speak" the former words of Prometheus that prove Jupiter to be the image of an outdated concept (I. 140 and 186). Unlike her son, who sees beyond each temporal moment, she speaks out only in the patterns of the current rhetoric, the discourse of grudging submission to old monarchies in which the human race presently interprets her. She is therefore urged to repress the primacy of self-projection and temporal change, and what urges her is "the language of the dead" (I. 138), the continuing influence of the old hierarchies once produced by those very movements. Soon, though, Prometheus reminds her that his original bursting out from and beyond her, the initial transfer of a shape from within her surface toward a different realm, is part of what she and her language retain in their memories (I. 157–58). The death of that movement within older shapes *creating* the "language of the dead" turns out to be one aspect of a basic Promethean drive surging out of Earth's surface to produce new mythic figures (thoughts about thoughts of the earth). By helping to remind her of that primal movement, Prometheus reopens her discourse to the succession of emblems that have been formed, by different "readings" over the years, from the way in which visible figures or "world"-orders seem to emerge from and rise beyond mother Earth. Now she is able to refer to the layers of interpretation piled up on her or driven into her depths, to such old productions of transference from Earth toward Heaven as the Fravashi of Zoroaster. She thus locates the figures that Prometheus wants to face again from his past in a realm of "shadows" buried beneath the current method of representing her in language.

This vast crypt of once-perceived and once-articulated "forms," including in it "all that faith creates, or love desires" (I. 196 and 199), is the cultural archive of former images—a knowing revision of the Temple in *Laon and Cythna*—which underlies the discourse describing the earth in the supposedly "latest" manner. Here lies the source of the Titan's inability *and* desire to break from the past. In this "dwelling-house of symbols," which Yeats has called the "Great Memory,"[35] rest the "writhing shade" of the Aeschylean Prometheus and the phantasm of Jupiter, "the supreme tyrant, on his throne / Of burning Gold" (I. 203 and 208–9). To these remnants of ideology, now blatantly mythographs, the Prometheus of the present still remains (and *must* at least remain somewhat) attached like a monument deeply anchored in subterranean foundations and buried philosophies. Yet the vast cultural mausoleum also announces how much its "ghosts" from many different times and systems are "united" only by the death of their sources (I. 199), left "vacant" of real conceptual force or truth and so able to be surpassed even while they are being repeated (I. 216).[36] The situation in which the Great Memory places one who would overcome it is inevitably double at all times. Any construct (such as Shelley's Prometheus) that takes a more recent or uncanonical figure (such as the Earth we now see or Thomas Paine's Jesus) as a point of departure, indeed a path of escape, finds itself at least half-repeating shapes in the repository of older forms that is the "ground" of the new figure (however removed from old power-plays) and, whatever happens, cannot be left entirely for dead.

Hence the Titan is this drama, once he faces his own curses as shoring up the Jupiter-phantasm and "repents" both his old works and his enthroning of a former self-image (I. 303), is not released from the Great Memory's bonds but actively assaulted by several of its other shadows, forced to deal (as Jesus confronting Satan) with many of the stratagems used to maintain the archive's influence over modern thought. First he must behold a version of "Jove's world-wandering Herald, Mercury" (I. 325), who frequently resembles the Hermes urging submission to Zeus in Aeschylus's *Prometheus Bound*. Though far more obsequious (and thus duplicitous) to this Titan than Hermes was to his, calling Prometheus "wise [and] firm and good" to his face as Milton's Satan does with Jesus (*Paradise Regained,* III. 10–11), Mercury argues that no power or origin is prior to the one possessed eternally and inherently by "the Omnipotent" (I. 362), even though Prometheus has already revealed the historical and derived beginnings of such a projected figure. The herald of the master text then asks the Titan for the sort of submissive "prayer" (I. 376) that would maintain the lie of a permanent originator not really engendered by a shifting process: "clothe . . . in words," Mercury advises, the "secret known" only to foresight (I. 375 and 371). This secret is not just, as in Aeschylus, the tyrant's future overthrow by his progeny (the resistance engendered by an imposition of power) but also the fact that Heaven's "sceptre" will inevitably undergo "transfer" to another place (I. 373), since that was the Promethean deed that first moved the sceptre to its current position. From Mercury's point of view, this motion must be immobilized if its transfer of power to Jupiter is to remain eternal. The incarnation of transposition (Prometheus) should be made to speak the "Nature" of that drive once and for all in a single statement, thereby turning a sheer movement between words into a referent, a static "essence," which one set of words can signify as occupying one unchangeable place "over there."

Fortunately, Prometheus has just the right response. He immediately identifies Mercury as Jupiter's "thought-executing minister," a sort of press secretary determined to kill any self-transfiguring thought that might transgress the limits of the reigning ideology (I. 287). In doing so, the Titan recalls Lear's famous cry asking the stormy elements to hurl "thought-executing fires" down from the heavens (*King Lear,* III. ii. 4). That speech shows Lear's desire for absolute power over his "ingrateful" children projecting itself outward and upward into the sky, a clear analogue to the self-serving act by which Prometheus once enthroned Jupiter.[37] Prometheus has answered Mercury by revealing the herald to be another product of the transference that produced both Jove and Jove's attempt to suppress his foundations. No one interplay, then, is "clothed in words" by the Titan. Instead, he assumes and rejects the posture of Lear, thus remembering and again repenting his making of Jupiter, and proceeds to transfer both allusive connections into the basis of Mercury's function. A single nature of transference is denied by a multileveled enactment of its process. Prometheus can therefore lecture Mercury on the many modes of transference there are (the *real* secret, whatever the herald of the Omnipotent may think). The Titan goes on to show how being "trampled down" by a superior comes from the victim's giving "all" his own power to another (I. 381–82). He then suggests that such created evil minds cannot escape the process creating them, despite achieving a sanction to dictate everything. They must "change good to their own [evil] nature" in order to control it, obeying the very interplay they would master and contain (I. 380).

As a result, to stop Prometheus from dissecting the oneness of the Omnipotent and so revealing the many exchanges underlying and undermining Him, some other old mythographs, the Furies, join Mercury in his assault and try to make the Titan "grow like" them by revealing another limitation in his movement (I. 450). Reincarnating old Greek nemesis figures who haunt younger generations with allegiances to or crimes against ancestors and former thoughts,[38] these caustic enforcers of history remind Prometheus (an impetus for change in human acts) of the past endeavors to which he remains attached and of the way these have always dwindled into the very restrictions and destructions he keeps trying to overcome. He is made to feel responsible for these fallings-off and still connected with them even when he would sever his links to them, whether they are the human-made "cities [that finally] sink howling into ruin" (I. 499), the "self-contempt" and "fear" left behind by unfulfilled aspirations (I. 510 and 516), or the "Kingly conclaves" produced in the end by what might have been republics (I. 530), all of which occurred in the hopeful and Promethean but then violent and tyrannical French Revolution (I. 650–55). Even the figure of Jesus à la Milton and Paine, to which Prometheus has allowed himself to be joined temporarily, contracts as the Furies present it into the always doomed fate (crucifixion) of those who try to cure the "Deep wrongs [of] man" (I. 595) and then into the misconstrued center of a dictatorial religion that "hunt[s people with] foul lies from their heart's [real] home" (I. 607). The Furies thus draw Prometheus toward believing that these entropic declines, these turnings of metaphoric relations into signs with fixed meanings, will be repeated henceforth without significant differences. Because the Titan transfigures the past *using* the past, all transfers (his and ours) will become hierarchies, all productions of life death, and all hopes fruitless, fulfilling the darkest forebodings of the Gothic sensibility; this is the "destined agony" of Prometheus and ourselves that, if we believe in it, gives "form" to the Furies (I. 471), to the human sense of being haunted by a primal state or sin that no revolutionary effort can alter or erase. The Furies thus suggest that nothing really changes as they enforce antiquated but dominant images of authority—so we might as well, they say, submit to what the most accepted ideology has enthroned, despairing of anything better, just as Mercury has advised. For the last time in act 1, facing this claim, Prometheus hovers between the attraction of that world beneath the "grave," where at least there is the "peace" of simply accepting outworn mythographs, and the determination to wait for entropy's other movement, its transformational answer to dissolution, at which point a thoroughly new system might be formed from old fragments containing "no [unaltered] types of the things which are" at the moment (I. 638–45).

But the submissive option is never really the likely choice of Prometheus. Though his self-transformation does decelerate after he becomes a Jesus figure, his shift between different myths continues surreptitiously even as the Furies try to trap him in a consistent pattern. Just after he briefly adopts and surpasses the role of King Lear, the very arrival of the Furies makes the Titan a pursued Orestes recalling the end of Aeschylus's *Choephori* and much of the *Eumenides*. Prometheus is then saved from Orestes's submission to the patriarchal hierarchies affirmed in the latter play[39] by the resemblance of Orestes (and thus the Titan himself) to the Acteon of Ovid's less authoritarian *Metamorphoses*. The similarity makes the bound Prometheus, in the eyes of the Furies especially, a "struck and sobbing fawn" pursued by "the lean dogs" of his personal guilt (I. 454–55). His own would-be confiners help him reestablish the principle of metamorphosis (Titan becomes Orestes becomes Acteon becoming a wounded deer) that Shelley wants to revive in recent and rigidified mythic systems and in the mistaken beliefs they encourage about the fixity of human character. At the same time the crucified Christ-image breaks off from the Titan and recedes behind the "Christianity" that Prometheus must disavow as a distortion helping the Furies to bind thought within notions of guilt and sin (I. 603–15).

Prometheus has kept his alteration going, we find, by playing out the role of the guilt-ridden ideologue only to turn round on it shortly thereafter and observe it from more of a distance. His is able—like Jesus in *Paradise Regained* (II. 466–71) yet precisely by *not* being the Son completely—to be "king over himself," a current thought subjecting previous thought to different interpretations, "rul[ing] / The torturing and conflicting throngs within," be they the Furies, other former mythographs, or feelings of resistance to old forms (I. 492–93). Concurrently, though, the Titan still gazes compassionately backward at all those enchained by the Great Memory as he has been himself; he especially "pities" those so enwrapped by old self-images, so unreflective about what past ideologies can produce, that they are not "tortured" by what the Furies point out (I. 633), by the fact that "all best things are [so often] confused to ill" (I. 628). Prometheus thus becomes transitional again, almost in the fullest sense. His removal from the past's dominance is still an effort to look at that past, and he tries to pull it (and not something else) toward a different future (a new combination of self-rule and sympathy for others). When confronted by a relation so complex as to beget such a nonjudgmental judgment, the rigidly judgmental Furies, who gaze only backward, must fall silent (I. 634), leaving the past still in the memory but far less in control of the will.

Now the once dominant cultural symbols in the collective unconscious can be denied exclusive power, and there can be a releasing from repression of the more "subtle" and mobile "spirits" inhabiting "the dim [innermost] caves of human thought" too long forgotten by the modern consciousness (I. 658–60). These "operations of the human mind" (to quote Shelley's Preface again, p. 133) are all passages between thoughts, or between locations of thought, where each pole is initially distant from the other in time or place or both. One form of this activity (a figuration of history) flees "From the dust of creeds outworn" toward the revolutionary moment crying "Freedom! Hope!," even to the point where the addition of a vengeful "Death!" to that cry is kept from gaining dominance by "the soul of love" bursting from the first crossing as its hidden impetus and later result (I. 697–705); another version (a mental traversing of life's known transitions) turns from a past "storm" seen as a "conquerer" to the redemptive calm that follows, while a rainbow "arch[es]" to lift the scene from violence into resurgent beauty or a sailor dying from the tempest gives "an enemy his plank" as he would never have done before (I. 707–22); and one more variation (a poet's sense of his basic process) sees imagination feeding "on the aerial kisses [the fading coals] / of shapes that haunt thought's wilderness" so that it may transmute an image of an image, a "lake-reflected sun" for example, into "Forms" that are "Nurslings of [an] immortality" being kept immortal by reinterpretations of them (I. 741–49). Such transpositions have been at least quietly at work, if sometimes only in "unremembered ages" (I. 672), throughout the whole span of the Great Memory's existence. The production of the domineering idols retained by that Memory would never have occurred had not these transfers of power between positions operated first, just as Prometheus has already told Earth. These transgressing movements compose the very "breath" in "the atmosphere of human thought" now and all through history protecting "Heaven-oppressed mortality" from total self-imprisonment and guiding it toward outgoing self-extensions, if often quite unconsciously (I. 672–76).

As a matter of fact, this atmosphere is so breathed *out* of the psyche to exercise its relational action in some other realm—fulfilling itself in "that which it resembles"—that the "spirits . . . inhabit, as birds wing the winds, / [The] world-surrounding ether" while remaining "human thought" (I. 659–62). The author has read in Berkeley, Volney, Erasmus Darwin, Sir Humphry Davy, George Dyer, and others that perceptions of what seems to travel invisibly from one object to another lead us to believe in an electrical fluid "always restless and in motion" that interanimates and "enlivens the whole [visible] mass," able "to produce and to destroy" by way of "forms it constantly sends forth and reabsorbs."[40] At least as early as the *Refutation of Deism*, moreover, Shelley has accepted such an ether as the conductor of "Light, electricity, and magnetism" and then seen all these as analogous to the "tenuity and activity" of thinking (*CW*, VI, 50). Now, in *Prometheus Unbound*, since the world exists even more for him only as it is perceived and continually reinterpreted, thought's primordial transference refigures itself as a "voyaging cloudlike and unpent / Through the boundless element," a transitional force in whatever seems to be outside it (I. 688–89). There is consequently an impulse for change (a redefined Necessity[41]) in things as they are, since they are but things as we interpret them. There is a Lucretian "floating," the movement of a Venus (or a love) producing relationships, projected into "all above the grave" of our past conceptions (I. 686). This force strives both to make "buds grow red when snowstorms flee" (I. 791) and to recover the age-old desires for "Wisdom, Justice, Love, and Peace" from within the prevailing rhetoric of power (the Mars) currently suppressing them (I. 796).

For the change to occur as it should, though, the "spirits" (or various transferences) of thought that envision this resurgence must first gravitate—because the past image must be the point of departure for present alterations—toward the foreseer who has always achieved dethroning transformations in Western myths of history. They must announce their "prophecy" but also the fact that it "begins and ends" in an unbound Prometheus (I. 690–91), the agent of actual transfer who first sprang from the depths of the perceived earth as they are doing and who can therefore impel what they desire by visibly shifting between forms and levels of being. He is what they see themselves as being: the "guide" and "guardian" of "Heaven-oppressed mortality" first projected by human longing in "unremembered ages" *and* "the thoughts of man's own mind" as they "Float through all above the grave . . . Voyaging cloudlike and unpent / Through the boundless element" (I. 672–74 and 688–89). Indeed, once the spirits approach him as images of thought's process trying to be reimaged in his release from self-denial, he briefly becomes the mirror-images of what they envision. The reader recognizes in him, particularly since he is the "reader" of the spirits' statements to him, the challenger of "creeds outworn," the giver of the "plank" to the "enemy," and the poet refiguring "haunting" thoughts in language,[42] each of which he is soon described as having been or begun in Asia's history of the world (II. iv. 43–79). The invisible crossings in our perceptions of existence thus further the slow unbinding of Prometheus from one configuration by revealing themselves, and seeing his movement, as the forgotten past behind the past's best-known constructs. They expose the projections by which such myths as "the ether" have always been created, and they show the connection between those constructs and the outreach of thought to all its "others" that, for Shelley as for many writers before him, is Love in the widest sense.

Shelley's Titan consequently moves closer to complete freedom by the end of act 1 but cannot finally be the self-liberating agent on his own. Just as the spirits heralding Love's (or Oromaze's) renewal must be read and reincarnated by Prometheus to become "what it is [their] destiny to be" (I. 816), so he must, as they fade into "echoes" needing his extension of them to remain in human consciousness (I. 805), reach for his destiny by calling out his love to Asia, the wife of Prometheus in some ancient versions (according to Herodotus),[43] who has been "far" from him (I. 808)—sequestered in the continent bearing her name—since the fixing of his identity under one male self-image stopped the Titan from "drinking life from her loved eyes" (I. 123). His self-transcendence must be reflected back in her thoughts and actions, as we saw in the previous chapter, especially since that was the case in the distant past after the Titan sprang from Earth toward Asia. Otherwise he cannot fully be again the becoming-self-by-becoming-different that he used to be when his "being overflowed" into her "chalice" and was there reshaped (born again) each time they made love (I. 809–10). The Titan here turns toward an image-pattern quite outside most of his previous ones. Again starting with but departing from the Aeschylean Prometheus, who begins the second half of *Prometheus Bound* by seeing his doom partly repeated and mitigated in the *telos* of the exiled Io,[44] Shelley's demigod recalls how much Wordsworth's speaker in "Tintern Abbey" is unable to keep recreating the past in more recent perceptions unless that entire process is extended by the Dorothy Wordsworth (the "Sister") of the final verse-paragraph[45]—though the process for Shelley is a more Lucretian and sexual pouring of backward-looking emissions into a soul that can redefine them. The new Prometheus, then, reconnects that kind of foresight to the stance Dante adopts toward Beatrice in the *Vita Nuova, Convivio,* and *Commedia.* What the versified Dante can become, after all, is simply not made known to him without her love calling him toward her from a great distance through the mediation of other women, visible icons, fading dream-visions, and other poets.[46] By assuming Dante's posture, Shelley's "foresight" announces plainly that his redemption must be completed by another being or figure, a "reader" of his present movement across figurations, residing in a different place and performing somewhat different acts (the second act of the play), yet turning back toward him to lift him out of his current state.

At the same time the poet intimates that no such outreach can finally be extended unless the figure giving way to his other foregoes his claim to one identity, or at least to one established range of self-definitions. Prometheus soon realizes that the major figures in a relation (for example, the subject and object in a sentence) must pursue each other through intermediate figures crossing the spaces between them, as in the Dante-Beatrice or poet-reader relationships. Prometheus and many of the mythographs confronting him have been partly interpreted for him, it turns out, by the intermediaries Panthea (literally a "crossing over [between] all [the different] godesses") and Ione (an "Io" fearfully contemplating the figures of her destiny, here combined with the Roman version of Isis transmitting love between different beings, as she once did in Bacchic rituals).[47] Hence, after noting to Prometheus the fading of the spirits (I. 801–6), these shifts between more complex transfers volunteer to carry the desires and tendencies of the Titan to their reenactment, extension, and transmutation by Asia. The Titan accepts their intercession by giving his longing over to Panthea especially, and she then foresees dimly (adopting his most famous quality) the remingling of Asia and Prometheus in the speech that closes act 1 (I. 825–33). Unlike Prometheus, though, who has too often sought a domineering selfhood, Panthea is so much an elsewhere-looking, selfless means of transmission that she can describe what is now occurring in the "scene of [Asia's] exile" before she even leaves the Titan to fly there (I. 826–32) and can give in to her deepest dream-memories of the Titan's hidden potential (II. i. 62–90), allowing the "presence" of his transmutation to "flow and mingle through [her] blood" (I. i. 80).

The turn between Shelley's first and second acts, therefore, belongs as it should to Promethean transference purified of its need to retain any one past "self" or the "central" position in a mythographic construct. Prometheus has begun his liberation from any "theisms" or plot-patterns that might still confine his drive by sending his primordial tendency away from the limitation of his name *and* his story in a feminine (not male-supremacist), pantheistic transfiguration that leaves some Western myths behind to form new links between those traditions and some from the Asiatic East. It is wrong, I think, to claim as some have that the whole of Shelley's lyric drama takes place in the mind of Prometheus or in some one mind by itself.[48] The ending of the first act leaps past such a restrictive frame to make Shelley's "setting" the wide cultural and intersubjective range of mythic shapes (or self-projections of human desire) that can be urged into momentary contacts, with "Prometheus" containing but some of the possible interplays and ultimately giving way to others by his own consent. In fact, that range is not really unfolded to the reader's awareness until act 1 ends this way and so, by denying that any fixed state of being can draw the present back completely into the past, begins to resolve the struggle between the mythographic archive and the possibilities of a future dance from mythic form to mythic form. Now the reader can focus purely, if only for a moment, on the surpassing of "identity" by the sheer movement between orders defining the self as male qualities turn female, despair turns to love, speaker turns to reader, self turns selfless, West turns East, and Caucasian summit shifts to Indian vale, all in the direction of mythographic relations far beyond the Aeschylean limits of act 1.

The Nature, Education, and Remobilization of Asia

But what does Asia, the focus of Shelley's second act, perform or carry through as this radical extension of Promethean desire? What impels and allows her, more capably than Prometheus can himself, to raise the forces that finally release him from the self-projections confining him and humankind in submissions to hierarchical ideologies? What, too, is her relation to these forces, especially to Demogorgon and his various emanations? Such questions must still be asked, given what act 1 has revealed and what the rest of the drama says. For Asia is not, as many suggest she is, perceived nature, Love, or the emotive-intuitive part of the mind divorced from the intellect by modern thinking and trying to rejoin it.[49] Though she does invigorate all things with a greater fecundity as a kind of Lucretian Venus joined to *Haysa,* the Indian muse of love,[50] she can hardly be separated from intellectual effort if Prometheus wants her to be his Dorothy or Beatrice, the "reader" of "his written soul" (II. i. 110), and if every dream-vision brought to her by Panthea prompts her to be a probing interpreter who can then question Demorgorgon quite philosophically about the final causes underlying the course of history. Moreover, she cannot be Love itself, which both she and Demogorgon refer to as a movement distinct from her (II. iv. 33 and 120), nor is she Mother Nature pure and simple, despite the Spirit of the Earth's reference to her as "Mother" (III. iv. 24). That Spirit has drunk its "liquid light / Out of her eyes" (III. iv. 17–18) mainly because that flow has first been poured into her by Prometheus out of his need to fashion (or even give birth to) himself by way of another figure. Asia is a redirection of another being's self-definition, so it is hardly surprising that she still needs to be redefined more than any other figure in *Prometheus Unbound.*

Her "nature," as it happens, can be clearly defined in Shelley's own terms. First, if her qualities echo the ones in any previous constructs, they recall some moments in Shelley's own *Alastor* and his further explanation of those in his essay "On Love" (written late in 1818 just before he began act 2). In being the "shadow of beauty unbeheld" (III. iii. 7) envisioned initially for the reader in a "far Indian vale" (I. 826), Asia replays the "dream-maiden" projected by the *Alastor* Poet in "a vale of Cashmir," where he casts outside of himself a feminized intermingling of his own memories and longings, "the voice of his own soul" reveiled behind a surface more beautiful than his. The basic impetus for such narcissism, we should remember, as we have seen "On Love" suggest, is simply "something within us [transference, the Promethean impulse] which from the instant that we live and move thirsts after its likeness." This drive from the start places so much more value on the likeness and so much less on the thirsting toward it that this other defines that "we find within our own thoughts the chasm of an insufficient void and seek to awaken in all things that are, a community with what we experience within ourselves" ("On Love," p. 473). Admittedly, we fear that this community may reveal but a void answering a void. Consequently, the "something within us," being a capacity for interrelation and still suggesting that an achieved likeness may provide the completeness that desire seems to lack, composes "an assemblage of the minutest particulars [in] our nature" as we have come to perceive them, being careful (since this Other must be the self as filled up, consistent, and worthy of value) to exclude "all that we condemn or despise" from this "miniature" of "our entire self" or self made whole (pp. 473–74). To this imagined "soul within our soul," this ego-ideal that we want to become but know only as a diminutive image of what we are not, "we eagerly refer all [our] sensations" to make them "correspond to it" (p. 474).

Concurrently, though, as this image is other than the self it would transform, we must hope that this "airy child . . . of our brain [can be] born anew within another's," within a different psyche that might validate it by repeating it and subsequently use it to fill the void in us (p. 473). This "discovery" of an "antitype," an "imagination" reimagining desire's imaginary object, thus has to become "the point to which love tends" (p. 474), much as Adam Smith has already argued in *The Theory of Moral Sentiments* (1759).[51] Yet that point is always "invisible and unattainable" (p. 474), a fact the *Alastor* Poet never quite realized. The other being's psyche can reconceive the desired image only by itself struggling to grasp the signs emitted by the image's projector. At best the Other can just start to approximate in a reading of the projector "the subtle and delicate peculiarities which [the projector has] delighted to cherish and unfold in secret" (p. 474). This is Asia's basic situation. As the chalice rechanneling the overflow of the Titan's quest for likeness, she is his assembled ego-ideal—the loving but non-Christian "savior and strength of suffering man" that he hopes "it is my destiny to be" (I. 816–17)—projected into an antitype (a Beatrice) who might thoroughly reshape the figure into a motherly embracing of the world and a gathering of Prometheus into that total fulfillment. She is also, consequently, the mere "shadow" of that ideal leaving it "unbeheld." She can only refer her interpretation of it back to Panthea's dream, which prophecies the future transfiguration of Prometheus that Asia must continue to "read" and flesh out. In Indian terms she is the goddess *Asa-devi* existing to fulfill *asa,* man's desire, yet she is that only in also being *Isi,* the great mother of the Hindu religion, who became herself by again embracing *Isa,* her once-distant consort, thus fulfilling herself only by way of another's fulfillment in her.[52]

At this point, of course, there might be a problem were Asia no more than an ego-ideal sought in the return gaze of a feminine counterpart. As the dream-maiden is to the *Alastor* Poet, the Maniac's lover is to him in *Julian and Maddalo,* or the ego-ideal is to the ego in Freud, she could become to her admirer the locus of power granting him the terms of his being quite as much as Jupiter has been to Prometheus for three thousand years. *Prometheus Unbound,* therefore, diffuses that threat as early as the first description of Asia, where very different previous images from Shelley are recalled to make her a will to generation transferring power into everything before her. By "investing" the "once . . . desolate" Indian vale with "flowers" and "haunting" it with "sweet airs and sounds" (I. 827–30), she revives the *Alastor* Narrator's sense of his own loving-to-love, the one flowing into and out of him through visible nature as a self-obscuring *Venus genetrix* quietly calling that love forth from him and making all things grow. In addition, as Asia makes the airs move "Among the winds and waters, from the ether / Of her transforming presence" (I. 830–32), she pours forth, as Prometheus poured into her, the fluid interpenetration described earlier in act 1. She takes into and sends out of her form the crossing of intervals in relational thought (the music of mind) after it has been projected from thought to become the crossing of the spaces and moments between transformations in nature. "On Love," after all, suggests that the impulse toward likeness reaches out only sometimes to one being and more often to "all things that are," looking for the "secret correspondence with our heart" in every motion it and we can contact (pp. 473–74). If we enter into these motions as "ether" supposedly can, we find "eloquence" transferred to "the tongueless wind" or human "melody in the flowing of brooks and the rustling of the reeds beside them," all of which intimate and draw us in toward a deeper, "inconceivable relation" between the "soul" in the object implied by "eloquence" or "melody" and the "something within the intelligent soul" projecting those qualities out there (p. 474). Asia, then, attempts the perfection of Prometheus that he wishes she would reconceive by turning that desire into this nurturing, penetration, and infusion of all visible things, a combination of traditionally feminine and traditionally masculine functions. The infusion thereupon urges the "things" to reflect subjective qualities and so to extend their supposed natures beyond the limits usually ascribed to them when they are seen as objects. Meanwhile, Asia herself becomes both the infuser of that transformation and a loving prober into whatever her process has infused. All that confronts her, from the vision of the Titan's potential in Panthea's eyes to the upsurging "mist" below a pinnacle on which she later stands (II. iii. 19), suggests to her a "shadow of some Spirit" lovelier still (II. iii. 13), a "soul" implied by "written" signs, that may be a version, as Panthea suggests, of "thine own fairest shadow imaged there" (II. i. 113).

Asia, we might say, even more than Prometheus, is for Shelley almost the epitome of a myth-figure before it becomes a mythograph. She puts former or potential relations back into interplay in the face of the written, isolated pieces they have long been broken into. First she is the casting of a subject's (or other myth-figure's) desired powers and unexplored potentials into a mobile figure outside the subject, as the Lucretian Venus always was. Then, the moment she starts to assume a particular shape, she becomes the dissolving outward of the initial transference. She turns into the relational motion darting between innumerable perceptions or constructions of language that have yet to seem connected in normal human awareness. In that way she disperses the projector's desire for self-transformation and self-other connections into "unapprehended relations" of subjects to objects, or parts of both to each other, generating interplays alien to or forgotten by the dominant culture's current ways of perceiving. She goes as far as to convert her projector's supposed range of identities into a male-female interplay, an Eastern-Western exchange of symbols, and a dissolution (though not disappearance) of the subject-object separation. Hence, unlike the Prometheus of act 1, Asia rarely crosses between different myth-figures in a gradual progression; as when she is *Asa-devi, Venus genetrix, Haysa,* and "ether" in Panthea's initial description, she spreads and trails (like ether) through myriad analogues almost simultaneously without one of them being fully dominant and without syncretizing them into a changeless consistency. Even at that moment late in act 2 when she seems most restored to her "essential" nature, reminding her sisters of how she first rose from the sea in "a veined shell" as "love, like the atmosphere / Of the sun's fire filling the living world, / Burst from [her], and illumined Earth and Heaven" (II. v. 23–28), she alludes (as Donald Reiman has noted) to that passage in *De natura deorum* where

Cicero contrasts the several existing accounts of Venus-Aphrodite's birth, some of which view her as the daughter of light and the sky *or* of light and *eros,* while others make her birthplace the sea, disagreeing on the exact location (near Asia Minor for some, near Greece for others).[53] Each version gets a hearing in this new birth of Asia, since all of them are made somewhat compatible by the sun appearing to rise from the East out of the Ocean. Yet the emphasis remains on uncombinable origins (fire, water, Greece, Turkey) that Asia seems to rise from, through, or between. Her emergence is thus primarily a relocation of her lover's birth. Like Prometheus, she is projected as first ascending from one realm toward another in order to make her supposed origins alter themselves (to make the sea produce some light, then a drive toward reproduction) and to initiate the human perception of the passage between these different elements. Such an ascent, after all, is the myth-making and remaking mode of thought that Shelley would restore to the West, this time from an East that seems more supple in its way of shifting myth-figures toward other ones, be they *Isi, Haysa,* or *Asa-devi,* all so similar and yet so different.

In any case, as a form of this mode Asia is eager to throw herself, though never completely, into any context with which her drift across figures has a slight, strong, or potential connection. When she and Panthea reach the pinnacle, for example, and there approach a "meteor-breathing chasm" pouring out the "oracular vapour" of Demogorgon, Panthea makes her sister remember how Euripides's Maenads, once they had drunk in the same type of "maddening wine" from Dionysus, screamed "loud Evoe! Evoe!" and made that "voice" a "contagion to the world" (II. iii. 3–10). Immediately Asia, already half-Dionysian in her generation of natural fecundity, falls into uncharacteristic, almost wild devotions: "Fit throne for such a Power! Magnificent! / How glorious art thou, Earth! . . . Even now my heart adoreth.—Wonderful!" (II. iii. 11–12 and 17). Then she is saved from the Maenads' destruction of other beings in the name of restoring the worship of a god by joining this role to another that she has slowly been assuming since the second act began. In her tendency to interpret oracular signs of "soul" and her journey to the demiurge's "vapour" by way of a deep forest resembling the Fortunate Woodlands in the Hades of Virgil's *Aeneid,* Asia becomes a variation of Virgil's Cumaean Sibyl, who initiates Aeneas into Hades, predicts the future, and resembles the Maenads, all by convulsively uttering the suggestion of a "breath" that rises from the depths of her cavern and dimly tells her what is to happen in realms beyond its own.[54] As a result, Asia turns from the emissions of the high "portal" (from what prompts the Maenad out of her) to their counterpart, the equally suggestive and upsurging mists below (the "underworld" that is our world). For them she prophesies in a semi-Sibylline fashion the eventual shaking of "nations" at their "roots" (their class structures and ideologies). She beholds in the sounds and swirlings of the mists the subliminal "piling" of "thought" on "thought" (the Promethean-now-Asian impulse) "till some great truth / Is loosened" from cultural efforts to freeze it "and the nations echo round" with the "contagion" of social revolution (II. iii. 40–42). At this point, of course, she is partially transformed into the prophetic figure of Liberty at a grand revolutionary ceremony. She recalls the role Cythna assumes in Canto V of *Laon and Cythna* and thus serves as an oracle-priestess revealing how the movement in the teeming fog of history's obscure unfolding can be made to evince a will to transformation as its dominant thrust.[55]

Now we can understand how Asia, in nearly being the self-extending myth-figure *par excellence,* can arouse the forces of change in ways that Prometheus could not by himself. Much as Love, turned into the fully sympathetic imagination, will try to do in Shelley's *Defence,* she carries out the Titan's step-by-step succession of breaks from a past still pulling him back toward Aeschylus by making his process enter, all at once, every height, depth, being, progression, *or* mythograph the psyche can observe, putting Promethean transfiguration "in the place of another and any others" in every direction (*Defence,* p. 488). Thought's pushing through its past limits thus comes to be accepted, again like "ether," as the "soul" of the perceived world's dim, sometimes violent, and apparently threatening drive toward change (the "truth" that is really a revolution on the way). Within "Asian" thought and its rapid, feminine shift through roles (Maenad to Sibyl to Liberty), in other words, every established, patriarchal way of seeing—hence the earth that each way perceives—is continually being covered, almost imperceptibly, by newer modes of thought-production that will first weigh down (like snow) and then bring down (like an avalanche) the reigning interpretations of existence that would keep us where we are.

Still, if all this is so, why is Asia's infusion of this activity into all forms of life unable, simply by occurring, to bring on Jupiter's overthrow as it wishes to do? Why is Asia kept from fully assimilating the vision of the Titan's unbound state passed along to her in the eyes of Panthea, "orb within orb" (II. i. 117)? Why is that "shade" as she beholds it suddenly cast "beyond [the] inmost depth" of those eyes (II. i. 119) and covered up by the "rude hair" of another dream (Panthea's and Asia's), where all the objects that ether might infuse write *"follow, follow"* on their surface or whisper it, as in a "farewell of ghosts" beckoning down to where they now reside (II. i. 158–62)? Why, too, once Asia and Panthea decide to follow those signs to where they beckon "down, down" to Demogorgon (II. iii. 61–62), do both sisters seem driven by a "mighty law" impelling Asia's infusions and desires from outside her, a "plume-uplifting wind" that appears to come from "the breathing Earth" and to force "All spirits on [a] secret way / As inland boats are driven to Ocean . . . while [the spirits] / Believe their own swift wings and feet / The sweet desires within obey" (II. ii. 43–56)? Moreover, if the breath and the law are Demogorgon's, what is he (or it), and why must Asia confront him? Why, finally, must she make the exact sequence of responses to him that she does before she can be unequivocally celebrated as the "life of Life" riding in the chariot of the revolutionary Hour that will bring on the freedom of Prometheus and humankind?

Some answers have at least begun to be apparent already. As a projected imagination interpreting her Titan's transference toward her by reading its shape in the eyes of an intermediary (Panthea uttering verses), Asia, despite the similarity of the Promethean process to hers, must see this orb within another orb as the emergence of a very different "shape" within a "shade" that intimates it (II. i. 120). Both shade and shape, too, within the orb sequestering them, seem cloaked, like a "cloud-surrounded moon," by the "radiance" of Prometheus's smiling love pouring forth in Asia's direction (II. i. 121–22). A transference—Asia—looking back on another—the Titan's—in order to draw the first one out of itself finds the object of its search always receding behind the several layers transmuting it, especially in the case of the many-shaped Prometheus reshaped again by Panthea's dream of his future and her memory of the dream. Asia must address the receding vision of her lover the way Shelley's speaker addresses Intellectual Beauty—"depart not yet!" (II. 1. 123)—and must then face the same problem when she emanates a similar infusion out beyond herself into objects and their future. What she sends into forms in nature no longer appears as exactly what it was once it is reconstituted by its new surroundings. That is why Asia must probe into the mysteries of the "depths" in objects, even though *she* has often provided them, and why the surfaces of objects must then beckon her to "follow" them toward the deeper impulses generating their self-veiling growth. To receive, be, or project a transference, even in Asia's case, is finally not to recognize the fact completely once the movement has occurred. It is, for a time, to see, as we have noted already, an implied depth elsewhere as possibly an absolute "Spirit," a self-generated, external essence facing a less self-contained interpreter, who must assume that depth to be the ground of visible surfaces as though it were king and they (and Asia) were its subjects. Indeed, Asia is tempted toward this view not just by the distancing of transfers from their projectors but also by her status as the overflow of the Titan's possibilities able to rework (though perhaps more lovingly) his moments of hierarchical thinking as much as his shifts into compassion and self-effacement. Hence, projecting or even beholding transformation in the world, history, or Western society (as Asia does) is not automatically to join, effect, or instigate that movement. It can be to fancy "out there," away from the projector, as we have seen "On Life" suggest, something "objective" with which the projector has no clear involvement and in which she may seem to have no function, place, or future. This supposition, as well as the more hierarchical concept of self-and-other relations, is as sure to keep Jupiter enthroned as the Titan's defiance of him or the Promethean sense of knowledge as power.

Such a tendency is even intensified by—but also able to find a solution in—the fact that transference is not the personal possession of any Shelleyan figure, Asia included. She is driven by transference to drive it out beyond herself in being an overflow of the Titan, a shifting across previous mythographs, the recipient (as well as the Julie-like embodiment) of fading Intellectual Beauty, and a configured explanation for what has always been perceived first (and nearly always as feminine): the flowing of fecundity or "sweet airs and sounds" between and among growing, intertwining, or entirely fluid objects of perception. Thus, much as Asia seems to cause this process (since she keeps reinfusing objects with it) in her first appearance, her hearkening to the "follow, follow," leading her in memory toward what really generates it, makes her submit to the "mighty law" of the "breathing Earth," which her own "desires" seem to project yet which now carries her to the source of its vapor. She both emits and ingests transfiguration, being unable to do the former without also doing the latter. Naturally, then, as unconsciously the agent of what she consciously projects, she cannot see how much of the process is unwilled and how much her will actually directs or contributes to it. Because transference thus obscures itself in its veilings, Asia is ignorant of its workings and potentials even as she employs them. That fact, most of all, is what tempts her to see herself as losing what is transferred toward her and to objectify transposition once she has taken it in or sent it forth.

As a result, Asia, an interpreting imagination created in language, has still to confront, with the heartfelt and philosophical understanding she should have, transference's production and operation, its being inside and outside thought, its subliminal movement underlying cultural history, and its exact relation to the personal desire for social revolution. Her need to face all these dimensions is what really stands in the way of her grasping and thoroughly extending Panthea's dream of an unbound Prometheus. Consequently, the other dream urging Asia to "follow" perceptions (or receding echoes of them) "down" to what actually pours their succession forth must interpose between her current state of awareness and a really free Promethean movement throughout an existence differently perceived. To pass that barrier she must descend to the primal drive that once made the earth exhale changes in the weather in classical and Renaissance meteorology,[56] to the basic movement that, for Shelley, has allowed human breath to be projected into the world's deep center so that it could seem to return as an emission of vapor from the Great Mother. If Asia can encounter that deep foundation and articulate its suggestions consciously to herself, she can arouse its ability to motivate the "Hours" of true revolution, the ones that could start to transfigure the most established Western perception of the proper relation between one being and another. These "wild-eyed," eager potentials of time (II. iv. 132), presently just waiting for the primordial urge to push them ahead rather than leave them where they are, are the last restrained transfers that Asia needs to help stir into forward motion, hovering as they are with their "wild and quick mein" at the limits of the second dream (II. i. 127–29). If she can prompt the full activation of these Hours, those limits can be surpassed, and she can rechannel the now obscured dream of Prometheus transfiguring himself and her far into the future.

Demogorgon, of course, is the power she needs to contact, since it/he is apparently the motive force at the center of the earth as perceived—or rather the possibility of all the thought-connections that construct (or could reconstruct) observed existence (as the Demiurge does in Plato's *Timaeus*). It/he configures the sheer drive toward conversion and projection, unformed and undirected in itself, which transposes receding interpretations of existence into future transformations that could revive, extend, or redirect their predecessors. As a result, when Asia first beholds this "Eternal" force "Filling the seat of power" usually assigned to an unchangeable entity, it resembles a dissolution, the "shapeless" blackness of Milton's Death in *Paradise Lost* (II. 666–73), turning out from itself to become "living Spirit" in "rays of gloom" that are changed fully into new life by the "feelings" of its hopeful perceivers (*Prometheus Unbound,* II. iv. 3–8). Demogorgon is Shelley's old "Gothic" sense of destruction changing to birth, recombined with Necessity and Power, both of which are mental projections of transference's crossing between differences—a crossing now made even more entropic by shining outward from the earth's turning in toward secrecy and decay. In Shelley's most immediate sources for Demogorgon, we should note, the pattern that emerges progressively, for a poet with the eyes to draw it out, is thought's casting of its self-altering process into primal, withdrawing mysteries so that a formative principle is seen to emerge within deformation. The *Timaeus* (28b–29a) proposes a Demiurge-artisan crafting the visible universe after a model that the visible form obscures and that is known only to thought's later probings into the obscurity; Boccaccio's *Genealogy of the Gentile Gods* suggests that this Earth-daemon in his cave open to visitors is an old mountain-rustic's fabrication that began "in the deepest and most secret recesses of the earth" when the inwardness of "darkness" and "silence" gave rise to "the suspicion of divine presence" and so to the filling of a gaping "absence" by an imagination interpreting the nothingness before it;[57] and Peacock's *Rhododaphne* (1818), which joins Western-Orphic to Eastern-Mithraic descents into oracular caves, defines Demogorgon as a construct reforming other constructions of thought, as a "philosophical emblem" of an already composed "principle" produced in order to give a foundation to "vegetative life."[58] Hence *Prometheus Unbound,* going one step further and blatantly using syncretism now to undermine syncretic conclusions, names Demogorgon initially as one of the tyrannizing idols in the Great Memory of the West (I. 207), only to press that figure down even more into the collective unconscious. At this deep level the figure recontacts a calling forth from self-retraction, one of the most basic and most metaphoric turns of transference, a process that once made possible all demiurges, all the transitions of Prometheus, and all the outpourings of Asia that now need to face their motivator. There is no reversal of history's direction, even by unchained mythographs—indeed, there is no thorough unchaining of them into radically different combinations—unless this formless figural movement is reunderstood and deliberately reactivated to the point of deposing what has kept it hidden, thereby returning all Western minds to what they have repressed in syncretic mythology.

But Asia's (and thus the reader's) reeducation cannot be achieved simply by her facing this conversion within all conversions. As one who has forgotten this action, she must be inducted back into it by passing through stages of understanding that reveal the different courses available to transference's basic turn. First, in the old tradition of seekers for causes, Asia, still obeying her more conservative tendencies, must ask the shapeless movement "Who made the world" and then shift into a Berkeleyan key to wonder "Who made all [the world] contains—thought, passion, reason, will, / Imagination," assuming the contents of all existence to be finally spiritual ones just as Berkeley does (II. iv. 9–11). Demogorgon must answer "God" and then "Almighty God," which is Berkeley's answer, and so reveal what it/he later says and several critics have noted: "I spoke only but as ye speak" (II. iv. 112); that is, I have converted your questions into the answers that the terms of the questions already assumed before the answers were given. Turns of transfiguration, even ones as simple as subjects of sentences proceeding toward objects or questions giving way to their answers, move only as far as the governing code of the dominant language allows, especially if the questioner is unaware of how bound he or she still is within an ideology of a certain kind. The only way out of this cul-de-sac is to shift to historical terms, eschewing most timeless universals in order to understand how the current ideology gained its temporary dominance. Asia therefore asks who brought about Jupiter's tyranny and its effects (II. iv. 19–28) and quite properly hears from Demogorgon the ambiguous "He reigns" (28). If Asia (or the reader) is to recover consciously a genuine, complex historical awareness, she must be offered the chance to resolve her question superficially using one simple name (Jupiter) but must also be invited to interpret the "he" as a product of transfer-relations over time irreducible to a single entity.

Clearly, she furthers her reinitiation by choosing the latter course and articulating her famous history, in which knowledge seen as power converts the earliest interplay of equal differences into conflicts between subordinates and the superior "knower." A war between superior and inferior induced by transference—Prometheus being the "he" transubstantiated into the Jupiter he hates and envies—becomes the underlying "meaning" of a vocabulary seeking a God at the heart of things. Meanwhile, within the struggle, the means for overthrowing a ruler supposing himself eternal begin to emerge as the supposed underlings develop sciences, languages, arts, and other modes for transmitting a love between equals under the guidance of the rebel Prometheus. This shifting from old methods of retraction and repression to more productive yet related constructs that drag down their predecessors: this sequence is history's enactment of Demogorgon's "nature." In that sense it/he is, as he later claims (III. i. 52), the "Eternity" in the process of time, the perpetual impulse bringing about the ideologies of the past, the present, and the future. His self-alteration, because it withdraws itself, can even be used, as we saw in Chapter 3, to create the hierarchical distance between what seems changeable and what seems permanent, especially if the retraction becomes a forgetting of itself as it passes from unconscious into conscious thought. Asia thus comes to realize that nothing but the continual repression of transference by its own methods can come from asking questions that have any kind of "mastery" or "slavery" in their ways of arranging words. Even to ask, as she does, "Who is the master of the slave," assuming Jupiter to be the slave of the system that has enthroned him, is to call for a "deep truth" that cannot be "imaged" in one formation if it is to be revealed as what it actually is (II. iv. 114–16). The "deep truth," since the very notion of one comes from a transference looking back through its self-concealment, is a self-veiling self-alteration and thus "imageless" in the same way that Demogorgon is. Because that depth keeps moving away from itself, Asia discovers that there is no single "voice" (as Coleridge would have it) inspiriting the power of change from the present toward the future and the "desire" of the Hour that brings on the revolution (iv. 115 and 169).

At most there is—and even this is a projection of thought's own basis into what it beholds—a turning out (a "revolving") from retreating depths or distances, a forming of "world"-making structures from the ever-mysterious "Earth" as in Hesiod, Heidegger, and the Prometheus of Shelley's act 1 (II. iv. 118),[59] wherein much remains concealed ("deep," unimaged) even as a succession of transformations appears out of the turn. This succession, instead of being rooted in one "secret" (II. iv. 115), can only be renamed and transformed further by various labels depending on the interpreter's predilections, by "Fate, Time, Occasion, Chance or Change," none of which can really be denied as underpinnings of existence as we perceive it (II. iv. 119). Moreover, if a ruler-subject logic continues in response to such partial interpretations of the process, "All things [become] subject" to those notions as though such forces were never underwritten by a movement prior to their naming (II. iv. 120). Fortunately, "eternal Love," the perpetual denier of that very logic, is not "subject" to them. It tries to make all beings will their own transformation in an erotic conjunction with others (iv. 121), in a process that supposedly nonmental Fate or Change have no desire to motivate on their own. Love is the only extension of transference that can channel Demogorgon's amoral turn toward the moral improvement of increased interrelations among all forms of life, the conscious revision of thought-patterns that such an expansion of vision would entail, and the social change that could be generated as these new priorities spread from mind to mind throughout Western culture.

Asia escapes at last from master-slave logic when she realizes this fact is announced by her own inner "oracle" even as she listens to suggestions from an oracular depth confronting her (II. iv. 123). She introjects Demogorgon, or rather finds him already operative within her own deepest impulses. It/he turns out to be a preconscious inclination in her that can be spoken forth as Love by the heart that wills itself to do so (iv. 121). By accepting this fact consciously, Asia keeps the "Darkness" from being, as "Fate" often is, a completely external principle that cannot be directed by its perceiver and so must be a sort of God demanding obedience. Demogorgon's suggestions about Love, in fact, are really just mysteries, meaningless potentials, until Asia sees them as *her* answers to her own questions, which she certainly can because she is the enactor of Love's continuous overflow. At this point she (as once more the reader of an obscure text) takes more control in an interchange between equals where each party operates both outside and inside the boundaries of the other. She practically demands that her last question be answered "As my own soul would" wish it to

be (II. iv. 125); she requests the time of her Titan's release, and, by calling out knowingly and directly for Eternity's shift to occur on behalf of Love, makes the Hour of
revived transference appear before her as she hopes it will. Now her awareness is as
expanded as the reader's should be. She comprehends the formless form of transference's basic shift, its existence inside and outside herself, its role in history and culture, what it will do depending on the assumptions about language she wills herself to
use, and how she can command it while being in many ways still under its incessant
command. Henceforth, though they still remain mysterious as transfers must always
be, she can help draw Demogorgon and the passage of time toward a dethroning of
the fixed hierarchies in a culture and a resurgence of her lover's activity completing
itself through her versions of it.

Only at this juncture does Asia emerge from exile as fully "herself" again, as
"Borne to the ocean" of relational movements from which she first arose to become
an "ever-spreading" song joining the now separate parts of the world (II. v. 83–84).
Consequently, the conclusion of act 2 is mainly a depiction of what that rebirth means.
It means, most obviously, a change in the secondary and passive position that she
certainly occupies when she first appears, in her waiting for Promethean inspiration
as the vessel of his overflow *and* for orders to follow signs to a source of understanding
that seems to be vaguely masculine. All this, the product of a Western ideology exiling
her—and "the feminine" in general—from the center of its culture into the "nature"
of an East being conquered by Great Britain,[60] is now denied by the voices that celebrate her spreading love (and thus her return to her primordial coming-forth). For
them her new enlightenment—the ascent of her new realizations, which she has
unconsciously felt from the start—now "illumine[s] Heaven and Earth" in the manner of the "sun" that has usually been the active, masculine giver of light and semen
to "Mother" Earth's fecundity (II. v. 27–28). Moreover, while remaining Prometheus's overflow and longing to recontact him in an unbound state, Asia is called to
by a distant voice very like his, yet one now transformed into the desire of all the
"spirits" in all the elements that need her infusion (II. v. 47). The voice begs her to
assume the role of "Life of Life," the outpouring of transference that makes even Prometheus possible in the first place (v. 48). As she once awaited the Titan's "burning"
through his current "limbs" while that very "atmosphere" shrouded him anew and
made him more desirable, so she is desired as the same operation by the voice now
crying for a west wind, a penetrating regeneration (II. v. 54–59 and 66–71). The almost
fully self-aware and well-educated "feminine principle" is now equal to the Promethean activity as a revolutionary and engendering force. That is true even when she
consents to being swept up in the sound of the transferred voice, "guided" by her
"instinct of [its] Music," and carried by transference toward a "Harmonizing" of the
perceived earth with the "Love" now moving rapidly through it and rising beyond it
into the heavens (II. v. 90–97).

Indeed, while the "boat" that she and her "desire" have become rises on the music
toward the transfigured "Paradise" that she and Prometheus have foreseen in their
different ways (v. 106), she envisions a new relation between the future and the past
that the Titan by himself could not have imagined in his attachment to the Great
Memory. She sees her own and the music's transformational ascent as passing through
age, manhood, youth, and "shadow-peopled Infancy / Through Death and Birth to a
diviner day" (II. v. 98–103). Her transfiguration seems to repeat that moment in Plato's *Statesman* (270c–273d) where the oracular "Stranger" predicts God's future

reversal of the earth's rotation. According to the Stranger, all earthly beings will grow younger and younger until they vanish to be reborn into a different nature, whereupon they will duplicate a much earlier transformation in which God drew people from the earth to begin the Golden Age of *Kronos*. Asia, however, must refuse the notion of divine intervention in that mythograph and especially reject the repetition of that Saturnian age, since people were there denied their birthright (their aspiration) in her own history of humankind. Instead, she must find revolutionary transposition—or rather its return from repression—to be a reversal of human development back to the sheer looking-ahead-by-turning-to-the-past, the forward-*and*-backward rotation of transference, forgotten by most minds since infant imaginations first turned perceived existence back on itself by populating what they saw with "shadows" recalling their previous perceptions. The death of past assumptions, Asia suggests, can become a birth that will "people" the world with transformed beings now "too bright to see" with our present vision (II. v. 108), yet only if the child's overthrow of one structure in favor of another using fragments of memory (as Asia uses Plato) is revived to produce a fluid and unrepressive ideology from materials gathered from what is now buried within the current language of the earth. A partial regression to the figural revolution behind all perceived changes (even taking the *Statesman* back to the rotation underwriting its "rotation") is radical forward progress at the same time. Asia can know that because she has undergone a rite of passage leading her movement to full self-awareness, to a recovery of the transference on which she is based, by the end of Shelley's act 2.

Transference Unbound in Acts 3 and 4: The Shelleyan Hope and Techniques for Projecting It

Acts 3 and 4, following that recovery, try to project what human language and thought might construct or behold if this regression finally succeeded and transference rose from its current self-repressions into a rapid furthering of its tendencies throughout perceived existence. Here is what might happen if "Demogorgon's mighty law" were channeled by many loving imaginations, each acknowledging transference *as* that law, into relations among perceptions, thoughts, and beings now forbidden by the present restrictions on discourse. Act 3 focuses on the transition of our time-bound awareness into this future level of interaction. It thus predicts how perceived objects, old mythic distinctions, and human interchange might begin to look to observers of this transformed existence who were conscious of the difference between transference suppressed and Prometheus unbound (transference released). To such eyes, even the longstanding biblical separation between the land and the waters would have to become questionable, narrowed, and blurred. From here on the Ocean lifting its face to Apollo, continuing Asia's drawing of the sea toward the sunlight that emerged from the waters at her birth, could be seen not only as "Heaven-reflecting" but as the changing of what it reflects into "fields . . . like plains of corn" borrowed from a more inland realm (III. ii. 17–18). After all, the sea would now be "unstained with [the] blood" left there by powers at war, powers that could barely recall how they once possessively tried to keep parts of the earth from flowing together across fixed boundaries.

The human "heart" of the future in *Prometheus Unbound* no longer needs to hide "the *yes* it breathes," the "sparks of love and hope" turning outward to other people and future ways of being (the conductors of those sparks into "electric life"). The "masks" of ideologically defined class-roles, "custom's evil taint," once projected before us by thought to situate the self and protect it from uncertainty, are now "floating" away, so the "yes" is no longer "trod out" by the contortions of a "firm sneer" subjecting both the self and others to the set dictates of the role (III. iv. 44 and 144–56). All human beings, and especially women, escaping the prison-houses of language they are locked within at present, now start to enact the continual self-transformation of Prometheus by way of other figures and beings as it was envisioned in Panthea's dream. The newly freed Titan himself, we must remember, asks the Spirit of the millennial Hour to breathe forth from a "curved shell" a "voice to be accomplished" by people (III. iii. 64–67), much as Ovid's Neptune asks Triton to blow a conch shell signaling the rebirth of the world after a deluge has returned existence to the primal fluidity of matter (*Metamorphoses,* I. 333).[61] The shell just by itself is a curving of once-repressed potentials out toward rapid and myriad reshapings of their tendencies, first because the figure crosses between Triton's conch, Apollo's curved lyre, and the shell of Venus' birth, and then because it is given originally to Asia, probably at that birth of hers so like the rising of Venus (II. v. 23), to symbolize her long-delayed "nuptial," her marriage to Prometheus, in which two self-alterations further themselves by turning toward each other (III. iii. 66). The "voice" or potential *in* the shell, meanwhile, is the power of its maker "Proteus" (iii. 65), the ancient sea-god amalgamated with both Triton and Prometheus by the syncretic mythologists,[62] who combines (like the Titan) foresight into the future with a restless tendency to change from one shape into another. It is this metamorphic impulse above all others—magnified by the shell's channeling of it in so many directions—that makes the human "yes" rise up against existing fetters. It unbinds the potential for being Promethean, Asian, and Protean latent in every mode of human thought and self-extension.[63] Consequently all beings, as they perceive themselves in relation to each other, are "changed to all which once they dared not be, / Yet being now, made Earth like Heaven" (III. iv. 159–160), as they, like Ocean, transfer to earthly behavior heaven's generous pouring out from itself, its raining of "fresh light and dew" in the manner of Asia emitting her "ether" back toward Prometheus (iv. 154).

By the time of the fourth act, though, written several months later, Shelley has realized the need to both reverse and extend the direction the third act takes. Especially when unfettered humanity appropriates the qualities of Prometheus, Proteus, Heaven, and Asia all at once, the emphasis in act 3 is on recovering self-transfiguration from the outward, mythologized locations of its action into which it has been exiled for so long. This taking of activities into the self to free the self cannot remain a loving transference, however, if there is no counter-movement from the self into all that seems "other," in the way the Titan has dissolved himself toward Asia and she has spread that dispersal into all perceivable things. Hence Shelley's closing sequence tries to assume that human beings have so sought each other out in love that they have become "a chain of linked thought," a common movement of desire instead of competing lusts for power (IV. 394). The fourth act then thrusts that movement, as the third act briefly promised it would be thrust, "Into the mysteries of the Universe" (III. iv. 105), into the progress of time and the music of the spheres, outer spaces beyond the present limits of scientific knowledge, so that thought's "singing [can] build, / In the Void's loose field, / A world for the Spirit of Wisdom to wield" (IV. 153–155).

The extension starts when the removal of masks in act 3, which throws off the dominion of a past seen as king over the future, reappears displaced as the fading spirits of former hours bearing the corpse of the "King of Hours" (IV. 10–20), the old notion of "Father" Time predetermining all that comes forth from him. The vanishing "shades" now withdraw into the "tomb" of time's former definition, thus making way for the long-repressed Hours of pure openness to the future that hope to "leap" beyond any past confines as "billows leap" toward nothing certain in the "beams" of a new "morning" (67–68). Then, since the rising succession of moments cannot impel its own movement by itself—all time being relative to, indeed created by, thought's perception of it—the unbound Chorus of Hours calls into its "mystic measure" the "Spirits of the human mind" (IV. 77–81) now released from the "caves" that kept them repressed in act 1. As the Hours thereby gain greater forward momentum from the continuing desire of the thought-spirits to cross intervals in space, history, and forms of language, the combined choruses strive to transport their interplay, partly into myriad experiments with verse-patterns not attempted in act 3,[64] but mainly beyond the apparent "bound / Which clips the [known] world with darkness round" (IV. 139–40). This extrapolation to superhuman levels of the state of human relations begun in act 3, this projection of an "unquiet Republic" of equals into the general realm of temporality (IV. 398), therefore extends itself again, this time into "the maze of Planets" outside the earth's atmosphere, to make even that interplay "a chain of linked thought . . . struggling fierce [like thought itself] towards Heaven's free wilderness" (IV. 400). Once this "colonizing" of the "hoar Deep" is achieved by the right kind of future scientist (IV. 143), the entire earth and moon can be brought down to mundane awareness as though they were being observed from a distant point above them. In addition, like the third act's self-altering and interacting human figures, they can seem to dance out an erotic pull of gravity between them and reveal all the transformations, historical and spatial, generating their newly loving actions from their previous movements. For each horizon approached by transferred projections in the fourth act, a farther horizon is at once proposed and constructed by the movement toward the first. Each additional circle proceeds to rework the interplay animating the earlier ones around which it is drawn, continually reentwining the "Bright threads" of desire "whence mothers weave the robes their children wear" (IV. 414).

At the same time, as many have seen, acts 3 and 4 are too canny to accept the relatively simple progressive perfectibility suggested by some of Shelley's Enlightenment predecessors—and by the younger Shelley himself in *Queen Mab*.[65] Even while both acts defer to future points, as one tendency in a transfer always does, they are close enough to act 1's struggle (the struggle of the Promethean impulse within the confines of present consciousness) to pull their forward-surging waves back with an undertow, to obey transference's self-reversing reflex always recalling its point of departure.[66] Instead of blithely claiming, the way *Mab* does, that "elements" left by the scattered "ruins" of the past will be "moulded" to "happier shapes" begetting "blissful impulses" when Necessity attains the convergence of all its progressions (*Mab*, II. 130–33), *Prometheus Unbound* sets its final rebirths squarely against "the melancholy ruins" of past "cycles" that ought to be "cancelled" (IV. 288–89), leaving those cycles (and their repressive masks) unscattered and still visible to the point of depicting them often in far greater detail than Shelley devotes to any portrait of post-millennial existence. By setting two such different states of being so side by side, in fact, the poet is indebted, even more than he was in *Queen Mab*, to several prophecies from Isaiah, especially the ones where "the palaces [of former rulers] shall [stand] forsaken" while their "forts and towers" become "a pasture of flocks . . . Until the spirit be poured upon us from on high, and the wilderness be a fruitful field" and "the wolf and lamb . . . feed together" in a sympathy as yet unknown (Isaiah 32:14–15 and 62:25).

This poet, to be sure, must keep the transitional force from becoming an absolute God, which he failed to do in *Queen Mab* (giving the role to Necessity). He solves that problem by using his famous "negations" to suggest the fruitfulness bursting forth without divine aid from the decaying palaces. He pictures unbound man as being "the King / Over himself," for example, by describing that state as "Sceptreless . . . uncircumscribed . . . unclassed, tribeless, and nationless" (III. iv. 194–97).[67] The present order is fully apparent and denied only by suffixes or prefixes forcing interpretation toward a vague opposite in yet another new version of Shelley's "Gothic" sensibility. Clearly the "spirit's" transition must be performed by Shelley's readers as they confront what they know now (circumscription) and turn imaginatively from that frame toward an utterly different arrangement of existence not entirely apprehended by any one at the present time.[68] Neither this lyric drama nor the "Necessity" in *Mab,* the creations of a consciousness very much of its own moment, can produce the transition they wish for unless a later and different consciousness—like Asia's interpreting the Titan's *or* Demogorgon's—carries subliminal impulses deliberately toward visible social change. Indeed, it would be wrong for *Prometheus Unbound* to forget the present as its springboard or to specify precisely what the future must become. Such tactics would simply revive the sorts of prescribed limits that give mythographs their power to bind the future to the past. Only a sheer deferral is really in keeping with the unmaking of current myths and the perpetual shift toward the present moment's "other" that this play has turned out to be in our reading of its first two acts.

Yet we must wonder exactly how the reader is pushed toward the most "fruitful" kind of transmutation in the later acts, pushed to such an extent that he or she must begin to perform the unending transference of thought that keeps breaking established limits of knowledge. Negations and the speed with which Shelley's verses toss them into the past can hardly promote that end by themselves, particularly since the reader's focus must remain unhappily attached (as in the Gothic sensibility) to the overwhelming "Sceptre" supposedly removed by the tiny "less" added on it. The ensuing profusion of similar figures rushing by does not really help either; though it tries to move beyond the sceptre, it only reinforces that image's power by making parallel notions the key syllables controlling the other words, admitting (as it should) that the assumptions of "class," "tribe," and "nation" do "circumscribe" what any present discourse is finally able to say. Most of the time in acts 3 and 4, it turns out, Shelley must augment negation with another technique, one that he has to produce very daringly out of yet another that also could have entrapped him as much as negation nearly does.

He begins with what Isaiah, according to his medieval commentators, is famous for participating in and (in some circles) inaugurating: typology, the process by which a scriptural figure recalls and completes another one from the scripture's past (as the "fruitful field" recasts the Garden of Eden, let us say) or by which the present figure forecasts a different one later in the Bible or world history that fulfills it by transcending its level of awareness (as the Second Coming of Christ, perhaps, carries through and alters Isaiah's millennium).[69] As a result, redeemed man's "king[ship]" over himself " in Shelley's third act refers to the Titan's effort to achieve the same self-mastery using the same words back in act 1. Prometheus, we should also recall, is there recasting the nonregal kingship of Milton's Christ, using a repressed form of "rule"—and further internalizing that—to counter the usual meaning of both "king" and "rule." The version in act 3 then completes that attempt by instilling the new alternative into every human heart after the unbinding of Prometheus, but this redaction also looks ahead to the future eradication of the very need to use "king" by subtracting from self-command (as even Isaiah would not) all overtones of hierarchy, "awe, worship, [and] degree" (III. iv. 196). Still, if such transpositions remain too strictly typological, be they too biblical or Miltonic, the poet risks what Paine warned Shelley against in *The Age of Reason* and what Leslie Tannenbaum has so clearly seen as the principal assumption of typology in Blake.[70] Were Shelley content just to apply typologically "the symbols from a previous text to a new context," to use Tannenbaum's words, the resulting world would have to reannounce "the value of the older text [the Titan's entrapment within the words of the kingship he would escape] by repeating the paradigmatic story both texts share," hence "reaffirm[ing] the pattern of God's salvic plan" running through all the uses of the type and making them connect. Shelley plainly uses such types to make them increasingly disconnected from their previous uses and to deny a preordained pattern of salvation that would keep the future attached to the types it must transcend. An additional, more radical device is necessary if acts 3 and 4 are to use typology to effect a series of unbindings instead of new entanglings of people within a syncretic system obeying an eternal center.

The best name for this added tactic, I think, is *parody,* though not in the sense of this word appropriate to, say, *Peter Bell the Third.* That sense sees a parodic figure only as a burlesquing of an older form determined to satirize it predecessor's weaknesses in the face of some standard that the earlier figure both reveals and violates. While *Prometheus Unbound* does employ this notion's gap between somewhat similar figures and its rejection of the past version by the present one, the third and fourth acts remind us, in the way Dorothy van Ghent did over thirty years ago, of parody's most literal signification, its placing of one "song [*ode*] next to [*par*]" another.[71] Almost every segment, or even set of words, in both acts is in some way a "beside-song" where a construct is positioned alongside (or at a slight distance from) the sources of its own, now reworked, materials. The newer formation presents those ingredients as radically disrupted and reorganized by a totally different gravitation between elements, "changed to all which once they dared not be" in a relational order that unleashes the repressed definitions that the older figures might have sought in the past but could never claim as sanctioned meanings. The emergent order is in no way complete, of course; its relations are too much in the process of resisting their old affiliations and facing the shock of newly possible ones that do not at first make sense according to established systems of discourse. Even so, this juxtaposition of similar groups of figures blatantly definable only by different lexicons or modes of interrelation is exactly what forces Shelley's reader into working out how the new logic could operate, thereby bringing it on in Western thought as mere announcements or negations can never do on their own.

Thus unbound man in act 3 is depicted as "King / Over himself," with bound Prometheus wanting that state in the past and a "sceptreless" form of kingship dimly beckoning in the future, only as this succession of types stands next to vacated "Thrones, altars, judgment-seats, and prisons" now emptied of their former power and standing as but hollow shells, "the ghosts of no more remembered fame" (III. iv. 164–69). In such a half-recollection of Isaiah and *Mab* (making this scene a parodic use of typology already), the "awe, worship, degree" connected to "king" are pulled off the word back into these "mouldering" relics, implying that they all should be "unregarded now"—save by the reader watching this parody develop—rather than "O'er thrown," a state far too connected to the revolutionary violence that is inclined to become a new tyranny repeating the old, just as much as traditional typology does (III. iv. 172 and 179). At this juncture, to prepare for imagining what an "uncircumscribed" rule of the self over itself might one day be, the reader must react to the way this withdrawal leaves only the long-obscured "just, wise, gentle" adjacent to "King" as they were originally supposed to be, especially in Milton's Christ (III. iv. 197). Lest the interpreter rest on a simple Gothic contrast, though, he or she must immediately consider how much the new kingship makes ruler and ruled one in the same person, how that "ruler" remains "subject" to such readings of Demogorgon's movement as "chance and death and mutability," and how this subjected being can still "rule [these 'masters'] like slaves," providing (s)he reads and employs them as forms of an impulse extending the self beyond the self (III. iv. 196–201). The distance between uses of the same words in the two different contexts widens the more the reader observes it, and the newer option seems downright incongruous, reconstituting and reversing old oppositions, if we continue to define those opposites by way of existing lexicons. On top of all that, the future side of this scene, in diametric contrast to the dead fixity of the relics, remains a *movement* between types of self-rule. It is a series of figures starting with Promethean desire and shifting by gradations toward the disappearance of the sceptre, with none of these forward-transfers (even the first) asserting the preordained center in most typological progressions. The reader must construct the new option, not just by proposing the redefinitions of "ruler" and "subject" that are needed, but by accepting, in the new logic that he or she makes, the incessant transformation of all the reworked terms by other forms of them, the *il*logic (by most current standards) that is humankind's best hope for future equality, free development, and social justice.

That is not to say, however, that all the parodies in acts 3 and 4 are exactly the same in basic structure and level of complexity. Nor does each one throw readers back on the same awareness of their own mental potentials for releasing the Promethean impulse into full play. Actually, in both design and effect they vary across a continuum that ranges from a one-to-one juxtaposition using its irony simply to rescue transference from our ways of forgetting it to denser and denser layerings of parody that force us to confront the several steps through which our rethinking of the world must proceed.

The simplest type is best exemplified in the third-act colloquy between Ocean and Apollo, especially in the fact that it takes place on the *"Shore [of] the island Atlantis"* now risen again from its fabled disappearance into the depths of the Mediterranean (*NCE*, p. 182). Shelley here alludes, again typologically, to the long history told by the title figure in Plato's *Critias,* where the island first appears as an indistinct turning of land toward the sea and sea toward the land, so much so that "the plain" from which Shelley's Ocean borrows its "fields" starts for Critias as both "in the center of the island" and "By the sea" (113c, trans. A. E. Taylor). Poseidon, says Critias, "receiving [this isle] as his lot" (113c), at first extends that commingling by desiring the land-maiden Clito, "ha[ving] to do with her" near her mountain on the plain and so producing a host of sons, one of whom is made king while the others become "sovereigns" of separate districts on this series of island-parts interspersed with waters (113d–114c). For a time this system, largely because of the cold and warm fountains generated by Poseidon at the island's heart, governs an abundantly fertile land that lies "open to the sun" (115c). But soon the interest of the sovereigns in their own power and produce—symbolized by their efforts to erect fabulous palaces shutting out the sun— turns them from fulfilling Poseidon's will toward the lust for local possessions that dooms them to the wars, earthquakes, and sinking ordained by Zeus as punishment for their pride (120d–121c). Shelley's third act clearly parodies this final state, apparently rescuing Atlantis by restoring the primal interaction of its separate areas. In addition, more precisely and anti-typologically, it breaks from Critias's controlling principle, which he announces well before he tells the story of Atlantis (as early, in fact, as section 109b). According to this premise, the entire earth is defined by boundaries given over to certain gods as theirs to control, by divisions that human beings project onto the earth (for Shelley) in order to justify their own wills to power with authorization from a height beyond themselves. Atlantis is violated, indeed raped, by this patriarchal injunction, since Poseidon comes toward the island with a sanction to take possession of it and its women. Shelley's restoration, particularly as it makes Ocean recline erotically but unaggressively on a shore reopened to the sun, pulls a briefly stated crossing of boundaries out of Critias's account to make it stand as the truer premise underlying yet refusing to accept its original frame. The reader then has the task of accomplishing this recovery without raising a physical Atlantis that might be worshipped as a land of monarchical splendours. The only way for a mind to accomplish that goal, Shelley's Ocean suggests, is to view any spot of ground with deliberate crossings of the separate senses into each other so that the mingling of sea and plain is produced and matched by heard "voices" made to feel "gentle" to the touch or by inhaled "odours" that are seen to "float" to the point of combining into "wave-reflected flowers" (III. ii. 31–33).[72]

The other extreme on the continuum is surely attained most completely in the Chariot of the Moon and the "multitudinous Orb" of the earth (IV. 253) as transference, projected so far out as to become the "deep music of the [entire] rolling universe," turns back into interpretable images (IV. 186), into a final erotic interplay of counterparts, before Demogorgon reenters to add his coda of warning at the close of act 4. There are innumerable parodies interwoven in this cosmic sequence, many of them parodies of each other as well as their sources, and the one that most clearly frames all the others is the disruption of the Chariot's form by the Orb's. Though both figures draw elements, as is well known, from Ezekiel's four "wheels" with wheels "in [their] middles" ushering in "the appearance of the likeness of the glory of the LORD" (Ezekiel 1:16 and 28), from Dante's reduction of that image to the "triumphal car of the Church" accompanied by rings of "ladies" alongside each wheel (*Purgatorio,* XXIX), and from Milton's "chariot of Paternal Deity . . . wheel within wheel undrawn" to which Christ ascends to conquer Satan's rebellious angels "Attended with ten thousand thousand saints" (*Paradise Lost,* VI. 750–67),[73] the Moon alone appropriates the "solid" structure of a triumphal chariot "seem[ing]" to bear a "Deity within" from which the entire figure's fixity of shape appears to emanate (IV. 214 and 226–27). That shape is actually produced—and committed to future changes—by a transference in process (the "deep music"). The figure first appears as a new moon (or "boat") carrying dim remnants of its predecessor while altering them as "shapes [are altered] in an enchanter's glass" (IV. 206–13). But prior to the Earth's later infusion of the Moon, the Chariot tries to ignore its true generator; taking its cue from what many older mythologists have done with the Moon, the figure makes a powerful center out of the point where the "orblike canopy" is displaced by white light (IV. 210). There "sits a winged Infant," as the Son of God sits in Dante and Milton, drawing into itself all the darkness around it as though it were the very source of night and of its own "gentl[y] dark" canopy. Its "two eyes" thus become "Heavens / Of liquid darkness . . . pouring" forth darkness visible (IV. 225–30) in a burlesquing of Milton that pours Hell's tyranny out of what seems the throne of God's Anointed.[74] Such a monolithic center, refusing an additional atmosphere, reflects the sun's light as a monochromatic, cold whiteness (the demeanor of a chaste, indeed unsexed, Diana) and ignores its own tendency to "Scatter [that light] in strings" of refraction so that it may turn its "moonbeam" into an undiffused "power" directing "the chariot's prow" on an invariable course (IV. 225 and 231–32). On its side, however, as it moves in tandem with this throne or judgment-seat projected into the heavens, the redeemed Earth critiques the Moon by adopting from the same mythic sources *only* the inter-involvement of separate but related spheres, only the wheel-like "orbs involving and involved" multiplied by the "ten thousand" that surrounded the divine charioteer in Milton. Here there are no charioteers or dominant, deep-eyed centers, just countless whorls of being developing from or turning back into one another around many different preconscious "sightless axles" that incline away from themselves toward the others nearby (IV. 248). In total contrast to the willed rule of the Chariot stands the unruled and unwilled transference of elements within and between themselves that give birth to and drive on (instead of being driven by) a reconstituted, hence infant, Spirit of the Earth no longer thought of as a godlike force somehow "guid[ing] the Earth through Heaven" (III. V. 7).

The Orb-figure has reached back through the yoking together of wheels, the enthroning of patriarchy, and the pouring forth of centers in Milton, Dante, and parts of Ezekiel to the disconnected, self-decentering, and self-obscuring relations of concentric circles to each other that control the Old Testament image until the "glory of the Lord" appears, control it even to the point of making that glory the "appearance" of a "likeness" of still another sphere beckoning beyond itself, wheel looking to wheel looking to wheel looking elsewhere without an initially visible ground that can stop this infinite regress. To keep this infinity from itself becoming the ground (or "LORD"), moreover, Shelley has created this restoration with the aid of many non-biblical texts, each of which he allows to parody some of the others so that no one among them will dominate completely. He thereby unleashes, as in "Mont Blanc" but more so, some rapid proposings and surpassings of existing theories about the world's foundations—another reason for his imaging of unfettered Earth as myriad and conflicting systems moving into and past each other.

First he frees the earth from having to have a singular and willful impulse underlying its rotation by borrowing Leonhard Euler's 1759 portrait of our globe as a mass of concentric spheres, each able to rotate in its own direction on its own axis.[75] The axis of the earth can shift, and thus Shelley's entire world can keep changing its position from the one to which it thought itself predestined, because the overall axis always combines the vectors of force asserted by myriad different axes playing off of one another in "self-conflicting speed" (IV. 259). Yet, at the same time, these various orbs are not only or strictly concentric, though some of them do subsume others because the others compose them. As they enter each other's path, are taken in by others, or take in others, all just for short periods that will some day come to an end, the "spheres" are crossings, carried forward from *Queen Mab* without their former grounding in the one "Soul" of Necessity, joining Lucretian *laminae* (be they atoms or whorls of atoms) to Leibnizian "monads" or "worlds" within worlds. The result combines a sense of the basic equality among all forms of matter, simple or complex, with a lack of complete equilibrium. Consequently, the forms keep swerving into each other and then dissolving their relationships, eventually "grinding" what they produce back to the "elemental . . . mist" from which they all came in *De rerum natura* (IV. 254–55). Meanwhile, though, since there is no *falling* mist here trying and failing to restore matter to the lifelessness of pure descent, this interplay of globules modifies the *laminae*-monad mixture toward the more modern molecular theories of John Dalton, Adam Walker, and Sir Humphry Davy, each of whom was an older contemporary of Shelley's read by the poet again and again.[76] In their systems the "spheres" can be atoms, combinations of atoms into molecules, or molecular combinations of all sizes. Now the oscillation is between the tendency in these parts to keep forming larger or more inclusive wholes and the drive in such formations to keep restlessly seeking other spheres with which the present ones can then combine. Indeed, all these theories hesitate, as Davy puts the matter, between emphasizing the integrative "motion of particles around [their governing] axes" and arguing for the far more unsettled "motion of particles around each other" in every object.[77]

But then again, Shelley's orb of orbs allows and revises both these options at once as the various axes "spin" to "destroy" themselves by twisting their motions abruptly "over" and into other spheres with different axes (IV. 246–50). This figure not only carries out the Promethean-Protean tendency now revived in all perceptions of matter; it also thrusts, into what Epicurus and Lucretius have called the "space between" little spheres of matter, some "unimaginable shapes"—some potential constructions of existence not yet fully conceivable by perception or imagination—which the process is slowly working toward as it dissolves its previous productions (IV. 243–44).[78] These potentials are known to the perceivers accelerating this process only in their preconscious or unconscious thinking (the levels where transference presses more rapidly beyond its current positions), and even there that awareness resides in the "dreams" of the "ghosts" of older thought-constructions as *their* preconscious sees such potentials constantly emerging out of the "lampless deep" from which all the interplays of "spheres" have developed (IV. 243–45). What past constructions have suppressed, as it happens, is how often the sudden, entropic projection of radical reshapings has instigated the transitions between the previous "cycles" of the earth we now perceive. When the reborn Earth-Spirit shoots a beam of enlightened archeological investigation into the earth's layered depths to "cancel" their excessive influence over the future (IV. 270 and 289), the probing reveals in these realms of decay the continual piling of unexpected and almost unrelated shapes on top of one another, especially when "The anatomies of unknown winged things" lie in fossilized form over different "prodigious shapes" from another time "huddled" together on their own level, all in "the dark black deep" (IV. 300–303).

True, in just the way some readers have noted, the poet is here repeating details from James Parkinson's *Organic Remains of a Former World* (1804–11) and its dependence on the "catastrophe" theory of the earth's abrupt and violent reformations throughout history advanced in the eighteenth century by the Comte de Buffon and Georges Cuvier.[79] The Dalton-Walker sense of molecular rotation is now parodied and extended by the tendency in Parkinsonian substance to seek an "amelioration of its [decaying] materials" in a "newly formed world" suddenly renovated by a new "affinity" between all its "atoms." Shelley, however, adds speed to that inclination by making each formation (or sphere) of earthly elements defer to its as yet "unimagined" ameliorations even before the current structure is completely achieved. Now "the melancholy ruins / Of cancelled cycles," natural and cultural (including the contents of the Great Memory), can reveal constantly—as the Spirits of the Mind could only wish such cycles would do in act 1—"the animation of delight," the loving colliding and "blending" that later "brings different [shapes] forth" throughout all perceived nature, as the basis of hope for all the students of history who can rediscover that movement in their collective unconscious (IV. 288–89, 322, and 344). Once that hope is celebrated as bearing ahead and not ruling the Spirit of the Earth, the "multitudinous Orb" can send it forth as erotic play to "penetrate [the] frozen frame" of the wrongly mythologized Moon (IV. 328). The latter's cold fixities can then be perceived as "loosened into living fountains" of desire and perpetual change, and the myriad transfers of the Earth's wheels within wheels can be mirrored in the new "living shapes" that appear to frolic on the Moon's "bosom" (IV. 357–65), all in a scandalous parody that turns the established Earth-Moon relation into the closing dance and consummation of a highly erotic comedy.

Clearly the reader cannot think out *this* future reversal simply by accepting and furthering the interplay of his or her perceptions, thoughts, and readings. Especially if he or she is to build any bridges over the gap in the text (at IV. 269) separating the interaction of the spheres from the earth's deep layers of fossils, the reader must, though "the Orb whirls, swifter than [any one person's] thought" (IV. 275), transfer that "self-destroying swiftness" into the cancelled layers to make the wheel within wheel cause and emerge from the "ruin within ruin" that at first just seems to lie there (IV. 295). The text does encourage that reading in the parallels connecting the two different passages set within "the deep" (IV. 243–50 and 300–15), but the reader must begin producing the link, given his or her bound position (like the Titan's) in one of the king-centered cycles that ought to be cancelled, by seeing what Demogorgan finally warns us we must see: the production of Hope's foundations and objectives from the "wrecks" of its own past endeavors (IV. 573–74). To have that insight in our present circumstances, we must exhibit the virtues of Shelley's bound Prometheus that will always be needed, even in a better future, whenever transposition is turned regressively into dominion (as it easily can be). We must "defy" the notion of "Power" seen as "Omnipotent" by offering as alternative standards or centers for being such forward-looking, outward-tending, and self-effacing stances as the "Gentleness" of an all-forgiving Dantean Beatrice and the "Endurance" of a nonviolent, ever-hopeful Christ (IV. 572 and 562). If enough of us open ourselves to transference to that extent, the "Bright threads" of our projective and interconnective "dream[ing]" will pass into, through, and beyond the apparently "cold mass / Of marble and of colour" left to us by the past (IV. 412–14), just as the Earth's interplay of spheres penetrates and recreates the Moon before it. When we can start or conceive consciously of such a movement, in fact, we are already installing the swiftness of the spheres into the succession of the previous cycles we perceive. The history that seems to bind us soon appears to provide the radical shifts that we can employ differently in newer "spheres" of social production to drive our present orders past themselves toward an "unquiet Republic" of free and continual self-revision.

The Reemergent Intertext and the Mythographic Lyrics

And yet a problem remains. Though Shelley wants his parody-typology to be continued by his readers outside the boundaries of his text, he knows that a mere attitude, albeit open to transference, is not enough by itself to keep the "Bright threads" of desire reweaving their constructions. The end of act 4 may provide suggestions for how humanity and what it perceives can start to recover transposition after that process has been made to repress itself. But the reader cannot perform the actual recovery unless there is an available mode of production to reuse, one that Western imaginations can always employ—despite frequent changes in its methods—to turn the wrecks of past human hopes into redemptive transformations of their features. Such a mode must be recoverable, first, in the deepest levels of the artifacts left behind by our culture's past and, concurrently, in the "back" of every person's psyche, in a preconscious mobility empowering changes in our conscious orientations. Ultimately these two "deep structures" must finally be one and the same. This mode must operate in the "dreams" of those "ghosts" residing in the "caves" of the Great Memory upon which every mind rests. By way of the mode's procedure, too, the constructs retained by that Memory must be drawn into those depths. There such figures can be reangled and recombined, all under the force of a subliminal impulse to merge existing distinctions that does not try to efface the differences to produce a settled unity. Moreover, this activity should not be the exclusive property of any one mind, group, work, or stage in cultural history. It must be reexposed as a culturally pervasive, if dimly apprehendable, movement in the background, out of which truly benevolent, revisionary, and relational thought can keep being formed.

Surely this mode and its required features are what Shelley intimates near the midpoint of act 3 when a reunited and freed Prometheus and Asia retire to a "cave" where they make "strange combinations" out of many "echoes of the human world" hurtling in from the different corners of the globe (III. iii. 10, 32, and 44). Here the cultural symbols "Prometheus" and "Asia" revert completely to their most primordial drives (their "dreams"). Now they can cross toward the "Shadow of beauty unbeheld" in each other's forms and so transfigure all they behold by entering into perpetual intercourse (verbal and physical) with one another. Meanwhile, the enclosure gathering in what they transform can become a deep conflation of the Great Memory *and* newer human perceptions by rapidly combining "echoes" of many earlier repositories that have all symbolized a comprehensive awareness of existence. The tributaries to this locus include Plato's cave of the various shadows we perceive; Homer's cave of the nymphs (depicted by Porphypy as figuring forth the basic elements of the sublunary world);[80] Zoroaster's cave of world-forms "in the mountains of Persia . . . florid and watered with fountains" (as in III. iii. 10–14);[81] ancient Greek and Roman temples open to "the ever-moving air" (III. iii. 18) to admit all the sights and sounds of city or country, land, or sea (see *L*, II, 73); the oracular cave of the Sibyl—or the locus of Demogorgon's pouring forth of transformation—whence the Earth sends out its vapor to be interpreted compassionately or cruelly (III. iii. 124–30); the retirement Lear hopes for, after he rejoins his long-lost Cordelia, in which he plans for them to "take upon's the mystery of things / As if we were God's spies" (*King Lear,* V. iii. 16–17); the Aeolian lyre, best described by Coleridge, here seen as receiving a wind already "enamoured" of the different sounds that relational thought can make from mere motion (III. iii. 36–37); Shelley's own "still cave" of Poesy attracted to all the "ghosts" flowing into it throughout "Mont Blanc"; and even "the mountainous ruins of the Baths of Caracalla," upon which much of *Prometheus Unbound* was written (if we believe Shelley's own testimony in his preface), wherein "winding labyrinths" (*NCE,* p. 133) offer "mossy seats" or "rough walls . . . clothed with long soft grass" (III. iii. 20–21) and yet admit the "sky of Rome" with the "new life" of an "awakening spring" (p. 133) that brings along the atmosphere of a brave new world resembling the one that is dawning all through act 3.

These monuments, memories, or quotations are not simply blended in the Promethean cave, however. In the manner of the myth-figures inhabiting the cavern, they remain "differences" impinging on each other without either "discord" or total compatibility (III. iii. 39–40), somewhat like the related strands of the already constructed lyre awaiting the influx of thoughts that "echo" the present state of humankind. Consequently, the incoming "apparitions" are "dim at first" as they are viewed through the lenses (or lines or strands) of established metaphors for how the world is interpreted (III. iii. 49). The "low voice of love" in each visitor is "almost unheard" (iii. 45) until each enters into the entire labyrinth of metaphors where the various gathered and half-blended old figures for knowledge modify and, more importantly, desire one another. The longing in each entering shadow, though, is not entirely fulfilled in a new "radiant" transfiguration of it (iii. 50) unless the attraction between the cave-figures is intensified and altered by the intercourse of Prometheus and Asia, the ultimate male and female enactors of transference. Only in what they do at the heart of the cave, at a center that "entangle[s]" all the cavern's ingredients in multiple and always intertwining combinations (iii. 30), does the "mind" acting through its productions "embrace" a "beauty" that turns the apparition from a dying "phantom" into a newly arisen "form" on which newly "gathered rays" of "reality" are "cast" (iii. 50–53). This sublime transumption does not occur because masculine Prometheus is "mind" making love to the "beauty" of Asia;[82] the feminine Asia has repeatedly longed for the embrace of Intellectual Beauty in the form of a self-altering Prometheus, even as the Titan has been a St. Preux-Abelard desiring the same motion in the visage of a Julie-Eloise. From the perspective of any character in this interrelational—and thus altogether androgynous—center,[83] an instant of thought in one figure is reshaped beyond itself by the process of the other's Intellectual Beauty. That process (the one composing the cave), after all, conflates different emanations or interpretations (the rays) of perceived life, transforms each of them by way of one another, and then focuses all the rays on a recomposition of every "echo of the heart" impinging on this glorious intercourse (iii. 47). In another parody, then, this one challenging the most established concepts of how people interpret life, a newly born thought-shadow is unaware of the full "reality" it can join until it has been read through all the lenses that can be trained upon it by thought or memory and so distended into its widest potential of relations with other thoughts.[84]

Some readers, of course, will point to that suggestion as proof that this cave incarnates the power of the individual poetic imagination, the true Shelleyan basis for future revolutions in the thinking of all humankind.[85] But Shelley has taken pains to locate this "entangling" outside the personal consciousness, though all minds (especially those of poets) can and should seek it out in every archive of the cultural memory. The products of time-bound imagination plainly come for self-transcendence to this "dwelling" exempt from much of the world's "ebbs and flows" (III. iii. 23–25), and, once the Titan and Asia are fully restored to self-extension and intercourse within this recess, it remains in Shelley's lyrical drama as part of the backdrop underpinning all the future parodic re-visions of acts 3 and 4 (*NCE*, pp. 189 and 194). For this poet there must be—and we should more consciously recognize that there is—a transpersonal level of sheer figures inhabited by all the world's mythographs irrespective of the systems they serve, in which each shape veers toward all the others it resembles (or would join to itself) without finalizing any combination until the conscious will calls one forth from its depths. Even syncretic mythography would be impossible without this preexistent interplay, yet the latter puts the former in question by eventually dissipating all syncretic conflations. To be unbound from a domineering system, even from the Great Memory, is automatically to return (as Prometheus does) to this serene but teeming clearinghouse of figural potentialities. To be Prometheus (or Asia) as well as being unbound is to dissolve into being the many-shaped, almost invisible, energizer, channeler, and performer of this vast mythographic interplay. No human conception, of self, society, or nature, can be transmogrified from what it "has been" to what it "shall be" until it has "sped" to, passed through, and reemerged from this Promethean-Asian "giving and returning" that waits to process all further thinking and is furthered by the processes of thought and art moving through it (III. iii. 40 and 60).

As in Asia's quest for Demogorgon, this eternal dance must be approached gradually by stages. A person can start simply by modeling domestic and social life on the small, loving community of the Promethean cave, fashioning a household of well-informed equals (men and women) who both retire into intimate, creative conversation and look out to the desires of humankind in general to find ways of giving them form and fulfillment in their intercourse.[86] The next step—the application of that pattern—at once dictates more retreats into authorial privacy and more immersions of the self in the long-term movement of political, cultural, and symbolic transformation. Hence Shelley writes (or pictures himself as writing) *Prometheus Unbound* alone in the ruins of ancient baths, in a space (since all roads lead to Rome) where past artifacts, present politics, natural decay, personal desires, and his individual crossing of ideologies dovetail in a serene semi-eternity subtly permeated by the mosses and air of change. Such surroundings emphasize the mouldering, covered-over antiquity, almost the near-irrelevance, of the poet's sources but also allow his mind to fall back on the playful combination of now groundless artifacts with newer perceptions, in which the former are redesigned to pursue the latter's desires.[87] In this situation the artifact Prometheus, with his companion-figures, is partly what he is in the "deserted . . . temple" standing "beside" and above the cave of act 3: one of the "Praxitelean shapes" with "marble smiles" remaining "unchanged" as a traditional symbol of the revolution that began with the bringing-down of fire (III. iii. 161–75 and 24). A statue in the style of Praxiteles, though, is "living imagery" for Shelley, a marble assertion of a figure's desire for additional motion, casting forth that "love" (like fire) into the "hushed air" around itself (iii. 164–67).[88] It thus draws the eye of the retrospective viewer, especially if it is a properly dynamic Prometheus, to the side of it and down toward the mobility surging up through its base, to the cave and its loosing of the statue's desire into the "infinite modes of expression" it can assume or link itself to.[89] At this stage of the poet's awareness, he rediscovers his ideal domestic society in the figural interplay underlying the already half-playful forms of antiquity. His own interlaced consciousness, his social sense, and his probing of the Great Memory all the way down to what it depends on and represses: these merge to glance between each other, thereby bringing the poet to a conscious knowledge of the cultural intertext and a need to challenge bounded myths deliberately using what the fluid base provides.

Once Shelley assumes all this, every sight, sound, feeling, political stance, or symbolic shaping of thought in his eyes must be opened out into all its knowable relations and contexts by being processed through this "labyrinth's" achievement of playful reconnections. In that expansion, as in Rome or the cave, the processed element must initially be referred to some analogous mythographs still visible, like Prometheus, in the temple of tradition. Beyond that, however, the set of allusions has to pull the elements into an intercourse among them and a seduction of still other traditions into that play, so much so that the consciousness describing the object must seem overcome and borne away by this activity, contained only by the limits that combined verbal conventions form in order to achieve a compatibility for the moment.

Such, in fact, is the governing procedure in nearly all the shorter poems written alongside the later acts of *Prometheus Unbound* or shortly after its publication in mid-1820. The west wind, the cloud, and the sky-lark, in the different pieces addressed to or spoken by them, all start out as half-Western, half-Eastern god-figures, ensconced in either chariots ("West Wind," l. 6), "skiey bowers" ("The Cloud," l. 17), or Yahweh-like "cloud[s] of fire" (the means by which "thou springest" away "From the earth" in "To a Sky-Lark," ll. 7–8). Yet each of these formations is translated again and again, not so much by the crossings of space urged on by the mobility inherent in winds, clouds, or birds, but by these already composite myth-figures sidling over to couple themselves to ones from many different contexts. The west wind has no sooner become the angelic, Protean, Triton-like, and Mars-like blower of the "clarion" or war-trumpet signaling cosmic, natural, and political revolutions (l. 10) than it is turned into the Hindu oscillation between Siva and Vishnu, "Destroyer and Preserver" (l. 14),[90] the visible effects of Dionysian superstition on the "hair . . . Of some fierce Maenad" in a frenzy of worship (ll. 20–21),[91] and the "Dirge / Of the dying year" from Coleridge's ode to the end of 1796 (ll. 23–24),[92] all the while leaving behind the most central gods of the various systems from which each of these is taken. The cloud, in its turn, speaks as the Nepheliads (or cloud-nymphs) do in Leigh Hunt's *Foliage* (1818)[93] only until it "wield[s] the flail of the lashing hail" as a sort of Boreas or punishing Neptune whipping his horses across the sky (l. 11). The latter analogue is then lifted out of the cloud, which thus becomes an enchanted boat like Asia's "piloted" by (not piloting) Zeus-Jupiter's "lightning" (l. 18), yet only as that electricity—suddenly Promethean—seeks an answering charge among the Oceanids, "Lured by the love of the genii that move / In the depths of the purple sea" (ll. 23–24). Meanwhile, the skylark is kept from assuming the oppressive functions of Yahweh by being made to recall the Hesiodic interplay of light and *eros* that first molded combinations from chaos "Like an unembodied joy whose race is just begun" (l. 15). This transitory and transitional motion prior to images of it, beginning chiefly as the "overflow[ing]" sonority (l. 30) of Wordsworth's "To the Cuckoo," thereby gains a license to dart over to and be "like" any self-transforming shape that thought can remember, be it a "glow-worm golden" or the "Sound of vernal showers" (ll. 46 and 56). Such an impetus can

make the likenesses adjacent to each other using the slightest of linking elements, such
as the glow-worm's "Scattering" of its "aerial hue" in the manner of falling raindrops
(ll. 48–49).

Shelley has not simply *wanted* to make analogies in these lyrics, though he does
again use such devices to help his objects escape from the godlike groundings of them
in his literary sources. Instead he has approached motions he has beheld or heard, as
"To a Sky-Lark" puts it, "Like a Poet hidden / In the light of thought, / Singing hymns
unbidden" (ll. 36–38). Much as he has tried to be accurate about what he describes,
even to the point of adhering precisely to the meterology of his own day,[94] he can get
to the objective base of what he observes only by a version of what he does in "Mont
Blanc," by probing to the foundations of his thoughts about these thoughts, since the
basis of what seems "out there" must really be the basic means by which it is observed.
Consequently, the poet has withdrawn so far into the interpretive process, which he
casts as a "light" on newer thoughts or perceptions, that he has given his will over to
the potentials for interaction among myriad stored-up cultural figures loosened from
older contexts ("hymns unbidden") that are already able to glance into each other and
need only some initial associations to prompt them into a definite interaction.

Indeed, if we believe the lyric voice—or really gathering of voices—in these
poems, Shelley longs to join his consciousness entirely to this self-extending dance of
potential connections far more than he is able to do in a formal structure fulfilling
(though also straining against by combining) generic expectations. He thus begs the
"impetuous . . . Spirit" of the wind or lark to become his very self some day ("West
Wind," ll. 61–62) once its dash across so many different frames of reference has established it as the Promethean impulse that composes the future relations of life from
Demogorgon's turning outward in the face of dissolution. In the present moment,
restricted to versifying one analogue at a time to suit the poem's governing meter, the
poet must find a "hidden want" in each metonym he uses to approximate the greater
motion ("To a Sky-Lark," l. 70). However close a figure gets to the pre-logical intertext that is a "harmonious madness" of "unpremeditated art" ("To a Sky-Lark," ll.
103 and 5), it still leaves the fashioner of the image pining "for what is not" yet imagined in the poem (l. 87), sure that there must be combinations of "sweet thoughts"
always "more true and deep / Than we mortals dream" within the limits of our individual psyches (ll. 82–83).[95] What might happen were consciousness to know the intertext fully is suggested in "The Cloud," where the speaker *is* the movement. The self
would seem the nexus (Prometheus in the cave) where all perceived elements and
mythographs about them would cross into and pass through each other onto other
states (as in ll. 67–75). In that situation Shelley would laugh (sympathetically, to be
sure) at the state of desire unable to surpass its earthly confines and especially at the
death of the body, or at least the threat of it, which makes a person feel trapped in
that pedestrian state. Every transition would be a shedding of that person's former
"cenotaph" (or strangling mythograph) in a continual resurrection, "like [that of] a
ghost from the tomb" (l. 83), whereby he or she would achieve the deathlessness of
the most constant change (l. 76) and the rebellious delight of being able to "unbuild"
whatever "pavilion" or "dome" is projected by desire into the reaches of heaven (ll.
78–84). But, since Shelley's speaker must usually admit he is a poet (soon to die and
thus able to name only some of the cloud's reformations), the most he can really hope
for is the death of his personal identity at the hands of the intertext's self-extension as
it uses him for a time and then passes beyond him, carrying what he has wrought along

with it. As Prometheus did at the end of act 1, the poet must ask a selfless and cross-cultural transitivity to "Drive my [present] thoughts," turning into "dead" reminders as soon as they become inscriptions of what he once felt, "over the universe / Like withered leaves to quicken a new birth" in a mind or minds of a different moment ("Ode to the West Wind," ll. 63–64). Unchained, interrelational, but self-transgressing mythography must take up Shelley's texts and make them incomplete crossings into states of awareness at distant times and places, else death will truly be the end of his efforts and his poems will be outdated generic exercises, not the "trumpets of a prophecy" he hopes they will be as they carry his desires over toward reconstructions of them ("Ode" l. 69).

In the meantime, for Shelley, it is only a growing cultural awareness of how this intertext operates and may be used to expand the range of Western thought which can give mythmaking any "redeeming social value," the moral worth so often and falsely located in "mythological systems." The way such an awareness can be developed, alongside the attitude urged at the close of *Prometheus Unbound,* is thus the concern, really the itinerary, of several 1819–1820 lyrics, particularly the "Ode to Heaven." In that piece the old strophe-antistrophe-epode stanza-structure, modeled on eighteenth-century modifications of Pindar, is pressed into taking the first needed step in the public's education. It offers a debate, with the different positions clearly contrasted at first, between the several different existing mythographs proposing a significance for that "Dome" we keep establishing over ourselves (l. 8). The reader must begin by seeing, as in Volney's congress of religions, that such proposals are debatable and partial stabs at the "abyss" (l. 37). Each borrows what it projects up there from the realm in which it actually operates (lending heaven "deep chasms and wildernesses" in l. 13), and each gradually reveals a class-based impulse to subjugate the average person onto "bended knees" (l. 24) so that even his or her "best glories" or notions of Heaven betoken the "presumption" of the "Atom-born" (ll. 34 and 38). Soon the reader should also start to notice the similarities between some images used by the different positions. As these resemblances multiply—for example, as "globe" or "world" figures appear in the strophe-assertion (l. 12), the antistrophe-stance (ll. 33–36), and the epode-response (ll. 46–47)—they undercut the attempted differentiations and make any concept of heaven no more than one "drop" or "sphere" in a larger collectivity of globes (ll. 41–45 and 51–53). The observer arrives, even this early, at some sense of a Promethean-Asian intercourse where figural patterns are torn between the impulse to blend and the desire to maintain their established distinctions.

Now the reader must be asked to step back a moment and confront the present political strength of each mythographic system. He or she must then decide, knowing the degree of public acceptance each position commands, which stance (and why that stance) holds out the most hope for genuine human improvement, following the poet's tendency "to attach himself to those ideas which exalt and ennoble humanity" most ("Notes" to *Hellas, PW,* p. 478). There is no problem in detecting the most widely accepted view, as a large "chorus" in the strophe celebrates a deistic "Presence chamber" or "abode" of "Power" (ll. 7 and 21). This is the vision revealed to "Reason's Ear" in Joseph Addison's 1712 "Ode" to the "The Spacious Firmament,"[96] even though Shelley's redaction tartly exposes such a realm as the Humean "glass / Wherein man his [self-enlarging] nature sees" and learns self-degradation at his own hands (ll. 21–22). A similar hopelessness emanates from the "remoter voice" of the esoteric Neoplatonists (such as Thomas Taylor) in the antistrophe. They see the first concept as a benighted "cave" of shadows obscuring a truer "world of new delights" that lies far beyond normal human comprehension (ll. 28–33). If this view, too, is rejected as excessively hierarchical, we are left with only the position most "remote" from the center of opinion: the stern skepticism in the epode, potentially stoic, gnostic, agnostic, necessitarian, *or* atheistic, which regards human beings or human concepts of heaven as but small elements in an "instinct" that really subsumes them both and "flee[s]" incessantly away from their inadequate apprehensions of its drive (ll. 41–42). Though initially as forbidding as the others in its ministerial castigations, this brand of Protestantism permits humanity to see itself as at least a portion of a rapid, progressive motion that may soon carry humankind beyond its current state. The "instinct," after all, is a motion not confined to a single conceptual or political order, and it even generates, on closer examination, the desire to pass to a higher plane in the other two positions. As soon as that possibility is accepted by the reader, in fact, it is as though a test has been passed when the epode moves on to its final stanza. The stern initiation here dissolves in favor of a gentler, gladder succession of figures, ranging from minute to immense, all of which view any metaphor for heaven (be it a "globe of dew" or an opening "flower" in ll. 46–48) as desiring reinterpretation within a larger or analogous scheme, whatever level of inclusiveness an image has attained. The reader's movement of individual desire extending figures into heaven now sees itself as joined to a vaster tendency of figural expansion reaching out toward more and more all-embracing textual frames. Heaven comes to look like the orb-upon-orb of the redeemed earth projecting itself outward in Shelley's fourth act. The "fading sphere" of the sky as temporarily perceived can unfurl happily out into "constellated suns" and "orbits measureless," all inclined to "tremble, gleam, and disappear" in the transfiguration of them by future systems and recombinations (ll. 50–54).

For his or her immediate welfare, though, the reader needs to get in conscious touch with such an instinct so that he or she can enjoy more than the mere pleasure of successive interpretations. This dynamic expansion turns out to be the perpetual basis of political and personal freedom, of that state held out at such a distance from the reader in acts 3 and 4 of *Prometheus Unbound*. Granted, Shelley defines day-to-day freedom as others do, as the capacity of the individual to act without being excessively constrained by other people. Then, too, he is not above mythologizing the notion, depending on his projected audience,[97] into a principle or feeling invigorating a people toward the achievement of their supposed potentials, either in the guise of a recurrent form (following Collins's "Ode to Liberty") or in the shape of an icon (the Athena-like Liberty in *The Mask of Anarchy*) leading the people against their oppressors in active or passive resistance. But all these versions depend on something like Demogorgon as Asia and Prometheus keep redirecting him. Such is the tenor of the "Ode to Liberty" and the "Ode to Naples" (the latter of which appears in *PW,* pp. 616–20), both written in 1820 to establish a broad context for brief new flurries of liberal reform in Spain, Italy, and other parts of Europe.

In both these poems there is a vast, mobile depth that sometimes erupts in the revolutions sproadically dotting human history. This movement is that of an age-old "spirit" entropically turning ahead that "makes chaos ever new," yet also creates restructurings of "delight," by linking existing perceptions of "life" to the regenerative desires of "love" striving beyond the existence generally perceived at a given time ("Ode to Liberty," ll. 89–90). No will to freedom could arise within the confines from which it has usually sprung, the reader learns, if the past or the present did not tacitly allow reconstructions of their orders within themselves, did not gestate turnings-outward inside their seemingly centripetal organization, "Like the man's thought dark in the infant's brain" or "aught that is which wraps what is to be" ("Liberty," ll. 55–56). Cultural freedom takes visible shape when this ever-disruptive potentiality arises in public forms that mock the "eternal dead" of older orders in mobile, "Praxitelean" reincarnations. That is what the entire Acropolis of republican Athens did "in derision of kingliest masonry" *and* in the loving, Asian, open-air outreach of its temples to all the aspects of the surrounding world as it was perceived ("Liberty," ll. 73 and 63–69). This kind of freedom, of course, lasts only as long as its "march" of "Earth-born Forms" stands "Arrayed against the ever-living Gods" of supposedly unalterable traditions. It must keep interpreting the surrounding elements anew, in the style of Prometheus, to help the Earth speak transformations of herself "out of her deep heart" ("Ode to Naples," ll. 127–28 and 8). Thus even Athens, like other political orders, may eventually find its dreams obscured behind increasingly systematic and hierarchical state religions. The individual in such surroundings, to become part of "what is to be" inside the frame of what "is," must consequently recover the "wrinkled image" of that looking-ahead in the "fleeting river" of history or the "caverns of the past" harbored by the collective memory ("Liberty," ll. 76–82). The aspiring person must then trace the "trembling" of this image in later risings of its qualities, however different the qualities become along the way, whether they appear in "Saxon Alfred's . . . brow" or the tribal leader Arminius freeing Germany from Rome ("Liberty," ll. 79, 123, and 196–99). That sense of an electric current leaping between poles, or periodically emerging at galvanized points from the underground stream of its "melody," will allow its perceiver to feel a constant yet changeable flow surging up in him or her from "the human spirit's deepest deep." He or she can even feel it as an answer to the charge electrifying poles outside the self, "The lightning of the nations" sent from "heart to heart" by recent revolutions ("Liberty," ll. 131–32 and 2–3). Freedom, before it is anything else, is the iconoclastic shifting of social and mental constructs toward transposed versions partly preconceived at the hearts of the older systems. Shelley's reader cannot know what he or she fights for unless he or she first submits to that interplay of mythographs, much as Prometheus takes his future shape from Asia and vice versa in the interplay of their cave.

Presumably, we could say, it takes this "depth" of understanding for the reader or poet (or Prometheus and Asia) to break at last from the mythic systems confining them most completely. It therefore seems strange that the odes to Liberty and Naples, even more than those on the West Wind or Heaven (the more traditional avenues for the descent of God), should insist on "Freedom's" being a "form divine" sent by a "Great Spirit" of "deepest Love, / Which [so] rulest and dost move / All things that live and are" that the poet cannot envisage his subject unless carried away by this "Power divine" ("Naples," ll. 91, 149–51, and 21). It would appear that Shelley has suddenly rigidified his sense of Christ's anti-mythographic God in the *Essay on Christianity* (1817). Now, it seems, that "collective," incoming "energy" of self-altering perceptions, social improvements across history, and material transmutations (*CW*, VI, 231) has become a "will" that "from [a] sphered shrine . . . yieldest or withholdest" liberty from particular societies ("Naples," ll. 169 and 174–75) in the fashion of any "Oppressor" created by the "enthron[ing]" of a person's "high will" ("Liberty," ll. 244–45).

This incongruity makes sense, nonetheless, as a kind of culmination gradually approached in the mythographic lyrics as they proceed from and hark back to the Promethean recess. To some degree all the lyrics echo the cave by interpreting the initial influx of basic memories or desires through the longest-standing metaphors for how the psyche receives what is temporally and spatially distant from it. Jesus in his demythologizing, we should recall, began by "accommodat[ing] his doctrines to the prepossessions of those whom he addressed," particularly in his use of the term "God" defined so very differently prior to his revision (*CW*, VI, 242). Shelley's speaker thus repeats the device, almost in the very words of Elijah and St. John's Revelations, by claiming to achieve his vision of Freedom's progress only when "The Spirit's whirl-wind rapt [his soul] from its station in the heaven of fame" ("Liberty," ll. 10–11). Yet these Shelley poems point more and more, as the cave does, to these standard frames as mere outdated figures from museum-piece rhetoric. After all, the whirlwind comes not simply from heaven but from a niche (or station) in "fame's" most exalted repos-itory, a heaven of well-known texts. The old saws, once exposed, then start to show how much they are already sliding into half-similar notions from different systems. Taking in the "wind" of "Power" in Pompeii, the speaker of the "Ode to Naples" feels borne up "like an Angel" by what first moves toward him as "The Mountain's slum-berous voice" and "the oracular thunder" (ll. 32, 4, and 6), modes of utterance typical of Greco-Roman "spirits" as they used to be received through "roofless [pagan] Halls" (ll. 3 and 5). The test of the reader in the "Ode to Heaven" has here been expanded to see whether he or she can grasp this mobile intertextuality going on inside and around conventional Pindaric or Christian inspiration. If the reader is perceptive enough to behold that irony rather than settling for some common definition of "The Spirit's whirlwind," he or she soon finds that awareness confirmed as the "spirit of deep and [collective Western] emotion" bears the poet over Italy on a cushion of airs from the "graves / Of the dead Kings of Melody," Homer and Virgil (ll. 37–39). On top of their tales of Italy's early hopes, other "prophesyings" soon gather to form the many-layered current driving the speaker's desire further on toward modern ana-logues of old battles for independence (ll. 48–50). By the odes of mid-1820, Shelleyan parody has been rigorously compressed. Instead of remaining a figural succession deferring to future transformations that simply stands alongside some hollowed-out order, the current of transference is placed at the core of that order, surrounded by its frame, to become its real motivator, its destruction from within, and a Power replac-ing monolithic force with "harmonizing ardours" ("Naples," p. 165).

In other words, this strategy asks that the order of the Western "state" come to center itself consciously on the revision from within that is freedom, on a deliberate production of revolutionary relations from older modes of organizing daily existence. Even more to the point, this decentering center should turn for models to the ever-changing cross-cultural intertext, the lovemaking between differences, which myth-making play has always been within and beside the mythographs that have seemed to hem it in. We cannot do without a tradition providing patterns for self-liberation, be they the remnants of republican Athens or records of biblical prophets interpreting an influx as having "flung" a "ray" back toward the "remotest sphere of living flame" ("Liberty," ll. 11–13). The key is to understand any such forecast, not just as a "trem-bling" toward different analogues in the river of time, but as a trembling, like that of Prometheus, at its own foundations, even in the "remotest sphere" that it takes to be its origin. Athens must be seen as having developed its "all-creative" mocking of the dead ("Liberty," l. 72) out of the havoc of Greece before the republic arose, out of an early "chaos" of differences becoming rivalries for power on the surface of the earth while "enchanted caves" in the earth's depths uttered "Prophetic echoes" of alternative social schemes (ll. 22 and 49–50). Before there was even the liberty set up by Athens, we must realize, there was the Promethean-Asian underground of ecstatic crossings between then-separate points, wherein lay the "deathless dreams" of "Art" that would soon burst forth in Athenian "stone" (ll. 57–58). Similarly, there could never have been a "remotest sphere" for Shelley to borrow from the prophets had they not assumed a Promethean "pav[ing of] the void," a sheer fiery crossing between Heaven and Earth ("Liberty," l. 13). For them, this transferring "swiftness," like the movement of a "ship" through water, sent a "ray" or shaft of "foam" behind itself, thereby pointing to something yet farther back in its wake (l. 14). That something then borrowed its nature from the mobility of fire that retroactively asserted it, installing that "living flame"—and thus the Promethean drive—within itself as the depth in its depths.

Hence, to see into that "sphere" in quest of the impetus that can free us from confining myths is to see, in the process (of the cave and the Titan) that once helped fashion mythic centers (such as the Delphic oracle and Jupiter), a means of flight, a turning out and away, from all the exalted spheres that have claimed to rule us from "above." A society can succeed in that quest if it accepts the fact that it will not find any one form, even Prometheus by himself, when it gets near the goal of its effort, "the inmost cave / Of man's deep spirit" ("Liberty," ll. 256–57). Freedom as a relational recombining can be drawn forth successfully from that intertext only as an element in a dialogue between tendencies, as would be the case if Prometheus were seized in that place. Leading freedom forth means bringing out a colloquy involving Wisdom, "Blind Love, and equal Justice, and the Fame / Of what has been, the Hope of what will be" ("Liberty," ll. 264–65). What else could be found in a subliminal cultural archive where the principal and perpetual task of figures in dialogue is to "Weave harmonies divine yet ever new, / From difference sweet where discord cannot be" (*Prometheus Unbound*, III. iii. 38–39)?

Free Mythography in Action: "The Witch of Atlas"

The pouring-out of this cave's constructions into the mythographic lyrics, however, is nothing compared to the darting between differences overwhelming the reader in "The Witch of Atlas." This half-comic epillyon, mostly composed over three days in August 1820, is Shelley's most intricate yet playful sporting among myth-figures, an apotheosis of near-total submission to Promethean intertextuality. Here the poet may very probably be filling out the features of his "Witch Poesy" from "Mont Blanc" *and* reworking with mythographs that rapid sequence (the genesis of poetic activity in thought) whereby his Intellectual Beauty becomes a "glance" upon the "heart" like "summer winds that creep from flower to flower" ("Hymn," ll. 4–7, as in "The Witch," ll. 521–24). But no single entity, static or mobile, adequately accounts for this goddess-wizard's headlong dance between sometimes incompatible aspects of Astrea, Venus, Juno, Minerva, Isis, Osiris, Persephone, Arion, Calypso, Pan, Apollo (her supposed father); Hermes at his most prankish (the subject of a Homeric hymn just translated by Shelley); Milton's *L'Allegro* nymph; Keats's Dian from *Endymion* (1818); Byron's "Witch of the Alps" in *Manfred* (1817) and Haidee in Canto 2 of *Don Juan*

(1819); Spenser's Una, Alma, Belphoebe, Amoret, and Phaedria; Dante's Beatrice or Petrarch's Laura coming to them in dream-visions; the Massylian priestess described by Dido as casting spells near Mount Atlas in Virgil's *Aeneid* (IV. 480–93); and the two sorceresses (one boating to Egypt) in Niccolo Forteguerri's Ariostan romance *Ricciardetto* (1813), not to mention Shelley's own Queen Mab, his dream-maiden from *Alastor*, Cythna, Asia, Panthea, the cloud, the west wind, and the sky-lark.[98] The Witch's successive deeds or states of being are therefore defiant of strictly sequential logic, especially if such a logic demands one underlying motivation behind—or causal connection between—the attraction of animals and nymphs to her Una-like "voice and eyes" (l. 103), her lying "in trance / All night within the fountain" next to her cave of "magic treasures" and "scrolls" (ll. 265–66, 154, and 185), and her voyaging out, following Herodotus on the topography of northern Africa,[99] into southern Africa's weather, the "Great Labyrinth[s]" of ancient Egypt, and the various dreams of sleeping Egyptians (ll. 425–72, 505–20, and 521–624).

Even Leigh Hunt's suggestive, and now much-repeated, argument that Shelley's lady-witch is an allegorical "personification" of the imagination at work[100] ignores the poem's perpetual incompletion and the author's own warnings against allegorical readings of the piece. True, the Witch's "thoughts [are] each a minister, / Clothing themselves or with the Ocean foam, / Or with the wind . . ./ To work whatever purposes might come into her mind," often to the point of crafting "pictured poesy" or "A living image . . . out of her hands" (ll. 210–14, 252, and 325–26). Nevertheless, she is not simply the "imperial faculty" that Shelley will soon depict in his *Defence* as creating an "order in which [the] beautiful, true, and majestic" can emerge in transformations of what we have perceived (*NCE*, pp. 483 and 494). Anything like finished and rounded-off orders are so much what she would avoid, more than Prometheus and Asia would (since they would at least "cast gathered rays" on one focal point, if only for a time), that "the lady-witch in visions [cannot] chain her spirit" and must immediately ask her productions to "extend again" the "outspeeding wings" she has given them so that they may carry her and themselves to utterly different surroundings and activities (ll. 419–22). To contain or center her in the face of that self-disruption, as Shelley cautions in his "Dedication" to "The Witch," would be to "crush" the free play of a "silken-winged fly" by forcing it to "tell [some definite] story false or true" (ll.9 and 4). Reading this poem in so traditional an allegorical way, he goes on (ll. 25–45), would make it seem too similar to Wordsworth's *Peter Bell*, just parodied by Shelley in *Peter Bell the Third*, too reminiscent of Wordsworth's Prologue, wherein the ascent of imagination's "little boat . . . / Through many a long blue field of ether" (*Peter Bell*, ll. 15 and 33) depicts the nature of pure poetic fancy and its forced encounter with the good poet's need to moralize the vagaries of down-to-earth life. Shelley, clearly refuting this pompous "mythological scheme" among others, thus climaxes his two-year unbinding of mythography with a display of what the exact relation should be (other than the vague submission already described) between the imagination and the intertext, both of which the Witch manifestly plays across as a feminine "Poesy" so entirely in transition that she incarnates no fixed principles, ideas, or faculties.

Consequently, one of the most fruitful attempts to locate the Witch in the movement of thought appears in an almost out-of-the-way article by Jean Watson Rosenbaum.[101] Taking its cue from Hunt's addendum that the Witch embodies the imagination "in its most airy abstractions," this piece claims that she is "a metaphor for the state of mind . . . a moment of total possibility . . . in which all irreconcilable things are present in the mind but are not yet unified," are "one step back from form." Sad to say, Rosenbaum goes on to maintain that this "moment" is one of "intuitive divine awareness" briefly knowing the absolute "being" from which all possibility comes. Yet prior to that lapse, which results in part from misconstruing the Promethean cave in which the Witch is born and to which she often retires (ll. 78–80 and 250–52), Rosenbaum nearly sees the Witch as what she is: an emergence from the cave's activity caught right in the process of her coming forth. She is a birth from numerous relations in the cave turning out at once toward all her possible contexts. She is, moreover, beheld just as she issues from that depth into imagination's willful reconstructions (some of which she attempts), yet she is allowed to continue the shifting through different roles that made her birth happen, all the while "attracting and assimilating to [her] own nature [the scores of] other thoughts" or texts brought in toward her.

The Witch's cavern, after all, is the Promethean one expanded to include myriad old "scrolls" of mythology, science, and the "inmost lore of Love" too often forgotten since it spawned the most primal relations (ll. 185–200). Across from these, still in the cave, lie "treasures" that are mainly memories of human sense perceptions "Folded in cells of crystal silence" until expanded on or reinterpreted by way of the scrolls (ll. 153–84). Pouring forth from all these ingredients as they start to interrelate, but also becoming the productivity that permits them to combine even more at later points, is the textual-sensual intercourse joining "one of the Atlantides," who brings along the history of her family's metamorphoses into the Hesperides and Pleiades, to Apollo, the "all-beholding Sun" replaying several of his pursuits of earthly nymphs (ll. 57–64). As if to complicate matters further, these figures are brought into conjunction by an allusion to the *aura seminalis* in Spenser's *Fairie Queene,* as should be the case when the scrolls are those of an "Archimage" (l. 186), albeit a "Saturnian" one borrowed from the old sage in Ovid's *Metamorphoses.*[102] The immediate result of this erotic (Promethean-Asian) fusion is the "changing" of the already metamorphic mother from "vapour" to "cloud" to "meteor" to "star" to a "dewy spendour" left to gestate in the cave (ll. 65–78), whereupon the Witch takes "shape and motion" from the "splendour" as a "form" of "embodied Power" (ll. 79–80), clearly the conduit of a force seeking innumerable other forms to transmit itself through and past. True to that birth, she at once draws all gazers in toward an "unfathomable might" of "love" where the "brain whirls dizzy with delight" if it tries to settle her ever-transmutable form within one structure (ll. 83–87). She then, being now at the level of imaginative formation and knowing the danger to earthly minds of continual immersion in the cave's process, repeats the relational "twining" that made her, as she will later in forming Hermaphroditus. She weaves a "subtle veil" obscuring her basis in "love" (ll. 151–52) out of perceived natural elements ("fleecy mist," "light") so that she may be reshaped by a semblance of her seen through different materials (ll. 145–47). At this point all her thoughts, like a poet's, must "clothe" themselves in those "Ocean foams" or "winds," and she thereby learns that the "power" of her "sire" demands that she "fly or run" beyond herself to help infuse with metamorphic energy "all the regions, which he shines upon" (ll. 214–16). "Poetry" (or poesy), the age-old movement across history and thought of which a poem is but one late product in Shelley's *Defence,* is here a succession swirling out from the intertext, from "a thousand unapprehended combinations of thought," which "enlarges the circumference of [every] imagination [through which the succession acts] by replenishing [each psyche's known ingredients] with thoughts of ever new delight" (*Defence,* pp. 487–88). As the progression of the

Witch, indeed, poetry "reproduces all that it represents" (including itself) by way of other "combinations" it can call in from the cave, "and [its] impersonations [henceforth] clothed in [that] Elysian light" remember this "gentle and exalted content" passing into and beyond them, passing because it forever "extends itself over all thoughts and actions with which it coexists" (*Defence*, p. 487).

Yet even this interpretation is in danger of becoming (as Witch Poesy) the sort of one-to-one allegorical equation resisted by the poem. Such readings, while partially accurate, must be modified by a sense of the piece as a kind of Panthea or cloud seeking an Asia reflecting the poet's Promethean desire back to him. "The Witch" was written at Lucca, the biographers remind us, just after Shelley returned from climbing Monte San Peligrino, at the peak of which was a little Catholic shrine containing, as such chapels must, a sculpted Virgin Mary surrounded by "Chrystal vials" ("Witch," l. 182), "cells of chrystal silence," and some "scrolls of strange device."[103] This holy place, claiming to offer a return to primal, virgin innocence not unlike that of the Golden Age in which Shelley's chaste Witch is born (ll. 49–53), was a widely known goal of pilgrimages supposedly sending its gracious influence down to all the areas below, much as the Witch extends her "sweet visions" to Egypt by descending the Nile (l. 524), whose source some mythologists did once trace to a "secret fountain" (l. 56) in the Atlas mountain range.[104] Shelley must have been led quite easily to these associations as the shrine on the peak recalled to him, almost simultaneously, the "Witch of the Alps," the "embodied Power" changing as it descends the river Arve from Mont Blanc, the "cave of the Witch Poesy" in the same poem, Virgil's priests near Atlas possessing "charms" to "free" oppressed "hearts" or control rivers or "bring trees [right] down from the mountains," the *magae* in the *Ricciardetto* assisting and inspiring loving questors to the point of carrying memorials of their love to Egypt, Herodotus's suggestions on why Europeans accept the mythic tracing of the Nile back to the Altas mountains,[105] Milton's Euphrosyne, akin to Venus, leading forth "The mountain nymph, sweet Liberty" (*L'Allegro*, ll. 12–14 and 36), the Lucretian Venus instigating playful relations among differences,[106] Asia interpreting Demogorgon's coming forth, and thus the mountain-cave of Prometheus and Asia making mobile and erotic reconnections from existing religious artifacts. This interaction of mostly pagan myths, to be sure, must have seemed sacriligious as a response to a Christian shrine. But nothing would have delighted Shelley more than to break Catholicism's hold, at least on himself at this moment, by making its symbols dissipate into the Promethean welter within the very kind of intertextual cave from which such playfulness comes. The central virgin figure in the recess, recast in all these other roles, could now be the performer, instead of the repressor, of a mythographic dance exploding official moral systems. She could externalize—or rather "create" in language—the sheer cascading of the intertext into, through, and past the poet's imagination. She is thus, as the title-figure of a poem or the poem itself, a pantheistic furthering of the Promethean impulse as it suddenly "distends and then bursts the [present] circumference of the [poet's] mind" (*Defence*, p. 485). She carries out this infusion into the imagination, using some of the latter's form-making capacities, across numerous mythographs so that the entire process can look out at a shape figuring its play back to the player. She is a sort of Asia, the oft-forgotten "female" process allowing a male poet to see his possibilities in an Other, but only as a reversion of such a figure to the unfinished swerving of many myth-fragments toward one another (the work of the womb/cave) that makes any such Other possible and needs an Other toward and through which its activity can be carried out.

If the Witch's poem is allegorical, then, it is allegory in the literal sense of that word, "a formal discourse always becoming alien from itself" (*agoruein* plus *allos*),[107] set against the equation-form that allegory has fallen into, as is the parodic typology of *Prometheus Unbound*. Every segment of this poem's text, such as the one where the Witch calls "ministering Spirits" to help her build "a proud pavilion" in the clouds from "woven exhalations" (ll. 459–66), looks elsewhere, not only to one other text (as in Patristic Christian allegory[108]), in this case to the erecting of Pandemonium in *Paradise Lost* (I. 710–711), but to a barrage of markedly different, though perhaps adjacent, other texts interpenetrating that one and becoming its analogues, even though few of them were closely related in their previous contexts. During this example, especially, the Witch occupies her cloudy "haven" by "playing" the "quips and cranks" of Euphrosyne in line 27 of *L'Allegro,* then summoning her spirits in "legions" recalling Milton's angels of Book V rather than his devils, and finally hearing in her "tent . . . all that happened new / Between the earth and moon" (ll. 453–78), replaying the godlike "spy" status sought by Lear and Cordelia in their retreat. Particularly with this last allusion, she blatantly pulls the entire collage back to the Promethean cave, a turning of texts toward additional texts rather than a central essence. Meanwhile, because that cave's process, acting prior to restrictive formations, glances between divergent stories, styles, and rules for generic decorum, each sequence must indulge in and even celebrate bathos, the abrupt descent to a lower from a higher stylistic register.[109] As a result, the moon, rising to end the Witch's pranks in the clouds, seems an aging prude, "like a sick matron wan," while it also "journey[s] from the misty east" in a grand mythic manner (ll. 454–56). A studied revision of this poem that would have smoothed such discrepancies into generic norms and tame compatibilities would have smothered that play of "winged Vision" much in the way Shelley's reviewers had suppressed other versions of that drive in his earlier works (Dedication to "The Witch," ll. 17–24). Hence Shelley's deliberate effort to write a poem in three days and to prevent it from being taken as a serious, decorous pronouncement. Hence, too, his choice of *ottava rima* for this piece, given his need both to seek a formal order in which mere figural play can become a definite text and to avoid the confinement of play by one literary standard. Such a stanza-pattern, already used by Shelley to translate the sprightly "Hymn to Mercury" (*PW,* pp. 680–99), was well established as cross-generic, bathetic, and seriocomic by its use in the Ariostan Renaissance epic,[110] Ariosto's often playful imitators (including the *Ricciardetto*), and many individual stanzas in *Don Juan,* which repeatedly plunge the romantic and pretentious into the sensual, hypocritical, or mundane.[111] Granted, "The Witch" compared to *Don Juan* is less aggressive and constant in its use of bathos. But then Shelley (as in *Prometheus Unbound*) is here concerned less with the distance between aspiration and "reality" and more with crossing visible gaps between mythic modes as they play out their impulse to transfer their properties.

Here, in fact, we find the rationale for the "unmotivated" shifts between activities and episodes in Shelley's apparent "story." His attack on "mythological schemes" by the time of the "Witch" does not strive to violate mere generic consistency (*ottava rima* being fairly official by now and already attached to epyllions). Trying to be more subversive, this poem does deliberate violence to the conventions of sequential narrative, in which all the dominant myths have been promulgated most effectively. Even in the Renaissance Christian epic with its "Witch"-like epyllion-interludes, in *Orlando Furioso, Gerusalemme Liberata,* or *The Fairie Queene,* the apparently disjunctive interruptions or interlaced plots, mixing the comic and grotesque with the exalted march of conquering principles and princes, carry out a divine will—or a self-complicating but emerging entelechy—that places all events on a connecting thread progressing through them, however much that thread criss-crosses itself, compares antitheses, and needs to be untangled for its thrust to emerge completely.[112] Shelley foregrounds, from this interlacing, the moments of apparently uncaused change in focus or setting, letting juxtaposed sequences form links because of only slight similarities within their progressions of figures.[113] He then installs that sheer movement between figures into the key transitions between blocks of action in "The Witch of Atlas," connecting the blocks only with a self-altering figure and a course for the Nile known to be fabricated from widely separated stories and analogies.

The epic tradition is thus pulled back toward the disjointed procedure of Hesiod's *Theogony* and especially Ovid's *Metamorphoses.* In those poems the principle carried from episode to episode, finally uttered in Ovid by one who hates tyrants and their habits, is but a "spirit [that] wanders [and so] occupies" every frame it pleases like "the pliant wax . . . stamped with new designs [that] does not remain as it was before nor keep the same form long" (*Metam.,* XV. 165–70). Modeled on such a spirit, Shelley's *maga* (and sometimes his Nile) is thus "wax" metamorphosed and undeified further into a shifting among metamorphoses that only half-emerges from the flux of all possible mythographic combinations in Western (fed by a little Eastern) thought. Consequently, she changes her course and makes her new fabrications—not having to battle previous constructs to the extent Prometheus does—*only* so that she can choose "different kinds of being" where different sorts of self-metamorphoses, or mutations of her earlier creations, can take place. There is really no other "causality" or "motivation" in "The Witch of Altas." The lady-wizard fashions Hermaphroditus, for example, shortly after lying repeatedly in a "well / Of crimson fire" outside her cave, in a molten liquid (suggesting perception flaming up into interpretive distentions of it) that makes the "star" above it look "bearded," the moon "mimic" itself, and the "snow" of winter melt into a blend of fire and water (ll. 278–88). There might have been a close causal connection between this pool and the hermaphrodite; even in Ovid, where there is a detailed episode revealing how the hermaphrodite of legend first became bisexual, this boy—for Ovid "the heir of Atlas" as the son of Mercury and Venus (two aspects of the Witch)—is joined to a girl passionately lusting for him, all in a "fountained pool," which henceforth has the "magic" power to make all who swim there "Half men, half women" (*Metam.,* IV., 231–60). Yet Shelley's poem almost completely divorces the pool from the making of Hermaphroditus, save for the narrative proximity between the two and the way the latter is "kneaded" into shape out of "fire and snow," a combination achieved in the well. To some degree, too, the Witch's metamorphosed "creature" (l. 341) is half-prefigured by the moon being half-in/half-out of its "mimicking" other form. But the "sexless thing" (l. 329) is still composed from differences drawn piecemeal from the well and Ovid, then "tempered" with "liquid love" (a combination of the well with the Witch's earlier Venus/Una-like behavior). It is further associated with, if only to "surpass" the prehuman androgyny recalled by Aristophones in Plato's *Symposium* (189e–193b), the sculpted Hellenic figure of a sleeping hermaphrodite seen by Shelley in the Palazzo

Borghese,[114] "that bright shape of vital stone / Which drew the heart out of Pygmalion" (a totally different episode from Ovid), and the "Creature" fashioned by Mary Shelley's Frankenstein (the "modern Prometheus") in an asexual act patching together mouldy fragments from many different sources (ll. 322–28).[115]

In "The Witch" the narrative procedure (or the lady's own process of fabrication) in each episode winds separate strands into what initially seems an ever-advancing thread, all the while doing so by breaking connections that were in the strands before they were brought into the weave of this poem. Then the poem cuts the new thread and begins again with a few pieces borrowed from the previous, now decimated, episode. The new moment interlaces these strings from several other contexts to produce a "grace" from hitherto distant ingredients (l. 331), much in the way Prometheus and Asia are made to become almost androgynous as they conflate differences in their ultimate state. At most a sheer tendency to metamorphose, to "beard" an often feminine "star," is carried over from segment to segment into other embodiments of that urge, as though "Poesy" were impelled by the basic transmutation of perceptions into metamorphic thoughts about them (the pool) toward a deliberate molding that reconfigures that change (the hermaphrodite) with the aid of other figures already moving in that direction.

Even in the new version, moreover, the impulse prevents any kind of achieved wholeness. For a moment, to be sure, the latest conflation seems to finalize the effort, to claim the apparent self-containment of a tale in Ovid, and even to press sexual and textual opposites toward a now self-consistent "purity" (l. 336). In this case, the witch's efforts appear to produce the androgyny desired by all those seeking to overcome the painful divisions that often arise from biological differences between the sexes. But the Witch, recalling the "Hymn to Mercury" or Ovid's grafting of "Wings" onto those who deny Bacchus in the segment right after the hermaphrodite-tale (*Metam.*, IV. 261–380), gives Hermaphroditus "rapid wings" that it never possessed in Plato, the statue, or Ovid and then makes its sleeping visage cover itself with "busy dreams, as thick as summer flies" (ll. 377 and 364), bathetically repeating an image of Venus in her temple (hardly a bisexual figure) from *The Fairie Queene* (IV. x. 42). Such continual re-metamorphoses give the Witch an agency by which her boat, already tending outward from its original setting, can be pulled or lifted toward the realms of her further "quips and cranks," many of which are also dimly potential in the hermaphrodite's incessantly metamorphic face. What is created by an instant of reweaving in this poem becomes the possibility of surpassing that moment, for the reweaving has already sought to unravel every old combination binding its best-known strands. Parts of the new form or episode (as in Shelley on Liberty) can so spring beyond its frame, in other words, that they are soon able to make its order disappear entirely, denying that they form a lasting link between current and later episodes in the poem. By the time the Witch forms her "haven" in the clouds to which Hermaphroditus has lifted her, he/she is no longer and never again mentioned in the text. The Witch herself at that point, of course, is already beginning to pass from the heavens to the Nile Delta onto her next adventure, chiefly because the next is "her choice sport," her metamorphosis of the next moment (l. 497). That new endeavor, too, generates departures from it, though it is the last one whose several versions are fully described in the poem. From "the pranks she played among the cities of mortal men" near the mouth of the Nile, she starts moving toward "entangling . . . sprites / And Gods . . . in her sweet ditties," remaking them "To do her will" (ll. 665–69). Yet what happens there is left a tale for a future time as the poem suddenly breaks off, unable to conclude, unable to finalize or neatly unite its broken narrative strands.

Meanwhile, as this narrative discontinuity becomes more and more apparent in the poem, it becomes increasingly bound up with more direct underminings of other continuities imposed on human thought by rigid "custom's lawless law" (l. 541). At first, with the leaps between differences only just under way, the attacks are so implicit as to go unnoticed by those who have read no more than a little Shelley. His jaundiced sence of the Golden Age myth as but the child "of airy hope," a "philosophically false" though psychologically attractive effort to propose a beginning of changeless harmony to which all later differences strive to return ("Essay on Christianity," *CW,* VI, 250), is scarcely visible when the Witch is conceived "Before . . . Incestuous Change bore to her father Time, / Error and Truth," who then chased away the "Bright natures which adorned [the] prime" of the earth (ll. 49–52). The reader, once attuned to Shelleyan irony, must later look back at this opening to see how much the Witch's parents during that prime, no less than time or change, are always and already metamorphic, discontinous narratives that shift incessantly away from their past forms by way of other figures. It finally turns out that there can be no moment prior to differentiation and relation across time, except as a retroactive proposal in a temporal sequence that draws the "shadow of [a] loveliness" back toward an origin that is somehow other than a shadow (l. 66). At around the midpoint of the poem, however, the reader has beheld enough shifts between differences producing points of origin that "mystic snatches of harmonious sound" coming out of the "upper air" (ll. 494 and 489) cannot be referred any longer, except laughingly, to the power of a high god (the usual assumption), even to one known to be a projection of human desire for power and knowledge into the heavens. Distant, changing, and unclear phenomenon, mythologically perceived prior to schemes of myth and mythography, must betoken conflations of differing elements in a temporary interplay, "quips and cranks" asking other "spirits" if the quips can "join [the spirits'] chorus" (ll. 491–97).[116] Such is (and thus the Witch is) the relational activity empowering any projection of a subject's desire toward an other than seems to be its object. Emerging from the Promethean cave to spawn such desire, this process makes possible all new interactions within and between our perceptions, the cultural memory, the workings of our imaginations, and the language (rife with "unapprehended relations") in which all such combinations must be formed. Now that the reader has seen so far into the movement generating and undermining myths, he or she is ready to observe it rising from the personal and collective unconscious to "pull / The old cant down" and license "all to speak / Whate'er they thought" at the moment of freedom from old ideologies (ll. 629–31). The poem therefore shifts in the later stages to the Witch's subliminal, subversive passage through the fluid foundations of Egyptian temples and the preconscious thoughts of Egyptians themselves. Though the piece styles itself as just a sportive "young kitten," according to Shelley's dedication, it gradually does "leap and play as grown cats do, / Till its claws come" near the end (ll. 5–7).

Indeed, during this final sequence the Witch's itinerary gains a clear sense of direction, redefining her drive all the way back to its beginnings. That occurs, however, only to the point of giving figural play, still endeavoring to further itself and to stave off complete systematic connection, some incipient social worth and political force, not a causality tying the sequence to a center. Granted, as we observe the Witch Poesy "Scattering sweet visions . . . through the peopled haunts of humankind" with a "soft step [that] deepens [the] slumber" in which she draws consciousness down toward her movement (ll. 522–24), we see, more clearly than ever, that she can do that because she floats freely beneath the surface of the Great Memory over which our conscious thoughts are driven by culture.[117] As a reincarnation of many older figures, she can easily find "her way," like Isis in the Nile, through the actually liquid "depths . . . Where in bright bowers immortal forms abide" (ll. 549–51). This "dizzy" intertextuality, seemingly so distant from the mortal world of hierarchies, repressions, and signs with supposedly fixed meanings, may attract some who can observe it from their fallen-off state into the Witch's free and loving intercourse of figures, as though she did hold out a Golden Age from which Poesy descends and to which it calls its readers. Yet "The Heliad [or sun-child] doth not know its value," nor do we, if it simply tastes "all blossoms" while being "confined to none" at the deepest level of crossings between existing formations (ll. 584 and 590); it is also in danger, at so far a remove from social life, of becoming an object of worship (like Una, the One True way). To effect changes that would truly "imparadise" mortal beings (l. 104), the Witch must force all sleepers from her "sweet wave" surging up within their depths (l. 595) to suddenly deconstruct (as Prometheus does) all absolutes or external restrictions that people have come to assume. Only thus can she reveal the joyous play of relations that once brought those limits about and that now arises parodically to dethrone them from permanent power.

Death, typically taken (as in *Alastor*) to be a total or sanctified end, must be thrown out of its coffins (transmutations of it that seal it within those grim assumptions) to become a transfer from restricted existence into the Promethean cave. In this latter "overarching bower," the dead one, now an "undecaying" figure among many others, can drift off into many successive "smiles" and "dreams beyond the rage / Of death or life" (ll. 599–614). Meanwhile, "priests" must also be made to "translate" their holiest symbols into leaps of interpretation from point to point. Then they will expose how much their established divinities are really based on that relocation from one level of being to another, showing the "god Apis" to be no more than a "bull" in the papal as well as the animal sense (not to mention the slang sense known in Shelley's day quite as much as in ours). A "king," in his turn, should realize that the man-beast hierarchy is first of all based on a relation, perhaps on an equality, between the two strata. He should therefore abandon hierarchy completely by putting an "ape" in his "seat," thereby announcing in the bargain how absolutism makes most kings brute "monkeys" with "mock-birds" responding to them (ll. 633–40). In addition, when human beings have been sufficiently impelled to change their priorities in such returns of the repressed, the metamorphic impulse should move on with further "subtle slights" to combat the gods people have created, perhaps at a time when thought can penetrate further beneath what we seem to see before us (ll. 665–72). Witch Poesy, redefined as she is in this poem, should not work only to enjoy the ease of her intertextuality or to be unveiled for "what she is." Using bathos, laughter, image-and-genre confusions, caustic irony, flat-out sentimentality (ll. 659–64), sleepwalking reversals of established behavior (ll. 641–45)—whatever it takes—her final destiny is to veil her already self-veiling emergence from innumerable relations in new reopenings of whatever denies her gaiety, sending thought back toward "unapprehended" transfers within it and beyond it. Only if they offer that "strange panacea" should refigurations of myth be allowed to imply that "some control / Mightier than life" can truly be the salvation of the "weary soul" (ll. 594–98).

The Social Role of Shelley's Anti-Myth

In suggesting that much—far more than has usually been granted to it, even by Mary Shelley (the target of the poem's dedication)—"The Witch of Atlas" completes Shelley's most strongly mythographic period by helping to announce a sort of political campaign in which such poems ought to participate. It becomes a kind of bookend temporarily closing a sequence of writings, whose counterpart, placed at the start of the succession, is the preface to *Prometheus Unbound.* Together these proposals, aided here and there by some of Shelley's prose writings of 1818 through 1820, sketch out the roles that disruptive mythography has performed in previous centuries and can perform again. In this way its function in social betterment, in fact its position in the entire sweep of cultural history, can be made clear to both Shelley and his readers, giving such writing a useful aim. Now the poet using mythographs to unchain them acquires a distinct moral mission with a series of tasks leading to its accomplishment, tasks that his poems from *Prometheus Unbound* to "The Witch" must try to fulfill or at least to begin.

The first task, intimated right at the start of the *Prometheus* preface and "The Witch of Atlas," is to take an oppressive, hierarchical myth (the Aeschylean Prometheus or the Golden Age) and press it back toward its probable genesis in ancient cultural history. What appears at that early point is usually a rebellion against the "common interpretation" of something debatable (Preface, p. 132). "In the beginning" was a rivalry between related figurations, such as Time and Chance or Prometheus and Jupiter, each of which had supporters claiming it to be the ground or father of its counterpart's being. The conflict turns out to have been resolved back then by each member of a pair inclining toward its opposite to the point where both deferred to a combined figure made from their relationship (Prometheus as Jupiter's progenitor *and* subject), as though most of that composite existed prior to them both (as the Golden Age supposedly precedes the Error and Truth spawned by Time and Chance). Getting to that early base clearly means beholding the most fluid, freely changing moments in the primordial cultures that produced the myths now in question. It means confronting, for example, the "flexibility" of Athens "between the birth of Pericles and the death of Aristotle" ("A Discourse of the Manners of the Ancient Greeks," *CW,* VII, 223) or the early period in Manichaean thought when "the good spirit" was manifestly an outward projection of "the principle of hope" rising up to counter the fear of destruction bedeviling the psyche ("Essay on the Devil and Devils," *CW,* VII, 87). The poet's next task, of course, is to reproduce that fluidity by drawing forth the relational interplay inside the established myth, yet only by opening the figure (as some Athenians did) to nearly all the analogues for it that have come into existence before, during, or since the myth's ascent to cultural prominence. That disruption should make possible unsettling comparisons—of Prometheus with Milton's Satan, say, or both together with the Aeschylean Titan and his "Oppressor" (Preface, p. 133)—leading to a passage of the main figure from counterpart to counterpart, each one partly accepted and partly rejected, to such a degree that the figure is free to play among myriad, even incompatible, figures for "the operations of the human mind" or "those external actions by which they are expressed" (p. 133). The poet can meet this objective only if he takes the most natural, yet oft-avoided, course and becomes a nonexclusionary thinker, unbound from one particular ideology. Then his mind can be Promethean, as all others could be if they only would; it can be "modified by all the objects of nature and art, by every word and every suggestion which he ever admitted to act upon his consciousness" (p. 135). In so recontacting the process of the cultural intertext as it increases in complexity since the days of old Athens, a mind can become a version of the Promethean cave, "a mirror in which all forms are reflected and in which they compose one form" of radically new connections (p. 135 again).

At this juncture the poet should also turn about to confront the relation between his own recasting efforts and the "contemporary" thinking around him cascading toward and being reflected, often unconsciously, in his receptive mirror (Preface, pp. 133–34). In that wide-angle vision he should see, as he would have in Athens but differently, minds (Byron's, his own) modifying nearby minds (von Schlegel's), and usually vice versa, to generate a "moral and intellectual condition" (including a sense of Prometheus as a very modern revolutionary) inside the older methods of production surrounding, and sometimes smothering, newly rising intellectuals (p. 134). This teeming interanimation underlying a surface conservatism in the social order is a precondition of a new freedom from the old methods and can bring on that liberation if there is enough "intense" questioning of the methods by those who interact, by a "cloud of mind" darting forth "its collected lightning" to expose the present distance between private desires and public "institutions" (p. 134). The poet should actively join that electric eruption by conveying his strange recombinations to "the highly refined imaginations of the more select class of poetical readers" (p. 135), the only audience educated enough to behold all his reworkings and therefore the counterparts to whom his portion of the new charge can be most easily extended. These readers, needing no more than a slight jog to behold separate parts of the Great Memory as interconnectable, should soon sense the movements of each key figure in the poetry rising into their own preconscious and consciousness from the most primordial and fluid levels of the collective symbolic unconscious. More than the surprised, even unwitting, recipients of the Witch's urgings toward fully relational thinking, such minds should then realize the ethical qualities demanded of them and others if they are to carry out in social activity the Promethean self-alterations they see impelling them toward a "going out of [them]selves" to all beings around them. They should begin to live out and promulgate a capacity to "love and admire, and trust, and hope, and endure" (p. 135) that can start to spread from these exemplary people to those who observe, hear of, and take up their example. From this coterie rediscovering and reenacting the movement of and through the Promethean cave—the dance of Poesy depicting man "not [as] what he is, but what he has been [turning toward what] he shall be"—a "fervent awakening of the public mind" should gradually spread and reach toward new possibilities of human being, shaking "to dust the oldest and most oppressive" myths that have kept the psyche bound to the class-systems of the past (p. 134):

> This, like thy glory, Titan! is to be
> Good, great and joyous, beautiful and free:
> This alone is Life, Joy, Empire and Victory.
> (The last three lines of *Prometheus Unbound*)

5

The Distribution of Transference:
A Philosophical View of Reform and Its Satellites

The Crisis of Shelley's Moment and His Gradualist Solution

Shelley, of course, knew that he was often too hopeful, especially about the spread of radical projections to an ever-expanding audience. Even as he was completing *Prometheus Unbound,* he was reminding himself of what he had realized years before: any address to "select classes" of readers, the ones already enlightened and at least half-radicalized, may lead only to coterie discussions in a sequestered Promethean recess where the lightning darting between participants stays within the walls of well-stocked private libraries.[1] He says as much when he writes to Leigh Hunt's *Examiner* in November 1819 to protest the conviction of the deist Richard Carlile for "blasphemous libel" against the state-sanctioned religion. The jury's application of Anglican standards to someone of a different faith, Shelley complains, shows how much the current "social order [is] in every respect [too] anomalous to create an alliance between the feelings of the untaught and suffering multitude" and the "cause of free enquiry" pursued by liberal intellectuals and poets (*L,* II, 146). "The rulers have [instituted] systems of public instruction according to their own tenets," thus dividing the middle classes (the members of the jury) from their own radicals. Then "misrule has [further] plunged its [poorer] victims into a condition of ignorance so profound and abject" that the only hope of radicalizing them lies in their "degradation" below the subsistence level where "superstition" once kept them obedient, a state hardly conducive to reading "The Witch of Atlas," despite the latter's attacks on a host of superstitions (II, 146). The opening in such poems toward more and more interrelations announcing a continual self-revision of thought cannot proceed on a large scale unless these class divisions are blurred by "some form of government less unfavorable to the real and permanent interests of all men" (II, 148). Harry White says it best in a recent essay that nicely corrects the most common misconceptions about Shelley's political thought. For this poet, he writes, "moral improvement" must "follow as a consequence of political reform"; it must be a second achievement after a more prag-matic one pointing the way to such later stages as complete "social justice and eco-nomic equality."[2]

Prometheus Unbound implies as much itself, even in its later acts, even in their wide, parodic distance between present hierarchies and future interconnections. That gap may be narrowed by imaginative remakings of the world in the minds of some sophisticated readers, but only to the point of giving those few a clearer sense of the ultimate goals toward which they should draw others. Were the distance to be hurdled in one sudden leap, most observers would read the new relations of figures by the standards of the present lexicon, just as Jupiter does at the start of act 3. All advances would be wrenched back into oppressive class rivalries (the basis of the current order) divorced from a true equality of understanding and the well-informed sympathy for others that all men and women should learn. The movement between such a present and future must be more like the development of Prometheus and Asia during the first two acts. Transforming the verbal orders that configure thought and reworking past myths to further that effort, the progression should be a gradual confronting, questioning, challenging, and altering of the discourse systems or institutions that determine the way we now see our personal identities and social functions. Those systems, we must remember, have been created by the Promethean impulse (or the entropic Lucretian *clinamen*) gathering its interplays into bounded, overarching schemes all the while it is trying to extend itself beyond this retrogressive turn in its drive. For at least "three thousand years," the impulse has had to pass through a myr-iad small struggles to form and then escape from the limits in which it keeps confining itself. Otherwise the human being carried forward by transference, in the words of Shelley's "On Life," would at some point be "what he is" (what he cannot be), a stasis beyond transference, not the wondrously eternal transitional figure who is "what he has been, and shall be" at each moment. Transference demands gradualism as much as it generates leaps toward total rearrangements of being, and so esoteric realign-ments of mythographs toward the "far goal of time" must be accompanied by exoteric plans, partial shiftings-ahead of transference, addressed at first to those educated lib-erals who can start to carry them out, for slowly emancipating the other classes into an equivalent state of awareness.[3]

Hence, beginning with his 1811 letters to Elizabeth Hitchener and T. J. Hogg, Shel-ley kept proposing specific, though always temporary, step-by-step changes in all the divisions of British government (secular, religious, and military). Though he did fall into self-involved periods when he seemed withdrawn from all political activity, he repeatedly tried to further or alter the proposals of the most liberal-to-radical reform-ers of his day: Paine, Volney, the Marquis de Condorcet, Godwin, Wollstonecraft, Bentham, Leigh Hunt, Henry Hunt, Sir Francis Burdett, John Cartwright, Robert Owen, Thomas Spence, David Ricardo, William Hazlitt, and William Cobbett.[4] The apogee of this effort, albeit unfinished, was the *Philosophical View of Reform,* started shortly after the *Examiner* letter, worked out in tandem with act 4 of *Prometheus* (as a means to the latter's end), and built out of notions either approached already in earlier, less comprehensive essays by Shelley or set up to be used later for slightly different ends in the "Essay on the Devil and Devils," some of the *Speculations on Metaphysics and Morals,* and the *Defence of Poetry,* all produced within the next year and a half.

Late 1819 and early 1820, after all, seemed to Shelley a climactic juncture, in view of both the number of once-divided interests turning toward each other to transform their common state and the tendency of these incipient coalitions to confront entrenched powers (the remnants of previous transfers) face to face. The teetering in a few continental countries between successful liberalization and the moves to crush it appeared matched in England by the post-war unemployed, the dispossessed farmers, the overburdended or underfed factory or mine workers, and most of the other disenfranchised classes linking their efforts during the second decade of the nineteenth century, often under journalist-leaders, to denounce numerous abuses: the government's foreign and trade policies; the inflation of the monetary system by government debt, taxation, and more paper money; the "rotten-borough" method for apportioning members of Parliament; and the channeling of industrial profits to a few aristocratic or bourgeois investors instead of the impoverished laborers—the methods of production most clearly responsible for creating and exploiting the very groups now trying to resist them.[5] Judging by the "Peterloo" Massacre and the Carlile hearings, Shelley saw the result as being a series of escalating confrontations between unleashed transference and the most forceful means of suppressing it, a natural view for the writer of a lyrical drama already organized as a succession of similar face-offs. The two opposites in his *Prometheus* "bedside-songs" were now head to head in daily existence as much as in his drama. He felt he must detail the exact, practical steps that might dissolve the repressive pole into the transfers that have made it possible and always sought to overcome it. If he and others did not do so, each competitor in each face-off would be in danger of overwhelming "the enemy" with the standard tactics of the tyrannical side. Mimetic desire could take over. The uneducated "populace" could adopt a stance of "savage brutality" vengefully "proportioned to the arbitrary character of their government," so much so that "tumults and insurrections" would quickly establish "the permanence of the causing evil"—the anarchy—they were hoping to overthrow (*Philosophical View, S&C,* VI, 1058).

The *View,* consequently, when it proffers specific remedies, proposes ones that share a different mode of transference, a suggested procedure far more visible in the radical writings of and around Shelley than in most recent interpretations of his political prose. Shelleyan reform asks for the partial redistribution of what have been and should be widely held capacities or currencies. As Paine or even Rousseau might say,[6] these possessions of the many—inherently inclined toward being transferred from where they are at any one time—have been given over to a few people quite alien from the rest in a relocation that the few regard as their natural right instead of as the delegation or theft that it really is. Thus the conflation of these elements into one center of power or exalted seat in a hierarchy must first be exposed for the unrepresentative hoarding that it is and then be made to transfer back, to disseminate and decentralize, much of what the many have ceded to its control.

The human "labor [that has] produced the materials of subsistence and enjoyment," for example, has been siphoned off from the laboring classes in many ways, with little returned in exchange, by "those [nonworkers] who claim for themselves a superfluity of these materials" (*S&C,* VI, 998–99), almost exactly as Cobbett has claimed in his *Political Register.*[7] The direction, apportionment, and equivalent value of that labor, all of which can be at least partly determined by those performing the work, are decided by "great landed proprieters" representing sparsely populated rural districts in Parliament, while some growing urban centers of labor have no one to speak for the needs of their workers (*S&C,* VI, 999–1011). In addition, to pay for the foreign wars against revolutionary forces undertaken for higher-class interests and not those of the lower orders, the aristocrats and bourgeois profiteers have contracted debts to the moneylenders of their own classes. As a result, they have urged the increased circulation of paper money without the old requirement that such bills be backed, immediately, by Bank of England gold, thereby expanding their ability to defer payment to their creditors while also inflating the currency that everyone else uses. At the same time, again to pay the debt, after managing to abolish the income tax in 1816, these profiteers have levied post-war taxes on some foodstuffs and other necessities bought by all the people and so drawn off a substantial portion of the already meager proceeds given to lower-class workers as compensation for their labor. The laborers must therefore work harder and longer for less money—money that buys less—and for sustenance that costs more, even as the upper classes work less for currency they can keep or expand instead of having to pay it back in taxes or to their creditors, as they have in fact agreed to do. Labor is thereby "defrauded" of its return and its "mark" (money) for the sake of "increased industry" that benefits only the rich (*S&C*, VI, 1010–13). There has to be a reversal of this one-way drain, this relocation bleeding off one side to fill up a second, since a genuine transfer is an exchange (between, say, a Laon and a Cythna) where any "giving" side in a relationship is given back at least some features or powers by any side that does the "taking." The estate-centered boroughs should therefore give back some of their "right" to "suffrage" at least to "the unrepresented [and industrial] cities" that provide the estates with many goods and services, and the national debt should be abolished along with the related taxes on essentials, permitting the worker to keep some of the returns for his labor that now pass over into the stockpiles of the wealthy (*S&C*, VI, 1050 and 1027).

These steps, to be sure, are for Shelley only hesitant beginnings measured against such final (and Godwinian) targets as the complete equality of possession among all men and women *and* the dissolution of all state government, even the representative kind (there being no class interests at this future point that might need equal representation). Shelley wants to prevent the hungry violence and uninformed "confusion" that could erupt from the masses in a sudden transition for which they were mentally unprepared. Hence his reforms rein themselves in to ask for only slightly fewer taxes on the poor at first and the extension of the franchise initially to those men in the cities now in "possession of [at least] a certain small property" and the informative education that goes with it (*S&C*, VI, 1050). The poet must admit how much his final objectives are deferred goals, "unattainable perhaps," used chiefly for inspiring, defining, and measuring the success of these "steps" that should all tend toward the attainment of those ends (*S&C*, VI, 1044). This great distance, however, does mean that every small advance must find its immediate value in the way it increases the number of people repossessing some measure of what they have transferred to the most powerful classes. Each widening of the present class boundaries, as in the extensions of earthly desires out into uncharted space in act 4 of *Prometheus Unbound*, can draw a new circle of inhabitants around the sphere of those who now possess more than they need, allowing the transference currently remanded to that "inner circle" to pour out toward the boundaries of the larger frame. Even those boundaries can be temporary, because the new expansions inside them should leak some hope and education to those still outside. The leaks should start to form a "majority . . . enlightened, united, impelled by a uniform enthusiasm," and this increasingly educated populace should then acquire a more "distinct and powerful apprehension of their object": the equality made to hover on the farthest horizon by the way the expanded frame keeps trying to include more beings in an even wider embrace (*S&C,* VI, 1052). Once the excluded classes come to "know and care" (VI, 156)—once women, for instance, become more self-aware and informed than even Mary Wollstonecraft has found them[8]—another extension of capacities and rights, providing they can now be wisely and effectively used by their new possessors, can be drawn around the one most recently attained in the march of Western society toward its ultimate goal. There are no reasons apart from ignorance, obsession with fixed identities, and the self-entrenchment of the powerful, all of which can be disturbed by "a small portion of . . . social improvement" (*S&C,* VI, 1022),[9] why this centrifugal spreading should not go on indefinitely in the sort of "energetic development [that] has ever followed [and] preceded a great and free development of the national will" (VI, 991).

For Shelley this giving and retaking, though often retarded by some of its agents, is finally "inevitable" (VI, 936); it is the movement of history itself. The *View,* as he has left it, starts with a thorough recasting of his old Necessity theory and a bringing-to-earth of the Promethean impulse to make that theory underlie the major transitions of Western history since the fall of the Roman Empire (already described by Edward Gibbon). In the important progressions during the last one thousand years, Shelley reveals, every attempted "domination and imposture" has borrowed its means and symbols (as Jupiter did) from an earlier mode of resistance (*S&C,* VI, 936). Moreover, each new hegemony has ultimately found its targets of conquest adopting aspects of that mode themselves to generate another counter-movement, a rebellious energy providing ammunition for both later forms of resistance and the new tyrannies they will face.[10] Thus James II in 1685 through 1688, imitating the rise of his beloved Catholic church during the Empire's decline (which Gibbon linked to Christianity), used a faith that was for Christ a hope for "liberty and equality" outlasting Roman dominance (VI, 963) to rekindle England's old and "unequal combat" between Catholics and Protestants, once the privileged and the excluded classes (VI, 967 and 969). The very fact of James' onslaught against hosts of non-Catholics made all those groups look back, as he did himself, to the stratagems of the Reformation that had risen up in answer to the "unequal combats" of the early Renaissance. This reversion reexposed what Luther found, a distance between "those professing themselves establishers" and the freedom-seeking "doctrines and actions of Jesus Christ"; that discrepancy brought on the Revolution of 1688 in which the "spirit of fraud" and "spirit of Liberty" reached a momentary compromise "limit[ing] . . . aristocracy and episcopacy . . . by [a] law" acknowledging "the will of the people" to be "the source from which [tyrannical] powers . . . derive the right to subsist" (*S&C,* VI, 967–69). One result, naturally, was a public acknowledgment that *"The Will of the People"* had the "right . . . to change their government,"* and this affirmation soon encouraged skeptical "enquiries" (Spinoza's, Hobbes's, Hume's) undermining the "popular systems of faith" long used to repress that will (VI, 969–70). Then, because such studies began to realize (though gradually) that "freedom and equality" had always been "the elementary principles according to which the happiness resulting from the social union ought to be produced and distributed," many eighteenth-century minds felt a "thirst for accommodating . . . to those rules of freedom and equality . . . [all] the existing forms according to which mankind [was still] found divided" (VI, 973). At the same time, most libertarians had to face the fact, as Paine did,[11] that 1688 really helped to produce "the existing forms" and divisions. The new emphasis on mechanical science, "increasing commerce," and rapid crop production (VI, 973–74), urged on by bourgeois individualism (the "will of the people" in another sense), had led, given the concomitant survival of some outdated hierarchies, to the formation of larger laboring and moneylending classes, the latter of which has now become attached to the Anglican church, the aristocracy, and the monarchy for the sake of advantages accruing to all four from the management of production (*S&C,* VI, 998–1002). The impostures of James II, repeating Catholic modes for appropriating the dynamics of revolutionary resistance, have been repeated themselves in the face of a different economy, and the result has since turned an "increase of the powers of man" into a "system of subtle mechanism . . . breaking to pieces the [laboring] wheels of which it is composed" (VI, 974).[12]

Consequently, the dispossessed should and will gradually recover what has been stolen from them, since their means of resistance and reorganization (exemplified by Christ) have made possible what holds them in bondage (Christianity, among other things). Moreover, resistance can best reassert itself, not by duplicating the recent violence of the monarchy but by borrowing monarchy's former ways of borrowing and attaching once-alien interests to itself. It must instigate widely inclusive and continual dialogues among different downtrodden groups, and this new interplay should model itself on the ways certain past societies (Periclean Greece, republican Florence, pre-Restoration England) once challenged domination with a "restlessness of fervid power which expressed itself in painting and sculpture" and the verbalized "energies of intellectual" genius (*S&C,* VI, 964 and 967). History for Shelley by 1819 is no longer a relentless linearity of organically productive causes and effects. It is a series of local, unstable, confrontations where attempts to gather and concenter elements around one source of power discover, at their very hearts, counter-drives (transfers away from the center) promoting the dissemination and equalization of power. In every circle of conflict, each drive depends on the opposing one to be what it is even to the point of drawing many modes of production (including rhetoric) from its antagonist, yet each also pulls ingredients or strategies from other circles, either earlier or contemporary— and not always from the side in the analogues most parallel to its own.

History when written is therefore both regressive and progressive, even when (as in 1819 and 1820) the ingredients of a given conflict seem about to burst entropically into a different configuration of the struggle. Pieces from earlier confrontations are always conscripted into both of the drives in a new conflict so that the newest tyrannies are dragged back toward "accommodating" former freedoms (if only in appearance) and so that revolutions have to blend "all that can be preserved of ancient forms with the improvements of knowledge of a more enlightened age" (*S&C,* VI, 1065). Shelley's narrative of those thousand years in the *View* therefore breaks up its initially progressive pattern to offer analogies crossing over differences in time and location, yet without abandoning a progressive thrust or denying the differences that time and place produce in similar structures. The history includes parallels between governments existing at different times, even reversions to eras already treated (when similarities to later ones become apparent), and these are placed alongside both the heterogeneous levels of enlightenment in countries of the same period and a sense that all the examples may soon see their tendencies continued and then recast in the present confrontations for which the *View* offers suggestions. The current crisis becomes a repetition of an historical pattern, a time when the pattern can be carried toward a recovery of the repressed energy it implies, and, even so, a distinct case with its own features needing solutions suited to them and to them only. The problems and desires of the moment are contextualized just enough to reveal history's tranferential movement surging into and through them, but, as repetitions always occur with many differences in any transfer of elements from context to context, the redistributive impulse of resistance must adjust its strategies to individual circumstances if it is to become the reforming "spirit of the [present] age."

In that "concrete universal," in fact, lies the chief problem for readers of the *View* and the other Shelley essays gravitating toward it. The continual oscillation (and the desired result) of a transference alternately confining and reviving itself can seem to progress on a level completely removed from the one in which gradual improvements inch toward a mutual give-and-take between members of different classes. Transference may insist on both levels and define the latter one more precisely by holding up the former as an objective and a hope, yet the distance remains unless some definite bridges are built between what is perpetual for Shelley and what is peculiar to his immediate time and place. Happily, I think, the bridges can be discovered and described, now that we have established the basic thrust of the *View*. I find that much of Shelley's later political prose works incessantly to make general principles into developments of action and behavior, carrying out what the poet could only urge in stanzas 4 and 6 of the "Hymn to Intellectual Beauty." Each large-scale idea, proposal, aim, or hope in these writings—be it equality and its greater representation, reciprocated labor, revisions of established laws, or the crafting of new reformist coalitions— is first probed in a manner that makes it reveal what kind of "going out of ourselves" and *it*self could be underway in its particular (but always outward-tending) case. Then each of these forms of transference is carried through to its consequences so that it manifests the social acts it encourages or resists, whereupon ways to bring its best results about are suggested in some detail, though only insofar as every benefit is furthered and none is shunted aside, as some could easily be in too hasty a revolution.

I therefore want to look more closely in the rest of this chapter at how those key concepts develop in this burgeoning fashion. For it is in these successions, I would also argue, that Shelley brings transference, for the first sustained time in his career, out from its hiding places in the undercurrents of thought, discourse, mythmaking, love, and social change. The poet now transports the transfer-motion into—and consequently finds it already within—such quotidian activities as voting, political representation, commerce, legal discourse, and the organization of associations agitating for reform. For Shelley transference in all these areas should be put even more into practice than it is so that its forgotten primacy can free those activities from current restrictions on them. The laboring over transferential procedures in his late prose, in other words, finally tries to make that operation a way of life, not just the subliminal impulse we have examined in so many versions. Granted, in presenting that prose as making such a case, I am writing almost as if unpolished, fragmentary material were more finished than any one piece of it really is, almost as if such efforts had achieved some worked-through sequences of thinking that even the *View* does not always attain. But, then again, the attempt at a fuller interrelation of the concepts composing Shelley's highly political ethics *is* one aim of his work at this time, one reason among many for him both to undertake a formal treatise augmenting or competing with other manifestos on reform and to add further paragraphs to his *Speculations on Metaphysics and Morals.*[13] Shelley, we can say, gives birth to transference as a practical *modus vivendi* by bringing that transformation progressively into being, area by area, across the process of composition in his later prose fragments. Each area of concern is formed as the poet gradually pieces together the previous concepts of or problems with it, isolates the kinds of transference that once made it possible, points out the need for changes in the area that transference urges upon older forms of the notion, and so leads that area, step by step, to the transfer-based use or manifestation of it that he finally wants to behold in Western attitudes. The *View* and the writings just preceding and following it propose a redistribution of transference from centers that presently hold it captive, then, only as Shelley slowly recomposes his own political ideals and the statements of others which, up until now, have kept too secret all that they could become, urge, and do.

The Real Function of Equalization

Few conceptions change in Shelley's thinking as much as his sense of "equality," the capacity and currency most repossessed by supposed centers of power and thus most in need of rediffusion by way of its own distributive activity. When Shelley writes in the *View* that the "grand principle of political reform is the natural equality of men . . . with relation . . . to their rights," he is passing from one definition of the idea toward quite a different concept, as he shows by making equality both "an elementary principle" at all times and a "goal" for the distant future ennobling those who currently "hope [for] and desire it" (*S&C*, VI, 1043–44). On the one hand, by using "natural" and "rights," he looks back to Paine's and Spence's definitions,[14] accepted in Shelley's letters of 1811 and 1812 (*L*, I, 127, for example). There equality is nature's endowment to men and women, the gift of a golden age from which we have fallen, a part of each person's being at birth that cannot be alienated from its possessors except in acts that violate the basic order of Creation. On the other hand, in one of the *Speculations* penned much later, though certainly before the *Philosophical View*, equality is an object of desire projected by human thought long after the birth of any individual. "Man considered in his origin, a child a month old, has [too] imperfect [a] consciousness . . . of other natures" resembling itself "to conceive of any relations," equal or otherwise, "established between man and man" (*CW*, VII, 74–76). Such relations, Shelley writes in an even later *Speculation* (probably after the *View*), come from involuntary "laws of thought," which make us "conscious . . . of our successive ideas, [then] of the existence of other minds," because "analogy" demands we view our succession in terms of another one "resembl[ing]" it (*CW*, VII, 61). Though Adam Smith (already noted as an influence on Shelley in these areas) argues very differently in his *Theory of Moral Sentiments*,[15] this "going out of ourselves" as we grow turns us from completely Hobbesian tendencies that at first desire the pleasure and "preservation of our individual being" alone toward an interest in an "accurate intimation of [similar feelings] as existing in beings resembling [the] self," the basis of what can later become a truly "disinterested benevolence" (*CW*, VII, 74–75). If civilization then furthers the development of a "cultivated imagination" envisioning the self's needs as the needs of others and vice versa, we "are impelled to seek the happiness of others" in the very act of pursuing our own, "to distribute any means of pleasure which benevolence may suggest the communication of to others" (*CW*, VII, 77). Equality becomes "natural" by the time of the *View* mainly in the sense that "benevolent propensities" born of transference's quest for resemblance "are inherent in the human mind" and are thus inclined to extend toward other human beings whatever one particular mind desires for itself (VII, 77).

Equality for the mature Shelley is therefore a future state eternally sought by "natural propensities" when they have developed themselves to the point of turning into the longings of sympathetic love. We now need to determine the status and use of this concept as Shelley finally works it out. For him, certainly, there is no state of earthly existence at which the movement toward more equalization should bring its spreading to a halt. Unless love's "desire that the feelings of others should confirm, illustrate, and sympathize with our own" becomes restricted to a single, dictating object or regresses to a fixation on one image of the self not really different from the self of the moment (*CW,* VII, 76), love's "extraordinary power over" thought and feeling (ibid.) should constantly ask us to identify "ourselves" with the [beauty we would find] in [any] thought, action, or person, not our own." As Asia does, we have to "put [ourselves] in the place of another and many others" over and over again, to such an extent that "the pains and pleasures of [our] species become [our] own" (*Defence of Poetry,* pp. 477–78). In this way "imagination," the means by which we see the world as if we were another, then many others, can become cultivated enough to desire and envision the spreading of pleasure throughout a "comprehensive circumference" including every "sentient" being (*CW,* VII, 79–80). Such a faculty must insist on something like Jeremy Bentham's principle of utility, valuing laws, acts, or social tendencies to the extent that they promote the greatest and most lasting happiness of the greatest number—but with the proviso that every number-limit reached at a given time be thought inadequate compared to the number that could be reached if the law, act, or tendency were some day modified to include the interested beings not yet covered. So that this principle can be pursued consistently, moreover, without "preference" for "those who offer themselves most obviously to our notice" (a restriction of the circumference), imagination must pour love outward alongside a semi-Godwinian "sense of justice" (*CW,* VII, 77). This impartiality of judgment not only looks to see if the "capacity of him that bestows" tends toward "the production of the greatest quantity of general good" (Godwin's chief requirement for justice);[16] it so considers other and similar beings when it focuses on any one being or any group of people that it "impel[s]" the distribution of capacity "in equal portions among an equal number of applicants" even if the number increases (*CW,* VII, 77). Barring our own suppression of what we naturally feel, we "desire that the advantages [apparently] enjoyed by a limited number of persons should be enjoyed equally by all," each person having an "equal claim" to the "pleasure" everyone wants (*CW,* VII, 77–78).

This continuous going-out to others beyond any present circle, however, must not aim at so much similarity between the self and its analogues that justice insists on a strict "uniformity of . . . conduct" among society's "members" (VII, 81). That would make the self, or at least one standard, the measure of any being placed alongside it. The result would be a tyrannical act pulling all others into the self, much in the way the Anglican church has become the official British faith trying to subsume all Christian sects under its umbrella. Such homogeneity would also rely on the evidence of a "superficial glance" that might not "distinguish" between different performances of the same kind of act (VII, 81). Imagination, as much as it can, should cross over entirely into the "otherness" of the other's situation, no matter how many actions of others it tries to comprehend. According to another *Speculation* written prior to the *View,* it should realize that anyone else's peculiar "frame of mind . . . impresses the

minuter elements" of thought with "peculiar hues" (VII, 82). For one thing, as Godwin suggests and as Shelley emphasizes in the preface to *Prometheus Unbound* (*NCE,*
p. 135), each frame is composed of many combined influxes (and interpretations of
some of them by some of the others) that can never be exactly the same from person
to person. In addition, as Godwin would not say but as Hazlitt would,[17] the "internal"
process that achieves the formation has its own mode of organizing influences, its own
developmental tendency like that of "hemlock" as opposed to the one in a "violet,"
which differentiates any species genetically from another with a "color [that] is in no
wise contributed to from any external source" (*CW,* VII, 82–83). For there to be a
crossing between positions, however alike, after all, the positions must be truly separate to start with, so much so that "no one action" can claim "an essential resemblance
with any other" of its type performed by another person (VII, 81). The deepest level
that "moral knowledge" should reach is a sense of the "differences" in people as these
translate outward into socially significant "tendencies" (VII, 82). The movement
toward equality should therefore encourage everyone to act out their differences, to
be similar by being different, and thus to oscillate perpetually between uniformity and
singularity without touching either pole. "All forms of opinion," for example,
"respecting the origin and government of the Universe" should be "equal in the eye
of the law" without having to recant any of their unique assumptions (*View, S&C,* VI,
1027). At the same time, Shelley's equal society, echoing Bentham again,[18] should prevent different inclinations (such as those of one church) from interfering with or subsuming other ones nearby. Society should judge the actions of its members, with a
scrutiny applied equally to all, by the "general effects" likely to result from continuing
the "peculiarities" motivating the actions (*CW,* VII, 82), by how much a person's act
is based on efforts to affirm or deny the differences to which every one else has a right.

The consequences of such assumptions are apparent at once, especially in the
View. Equality in basic sustenance, material possessions, and opportunities for happiness should be the personal desire of everyone for everybody else, provided that
every mind's "natural propensities" are developed into the sympathy for others incipient in each mind and assuming that the primal differences setting human beings apart
do not make one group of people insist on their distinction by drawing to themselves
all the products and privileges of the other differences. The latter perversion has
occurred for centuries, of course, in the divisions of labor recently exacerbated by the
"greater number of hands . . . employed in the labors of agriculture and commerce"
while others receive the proceeds and the right to hire more hands (*S&C,* VI, 998).
That blatant immorality, denying most people a fair exchange for their special skills
(and thus ignoring their differences), should be challenged by at least a Parliamentary
reform granting the lower classes created by this division a number of representatives
in the Commons equal, theoretically, to the number that speak for the special differences of the aristocracy.

Yet instead of finally arguing, as he wishes he could, for five hundred "electoral
departments" apportioned so evenly that each elected member is "the expression of
the will of 40,000 persons" (one five-hundredth of the British population), Shelley
must acknowledge class and personal differences so much, projecting himself into the
psyches of beings very different from himself, that only those of a "perfect understanding" not far from his own—those who can therefore give the deliberate "consent"
needed to transfer "sovereignty" to a representative—can be included in his initial
voting public, thus letting out "women and children" and all the uneducated classes

until much later (*S&C,* VI, 1046 and 1042). To promote universal suffrage right away would be to ignore the present obscuring of difference that has imposed the "military habits" of the monarchy on the minds of "the mass of the nation" (VI, 1041). It would grant the vote to many a mental "slave" whose "will" could not be "guided by his or her own judgment," who would simply take over the self-centered hauteur of the monarchical attitude "taught to despise human life and human suffering" aside from its own (VI, 1041). Reapportionment cannot represent all the classes until a small amount of it, accompanied by the dismissal of the King's standing army (VI, 1027), has helped to restore two factors: distinct "frames of mind," each requiring its own representatives, and the sympathetic understanding of different beings (what a representative must always have) now repressed in so many minds by the very differences it should cross between. Equalities among differences can neither remain equal nor maintain the freedom to be different unless each step toward equalization can manage to keep alive the primal and relational modes of thinking that demand both difference and similarity among human beings.

The combination of recollection and progression in Shelley's history of the West has again revealed itself as vital, this time to the ultimate cessation of the conflicts among different nations, sects, and classes. Given humankind's age-old acquiescence to various forms of aristocracy, generated by the "imbecility of their own will and reason" when both faculties chose the wrong form of transference, the reformer should encourage present-day "land proprietors and [large-scale] merchants" to remember the "bond of union" prior to 1688 pitting "the aristocracy and the people" against a "royal power weigh[ing] equally [down] upon all denominations of men" (*S&C,* VI, 1001). This memory might restore existing aristocrats to an awareness of their long-standing function as "receive[rs] and interchange[rs]" in an economy involving other producers and consumers with whom they are thus interconnected and inclined to be sympathetic (VI, 1016). They might revive their *noblesse oblige* of old, that "generosity and refinement of manners and opinion," by which they sometimes felt responsible for the people whose labor they directed and whose produce they processed, owned, and profited from (1016). Shelley, being of the proprietor-class, a manipulator of its privileges, and attuned to Leigh Hunt's nostalgia for the "social wisdom" of the "middle gentry" now smothered by the "commercial and jobbing spirit" of industrialism,[19] naturally leans toward this outdated ideal even while disparaging aristocracy in general, much as his grandfather Bysshe had so often done as well.[20] Nonetheless, the nostalgia is aimed at regrounding the aristocracy in the most basic, most transfer-oriented patterns of thought and economy that once secured the aristocrat's position and now deny "the permanence of hereditary right" (*S&C,* VI, 1001).

After the execution of Charles I, in Shelley's view, aristocrats severed that bond linking them to the masses. First they transferred their loyalty to the Crown to counter a rapid increase in the size (and thus the potential power) of the working class. Then they started drawing funds, as Hume saw,[21] in the face of an agrarian economy shifting toward more urban methods of production, from "attornies and excisemen and directors and government pensioners," who have since gained aristocratic levels of income and influence without the "chivalrous disdain of infamy connected with [being] a gentleman" (*S&C,* VI, 1016). This redistribution of power toward the top and toward an adjacent parasite-order, one created to increase "that class of persons who possess a right to the produce of labour . . . without [undertaking] any labour in return," must be dispersed or at least "enclosed within the narrowest practicable limits" so that aristocrats cannot keep bleeding the people they once sustained (VI, 1015). For a start, to extend one of Cobbett's suggestions,[22] the national debt should be ended, as Shelley sees it, in a transfer of property from the indebted aristocrats to the *nouveaux riches* who are their creditors (*S&C*, VI, 1029–30). Such a freeing of the masses from a part in the transaction would be a restoration of "natural propensities." It would make a one-way transfer (from the people to the government to the money-lenders to the aristocrats) a restricted, face-to-face, two-way exchange (from the aris-tocrats to the moneylenders in return for the latter's money *and* between lenders themselves, since many of the *nouveaux riches* are borrowers too). There would also be some dissemination of hoarded resources to realms outside this circle of two aris-tocracies. The "public creditor" ("whose property would [be] included") would orga-nize the exchange by auctioning off the "mortgaged" property. He would therefore be entitled to satisfaction for his services, some "proceeds" going presumably to the pub-lic coffers, except for the principal and perhaps some interest owed to the lenders (VI, 1029). Meanwhile, by losing perhaps "a third of his estate" or "a fourth of his [invested] funds," the aristocrat would be forced down to a station closer to that of the average person (VI, 1030). In time he might again sympathize with lower-class beings now more similar to himself. He might recover his former generosity of vision, lost when he gave some of his aristocracy away to the "usurers" and "stock-jobbers" (VI, 1016). He might even look at the situation of laborers (perhaps now at his own need to work) enough to see that "Labour, industry, economy, skill, genius, or any similar powers honourably and innocently exerted are the foundations [of] property" in the truest sense (VI, 1033)—that work is a right to a return for it that no nonwork-ing person should be given the license to appropriate for himself.

The Shelleyan impulse toward equality, when thoroughly understood, is thus not the mere leveler in the later prose that some have taken it to be.[23] Because it proceeds from self-interest becoming repeatedly transferred to the level of desiring for all what remains a desire for the self, it is useful mainly as the calculator of how much or how little interplay is going on at any one time between givers and receivers. The mind, we should recall, must be "cultivated" if it is to turn "natural propensities" toward equal distribution, and such a mind is aware that the dissemination to everyone of the various materials conducive to happiness cannot occur in equal portions at any single point because materials are limited and different people have different needs depending upon their different locations. Hence all civilized men and women, though "intrinsically" moving toward the desire for equality in their personal thinking, must accept the social division of labor necessitated by the scarcity of resources in some places and the basic differences between scattered people. They must "forgo the asser-tion of all [the rights and possessions they might claim] that they may more securely enjoy a portion" of what is available, while the other men and women around them enjoy a different portion, ideally in equal profusion (*S&C*, VI, 1026). The right to manage and defend the land may have to be given away by some of the workers on it so they can do the actual work (the beginnings of aristocracy); the results of some labor must often be given up so that the products of other kinds of labor can be purchased from their possessors; and a person in a large society, in danger of being drowned out in a crowd of many competing voices, must grant his or her right to speak for his or her interests to a representative of that and other interests, a synecdoche ideally ges-turing back toward and announcing a large (but specific) conflation of concerns and people. In other words, there are choices to be made, both at the start of a civilization and at later stages in it, as to how much of anyone's possible capacities or possessions must be invested in another being or group in order for everyone to have some measure of what all people desire.

The possibility of equality for Shelley, in an almost Benthamite calculus,[24] starts to be impeded when a person or group's resignation of various means to happiness is clearly more extensive than the return of other such means to that person or class. At such times the selfishness of the very earliest impulses uses the excuse of *any* difference permitting the transfer of several means toward the self to justify the gathering of all those means into one location without sending a similar amount back to the source from where they came. Equalization can be approached, then, when a fairer exchange between different people or groups begins to operate more regularly. That adjusted transference can happen when the aristocracy submits "to a diminution of [its] luxuries and vanities" as the income of those producing them increases with less taxation; when those performing a task in name only lose the government sinecures keeping the full cash value of labor from the true laborers; and when representatives "consult the interest of their electors" because they genuinely respond to the many voices of their districts, not just to the owners of the most property in the region, as though the latter stood for everyone there (*S&C,* VI, 994–95). At some distant moment the exchange may be so equal that the differences between people could become as minimal as physical limitations and modes of production allowed. In one of his notes to *Queen Mab,* Shelley foresees a time when each day for each person would intersperse a "share of labor" and a "portion of leisure" devoted to pleasure and self-education (à la Godwin and Herbert Marcuse) instead of leaving those activities unfairly divided into the tasks of one class and the privileges of another (*PW,* p. 805). Until then, though, the idea of equality must be an advocate for the depleted side of any social duality, trying to turn that bifurcation as much as possible into an exchange of equal amounts. Equality must keep promoting the ever-wider distribution of a *double* capacity of transference, which should first take hold among the educated and spread out from there: the ability, on the one hand, to possess all that other people are able to transfer toward the self, and on the other hand, to return that ability to every known person of every sex, race, or class.

The Realienation of Work— And the Limits of Shelley's Proto-Marxism

Even so, "Labour," that going-out-of-ourselves most often denied a fair return in an unequal world, remains a problematic notion, even after the equalizing impulse has established the worker's right to an equitable exchange for his work. In claiming during the *View* (with Cobbett[25]) that "Labour and skill and the immediate wages of labor, and skill," form a "property" to which the laborer has "a sacred and indisputable right" (*S&C,* VI, 1036), Shelley seems to restrain the movement toward exchange implied by what labor is, the transfer of effort into the making of a product that others might want for themselves. He urges the worker either to keep his product as "properly" his, almost as if there were no transfer going on, or at least to possess, without its being subject to further transfers mandated by others, the equivalent (or wage) of the productive process that allows the worker to replenish what he has expended. Concurrently, though, this poet accepts the need for money, the "sign of labor," because it is a commonly held medium (similar to words) permitting the transfer of the ownership for which it stands in "some representation of property universally exchangeable" (*S&C*, VI, 1013). Such a "sign" automatically extends the earlier transformation of labor into its product, this time making labor's reward depend on the relation of similar signs (coins or bills) to one another. This new context determines the price of the product more by values in the monetary and market system than by the amount of labor expended, thereby denying the laborer the full ownership of his work and thus his right to set the cost of what comes forth from him.

Shelley seems attracted here, as he was in the *Queen Mab* notes (*PW*, p. 804), to Hume's and Adam Smith's sense of labor as the unchangeable, perpetual "quantity" always represented in any product or commodity or in the money paid, either by the consumer to the laborer or by the laborer once he is compensated for his now-concealed efforts.[26] Being the significance of all produce and of the price paid for produce allows labor to be the "meaning" of the buyer's payment even before the product is delivered. A purchase—or wage, for that matter—can thus be a reference (in Smith's words) to the product's "real price," to "the quantity of the necessaries and conveniences of life which are given up for" the product by the laborer during labor and then by the purchaser in return for what he receives. Yet any such submission to Smithian free enterprise must acknowledge, with *The Wealth of Nations,* that the real price differs from the "nominal price," the "quantity of money" actually charged for the product, which varies according to the "market price" determined by a product's "exchange-value" (not its "use-value") in a momentary relation of supply to demand during a time of greater or lesser inflation of the currency. In addition, as Ricardo (the most widely known British economist of Shelley's own time) emphasizes even more than Smith, the labor-value in most products is an accretion of many acts of labor and contributions of capital, not all controlled by one worker. These estrange the product from, and even obscure, any single base, so much so that the wages owed for each contribution may not be equally or fully reflected in the market price of the product, especially given "alteration[s] in the value of money."[27] Shelley seeks to relocate this process in its basic performer even though he has to acknowledge how much labor is a transfer of itself across many different systems of exchange and their different interplays of forces. He must work out a rationale for such a backward look, therefore, in the face of a progressive alienation he confesses, indeed in the face of shifts between contexts that one would think he would celebrate, if his previous writing is any indication.

In his solution, to be sure, Shelley still ends up promoting transference as a transposition from place to place and an interrelation between those positions. But now he does so, as he never has before, by distinguishing true from false transference both in the history of economic change and in a critique of economic theory. The *Philosophical View* echoes Smith only up to that point in the latter's system where the worker is assured, whatever the variations in the market price for his product, of "a competent share of the decencies of life" (*S&C*, VI, 1019), a transferring back of what his effort (for Smith) "must always lay down" or risk: "health, strength and spirits . . . ease . . . liberty, and . . . happiness."[28] More often than not, Shelley finds, that minimum was achieved in rural and factory labor prior to the abandonment of the gold standard in 1797. It was *only* a minimum and never close to an equality between the classes, "depriv[ing] workers] of those resources of sentiment and knowledge" available to the upper crust. Nonetheless, a "competency in . . . external materials" sufficient to sustain the worker for labor without ravaging his body or family did transfer to him enough means or fuel to replace most of what he had given away or depleted, at least until the next exchange (VI, 1019).[29] Smith, however, would let the "market price" of completed work fall far below the "real price" without government interference, assuming that laborers would adjust by shortening the supply or changing occupations, even though the time needed for these changes might encompass, and thus damage, the entire "lives of some of the workmen who were bred to the business."[30] Shelley is horrified at this prospect, in part because he sees the damage being wrought all around him by the inflation of the currency driving the "real" price of sustenance up while the wages of labor fail to keep pace, despite the fact (as Ricardo saw) that "market prices" are going up too. Now "the worth of labor," the money for the "food and clothing" needed to keep workers at least alive, requires "twenty hours" of work (Shelley estimates) for the same "competent share of the decencies" that came from only ten hours of the same effort before (*S&C,* VI, 1020). The control of labor's products by other contexts of relations is refusing to send *any* real equivalent of labor's expense back to the laborer through this series of displacements. Adding taxes, furthermore, to increase the drain outward and upward, as even Smith would admit, simply makes labor a total depletion of itself to other points, a "carrying over" entirely cut off from the two-way exchange between levels that should always come with an act of transference.

What promotes this false transposition, to be sure, seems to be something Shelley might value: the divorce of paper currency from its old basis in gold so that the value of notes seems determined by the relation between them instead of some set amount to which they all refer. But the poet, developing the arguments of Ricardo and especially Cobbett,[31] sees this mutation of the "sign of labour" (gold) into the sign of that sign (bills signed by buyers claiming the backing of gold without having to produce the gold itself) as a centralization of purchasing power into a restricted location from which little returns, not a decentering from its base of a commonly held piece of paper (*S&C,* VI, 1010). To begin with, a "man may write on [that] paper what he pleases; he may say he is worth a thousand when he is not worth a hundred pounds" (VI, 1010). The key to the receiver's acceptance of this sign-of-a-sign is a belief that the signer "possesses this sum," an amount of gold that remains withheld, perhaps never to be transferred to the holder of the note (VI, 1011). The belief, in turn, obviously depends on the apparent class of the signer, the assumed "authority of the possessor expressed upon paper" (VI, 1010). The seller gives that authority to the buyer by interpreting through the lenses of the class-system one who could be no more than the "author" of a fiction, as Shelley knew from signing notes he never did repay. A hierarchy is thereby implanted in a place that could be empty (the place behind the visible sign and its signer), allowing the sign to refer up to a "right to so much gold" that itself refers back to a "right to so much labor" supposedly at the buyer's "command" (VII, 1010). Worse yet, although the note's receiver has thus transferred the dictates of an ideology to the signer, the signer has transferred nothing; he has simply taken in, as Jupiter did, the power given to him by one who would "know the truth" and raise it to the level of "authority," and he has used that gift to make himself entitled to labor, its sign, and the sign of that sign. If a "labourer or artisan" is the seller in this case, he is "defraud[ed]" of any "advantage attached to increasing the nominal price of [the] labor," for, whatever the price, it is deferred, through the signed note, to a parliamentary writ declaring "that the persons who hold the office for . . . payment," the Bank of England and the buyer, [can]not be forced by law to pay" (VI, 1013). All "increase" of "industry," urged on by inflated prices, is therefore pulled by such buyers toward themselves and their class without the slightest property or right to property (what gold has always been) having to move the other way to those who produce the increase.

The gold standard, or at least Ricardo's proposal for reducing the number of usable notes until the "remainder [are] of equal value with the coins which they represent,"[32] is consequently a fairer basis for exchange. That is not just because it would lower the rate of inflation but because the coin (or note equal to one) is more likely to remain a crossroads—a center only in that sense—through which all the directions in any exchange are in motion simultaneously. To begin with, unlike paper money, which may be the mark of nothing, a gold piece has to be a "sign of labor" like all the commodities it pays for. It is molded from "precious metals" by a process of mining, extraction, combination, and conversion (*S&C*, VI, 1004 and 1010) and so objectifies a labor process, as Ricardo puts it, "produced with such proportions [of labour and capital] as approach nearest to the average quantity employed in the production of most commodities."[33] Even more to the point, the fact that the pressed metal is affixed with a "stamp" by "the [government of] a country" establishing the result as legal tender (VI, 1004) makes this highly typical commodity the embodiment, the channel, of the entire exchange process. The coin becomes the conduit of a motion transferring products to their destinations and giving the producers, in return, the power to buy products from their consumers or other producers. When Marx finally carries out the tendency in this token, he therefore sees gold in its "money-form as but the reflex, thrown upon one single commodity, of the value-relations beween all the rest."[34] Stamped gold, to keep quoting Marx, is the ultimate "fetishizing" of the many interplays into which labor's produce must pass; it is "the objective appearance of the [entirely] social [rather than individual] characteristics of labour." On top of all this, the sanctioned coin is the most metamorphic of products, and not just because its basic material is among the most malleable, divisible, and recombinable of metals. It can be (as a price) what commodities are converted to and can be immediately (as compensation) converted to what labor produces, thus allowing Shelley to grant the same legal "advantages" to the possession of "gold and silver" and the possession of "goods" (*S&C*, VI, 1011). Because labor leads to it, the product of worker effort, gold (like goods) entitles any worker possessing it to an immediate (not delayed) "command [over someone else's] labour" and the goods that labor generates (VI, 1010).

A coin, we must conclude, if unalloyed and undebased, is a double transfiguration available to everyone, a turning of labor's product into the synecdoche of all labor relations which also transforms labor-for-others into the right to the labor of others. Consequently, it holds out this right to every member of every social group, gold being common coin, not a certificate conveying "authority" only to members of the upper classes. Granted, since its tracing of the relations conflated by it can disappear from its surface and use, as they can from any fetish, these potentials in gold can too easily be suppressed to make it one class's "title" to "unequal distribution" (VI, 1004). Even prior to paper money, coin can be gathered by the few in tribute or stamped with the mark of a sovereign licensing and "mask[ing] the power of the rich" to tax everyone else (VI, 1002–3). But gold never signifies what bank notes do: the indefinite deferral of the receiver's power over labor. It betokens right away the power to set the entire range of economic relations into a give-and-take surging toward and through the possessor.

All this, admittedly, is not to say that Shelley simply advocates a return to the outlawed gold standard. Actually, like Cobbett, he is more interested in dissolving the national debt that seems to have brought on the recourse to paper money and thereby removing the fear that there is not enough gold to pay for the principal and interest that the wealthy owe the wealthy. The real issue is how long, to what extent, and by what means the effort of the laborer can be transferred into the power over labor, the "other" to which the worker is entitled but which non-workers too often possess. How, Shelley is asking, is power over others to become everyone's common recompense so that no one has a monopoly on it, so that "power" can become no more than the most daily give-and-take, an always shifting transfer of power between both sides of an equal relationship? The reassignment of labor's alienation to the laborer, though the alienation remains, is Shelley's method for disseminating the power over labor beyond its present holders, whatever form (gold or not) such power finally takes. What he wants workers to possess, according to passages already quoted, is "property," yet not in the mere sense of something owned that never leaves the laborer's side. Shelley is again being literal and, recalling Locke's political writing, taking "property" back to what is "one's own" as a result of what is "particular" to oneself *(propertius)*. The "exertion of [anyone's] own bodily and mental faculties," he writes just as Locke did,[35] should be mirrored by "the produce and free reward from and for that exertion" (*S&C*, VI, 1036–37). It is as though the product and payment for it were both metaphors (as well as metonyms) reflecting a significance from another realm, that of commodities, back to an earlier expense of labor-power that has no meaning on its own. The exchange retransfers the labor-power that commodities signify for everyone into the hands of the particular worker in response—and in some proportion—to his particular exertion. Were every person to gain this sort of ownership from such an alien place in such a two-way manner, each would find that this "privilege of disposing [at] will" of a power over another's labor (a commodity or coin) would be equivalent to another's power over the laborer's work (another commodity or coin). Everyone would see that there never should have been and never should be again "any great and invidious inequality of fortune" (*S&C*, VI, 1034). Even if "industry" and "economy" on the part of some producer-consumers led to slight inequalities of ownership for brief periods of time, the temporary "accidents" of scarce materials and changing demand would later "level . . . that elevation" (though not reverse it as completely as Smith would allow), and the "signs of property [most of the time] would perpetually recur to those whose deserving skill might attract and whose labor might create it" (VI, 1034).

The distinction between gold and paper money, it turns out, is but a symptom of the more basic difference between real and false property. The most equalizing qualities and potentials in gold are all aspects of the "true . . . species of property" just described (VI, 1033–34). That sign of labor-power, in fact, given gold's potential for abuse, is discussed mainly as but one present avenue to a better future, something that need no longer be (and is not) mentioned when that future is finally proposed. Paper money, meanwhile, because the bearer signs for an amount to which he may have no real title and which he may not have labored to earn, is the latest synecdoche pointing to the other sort of property "which has its foundation in usurpation or imposture"

(VI, 1034). Here Shelley locates most of the "property enjoyed by the aristocracy and by the great fund holders" (VI, 1034–35). It ranges from grounds or houses acquired from sovereigns as rewards for conquests elsewhere to "lands" repossessed from the suppressed "Catholic clergy" and then to "products of patents and monopolies." The last of these iniquitous exchanges points to the proceeds of large-scale factory labor that go in large part to an investor or an inventor's patron, even an absentee owner, who has more often signed his name to an exclusive-rights document than performed the day-to-day work in the factory (VI, 1035). In all these cases the power over labor has been stolen by a party divorced from the endeavors of the many who actually developed the property itself. The transfer each time is illegitimate for Shelley—quite literally, since the official "parent" is in no case the real one—because the owner has never turned his energy or being (as a writer does) into what is regarded as his product. The product cannot reflect him, for it has been transferred from its true base back to him, not back to the workers that it really represents. It is the sign of a sign (or of the usurper's title, deed, or signature) rather than the sign of a metaphor (of labor's exten-sion of itself into its product). In addition, for this usurpation to occur, those entitled to the property must be divested of most of it, as laborers (or poets) are cheated by the paper money that promises what may never be paid to them in full.

The descent of such property through the eldest son (Shelley's "expectations" not-withstanding) is no legitimation of this tyranny, as Edmund Burke has said it is,[36] though it has granted this usurpation "the property of a snowball" for many years (S&C, VI, 1036). As Shelley sees it, "absolute right becomes weakened by descent," even when the descendents look back to a first owner who "created [the property] by his labor or skill" (VI, 1034). The descendents usually have not contributed their own effort and so might as well be usurper-aristocrats. In them, "the principle upon which all property rests . . . becomes [quickly] disregarded and misunderstood," the perpet-uation of a mere ideology giving an heir "discretion . . . in matters of property," an ideology now separated from the labor that gave a particular person that discretion in the first place (VI, 1034). Shelley does hesitate, we should note, when he denies that discretion to the true laborer who leaves his property to his children. Yet he has no qualms about urging the public redistribution of property descended from heirs or suggesting the graduation of future taxes according to the type of property, earned or inherited or owned, which each person claims as his. Any sudden need for "a tax on capital" should not rob labor of the proceeds reflecting it but should usurp only the property of those who have usurped, paying both the real owner and the false one back in kind (VI, 1037).

The future that such devices should open up for workers, however, is not the one that we might expect from an author who seems (and is) such a proto-Marxist. Shel-ley's hesitation over "discretion" is quite telling, mainly because of the contradictions it indicates. On the one hand, it reveals how much he tends toward a return for labor unrelated to any sort of class system, almost a stance of "from each according to his ability and to each according to his need." On the other hand, the poet admits (with Godwin in *Political Justice*) how very personal property is for him. There is no com-mon pool of labor's produce from which everyone draws equally without personal ownership, as they do in Marx's communism (which Shelley could not know) and in the state socialism of Robert Owen (which Shelley certainly knew).[37] True, the alien-ation of the product from labor is, in the end, a positive development in all these philosophies, even in Shelley's where the alienating act (production) creates a system (commodities) for defining, socializing, and returning the expense of the self. But in Shelley's version this alienation is the sort of transference of the self into the other where the self tries to discover, even create, its own nature by way of a reflector "which it resembles" and so would recover for itself. This reading of the self "out there" in order to have an identity at all is not simply narcissistic, though it surely is that; it is semi-bourgeois (as Godwin is), despite, indeed because of, Shelley's aristocratic effort to bridge the gap between his class and the proletariat in a revised *noblesse oblige*. To say that the individual producer becomes what he or she is by coming to own the proceeds in which the product is alienated is almost to adopt the ideology that the entrepreneur has the right to be what he makes of himself and to have what he gathers to himself from what he sells, even though Shelley would want to add that each producer wishes the same capacity for everyone else. Much as this poet pays attention, encouraged by Owen, to the wider social interplay and inequities drawing in and returning (or *not* returning) labor-power, only money for Shelley—not the labor process itself—"fetishizes" the entire context impinging upon it. What applies to an unbound mythograph, its scandalous playing across ideological formations from different quarters, applies only to certain aspects, the circulating signs, of day-to-day labor, at least at present and in the immediate future. Consequently, recoiling with Leigh Hunt from the current "wheel" of society's mechanism driven by moneylenders so they can gather the spin-offs of centrifugal force, Shelley envisions almost cottage industries in his equalized world of tomorrow. He does not accept what Marx would later have to: the massive network of job functions, partly similar and partly different, that work would increasingly become as industrialism accelerated. Even the city at its best to Shelley would be a series of "tradesm[en] who [are] not monopolists . . . [of] surgeons and physicians . . . artists and farmers, all [of] whose profits spring [more] from their own skill and wisdom or strength, [from] honestly and honorably exerting, than from the employment of money to take advantage . . . of the starvation of their fellow citizens for their profit" (*S&C,* VI, 1032).

But, then again, Shelley as laborer/writer was a crossroads of contradictory ideologies himself. The *noblesse oblige* of the aristocracy he inherited came to him colored by the bourgeois acquisitiveness of his grandfather Bysshe, the son of a tradesman who became a self-made landed gentleman and baronet (with the aid of shrewdly lucrative marriages).[38] Partly because of his mercantile attitude, Shelley was brought up to be a Whig, a member of that high- to middle-class party itself divided between acquisitive and estate-centered aims.[39] Even his reading after he broke from the conservative and moderate Whigs turns out to have offered him different images of the working self projected by different class orientations. Volney holds out the aristocrat-scientist rescuing advanced empirical inquiry from the mystifications of lower-class religion; Leigh Hunt the reasoned compassion of the "middle gentry" actively improving its estates and its tenants; Hume the bourgeois experimenter with noninherited assumptions gradually acquired and modified by practical experience; Smith and Ricardo the independent producer reinvesting earned capital into the expansion of his enterprise; Rousseau the petty-bourgeois tutor retiring from the urban class struggle to the genteel cultivation of natural gardens; Cobbett the rural laborer with "natural ability" producing all the resources of civilized life; and Godwin the unclassed and steadily improving but frugal and rational man (the son of a dissenting minister, as he was) keeping only as much as he needs in his private sphere while everyone else uses the same amount in theirs.[40]

It should therefore come as no surprise that Shelley's *View* attempts a composite figure for labor that uses pieces of all these ideals while trying to minimize the quirks peculiar to each class bias. The "tradesman" of his hopes, while maintaining the individual "discretion" that each of these images demands in some way, joins aristocratic "honor" and well-educated "wisdom" to "plebeian . . . utility," agrarian "strength," and a businesslike drawing of "profits" from "skill" rather than traffic in other people's money (*S&C,* VI, 1032). Fredric Jameson has rightly called this kind of construction a "romance" in that it strives to resolve intricate class conflicts in a fictive act of desire, all the while intimating a "political unconscious" aware of how pervasive the conflicts are in the fragmented world that the romance tries to heal.[41] Shelley's attempt is a good case in point because it announces the very polyglot system that it tries to level and cure. It proposes an almost bourgeois, class-based ideal in order for its equalized figure to dispossess the aristocracy and elevate the poor above subsistence. In avoiding much of what Marxism finally projects, the *View* still confirms a Marxist analysis of authors (Jameson's in particular) and reveals the Promethean intertext very much in operation behind the surface argument that would contain its multiplicity.

What remains special about this poet's sense of labor, nonetheless, is how deftly he exploits his duplicity in his half-centripetal/half-centrifugal images. Transference, by being both unifying and disruptive in its movement, allows Shelley to fashion composites that argue against double standards even while employing some, admittedly in the hope of extending real self-transfiguration to a larger range of people than now have access to it. The portrait of the honest tradesman in the *View* employs the word "profit" twice, partly to distinguish once more beween false and true variations. Profit in its worst sense resembles Marx's "surplus value," the price added to a commodity only so that those who market it can make money over and above the amount they expended in the production phase. The stock-jobbers and lenders as Shelley presents them take this "greater abundance" as their be-all and end-all. They value increased "capital" as an end in itself instead of caring for the "exertions" it buys and costs; hence these sorts of people work to lower or fix the wages of labor whenever they can so that their profits from sales can rise beyond the expenses of production (*S&C,* VI, 1032). "Profits spring[ing directly from] exert[ed] skill" must not be confused with such a rapacious "starvation" of workers; this second type of profit should be the later abundance coming to the laborer that somehow answers labor's increased output of "skill and wisdom and strength" as these qualities all strive to make better products (1032). "Surplus value" is castigated by Shelley if it is used in the sense of a greater capital return on a smaller capital investment, yet such a value beyond the value of the time and energy expended by labor is made the worker's rightful property if it comes back to him instead of going on to some other investor or seller. Shelley reinstalls "progression to a point beyond the *status quo,*" which is the very basis of "profit" (the meaning of the Latin *profectus*), into the succession of worker-buyer relations from which merchants and moneylenders have stolen it, all in an image that is both a celebration and a rejection of bourgeois economics. The further translation of already transfigured labor into the payment for the product is here the repetition with a difference, the third term, that it always ought to be. Yet this is true in the best sense for Shelley *only* if the payment translates labor's earlier exertion of itself into a power over other labor greater than the worker had when he first expended his energy *and* if that extension empowers the laborer's additional transformation by being invested in an expanded mode of production that he can use, not simply congealed into capital for the sake of making more capital. Such a modification of the initial term (the worker's expense) cannot occur if the subsequent transmutations of it are referred to another agent (a different basic term). Nor has a genuine sequence of transfigurations really happened if an entity (money) changes its form for a time only to be turned back into a larger amount of what it already was. Some day, Shelley concludes, labor should become what it really can be for every individual: a daily reinvestment of effort and resources seeking a greater return that labor can reuse differently. Then work can become an expansion of each person's capacities at every stage in its development. Only in that self-renewing process can the "one harmonious soul of many a soul" desired near the end of *Prometheus Unbound* (IV, 400) come into being as a harmony of equals, maintain the many differences in its population, and draw circle after circle of human achievement and possibility around the existing limits of labor now striving beyond themselves.

How the Language of Legality Can Free People from the Law

There is a well-entrenched obstacle that labor must neutralize to reach that long-deferred point, however. There is "the Law," one of the bodies of "visible symbols which express the degree of power [claimed] by [the dominant] party [or classes]" (*S&C*, VI, 966), that set of supposed standards that can give rise to a writ declaring that signers of bank notes need not be forced to pay creditors or laborers in gold. Law has become a strikingly effective shield for concealing high-class power plays from the eyes of the wider public, for it wrests language into what seems a "durability . . . of forms within which the oppressors entrench themselves" as though the forms were grounds of being (VI, 1058). Paper money's illegitimacy must be sanctioned by law because both it and law are signs of what can only be signs (in law's case, signs of legislative action), and yet both types (especially laws) are set up by declarations, using the cover of the official edict, to be commands apparently uttered from an unimpeachable center of authority. If there is anything grounding law besides such a center, it is supposed to be the unwritten British Constitution, or what Shelley would call "that legislature created by the general representation of the past feelings of [Englishmen]," a nationalized version of the Great Memory recast as an often-altered ideology of social and political mores (*Speculations, CW*, VII, 82).[42] This "basis" is of course a many-layered concatenation of class-based traditions and maneuvers from different historical moments, all now so removed from their complex foundations that those origins are even more obscure than they were when they existed. That palimpsest may seem to make the law more groundless and confused than it usually claims to be; the young Shelley even delights in the Constitution's "indefiniteness and versatility" because its malleable elements might be reinterpreted (as in *The Mask of Anarchy*) to "accommodate" reform ("Address to the Irish People," *CW*, V, 244n.). But the Shelley of 1819, as we shall see, often finds that the Constitution shores up the law's power by obscuring the conflicts that brought most laws about, even the conflicts of recent years, which are often justified by those in power as natural outgrowths of the Constitution. Thus he accepts more and more Godwin's paradoxical definition of law in *Political Justice* as an "unbound multiplication" of claims based on "uncertainty" and yet a reduction of people's "actions . . . to one standard," a "sophistry" that stops the self-expansion of the mind, making it "look to some foreign guidance for the direction of its conduct."[43] Shelley agrees with the last part of that definition as early as his letters to Godwin in 1812, where he sees that the human attachment to signs without a critique of their actual generators and referents licenses "the growth and establishment of prejudice: the learning of *words* before the mind is capable of attaching correspondent ideas to them" (*L*, I, 317, my emphasis).

The reformer, as a result, has to square off against law and its language if he or she is to alter the realms of labor it regulates and the structure of classes it serves. Moreover, he has to do so within the language the law employs. There is no other means by which the challenge can be articulated and no medium so able to reveal the repression of its own real foundation: the transference, if only of desire into words, underlying the law's supposed permanence and power. In general, then, the assault on law as it presently exists can best be waged from two directions at the same time. One of these, argued most forcefully in a Shelley fragment usually called "A System of Government by Juries" and dated in early 1820 (right after the *View*), tries to break down the construction of law into the layered acts that have produced its present language. It sees that "government," however rudimentary, begins when "masses of the product of labor are committed to the discretion of certain individuals for the purpose of executing [the product's] intentions, or interpreting its meaning" (*CW*, VI, 289). That transfer is from the start a linguistic act giving the authority behind the product and the product itself (like a written text) into the hands of interpreters, allowing them both to determine its intentions and to take on the authority granted to "meaning's" true announcers. This initial move and its inequities are forgotten when the class structure begun by this delegating act turn into seemingly "permanent forms which regulate the deliberation or the action of the whole," whether the resulting "state is democratical, or aristocratical, or despotic, or a combination of all these principles" (*CW*, VI, 289). Indeed these forms ensure the veiling of their impetus, and even the concealment of their own dominance, by overlaying themselves with "the necessary or accidental" parts of government—almost an ideological superstructure interpreting and concealing a more "fundamental" base. Chief among these "parts" are the "constitution," the "traditions which determine the individuals who are to exercise [the] discretionary right" that all laborers should have in equal measure, and "Law," the "mode of determining those opinions according to which the constituted authorities are to decide any action" (VI, 289). Once this succession of masks is made fully apparent, law can be exposed as the mere "collection of opinions" that it is, divorced from the natural origin it tries to give itself and unveiled as "opinion" conceived "for regulating political power" (VI, 290). At this point the initial transfer of discretion can be recalled and reversed, at least to the degree that some nonauthorities (as the Constitution would define them) can become interpreters—local juries, in fact—if they have a sense of history and an awareness of what current economic options suggest as the most fruitful human beliefs. Now the judgment of actions can start becoming more a relational instead of a prescribed mode of analysis, more open to the full interplay of all the "arguments" and "particular[s]" impinging upon a particular situation (VI, 291).[44] Even the average mind can refuse to believe automatically in established "forms" that are no more than old (though widespread) "superstitions." If that happens, "the most exploded violations of humanity," still ordered by judges today on the basis of "obscure records [from] dark and barbarous epochs," can no longer "maintain their ground in courts of law after public opinion has branded them with reprobation" (291).

The other general plan of attack on the law should be a new understanding of the mind-language relationship, one that accepts Shelley's view, discussed in my introduction, of how thoughts and verbal patterns generate one another out of the continual pressure for expansion that each exerts on its counterpart. In the first place, more people should analyze that dependence of the mind on the word which Shelley points to so often in 1812 and after. Laws, they should see, would not gain the power to make people regard them as historical and absolute did not thinking depend on and desire a sign-system to give it shape—and mistakenly assume that system, later, to be independent of what it shapes. This tendency, almost a necessity, permits thought to pass its own responsibility over a widely used order outside itself that can hide the influence of personal and class priorities on verbal assertions about social arrangements. Words, on their side, suit that desire because they really are as transpersonal, as interreferential between themselves and rules for their use, as they are attracted to constructions of thought, society, or nature that their syntax can be enlisted to signify and create. Thus, especially when they drift beyond the referents urged on them by earlier hierarchies and contexts of opinion (which they helped to manufacture), words can seem to dictate their best-known directives from a place outside all the efforts of people at particular moments. They can appear "magic" and incantatory, calling their receivers to accept their transcendent truth and suggesting that "any given form of words" can be made to "persuade" anyone of anything, provided the hearer has a need that those words can answer (*L,* I, 91; April 6, 1819).

Concurrently, though, this same analysis should realize how much that need is one of the drives in language as well as people. Words perpetually differ from themselves and each other because they are always hearkening to other words that have their own deferred reference points, always more desired than attained. Linguistic symbols therefore gravitate into contexts to give individual forms specific functions and limited ranges of significance, yet each formation, to complete and further itself, to bring itself nearer to its ever-receding referents, needs other contexts different from its own that often exceed the present frame of reference and many of the significations it suggests. Hence language is both in pursuit of a thought system to construct and obey, deferring its own responsibility, and inherently "susceptible of more various and delicate combinations" of its symbols at any given point in its history (*Defence,* p. 483). That "flexibility" for Shelley is nearly always responsible for and indicative of revolutionary shifts in the thinking of a culture. Throughout the *View's* survey of civilizations, language's capacity for refracting its patterns into a "many-sided mirror," a series of different contexts or arrangements that could reflect the same thought in different ways, helps thought to see itself as (and make itself) "ever changing" and so to incorporate a "severe[,] bold, and liberal spirit of criticism," even self-criticism, into its assertions (*S&C,* VI, 982). When this resurgence attains a real "comprehensiveness," as it soon may in England, a society can fight against, though only from within, the "erroneous and illogical" restrictions on "intuitions into truth"—such restrictions as old laws in particular—to a point where "panic stricken tyrants" may have to promise "that their governments [shall] be administered according to republican forms" (VI, 981–82). After all, it is the malleability and deferral, in addition to the universality, of language that once permitted class interests to appropriate its methods for composing contexts of words restricting what those words could mean. It thus has to be that same fluidity, rediscovered and reawakened, which is used to undermine the "obscure records" of law. Reformers, as a result, must adopt tactics that reveal how much law is contingent on economic, historical, and linguistic change, and these gambits must begin by exposing the old transfers and the persistent transferability in the present articulations of law that still try to mask what brought such edicts about.

These general strategies, in other words, dictate some specific ones acting within or upon the language of the law to make the law disperse the centers of power it creates. One ploy that Shelley recommends urges people to ask the law first to interpret all phenomena by the strict letter of itself and then to carry out the literal interpretation of its own words. The two aristocracies of high-class borrowers and lenders, for example, should be read as the civil courts might read them, as having "mortgaged . . . all land in the nation . . . for the amount of the national debt" (*S&C,* VI 1029). That contextualization, the law's usual method for restricting a phenomenon's range of reference in order to control it, should now be forced to insist on the legal consequences: "to use the language of the law, let the mortagee foreclose" (VI, 1030), let the debtor's collateral pass to the creditor, let there be a "transfer among persons of property" reversing the direction of the one that has already taken place. When the law's language is insisted upon and simultaneously parsed to expose its roots, everyone discovers that there is no "literal" base. The base if anything turns out to be a metalepsis, a concealment of one transfer (between two wealthy parties) by a very different one (a debt charged to the entire population).

The law can also be trapped in another way because it is tied by its own rules to the validity of its prior commitments. Once the earlier of these two transfers has been uncovered, the law must reinterpret the later version according to the dictates of the one that is prior. The law must thereby confront its basis as always a kind of mortgage, an alienation of property (or risk of its loss) by the people in return for the power to acquire this property and more, unencumbered by present limitations. In Shelley's eyes the law announced that exchange as its foundation in 1688. It acknowledged that government was a delegation of the people's will to a few representatives—and thus a risking of that will's usurpation—to ensure "the benefit of the people" that mere individuals could not secure without a government, but with the limitation that people had the *"right . . . to change their government"* if the benefit were withheld (*S&C,* VI, 968–69). Since then, the usurpation has actually occurred, along with foreign wars in the people's name without the people's consent and at the expense of the public benefit now being taxed away instead of being distributed to the public. What that means legally is that the governing classes are now required to return sovereignty to those who mortgaged it away, since government has kept what it initially promised to give to its debtors, breaking its side of the mortgage contract, and has also ignored that contract's proviso, which can now insist on the change of government it holds in reserve. Meanwhile, all the actions on both sides of this contract over the years have been made to reveal their dependence on the mortgage-notion's ability to shift between contexts (from the financial to the governmental to the legal to the reformist). If that could not happen, law could not apply to all the other realms it conscripts, and because it does happen, law can be made to release that notion back into its free drift across meanings and classes.

Still, there is no harm in pursuing other stratagems while this one is being played out, especially if they tend toward a similar scattering of what has been contained and concealed. Another tactic that Shelley recommends would take advantage of law's confused "multiplication" on top of a "ground" that is only a transfer of desires and needs between people. In this strategem members of all the classes would exploit the veil-upon-veil of legal language that bases law's power on the obscurity of its expression, the obfuscation of its uncertain base. Great numbers of people would "confound the subtlety of lawyers with the subtlety of the law" in a barrage of petitions and suits forcing Parliament and the courts to defend, and thus clarify, the stances they seem to have taken (*S&C,* VI, 1059). A clarifiction would have to reveal the fact of the obfuscations upon which legality rests, forcing government officials to put in question the "durability of those forms within which the oppressors entrench themselves." In that way the law could be made to accept its relation to uncertainty, historical change, and the mutability of its own language—all the things that leave it open to different interpretations. Law, by being questioned, could finally emerge as constantly in need of self-revision without having to assume a rigidly static core. It could come to be regarded a self-reinterpreting order very like those it tries to interpret, like the personalities and social conditions around it that always try to define themselves through it in order to gain a greater good for a greater number. At the same time, the upper-class resistance to these changes, still claiming that its "durability" is licensed by the public opinion that once granted it power, could come to behold the widening gap between that very opinion and the supposed center of law: the British Constitution interpreted as transferring the rights of everyone to the upper classes. The more an "overwhelming multitude of defendants" raises "doubts" about taxation, government, and "jurisdiction" in "courts of common law," the more "the existing depositories of power" might see that their methods of production have become outdated by rising forms of endeavor and thus by the "active and vigilant . . . opposition" coming from "large bodies and various denominations of the people" (*S&C,* VI, 1058–59).

Hence all the interests that the Constitution and many of its laws have tried to keep separate (in "various denominations") should now present themselves as drifting together in legal petitions to form interrelations that legal language would like to prevent. Alongside its uncertainty, historicity, and divorce from social mobility, the law must be made to see how the "subtlety" it employs can cross between the boundaries that it has created itself. Good petitions should therefore show the law "the diversity of the convictions they entertain," pressing law to face up to the differences in people that it often works to forget. Then these expressions of conviction should propose such "connection[s as the one] between national prosperity[,] Freedom and the cultivation of the imagination" (VI, 1059–60). These interplays, once verbalized, would link acquisition, decentralized government, and a greater "going out of ourselves" in a fashion that the language of the law has resisted for many thousands of years (VI, 1059–60). It is as part of such a petition drive, in fact, that the best refashioner of language, the poet, should find his place in the reformist movement. While others file suits, appeals, and protests in abundance, starting to confront the law with the unsteadiness of any language system, the writer should pour forth public "memorials" insisting that this fluidity seek the "unapprehended relations" of unsanctioned verbal interplays, at least to expose the "blindness" or begin the "confusion" of those who uphold the fixity of the law (VI, 1060).

Indeed, all Shelley's proposals for undermining the law augment themselves by redefining the range of those engaged in the legal process, as should be the case in a *Philosophical View* arguing for the wide redistribution of sequestered and specialized powers. Shelley urges large segments of the public to invade the hallowed halls of the law legally and legalistically in order to pull formal decisionmaking about proper conduct and the order of the state into the public sphere, into a quasi-Athenian meeting of the *polis,* where the public eye can judge the process of judgment by how much it considers the larger public welfare that law was created to protect. At some stage of true reform, the various interest groups should come to a broadened space of debate and begin "a process of negotiation" starting with "the oppressors . . . imperfectly conced[ing] some limited portion of the Rights of the people" and the people realizing they must sometimes "pause until by the exercise of those rights . . . they become fitted to demand more" (*S&C,* VI, 1060–61). This off-and-on conclave may "occupy twenty years" or more, yet it will prevent "civil war" and open up the possibilities of social reorganization by experimenting with the very language of law so long resistant to this kind of change (1061). As a result of such a forum, law, a public mode of discourse, now returned to its self-transformative nature, may arrive at new definitions or repositionings of the people and groups it has already named. Such reformulations in language could even interpret the tension between the negotiating parties so as to balance the need for both equality and conformity with a respect for personal differences. "In [such an] instance," the notion of an underlying "Constitution" might return to being what some "approved writers," Godwin in particular, think it once was and might be again (VI, 1061).[45] It might become no more than an unstated assumption "declaratory of the superior decisions of eternal justice," an insistence that all negotiated decisions now and in the future aim at an equal allotment of resources and potentials among the different types of people (1061).

And yet, given the law's self-protective ability to keep its power hoarded by its agents and minions even in public sessions, this kind of forum may still be far off, much as it may be approached very briefly in some court cases, town meetings, and parliamentary debates. The attack on law, then, should probably fall back to inch toward that and other possibilities with smaller forays in local areas, each committed to achieving the same kind of flexible exchange. One arena for Shelley that should be altered as soon as possible is the district elections for members of Parliament, assuming that some reapportionment has begun to draw national representatives toward confronting the larger populations of more and fairer districts. Such elections in the past have usually been small meetings where higher-class male electors have cast open or secret votes with little discussion. The candidates themselves have often been present, as have the wealthy patrons who have set up some of them as placemen, and the votes have usually been tallied before them all, whereupon the winner has been declared and celebrated.[46] Bentham's *Plan of Parliamentary Reform* (1817), at times a model for the *Philosophical View,* has urged much greater secrecy, in addition to a vast expansion of the electorate, to protect the voter from the pressure applied by candidates and patrons who may stand glowering right in front of him.[47] Shelley, however, discounts Bentham's assumption that the elector is ideally alone with his own will and not at all subject to the will of others; in the *View* the future voter, partly following the example of the "small parish" citizen in Godwin's *Political Justice,*[48] should attend a meeting of electors (carrying the old practice forward to intensify its public aspect) and declare his vote along with his "motive" while everyone else does the same in a vibrant "popular assembly" (*S&C,* VI, 1047). This procedure would make private opinions, too inclined to be antisocial if they are kept secret, test themselves in a give-and-take with others to discover how much each personal view has

considered the needs of "another and many others." As the voter's sense of his difference is modified immediately by the differences and similarities expressed by those
nearby, the "sentiments" of each participant could be expanded in a "going out" of
the self toward every opinion in the room. "The imagination would thus be excited"
toward the formation of a "common sympathy," a "mass of generous and enlarged
and popular sentiments," that would draw the entire electorate, including the candidates, into the pursuit of the common interest (VI, 1047). Along the way the "elector
and the elected [would] meet one another face, to face [*sic*]" in a fashion whereby they
could "interchange [their] meanings by actual presence and share some common
impulses and in a degree, understand each other" (1047). Here Shelley may be recasting Socrates' defense of oral dialectic in Plato's *Phaedrus* (277–78), emphasizing how
"actual presence" is more likely than written ballots to represent the needs and desires
in the body and thoughts of each voter. Even so, the poet's chief hope is that "representation" in the parliamentary sense will henceforth mean a member's recollection
of a thorough transference between himself and his constituents. From this verbal
interplay at each election, Shelley imagines, the representative will grasp the nature of
his common ground with the voters and be sympathetic to the "degree" of difference
(and similarity) between his understanding and theirs, so much so that his votes on
laws will try to serve the majority interest without harming members of classes other
than his own.

   Meanwhile, if this electoral process still fails to bring on the "negotiation" it
begins, that goal can be pursued in the legislature itself by a change in Parliament's
construction that would make it more like those local meetings. The *View* thus offers
the brief, almost cryptic, proposal that the people's delegates "unite . . . the legislative
and executive functions" in all they do (*S&C*, VI, 1043). As the government now operates, the lawmaking functions are divided, first between the crown and the Parliament,
then between upper and lower houses, and even in the Commons between House and
the ministries, which members frequently occupy to serve upper-class interests often
removed from the concerns of their districts. The results of deliberative interplay (the
legislative function at its best)—already inhibited by the way each debate refers to the
interests of the parties either in or out of the ministries—are consequently given over,
like labor from the laborer, into the hands of authorities (the executive functionaries)
who may change or enforce a new statute to shore up their own positions rather than
solve the problems addressed by the law itself. To be a true extension of deliberation,
enforcement would be no more than a relocation and redirection of a transfer-filled
discussion, one that keeps restoring the dialogue, the play of differences in that interchange, rather than asking it to disappear in favor of a monolithic dictate. Consequently, Shelley decides that legislation and administration should be performed by
the same representatives without some of them dividing into member/minister, without there being a "chamber [devoted only to] hereditary aristocracy," and without any
establishment of a "King" as a "rallying point" for the interests of the upper classes
(*S&C*, VI, 1039). The recommendation is largely Godwin's: the creation of an interim
republic governed by one congress and no other institution (1039) or, as *Political Justice* puts it, "a modified species of national assembly" in which "arguments and
addresses" brought up from and sent back to local meetings in the parishes would
come so close to being "commands" to the entire "confederacy" that the distinction
between lawmaking and enforcement would disappear.[49] Shelley and Godwin both
admit that the passions begotten by party divisions may remain in a nation with a

reformed assembly, to the point of forcing that body to issue orders for a time repressing their real grounding in face-to-face discussion. But as these remnants of the present order fade, the national legislature can become the open forum that Shelley wants it to be, a clearinghouse for public concerns verbally "persuading" its members and their constituents (Godwin's word) to labor for the larger public interest within a climate of interchange and accommodation gradually producing a common sense of the common good.

Nevertheless, the realm or body for Shelley that most needs to become, and can soonest be, an open conclave right away is still the courtroom jury supposedly made up of those "twelve contemporary *good and true men,* who should be the peers of the accused [in a criminal trial], or, in cases of property, of the claimant" in a suit ("A System of Government by Juries," *CW,* VI, 292). On the one hand, in Shelley's eyes this "assembly" has been employed more and more to sanction and cloak the despotism of the aristocracy, the church, and the upper bourgeoisie, particularly in the Carlile case. On the other hand, the existing language defining juries states that such power plays, even when concealed—and particularly when they divide the symbolic systems of juries from those of defendants—contravene the letter and spirit of the law governing jury trials. If a person is really to be tried "by a jury of his *peers*" (my emphasis), writes Shelley in yet another effort to trumpet the "strict legal import of [a] word," the verbal rendering of the defendant's actions should be subject to the interpretation only of "men of the same station [or] denomination with himself." Such "readers," though Shelley does not use that word here, will have enough "sympathy" for the basic situation of the accused to avoid "commit[ting an] injustice towards him" unless they can read him as having violated the "interests[,] habits, and opinions" that he and they share in "common" (*L,* II, 137). Such reciprocity can be compromised a little, as when some Englishmen sit alongside some foreigners to judge a defendant from outside England, especially if there need to be mediators between "inexperienced" defendants and an understanding of British pressures on foreigners sufficient for "knowing and weighing the merits of the case" (II, 137). But in general, English jurisprudence should be forced to revive the guarantee already in the language of the law that the accused and his judges will always speak a common language with agreed-on definitions for words in which can emerge the defendant's exact relation to the particular social context by which he is already defined. If this return of a now-repressed interchange fails to occur in the near future, juries can keep doing what the recent one did to Carlile and try him by their Anglican definitions of the words applied to a deist, using the law's language as an "instrument" of war against a "theological opponent" (*L,* II, 154).

In the end, law will never be fair or flexible for Shelley unless its enactment becomes at least a jury-discussion in "every possible occasion of jurisprudence" (*Philosophical View, S&C,* VI, 1028). There must be so little restriction on this free exchange by fixed statutes or high-class dictators and so much reason[ing, so much] hear[ing of the] arguments of others upon . . . the life, or liberty, or property, or reputation" involved in "each particular case" ("A System of Government," *CW,* VI, 291) that each judgment can be determined one at a time by a group interpretation of all relevant factors and a decision as to whether these factors encourage or impede the distribution of beneficial pleasures beyond a small group of people. In such an activity, law could become less a collection of axioms and more a community process of understanding and caring, always revising its conclusions as more factors are considered.

Surely, by calling that late fragment "A System of Government by Juries," Shelley is reworking Godwin's dream of confederated boroughs, each of which would center on a panel of very different but well-educated men and women evaluating all debatable acts in their particular region.[50] The national assembly, if one were necessary, would be a more comprehensive but less often used arena for deliberation and would defer as much as possible to these local conclaves so that they could work out the ethics of their societies in a thoroughly relational interchange of proposals. These face-to-face encounters could blend into a national negotiation if problems remained in the distribution of equality. Or perhaps that negotiation need never be carried out, should society dissolve into equal sectors, all determining the order within themselves by roughly the same decision-making process. At this point, of course, Shelley's deferred hopes become as vague, incomplete, and blended as such projections must always be. Yet the general image of a wide-open public forum of continual negotiation still hovers in the distance before us, with only an awareness of history and experience as its guide and the malleability of language as its principal tool. We can drive on past the present tyrannies using law as their cover by urging all current practices of law as far toward that target as they can be made to go. Even within the present language and the dimly remembered aspirations of law, methods of transfiguration are already there to help effect the change. All that is needed is a persistent and collective effort to free that mobility from the containers it has fashioned.

The Unbinding of the Political Association

How that effort can be made collective remains a nagging quandary in Shelley's political programme. Throughout the *View* he is sure that the true reformer must somehow "rally . . . the divided friends of liberty and make them forget the subordinate objects with regard to which they differ" by promoting "such open confederations among men of principle and spirit as may tend to make their intentions and efforts converge to a common center" (*S&C*, VI, 1053). But what form would such "confederations" take, given the recent and compelling but tortured history of extraparliamentary associations in England and Ireland? Godwin has condemned nearly all such groups—warning Shelley against them during the poet's crusade to Dublin in February and March 1812 (see *L*, I, 267–69)—because the past has shown them to be, as *Political Justice* claims, irrational, rabble-rousing, prone to party rivalries or violence, and inimical to free communication across class boundaries because of monolithic party lines that associations must promulgate in order to have a center and an aim.[51] Shelley has probably taken some comfort in his mentor's early support for the London Corresponding Society and the Society of Constitutional Information (now against the law);[52] in the concession during *Political Justice* allowing loose associations in times of crisis (such as now) to protect the persecuted and prevent public anarchy;[53] and in the tradition established by the United Irishmen, despite their suppression in 1803,[54] who once presented their goal as the embracing of widely different interests from Catholic emancipation to parliamentary reform, all in an atmosphere of "public discussion, ardent love of liberty, and greater [personal] independence [from centralized] government."[55] Nevertheless, evidence of Godwin's fears surrounds the poet everywhere he looks throughout the second decade of the nineteenth century. The Luddite uprisings of 1811 and 1812 and the large-scale, sometimes riotous meetings of the unemployed and disenfranchised from 1816 onward have only allowed the government to polarize the nation by brutally suppressing the "evil" of incipient violence in the name of the Constitution and national security. The secrecy of other such gatherings or groups has also encouraged the same "insincerity and concealment," hence selfishness, of motive that Shelley later fears in the use of secret ballots (*CW,* V, 259). It has even opened those societies to the government's imitation of their secretive tactics, to undercover agents of the Tories who have led malcontents into the open defiance that permits troops to close in on their meetings and courts to prosecute their leaders and publicists.[56] Worst of all, the ranks of the reformers have become severely "divided" into camps, particularly into the liberal Whig and urban moderates (Burdett, Leigh Hunt) on one side and the radicals (Henry Hunt, Cartwright, Cobbett) on the other, with the latter's rural base connecting them more to peasants, tenants, and small farmers. The journals in each camp, especially Hunt's *Examiner* and Cobbett's *Register,* have spent almost as much time attacking one another as they have urging the government to extend the franchise. Each has a class-based agenda so specific, votes for the mercantile bourgeoisie on one side and universal suffrage (except for women) on the other, that neither faction holds out a sufficiently classless, Godwinian objective beyond the winning of the most immediate goals.

For Shelley the solution naturally lies in a compromise among the factions and a search for a cause drawing them together with a unifying sense of purpose. But all this means that he must redefine the notion of "a common center" even as he describes one, since it is groups gathering around such cores that divide and defeat the movement toward reform. Up to the time of the *View,* nearly every opposition group has set itself against the government as though the group were an alternative circle of being with a center opposed essentially to the center of government's process—despite the fact that government did not really begin as a centered circle at all. Actually, when the products of labor were first "committed to the discretion" of various distributors, these "delegates" drew their different interests together centripetally toward a center that then came into existence as a fabricated ground for the nonlaboring classes, a supposed "Constitution" raising up a crown and then presenting itself as based on that authority. To avoid being as oppressive as that conflation has become, or at least to keep from imitating its self-enclosing procedure, opposition groups should keep stepping away from any one set of ideas or strict mode of organization they happen to attain. They should never say, as Cobbett has, that the government's effort to divide and destroy reformers means that the radicals' "main principles must be adhered to inflexibly."[57]

Shelley has found all this out the hard way by proposing a series of political associations throughout his career only to be forced by his own perceptiveness, as he was in his early philosophies, to modify every suggestion as soon as he makes it. The *View,* after all, is preceded, insofar as it offers new methods of association, by several shorter essays that articulate the need for purposeful groups, work out actual designs for them, and suggest at least some solutions to the problems that associations have always presented. In each piece, however, the urgings of transference toward interrelation that initially make each association desirable end up putting in question the form of association proposed and looking beyond the limits of that form to a different and broader-based interplay of people and objectives. Consequently, each essay keeps giving way to its successors and thus to further attempts at resolving the quandaries that remain—until the *View,* that is, responds to the quandaries with a two-pronged strategy: with a vision of fluid, nonviolent associations opening themselves to continual revision or expansion *and* with a style of argument that makes existing interest groups turn toward each other to revise the entire notion and process of association. To understand Shelley's final recommendations in this area, as well as his putting of transference into action, we therefore need to trace the self-revising movement in that essay-sequence as it builds toward and becomes the key to the theory of association in the *Philosophical View.*

The self-revision is apparent as early as the poet's very first proposals for associations. The initial one, at least among those he puts in writing, appears in an 1811 letter to Leigh Hunt written to congratulate the editor and his brother on their recent acquittal from charges of seditious libel. Here Shelley suggests that he, the Hunts, and other liberals "form a methodical society which should be organized so as to resist the coalition of the enemies of liberty which at present renders any expressions of opinion on policies dangerous to individuals" (*L*, I, 54). As P. M. S. Dawson points out, the nineteen-year-old poet is probably hinting at "a kind of insurance scheme for journalists, by which the costs of standing trial and paying fines would be defrayed from a fund raised by regular contributions."[58] Yet such a group designed for "mutual indemnification" (*L*, I, 54) might resist an "enemy coalition" by becoming one itself. Granted, Shelley tries to give his "committee" a position morally superior to that of England's ruling parties by half-modeling the group on the Spanish society of the *Illuminati* founded in 1776 and described to the poet's delight as a hotbed of heresy in Augustin de Barruel's *Memoirs, Illustrating the History of Jacobinism* (translated in 1797). But the greatness of that sect's vision, its commitment to the individual as the true "*sovereign* of his actions as of his thoughts," is negated by its members' pledges of secrecy, their oath of allegiance to an absolute leader patterned after Jesuit practice (a target of the society's resistance), and the leader's orders to them, according to Barruel, to "employ the same means for a good purpose which [others] employ for evil."[59] These tactics involve the individual *Illuminati* less in a "going out of themselves" to the needs "of another and of many others" and more in a conflation of rebellious feelings into and toward a center of near-monolithic consistency determined mimetically— and thus really submissively—by the standard of the order being opposed. For the individual to be a *"sovereign"* in this context is not for that word to be as utterly redefined as it would be in a Promethean future, but only for the resistant self and a group of such selves to try to duplicate, all too exactly, a tyrant's claim to absolute power. Shelley therefore retreats, even in the same letter, to the Godwinian model of a mere discussion group far less inwardly directed, one that should try to determine in nonviolent conversation how *"rational liberty"* can become the basis of what the *Illuminati* claim to desire, "a completely equalized community" throughout an entire civilization (*L*, I, 54).

In his next written plan, the "Proposals for an Association of Philanthropists" that immediately follows the "Address to the Irish People" in 1812, however, Shelley starts out with this last model only to discover that he must both expand and contract the scope of the idea if he is to be true to the tendencies within it. The new group should look beyond itself enough, he writes, to "corroborate and propogate philanthrophic feeling" in wider and wider circles beyond the association (*CW*, V, 256), and at the moment the present circle should begin such a process with contributions promoting "Catholic Emancipation" (hence religious freedom) in Ireland and a repeal of the Union Act that now allows English marketplaces to "suck the veins of [Ireland's] inhabitants" by profiting from Irish labor and returning little to the laborers (V, 268 and 255). Almost at once, though, the pursuit of these objectives must redirect the group toward reforming the wider systems that contain and cause these immediate problems. The association should eventually find ways to better educate the Irish masses so they cannot be as easily exploited, and that expanded concern raises the question of how to reorganize Western education generally, a question that should at some point face the pervasive social "principles" that determine the educational system as it stands (*CW*, V, 257–58). The outreach of the group may, in fact ought to, become so self-expanding and diffuse that Shelley admits:

> I am thus indeterminate in my description of the association . . . because I conceive that an assembly of men meeting to do all the good that opportunity will permit . . . must be in its nature as indefinite and varying as the instances of human vice and misery that precede, occasion, and call for its institution. (V, 257)

Here, quite clearly, is an early version of the flexible and self-altering association that Shelley will later promote in the *View*. Nevertheless, the objectives in some of the many and changing goals in the "Proposals" demand a contraction of this indeterminacy that could set boundaries to its perpetual expansion. For one thing, if the new association keeps making Irish problems the merest stepping stones to wider prospects, the group may be colonizing Ireland for larger purposes almost as cruelly as Great Britain has and might be passing over the pressing needs of Irish workers, as Shelley occasionally does in his Dublin "Address."[60] No such transfer of attention from a local need to a wider one is really helpful if the smaller problem is left unresolved by the shift. Then, too, such an indefinite agenda might make the reformers lose sight of the principal "end" to which they first committed themselves. Since attention can always be transported from localized concerns to any number of general causes, the discussants might easily fall into "controversies concerning the nature of th[eir] end." These would "serve only to weaken the strength which for the interest of virtue should be consolidated" (*CW*, V, 267). Perhaps group discussion should be restrained so that the participants work to make their possible charities "converge to one point," even "though . . . what point that is may be hidden" at first until the members of the association work it out gradually in exchanges and compromises with one another (V, 267). Still, such an attempt at defining "principles" on which "none disagree" (V, 267) may go so far as to halt the group's attempt to extend its own awareness and philanthropy to those with initially different interests. In a letter to Godwin just after the "Proposals," Shelley admits that his "friendly discussion" might aim at producing such "unanimity" that "the minority whose belief [can]not subscribe to the opinion of the majority [on] any question of moment" might have to "recede," even if this meant that the resulting group "might by refinement of secessions contain not more than three or four members" (*L*, I, 267).

After his first two proposals, in other words, Shelley's view of associations is caught between centrifugal and centripetal tendencies. The transfer "out of ourselves" encourages both impulses, being always as double-edged as we have seen it to be in previous chapters. It can make us either change our object of focus for another elsewhere or connect other aspects of thought, perception, and social interplay with a particular focal point. As a result, a reformist coalition may try to disseminate its desire for increased transfers of power, yet it does so, and even forms a sense of that desire for its members, only by transferring individual interests toward a single group concern. Shelley's later approaches, then, to what associations can do have to start with a paradox and resolve it without denying its continuing existence. That fact is certainly acknowledged and dealt with, I find, in Shelley's pamphlet of 1817, distributed to liberal journals as "A Proposal for Putting Reform to the Vote Throughout the Kingdom" and directed at various "Friends of Reform" (moderates and some radicals) to suggest a method by which they might start "to settle those subjects on which they disagree" (*CW,* VI, 67). The answer here, broadly speaking, is an organization that becomes very concretely centrifugal before it can become centripetal enough to link its members too tightly together. In this idea, even at those late moments when centripetal tendencies might take groups over, the entire gathering-process should be transported from its earliest kind of assembly into a different and wider arena that must also relocate its interplays in yet another conclave to which the first one in the series must finally be drawn as well.

At first, to be sure, Shelley's basic "step towards reform" in this pamphlet seems as drawn inward as a gathering of liberals could be. He calls for a well-publicized meeting "to be held at the *Crown and Anchor Tavern*" in London (*CW,* VI, 64), which recently housed "a convention of delegates [brought in] from the northern [and radical] Hampden Clubs" that rejected the more "moderate [reform] proposals" and passed inflexible "resolutions [calling for] Universal Suffrage, Annual Parliaments, and the secret ballot."[61] Even so, Shelley's meeting would use the same location to invert the Hampden Clubs' imitation of the government's procedures and priorities. Rather than fixing group opinions on the spot in order to promulgate them to others not at the meeting, his gathering would almost immediately send those present back out to the public at large to conduct an opinion poll on whether members of the Commons should be elected by methods more representative than those now in use. "All animosity and discussion" between the pollsters would be deferred until they could assess "the will of the majority of the individuals of the British nation" (*CW,* VI, 65). True, the poll would involve delegates taking signatures on a "Declaration" stating that Parliament as it stands "does not represent the will of the people" (VI, 66). But Shelley's hope is still that delegates from an association will become delegates expressing opinions from the wider public, delegates transfigured into synecdoches of many figures, before the association is fully formed in any true sense. The return to the people of the sovereignty they have inadvertantly signed away should not be demanded by any set of representatives unless the people advertantly transfer their right to seek it to those delegates on a series of petitions that only then becomes the "sense of a meeting." When the delegates reconvene, moreover, Shelley would have them avoid any of the "revolutionary and disorganizing schemes" that Godwin and others would attribute to the Hampden Clubs and that only some of those attending the meeting could accept (VI, 66). Instead, the reformist factions should acknowledge that a widespread sentiment, already diffused far beyond them, has been transferred toward them to the point of urging them into a reconciliation among themselves for the sake of the people they now represent. Even then the unanimity that is reached should be announced only as a transferred impulse to make another transfer of representative signs. The association should have no more than a "duty . . . to petition" Parliament for the people and to call on the "House" for a "measure of reform" proportionate to the request that many people have signed (VI, 66). For the Shelley of 1817, the final discussion of this series of re-presentations should be held inside a center of power, yet one now made to resemble the association (though not entirely) by being opened up to the will of the "outside" that was its foundation centuries ago.

At this point Shelley need deal only with the problem—though admittedly a major one—of how this deft oscillation of transfer-based impulses can be made to operate in the day-to-day formation and activity of associations, most of which will not be organized at just two meetings or for the sake of just one massive approach to Parliament. The solution is offered, finally, by the *Philosophical View* when it asks its readers to "promote open confederations" like yet unlike those of 1811 and 1812, ones that tend simultaneously toward both the unforced "converg[ence]" and the constant dissemination of the most compatible reformist beliefs (*S&C*, VI, 1053). Here Shelley asks people "freely to exercise their right of assembling" in loosely organized, perpetually different, and numerically limited (though not restricted) groups (VI, 1053). Each of these gatherings should be nonhierarchical in organization, small enough to promote interchanges among everyone present, and sufficiently moderate to draw people from various walks of life, some of whom have not habitually attended anti-government rallies. A fluid public forum would then be underway with the right degrees of focus for, oscillation in, and expansion of its membership, particularly if each assembly, in proximate but different places, retained some previous participants and gradually kept drawing new ones gently into the exchange. Closed pressure groups would be unlikely to form in such a decentered process of drawing many people toward a center of interest, and public understanding would increase just rapidly enough to prevent any kind of rabid mob psychology from taking shape and pursuing some vaguely focused revenge in imitation of the government. With the separations between reformist factions obscured by this "going out" of local groups with fluid boundaries, it would also be easier for highly determined reformers to "appeal . . . to that respecting which they are all agreed," since no set of principles would be imposed on anyone from outside or from a center of the process, and the "subordinate" differences between areas and peoples would be respected while the common ground was being agreed to, moment by moment, in noncoercive local discussions (*S&C*, VI, 1053). Gradually, a staunch but considered, rather than angry and sudden, "resolution" should develop across an increasing group of protesters as discussion builds up a clear rationale and program for change, one eschewing factionalism, class consciousness, rivalry, and violence as necessary elements (VI, 1054).

Such an open, even loving effort to disseminate more and more transfers of the desire for freedom among more and more people can ultimately draw in, by its avoidance of hard-and-fast distinctions between people and groups, individuals thought to be entirely outside the circle of those presently calling for reforms. Once this conversion process were well underway and even if the government then were to try to provoke inter-party conflict and punishable acts of violent rebellion, Shelley ventures to hope, the now undogmatic and calmly resolved "multitude" would stand "unresisting," just as Liberty recommends in *The Mask of Anarchy,* with a "temperance and courage" that would convey no more than "the [nonincendiary] assertion of their rights" (VI, 1054). The average soldier asked to attack such an assembly, the way the troops attacked at Manchester, would find the group, unlike the Peterloo mob, refusing the option to "fight" and the postures of "conflict" that allow an attacker to place himself in the differentiated position of enforcer and opponent (ibid.). A clear distinction between the soldier and those facing him could not be maintained in such a situation. Now a sympathetic feeling of equality, already disseminated among the people, should pass over to—or be restored from repression in—the soldier before them, who would then have to see himself as "a man and an Englishman" linked to every person he beheld (*S&C,* VI, 1055). At that point, should enough soldiers feel this way, the enforcement of definite class distinctions and government only for the privileged would no longer be possible. The militarist would join the multitude and be further reeducated and reformed without coercion alongside others in a large crowd that would by now have become an unmilitant, unranked, and still-expanding association unlike any, and more effective than any, in European history.

The reformer-writer, though, cannot set that process in motion—especially since it is enacted in public, linguistic exchanges—unless he first makes a blurring of differences occur in the language that he and all political associations should use to "create thought." Language itself insists, as Shelley has seen already, on such attempted (though never total) conflations of separate figural patterns. Consequently, the *View* makes a point of aping well-known prose styles already employed by explicitly political writers, yet only to make those modes compound themselves with others after the different styles have been clearly announced. Shelley's history of Western freedom, after all, imitates Condorcet's "Sketch for an Historical Picture of the Progress of the Human Mind" (1793), especially in the way the *View's* narrative intersperses the (usually) general details of political and governmental advances with sweeping assessments of how "the abstractions of thought" urged in a given era assist or prevent the arrival of "a future and more universal advantage" (*S&C,* VI, 972). At the same time, this very survey echoes Paine again and again; it first makes all people entitled to certain rights once those rights have been even half-asserted by small groups at particular moments and then throws examples of achieved rights in the face of existing power brokers, finally holding up Paine's vision of the United States as "the first practical illustration" of "true representation" (VI, 974–75). Such a juxtaposition of views allows the sometimes quietistic confidence in social progress argued by the French Enlightenment to begin an accommodation with the fervent colonial demand for usurped rights. It thereby rejoins rhetorics separated by the French Revolution, which finally sent Condorcet (and rational historiography) into hiding while its demands erupted into murderous mob violence.[62] This realignment should help unite the disenfranchised by making them see their desires in an historical, hence gradualist, context, and it ought simultaneously to make all usurpers confront reformist demands as the inevitable rising of historical transmutation, as a version of Demogorgon called the public will (*demos,* meaning "the people," added to *gorgon,* meaning "terrible").[63]

In the meantime, more immediately, these maneuvers of style must heal the breaches in the ranks of the reformers by forcing the typical language of each faction to speak alongside and even within the language of the others. The *View* can be as blunt and inflammatory as Cobbett, as when it finds that "the rich, no longer being able to rule by force [since 1688], have invented [the] scheme [of public credit] that they may rule by fraud" (*S&C,* VI, 1003). But, in trying to solve such problems, Shelley is far more genteel, measured, and calculating than any of the railings against the national debt in the *Register.* Analyzing paper money as the tool of credit in the paragraph following the foregoing invective, he falls into one of Leigh Hunt's half-jocular, half-caustic comparisons across Western history, seeing credit as "extorting from the people far more than praetorian guards and arbitrary tribunals ever did" (VI, 1004).

Then (after crossing out an elaboration of this last point in his manuscript) he shifts to Ricardo's almost neutral, explanatory summarizing of the facts about gold as the "signs of labor" (VI, 1004–10). All the while, though, he never leaves the radical barb behind. If gold coins are "signs of labor," he writes, they are just as much "titles to an unequal distribution of [labor's] produce," something Ricardo would never claim (VI, 1008).

No stand is ever taken in the *View* without being modified at once by a posture from another quarter. Even the list of reformist demands at the midpoint of the piece combines Cobbett's assaults on rural tithes and the national debt, Bentham's and Leigh Hunt's very pragmatic opposition to sinecures and placemen, Burdett's and Hunt's feelings about standing armies and the equality of religions, Paine's call for "speedy" trials, and Godwin's hope for the ubiquity of a jury system throughout England (VI, 1027–28).[64] The individual demands, as often as not, are also qualified within themselves: "We would . . . abolish sinecures" only "with every possible regard to the existing interests of the holders," presumably to avoid degrading them so much that they descend to poverty and society loses the beneficial aspects of their gentility and influence (VI, 1027). Hunt and Burdett are speaking here before Cobbett and Bentham have even completed their sentence. And of course that dance between voices must continue when Shelley adds his suggestions for parliamentary reform. He has already tried a simple compromise in his 1817 "Proposal," which accepts the moderate extension of the franchise to educated male property owners (as the *View* does) alongside the radical demand for annual parliaments, a way to teach voters in a yearly repetition "to cultivate [the] energies" of democratic give-and-take (*CW*, VI, 67). By the time of the *View*, however, the poet endorses the moderate plan for "triennial Parliaments" (still a reduction in the maximum seven-year life of one House of Commons), deciding that all steps must be equally gradual so that frequency of election can better match the extension of education among more and more voters (*S&C*, VI, 1050). He must therefore keep his discourse from becoming factionalized as the stand of a strictly upper-class liberal. He must strengthen his radical affiliations as much as his moderate ones, this time by parceling out moderate and radical rhetoric among a series of conditional clauses (a favorite device in his poetry). Now the "moderate" program is recommended only "if reform could begin from within the Houses of Parliament" as Hunt and Burdett hope, if those in control would inaugurate a "period of conciliation" leading to the "negotations" that Shelley advocates elsewhere (VI, 1049–50). But it is quite "possible that the period of conciliation is past," as the radicals insist, perhaps because "the petitions" of "two years ago" (the time of the "Proposal") have been "rejected with disdain" by a government that has strengthened libel laws, suspended habeas corpus, and stepped up the use of *agents provocateurs* to encourage reformers to risk the hangman's noose (VI, 1049).[65] If such is the case, "if the Houses of Parliament obstinately and perpetually refuse to concede any reform to the people," Shelley's "vote is for universal suffrage and equal representation," the principal demands of the radical position (VI, 1051).

In both the word-patterns of its argumentative strategies and its vision of many expanding conclaves, then, the *View* has taken the revisionary drive motivating the poet's earlier shifts from proposal to proposal and made it, at last, the manifest basis of pressure-group formation or expansion and of the language in which a coalition of such groups should be sought and fashioned. Now we can specify Shelley's final redefinition of the "common center"—which is no longer a center—of extraparliamentary associations. He proposes a multiple, fluid, and ever-expanding set of interactions between different interests and needs that lack an initial core of entirely fixed principles. This outreach from different groups of people toward more and more interrelations with others should work to fashion a series of common aims and projections that can draw even more thinkers into the group and still leave room for divergent desires, abilities, and means to ends. Such a conflation at its best can be unabashedly centripetal and centrifugal at the same time. It can bring together, compound, and focus the longings of people toward a future equalization of property by appealing to the tendencies toward transference in each person that naturally seek such a goal if developed. At the same time, such a coalescence can also disorganize itself somewhat, at regular intervals, to reach out to the needs and opinions of groups not yet acknowledged or understood by many reformers. Only if such a procedure is followed in future attempts at "confederation," Shelley concludes, can political associations truly avoid miming what they oppose. In his program and his prose, the more recentralizing the edicts of tyranny try to become, the more decentering, self-disruptive, and nonviolently disseminated across the population the organization of reform groups can and should be—hence the more reformers can insist, with their own example, on nearly total decentralization of present government powers.

The "open confederation," it turns out, should expand its boundaries progressively much in the way Shelley changes his definition of "association" from 1811 to 1819. The process should start small, as Shelley tries to make it start in 1811, among half-affiliated intellectuals who link up to protect and further their local efforts against the inequities of the moment. Then almost immediately, because of the compassionate "going out" of the group's members beyond the group, this circle must retool itself to target the most perpetual abuses against the entire nation by discussing, even forming, some visions of a freer state toward which the existing system must be pushed. Lest that future be but the projection of a few denying the different hopes of others, however, the association must assess the desires of many people, before it refines the structure of the confederation, so as to make the group's endeavors a large-scale transfer of society's general desires toward reform proposals that at least begin to satisfy such longings. Indeed, the group must always keep installing what is outside it in its basic *modus operandi* by dispersing the combined interests it has created into many gatherings of different and changeable groups, all dedicated to an interplay that more widely socializes the local, class-based desires of everyone who attends. As this unregimented gathering and regathering becomes even more fluid and continuous, many of the oppressors themselves may no longer resist being drawn into the ever-expanding spheres of liberal-to-radical reform. Clearly, more than any other in Shelley's writing, this prospect as he presents it, this day-to-day and informal but focused set of conversations, is the image that makes transference seem a continuous and disseminated practice of personal and social behavior instead of just a subliminal impulse kept only subliminal. For Shelley the logic tending toward such an image exists already to a degree in the most outward-tending, foresighted (or Promethean), and least factionalized endeavors of reform—if only there were more of them—and these can attain greater fruition, even in the near future, perhaps, if the style and practical proposals of the *View* can be transplanted into the many reform debates of its own era.

Transference Made Practical:
The *View* as an Epitome of Shelley's Career

As events turned out, the soil was not ready for the transplant. No London publisher, however sympathetic, would risk the prosecution that might well have come from distributing the *View,* especially in the face of Parliament's new Six Acts and the intensified sedition laws applied in the Carlile case.[66] Moreover, Shelley admitted while writing his "Octavo" that the "struggle" he would resolve was being "postpon[ed]" by "the passion of party" (*L,* II, 164). Since the Manchester Massacre and the trial of Carlile, the confrontations between oppressor and reformer had receded behind the arguments among reformers themselves and between factions in the government debating trivial matters or finding less visible means to snuff out reform. This cacophony dissipated the face-off with authorities that was needed to provoke true unity among the reformers and broke Shelley's audience into splinter groups just when he was hoping to draw them together. Hence, as early as December 15, 1819, he suspected he might "not trouble [him] self to finish [the *View* this] season" (*L,* II, 201). He probably abandoned the treatise in early 1820, deferring some of its notions until later prose fragments and resublimating transference in poems on love, death, history, and the fading of the visionary, world-reforming impulse.

Nonetheless, the die was cast, even if the public of Shelley's time never had a chance to read the best evidence of that fact. In the *View* and the prose connected with its argument, transference is increasingly (if gradually) redefined and restyled as visible, daily social activity. The transfer process climaxes its nine-year struggle across the development of Shelley's writing to emerge into the light of common practice from the often obscure depths of perception, thought, language, and cultural progress. Seen in this light, the *Philosophical View* could be said to encapsulate Shelley's writing career from 1810 to 1820. Beginning with a history heavily indebted to similar accounts by earlier writers (as was much of Shelley's juvenilia), the piece sublimates transference, enough to seem unaware of its primacy at first, in a series of that movement's self-concealments, restrictions of it that avoid their real foundation, similar to those in Shelley's early theories about the *natura naturans* and how it works. Each segment in the history, as though it were a moment in Shelley's early life, thus presents a people's (or a person's) continuous reflection in a series of mirrors (commodities, cities, other people, beliefs, gods, or governments). These are first "many-sided" but become compressed into a monolithic structure (like the dream-maiden in *Alastor*) that gives other beings or forms absolute power over the self or selves setting up the reflectors. The more the history proceeds, however, the more it exposes the actual process behind and within its many transformations. It shows that cultural and personal change, often ascribed to what a static absolute (such as God or nature) can impose from on high, comes from incessant interplays in thought and action between apparently "internal" and "external" notions (recalling the poems of 1816). We therefore know that "the means and sources of knowledge [have always] increased together with knowledge itself [and] the instruments of knowledge" as the sources and instruments have created one another by playing off of and changing their counterparts (*S&C,* VI, 973). Now transference can be detected, though obscurely, in both the movement of natural and cultural transformation and the constructions of human thought that create and interpret the movement. "Power," however conceived, is thereby "stripp[ed] of its darkest mask," of the veil that covers the underlying motion, and we become aware of brief moments in history when that drive has broken through the veil into consciousness (in the manner of "Intellectual Beauty"), as when the United States created a government that kept adjusting its laws (or so it seemed) to the less visible "progress of human improvement" (VI, 976). For those with the insight to see it, transference soon appears dimly operating everywhere: in the under-currents that have established nations, in resurgent attempts at liberty within confin-ing systems, in Enlightenment philosophies revealing causality as an interpretation of relationships, in the very inevitability of cultural transmutation, and in the way poets can always recover the "electric life" in existing works, enough to make flexible lan-guage relegislate the "order" of the "world" we perceive (VI, 993).

True, the argument must backtrack slightly once the modern situation has been reached by Shelley's history to reveal the various ways transference is partly respon-sible (with the will's assistance) for establishing the current class structure oppressing the will (*S&C,* VI, 997–1022). But this revelation mainly shows that the way to unset-tle that structure is to wrest transference, especially its potential disruption of the signs it has composed, from the symbolic forms that hierarchy uses to maintain itself. Those forms, like the myths reused in *Prometheus Unbound,* must be shown to be temporary, malleable, and recombinable, as are the ingredients of any linguistic construct. The self-obscuring language of the law, for example, must be exploited and reinterpreted so that it comes to insist on scandalous exchanges (transfers of property among the debt-ridden wealthy) that were always potential within the language but have been kept under wraps to keep current supremacies—and the taxes supporting them— exactly where they are. Alongside this critique and its playful recombinations, there must also be a gradual confluence of practical proposals for changing the social order upheld by stultified myths. The rhetoric of reform always impelled by transference should use that drive to join revolutionary styles and proposals in a nonviolent give-and-take among these differences that aims them all at the ultimate accomplishment of fully distributed benevolence, knowledge, and property. This last effort is the func-tion of the *View's* final chapter and of the treatise as an unfinished "whole," provided both pull together the previous essays that have tended in their direction and both hope for the playful and equalized "harmonious [society] of many a soul" envisioned in the demythologizing poems of 1819 and 1820. The way for the individual to begin approaching that vision, Shelley now sees, is to open himself or herself to the trans-ferential impulse moving across Western history into the current moment. A person must gravitate toward the ways of "another and many others" in successive, flexible, gradual discussions and actions, becoming a wider-ranging being under the influence of others and joining with others in proposing and forming the kind of equal society that meets everyone's needs.

Looking back through this poet's major achievements, we find, from where he has arrived in the *Prometheus* volume, "The Witch of Atlas," and the *Philosophical View of Reform,* that his readers need no longer be troubled by the distance between day-to-day and eternal transference. These middle-to-late works see that gap as a problem and work to solve it in ways provided by the subliminal movement that Shelley has uncovered already. The "Hymn to Intellectual Beauty" could urge the connection between these levels only because it too simply saw the shadow-reveiling-itself as inherently becoming "Love" and "hope" out of the relocation of "Power" that must "float" beyond any mind it infuses. The efforts I have just named from two to four years later accept that tendency as always potential and ideal, but they must face the discoveries in intervening pieces that show how that movement has introverted itself and become, by its own means, hierarchical instead of communal, thus establishing the gap between beneficial transference and everyday life. Hence Prometheus, the Witch, the reformer, and the poet depicting them all must perform willful acts to reverse that perversion and reconnect the moments in Beauty's succession. They must deliberately replay and rearticulate the backward-looking and forward-tending directions in which transference always draws the thought and actions open to it. In the first place they have to try to recover the self-transmuting impulse in their personal, cultural, and linguistic unconscious, the repository of transference's previous achievements. They must draw it up again from, and so deeply investigate, all the places where it has continually operated: the versions of the Prometheus story, the changes in particular myths, the Promethean cave of intertextuality where those shifts are always possible, personal memory, dream-play, the ideal "other" of the self envisioned by the self, the moment of falling in love, the process turning the results of labor into commodities for exchange, parts of earlier social revolutions, and the drive of words toward deferred referents by way of other words. These movements, transferred toward one another as much as possible, should provide flexible models on which a *praxis* can be built. Unfulfilled as they are, they should now be restaged in conclaves among people (or text-reader relationships) wherein the current orientations on all sides are changed from what they were, by way of adjacent differences, toward an equality of understanding, feeling, and objective. The repressed mobility of the past should be remade into future social action and so pour visibly from the depths of dreams and social history, where transference has always operated and always will. To be discussing reform in a centerless collective or to be working with another being to change both your characters toward greater sympathy for each other and others beyond you: these actions *are* universal transference in particular guises, in willed, practical reworkings of our deepest cultural and mental impulse.

Perhaps the image of the individual in a larger scheme that Shelley's work up to 1820 wants most to encourage is the one built up quite gradually in Shelley's "Essay on Christianity," written almost midway between the "Hymn" and the works of 1819 and 1820. There his reinterpretation of Christ's pronouncements, designed to force them back toward their most beneficial thrust and away from the Church's twisting of them into dictates from above, situates the psyche (*any* psyche, not chosen ones) at the crossroads of all the "streams," internal and external, past and present, that try to transmogrify all established aspects of themselves "into the purest and most perfect shape[s] which it belongs to their nature[s] to assume" (*CW*, VI, 235). Those streams, of course, as "the collective energy of the moral and material world"—the transference moving through history, economics, language, feeling, love, visible change, and great poetry—are as much of a God as Shelley is even close to accepting and surround the soul with all potentials and tendencies in existence "like the atmosphere in which some motionless lyre is suspended" (*CW*, VI, 231). Once the lyre becomes cognizant of that motion already flowing through it before consciousness feels its force, it has the choice of "represent[ing]" it as "Providence" (a supremacy of knowledge that the psyche wishes it possessed) or as a "merciful and benignant power who scatters equally upon the beautiful earth all the elements of security and happiness, whose influencings are distributed to all whose natures admit of a participation in them"

(*CW*, VI, 232–33). At that point of awareness, it becomes quite possible to choose the latter alternative and give in to a "participation" that lets the self be a conduit for transference. Existence thus perceived insists that the desire to fulfull the needs of the self be carried by the flow toward others as well, bringing along that drive's effort to transfigure and perfect every being through which it moves. That realization makes each person who carries out the movement an unacknowledged legislator for himself or herself and for all other people, someone who wants and works for the absolute justice of equally distributed (and increasing) property, sustenance, and profit. However much and however often the direction of "the Power" is perverted by others, the compassionate believer forwards his or her attempt at a fair dissemination of transference's benefit "until the mutual communications of knowledge and of happiness throughout all thinking natures constitute a harmony of good that ever varies and never ends" (*CW*, VI, 235–36).

6

The "One" in the Later Works: "Thought's Eternal Flight"

A Late Reorientation?

Despite the progression that I have just presented, there appear to be some marked changes in the poetry and prose of Shelley's last two years (summer 1820 through summer 1822). One of them is simply tactical, a change in his stance toward his own opinions in the face of increased opposition to them. Though "I cling to moral and political hope, like a drowner to a plank," he writes in 1821, "my disappointment on public grounds has been excessive" (*L*, II, 291). He is now painfully conscious of his inability to find many readers and of the principal reasons he cannot: the government's skillful division and diversion of the reformer's potential audience, the desire of many readers to ignore social problems under a guise of higher, more pious concerns (promoted by Wordsworth's later poetry), and the widespread, virulent attacks from Whig and Tory circles on the immorality or downright insanity of Shelley's published work, especially the volume headed by *Prometheus Unbound*.[1] Consequently, as Marilyn Butler points out, Shelley and his closest associates (a small political group of higher-class intellectuals already divorced from many of the classes they would help) revert for the present to esoteric exchanges only among well-educated liberals. Henceforth avoiding such direct political statements as the *Philosophical View*, they attempt more sophisticated, intricately wrought recastings of complex genres and "devices by which such groups [can] define themselves flatteringly to one another [and thereby work from within the circle that expertly manipulates poetic forms and mythographs to] enhance [gradually the] prestige [of radical poetry] to the world outside."[2] The result in Shelley's case is a stylization and introversion of his lifelong quest for reform, a subtle building of his iconoclasm into careful recastings of longstanding verse-forms that have supported ideologies very different from his own.

Another change, though, seems far more radical, particularly as it has been rendered in some attractive interpretations of Shelley's "later poetry." Indeed, this swerve, should it really be present in the way those redactions claim, denies some aspects of what I have argued from the outset of this study, above all my contention that Shelley eludes any attempt to ground any of his works in a unified absolute entirely and perpetually at one with itself. More often than their predecessors, so this view argues, Shelley's later efforts reveal the hidden basis and goal of his (or his speaker's) desires to be a kind of "One," apparently an "undying" and "Fathomless" level of unity uninhabited by the differences that alter repetitions across time. Compared to it, all of transference's changing and passing is "but a vision" unable to "look [clearly] on that which cannot change" behind and beyond experience. The evidence for this reorientation does seem considerable and even overwhelming at times. The words I have quoted are spoken, after all (at ll. 766–85), by the age-old Ahasuerus in Shelley's *Hellas,* the lyrical drama of late 1821 modeled on the stagecraft of *The Persians* by Aeschylus. In this piece the possibility of a resurgent, free Greece, trying to revolt against the Ottoman Turks even as Shelley writes, can reveal the general tendencies of history only when Ahasuerus turns our attention beyond whatever is mutable to "The stuff" that has least "to do with time or place or circumstance" (ll. 799–802). *Hellas,* we must confess, could have devolved completely—and really does in various places (such as ll. 41–63)—on the memory of ancient Greece's self-transfiguring tendencies that keep the potential for revolution alive in the "Ode to Liberty" and *Prometheus Unbound.* Yet by the end of Shelley's last finished play, the "fragments" of Greece can "build themselves again . . . / In a diviner clime" (ll. 1003–05) only as "mutability's" weaving of what "cannot die" (ll. 797–98), as "idle shadows" that at the truest level "have no being" at all (ll. 783–84).

If we accept this perspective, the writing of Shelley's last two years appears to be an explicit argument for approximating this One in his and future poetry. The initial statement seems to come in "The Sensitive-Plant" (finished by the early summer of 1820). Here the wearisome changes that a loving but easily hurt *mimosa pudica* (perhaps a figure for the unappreciated, inward-turning poet) undergoes in striving to receive and return the effusions of its fellow plants, an Asia-like attendant, and the "vapours" in the garden all around it (Part First, l. 90) turn out to be the merest "shadows of the dream" that is our conscious, shifting existence in the world of appearances from which we must wake to attain a more ultimate knowledge (Conclusion, l. 12). Mutation, death, "error, ignorance and strife" exist "where nothing is," being at most the "mockery" of something else, when set against the "love, and beauty, and delight [residing where] / There is no death nor change" in a "might [that always] / Exceeds our [sensory] organs" (Conclusion, ll. 10–11 and 21–23). It would seem from this time on, then, that any truly poetic response to perception and feelings must quickly surpass them to approach a far more glorious and changeless level on which they are based. According to the *Defence of Poetry* (spring 1821), the poet must "ascend to bring light and fire from those eternal regions where the owl-winged faculty of calculation dare not ever soar" (p. 503). Imaginative effort should be defended against Peacock's sense, in *The Four Ages of Poetry* (1820), that poetry's use-value declines with historical changes in social priorities.[3] Shelley's retort is that a real "Poet participates in the eternal, the infinite, and the one [and] as far as relates to his conceptions, time and place and number are not" (*Defence,* p. 483). The true poet-prophet apparently overleaps his own limits on the way to a greater unity, whether his conceptions receive the infusion of an "eternal music" outside the imagination or his imagination produces a new complex of relations after that onslaught, since every imaginative composition of "other thoughts" from earlier "elements" in perception must leave each new construct "containing within itself the principle of its own integrity" (pp. 485 and 480).

At every poetical moment in a work, therefore, it appears that the poet's projected or remembered images or phases must look ahead, inward, or back to "unchangeable forms" more universal than the connections of "time, place, [or] circumstance" in unpoetical "stories" (*Defence*, p. 485). Hence the "Emilia" addressed in *Epipsychidion* (early 1821), though based on an actual, temporary love-interest renamed after the heroine of Boccaccio's *Teseida* (*NCE*, p. 371), must be depicted, like Dante's Beatrice or Petrarch's Laura, as "veiling beneath that radiant form of woman / All that is unsupportable in [her] of light, and love, and immortality" (*Epipsychidion* ll. 22–24). The dead Keats of *Adonais,* Shelley's great elegy of the summer of 1821, must "burst" toward "Heaven's light" in the manner of a Lycidas or a fallen Greek hero and so be carried to the level of "stars" in "the firmament of time" by the "one spirit's plastic stress" as it strives to return to what seems to be its origin, the "white radiance of Eternity" (*Adonais,* ll. 386–87, 388–90, 381, and 463). And finally the shade of Rousseau in the unfinished *Triumph of Life* (1822), the new Virgil interpreting the grim array of Life's prisoners for Shelley's Dantean speaker and dreamer, must direct his ghostly awareness back to the instant when his own forgetfulness (a drink of Nepenthe) turned his early vision of a "light diviner than the common sun" into the "cold light" of Life's approaching Chariot, "whose airs too soon deform" (*Triumph,* ll. 338 and 468). Probing into the very foundations of how the dream-world we see every day covers over a more primal and beautiful level, Rousseau must recount the one dream, the most clearly Platonic one in the poem,[4] in which he seems to reach a "place ... with many sounds woven into one," a realm where a "shape all light," another "splendour" of the firmament, makes "All that was [in daily observation] seem ... as if it had been not" (ll. 339–40, 352, 359, and 385).

Particularly after 1817, we must remember, as Timothy Webb has shown better than anyone else, Shelley engaged more and more in reading and translating Plato, some ancient Greek hymns attributed to Homer, the pastoral elegies of two other Greeks (reputedly Moschus and Bion), Petrarch and Dante himself, the Spanish playwright Calderón de la Barca, and the *Erster Teil* of Goethe's *Faust*. All these writers and works, even now, seem manifestly obsessed with drawing the sharp line proposed in the *Republic* (VI, 509d–510a) between transmutable appearances or half-conscious intimations offering "a pale reflection of celestial light" (an image from one of Calderón's *autos sacramentales*[5]) and the "All-sustaining" itself that permits "Eternal stars [to] rise" (Faust's claim to Margarete in the *Marthes Garten* scene[6]) or allows the "apotheosis of Beatrice in Paradise by which [Dante] feigns himself to have ascended to the throne of the Supreme Cause" (Shelley in the *Defence,* p. 497). Given this constantly accelerating immersion in Platonic or seemingly Platonic visions of the ultimate state, it is natural for Webb to maintain (and hardly by himself) that Shelley, "towards the end of his life, was beginning to chafe against the restrictions which time and space impose on the poet and to aspire towards an ideal kind of poetry where time and space can be temporarily abolished."[7] Had not this poet's efforts to expose the most primordial energies *within* time and space led him only to exile, bad health, the death or loss of several children, quarrels with Mary, estrangements from friends, rejections from readers and publishers, and a wrenching sense that his poetic genius (which he also doubted) might have no connection with his social influence as a man?

The "only relief I find," he confesses in a letter dated June 8, 1821, "springs from the composition of poetry" as it "necessitates contemplations that lift me above the stormy mist of sensations which are my habitual place of abode" (*L*, II, 296).

Nonetheless, this widely accepted view only seems to be a complete negation of the one advanced throughout this book. It does not take exhaustive general readings of the later texts—it requires only a closer look at the segments in them claiming to intimate oneness—to reveal how small a breach there is between Shelley's developing sense of transference and the increased allusions to the One in the major works of his final years. To be sure, I do admit some change of emphasis in his later work, aside from his sublimations of the reformist impulse. His increased sense of being ineffectual, incomplete, and exiled does make him consider more often how much transference keeps seeking higher amounts or degrees of relationship among differences, a greater and unending thoroughness of anological interplay that might create the "one harmonious soul of many a soul," the future "chain of [totally] linked thought" in act 4 of *Prometheus Unbound* (ll. 400 and 394). He therefore resuscitates some aspects of his old Gothic sensibility just enough to write in a letter of April 1822 that "Perhaps all discontent with the *less* (to use a Platonic sophism) supposes the sense of a just claim to the *greater,* and that we admirers of Faust [or unceasing Faustian striving] are therefore on the right road to Paradise" (*L*, II, 406). The texts he now translates both encourage this view and draw his interest—or reattract his attention from earlier exposures to them—because they manifest how this urge has been carried through or depicted by brilliant poets and stylists, sometimes within the rhetoric of hierarchical and God-centered systems. All the while, though, Shelley knows these systems, as he has known them previously, to be as oxymoronic as a "Platonic sophism." They are all dependent for their ultimate unities on some of the mobile, disjunctive modes of logic they claim to refute and immobilize, as when the striving for "the greater" shows itself as the belated product of a discontent with "the less" moving away from its own position. Shelley's later writing, therefore, in the general manner of nearly all his efforts from *Alastor* onward, works rebelliously to redefine the concept of the One that it seems to repeat, even when the result uncovers and acknowledges the reasons for the human psyche's inclinations toward oneness. Instead of the One drawing him away from transference, I want to argue in closing, the poet draws the One back *toward* transference and reinstalls that notion at the heart of the One's various forms of existence as he reworks these from the earlier writings in which he finds them.

The Translations as Recoveries of the Repressed

Much of the evidence for my view, to begin with, appears in the very texts that are the evidence for Webb's. Throughout his translations or the commentaries connected to them, Shelley repeatedly disavows the most absolutist assumptions in the Platonic and Catholic works he anglicizes throughout his later years. He tries in each case to foreground what empowers yet questions those assumptions. He keeps emphasizing the displacement of one trace of a distant point by another trace (a thought about a thought) that increases the distance while longing to bridge it in a future transposition that might attain something like the lost foundation of the earlier trace. Shelley's preface to his 1818 translation of the *Symposium* finds that Plato's manifest "theories respecting the government of the world, and the elementary laws of moral action, are not always correct" and so have become exploitable shields behind which a "variety of superstitions have sheltered their absurdities" down through the ages (*PS,* p. 402). What Shelley values more in Plato is what seems to the latter the most uncertain of foundations: the "intuition" of Socrates, that not strictly rational quality in great poets criticized as divorced from knowledge in Plato's *Ion* (also translated by Shelley, probably in 1821).[8] Because each dialogue submits to it after Socrates' example, a "Pythian enthusiasm of poetry" animates and unsettles Plato's otherwise "close and subtle logic" as Shelley reads it, and the result is an "irresistible stream of musical expressions" tending away from what it would intimate, tending to see the basic "nature of mind and existence" as "obscure" or self-concealing even in the ostensible signs of its "profound" depth (*PS,* p. 402). Shelley is interested in Plato (or Socrates) the ironist, who suggests, as he finds more accepted assumptions inadequate, a radically different Other—as far as language is concerned, the otherness pointed to by all symbols— beckoning far behind or ahead of, but also dimly infusing, any thought, utterance, image, point of discussion, or person.[9] As though the process of dialogue were the generator of the concept, the One is the projection spawned by a basic otherness-from-themselves opened up in every word or statement as each turns for its completion toward other ones or different versions of itself. That ultimate level is proposed mainly by contrast to the statements of those interlocutors whose claims first deny it and then come to depend upon it as their words give way to Socrates' redefinitions. Even in the great gadfly's rejoinders, the One is intimated as the far-off completion of his words, all of which emphasize it by explicitly not being it, casting it off from them so as to make it their faintly recalled and vaguely anticipated ground. At most, oneness is therefore a withdrawal and "coming down," a relocation of the temporal shift between figures as they make their own otherness-from-themselves their ultimate reference point lying far behind or beyond them even as they all suggest it.

It is the poet's attraction, we must realize, to this half-forgetting/half-remembering in Plato, this dislocation looking backward and forward instead of the fixed *eidos* at the ultimate level, which decides what dialogues Shelley translates and what moments from them he singles out as his special favorites. These touchstones naturally include the rush of mad inspiration toward the rhapsode in the *Ion* (533d–534b) through a series of magnetic rings displacing one another in a transportation of Phythian energy from a far remove (reworked in the *Defence,* p. 493). Then, too, there is the suggestion of *anamnesis* in the way a person "not only becomes conscious of [the] thing [observed] but also thinks of something else [beyond it] which is the object of a different sort of knowledge," all in a segment from the *Phaedo* (73c, trans. Hugh Tredennick), which Shelley is known to have read aloud at Oxford and to have translated himself some years later (though we do not have the final version).[10] And of course there is the definition of Love in the *Symposium* as "desir[ing] that which is absent and beyond its reach, that which it has not, that which is not itself" (Shelley's translation, *PS,* pp. 442 and 440). Shelley's "On Love" quite unplatonically takes that transposition from incompleteness toward fulfillment and raises it to the primal and even casual level of the ultimate forms that *eros* pursues in Plato's dialogue. The "point to which love tends" now becomes a form of dialogue itself: the projection of love's process (of transferring the self) out to another being whose responsive "nerves" may carry the lover beyond himself into the erotic aspirations of a different "imagination" ("On Love," p. 474).

Shelley thus approaches Plato in the later years with great ambivalence, especially when the *Republic* is the focus of renewed attention. On the one hand, Socrates in that work, guided by his hierarchy of levels of knowledge leading only some to an apprehension of the good and the beautiful, places "limitations" on equality by flirting with a vertical class structure (though admittedly a meritocracy elevating intelligence) in his "just" society. On the other hand, he makes guardianship potentially open to all adults from both sexes, because all minds, despite different ranges of understanding, are grounded in the same remembering/forgetting, a level of thought "comprehending at once the past, the present, and the future condition of men" (*Defence,* p. 496). We can therefore say, in Shelley's view, that the "principle of equality has been discovered and applied [as well as endangered] by Plato in his Republic" (p. 496)[11] and that this achievement is apparently one consequence of assumptions frequently articulated by Plato's teacher, as the poet found in reading Xenophon's *Memorabilia* as well as several Platonic dialogues. According to Socrates, Shelley writes in a translation of Xenophon, "a supernatural force" inseparable from inspiration, anamnesis, love—hence transference—"has sway over the greatest things in all human understandings [so that] the uncertainty belonging to them all," something that makes us equal because we all share some sense of it, comes from "the intervention of that power" as it transfigures itself differently in its various conduits (the 1819 fragment "On the Daemon of Socrates," *PS,* p. 507).

After all, such self-transforming, boundary-crossing, joyful, and un-Christian powers animating and interrelating the parts of nature that we perceive are for Shelley characteristic of the ancient Greek mind at its best, if we believe his post-1818 letters and his translations of Greek hymns and elegies. Webb himself has demonstrated this increasing fascination with a Grecian "spirit of beauty" pouring its power of self-reformation into all natural and human-made constructions. He accurately notes that Shelley saw Greek temples as calling this movement to them through "the interstices of their incomparable columns" (*L,* II, 73), that the poet used this now-repressed infusion as an effective means of undermining its Judeo-Christian replacement, and that he regarded this belief as more "life-enhancing" than later ones because the playful divinities in it, though admittedly "capricious," combined a disruptive "swiftness of action [with] benevolence of intention" in a self-altering "blend of energy and control, of animation and tranquility."[12] Yet Shelley's attraction to such qualities in their mythologized forms is sparked mainly by the transmutation they share with the Lucretian Venus derived from them, the "interfused" and interfusing "God" of the *Essay on Christianity* or the "Hymn to Intellectual Beauty," and the transfiguration/diffusion of Prometheus and Asia, especially when they are restored to their pre-Aeschylean states. As Webb does not quite realize, it is less the exalted divinity and more the free, serene, eagerly awaited, and often feminine self-displacement of Greek daemon-figures that interests Shelley, in search, as he always is, of the transferability that makes daemons or gods half-visible and thus dimly possible for human belief.

Without exception, it is this reconfiguration of inspired descents by their own counterparts that pervades the ancient hymns and elegies that Shelley translates. It is as though that impetus within them insists on *translatio* (the Latin word for a metaphysical and verbal "carrying over") and thus on Shelley's transliteration of them into the English language. Apollo inspirits poetry in Shelley's Homeric "Hymn to Mercury" only because the sun-god's "amplitude" of "mystery" is first refashioned by the thieving messenger's lyre "soothing the mind [of the poet] with sweet familiar play" (ll. 637–51; *PW,* p. 696); the circle of light in the translated "Hymn to the Sun" must radiate, not as a self-determining center but as a network of relations, "Of woof aetherial delicately twined," which is kindled into brightness by an ever-moving "wind" much like the power that revives the fading coal (ll. 18–20; *PW,* p. 701); and the spirits in all created things must weep for Bion, in Shelley's version of the elegy on him attributed to Moschus, by pouring "liquid sorrow" through something else, through every "tender herb," or breathing out a "melancholy sweetness" that "diffuse[s] its languid love [as Asia does] on the wind" (ll. 4–8; *PW,* p. 722). Like later cultures, to be sure, classical Greece could prevert these intimations in "monstrous superstitions," hierarchical religions and class structures, or debasements of women in the midst of an otherwise "enlightened philosophy" of love.[13] But Shelley can condemn such abuses even in the Periclean Greeks while celebrating how suggestively Greece in general "opened as it were the doors to the mysteries of nature" ("A Discourse on the Manners of the Ancient Greeks," *PS,* p. 405).

The same double attitude appears in Shelley's stance toward the later figures he translates and finds driven in their own ways toward beliefs in a heavenly One. Calderón loses more than he gains for Shelley by "substituting rigidly-defined and ever-repeated idealisms of a distorted superstition for the living impersonations of the truth of human passion," and Dante, like Milton, in Shelley's eyes, is often so "enveloped and disguised" by "distorted [Catholic] notions of invisible things" that his work has contributed to the cruel, restrictive process that has "conferred upon modern mythology a systematic form" (*Defence,* p. 498–99). This circumscription of an author by his church and his early interpreters is especially sad in Dante's case, again as in Milton's, because that fervent Italian republican was to Shelley a "religious reformer" trying to redirect the theologians around him toward notions of being and value that only later readings of him can draw from his words (*Defence,* pp. 497–98). Yet, with all this being so, the lines of both Dante and Calderón as Shelley reads them, like those of Wordsworth and Coleridge even at their most religious, can be construed as depending upon (as the transitional force behind their movement) and calling forth from their readers (as an immediate, visceral response) an "electric life" of desire without a clear origin transferring itself between mental and verbal states, levels, or locations. Dantean and Calderonian verses often resemble those of Petrarch and the Provençal *trouvers* in drawing "the grief of Love" (its sense of incompletion) toward the "foundations of delight" projected beyond desire from the very core of erotic longing. The sensitive reader of all these efforts is inevitably called out of himself, finding his own outpouring of *eros* echoed in what he beholds, to "becom[e] a portion of that beauty which we [start to] contemplate" in the distance, to approach what he could yet be by way of another figure or person (*Defence,* p. 497). Indeed this primordial interchange affects both figures in each version of it (poet and goal, poet and text, text and goal, text and reader, reader and goal), refusing to leave a "higher" figure constant while a "lower" one simply approaches it. Dante nears Beatrice by "gradations of his own love *and* her loveliness" leading on from one grade to the next because each side of the duality gains brightness by reflecting the increasing love in its counterpart (p. 497, my emphasis). In any case, the feeling or impulse that begins this outreach is already undergoing multiple transformations, even "carrying [itself] over" from its initial sensory location, before awareness can interpret it as having divine or evil roots. It is this continual relocation of desire to which Shelley points by choosing to translate such pieces as the First Canzone of the *Convivio* and some scenes from *El Magico Prodi-gioso* during his various attempts to anglicize Dante and Calderón. In the words of the Justina in Shelley's *Magico,* the "Melancholy Thought" of longing becomes "flat-tering and so sweet" in both these works because the self-obscuring "cause of [a seemingly] new Power / which doth my fevered being move" keeps "overflow[ing] from [the] heart . . . Into all the senses" and beyond (sc. III, ll. 35–44; *PW,* P. 744).

The transference in Goethe, when Shelley turns to it, however, need not be released from repression in the same way at all. Part 1 of *Faust* just as it stands rescues mobile interplay and self-extending desire from the Judeo-Christian tradition that would make both drives the effects of either Satan or an emanating One. When Faust proposes his "All-Embracing" in the *Marthes Garten* scene, he does so mainly to counter Margarete's slavish devotion to the dictates of Catholic priests, somewhat in the manner of the speaker in *Epipsychidion* as he addresses an "EMILIA . . . NOW IMPRISONED IN A CONVENT" (*NCE,* p. 373). Once free of these dictates, Faust's All-in-all can emerge as a teeming expansion widely infused, thoroughly diffuse, and always transmigratory between and within its conduits. It can be operating, as Faust would have it, in the way lovers "look into each other's eyes" and in the "surging to your heart and head" of "all [that is] in you," accelerating in everything only to change and divert itself from whatever forms it has taken and so perpetually "weav[ing thus] in timeless mystery."[14] Such a heresy, so like the one in Shelley's "Essay on Christian-ity," must be a principal reason why he finds *Faust* irresistible, why it "both deepens the gloom [or dark obscurity] and augments the rapidity of [his] ideas" (*L,* II, 406; April 10, 1822). It insists that human effort, to be "on the right road to Paradise," suit the interplay expanding itself even at the heart of observable things by striving, just as that drive does, beyond the point most recently attained, again from "what [a person] has been" to "what he shall be," always "scorn[ing] the narrow good we can attain in our present state" (*L,* II, 406). Shelley must have hastened, then, to translate Goethe's "Prologue in Heaven" the way that he did, since all he needed to do was intensify the "eternal motion" in the Prologue's hymn to creation and thereby depict an "emulation [of spheres by] brother-spheres" and an "inconceivably swift . . . adornment of the earth" by the way it "winds itself round" from state to state.[15]

As he often has, even in earlier days, this poet extracts from his literary ancestors the tendency in transference both to obscure its operation and to extend its range in quest of an eventual totality of interplays. The first of these impulses, by hiding its actual basis, opens up the possibilities of an origin for transference completely outside it. A oneness that might be discovered at that source, however, is supposed only because transference in extending itself strives always for more interconnections than it has so far encompassed. Consequently, Shelley can expose in those he translates a basic displacement that searches for its own beginnings in its future transformations and counterparts. No sort of One can exist in these recast authors entirely outside the succession of passing and changing that desires it, except as such a One is forced to beckon ahead of or behind the movement by transference's need to urge its "grada-tions" of connection beyond the existing limits of understanding. If a One can be spo-ken of, Shelley reveals, at least in his versions of Homer, Plato, Bion, Moschus, Dante, Calderón, and Goethe, it is *either* as the projection, nostalgia, function, accumulation, extension, or unsatisfied desire of a self-altering and self-concealing passage between differences *or* as the displacing drive that makes translation conceivable and permissible, despite—in fact, because of—its uprooting of past conceptions from their own temporary groundings. Indeed, most of these authors have generated their ultimate unities by themselves dislocating the Ones in their predecessors. The "imperfections" in the religious and political "schemes" achieved by "Athenian society" have been "erased" from "modern Europe" by "Chivalry and Christianity," especially in the way the latter has "divulged" hidden potentials in the "wisdom of antiquity" by both "supersed[ing]" and "incorporating . . . a portion of that which it supersede[d]" (*Defence,* pp. 488 and 496). The potential for being redirected yet again is therefore dimly present in every new poetical "notion of invisible things," making the poetry in the new "system" the expander of imagination's existing "circumference," the possible "refutation" (as in Dante and Milton) of the codified order it usually seems to "support" (*Defence,* p. 498). Shelley's penchant is for drawing out that refutation— the "electric life" awaiting a different conductor—by presenting it as already a translation within his own translating act.

When the results of his translations, then, are reemployed in his later works, the One never remains firmly attached to any one of the contexts from which he has borrowed the notion, even though many portions of these older orders are carried ahead, if only to further their desires for contexts they could not attain on their own. Instead, the One increasingly becomes, like the Witch of Atlas, transference in the process of expanding its range of interrelations and projected reincarnations. True, Shelley acknowledges the division between our local, immediate sense of change or desire and an awareness of this subliminal-historical movement, the one that perpetually generates change and desire. But, as we saw in Chapter 5, this apparent distance does not mean that the more forgotten of these levels is actually divorced from the qualities in felt or perceived transitions. On the contrary, it must be seen as what eternally but always disruptively makes possible what the human race "has been" and what it "shall be" in its many ways of interpreting and reinterpreting human inclinations now and throughout history. Shelley's later writing, in other words, must be conscious enough of history to see that this One demanding so many alterations is really a series of very different views of it, each displacing some predecessors as Christianity displaced Greek mythology. In each work I am about to treat from the later period, Shelley's speaker must approach one type of oneness (occasionally more than one) as a point of departure for his revision of the notion. The work, or sometimes series of works, focusing on a particular type must then expose what is really responsible for the way this One has been constructed. At that point, the exposure must lead the notion to redefine itself on the basis of its own long-hidden impetus. What the earlier form (or forms) of the One did not grasp about its foundations is now brought out and set alongside the older concept, as in the parodies in the last two acts of *Prometheus Unbound.* More and more in the later works, too, the One thus redefined is shown to be a version of other redefinitions of it, so much so that a new general sense of the One as a transfer-process emerges to be compared with the absolute center in the forms of oneness that Shelley reuses and critiques. By the end of this succession of writings, we find that we are being left with a choice. We discover we can either still believe in one or more forms of the center or decide to embrace the potentials of thought's foundation seen as a perpetual transference, all the while knowing—if we read Shelley's last works with care—that a transfer-process underlies both the projection of an absolute One and the redefinitions that can free us from that construct.

The One as Progressive Conflation:
"On Life" and the *Defence of Poetry*

The first sort of oneness that the later Shelley approaches in this fashion is the supposed end result of a steadily increasing interplay among differences that produces a greater and greater sense of resemblance among the diverse forms. The more the perceived similarities emerge and the differences recede, and the more the similarities among some forms are felt to be the common ingredients among them all, the more the sense of distinction dissolves into an awareness of the unity, the common ground, of which the forms are but portions that reflect it locally and refer to it ultimately. Plato's *Republic* advances such a procedure as reason's basic ascent from observed appearances toward an apprehension of the unities behind them. When we examine "various multiplicities" and go on to "give the same name" to those which seem variations on a certain "type," Socrates maintains, we are "positing a single idea or form" that all the variations both repeat and anticipate (*Rep.* 596a, trans. Paul Shorey). In addition, William Drummond, Shelley's favorite empirical skeptic, having established that all things exist only as perceived, argues that the inseparability of "world" from "thought" or "substance" from a "Power" assumed to be within it means that there is something to the ideas of Parmenides as presented in another dialogue by Plato. In the words of Drummond's version, three must be "one that is all, which is the principle of all, by which extension and mind exist," and only to the "inattentive" does "the nominal difference between physical forces, and mental faculties, conceal . . . from the . . . observer this common origin and real similitude."[16] Shelley clearly finds these statements suggestive even before the summer of 1820. In the late-1819 essay "On Life" so very indebted to Drummond, the sense that all perceptions and reactions are similar in being thoughts leads to a belief that the thoughts in one psyche are not essentially different from those in another. "Pursuing the same thread of reasoning," Shelley writes, "the existence of distinct individual minds . . . is likewise found to be a delusion. The words *I, you, they* are not signs of any actual difference subsisting between the assemblage of thoughts thus indicated, but are merely marks employed to denote the different modifications of the one mind" (*NCE*, pp. 477–78). It is from this "thread," less than a year and a half later, that Shelley weaves his sense of exactly how the true visionary "participates in the eternal, the infinite, and the one" in the *Defence of Poetry*. A poet does so, the *Defence* claims, by receiving and then adding "links" to that age-old "chain" of poetic writings that has continuously generated "unapprehended relations" from the potentials in established discourse. The writer in this way contributes "episodes to that great poem, which all poets, like the co-operating thoughts of one great mind, have built up since the beginning of the world" (*NCE*, p. 493).

Yet Shelley makes more than his sources do of the "building," "co-operating," "projecting," and "positing" in his notion, so much so that his revised version is a One with almost no precedents in Western thought, even though the foundations of the revision are all present within its ancestors. The "one mind" of "On Life," we should note, is first a revision of an earlier Shelleyan figure: the final state of Cythna's psyche after she has been kept many months in that sea-cave mentioned earlier and has become, in response to her memories and to all those "shells engraven / With mystic legends" from the past, "the book of all human wisdom" and in that sense

"One mind, the type of all, the moveless wave / Whose calm reflects all moving things that are" (*Laon and Cythna,* ll. 2940–3105; *CPW,* II, 203–8). Though such a portrait anticipates the poet-prophet's mind (as Shelley sees it) withdrawing into deep contact with the Promethean intertext, this part of *Laon and Cythna* is in danger of making one *person's* mind the repository of all previous and potential thought and thus a single "type" serving as the standard for others, a possible center of tyrannical power that Cythna herself would surely (yet can hardly) resist. "On Life" therefore turns that centripetal gathering inside out by constructing oneness from a series of transitions in reasoning, most of them Plato's and Drummond's, which transport the ingredients of personal psyches more and more outside personal limits.

The key to the transitions, Shelley finds, is the gaps they cross even in his precursors. Plato makes a point of reason moving from "multiplicities" to qualities in common to the common name, only to leap suddenly to a "type" that is projected beyond any personal consciousness as the distant "signified" to which the name refers. Drummond, in his turn, has to admit that the One, like his Power, must be boldly hypothesized as "out there" after repeated mental sightings of recurrent connections between differentiated elements (such as "feeling" and "substance").[17] The Shelley of "On Life" consequently foregrounds distance as his concept's most basic ingredient, denying, as in Drummond, any total difference between "ideas" and "objects" but affirming, as in Plato, that the "one mind" is projected elsewhere ("posited" or placed) from the position of some "different modification" that is not identical with it. To keep its "one mind" removed from Cythna's, "On Life" must say that "I, the person who now writes and thinks, am [not] that one mind," only a "portion" looking to other portions ("you" and "they") to begin approaching oneness (*NCE,* p. 478). Seeing that difference reopen when it appears to have been elided should remind Shelley's reader of the rather wide logical spaces in the same paragraph between the "nominal" difference among "classes of thought," the "questioning" of "distinct individual minds," and the assertion of a "one mind" partially denoted by the "marks" of its "modifications." Each of these makes its successors possible, but not absolutely necessary—all these notions remain more separate than equivalent—and even the final step spreads out "the truth" into three different levels (the "marks," the "modifications" they refer to, and the ultimate referent of these referents), leaving thought unable to dissolve into the unity toward which the entire paragraph moves.

Shelley's playing of Plato and Drummond off each other this way results in a concept far more skeptical than either of theirs, albeit on the basis of what makes theirs possible. That basis is stated fairly explicitly in Plato's *Parmenides* when the title figure admits that the "One" behind all universals "must be both in itself and in another" before it can be the "one being" (*Par.* 145e, trans. F. M. Cornford). The "one mind" must be intimated only by "modifications" other than itself transferring themselves toward it by way of each other, yet it must be at a distance from them off by itself as the point toward which transference presses them all without really attaining a oneness-with-itself. That is why the notion is presented as the result of a later-stage leap across spaces in logic wherein degrees of transference shift toward greater degrees (a similarity of thought and object becoming a similarity of one thought to another). The "One Mind" must announce itself as the other side of a gulf that transference is trying to bridge in order to further its capacity for producing relations. For this reason Shelley has to pull back from completely affirming the idea as more than a desirable hypothesis; he must say, just as thought makes its projection ahead of *"I, you, they,"* that "we are on the verge where words abandon us" and "we look down the dark abyss of—how little we know" ("On Life," p. 478). The drive of transference toward greater interconnection is always wrenched backward by its status as a transition between differences and distances, and that undertow means that the distance must be reannounced even as it is crossed so that the chasm, the bridge, and the other side all hover in thought together, the common cause and factor being transference rather than the total unity sought at the end of the sequence. It is no surprise to find that "On Life" was written during the very months that spawned act 4 of *Prometheus Unbound*. The "one harmonious soul of many a soul" in the latter, a "Sea reflecting Love" between innumerable tributaries (l. 384) instead of the "moveless wave" of a single master intelligence, is what we can build up to in steps, as "On Life" does, by adding myriad further connections to whatever "chain of linked thought" we have at the moment, yet only in a "struggle [carried out of the self by love] towards [a] free wilderness" of the future where the struggle continues (IV. 394–99).

The *Defence of Poetry* proceeds so much from this basis that it both intensifies the radical change in the idea and extends the motion's forward momentum to make it an impetus involved throughout all levels of the poetic process. The reader is set up for an iconoclastic shock when the essay answers Peacock's portrait of the modern poem as almost completely nostalgic with the claim that all true poetry in every age adumbrates what is most universal and eternal. Shelley here seems at first to repeat the Plato, Aristotle, Horace, Sidney, Johnson, Wordsworth, and Coleridge from whom he does indeed draw parts of his rhetoric.[18] But he does that in an explicit effort to redefine their terms so as to free such words from the highly monolithic, even tyrannizing transcendentals that he must have found in most of the theories of poetry prior to his own.[19] When he reuses Aristotle's distinction between poetry and sheer narrative, he maintains that the former "is the creation of actions according to the unchangeable forms of human nature" only in the sense that poetry "contains within itself the germ of a relation to whatever motive or actions have place in the possible varieties of human nature" (*Defence*, p. 485). In this context "unchangeable forms" cannot be underlying entelechies, "stabilities of truth," assertions of a quasi-divine "I AM," or fixed predilections in different types of people. They are now potentialities or sparks or seeds ("germs"), too often "unapprehended" in everyday perception, able to grow (as poets render them) toward relationships with many forms of human being and effort, some of which already exist and some of which are still to arise. The "germ" of this sort of universal, we could say, since the *Defence* does place the generation of these seeds in a psyche "which is itself the image of all other minds" (p. 485), lies in the "one mind" of Cythna as it starts to realize how much its conflation is not a completeness within itself. Such a mind makes itself "[rear]range [the existing] woofs, as they [are] woven, of [its] thought" to compose as yet unapprehended relations, "a subtler language within language wrought" (*Laon and Cythna*, ll. 3109–113; *CPW*, II, 208). As a result, such universals in the *Defence* transcend the past only as they (like seeds) become what they always could have been but have yet to be. Being unfoldings of possible interconnections or rearrangements, potential traits of personality constituted mainly by their continual transferability among a number of persons, Shelley's "germs" are crossing from past and present existence as it has been perceived toward arrangements of life waiting to be conceived, even toward "varieties" that can make those arrangements widespread by carrying them through repeatedly in different forms. "For the [Shelleyan poet] not only beholds intensely the present as it is, and discovers those laws according to which present things ought to be ordered, but he beholds the future in the present, and his thoughts are [in that sense] the germs of the flower and the fruit of latest time" (*Defence*, pp. 482–83).

The transitivity in this opening-toward-eternity operates even at early stages in the gestation and composition of poetry. It is active in the basic moment of imaginative reorganization, the instant when that "faculty" transfigures and reassociates thoughts that have already been arranged by the reason into basic relations and classes. At that point, to be sure, imagination becomes "mind acting upon those thoughts so as to colour them with its own light, and composing from them, as from elements, other thoughts, each containing within itself the principle of its own integrity" (*Defence*, p. 480). Many have read this procedure as though it were proposed by Wordsworth or Coleridge, as if it were simply the organic wholeness of a self-contained presence at the heart of thought making thought's new ingredients whole within themselves—and thereby raising them to the "Elysian light" of a greater oneness (to quote p. 487). The imagination for Shelley, after all, is the "spirit" in the "body" of thought, the "principle of synthesis" striving to establish not just relations but a "harmony" among them (p. 480). Yet such readings forget how much this poet, by composing "integral unities" from "elements" in a manner that generates light, is alluding most immediately to chemistry and its most common operation on elements, the one that produces chemical compounds with their own new laws of interconnection giving off light and heat during the period of their formation. In fact, at this juncture, since Shelley has never stopped his voracious reading in the sciences of his own day, he is very likely repeating the following passage from Sir Humphry Davy's *Elements of Chemical Philosophy* (1812):

> The fire produced in a number of chemical processes, particularly in combustion, can be ascribed to particles sent into free space, in consequence of the repulsion exerted by other particles at the moment of their entering into chemical union. . . . [This sort of] circumstance is favorable to the idea of the possibility of the conversion of common matter into radiant matter.[20]

Imaginative re-creation being this kind of "conversion" for Shelley, it cannot develop out of an existing wholeness or "colour" its product with a light born from simple unification or sent from Elysian realms. Instead, the imaginative act must be a fiery reaction of thought-elements to each other that forces the elements together in configurations that alter their older relationships for the sake of new realignments. The resulting formation must also project particles outward (hence the radiance) as the differences in the related elements insist that confirmations and extensions of the new relations be sought in different conflations outside this one, variations toward which some particles now dart into "free space." The "principle of integrity" in each part of this construction is a centripetal compression that is centrifugal too, as we have now come to expect, sending off at each moment toward other unities some of the very parts that are being made "integral." The "light and fire" to which all this rises, too, are products of the reconstruction and expulsion in action, bright emissions at the level of a forward motion to which merely generalizing reason can never ascend on its own.

The specific creation, the "germ," achieved by this compounding action consequently demands a deferral to the future, no matter how many ingredients it wrests into a network of interconnections. What a poetic conflation usually "collects," Shelley avers, are "the brightest rays of human nature" given off by humanity when empirically observed or remembered, and imagination touches these "with majesty and beauty" (its higher light) by making each one reflect and refract the others, altering "the [existing] simplicity of these elementary forms" (*Defence,* p. 491). The result is "a prismatic and many-sided mirror"—the "germ" as always and already a succession of transfers between frames of reference—where apparent human actualities, blurred together and newly connected by reflection and interreflection, become the myrid and linked possibilities that they could always have enacted and might one day fulfill (p. 491). This mirror so "multiplies all that it reflects" that its achieved interplay of tendencies immediately starts expanding its number of variations and looking for further reflectors. That restlessness, basic to its very conception, thereby "endows [the germ] with a power of propagating its like wherever it may fall" (p. 491). By its very nature as a turning from what people seem to have been to what they could be, the constructed universal *has* to be transferable "to whatever motives or actions have place in the possible varieties of human nature." That is what Shelley means a few pages earlier when he writes, as we have noted, that "Poetry enlarges the circumference of the imagination," never leaving it in some initial state of contained unity, "by replenishing it with [unforeseen] thoughts of ever new delight, which have the power of attracting and assimilating to their own nature all other thoughts, and which form new intervals and interstices whose void forever craves fresh food" yet to be found.

If this self-extension sounds like the continual reopening of words toward words, sentences toward sentences, and the text toward a reader in a written piece of poetry, that is because Shelley sees this oneness of process appearing quite visibly in the verbal work produced by imaginative composition. He supports his view that "time and place and number are not" in poetic projections by claiming that the "grammatical forms which express the moods of time, and the differences of persons and the distinction of place are convertible with respect to the highest poetry . . . and [that] the choruses of Aeschylus, and the book of Job, and Dante's Paradise . . . afford, more than any other writings, examples of this fact" (*Defence,* p. 483). This "conversion" in lines of poetry takes the strictly time-bound tenses and specific persons or settings on which "normal" discursive sentences depend and lifts those differentiations into an almost timeless present tense, free of one particular past or present or future. At this point people dissolve into the we/they of "mankind" (as in act 4 of *Prometheus Unbound*), and their location becomes a "here" as "everywhere" spreading out in all directions (like a sea) wherever it positions itself. Yet the examples Shelley offers never entirely transcend time or forget that the spreading must pass from figure to figure and place to place. The choric songs in Aeschylus's *Prometheus Bound* announce the eternal nature of things usually by questioning, hoping for, or anticipating tomorrow from the perspective of today, as when the chorus sets itself off from defiant Prometheus by praying that "Zeus, who disposes all things," may "never exert his power to crush my will" as he has with the Titan (ll, 526–27); the lamentations of Job and his interlocutors enunciate an unlocalized present condition only to see that state as intimating an inaccessible other one somewhere else, forcing them all to exclaim "It is as high as heaven; what canst thou do? deeper than hell; what canst thou know?" (Job 11:8); and the conclusions from his journey to Paradise that the poeticized Dante can best put into words say mainly, as he utters them, that "Hope" for "grace" and "dessert" is the only "certain expectation that the heart / Has of future glory" (Paradiso, XXV.

65–69).[21] In each case the conversion toward atemporality escapes one moment in time because the new tense is a slippage from the present toward the future, a sliding of desire that is always present as an eternal aspect of verbal temporality. Meanwhile, persons and places blur on one level only as that level nearly gives way to an unattained context offering a fuller interrelation of those differences in another state very different from this one. Only if language can be made to realize and draw out this potential that is always within it does the poet have an effective way of both "behold[ing] . . . the present . . . intensely . . . and discover[ing] those laws according to which present things ought to be ordered" in days to come.

All this while, though, Shelley never lets us forget that the poet cannot will "unapprehended relations" on his or her own. He or she does so only by unleashing the possibilities of analogy unexplored in the history of poetry (the Promethean intertext) or recovering the "chaos" of connections just in the process of formation that was achieved in the old "cyclic poem" before such play was restricted by "lexicography and the [more recent] distinctions of grammar" (*Defence,* p. 482). Such oneness as the poet attempts is forced from him by his being one link in a longlasting "chain" approaching him from the past, almost imperceptibly, to call his imagination into a "finer [state of] organization" (*Defence,* p. 493). For Shelley, as in the *Ion,* though not as irrationally, "Poetry" is "a magnet [of] invisible effluence" outside any one imagination, attaching itself to potentially "great minds" in the revival of the "fading coal" so that the glow of energy through "sacred links" can continue as an expansion of relations "which at once connects, animates, and sustains the life of all [interpretive activities]" (p. 493). It is by way of this infusion—which makes imagination less an originating power and more the conduit of a perpetual transference reenacting itself in individual schemes of transfiguration—that the poet's efforts become "co-operating thoughts [in that] one great mind," the renewed "echoes" of an "eternal music"—or "life of truth"—that keeps trying to "unveil the permanent analogy of things [as perceived]" so that more interconnection can be seen by us all (*Defence,* pp. 493 and 485). The poet's "majestic rhythm" must be rooted in this impersonal transmigration away from any clear origin (just as the *Ion* says) if it is to be the iconoclastic "strain which distends, and then bursts the circumference of the hearer's mind," for only in that case will the poem's music pour "itself forth together with [the reader's expanded thinking] into [a] universal element [of rhythmic movement] with which [the poem] has perpetual sympathy" (p. 485).

Yet even this overarching One, as it further removes oneness of mind from any single psyche, is no more organic or unified inside itself than an act of imagination or the "reasoning" toward the possibility of oneness in the piece "On Life." The apparently "one great poem" of "co-operating thoughts" must be "built up" repeatedly in restorations of depleted energy, as though the cooperation were an entropic process of stultification, then sudden reorganization, rather than an uninterrupted growth leading one sort of work to reappear with the slightest change in another guise. Poetry's history in the West as Shelley sees it, we should remember, shows each emergence of "unapprehended relations" during and since ancient Greek times "troping down" (to quote Harold Bloom[22]) into "signs" referring only to circumscribed "portions or classes of thought," into set relations of certain words to certain angles of reference that try to limit, even halt, the expansion of analogy and thus restrain the "going out" of what has been imagined into additional associations and "many others" besides.

"The sacred links [of poetry's] chain," however, are almost but "never . . . entirely disjoined"; a few "seeds" or "sparks" flying "into free space" from old poems toward the distant ground of their "own and social renovation" revive the "fading coals" in other and later psyches. Once they start to interact, these different repressed potentials (be they textual, cultural, or personal memories) strive together toward the "true and the beautiful" gradually projected by the transference that the revival inspires, "first between existence and perception, and secondly between perception and expression" (*Defence*, pp. 493 and 482). This entropy continues, moreover, even in these latter two transitions, as the new poet's reconception rises out of and leaves behind the fading coal, the Promethean intertext, and the "peculiar relations" of his moment in time. Since the transference inaugurating the coal's revival conceals and transmutes itself in doing so, the "very mind which directs the hands in the formation [of a work becomes] incapable of accounting to itself for the origin [or even] the gradations [instigating] the process" (*Defence*, p. 504). The self-obscuring "decay" of the coal's new brightness must be "redeemed" in the "veils" of "language" or "form" that revive and explain the fading only as they are drawn into the poem from earlier, different retractions and changes that they dimly recall. The veils, therefore, can suggest but never reveal some "inmost naked beauty" behind them; they depend for completion on their own deferral to the reader's responsive "chord," always differently tuned, on "the bridge thrown [especially by the most progressive thinking] over the stream of time" that will never run dry (pp. 504–05).

To "participate in the eternal, the infinite, and the one" for Shelley, we have to conclude, is never to fulfill a self-consistent unity or promote a conflation of differences that will really blend all its ingredients together at a final point. It is to contact the transportability, sometimes translatability, of actual or potential conceptions or word-patterns between different minds, moments in history, poetic contexts, and states of social organization.[23] This drive toward conversion in poetic thoughts and forms—the ultimate generator of the revolutionary "light and fire" to which imagination is able to rise—carries incipient or established relations over into different but expanded orders of relationship, orders that seek a common ground uniting the analogies within or between different constructs yet realize how little total unity can be achieved in any one leap beyond existing interconnections. Such a process preceding, infusing, and surpassing any poet, as both a motion or train helping to fashion his or her thoughts and a level of enlightenment that his or her thoughts should try to attain, is perpetual enough and has enough procedures common to each advancement of itself to be "one" as opposed to many kinds of movement and to be "infinite" in its possible range of connections as well as "eternal" in its operation. But it is a oneness that transmutes all that it retains, so much so that it cannot be said to remain what it is or where it is at any point. What it retains, if anything, is the once-unexpected transposition turning to another iconoclastic interplay that should recreate, not just the first one's present or apparent ingredients, but the activity of "going out to many others" that made the earlier relationship possible. Were Shelley not to advance this "unity" of minds, thoughts, and discourses continually differentiating what it would and does conflate, his "One" would have to endorse the constant quality of Essence in things projected "out there" by nearly all hierarchical, patriarchal, syncretic, and imperialist ideologies. Shelley must avoid such a stance while still pursuing an expansion of equality that spreads common interests among all human beings, so he opts for a "One," in this instance, that allows minds or poems to read their ingredients or predecessors from a different perspective at each moment and to send out their own redactions to listeners and readers who have a chance to transmogrify such figures from their own angles of approach.

The One as a Fusion of Opposites: *Epipsychidion*

Nevertheless, this "older, wiser" Shelley retains enough aspects of his earlier Gothic sensibility to focus simultaneously on a somewhat different kind of oneness as an object of desire in his later work. Recalling what his younger self did with the "amyranth bower" that "points" all states of existence to a level of total satisfaction far in the past or the future, the mature poet seems to hypothesize a sequestered condition *not* attainable in a gradual expansion of interrelations where the interval between human desire and its objects would abruptly disappear and the poles would fuse, difference becoming Sameness and plurality Unity. Diotima in Plato's *Symposium* seems to revive the appeal of this fantasy, upholding Shelley's adolescent connection between that projection and erotic longing. She defines *eros* as the ardent passage from a sense of privation and lack to a distant Plenty that is both the father and the desired completion of love's quest (*PS,* pp. 442–43). Desire is now more, and more clearly, the pursuit of the primal and all-fulfilling "good" at a great remove from the incomplete self, and longing can start to reach that goal through intercourse with the beautiful bodies and thoughts of other beings, the visible conduits in the world of appearances (or dreams) to that conjunction with the ultimate Unity. Dante and Petrarch modify this myth slightly by elevating its principal woman-figure, the "ignorant and poor" mother of *eros* (*PS,* p. 443), to the place of Diotima the wise interpreter and Venus the most beautiful embodiment of the good, near whose threshold Poverty once desired Plenty to the point of spawning the love that currently moves between them. The two giants of Italian poetry thereby locate their pathway to the One in the once earthly and inviting, but now heavenly and all-knowing, woman surpassing all women, "who art [therefore] the only virtue whence / Mankind may overpass what is contained / Within the heaven of least circumferance" (*Inferno,* II. 76–78). Shelley's *Epipsychidion* then furthers this succession of love-visions by styling the "Emilia" it addresses as the supreme synecdoche that opens out into all the various qualities the speaker-lover wants to possess, enact, or be. She is the figure leading desire to a Plenty of countless interfused ingredients and variations from "light and love and immortality" to "a well of sealed and secret happiness," or at least to "A cradle [containing] young thoughts of wingless [but potentially winged] pleasure" (ll. 58 and 68). The lover, perceiving "mine own infirmity" as a diametric contrast to what the lady seems to offer (l. 71), seems to wish that all beings, terms, times, or states in his mundane existence could press toward the fuller opposites that ultimately contain them and that might finally, as a consequence, carry them away from their insufficiency. He wants "Night [to be subsumed] by Day, / Winter by Spring, [and] Sorrow by swift Hope," to name a few examples, so that his separate "sphere" will be able to approach Emilia's in a realm beyond desirous lack and to "become the same" as that "Spirit," to "touch, mingle, and [be] transfigured" with her (ll. 73–74 and 574–78).

Yet Shelley writes this poem deliberately in the tradition of the *Symposium* and the *Vita Nuova* so that he can reconstitute all their originating centers and ultimate points, which are usually the same location or being: a One of absolute power. He objects, as we know, to any notion of love as stemming only from a self-sufficient Father or even from a raised-up daemon or goddess calling the seeker up the steps of knowledge to a monolithic Supremacy beyond all interplay. "Love [for Shelley] makes all things equal," not hierarchical (*Epipsychidion*, l. 126). Moreover, as it pours forth from the human "heart" or "spirit" in its quest for an answering quest from another quarter, it "creates" (not "finds") the desirability of any "object" or conduit it seeks or employs (ll. 170–72) *without* its desire having to have been created first by a preexistent deprivation or fullness (even though it does feel the former as the product of its need for something outside itself). Diotima, much as she tries to deny it later, suggests that possibility when she defines *eros* initially as a positing of "what it does not possess," a valuing of that object because it seems to harbor the sheer, unspecified opposite that would complete desire (*PS*, p. 439). The desired other as the reflector of a projection is intimated even more at the start of the *Vita Nuova* when Beatrice's first appearance to the nine-year-old Dante is described as the moment "the glorious Lady of [or already in] my mind ... appeared before my eyes."[24] As a result, Shelley's speaker, using both authors against themselves by exaggerating the change that Dante makes in Plato's concept, seeks Emilia (in l. 238) as the "antitype" of the "soul out of my soul" defined by the essay "On Love" (Shelley's revision of the *Symposium*[25]), as the reincarnation of "Youth's vision" (l. 42), the imagined ego-ideal of *Alastor*, finally embodied by a physical being who approximates the relational process of thought that brought the dream-maiden about.

The Greek title *Epipsychidion* means "About" or "Toward" the "Little Soul," we should recall,[26] and so refers, as "On Love" does, to the lover's miniaturized creation of his own more perfect form. For Shelley (as for his *Alastor* Poet or Maniac), the psyche's "thirst after its likeness" makes it interrelate the most "excellent ... particulars" of the perceived self into an "assemblage" or small "soul within [the] soul"; that complex of related transfers is then projected beyond the self as the projector's "proper Paradise" to be approached through someone else's "imagination[,] which [may] enter into and seize upon [such cherished] peculiarities" in quest of its own better self (*NCE*, p. 474). The dream-ideal of youth, too, as much in this later version as in *Alastor* or *Julian and Maddalo*, is fabricated to incarnate that "assemblage" in an image of the other sex, since the better self by definition must be the opposite (therefore the gender-opposite) of the insufficient lover. As such, the envisioned figure, again recalling *Alastor*, must itself be an interaction of perceptions and sensations drawn from various sources, so much an emerging "voice" in "whispering woods ... fountains, and the odours deep / Of flowers" that she is never fully "beheld" as a settled body halting the interaction (*Epipsychidion*, ll. 200–203). This spreading transmutation, trying to rework another one transferred toward it by its projector, is what lies within or behind "Emily" perceived as "youth's vision made perfect" in a tangible person (l. 42). Being thus a "bright Eternity" different from Plato's and Dante's, since it is the "shadow of [a very mobile] golden dream" (ll. 115–16), the movement—the One—trembles through [Emilia's] limbs" as a "liquid murmur" recalling the "music" of a former "trance" and "issuing" outward as an "unentangled intermixture, made / By love, of light and motion" (ll. 77–78, 84–86, 91–94). Moreover, this new Asia-like process must flow back toward the projector of the "little soul," "call[ing his] Spirit" as he calls to hers (l. 337). The real source of her possibilities lies in the succession of transformations of himself that he has imagined, even as his ultimate potentials lie in the better alternatives toward which he can expand with the help of her spreading "intermixture."[27] Hence the originating drive in both the generative center (the heart or soul of each lover) and the eventual objective (the potential that each imagines in the other) is "one intense Diffusion" of transference, an "Omnipresence" only in the sense of "one [process] whose flowering outlines mingle in their flowing" toward the achievement of further relations, the goal that sparked Love's quest to begin with (ll. 94–96). No wonder the Plenty that this Beatrice offers is an endless array of different human potentials or myths of possible existence. As the outward-tending and relation-seeking lover perceives her, she must dissolve, as his dream-figure did, into a host of possible analogues for existing analogues, "A Metaphor of Spring and Youth and Morning" and more (l. 120). It is only in this way that she intimates "all that is insupportable" in her bodily form of the "light, and love, and immortality" that transference keeps generating and moving toward.

The consequences for what is now left from the quests of Plato and Dante, in fact, are even more disjunctive by their standards than this mere replacement of an emanating center by a decentered and self-decentering "diffusion" among beings. As right as both the lovers in *Epipsychidion* are to say "I am a part of *thee*" (l. 52) in a mirror-relation that keeps expanding into multiple refractions of it, they can never "become the same" to the point of eliminating all difference or opposition, if Shelley's vision of the unifying force is to prevail over the ones he revises. For one thing, since the "Spirit" of the early dream-vision is a multifaceted, unstable "shadow of beauty unbeheld," her nature and special value cannot be desired by one who really understands her difference from a commonplace object of thought unless (somewhat as in Plato) her spreading interrelatedness is re-beheld from the position of what it is not, in seeming reflections of it that turn out to be as distant from the true "Sun" as Poverty is from Plenty. The dream-woman, composed from myriad observations or memories as a "Beauty furled" from the beginning (l. 102), must quickly vanish, as the *Alastor* Poet did not comprehend, behind "the dreary cave of our life's shade," the source of some of the perceived ingredients producing her diffuse image (l. 228). As she recedes, repeating Asia, the *Alastor* maiden, and the Maniac's "Leonora," she must seem for awhile to become what Dante and Petrarch posit, a kind of "God throned on a winged planet" setting a standard that can be pursued only through lesser "mortal forms" (ll. 226 and 267). To approach this newly unified, objectified, and uplifted absolute, the speaker must rush into a quest from one "shadow"-woman to another (ll. 246–71), all of whom seem to harbor a few of the standard's qualities (making each attractive) yet each of whom soon reveals a lack or perversion of the rest, driving the seeker away and onward. Indeed, the dream-ideal's myriad ingredients, forms, and potentials force the lover, so that he can come closer to encompassing their multiplicity, to increase the number and variety of "screens" he tries far beyond the smaller number in the lover's autobiographies of Dante and Petrarch. That bewildering succession, moreover, starts to establish how radically separate the standard really is from goddess-hood and simple objectivity. "Wounded," like Prometheus as Acteon, by the disappointment that must result from any quest for a supreme form by way of inadequate substitutes, the speaker stands "at bay" by "turn[ing] upon [his] own thoughts" (ll. 273–74), by confronting the fact of the basic and projective psychic process that looked to an Other of itself to complete itself in the first place.

Still, the dream's difference from the hierarchical objectification now tormenting the speaker's infatuations is not entirely clear until he, like Endymion, falls in love with a "Moon" (a version of Mary Shelley after 1818[28]). This substitute is much more like the "glorious shape" than any of the others, particularly since the shape has already been described as partly analogous to "the eternal Moon of Love / Under whose motions life's dull billows move" (ll. 278 and 118–19). The new surrogate "Queen of Heaven" (l. 281), providing a comforting serenity after the many painful breaks with earlier screens, seems happily, at first, as full of "changes" as is the "eternal Sun" (ll. 279–80). But these shifts finally stop expanding their range. They "ever run / Into themselves" exactly as they have been before, repetitively "waxing and waning . . . According as she smile[s] or frown[s]" her approval or disapproval in response to the speaker's feelings or acts (ll. 279–98). She becomes too completely like an enthroned figure announcing the judgments by which his very being is deemed worthwhile or worthless, as in the Maniac's vision of his lady in *Julian and Maddalo*.[29] The movement of the lover's waves becomes so dictated by the expression on his Queen's "pale," Diana-like "lips" that her "cold" absence or "chaste" disdain for any period freezes him into an icy death-in-life, an effort not to feel (ll. 309, 281, and 316). Now the speaker can plainly see that any sort of completely external and heavenly Beatrice is precisely what the dream-vision never was and must never be interpreted into becoming. Not surprisingly, at this moment, the vision reappears reincarnated much as it was initially, as a "flash[ing of] motion," a "respiration," and a "Dissolving" through perceived elements of nature, all of which "Govern[s]" the speaker only by "penetrating" him with the "light" of his potential metamorphosis into a "sphere" of "brighter bloom" (ll. 324, 329, 334, 361, and 367).

The transfiguration that makes its projector/counterpart become other than himself by way of numerous analogues—the feminine Other that is man's repressed and sublimated capacity for transporting his desire through and across whatever is outside him—rises from "obscur[ity]" by being the opposite and the foundation of its Platonic and Catholic antithesis (l. 321). "She," like the witch of Atlas now, is "the intense, the deep, the imperishable" in "me" that must always seek (and return from) another version of itself (ll. 391–92). The speaker must press for reunification with that level of thinking and being now that he knows its differences from the too commonly accepted world of "veiled Divinity" (l. 244). He must strive, at least figuratively, to transport himself and that level's best reincarnation to a realm like the "fairy isles" of his youthful "dream" made partly, as the Witch is, from elements "of antique verse and high romance" (ll. 193 and 210). There strictly demarcated elements, objects, minds, beliefs, and sexes need not remain in their usual segregated and hierarchized states but can instead live out an "Omnipresence" of intertransference, each "Possessing and possest by all that is" (l. 549). He thus proposes an escape to "one of the wildest of the Sporades" ("Advertisement," *NCE*, p. 373), choosing an unsettled island between Greece and Asia Minor that is almost (like the birthplace of Asia nearby) unrestricted in its potential combination of Western and Eastern mythologies outside a fixed order. This paradise even lies "under Ionian skies" (l. 422) near the original homes of Homeric poetry and ancient Greek romance,[30] thereby drawing Platonic, Dantean, and Petrarchan writing back to the primal "chaos of the cyclic poem" in which types and levels of being mix freely with one another, be they gods, heroes, objects, or perceptions through different senses. Only here, where the vision of youth is revived with the aid of the oldest interplays in the forms that once helped to create the initial dream, can the speaker and Emilia be liberated into a "Love mak[ing] all things equal," a movement surging around and through them constantly and consciously instead of surreptitiously and subliminally. Only here can the logic slotting self and other, man and woman, or opposition and transference into separate spheres be replaced by the relational logic of "the blue heavens bend[ing] to touch their paramour" as the island rises toward them (ll. 544–45). Such a total interplay, transferred into every figure or being that enters this setting, can revive the sense of a "soul that burns between" the separate lovers and pull the two "spheres instinct with it" into constant mental, verbal, and bodily intercourse with each other (ll. 568 and 577).

Yet even in this Elysium, because it is so constituted, because its ingredients and residents are free to alter themselves in their loving of one another, there can never be a conscious fusion of differences to a point where all difference disappears, not in an "amyranth bower" or any other location. The island, first of all, though it restores relational fluidity to thought and behavior, is still a desired recreation of constructs remembered from days long past, the days of the speaker's early fantasies, not to mention Ionian poetry. Consequently, this far-off goal must be "Beautiful [only] as a wreck of Paradise" and formed out of "motion[s,] odour[s] . . . and tone[s that] seem / Like echoes of an antenatal dream" (ll. 422 and 453–56). The "soul within the soul," its ingredients, and its surroundings lie more in the past the more they are approached in present and future remnants of themselves. Desire's object still hovers partly elsewhere in any future embracing of its form, so much so that even in the speaker's arms Emilia is "a well of sealed and secret happiness," a flame that "point[s away] to Heaven" *from* a supposed heaven on earth (ll. 581–83). Such would have to be the case even in a fully restored past—an impossibility, to be sure—since the original dream projects but an image of a desired perfection never fully beheld at any time or in any antitype. There is no final surpassing, though there may be a narrowing, of the distance between desire and its ultimate goal, especially since that goal is the expanded transference of desire. The attainment of that transfer's best intimation shows the objective to be somewhere else yet again, reinvoking the separation between self and its "other" one more time.

Giving selfhood up suddenly, then, to the primordial intertransference of reverie means launching desire, with its sense of a gulf to be bridged, into a series of relocations where that sense remains even while it is being "transfigured" (l. 578). The interrelating island, which itself keeps changing its combinations of ingredients, contains quests of parts toward other (or previous) parts that keep turning toward other such quests, drawing some of their own parts toward still others. The lovers in such a realm, clearly possessed by and possessing it, must follow that never-completed course, especially when they make love. The "melody" that each lover sings to the other, however similar it may be to what answers it, must "die, / In words" because the "thought" it carries forward wants to "live again" in other signs of its expression, in the lover's "looks" (for example) that can then dart their appeal into the "heart" of the other person's being (ll. 560–63). Beyond that, should this darting by both lovers succeed in making the "veins" of both "beat together" in a common rhythm indicating a commonality of soul (l. 566), the "lips" of the two, further displacing the "eloquence" of the "words" they once attempted, must "eclipse the soul that burns between them" if the two "spheres instinct with [desire's heat want] to become the same" at last (ll. 566–68 and 577). No shared state or feeling comes into existence here without being abruptly supplanted and "eclipsed" by another in a manner that places what the lovers are about to share "between" two figures, one on the rise and one receding. Plurality and temporal difference reemerge in every achieved singularity, leaving "One passion [divided among] twin-hearts, which grows [in one way now] and grew [differently at an earlier time]" (l. 575).

That being the case, Shelley can raise physical intercourse, as Dante and Petrarch emphatically could not, to the height of "passion's [future] golden purity" (l. 571), this poem's equivalent of the point in the *Paradiso* where Dante's eyes move past Beatrice to "pierce / Into [the] splendour" of the "Primal Love" itself (XXXII. 142–44). In the sex act at its best, the "expanding flame" envelops both lovers, urging them to be as ultimately equal as Shelley insists they be, but only as it pours forth from "two [distinct] meteors," two members of still different sexes (l. 576),[31] whose friction with one another increases the heat so that they can be "transfigured" to the fiery level that "eclipses" the earlier burning between them. With this becoming-one-by-remaining-two-bodies elevated to the supreme fulfillment of *eros,* ultimate oneness is itself transubstantiated into one figure's continual "finding [of] food" in "another's substance" (l. 580). *Epipsychidion*'s final fusion therefore dissipates into the paradoxes that intercourse has always tried and failed to resolve: its being a great pleasure by making some use of painful friction, its holding out a final objective that begins to recede as soon as orgasm has been achieved, its efforts to make somewhat different preferences compatible, and its being both a "little death" *and* a possible inseminator of future life (the closest the body comes to realizing immortality in the *Symposium*). The "two spheres . . . becom[ing] the same" thus refer in fact to myriad opposites defining themselves in terms of their counterparts, even by half-introjecting them, while also maintaining something like their present shapes and definitions. The merging of the lovers is "One hope within two wills, one will beneath / Two overshadowing minds [each holding on to some independence], one life, one death, / One Heaven, one Hell, one immortality [that is also an] annihilation" (ll. 584–87). None of these entities or levels can be "one" without being connected/opposed to the others, so oneness is no more than this concatenation of relating differences, each of which is similar to or distinct from the other in varying degrees.

As it turns out, what this "unity" most resembles is a composition made of words (the poem itself), of differences turning ahead and back toward the meaning they all desire by way of other such differences they may try to join but cannot ascend beyond by themselves.[32] Hence, just at the moment when he most clearly confronts the incompleteness and difference in a version of the ultimate coitus, Shelley's speaker recalls how much it is mainly "winged words on which my soul would pierce / Into the height of love's rare Universe" (ll. 588–89). He remembers that the courtship and foreplay in *Epipsychidion* have been, from the start of the poem, an extending of "votive wreaths" and roselike "songs" toward the "twin lights [Emilia's eyes, which her] sweet soul darkens through" (ll. 4, 9, and 38). As in the courtly love tradition, the hope in this outreach has, of course, been that tears or smiles sent back by such an emanating beacon will lift the word-blossom up, as it dies, to a new blooming-forth in another state (something like that of the great Rose in the *Paradiso*), a sudden elevation of the "sorrow" in the text's incompleteness to the "ecstasy of Youth's vision . . . made perfect" in the way the poem is read by what seems "A lovely soul" (ll. 39, 42, and 57). But an ascent attempted by words, which can gain its will to meaning only in the passage from sign to sign, depends primarily for its first satisfaction on the responding signs in some reading eyes that intimate a deeper soul "through a glass darkly." In that soul may lie, the speaker hopes, a reincarnation of the ideal prototype of the self.

Yet the pathway to it (her visage) is merely the "shadow of some golden dream" to which words of appeal must defer themselves only to behold another mere sign and to feel their own "mortality" as the shadow recedes beyond them (l. 36). Meanwhile, the desire in the words is usually carried away from them and their author by another body of signifiers, a "cradle of young thoughts" (the text), which is deferred to a still more removed and invisible set of points.

Here Shelley radicalizes, by making explicitly verbal, the instant when Dante nears the "Light Eternal" only to find that "the principle escapes him still" because the "force" of the human "imagination" has "failed" even as "The Love that moves the sun" has carried off the seeker's "desire and will" (*Paradiso*, XXXIII. 124–45). There consequently have to be "chains of lead around [*Epipsychidion's*] flight of fire" (l. 590), because such a desirous sequence of words must fall back, at least partly, into its printed shape and remain both earthbound and never wholly coincidental with either any succeeding sequence or the work's eventual referent. The entire text, as an opening to Love's movement into, through, and beyond it, depends on a receptive mediator carrying the verbal drive past the poem (which stays where it is) much in the way the poem mediates between the speaker's longing and the eyes he so passionately addresses. Like the climax in intercourse, therefore, which resembles the close adjacency of words gaining as much response from each other as possible without dissolving together, the end of this poem must begin a withdrawal and a dying-back of the unifying flame just at the moment when either self's engulfment by the other seems most complete. In a closing cry parallel to slightly earlier breakings of intercourse's unities into many dualities, the speaker must admit the necessities of verbal expression with an orgasmically breathless exclamation, "I pant, I sink, I tremble, I expire!" (l. 591). He must both celebrate and lament the outreach of a deferred reference (the speaker's text) as it half-succeeds and half-fails to drive one transference of figures completely into the movement of another (the "Love" of the reader, in this case of "Emilia").

Finally, this kind of oneness, when carried through enough to be exposed for what it is (though it can never exactly be "attained"), reveals itself as an alternation between the attempted merger of incomplete figures (physical, verbal, or mental) and their continual reseparation into different forms still in a state of desire for other forms. Each version of this oscillation must naturally look ahead to seek another location for its reenactment, such as the island or the reader(s) of the poem. Each must thereby break beyond any closed circle of strictly two-sided oppositions or connections in order to disseminate the linkage of differences to many possible forms of relation. Once the spread becomes inclusive enough, this drawing-together that only disperses itself must emerge as the governing energy that always has pulled and will pull opposites toward and away from these interconnections. At that point we must realize completely how much the fusion of opposites has needed and will always need opposition. It is not just that desire seeks to "become" its satisfaction, as in night seeking to be day; winter, spring; sorrow, hope; and the self its greater prototype. It is that each term in a pair requires the other as its reverse-mirror even to be what it is; hence for Shelley the need in a person for one of the opposite (rather than the same) sex, the need of a word for a different word or for a reader, and the need of transference for its repression if it is finally to be revealed as more fluid by comparison. There is no object of desire without the pointing toward one from another desire outside it, no better state without one to rise beyond, and no "prototype" without an imperfect psyche to project it as a better self. Each referring subject or sign is *in* its so-called object or referent, finding its own "soul" reflected in the soul of another being or form, precisely in order to be an "I" not fully possessed by the form in question. Yet to be a part of the other therefore means to be partly transferred into it and partly not, like a word relating to other words. It means knowing that neither similarity nor difference will be eliminated in any union, unless of course the Love (or transference) giving the poles value and relationship dies out completely, as we hope it never will. Even if we arrive at the "circumference of bliss" that it seems we have always wanted (*Epipsychidion,* l. 550), we will find unification redividing at the moment of achievement, forcing us to separate the oneness we have sought into different moments and versions. "We shall become the same, we shall be one," Shelley's speaker tells Emilia in a seemingly redundant pair of phrases that nonetheless make "becoming the same" and "being one" distinct in style and different in position, not to mention far off in time (what we "shall become") as one projection looks on to another. Any sort of oneness between people, after all, must become "One passion in *twin*-hearts" for Shelley (my emphasis), leaving a total fusion forever deferred. Different figures can approach a Shelleyan unity of equals only if neither figure is subsumed by the other and if no distinction is erased altogether in favor of one dominant sex, form, or being.

The One as Another Plane:
"The Sensitive-Plant" and *Hellas*

Meanwhile, there is a third sort of oneness in Shelley's later writing, and compared to the others it undergoes a faster alteration as the poet wrestles with it for a year and a half. It starts as what "Exceeds our organs" in the Conclusion of "The Sensitive-Plant": an apparently Platonic or Zoroastrian level at which the essence of each "shape or odour" in the ever-changing world of observable "shadows" apparently lives unaltered where "There is no death nor change," as do Plato's Ideas and Zoroster's *Fravashi*. Here Shelley makes his most blatant use of the One in Plato especially, despite the contradiction in the idea of a unified, undifferentiated state containing an array of separate forms, each of which is the origin of the perceptible variations on itself. The poet seems to accept the oneness that is constituted in the *Parmenides* as both "indefinitely numerous" and unaffected by the "'coming to be' and 'ceasing to be'" in visible existence (*Parmenides,* 144e and 163d). It appears, then, that Shelley is also following the Socrates of the *Phaedo* in urging a reassessment of our usual perceptions and assumptions, since they are "themselves [so] obscure" as to make us and "ours [seem to] change" while "truth" itself apparently remains constant (Conclusion to "The Sensitive-Plant," ll. 19–24). We must regard the sensible world as a "mockery," Shelley's speaker seems to say, in the sense that it is an "unreal" sign of what is most real. This sign first shows us how much "sensible equals [ie., similar objects] are striving after [an] absolute equality" making them all essentially the same and then "distracts [and] prevent[s] us from getting a glimpse" of that absolute level, intimating that "the wisdom we desire . . . is only possible after death" (*Phaedo,* 75b and 66d–e).

This philosophy is reinforced for Shelley, we must admit, in the speeches of many heroes in the plays of Calderón. But shortly after Shelley completes "The Sensitive-Plant," at which point he reads these plays more earnestly than he did before, he starts using such soliloquies to expand this concept of oneness by turning toward the special emphasis in the Spaniard's version. As Webb (again) brings out, one of Shelley's later notebooks contains a translated passage from Calderón's *Life Is a Dream*, in which the hero, Segismundo, sees "this life we covet" as "A vain and empty shadow" wherein man "dreams of that he is / And never wakes to know he does but dream."[33] Here what lies behind each shadow, divorcing it from its "higher" foundations, is primarily "the memory of other dreams." Earthly consciousness looks back more to an unfathomable pouring-forth and succession of shadows than it does to a phalanx of clear and eternal Platonic archetypes. It is this possibility that is most echoed in Shelley's *Hellas* when Ahasuerus posits "the unborn and the undying" beyond the "bubbles and dreams" of our visible perceptions and histories. For this sardonic reembodiment of the Wandering Jew (now beyond one racial identity), it is dreamy "Thought," rather than some extramental or more abstract level, that forms the "cradle and grave" of the "idle shadows" as he defines them (ll. 781–83). *Hellas*, moreover, exploits this option repeatedly, encouraged by the skepticism of Drummond, in order to deepen and sophisticate the shadow/truth dichotomy in the fairly simple temporal/timeless split proposed by "The Sensitive-Plant." Whenever *Hellas* turns from the incipient revival of ancient Greek freedom toward a general theory of history, Shelley has his characters claim that the "quick elements" of "Thought / Alone," not ideas beyond thought, form the "stuff whence mutability can weave / All that it hath dominion o'er" (ll. 799–800), to such an extent that thinking both generates "worlds, worms," or "the coming age" and remains aloof (as "the One") from any particular "time or place or circumstance" (ll. 700–05).

The rapidity of this change, in fact, means that Shelley finds it relatively easy, as I read him, to reconstitute and relocate this kind of oneness away from the static superhuman state that he finds it to be in most previous incarnations. He need only take the change from Plato's concept to Calderón's one step further and do so by combining terms once kept separate, either in these very sources or in others related to them. Indeed, I would argue that this procedure is the one Shelley follows with this concept all the way from mid-1820 to late 1821. Even "The Sensitive-Plant" attempts a subversive repositioning, especially when the Conclusion maintains that "there is no death nor change [at the most fundamental level] / For love, and beauty, and delight." First, there is the announced irony that this prospect is only a "pleasant creed," a hopeful projection that may be a fiction, one tempered, even, by the "modest" awareness that it is not uttered by a thinker whose mind consistently reaches that level of understanding (Conclusion, ll. 13–14). More significantly, too, there is the irony of what Shelley does here with the philosophy he seems to repeat. The terms love, beauty, and delight are often employed in Plato's dialogues, but his most knowing speakers never place those three together on the same or the ultimate stratum. The Socrates and Diotima of the *Symposium* make beauty the "eternal, unproduced, indestructible" oneness at the level of every *eidos* toward which time-bound, lack-filled, entirely transitional Love struggles to rise as it spreads "from the love of one form to that of two, and from that of two, to that of all forms that are beautiful" (*PS*, p. 449). "Delight" in this scheme, as in several others, comes when the lover "touches the consummation of his labor" (p. 449), and that moment in the *Symposium* is a hovering between the sensual embrace of a love-object and the passage through that sensation toward a "contemplation" of the "supreme beauty itself" (p. 450). Shelley rear-

ranges these portions of different levels into points on the same plane, then changes
and blurs the order of succession as well (from love to delight to beauty to "love, and
beauty, and delight"). He thereby draws love's and delight's in-betweenness and
motion-beyond-themselves into the sphere of eternal beauty, much as he did (albeit
differently) in the essay "On Love." Beauty, placed between the other two drives, is
thus pulled into their endless passage between different beings or positions. It becomes
the movement from the love of one to the love of two as that transference diffuses
itself further, the way it does in the *Defence of Poetry,* to love yet "another and [then]
many others."

Such a metamorphosis turns out to be basic to the logic that pervades "The Sensitive-Plant." Shelley claims that the mimosa's "garden sweet [and] lady fair / And all
the sweet shapes and odours there . . . have never past away" (Conclusion, ll. 17–19)
and therefore lie at the changeless level occupied by "love, and beauty, and delight"
as he defines them, despite the lady's apparent death and the garden's "ruin" during
the winter of Part Third. That is because there is a self-transferring rather than fixed
beauty in all these "shapes" and sensations throughout Parts First and Second. Beauty
appears in the "lady fair" as a "tremulous" and "flush[ed]," even flowerlike, outpouring of "dilating" sympathy (Part Second, ll. 14 and 8), the disseminating overflow of an Asia or Emilia. This lady even recalls, as in Calderón or Shelley's Cythna,
"dreams" of a "bright [male] Spirit" (her ideal ego). Needing analogues (as we all do)
for that conception, she attempts, as did Spenser's Una, to reembody and extend that
longing in everything she beholds with loving acts of goddesslike "grace" that give
renewed life and hope to each plant in the garden (Part Second, ll. 16–17 and 2).

All this, the poem does say, is what the flowerless mimosa "desires [but feels it]
has not—the beautiful" (Part First, l. 77). Yet as its "deep heart" brims over with the
love it cannot blossom forth, as its longing resembles the desire of a poet whose verses
may be stillborn or go unread, its invisible effusion can choose to feel itself encountering "ocean[s] of other dreams" and "ministering angels" of love, either at the hands
of its guardian angel (the lady as projected ego-ideal) or in the "quivering vapours"
sent forth from other "sensitive" figures (Part First, ll. 76, 103, 94, and 90). It is this
entire, subliminal, intersubjective "deep language" of possible interplay that can and
should be seen as eternal, at least in a hopeful "creed," and so as lying behind and
beyond our nightmare-fears of material change and wintry death. We can "awaken"
to this awareness if we give in to the way fading perceptions can always be carried
over to their reconstitution by other forms or objects or locations of desire. As the
speaker of the "Ode to the West Wind" does but as the wind-blasted and unrequited
mimosa (the poet in a mood of despair[34]) may not, we can realize that "If winter comes
. . . Spring [cannot] be far behind." We can feel that drive toward renewal especially
if we recontact the repressed "spirits" within us who perform this forward transfer in
act 1 of *Prometheus Unbound,* the ones that keep urging us to generate projected Edens
from the wrecks of our past hopes. Even if we fail to recover these eternal drives in
our deepest cultural memory, we should at least realize that "Tis we, tis ours, are
changed—not they" (Conclusion to "The Sensitive-Plant," l. 20).

Though never going as far as *Hellas,* "The Sensitive-Plant" clearly anticipates it in
making thought's most basic process the underlying impetus in all the supposed
"strata" of being. Distinct levels, if they remain at all, become no more than different
depths of awareness, some less and some more in conscious contact with the loving,
beauty-making, delightful transference out and ahead that keeps refashioning and

desiring ego-ideals and visions of the future expansion of the self. The deepest awareness of this movement, the one most "exceeding" the use of our "organs" and thereby
surpassing the ways we make their perceptions "obscure," perceives nothing more
fixed than a fluid, continuous unfolding and transformation of potentials. That is particularly true when we reconsider Shelley's link in this poem between the Platonic One
and the "pre-existent . . . spiritual powers" of Zoroastrianism.[35] The joining of the
former to the latter figure in the "creed" of the Conclusion transports Plato's *eidos*
into primal levels of Zoroastrian change, in which the destructive Ahriman is forever
turning into the restorative Oromaze, just the way any principle or form is always
becoming another. Now all such transformations clearly take place on a mental plane
of hopeful suppositions where nothing finally dies, existing forever as self-altering *Fravashi* beyond and beneath each act or perception in everyday life.

The consequences of this iconoclastic coup are many, particularly if we consider
the effect of "The Sensitive-Plant" on the self-deceiving "dreamer," the reader (or
poet), who has not yet awakened to (or has forgotten) primordial transference. In the
first place he or she must accept, without going beyond "a modest creed" into a slavish
belief, the fact that dying forms or fading perceptions are but synecdoches (or "mock-
eries") of a larger, continuous regeneration carried ahead by transference in all the
outpourings of love and formations of beauty that human thought can imagine (Conclusion, ll. 13–16). In the second place the reader (or mimosa) should realize that this
restless but deathless level, particularly as it has been enacted in mythology and writing through the ages—and is now rendered again in the present poem—coincides
almost exactly with the constant expansion and interplay of the deep Promethean
movement among texts described in my fourth chapter. It is this connection between
transference and intertextuality that encourages the One of Plato to dart toward the
eternal "fields" of Zoroaster. It also allows the "lady fair" and her garden, seeing as
they exist primarily in a poem, to resemble so many older goddess-figures in so many
poetic gardens of earthly or heavenly delights.[36] Such an associability among figures,
in any case, is what accounts for their ability to revive themselves in an "intercourse"
with different forms, the poetic relocation that keeps nearly all of them from "passing
away" entirely.

Indeed, as a third consequence, the "dreamer," after he or she acknowledges this
capacity at the most basic, collective, and preconscious levels of his or her own
thought, must see that he or she has been granted the ability, as an interpreter of a
mere text not complete in itself, to make the poem's dead or dying figures live again
in a reworking of the dream of the moment, which admittedly must always end with
its own dissolution. By adopting the attitude of the mistress of the garden, who carries
through her "bright" memory of a Promethean "Spirit" by "lift[ing] all the plants with
her tender hands" as Prometheus raised humankind from the earth (Part Second, l.
37), the reader (like Asia as reader) can bring the "lady's" process back to the poem
after it seems to die in the poet's cryptic words, fearful as these words are (as is Shelley)
of being left unread. The reader, now very much a maternal nurturer of "germs," can
bring about, aided by the potentials for additional relations in the collective mythographic unconscious, the "dream of [a] life to come" that every bud, cocoon, or dying
plant, animal, myth, or person—every "antenatal tomb" (Part Second, ll. 53–54)—
projects as a future possibility without being able (as the mimosa is unable) to achieve
it in the absence of a "reading" that transfigures existing forms. In sum, this poem's
readers should step into and carry further the drive of transference that has animated

the garden and then passed beyond it, leaving it fixed in a death of former relation-ships. That drive is what lasts and can keep being reproduced, provided that we, as well as the poet, accept our role in the process. We must become conscious of that transpositional "might / Exceed[ing] our organs" that keeps extending the "love" in its elements. In that way we can help draw those conduits toward the recreated "beauty" and "delight" that they may always attain in a context beyond the one in which they now appear.

As we might expect, it is on the basis of this last suggestion, used as a potential to be carried further, that the vision of a One overarching history in *Hellas* makes its principal advance on earlier versions of that idea, including the one in "The Sensitive-Plant." For this play's Ahasuerus, to be sure, "Thought is [the] cradle and grave," as in Drummond, of all the Calderonian "bubbles" (or dreams) that "have been, are, or cease to be" (l. 779). But this Teiresian "sage" (l. 155), drawn to the deepest levels of thought's movement by "dwell[ing] in a sea cavern" much as Cythna did (l. 163), uses his Drummondesque words in a radically skeptical fashion that sees each human con-ception as a process of entropy, as always about to wind down and explode into a thorough reorganization of its ingredients. Ahasuerus forces the *Academical Questions* beyond where even Drummond wants to go and reworks Calderón's dreaming of pre-vious dreams at the same time, all by making each thought-about-another-thought at bottom the Ovidian birthplace of its own metamorphosis.

The notion of thought being the beginning *and* the end of its mutable variations, we should note, is accompanied in *Hellas* by two other surprising statements: "Nought is but that which feels itself to be" and "Dodona's forest to an acorn's cup / Is that which has been or will be, to that / Which is—the absent to the present" (ll. 785 and 793–95). Ahasuerus is suggesting that a moment of thought, on one level, can be vir-tually nothing (or "nought"). At that level it is only the death or husk of a previous sensation, "bubble," or dream, especially if it does not "feel itself" (or is not felt by another stage of itself) "to be" an additional configuration that brings forth a new life from the fading vision or sign. Consequently, all formations of existence as perceived, such as the Dodona forest of oaks on the Greek isle of Epirus once interpreted as the oracle of Zeus speaking through rustling leaves (*NCE*, p. 432n.), must have come from and left behind "acorns" that are partly just inert shapes and yet partly containers that could launch germs of future growth. This double tendency at the base of thought, if the shift from one inclination toward the other is "felt" as the transition it can be, empowers the recasting of Dodona within a different context (such as this one) after its status as oracle has decayed. The reader cannot draw out the dream in "The Sen-sitive-Plant" or behold the "might" that has produced it unless he or she has con-fronted (if subliminally) that ever-present "in-between state" in any act of thought where a disappearance turns into a nonexistence about to come to life, all by way of an intermediary movement that is meaningless on its own.

In itself the eternal repository of this thought-transition is empty—the "acorn's cup" without the seed—because the germ it receives and then sends ahead is in motion from a parent-form toward a future reincarnation. This "cup," in other words, is constant in being no more than a drive or facilitator turning what recedes toward a different repetition of a previous form. To attach oneself obsessively to the visible products of this sheer transition is to make the eye "sick" from gazing too long at temporary "motes" (l. 781), at mutable specks (the "false nature" of Segismundo) sent forth from and transformed by a mutability darker, deeper, and more lasting. Insight, then, into what really urges history ahead, or what temporality can bring about from what has existed already, comes from gazing on the ever-"present" cup of transposition troping some now-buried constructs from the past toward the birth of new variants equally "absent" in the present moment. Yes, that moment or locus happens or exists in, and is kept in motion by, "Thought / Alone, and its quick elements, Will, Passion, / Reason, Imagination," giving them all eternal life outside the single person (ll. 795–97). But all this is true only if that "Which is" eternally is a basically senseless turn, able to be "felt" toward another state, which underlies each of thought's variants as what can be developed and even asserted by them. The "One" in *Hellas* is therefore called both "The Fathomless" and "thought's eternal flight" (ll. 764 and 784). It is "fathomless" in that it reconceives Shelley's own Demogorgon, a sheer emergence from decay into vague potentials (an imageless deep truth) that waits to be interpreted and felt as some definite inclination. It is an "eternal flight" in always being a passage across, like Shelley's sky-lark or Witch of Atlas, able to become and generate innumerable recombinations of older forms in the process "whence mutability can weave" all the "dreams" of "time, place, and circumstance."[37]

If a reader or observer interprets the course, or tries to predict the future, of history with this understanding, *Hellas* goes on to suggest, the interpreter finds that, because of such a One, the "coming age is shadowed on the past / As on a glass" (ll. 805–06). Indeed, this pronouncement turns out to be true in two different ways, depending on the attitude that a person assumes toward past thoughts in flight. The first way is the one that Shelley's Ottoman sultan Mahmud confronts as his own preconscious choice when he summons Ahasuerus to help dredge up and interpret one of the sultan's "strang[est]" dreams, the one that has left recollections of a "tempest [but] no [exact] figure upon memory's glass" (ll. 130–31). The old seer's account of the eternal One in mutability suddenly jogs Mahmud into visualizing his ancestor "Mahomet the Second [at his moment of triumph over] Istanbul" (ll. 807–08), seized in 1453 from the defending garrison of Christian Greeks in a bloody conflagration that for Edward Gibbon completed the fall of the Roman Empire in the East.[38] Mahmud is made aware that intended prospects or incipient events (such as the conquest he plans) always reorder precursors after a movement through the "cup." He believes now in faded memories being able to "feel themselves" reembodied, "to assume the force of sensations" as they do before his eyes ("Notes on *Hellas*," *PW,* p. 479). He therefore comes to see, manifestly instead of dimly, how much the triumph he anticipates over an enslaved but rebellious Greece is a semi-reenactment of Mahomet's hard-won victory.

For Mahmud this reworking is so much a repetition that it brings along the ironies that Gibbon saw in the earlier event. As *The Decline and Fall of the Roman Empire* tells the story, Mahomet himself, on contemplating the Eastern Empire's demise, had to reflect, in public verse, "on the vicissitudes of [all] human greatness," including his own. As a result, it would seem, Mahmud must hear the recollected image of Mahomet, seen as a "portion of [Mahmud] which was ere [the sultan] / Didst start for this brief race whose crown is death," proclaim that "A later Empire [Mahmud's Islam] nods in its decay" even in prospective victory; "The autumn of a [once] greener faith is come, / And wolfish Change" is now "strip[ping] Fame" of its "foliage . . . while Dominion" recedes into memory, just as Rome's and his own did in Mahomet's oration (ll. 855–56 and 870–74). The incipient undermining of power at its peak by a version of the will to change that once brought power about—another moment of attained fullness dissipating and turning toward an alternative—is manifestly repeated here from Rome's example, with only the slightest differences, first by the conqueror of the Eastern Greco-Romans and then by a descedent who struggles to keep the descendents of pre-Romanic Greece in subjection. Mahmud, now believing all this consciously, must despair, even when—indeed because—the Greeks are again defeated. He feels that "The future must [simply and always] become the past" and thus that the Ottoman Empire must fall in the aftermath of his victory, as though the One can permit no real change in the contradictions of previous historical moments (l. 924).

Perhaps because it begins as a preconscious decision, this way of restating the One's drive toward repetition assumes, without reflection, that later reenactments of major political change duplicate *exactly* the combination of ascent and decline in earlier conquests. Such a presumption can seem to be true only if thought's "flight" is "felt" as a command from the past that enjoins its present and future counterparts to construct themselves according to the previous pattern. This view is both the one that the Great Memory tries to impose on Shelley's Prometheus and the attitude assumed by the Ghost of Darius when it is called forth from the "Shades" in *The Persians* of Aeschylus. In that play all the defeated and lamenting Persians, especially the reawakened Darius, father of the current king, explain the Athenian victory as "the issue of oracles" that predicted that the "suffering" of the Persians would follow the "sacrilege" of their earlier attacks on mainland Greece. The Persian defeat is "evidence to trust / Divine prophecy [from the past], which shall surely be fulfilled / To the last jot" (*Persians,* trans. Philip Vellacott, ll. 739–832).[39] Mahmud accepts such predestination, thereby believing in what Shelley must have seen as no more than the "upthrown" projection of Athens's own will to power. The sultan does not question the Mahomet-phantom's placement of itself (now) and Mahmud (in the future) on the "throne[s of] the abyss" from which such "Anarchs" seem to "rule the ghosts of murdered life" and the "fragments of the power which fell / When [the Anarchs] arose" (ll. 867, 879, 882, and 866–67). Mahmud allows such shapes of former tyrannies in the Great Memory to maintain their permanence as standards for future rulers, even though such exemplars reveal their inevitable decline and point to the resurgence of "strange [revolutionary] voices" in the fragments surviving from the older orders that these tyrants overthrew (ll. 878 and 867–68). For one who insists, as Mahmud does, on seeing transformation as such a repetition of sameness, the resulting torments and subsequent laments for the "destroyers" as they become the "destroyed" are simply a just reward in Shelley's eyes (l. 895). There can be no other recompense for believing in the Great Memory as determining the future, since the construction of such a past as dictatorial has formed the ideological base for a long line of foredoomed tyrannies ranging from those of the Persians and the Romans to the brutal repressions of Mahomet and Mahmud themselves.

Yet, just as Asia discovers while interpreting Demogorgan (whose movement depends on how the interpreter frames it), the construction of the future from past inclinations can refuse to believe in predestination if the past's deferral ahead of itself is differently felt by present thoughts about it. Ahasuerus defines Mahomet's phantom as only a "portion" (or germ) of what Mahmud might be or enact, and the phantom even chooses to imply such a relationship, emphasizing the distance between a potential and the later growth that retains it as but one of several ingredients. The shade reveals how the "dry[ing]" of a previous plant sends forth a "seed" that must "Unfold itself [reconstituted] in the shape of that / Which gathers birth in [the] decay" of the growth (ll. 890–91). As the image of the acorn's cup suggests, there must be a remainder of a past life spawning its future conterparts, but that past must also recede while its vestiges burst ahead to reground themselves in different contexts by sending down roots in a soil that exists partly because the old form has mouldered and dissolved. Here, after all, is the best available image for the connection between *The Persians* and *Hellas* itself. Shelley's drama, right at this point, models the phantom's role on that of Darius's "Shade" yet goes on to question many of Darius's assumptions in the very words of the phantom, as though the "source" of this moment were as outdated and superceded as it is procedurally useful.

We must not be too surprised, consequently, to hear the chorus of captive Greek women in Mahmud's seraglio sing out an alternative to the repetition of sameness, a counter-song that thoroughly recasts the roles of Greece and even women in the "acorn" left by Aeschylus. The freedom-seeking Hellas of old, the chorus claims, can perpetually "Rule the present from the past" with remembered "foundations . . . Built below the tide of war" (ll. 701 and 697). That undercurrent means that Hellas must return from repression, as in the "Ode to Liberty," by employing postures of temporary defeat, continued nonviolence, and even gentle and loving resistance to tyranny, not by pursuing ordained and rapacious victories over Persians or Turks. The aspirations of Hellenic Greece, left hearkening ahead even in their own day, should be viewed as self-reconstructing, not destructive, waves still moving in the "sea / Of [collective Western] thought" (ll. 698–99). These waves must be encouraged by those who remember them to draw the submerged but "springing Fire" of aspiration and of "Love [with] its power to give and bear" out of the "hoary ruins" of Athens that still "glow" in the memory since Greece fell to predestinarian thinkers (ll. 56, 45, and 84).

Moreover, this revival of a fading coal must follow the lead of the "springing Fire's" arc away from its ancient fuel. The "fragments" of old Greece recalled by her current "nurslings" must not be "reassemble[d]" exactly as and where they were, lest they slip back into what confined their energy and be no longer "springing" into the "New shapes they may still weave" (ll. 1003, 87, and 207). Instead, since so much of Europe, even England for Shelley, aggressively or tacitly supports Ottoman oppression, the fragments, reunited though not completely recovered by transference, should "build themselves again . . . in a diviner clime," such as the one that prevails in the United States as the *Philosophical View* has envisioned its possibilities (ll. 1004–05).[40] At that point, too, the semi-restored "golden age" (l. 1061) should recommit itself right away to overcoming all remaining limits on freedom (the real drive of Greece at its greatest) so that this other "Athens shall . . . to remoter time / Bequeath [its] splendour" and make the "earth . . . like a snake [ever] renew her winter weeds outworn" (ll. 1084–87). As nonmilitaristic women can see better than power-hungry men obsessed by the Great Memory—feeling, as marginalized women often do, the drive of hopeful love suppressed by that repository of the past—the reflection of the future on the "glass" of the past or the present reveals an eventual reversal of longstanding, patriarchal hierarchies. Such a reversal even uses the most established reflector (the recent defeat of Greece) to deny that mirror's assumptions, much in the way that Shelley uses *The Persians* in *Hellas*. The current mirror-image can thus be viewed as ultimately altered by a turn (that of the cup) already underlying it, so much so that the image seems destined to rechannel "false times and tides" away from the "awakening night" of our present situation while that situation is still in existence (ll. 481 and 1038).

This kind of One-in-the-many, then, as Ahasuerus has concluded long ago, makes sure that "All is contained in each" (l. 792) no matter what set of natural or historical particulars are the focus of attention. To pass from any mere "shadow" (or particular thought being rethought by others) to the most eternal aspect of existence behind thought (its cradle and grave) is to discover a sheer point of passage into which all previous forms and connections of the shadow (the "other dreams" behind the dream) have spilled and out of which its potential reshapings may stream without any of the later formations being determined entirely by one of the previous versions. No state of being-as-perceived is final or static on this plane; there is for Shelley no Platonic *eidos*-form for anything. Even death or a temporary loss of sustenance or visible affection, as in Part Third of "The Sensitive-Plant," is but one bubble on the rapid stream of "love, beauty, [and the quest for] delight" as all these desires spring ahead of wherever they are—at the basic passage-point—to find their satisfaction in the rebuilt wreckage of their own past hopes. An accurate reduction of this "eternal flight" to its heart, *Hellas* goes on to say, can arrive only at a cup-shaped redirection, "unborn and undying," on which all flights of thought and their manifestations depend, particularly when a set of dreams wants to be reconstructed in a "diviner clime" far beyond itself. Clearly the transferability of dreams or reflections in Shelley's *Defence* and the need for desirous feelings or figures to behold and embrace their distant reversals in *Epipsychidion* cannot be set in motion without this strictly transitional conduit transferring the ever-shifting "germ" of longing from place to place. This One, we could say, is the endless process that, in certain ways, underpins the other Ones we have noted thus far in Shelley's later writing. Since it is so much a pure transference, too, we can never get to its "bottom" or all-explaining basic form, except when we perceive it as an activity looking before and beyond itself at the same time. This rush constantly "feeling itself to be" over again is the real "tempest / Of dazzling mist" that Mahmud feels in his dream and then wants a single, unshifting figure to incarnate and explain (ll. 786–87). Ahasuerus's explanation of the tempest, however, much as Mahmud tries to reduce a sheet relocation to one event's repetition of itself, forces the sultan to view "all things [he thinks] surest, brightest, best" with the "Doubt [and] insecurity" born of seeing so many potentials circulating in and out of any supposed "foundation" as it looks back to the "cup" at its base. It is at least to this state of mind—and then to a sense of open and changing human potentials—that Shelley's poems about the "plane" of the One try to lead most readers. What else can we expect from writing that so fluidly combines Plato, Aeschylus, and Calderón with Edward Gibbon and William Drummond, if not an idealism so skeptical that it finds no single idea on which to rest and a skepticism so idealistic that it has to affirm the perpetual fall and rise from idea to idea?

The One as the Image of Death: *Adonais*

At the same time, the fact of an eternal passage-point cannot explain why the movement through the "cup" operates as a fall and rise. Why does that motion, in the words of *Adonais* (ll. 382–84), decline into a "dross" that "checks its flight" only to "Tortur[e that] dross" into "new successions" that draw our perceptions of the "dull dense world" toward transformations of themselves? There is still the problem, we have to admit, of why the One as eternal transference must keep springing out of its own death, must constantly reform perceived existence from the dissolution of the previous relations that transference has helped produce. *Adonais,* the only long poem that Shelley completed between the *Defence of Poetry* and *Hellas,* tries to answer that question while establishing a perspective in which a dead poet can be said to outlive himself. Indeed, the answer is so much the basis of the perspective that both reveal the eternal principle—the one *within* the "cup"—that urges that death be interpreted as a resurrection even when Christianity has been disavowed. The most prominent statement of the answer, of course, is the stanza describing the "one Spirit's plastic stress." This drive, like the "God" redefined as a transfer process in the "Essay on Christianity," works prior to yet through poetic imaginations to "compel" the "flight" now suppressed by the "dross" into "bursting" out of and shifting beyond its present (and dying) forms (ll. 384–86). It thereby lifts the perceiver's "heart above its mortal lair," makes the flowers (or Keats poems) that betoken death reappear as stars in a "Heaven of song," and so allows Keats/Adonais (with other poets like him once they die, Shelley hopes) to "outsoar," in the minds of readers, "the contagion of the world's slow stain" (ll. 393, 413, 352, and 356). As too many critics will not admit,[41] this action, in different forms, empowers the resurrections throughout the poem, before and after it is named as doing so. "The leprous corpse," while it is mourned earlier in the piece, is "touched [enough] by this spirit tender" that it, like Keats in a poem, "Exhales itself [in a transfer of locations,] in flowers of gentle breath" (ll. 172–73). Then, too, when Adonais reimaged as a star is elevated to join the "enduring dead" near the end (l. 336), he is carried there by the way in which the "stress" and the "hopes" of the speaker transfer the "light" of a fading coal (or flower) beyond the reader-responses of the current "revolving year" to a point surpassing even the lifetime of the speaker. At that point the "fire" of both poets' desires should be "mirror[ed]" back by distant receivers filled with the "sustaining Love" that keeps reviving the forward extension of transference (ll. 470, 472, 484–85, and 481).[42]

Still, though we have located a few versions of the answer, some questions remain. We have to ask what makes the stress "plastic" in the sense that it is driven (or drives itself) to refashion vestiges of death automatically and repeatedly. What is it that sets this kind of oneness in motion? We must also wonder, surely, how this process is related to the poetic form—hence the perspective—that Shelley employs to solve this problem and give eternal life to an analogue of himself. After all, more than in most of his previous forays into long-established genres, Shelley in *Adonais* emphasizes how precisely he repeats the conventions of the pastoral elegy. He practically underlines his many echoes of the accommodation and relocation of death in ancient Greek idylls and laments, Latin eclogues, and later Christian elegies, a tradition lasting from Theocritus and Bion through Virgil and Ovid to Spenser and Milton (all of whom Shelley repeats). Why does the poet go to such lengths to be fervently generic, especially since his more usual procedure is to shift the elements of one genre toward those attached to others?

I think there is an answer, or at least a series of related answers, to all these questions. Shelley in *Adonais,* I would argue, presses elegiac conventions so hard because he wants to drive them back to their most fundamental maneuvers, whereupon these can reveal the most basic drive, or "stress," in memorial tributes, a drive that demands verbal movements beyond single genres.[43] He wants to expose what really makes possible, before and within Platonic or Christian salvation, the resurrections in previous elegies—and, all the while, what produces his "Gothic sensibility," here at least half-revived. What he uncovers is an eternal "stress" of transference going on in death itself and in the many symbolic interpretations of it. As this artful poem proceeds, that motion is drawn forth as the repressed and saving impetus behind all articulate mourning. It surfaces in a new concatenation of old elegies, in fact, to show how much the One as the later Shelley reconceives it is bound up, at its very heart, with the facing of death.

The concept of the "Spirit's plastic stress," to begin with, is a supreme example of how this poem forces all its source-material back to the assumptions in earlier pastoral elegies and even to the partly hidden roots of those assumptions. As Anthony Knerr has reminded us,[44] the very words of the phrase recall Coleridge's "Plastic and vast, one intellectual breeze" infusing minds and perceived objects as "the Soul of each, and God of all" ("The Eolian Harp," ll. 47–48). By the time of *Adonais,* moreover, Shelley has noted the "*Esemplastic* power" of the imagination in the same author's *Biographia Literaria* (1817), which has itself developed the idea by combining the writer's earlier Christian pantheism with the transcendent "creative force" that inspirits all artists in Friedrich von Schelling's *Relation of the Plastic Arts to Nature* (1807). Shelley clearly wants to base the genesis and survival of poetry on something like what the divine "I AM" becomes for Coleridge when its creative will is reenacted by the will of particular poets: a drive that "dissolves, diffuses, dissipates, in order to recreate" and so makes "vital" new forms from perceptions now "fixed and dead" by "struggling to idealize and unify" the fragments of faded life with which it begins.[45] Yet, just as we saw in examining the "Essay on Christianity" and the *Defence,* Shelley still wants to deny that imagination recalls or seeks a transcendental Ego or identity as the seed of an organic oneness in poetry. By 1821 the "imperial faculty" for this poet does not "shape into one" as in Coleridge (as in the "root meaning" for the "esemplastic" he coined). Instead it gives into, extends, reconstitutes, and disseminates the preconscious self-displacement of transference, especially its departure from its fading past, much in the way the poet submits to the action of the "Destroyer and Preserver" sweeping through his perceptions in the "Ode to the West Wind." Hence the impulse governing imagination's and poetry's movements before and after the death of poets in *Adonais* can be "plastic" (or able to reshape and remold itself) only if the psyches of poets and readers open themselves to—or "bear [their] part" in (ll. 380–81)—a primordial movement more like the one in the most ancient elegies that Shelley has translated, particularly from the Greek of Bion and (supposedly) Moschus.

In those pagan poems, since they assume a transmigration of daemonic energy from one form of being or desire to another, human "sorrow" for a death can be "breath[ed]" through "herbs" to be carried further by a wind, "springs their waters [can] change to tears," a mournful "hyacinth" (perhaps a remnant of a death that was its seed) can "Utter [a] legend" or leave "letters" for an "heir" to recast, and cyclic regeneration can allow dead forms to live again differently at later points, making itself seem both analogous to and distinct from human reproduction and memory.[46] This sort of metamorphic dislocation allows a sense of death, and even a deliberate dissolving of the past, to be instantly reconstituted, always as restorative images, outside a belief that all forms must slavishly repeat and maintain a single anthropomorphic Essence. Here a dead being becoming a flower that then "exhales" itself is simply a natural metamorphosis, one that can be said to pass through a decline only as long as death is interpreted to be a loss. That interpretation is driven to alter itself by the movement in what it interprets as the signs of loss, regardless of the observer's conscious will, are reconstructed and repositioned away from their initial locations. Shelley wants to preserve Keats's memory, thoughts, and writings by submitting them to this non-Christian process of destruction and preservation, so the resulting elegy returns to its Greek precursors and attaches the Coleridgean "breeze" to their Dionysian transference. The "plastic power" passing into and through both the dead and the living poets thus comes to resemble, first, the eternal but changing return of the slain Adonis in the flowers and ceremonies of future Springs (the consolation in Bion's "Lament for Adonis") and, second, the displacement of the surviving poet's grief into objects he observes and other passions he feels, the transposition that allows him to anticipate and desire his own transportation to the distant level attained by the deceased (the logic of the "Lament for Bion" attributed to Moschus).[47]

Meanwhile, *Adonais* follows an equally backward-looking procedure when it echoes the transportation from earthly death to "blissful Paradise" in Milton's *Lycidas* written in memory of Edward King and Spenser's *Astrophel* memorializing Sir Philip Sidney (which I quote from l. 67 of Clorinda's final lament). Both of these poems, naturally, find the cause of the relocation not in the transmutation of one physical form to another but in "the dear might [or restorative grace] of him that walk'd the waves" (*Lycidas,* l. 173). Shelley employs yet revises this sense of abrupt exaltation by heretically splitting up the powers of "dear" Christ. The moral force of Christ's outward-tending and world-transforming love is almost entirely transferred by Shelley into the sympathetic imagination of Adonais/Keats as he is read and remembered by present and future readers. Because his poems have transfigured the "loveliness" of perceived existence into interpretations still "more lovely," always with such power that "His voice . . . is heard [henceforth] in [Nature's] music" by those who know his work, Adonais now becomes what Jesus is supposed to be to those who believe most strongly in Him: a "presence to be felt and known / In [the] darkness and [the] light" about which the poems were written (*Adonais,* ll. 373–74). The "walk[ing]" might that drives relocation, however, is wrenched back toward pre-Christian forces so that it resembles the often impersonal Greco-Roman action that empowers figures born from or standing on the decaying earth to rise toward heavenly reembodiments of themselves. This action is the one described most succinctly by Ovid in the *Metamorphoses,* where all the natural elements complete their natures only by changing into other elements. In such a process, "the element of earth, set free [by its own desire], is rarified into liquid water, [which itself] changes into wind and air[; t]hen . . . this air, already very thin, leaps up to fire, the highest place of all" (*Metam.,* XV. 245–48). Driven by this kind of self-transforming energy, the "new successions" prompted by the "stress" in *Adonais* can spring, almost the way Astrophel and Lycidas do, toward "Heaven[ly]" reincarnations of earthly forms, especially of Adonais/Keats and poets like him. Yet these reincarnations do so only as the stress, once its Ovidian transfiguration is sensed by the imagination, emerges with no divine assistance out of the earth-bound objects through and across which it moves, lovingly urging each form to make a turn toward "another and many others." It is only because of this transference within perceived forms compelling them to recast themselves in other observable entities that we find the force that "walks the waves" continually "bursting in its beauty and its might / From trees and beasts and men into the Heaven's light" (ll. 386–87).

This revision of Spenser and Milton, we can even say, draws their figures back, quite ironically, to the poems most regarded by Catholic and Protestant allegorists as the true mediators between pagan and Christian pastoral poetry: the *Eclogues* of Virgil, especially V, VI, and X. The abrupt translation of Adonais from flower to star recalls the colloquy in the fifth eclogue, which itself recasts some similar conversations between two speakers in the Greek *Idylls* of Theocritus, including a dialogue responding to a festival for Adonis.[48] Virgil offers two interlocutors deciding how best to sing of "Daphnis cruelly slain." One of them emphasizes the consequences of the loss, but the elder of the two offers a countering hope. He simply decides to "praise Daphnis [literally] to the stars," particularly in view of the many existing stories where the stars or constellations are heroes and demigods "enskied" after their deaths (*Eclogues,* V, 50–52). The distance between the fallen and reembodied states in this piece is not bridged by anyone or anything except the will of one poet revising the will of another,[49] and the will to revise is not so much self-generated as repetitive of a tendency toward transfiguration "stressed" in a long succession of previous tales. In addition, Shelley's analogy between the "stress," "sustaining Love," and the passage of a dying figure's drives into both the self-renewal of nature and the feelings of the eulogist emulates the tenth eclogue focused on the passing of the lovesick Gallus. There the enduring power of overflowing love makes that now-dead worthy seem to dissolve, as the living remember him, into his old, restless wandering "among rocks and echoing groves" and then into the flow of outgoing feeling inspiring the speaker himself, "which grows in me as fast . . . as the green alder shoots up when spring is young" (X, 58–59 and 73–74). Such a transmigration, much to Shelley's satisfaction, turns out to have been motivated for Virgil by the half-Epicurean "forcing together" that has united the different "seeds" of "all things" since the beginning of time, that has inspired the pre-Lucretian song of Silenus in the sixth eclogue (esp. ll. 31–36), and that has been interpreted by Gibbon, writing on Virgil, as a "metaphysical [instead of] a theological" foundation governing the "powers of matter" from inside their deepest inclinations.[50] To force Spenserian and Miltonic figures to manifest these precursors of them is to reground transfiguration in several kinds of earthly transference at once, each seen as reinforcing the other. It is to root the Christian elegy in reinterpretations of one death by different perspectives, patterns of transubstantiation repeating themselves (with differences) from text to text and verse to verse, inclinations in pre-Christian figures to reassert themselves in the later mythographs designed to overrule them, and metaphysics that encourage constant textual transmutation by centering themselves on a mobile play among differences instead of an origin at one with itself.

Adonais suggests, as a matter of fact, that this last way of disrupting Milton and Spenser is already occurring in their texts—indeed, in virtually any elegy (Christian or pagan) configuring a death. Shelley's stylized manner in this piece reminds us that *Lycidas* is justly famous for what Samuel Johnson disliked about it[51]: the affected, formal distance of elegiac discourse from its subject (physical death and a very personal reaction to it). Milton's grieving "swain" indicates the reason for this posture right away when his "forced fingers" start to pick laurel and myrtle "Berries" to serve as signs of tribute to the drowned young poet (ll. 1–4). Ostensibly to match the fact that Lycidas died before his "prime," the swain chooses berries that are "rough and crude" (unripe) and thus unable, especially when violently pulled off the parent stem, to refer to the ultimate future significance (or to the lost origin) toward which they are inclined (ll. 8 and 3). They cannot even refer to Lycidas directly in their manifest difference from his water-laden body and from his more mature ability to "build the lofty rhyme" when he died (l. 11). Signs, and thus words, for Milton here are primally divorced from any proximity to ultimate origins or referents and so from any "other" they would approach. Consequently, their deferral to another point can look only to other announcements of that deferral (other mere signs). The tribute of berries in *Lycidas* must give way to tossings of flowers, and every flower must prove so inadequate a symbol that each needs several others to continue its symbolic act of reference (hence the "Catalogue of Flowers" at ll. 135–151). The only way such figures employed by fallen humankind can prompt a leap beyond their own shifting between their differences is for them to assume a raising act of grace outside human language, to the vague "might" to which mortal words must not aspire on their own but which can complete the movement beyond temporal displacement that is always being sought as word leads to word. By denying this transcendent aid while using many of Milton's pastoral formalities, Shelley forces the distance in elegiac language to confront its own grounding in transference at every stage, even in *Lycidas*.[52] Words about death even for Milton, Shelley suggests, must be exposed as "killings" of their connection to their foundations (tearings from the stem) and yet as repetitions of this basic displacement of death that mainly revive the need of signifiers for other signifiers. To symbolize Adonis, Shelley therefore writes in one of his Miltonic moments, we must use "The broken lily" and other incomplete signs that have already done violence to, or are cut off from, their own acts of reference, and these figures must all look back to a figure who "Died on the promise of the fruit," who (having been a young poet) is regarded as a sign deferring to—or promising—figural outgrowths of him that he never attained while he was alive (*Adonais,* ll. 53–54). The only metaphysical ground truly analogous to this basis of the elegiac form is a "plastic stress" of natural and poetic "new successions." This sort of grace operates much as language does in its crossing between successive terms to redefine the inaugural ones. Both drives rely on no causality aside from the tendency to dislocate the signs of death from their initial positions. Perhaps the ancient elegies that affirm this type of process as the basis for their senses of loss and hope have but projected a movement supposedly prior to elegies out of, and as a result of, the movement of elegiac signs.

In any case, Shelley also manipulates his allusions to Spenser so as to uncover a similar admission in the texts of this other precursor. The very title of Shelley's poem, assisted by the dead Keats's early transformation into a "pale" version of the flower that Adonis became (l. 49), recalls the sequence in *Astrophel* when "Stella" and her fallen shepherd suddenly resemble Venus and her wounded Adonis in a great many ways. *Adonais* forces us to remember that Astrophel is gored by a "cruell beast" (*Astrophel,* l. 116), as Adonis was and Adonais will be; that Stella, as Venus did and Shelley's Urania will, bathes her love-object's "deformed" figure with "teares" that feed the "flowre" he soon becomes (ll. 152, 165, and 184); and that the Astrophel-flower itself reworks the eternal withering and seasonal reappearance of Adonis in the way it "doth fade" into the color blue and "growes red" when it blooms year after year, all at the urging of higher powers that take pity on Sidney and Stella (at Spenser's ll. 181–85) much as such forces under Venus's command took pity on Adonis when they turned him into a perennial blossom. By emphasizing these connections in drawing us back to Spenser, Shelley makes his source refer, on two different levels, to an eternal process of revisionary transfiguration—one very like the movement in the caves of *Prometheus Unbound* and "The Witch of Atlas"[53]—definitely stated in Spenser's own words, despite his Christian stance. On one level we are reminded that the Ovidian process of reformation in the *Metamorphoses,* the primary source for the details in Spenser's use of Venus and Adonis,[54] grants metamorphic powers to the poet as extensions of the universal drive of metamorphosis. Just as the general tendency uses analogy and displacement to transmute a dying figure into a different form of being, the Ovidian poet can use analogies between tales of metamorphosis to combine older transubstantiations, or embed one within another, thereby altering the received forms of tales (as when Ovid has Venus warn Adonis by telling him the story of Atalanta and Hippomenes in *Metam.,* X, 560–680). Shelley's heretical recasting of Spenser in the "pale flower" mourned by Urania, licensed as the alteration is by a resurrection of Ovidian metamorphosis (physical and textual), points to the revival of that process in *Astrophel* itself, especially to the moment when that piece transforms both Stella and her shepherd into the blue-and-red flower. There Sidney's exaltation of his love-object into a star throughout a sonnet sequence comes to be embedded as the flower's white, starburst center "Resembling *Stella*" as Sir Philip portrayed her in verse (*Astrophel,* ll. 182–88). *Adonais* recovers Ovidian transference from its apparent suppression in Spenser by reenacting Spenser's own employment of metamorphic intertextuality. Shelley's further whitening of the Adonis-flower and his relocation of it under the eye of the heavenly Miltonic muse (Urania instead of Venus) resembles Spenser's joining of Adonis's reembodiment to Sidney's longing for a union with his "star" in the sonnets of *Astrophel and Stella.* This earlier conflation of very different texts, itself driven by Ovidian transposition, appears almost to demand a later one that violates its predecessor.

The irony becomes even more complex when we notice, as Shelley certainly does in *Adonais,* that Spenser, on another level, extends this metamorphosis of Venus and Adonis to the point of making it an eternal activity (in yet another emulation of Ovid). First, *Astrophel* depends on the stargazer's quest for his star being transformed into a flower—or rather on his desire for a projected ego-ideal being transferred into a substitute form of its completion—to lift the Sidney-blossom, with God's grace, to a "blisfull Paradise" replete with flowers (ll. 68–72 of Clorinda's plaint), a very pagan eternity of fecund mutability (including "day and night" at l. 74) where the constant insemination of new forms of beauty, anticipating the Eternal Garden of "The Sensitive-Plant," is almost as likely as a static Christian deity to be the timeless essence of the One. Then, too, Spenser makes the likelihood even greater when he restyles his allusions to Ovid and his ultimate "bed of lilies" (l. 70) to produce the Garden of Adonis in Book III of *The Fairie Queene* (Canto VI, stanzas 29–50).[55] In this "first seminarie / Of all things" (stanza 30), resurrected Adonis, in part because he periodically reunites himself with Venus and the energy of her reproductive love (thereby resembling Shelley's Prometheus in the cave), engenders new mortal reincarnations for shades that "returne" from earthly life to the Garden through the "old and dride . . . gate" of death (stanzas 31–32). Adonis so transfigured is the "Father of all formes," insofar as his nature, clearly a capacity for transubstantiation, is "Transformed oft, and changed diverslie . . . And [thus only] by succession made perpetuall" (stanza 47). For Shelley, then, to claim that his dead Adonais is taken up by and restored to an eternal plasticity that turns old forms into "new successions" is for him to link the mourned Keats, in the stanza-patterns of *The Fairie Queene* instead of those in *Astrophel,* to the ultimate state of Adonis in Spenser, a state both "subject to mortalitie," always beginning anew with figures left by death, and "eterne in mutabilitie," perpetually connected with the radical reconstitution of figures left over from a fading past (ll. 4–5 of stanza 47). In fact, while Astrophel can become no more than one eternally transmutable flower *(Amintas)* in the Garden of Adonis (stanza 45), Shelley's fallen poet can be renamed so as to become a part of the very power of "diverse" restoration that is most able to transform death into a revival of poetic life.

When the disembodied "spirit" of Adonais, in other words, "flow[s] / Back to . . . whence it came" in Shelley's poem, it is not to a "white radiance" that emanates from a fixed, Plotinian / Dantean center of light; it is to the forward-looking overflow of a "burning fountain" (l. 339) where the central point, as with Demogorgon, is a perpetual turning outward from what recedes (or burns up) in death and a crossing (or gushing forth) toward future transformations of all surviving vestiges. Such is the repressed One that must be recovered, Shelley maintains, if elegiac rhetoric is forced to return to its foundations. The writers of the earliest Greek elegies, and Virgil and Ovid after them, hearken back to the Hesiodic emergence of life-giving fecundity from chaotic dissolution at the beginning of time. Like them, the speaker of *Adonais* depends on his perception of "A quickening life from the Earth's heart [that] has burst / As it has ever done, with change and motion, / From the great morning of the world when first [a transpositional] / God dawned on Chaos" for the sense that "All baser things pant with life's thirst" even as they die, so much so that every "corpse . . . / Exhales itself" to "illumine death" from a position of "renewed might" outside the body (ll. 164–75). This assumption is both urged and reinforced by an elegiac mode of discourse that always sees the signs of death as at least potential resurrections in themselves, as transfigurations that insist on revising their figural ancestors just in the way any vestige of death inherently "bursts" beyond its past. Consequently, as in no other English elegy before it, *Adonais* demands that we confront a longstanding, non-Platonic, and pre-Christian compulsion urging any dead or receding figure to undergo a metamorphosis that draws elements within the figure out to another place. Whether that tendency is viewed as a transcendent, though physical, movement or as the figural basis of the relation between successive myths or texts in a tradition, it offers a liberating answer other than Spenser's or Milton's to the key question, the one most related to the Adonis legend, worded this way in *Astrophel:* "What is become of him whose flowre here left / Is but the shadow of his likenesse gone[?]" (ll. 57–58 of Clorinda's lament).

Shelley's greatest coup in *Adonais,* however, once he pulls so many elegies together and back toward their underlying principles, is to announce what makes a Bion, Virgil, or Spenser ask such a question in such a way and thus what gives rise to the principles themselves and the elegiac mode generated from them. The key insight, the one that Shelley has not really sensed until now, not even in the "Ode to the West Wind," is the fact that death is always perceived as "the shadow of a likenesse gone" the very moment there is a death of any sort. Shelley's speaker says exactly this as early as the first stanza of *Adonais,* crying out that the "fate and fame" of the poet cut down by the violence of conservative criticism is automatically "An echo and a light unto eternity" (ll. 7–9). The "fate" composed from his sufferings has become their "echo" right away and therefore a "fame" coloring future recollections even as the pain itself has receded from sight along with the living body of John Keats. There must be a multiple metamorphosis of death, the echo must become a light or the poet a flower and star, because observable death is itself an image being reconfigured and thus an

already layered stand-in for a loss, if only as a body about to be embalmed or
entombed.[56] "Death," Shelley writes in his eighth stanza as if his speaker were looking
dissolution in the face, appears as "The shadow of [its] white" visage, veil upon veil.
"At the door" of this shadow, "invisible corruption," another and incipient refashioning of the image, "waits to trace" its further reconstruction with the intention of chis-
eling down to Death's "dim[mest] dwelling-place" (ll. 66–68). Death is a transference,
Shelley reveals, even at the heart of its destructive nature. Its core is apprehendable
only in the "dwelling-place" that is its refiguration, and the dwelling is always in the
process of reappearing in some other container or form of itself.

Even the title of Shelley's poem, and thus the name of the figure he eulogizes,
emphasize death as a metalepsis, the metaphor of a metaphor. True, the connection
of Keats to Adonis is prompted in part by a "beastly" critic's goring of *Endymion* and
in part by the dead poet's own writings, particularly by the goddess-hero relationship
in *Endymion* and "the pale flower by some sad maiden cherished" in "Isabella"
(*Adonais,* l. 48). Yet, by restyling Keats to make him "Adon*ais*," Shelley not only
raises him to something like the final status of Virgil's Daphnis, Spenser's Sidney-
Astrophel, or Milton's King-Lycidas; he also draws Adonis, the basic analogue for the
fallen worthy, toward his alternate Greek name *Adonai* and again toward the word for
the Greek mourning ceremonies or festivals once devoted to that slain hero: the *Adonias.*[57] The resulting composite, as a shifting across successive forms, points to the inevitable conversion of the dead person into several metaphors for what he was or still
seems, into alternative figures for what is already the sign of an absence (the body)
looking to other signs (other memorials: epitaphs, gravestones, eulogies) as the only
available counterparts to which the remnant can refer. Such a name goes so far as to
transport the reconstitution of the dead into the ceremonialization or memorializing
rhetoric that must always follow death if death is to be interpretable.

Death, after all, is a self-division in which the supposed vital principle is retracted
while the body or "dwelling place" goes on to welcome changes in its form (such as
decay). Any symbolic announcement of this process, if it is to be accurate to what it
portrays, should specify the inaugural breach and refiguration, either in a sequence of
related names like Adonis/Adonai/Adonia or in the multi-leveled "twilight chamber"
(of Shelley's ll. 65–68). In addition, the divisive process must be positioned and
framed precisely to keep the gap that opens between life and the body from spreading
to other people too rapidly or senselessly.[58] Indeed, this covering of what is already a
concealment—usually an inscribed grave encrypting the body—must insist on
another version of itself in another symbolic formation where a relevance or sense can
be found for it aside from its act of mere figural substitution. The tomb or metaphor
placing and naming the dead must exist primarily to be "read" by interpreters or by
other such metaphors. The latter figures, in turn, must long to revive what the chamber conceals and then begin the revival by transporting aspects of the dead figure
(Keats) and its cover (*Adonis/Adonai*) into an organized context of related figures,
formalized and ritualized *(Adonias),* where those aspects can be drawn out of themselves into an ordered development of multiple meanings and sign-relations. Shelley's
title and title-figure really must be named so as to suggest all the steps in this development, for this series of shifts is the basis of any meaning that might be drawn from
the deceased's life and death. "Naught we know, dies," Shelley writes in the twentieth
stanza of *Adonais* (l. 177). Only if what seems dead becomes "known" as an element
in a system of related figures granting it a superadded significance can we say that

"The leprous corpse [seemingly] / Exhales itself [Adonis-like] in flowers of gentle breath."

It is this continuous, layered displacement, Shelley makes us see, that really underwrites, permits, and encourages all the conversions of the dead into resurrected states throughout the ancient and Christian elegies that *Adonais* repeats and regrounds. The automatic existence of death as an interpretable image sundered from the withdrawn life is what demands a language of ceremonial distance in elegies. The very "style" of death, if true to its subject, must keep its referent entirely "other" (as the dead being must always remain), yet it can also take that divorce from the parent stem as a license to reposition and transfigure each sign of death (just as those signs urge themselves by so explicitly being figures). Such a movement of loss that also defers itself, moreover, generates the Theocritan-Virgilian dialogue between regret and hope—and now the famous two halves of *Adonais* shifting permanently at stanza 38 from the forms of the speaker's mourning to a celebration of what can be said to ensure Keats's resurrection. On the one hand, death's self-division offers signs of loss that seem to pull observers sadly toward a desirable but irrecoverable past. On the other hand, those beckoning memorials are also uprooted signs calling for their own recontextualization. In their immediate reference to forms from age-old rituals, they show their longing for contexts replacing the one (the life) they have lost, ones that can transport retrogressions into a surviving and resuscitating order of symbols. This transpositional drive, we can even say, is the impulse that motivates the elegist, as in the "Lament for Bion" or Virgil's tenth eclogue, to take upon himself, as his own flow of feeling, the dead figure's attempts to strive beyond the existence he knew in his lifetime. Inclinations that are losing their connection with a receding absence inherently look to analogues for themselves connected to what seems a surviving presence, so Shelley feels free (almost scandalously, for some people[59]) to liken the sorrows of Adonais more to his own than to Keats's, even to the point of including among the brother-shepherds who mourn Adonais a "phantom" of himself weeping "his own . . . in another's fate" (ll. 272 and 300). The opening-ahead when the signs of death seek an interpretation can be furthered only if the interpreter takes this movement, framed by and receding behind the remnants of dissolution, into his own frames of reference and the range of analogues for the movement that he is able to comprehend within those frames.

In fact, every elegiac metaphor, gesture, or claim in Shelley's journey back through the pastoral tradition turns out to be rooted in, even motivated by, the mobility of death turning into a figure for itself. It is again this movement which really insists that a principal analogue for it be the perceived cycle of dying and self-reseeding plants, the pastoral metaphor by which Adonis has been resurrected so often—and one means by which Adonais, through his poems/flowers at least, can be "felt and known" as an impulse for renewal "spreading" through our perceptions of "herb and stave" (ll. 373–75). Since death is a rupture "exhaling" a desire for later and distant transpositions of it, it sends forth to interpreters a germ or seed, however metaphoric, be it a corpse, an inscribed tombstone, or remembered words and deeds. Such an ejection resembles a similar "effluence" (*Adonais,* l. 407) given off by a plant through its flower (already an effluence). This similarity allows the metalepsis in death to be transfigured quite readily into the self-renewal of botanic life, since the metalepsis is embodied quite well by the way a flower loses its past life while giving off seeds.[60] Then, too, the same sort of logic encourages elegies to suggest the reappearance of a mourning natural object within some other pastoral location. Just as a sign of death (say, a corpse) must be read as searching for its meaning in signs from what is really another context in the culture (a verbal ritual, perhaps), so the taking of a natural entity to be a token of regretted loss must find its fuller significance, and thus a remedy for the loss, by turning toward another form or process also subject to fading and revival. Even the grieving speaker in elegies, having drawn the unsatisfied longings of the dead one into himself, needs a third figural place into which this transfer and the longing can be transported so that both can come to know themselves "in that which [they] resemble." The perceived natural object is the most logical place, since it is both a sign of the object's distance from (indeed, death in) the perception and a reference to a dying and self-regenerating process apparently going on over time in the object itself. That is why elegiac speakers make perceived objects (such as broken lilies) the analogies most embodying their own sense of loss. Once this transfer has been made, the observed form can provide, first, an analogue for mourning that can help it find a shape and then, almost at once, the consolation of deferring to yet another natural thing that continues yet surpasses the initial mourning. The transposition of the dead person's signs in most elegies disseminates that reproductive process throughout the whole perceivable world, from dead body to observer to immediate natural object to more distant objects, because death-as-image is such a drive in and of itself, demanding and finding new extensions of its motion the moment any one of them has been achieved.

The supreme example of what this drive insists on is the sudden, Virgilian raising of the image from earthly forms to heavenly counterparts. An image of death does not transfigure itself sufficiently if it simply defers to a further image on the same level, as when one dead body is made analogous with another. To approach a significance outside of sheer dissolution, as in the early stages of Shelley's Gothic sensibility, the death-figure must be transported to an utterly different (almost opposite) translation of it, one that is at least as much a radical shift as the basic one, where a visible body is put forward by death's invisible retraction of life. That search for a difference must be continual, in fact, even when transpositions have already occurred. A dead person (specifically an Adonis) can be reincarnated as a flower because the latter form "mock[s] the merry worm" devouring the body (*Adonais*, l. 176), in the sense both that a blossom is a resurgence of life from a plant fed by dead matter (thereby ridiculing death's presumed supremacy) *and* that a flower is doomed to die as it ejects seed (thereby imitating death's "exhalation" of an image). The resulting repetition of death inside something differing from it, however, means that the differentiation can eventually be pulled back, when the flower dies, toward a resemblance with what it would transcend. A mirror of the flower reflecting and yet reversing the flower's nature must be found before the blossom becomes a dead sign of death, almost no transference at all. Stars are such mirrors, Shelley points out, to such an extent that flowers can be seen as "incarnations of the stars, when splendour / Is changed to fragrance" (*Adonais*, ll. 174–75). Both of these star-shaped forms look to each other, to their heavenly or earthly opposites, for the reembodiment that brings self-realization, so much so that each contains a version of the other within itself, as a center for itself, the way the blue-and-red flower contains the star-burst in *Astrophel*. Consequently, the inversion/reflection of death in the flower has to spring toward the reflection/ inversion of the flower in the star. Here is the main reason why Shelley wants to move this process back toward its Greco-Roman "bursting" from a drive that moves through and within earthbound forms. That relocation of the saving grace shows that the "bursting" (even "from" the earth toward "Heaven's light") is endemic to the sheer image of death and does not need divine assistance to occur in human thought, only the submission of imagination to a death-figure's search for a counterpart it already half-includes.

That relentless search, in any event, also explains the self-renewing succession of elegies since ancient times, particularly the effort in so many such poems to revise their predecessors in order to revive the dead person. When Virgil recasts the Theocritan dialogue to emphasize competing perspectives on the passing of Daphnis (as Theocritus did not), when Ovid sees numerous tales of death as partial analogues of earlier ones that now need to be retold in their new contexts, and when Spenser combines star-flower images from Bion, Ovid, and Sidney to produce a new variation on the blossom of death, these elegists are all extending the revisionary process in the image of death itself. As we have seen, the image recasts the withdrawal of life into at least the sign of an absence (the body, something different from the withdrawal), which is then encrypted by symbolic forms and enclosures that are themselves reinterpreted by readers of them with the aid of thought-patterns recalled, but also updated, from previous ceremonies of mourning. If there is not both a harking back to and timely revision of that nostalgia, the dead one is not made to live again in the current (though derived) frame of reference demanded by the image's transposition away from receding death. The two directions of reference in death's image must be matched in interpretations of it by both a repetition and reorientation of tradition, seeing as the symbolic forms waiting to be repeated have themselves been enacting that same regressive/progressive drive.

Adonais revolutionizes its genre by exaggerating both thrusts at once more than most elegies do. It forces the pastoral tradition back not simply to its earliest metaphysical assumptions but to the drives in visible death making those assumptions attractive and subject to revision. It then uses the basic energy in the image of death— and especially its drive toward repetition with a difference—to challenge the most current presuppositions on which the elegy rests. Christian resurrection is apparently repeated but in the most disruptive of ways, so that it looks back and ahead to another kind of leap beyond bodily decay. This transcendence carries the dead poet to a "burning fountain" of restless future revisions where "the dead" do not become fixed stars but, more like ancient daemons, "move [ahead] like winds of light on dark and stormy air" (l. 396). On the way to this metamorphosis, too, Shelley's elegy revises its generic stance more than once, precisely by taking the elegy back to its roots. By appealing at first to all the conventions of pastoral mourning in the face of a "frost which [now] binds" Adonais/Keats (l. 3), the speaker discovers that death is both recast in and irreversibly sequestered behind its image and all readings of it, to such an extent that "our tears / Thaw not the frost" (ll. 2–3). Death's "mute voice" so escapes the lamentations about it (l. 27) that all the mourners pursue their desire for the lost poet's restoration only by failing to reach him in his "chamber," while death itself (if there is such a thing) eludes all scrutiny and attack as the distant "other" of every representation. The feelings of the current "sad Hour" can only "rouse . . . compeers," other responses to death, and "teach them" versions of the old "sorrow" (ll. 4–6) unless a diversion of the reference to death can establish a different object of attack. Such an object is finally chosen when death as the dim cause of Adonais's departure is made to point to *its* cause: the "deaf and viperous" conservative critic (l. 317). Now there is an accessible target, and the poem veers briefly into satire (ll. 316–35) until the speaker returns to the process of death as the best counter to the power of criticism. Death becomes valued for eluding the contemptible critic as well as the signs of the elegy, since the shifting of sorrow between successive hours and interpreters, the transference spawned by death's inaccesibility, permit all memories of the dead poet to outlast the prejudices of the moment ("the shadow of our night" at l. 352). Henceforth the vestiges of Adonais can be envisioned as joining with the "transmitted effluence" of other great and dead poets who have had "hopes [that have] gone before" their lifetimes and so have survived beyond their eras and should defy prejudice well into the future (ll. 407 and 470). Elegy has become satire, then prophecy, revealing the latter two modes to be incipient in the former, all because *this* elegy has uncovered the dynamic in death's image and allowed it to drive the poem backward and forward though the "stress" of poetic "successions."

The "one Spirit's plastic stress" for Shelley, it turns out, is the compulsion toward "new successions" emerging in and from all forms of death at many different levels of what we perceive. It is the eternal action of (or in) the image of death, we now can see, and it therefore makes possible all the redemptive movements that I have just enumerated: the consolations in the oldest (and even most recent) elegies; the deconstruction of later elegies to reveal a more primordial and liberating figural activity; the analogies between dying and surviving natural objects; the relocation of a dead person's longings into the interpreter of the death; the figurative transportation of the deceased into an earthly object, then a ceremony, then a heavenly analogue; the distance of death's representations from the withdrawal of life; the revision undergone by images of death as they give way to others the way death gave way to them (thus revising its own movement); and the survival of dead people, not as their own identities but as the present and future series of ceremonial, allusive, and revisionary readings of the already revisionary signs they leave behind. On all these levels the "one stress," just as *Adonais* says, "tortur[es]" the signs of death that seem to signal its demise into "its own likeness, as each mass may bear" (ll. 384–85). This one process in death's image, particularly if our imagination becomes aware of it, takes forms that seem to indicate a cessation of process and distends, then displaces, them so that they reenact its continual transference in the different ways possible for different forms of death. Such a "stress" is really figural before it is anything else. It is a drive to represent an inaccessible "other" that recovers this referent only by continuing to lose it in "new successions" of the drive itself.

Now we can see why Shelley's revisionary One—or cup-shaped process of fading and reformation—must involve a facing of death and even the momentary death of the One's manifestations. For one thing, an image *is* a death, the disappearance of its referent, quite as much as death is always an image. Moreover, as Shelley started to see when he revised Wordsworth's sense of memory in 1815 and 1816, there needs to be a death of the past behind personal recollections or behind figurations left by a dead person if those signs are to achieve a significance lasting beyond a brief span of time. Signs of death cannot be resurrected in surviving contexts unless the hold of the dominant previous context is broken enough for the figures to shift away from it.[61] Indeed, the ability and longing in such signs to outlast the death they have come to embody insist on a separation from what they betoken so that they may "transmit an effluence" to a "fire [that] outlives the parent spark" (*Adonais*, ll. 407–08). The poems of Keats himself speak frequently, Shelley reminds us, of the poet's desire to "outsoar" the time of "A heart grown cold [and] a head grown grey in vain . . . when the spirit's self has ceased to burn [and] / With sparkless ashes load[s] an unlamented urn" (*Adonais*, ll. 352–60).[62] For them to break from that moment even while intoning it is for the writings of Keats to finally achieve their aim, to be free of what they mourn— hence for the signs of him to "wake" and "live" elsewhere, to leave death itself far more dead than Adonai/Adonais, the layered sign of the dead poet shifting toward related signs (ll. 357 and 361). Language wants to carry though the same disruption, since its figures are always mourning the referents not present in them and countering that regressive pull by making words defer to other words in a deflection of referential desire that allows the desire to survive what it loses.[63] Elegiac discourse foregrounds this dimension of language and thereby allows the image of death to announce itself clearly as a sense of loss and a turn (or troping) away from loss at the same time. The fact that Adonais/Keats has sought that figural process, has died having set it in motion, and is now mourned by a version of it that returns itself (and his signs as well) to its most basic drives: all this joins him to an eternal stress moving through and across the history of language, the tradition of the elegy, and the metaphysics projected by elegies from their figural process. True, this plasticity does engender products of transference that eventually become "dross" or mere dead letters, "unwilling" to accept refiguration by past and future versions of the current image (l. 384). But this "checking" of "thought's eternal flight" is also what allows the flight to continue its "bursting" beyond its past while the past still calls out for the restoration it receives from the change. For the "fading coal" of Keats, in Shelley's eyes, there could be no greater or more lasting salvation.

Adonais as the Confluence of Two "Eternal Flights"

The salvation, too, seems all the more complete in this poem when we realize that the eternal "stress" underlying any image of death for Shelley resembles the transferability of universal potentials that keeps building the "one great poem" in the *Defence of Poetry*. When the elegist portrays the death of Adonais behind his writings as an "effluence [which] cannot die / So long as fire outlives the parent spark," he virtually repeats Shelley's narrative of how the gestation of poetry produces a fiery, prismatic "germ" and then projects it toward future transformations that are urged to reconstrue it. The resemblance is not surprising. Poetry in the *Defence,* as a quasi-chemical interaction of fading memories that produces new combustions of "unapprehended relations," always starts as a process reconfiguring vestiges of a dead or dying past. That is true whether poetry is viewed as a reworking of a "fading coal" already half-rekindled or whether it is taken as a disruption of dead letters that generates revivals and revisions of now-buried associations. In the context of *Adonais,* which focuses on poems as figures for the death of an actual poet, poetry therefore becomes the most visible embodiment of what death-as-an-image is, does, and can produce. Poems that survive their author are obviously "exhalations" of him that keep him breathing out after— and even *because*—he ceases to breathe. They provide a continuing life for the deceased by making him their referent or point of departure, yet they also leave him behind so that the interactions of the words can incline, in part, toward contexts distant from those closest to the author. Far more than in most deaths, a fading that leaves poems as its epitaph reveals a dying process that is already figural (a poet who transfers his "breath" into written words) leaping over a widening gap (between the receding life and the words seeking readers) to find conductors for the surviving electricity (in the future readings and reworkings of the readable signs). The "One" in *Adonais* is a renewal by transference, then, only as it combines two different eternal and figural movements, the one in death's image and the flight of imaginative "sparks" across the history of truly progressive poetry. Keats, as a matter of fact, makes that interplay almost inevitable for an elegist who is sensitive to the best pieces published in *Lamia, Isabella, The Eve of St. Agnes, and Other Poems* (Shelley's favorite Keats volume), issued in 1820.[64] In several prominent passages throughout that collection, Keats not only seeks a movement through and past death; he also calls half-lovingly to it in "mused rhyme" just so that the process of dying behind verse will "take into the air [his] quiet breath" and "pour forth" a "song" in another form that flies on ahead while the poet falls back to "become a sod" ("Ode to a Nightingale," ll. 52–60).

Consequently, *Adonais* matches its iconoclastic journey back through the tradition and grounds of its genre by continually linking the transpositions in death and genuine poetry. The result is an intimation of why some poets are carried ahead by "the One Spirit" and others are not. On this level of his elegy, Shelley exposes the process that actually makes the best dead poets (including himself as well as Keats, it is hoped) live forever in a "Heaven" of "song" as "winds of light on dark and stormy air." This further eternal movement, we discover, begins each revival of itself in human thought, somewhat as revisionary mythography does in *Prometheus Unbound,* with a longing for past foundations that can never be fully recovered yet must be sought if the past is to be meaningfully continued in a different form of its tendencies. Such a regressive gaze, when fervently pursued, however, must finally see that what is desirable in the past is made attractive by the longing in the gaze rather than by powers that receding figures supposedly still possess. The gaze, especially if it is a poem, must then realize that it is denied any real fulfillment of its desire, indeed is drawn toward the very withdrawal into stultifying death it is trying to reverse, if it chooses to regard past forms as forcing interpretation to obey them and so fails to view them as incomplete images already starting to transport themselves from the death they embody. To avoid being confined only to the tyranny of the past over desire, the gaze must critique the illusion of self-contained power in remnants of the past and reconstrue all remnants as rebellious leaps beyond death longing to be seen as such and joined to other such rebellions. At this point the poetic "reading" of the image of death can see the image as enacting the pursuit of "unapprehended relations" that is the aim of poetry itself. That quest in the image, therefore, can be brought out by a new poetic rendering of its poetry that does in fact link the signs of death to other figurations of resistance to the past. The attempted revolutions sought by all these related figures, though their individual methods may differ, thus turn out to be the driving activity that makes them all outlive themselves as the "co-operating thoughts" of what appears to be "one great mind" in continual progress. For an elegist to try reading signs of death in this supremely poetic way, moreover, is for him to want to join that movement into the future, even if that means he must long to die into and behind his own poetry. The definite stages in the structure of *Adonais,* its mournful turning-back toward death's "dim dwelling-place" and then its eager pressing-ahead to join its development to the "plastic stress," follow the exact course they do because they carry out this logic uniting the image of death and the poetic "seed" of future possibilities.

The early steps in that logic manifestly start to drive the poem from the moment the main image of death is most clearly the poetry of Keats/Adonais. His first redeemers for Shelley are indeed his versified conceptions (or "quick Dreams" at l. 73) as they turn back toward their supposed progenitor to seek and recover what appears to be their lost origin (esp. at ll. 73–126). The problem is that they initially misconstrue the kind of resurrection they can perform. At first they all try to say that "our hope, our sorrow, is not dead" as though such exclamations could draw the one who infused them with those emotions out of his grave to be preserved as what is clearly "ours" and not "his" (l. 84). At this stage the "Dreams" are oblivious, in their unexamined nostalgia, to the irony that their possessive pronoun no longer includes Adonais. "Our" actually points to the retroactive attempt of his "passion-winged Ministers" to reembody him as the emotions taking flight from him in the poems (l. 74). One of the "Dreams" even ascribes a vision like herself to the decaying "brain" of the buried poet. She claims, in her reading of a tear that seems to glisten on the eyelids of the invisible corpse, that "some Dream" still impels an overflow from his mind (ll. 85–87). Yet a careful reader of *Adonais,* itself a reading of her reading, sees that her conclusion is her own longing projected onto the dead poet without her being aware of the fact. "She knew not," we find, that the tear prompting her reading was "her own" (l. 89). Such myopia, by its very nature, does not see the sort of revival it is and so fails to achieve the resuscitation it seeks, encouraging the woeful lamentations that join it in the first half of the poem.

This almost willful blindness has definite causes and consequences. The "Dream's" projection backward and the need to conceal it, to be sure, are demanded by the fact that the referent is a buried withdrawal and not an interpretable object. That disappearance, since it does leave a beckoning vestige (a body), implicitly asks the interpreter to cover the remnant with an additional mark (the tear). What results is a layering of signs that produces a sense of depth (signifier masking signified), and this sense calls forth a reading of the death that regards its signs as harboring an essence (or author). Meanwhile, this request also asks the interpreter to forget the request was made so that the interpreter's way of seeing, the source of the sign (or tear), will read the mark and what it covers simply as objects to be probed by the perceiving subject. As this sequence works through its progression, however, the sheer and potentially meaningless withdrawal of the dead becomes increasingly visible the more it is exposed as needing added elements from the observer and as being implanted with a motivating mind that is but an effect of the poet's "exhalations." In addition, the speaker's reading of the tear, which translates the droplet into the "lost angel of a ruined Paradise" (l. 88), can only relocate the sign and not resurrect the mind, since the latter remains just as "ruined" as it was and "lost" to the fallen "angel" cast out from it. The reading, too, must say all this using the Miltonic imagery and rhythms so often employed by Keats in his poems. Such diction draws the leavings of the dead poet back toward the equally deceased "Sire of [Adonais's] immortal strain," a father-figure already remembered as swallowed up by "the gulph of death" and now seen as taking his progeny with him, leaving only memorials of a Paradise lost as epitaphs for them both (*Adonais,* ll. 30 and 35). On top of all this, the Miltonic/Spenserian style of the eulogist's lament makes the image of death a repetition of past poetry and not the reconstruction of the psyche that the "Dream" seeks to raise from the tomb. Another kind of deflection is needed, albeit still a poetic one, if death is not merely to "blot / The brightness it may veil" (*Adonais,* ll. 391–92).

Perhaps the tradition of poetry should be the deflection. Perhaps the displacement of a fading originator into a stream or chain of linked poems spanning Western history may offer the dead figure incorporation into a perpetual revival, a more lasting form of resurrection, as it makes Adonais's "dreams" seem "episodes [newly added] to that great poem" constantly building upon itself as a succession of "co-operating thoughts." The speaker of *Adonais* realizes and broaches this possibility, without a doubt, in his "lost angel of a ruined Paradise" and elsewhere. Yet initially he makes an inaccurate choice in specifying the nature of that tradition, both in misdefining what makes that tradition survive and in wrongly specifying what in Keats's poetry actually links him to the most eternal tradition. Tying himself stringently at first to longstanding and precisely codified verse-forms, as did the younger Keats once lamented by Shelley as "entangled in the cold vanity of systems" (*L,* II, 31), Shelley's speaker takes Milton's apparent status as the "Sire" of Adonais seriously enough (again in the manner of Keats before 1820) to make the departed poet a link in the "chain of thought" inspired solely by Urania, Milton's "Heavenly Muse" and the "voice divine" ruling all the Muses as the favorite child of her "Almighty Father" in Book VII of *Paradise Lost* (ll. 1–16). The attempt here is multi-faceted. To begin with, the longing for lost origins in the image of death and the tear that overlays it connects the sign's loss of its referent with every person's longings (including Adonais's and the speaker's desires) for the "original" place, the body and embrace of the Mother, to which Freud claims we seek to return in death so as to reach a state prior to our differentiation from the womb.[65] As the "mighty Mother" spawning and continuing the line of the "Sire" in Keats/Adonais, Urania is therefore called to embrace her "gentle child" in "the death chamber" (ll. 235 and 217). At the same time, the speaker tries to enfold the dead poet into a long-lived order of poetic style that once had enough transformative—and thus restorative—power to make "camps and cities" seem "paved . . . with flowers" that recalled and foretold a forgotten but eternal Love (ll. 209–16). The mother of what seems the literary tradition behind Keats is thus summoned from "her Paradise" (apparently the "lost" one) to "weep" the loss of her "last" hope for the survival of her descent (ll. 14–20), much in the way Keats's Diana came down to Endymion, Ovid's Venus or Keats's Isabella watered the Adonis-flower with their tears (*Adonais,* ll. 48–54), and even Spenser's Urania in *The Tears of the Muses* wept to find that "th' heavenlie light of knowledge is put out" in human thought (*Tears,* l. 488).

So much frantic effort on her part and the speaker's, however, shows that she is no longer a renovating "plastic stress." She is more like some grasping mothers, or like Mercury and the Furies in *Prometheus Unbound,*[66] when they strive to bind a tendency toward transformation exclusively to the commands of past ideologies. She tries to draw Adonais into the old, hierarchical fashioning of the poet as the Warrior-Son of the Muse-Mother who is herself fathered by the Most High. Urania's own lament for the dead poet wants to see him as a "god-like mind" that "soar[ed] forth" like the "sun" from the "heaven" it "veil[ed]" but was crucified before its full brightness could make "The monsters of life's waste [flee] from [it] like deer" (ll. 259, 253, 260, and 243). Shelley's Urania, we must realize, is but a "fading Splendour" (l, 198), "chained to Time" and so doomed to retire to the Great Memory of "listening Echoes" in which she must sleep with all the other incarnations of receding assumptions (ll. 234 and 14).[67] Such is the realm of mere ghosts, the "Paradise" of the lost, from which Urania is called near the start of *Adonais* (ll. 12–16 and 194–98). That collective unconscious is so disjoined from the "electric life" in the movement of progressive thought that any new attempt in Urania's dated manner to "pave" obdurate "camps and cities" with "flowers" is sure to have no transformative effect, with "human hearts . . . Yielding not . . . to [a] tread" that has so often been used to underwrite the most entrenched ways of seeing (ll. 210–11). For Adonais to die simply into her embrace or to be revived as she wishes would be for him to become, as Urania fears he may, an "ephemeral insect . . . gathered into death without a dawn" (ll. 254–55), a merely conventional poet of the moment destined to die in the Western memory without the new day of later revivals. Then, too, the danger is just as great if the dead poet's "Dreams" or interpreters become fixated on his (and their) possible return to the biological Mother. To be held by such a longing, though it always tempts us in our responses to death, is to seek a melancholic, stifling regression—one doomed to failure in any case—toward an infantile attachment that would discourage both personal development and any reconstructions of memory-traces that could free the self from the domination of the past.[68] It is to be a "nursling" who is never seen to bear the "fruit" of the "hope" for a better future pursued by "true love tears" and the projection of ego-ideals (ll. 47–53). The call of Urania, however it is read, tries to pull the remnants of Adonais into the receding blackness of several kinds of death instead of outward to the transposition most naturally sought by the remnants themselves.

Whatever surviving power Urania has comes not from the older supports to which she would link her fallen "child," but from the way the "Echoes" of, in, and around her, "listening" for revivals of her, hear themselves somewhat confirmed and remade in the "melodies" left by Keats/Adonais (l. 16). The posterity, rather than the supposed origins, of this Great Mother is what keeps her alive, particularly when the partly rebellious progeny of her progeny (Keats in his later work) alters ancient formulations of her into such "descents" as "veiled Melancholy" (an enshrined goddess "'Mid listening Echoes" in stanza 3 of Keats's "Ode on Melancholy") and the voice of the nightingale once heard in "fairy lands [now] forlorn." Even the speaker of *Adonais* can really describe Urania only by reattaching these versions of her to her decaying form in the "veiled eyes" and "lorn" reclusiveness used in the elegy's first portrait of the figure (ll. 12–13). True, this reactivation of Urania makes her feel "stung" by the "snake Memory" into reading her buried descendent according to the standards that she tried to impose in her days of mythic power (l. 197). But she acknowledges the irony in her attempt to repossess a newly dead figure on which her very survival depends by calling to the dead poet's reanimation of her as Shelley calls to Intellectual Beauty ("Leave me not!") and by asking for a kiss from his dead body so that her decay-ridden, "heartless breast" can have some "food of saddest memory" to fill up the emptiness now that "all thoughts else" once connected to her have lost their connection with a dominant ideology (ll. 224 and 228–29). Confronted with this reassertion of her old hierarchies alongside an admission of their lifelessness, the "Death" claiming Adonais ultimately smiles and embraces Urania as she embraces her fallen disciple (ll. 217–25). Since she can no longer transfigure Death into "new successions" as she once did, Death shows that he subsumes her outdated attempt to draw Adonais back into the life of a worn-out set of traditions. Quite clearly, to empower a deceased poet's resurrection by forcing him back into superceded modes would be to consign him to the fading and vanishing of transference in the dead letter, only one of the two

inclinations in the divided movement of death's image. There cannot be any true elegiac redemption unless both the nostalgiac and the revisionist drives are active, notwithstanding the constant tug-of-war as they strain in opposite directions.

For Adonais to be reborn within and carried off by the "build" spawning stage after
stage in the "one great poem," then, he has to be partly dissociated from dying orders
and connected with a "vitally metaphorical" resistance to them, to quote the *Defence*
once more. This latter drive is the impulse in true poetry for Shelley that has kept
generating revolutionary interrelations of figures out of, in defiance of, and in flight
from the most established political and symbolic systems. Only if Adonais is linked
to that disruptive "tradition" can his resurrection by poetic means equal and thus
blend with the way the "plastic stress" of death's image compels "dross" into "new
successions." Hence Shelley's speaker soon turns away from his initial call to Urania.
He now configures Adonais as either parallel to or repetitive of those poets who,
through subversive poems or their known political stances, have recovered the
repressed drive for "unapprehended relations" in the hegemonic dead letter while
enduring the full force of hegemony's attempted domination. Keats is thus restyled as
primarily a successor to such long-dead champions of liberty as Lucan ("by his death
approved" because it resulted from his opposition to Nero), Sir Philip Sidney/Astro-
phel (who "fought" and "fell" while resisting tyrannical Spain and the privileges of
his own rank),[69] and the republican Milton (imprisoned by the royalist "liberticide"
he often wrote against), who used Urania to deny or redefine battle-hungry and aristocratic notions of epic heroism (ll. 401–05 and 31–34). The fallen poet is also remembered as one figure in, outgrowth of, and remembered example to the community of
his principal mourners, all of whom are liberals noted for various forms of resistance
to reigning authority and so are filled with grief for a fellow "shepherd" who was part
of that effort in their eyes (ll. 262–315).

Keats/Adonais is aligned most completely, of course, with that "herd-abandoned
deer," so like Shelley as well as Acteon, who comes to the graveside already bearing
wounds from "the hunter's dart" thrown repeatedly by upholders of the most established ideologies (l. 297). This parallel, if the reader accepts it, connects Adonais with
one of the most iconoclastic of stances and styles. The wounded and hounded figure
of "Love in desolation masked" is forced to "wither" in the "killing sun" of current
religions and hierarchies because he fervently refuses and reshapes the usual postures
of the Christian mourner. Insofar as he looks to the past for models of self-fashioning,
he adopts the features of a worshipper of old Dionysus (a true Spirit of "plastic stress"
within observable forms), defiantly carrying a "light spear topped with a cypress cone"
and revealing a "head [entirely] bound with pansies" (ll. 281–91). The composition
of this poet-figure is not only a disruption, even a parody, of conventional lamentation; it also resurrects the ancient Dionysian rituals designed to bring about renewal
after death, ones that fashioned reincarnations, as does the "Ode to the West Wind,"
in a highly physical and metamorphic fashion far different from any that the tradition
of Urania would recognize. As a result, when Adonais becomes a version of this transference from a past into a present that proposes to alter future postures of mourning,
Urania "scans" (presumably the poetry of) this "deer" who "sung [the] new sorrow"
and, unable to grasp who he might be or incarnate, retires from the battle for the
possession of Adonais, declining to be mentioned in the poem again and leaving the
dead poet to be drawn into the succession of revolutionary writers and prophets (ll.
301–02).

Granted, *Adonais* may appear to be making it easier than it actually was for Keats to be seen as another subversive turn in the stream of poetry's radical self-revisions. The speaker does choose to develop Shelley's conclusion, despite available evidence to the contrary,[70] that Keats's consumption began as a reaction to "savage criticism" from the Tory *Quarterly Review*. We also seem asked to believe that this attack was leveled against Keats because he was more like Shelley than he ever thought himself to be.[71] Presumably, as with the "herd-abandoned deer," Keats's form of skeptically unsettled and self-questioning verse made him analogous for many to a "woman taken in adultery" over whom self-righteous purveyors of more absolutist thinking (really "prostitutes" to established interests) felt they could stand in judgment as did the judges of the quiet rebel Jesus Christ (Preface to *Adonais, NCE*, p. 391). Shelley might even be said to have skewed the political position of Keats by mourning him in an elegiac poem reinvoking the foundations of the pastoral tradition. Pastoral poetry, far from starting as the songs of country folk, began (probably in Alexandria) as the sophisticated work of disaffected city-dwellers who faced the decline of the ancient city-state, increasingly anti-rural urbanization, and thus the alienation of work and leisure into vast market systems controlled by a hierarchy of profit-seeking merchants.[72] The position of the pastoral speaker was initially and has often remained that of an ironist speaking from inside a system he would critique as though he were outside it in a world of *otium* (country leisure) instead of the *negotium* (the "getting and spending") that actually engulfs him. Ideologically uniting (as Shelley often did in himself) the stances of the devalued aristocrat and the exploited rural laborer, such a speaker's style of appearance and versification, like Shelley's *Philosophical View of Reform,* frequently strikes at the core of ascendent social mores and economic patterns, not to mention their effort to maintain the power of hegemonic urban groups. The pastoral poet or character is thus very like the itinerant Old Testament prophet from outside the city uttering his counter-statements in the very marketplace he resists. The attachment of that attitude in *Adonais* to the speaker, the dead poet, and the mourners aligned with him firmly places them all in that iconoclastic posture. Such a link is especially evident in the "deer" who has "gazed on Nature's naked loveliness" to the point of seeing the actual process in perceived existence (l. 275) and so is pursued by the dominant, urban thought-patterns that want to hide that process behind the symbolic forms taken by their power plays. For Keats to be paralleled to such a figure—and set up for such an analogy in a pastoral poem—is perhaps for him to be inaccurately credited with and forcibly saved by a radical, and indeed Dionysian, attack on established beliefs that he never quite undertook.

Still, however self-serving he may have been, Shelley has genuine grounds for conscripting Keats into this pattern. The poems of the 1820 volume are often as revisionist (or *nearly* as radical, with some help) as Shelley would have them be, and it is just those moments from which *Adonais* borrows words or image-patterns most frequently in order to make the signs of the dead poet images of death that link him to eternal revolution. To say that Adonais "is made one with Nature" in the sense that "there is heard his voice in . . . the moan / Of thunder [or] the song of night's sweet bird" (ll. 371–72) is to recall the way the tempest in, say, "The Eve of St. Agnes" is transformed by Porphyro's restyling of the "gusts" into the "elfin-storm" of Madeline's hopeful dreams ("Eve," ll. 327–45) and the way the song of Keats's nightingale once heard in the Bible and "fairy lands" is made to pass beyond those renderings of it, and beyond the present one too, to be "buried" again in the "melodious plots" of "valley-glades" further on ("Ode to a Nightingale," ll. 65–70, 8, and 77–78). In giving a revisionary turn to existing sounds that drastically alters their ranges of reference, Shelley suggests, Keats adds a layer of revoicings onto existing vestiges of voice. The layer is so re-definitive that it cannot be separated henceforth from the all the ways we will come to hear the same sounds with the aid of existing interpretations. Moreover, Shelley's sense that loss begins renewal quite as much as fruition initiates a decline—that "the swallows reappear [when] Winter is come and gone" even as "grief returns with the revolving year" (*Adonais,* ll. 154–57)—plays up the "gathering swallows" that fly off toward their Spring return in Keats's "To Autumn" (l. 33) and the "dwell[ing] with Beauty [foredoomed to] die" that is the double nature of "Veiled Melancholy" in the "Ode on Melancholy" (ll. 21–26). *Adonais,* to be precise, takes the persistent turning-toward-death, the revisionary understanding of metamorphic process, in so many Keats images and extends its basic drive to make such figures more two-directional in their change, more inclined to see death as turning toward Beauty and thus as veiling Melancholy with hope while hope also faces its mortality. In that way the Autumn that is asked by Keats's speaker to "Think not" of "the songs of Spring," though Autumn clearly does think beyond its situation in Keats's poem, can come to launch its swallows into "skies" of future possibility despite the prohibition ("To Autumn," ll. 23–24 and 33). Seasonal change as poetically rendered can now be seen as pursuing the renewal of death's signs so clearly desired by and yet so muted in the later poetry of the fading Keats.

The most revolutionary allusion to him in *Adonais,* however, and one that needs to revise his figures very little, turns out to be his amalgamation with a nontheistic and Ovidian "plastic stress." At this point Shelley is echoing the metaphysical pre-suppositions declared in *Hyperion,* the long fragment that closes the 1820 volume and the semi-Miltonic poem that Shelley regarded as far and away its author's greatest achievement.[73] In the Second Book of that piece, the God of the Sea (the expanse upon which Shelley's speaker will finally launch himself) reveals to the fallen, even decaying Titans how much their past and present states are "not the beginning nor the end" of perceivable existence (l. 190). This speech assumes, just as *Adonais* will, the Hesiodic emergence of primal "Light" from a multiple, not singular, "chaos and prenatal dark-ness" (ll. 191–92). Such an emergence was then and still is perpetually a "ferment . . . ripening in itself," one that extends the bursting-ahead of light by urging light to turn round on "its own producer" (any pull toward dissolution) and to "engender" in it new forms of observable life that repeat the image of death with some differences (ll. 193–97). Because this process is so basic to the senses of natural and historical change—or really the mythological successions (hence the history of poetry)—on which Western thinking has long depended, "a fresh perfection [really] treads" on "the heels" of any fall, including the overthrow of the Titans, and the result is always an emergent "Power more strong in beauty, born of" past formations "And fated to excel" them (ll. 212–14). All this his fellow Titans must finally admit, the Sea God concludes,

> For 'tis the eternal law
> That first in beauty should be first in
>   might;
> Yea, by that law, another race may drive
> Our conquerors to mourn as we do now.
>   (ll. 228–31)

This non-Christian, decentered, self-revising, and ever-disruptive action, quite clearly a transference inherent in all thoughts about fading thoughts, really pervades the assumptions of Keats as far back as his early poetry, notwithstanding his later concentration on transformation as inevitable destruction. Even in a Keats sonnet of 1814 (one echoed in *Hyperion*, II. 286–88), "from the darkening gloom a silver dove / Upsoars, and darts into the Eastern light, / On pinions that naught moves but [the] pure delight" of the movement itself ("As from the darkening gloom," ll. 1–13). The images left by Keats when they are revived in *Adonais* do not have to be wrenched into "bearing a part" in a "bursting" of "new successions" uniting "might" with "beauty." For Shelley that exact—and revolutionary—vision is struggling to be born again in the very best poetry that Keats dies into. The "Spreading . . . Power" of the transpositional One, even before *Adonais* announces its existence, has "[already] drawn [Keats's] being into its own," and Shelley need only carry out and further that operation (*Adonais*, l. 375–76).[74]

Because such rebellious and "lofty thought" has so "lifted a young heart above its mortal lair," in fact (ll. 392–93), the immortality to which Keats rises in *Adonais* is the kind held most in common by the image of death and the "one" tradition of iconoclastic poetry: the perpetual movement of "burning" and "bursting" through and beyond the dominant sign-systems of the moment. Shelley's speaker, to be sure, describes Adonais as elevated to a level of everlasting "splendours" that are "extinguished not" (ll. 388–89). There the dead poet as transfigured in his writing is "gathered to the kings of thought" who beckon beyond the elegist "where the Eternal are" (ll. 430 and 495). Such images are borrowed, as several have seen,[75] from the ascents of Dante in the *Commedia* and *Convivio* and from the soliloquies of Calderón heroes seeking the eternal light beyond the veil of decaying life, not to mention the leaps to lasting fame among the stars intoned by elegists from Moschus to Milton. But Shelley transports the temporal struggle against such absolutes (the drive in Keats linking him with the "One spirit") to the ultimate levels in these sources, thus altering the nature of the "Eternally" poetic yet again and firmly recanting his own temple of "the Great" in *Laon and Cythna*. The "dead" resurrected at the greatest height now "move like winds of light on dark and stormy air" because they all—Lucan, Sidney, Milton, Keats, and even the "agon[ized]" Chatterton (l. 400)[76]—"have waged contention with their time's decay" and thereby serve as permanent examples for poets who will and should do the same in present and future circumstances (l. 431). What never decays, though poets do, is the windlike effort of their poetry to blow imagined potentialities beyond the storm of contending power plays in a particular historical period. All else will die eventually save this splendorous "white radiance" or rebellious sending of light ahead. The truly poetic "dead," now including Adonais, "live" forever in the sense that they "*move* like winds of light" (my emphasis); they transfer their materials away from established contexts, amid the "darkness" of repressive systems, even for future readers. Such poets are (or become) "kings of thought" only insofar as "they borrow not / Glory from those [autocrats] who made the world their prey" (ll. 428–29). Like Christ and Shelley's Prometheus, these radically different types of kings "rule" thought by holding out and calling us to the "Light [of imaginative aspiration] whose simile kindles the Universe" into flames of new life and the "Beauty [of thoughts transforming thoughts] in which all things work and move" throughout existence poetically perceived (ll. 478–79). These possibilities are extensions of basic human "hopes [that] have gone before" (or projected themselves past) mortal existence, and so the really eternal poets lie ahead of us as "mirrors of / The fire for which all thirst" (ll. 484–85), as stars offering the "radiance" to which we poor moths do and should aspire, even if the quest means dying in the process of pursuing that level.

Consequently, once this "fire" becomes the mobile destiny (or "plastic stress") into which Adonais has been carried and to which the elegist now longs to follow him (as Moschus supposedly longed to follow Bion), the interplay of the "flights" of poetry and death's image becomes so total and continuous that an explicitly poetic dissolution turns out to be the main object of the surviving poet's desire. Indeed, from "the world's bitter wind" of repressive ways of seeing, the speaker suggests, we may all want to "Seek shelter in the shadow of the tomb" (ll. 457–58). "What Adonais is" now, he asks, "why fear we to become?" (l. 459). Yet this quest must not seek death as the passage to a projected and static Absolute sought so regressively by the *Alastor* Poet, the followers of Laon and Cythna, the Maniac of *Julian and Maddalo,* and Beatrice Cenci. In the first place the survivor must pursue his demise in some measure as Keats did throughout his writing. He or she should face death directly enough to fashion images of its coming (or shadows of the tomb) that will outlast death the way such an image usually does, and he or she should make that attempt in an overturning of poetic traditions that employs the disruptive means provided by those traditions, all of which *Adonais* strives relentlessly to do. In addition, all seekers after the imaginative "fire" that rekindles wrecked hopes should be very conscious of aspirations as mere projections and as distant possibilities that no one mortal being can hope to attain on his or her own, even in the death of the material body. To "know [ones]self and [Adonais] aright," the aspirant, addressed with the familiar "thou" by Shelley's speaker, should

> Clasp with thy panting soul the pendulous Earth [and]
> As from a centre, dart thy spirit's light
> Beyond all worlds, until its spacious might
> Satiate the void circumference: then shrink
> Even to a point within our day and night;
> And keep thy heart lest it make thee sink
> When hope has kindled hope, and lured thee to the brink. (ll. 417–23)

The seeker should, quite clearly, make an imaginative kind of love to the perceived natural world that may reabsorb the self in death. But desire should attempt that embrace of death's image only to the point of using this center of attention as a point of departure (not as the ultimate, maternal object of a Freudian desire). The "light" generated by imagination's transfigurations of observed natural objects, with the latter already revised by thoughts about them (as the image revises death), should not so much penetrate the known world as extend the transformative drive into, out of, and beyond the initial center—ultimately to the point of surpassing the limits of perception (or senses of "the world") by which objects have been previously defined. This "darting" of light should strive to reach the farthest "circumference" or limit of the universe known to have been drawn by human interpretation upon the "void." Then the projection of ultimate potentials should try not just to satisfy that circumference but to fill it up to the point of exceeding its limits (to "satiate" it rather than obediently attain it). All this while, though, the aspirant, like the skeptical empiricist who starts believing in "one mind" during the essay "On Life," should accept a small personal place well within the supposed limits of time, perception, and knowledge, beyond which place lies a gaping distance separating desire, and even imagination, from its greater and more interrelational projection. Such a realization will keep the longing heart "light" in the face of the projection's unattainability as hope presses on from one version of it to another only to near the "brink" of death—or the edge of mortal awareness—that seems to stop the quest of the individual before it is fulfilled. The poet/thinker will know that the light, which he or she has at least continued, will aspire onward to urge revisions of the present construction and placement of the hanging (or "pendulous") world despite the limits and the death of the self, particularly if the death leaves poetry as its image. Here lies the process that makes Keats/Adonais what he now is and what we need not fear to become. The poetic effort, as the *Defence* maintains, can be "at once the center and [ever-expanding] circumference of knowledge" if the imagination can see its personal smallness and demise as but "points" from which transference springs once more to outlive and transform its products, obstacles, and purveyors.

Certainly *Adonais* does end with assertions of this very kind of skeptical idealism. The speaker now calls his readers to the *Cimitero Acattolico* (the "un-Catholic" cemetary) at Rome where Keats is—and Shelley himself will later be—buried. There we see the image of Adonais's death surrounded by old imperial forms that (like Urania) would fix death into the immortality of one ancient and tyrannical pattern. We behold especially the pyramidal tomb of Caius Cestius incorporated into the Aurelian wall, wherein the rising of desirous "flame" is "transformed to marble" in the shape of an immobile "wedge sublime" (ll. 444–47). The possibility that Keats/Adonais could be attached to such a freezing (albeit a creation) of transference, however, is denied by his placement among the "newer band" at a slight yet ironically pastoral distance from the pyramid, at which point, "like an infant's smile, over the dead, / A light of laughing flowers along the grass is spread" (ll. 448 and 440–41).[77] Pastoral nature's absorption of one of its lovers bent on transforming all perceptions of it results in a happy rebirth (or new infancy) of the scene, causing the ground to sprout fresh poetic potentials (or growing flowers). This resurgence counters the restrictive presence of the ruins of empire, the "shattered mountains" that pull Adonais toward a Uranian Great Memory (l. 435), by both contrasting with the decaying "grey walls [that] moulder round" (l. 442) and starting a new version of the process that will overgrow the ruins. The "wrecks" of the past, even now, are coming to seem the mere "bones of Desolation's nakedness" calling for the flowery covering of a very different new world (ll. 435–37), and so the incipient flora spawned by the "new band" of the dead are the beginnings of transformations that will finally surpass whole "ages, empires, and religions," the flowers themselves included (l. 426). The initial posies/poesies in the grass over Keats's grave may be small and fragile points of departure that cannot complete this revolution by themselves, but they can kindle a "light" that restoratively "laughs" at the death behind them and then opens itself to being extended by later forms of poetic disruption.

The same can be said of the very words of the elegist as they reach out for the projected status of Adonais "where the Eternal are" and find it "darkly, fearfully, afar" at a great distance from the present poem (ll. 491 and 495). Like "flowers" and "ruins," poetic "words" indeed "are weak / The glory they transfuse with fitting truth to speak" (ll. 467–68). That is because they can only reorient previous words or uses of themselves, and only for an instant, after which they must defer to other locations and instants. Yet in that way they "speak" and carry on the "light" (or "glory") of the "plastic stress" by instilling it with a "fitting [revisionary] truth" of the moment that allows the movement to drive through and then beyond the words of the past *and* the present.[78] To employ and even to die behind the deferral of such words, as the elegist hopes to do, is to reach for the revisionary "tempest" that *is* the eternal condition of the dead poet's deferring words (l. 490). It is to be "borne" by the transpositional "breath whose might I have invoked in song" at least some distance "from the trembling throng / Whose sails were never to the tempest given" (ll. 487–90), whereupon the speaker can feel at least closer to the "Light," the "Beauty," the "Benediction" (l. 480), and the "sustaining Love" of the perpetual transference that "wages contention with time's decay" in the poetry left by the dead.

The stages of Shelley's *Adonais,* we can surely say (partly as others have for years), appear to rise through the levels of Christian allegory as listed and applied by Dante— the literal, the allegorical proper, the moral, and the anagogical—so as to arrive at an ultimate vision of the "radiance" that promises to incorporate the dead poet, his living counterpart, and the longings of all true poets and their poetry.[79] At the same time, though, Shelley suggests, if such a poetic process is employed only within the confines of Catholic (or any official Christian) theology, it makes ultimate "Life" seem no more than a "dome of many-colored glass" (*Adonais,* l. 462) as it seems in St. Peter's Basilica of Rome, which is covered by glass mosaics throughout the domed interior. This limitation of vision, like the immobilized fire on the pyramid, "Stains [our perception of] the [true] white radiance of Eternity," so much so that a poetic sense of what "Death" really means must be employed to "trample [Christian suppressions] to fragments" (ll. 463–64). The succession of death-images that we have just reviewed in *Adonais,* then, is a use of allegorical procedures to redefine each level in the Catholic version. In that process, these alterations challenge the basis of Christian redemptions from death by substituting the "otherness" of poetic allegory for both the main problem (death) and the ultimate referent (the God) of orthodox theology. The mournful early stages of Shelley's poem, after all, seem obsessively "literal" at first, since they try to recover the lost "shepherd" by picturing such movements as the process of decay in his unseen body and the longing in his poems for the physical existence of their author. But the more literal the initial images try to be, the more they find their referents to be "allegorical" already, to be "forms other than" themselves, in that they are figures of death reconfigured, ones on the way to being reconfigured yet again. The medieval sense of allegory "proper" as one text referring to another (such as the *Commedia* to the Scriptures or the New Testament to the Old) now reappears as it did in "The Witch of Atlas," again with a vengeance against Church fathers. It becomes, first, the reference of death-image to death-image and, second, the reference of each image to textual versions of it (such as the mourning of Urania) that have long existed—and have variously contextualized the image—in the tradition of Western poetry. The allegorical and intertextual act of seeing the death of a recent poet in the language of an ancient elegiac form now shows that its "literal" subject is the "allegorical" movement of death becoming poetic images *and* of these images revising themselves by way of others, just as the pastoral "flocks" mourning Adonais transform their earlier natures by being and repeating Keats's poems. This view of death quite literally tramples its Catholic counterpart to pieces, because here the single main symptom of fallen human nature becomes a deferral from one figure (or fragment) to another and then to another.

For such an allegorical otherness to revive the dead figure poetically, it must not depend on a power entirely separate from its own movement or from the "succession" of death-images prompting and revising each other throughout the history of the elegy. It would be immoral, in fact, a violation of allegory's self-transfiguring nature, for *Adonais* to propose a beginning or end of mourning that would be a self-sufficient and self-contained death or Heaven. The "moral" interpretation of death's refigurations for Shelley must see each image as a "bursting" from whatever confines draw it back toward the dying past. The dead Keats in his poetry, for example, must be read as a rebellious questioner of the assumptions most accepted in the age-old conventions he often uses. Such a reading establishes the morality of the elegy's dead subject *as* his figural eruption out of and away from forms that are dead or dying. In addition, his apparent acceptance of that drive shows him submitting to a self-displacing movement of successive figures that precedes and continues his conscious effort to extend it. It precedes him in the sense of revising itself throughout the history of previous poetry (especially elegies) and surpasses him in the sense of encouraging new sign-relations to emerge in his verse out of established verbal patterns. These revisions, especially if the author dies behind them, should "burst" ahead of existing formations and strive to complete the deferral beyond their present situation primarily in future versions of a similar rebellion. To see the poetic remnants of Keats/Adonais as dissolving into this revisionary—and mainly linguistic—"radiance" is to see him raised to, or devolving back upon, an "anagogical" provenance of eternal transference. The very allegorical process in the image of death, supposedly the opposite of the undying Absolute in Catholic mythography, reappears perpetually displaced in the ultimate force providing genuine poets with salvation beyond the horizon of the waters over which we voyage to meet our ends. Such is the only result that could finally emerge from a crossing between the Shelleyan image of death and his conception of poetry's eternal self-extension. A oneness of either sort seeks a counterpart, we must remember, because of the very analogical—hence allegorical—impulse underlying each type. Consequently, the combination must reveal this urge to be the primordial one "Which wields the [perceived] world with never wearied love, / Sustains it from beneath, and kindles it above" (*Adonais,* ll. 377–78).

The One as Its Different Forms in Tandem and as a Poser of Questions: *The Triumph of Life*

Yet if *Adonais* radicalizes so many older notions by combining just two versions of this poet's revisionary One, the results are even more revolutionary—and unsettling—when all the versions are finally made to interact in one poem's central mystery. Shelley achieves that conflation in the dream-within-a-dream within his last piece of extended narrative verse, *The Triumph of Life,* the allegory famous for reworking Dante's own *terza rima* and breaking off right after the start of a line just before Shelley really did set sail into the gulf that claimed his life. To be sure, the "scene" of interwoven sights and sounds apparently dreamed, prior to the narrator's dream, by the shade of Rousseau is styled and positioned as though it were recalling the almost-forgotten basis of the "wretchedness" in the parade of Life's victims as it has been perceived by Rousseau and the speaker (ll. 336 and 306). In the first place, the "woods and waters" emerge beneath a "yawn[ing] mountain," and the lovely "shape all light" refracts "the Sun's image" to the point of unfurling a rainbow across the "invisible rain" of "Dawn" (ll. 336, 312–13, 345, 353–54, and 357). In doing so they replay the earthly paradise or nearly recovered Eden waiting across the river Lethe of Dante's *Purgatorio* and the figure of Matilda there who draws the observer toward the veiled light of Beatrice because this new Persephone has been "warmed at the radiance of Love's fire" and so can "dispose" with her "hands" all the "colors" of the setting that lead to the brightness behind them (*Purg.,* XXVII. 1–102).[80] Both the impulse generating Rousseau's basic longings and the cause of his forgetfulness are thus connected to something like the supposed dawn of existence and the human race's earliest "fall" from those desirable beginnings.

Meanwhile, the apparent emergence of the "shape," the stream, the objects it feeds, and Rousseau himself from a vaginal "cavern high and deep" in the mountain (l. 313) points, as others have seen,[81] to memory-traces from the time just after and the years immediately following a person's biological birth. The years, in fact, encompass the fairly long sequence in Wordsworth's "Immortality" ode, where the light "trailed" from Heaven in a child's perceptions "fades into the light of common day" as mother Earth fills consciousness with "pleasures of her own" ("Ode," ll. 64, 76, and 77–84).[82] Admittedly, the "trailing" in Rousseau's vision denies that it can recall a Dantean Eden or a Wordsworthian "imperial palace" ("Ode," l. 84), except perhaps in a retroactive "Heaven which I [later] imagine" and then only with the admission that "I know not[hing]" aside from a tendency to hark back to some "life . . . before" (*Triumph,* ll. 332–35).[83] But the moment and the scene are still as primal as Shelley can make them, a fact agreed upon even by critics of the most different persuasions.[84] Rousseau is offering the narrator an explanation of what both have seen as "Life" and how a certain way of seeing, chosen long ago in personal growth and the history of civilization, has really brought about the Death-in-Life that presently engulfs most people. That is true even if we notice the all-effacing entry into an "hour of rest" at the start of Rousseau's vision (l. 320), which establishes the scene as what Rousseau confronts when he awakens from having died.[85] In an ostensibly medieval and quasi-Italian dream-allegory recalling Dante's *Commedia* and Petrarch's *Trionfi,* death begins a figure's reading, in a figural narrative encapsulating his life, of the real "essence" of his nature established at and after his birth. The shade of Rousseau, like Dante's Virgil and Beatrice, now speaks from a position of having uncovered actual "causes" far more than the narrator has, even though the latter's dream is beginning to expose what waking life too often hides. Death in this mode of writing faces a person and all those who hear him—or her, when the dead Laura speaks to Petrarch in "The Triumph of Death" (pp. 60–68)[86]—with exactly what key decisions were made after birth and what the personal and social effects of those decisions have been.[87]

Here Shelley, however, is again performing his most iconoclastic maneuver, the one he first used extensively in *Alastor* with its cradles of civilization, its vale of Kashmir, and its Edenic *locus amoenus* near the headwaters of the perceptible world. He is deliberately placing loaded settings and figures in initial, causal, and final positions, all the while recalling such "shapes" in earlier works and how they were positioned so as to announce an entirely unified oneness beckoning behind them. At the same time, he is troping those figurations, using the fading and shifting already going on in them, to make them reveal a mobile and ever-changing oneness that keeps crossing between figural differences and revising older figures by connecting them with other (and often newer) ones. Now he carries out that turn more thoroughly than he ever has—and truly makes the "scene" a locus of "many sounds [or previous utterances] woven into one"—by reworking these forms, especially the "shape all light," into enactments of all the transgressive Ones that he has proposed since 1820. The shade's memory of the "shape's" genesis and continual relocation even proceeds through the four notions of the One that I have defined, following roughly the order in which Shelley has developed them and thus the order I have used in this chapter.

The shape first comes into focus after some radiance from "the Sun's image" is reflected back from and adds a golden glow to "the waters of the well" in the mountain's "cavern" (ll. 344–47). The result, unlike Matilda (who appears outside all cave-like enclosures as simply an effluence of one light alone), is an image combining several rays in the watery medium on "the vibrating / Floor of the fountain" (ll. 349–51). This figure undergoes birth in a version of Cythna's cave-mind partly filled with water and thus in a "womb" of imagination (a cave of poesy) where perceived radiations are brought into a close relationship after being refracted through different media. As the interplay intensifies, it gives off more light generated by the process, just in the way of *Defence of Poetry* claims—light that flashes outward in many directions even before the image is fully shaped and so "thread[s] all the forest maze / With winding paths of [now] emerald fire" (ll. 347–51). Here again is the imaginative taking in, acceleration, and pouring forth of transfiguration that both produces a figure with some "integrity" and "multiplies all that it reflects" so that the light is sent outward to be transformed further (even recolored "emerald") by new media (green woods) with their own reflectors, "intervals[,] and interstices." Like Shelley's sense of poetry in general, this process is neither self-contained nor subservient to another container. It reflects several forms of the "Sun's image," but only as some of these are already starting to interact outside the power of the cave or fountain (ll. 308–11) and only as the Sun is forced to see *him*self as a reflection of the feminine shape, which stands "Amid the sun, as he amid the blaze / Of his own glory" given back by the floor of the fountain as it becomes "paved with flashing rays" (ll. 349–51). In this looking back to yet commanding refraction of the sun's brilliance, the shape's oneness extends backward and forward in both time and space as it channels the passage of interreflected elements from the past toward the future and from one set of existing but distant figures toward others that go on to seek the receivers of the poetic "germ."

Then again, the "shape," though it does keep the "integrity" of being "all light," seems to realize that there is no continual extension of transpositional oneness unless there is a perpetual redifferentiation of the kind we observe in *Epipsychidion*. Again unlike Dante's feminine figures (Matilda and Beatrice), who can alter their appearances only within the limits of precisely role-bound body-languages, Shelley's focus of interrefractions seem inwardly compelled to become a layering of different figural veils covering previous veils. As soon as the sunlike "shape" rises from and out of the fountain, she starts playing the role of Dawn flinging a "Dew on the earth," whereupon that rain differentiates its tangible dampness into audible "silver music" (ll. 354–55). Then she reappears as "Iris" the rainbow "before" her other layers, as though she were her own "coloured scarf" as well as the light and the wetness that it masks (ll. 356–57). Clearly her initial combination of perceived fire, air, earth (the cave), and water cannot complete the union of its parts until it projects beyond itself arrays of raindrops, songs, objects, and colors that both differ within their separate realms and emphasize how different each realm (dampness, sound, and sight) is from the others.[88] In addition, this self-transfiguration undergoes a partial loss, even forgetting, of itself as it/she glides between the differences that she continues to shift across. She carries a "chrystal glass / Mantling [or brimming] with bright Nepenthe" (ll. 358–59), the Egyptian drug of forgetfulness, "free from gall," given by Helen of Troy to Telemachos in Homer's *Odyssey*.[89] As or because she does so, the shape lets her sun-reflecting "splendour / F[a]ll from her as she move[s]" to leave the "cavern" behind, thereby freeing herself to become "like a willow" as her "fair hair sw[eeps] the bosom of the stream" that pours out from the well (ll. 359–65). Reworking the vessel she bears, she comes to resemble the eternal "cup" that is the "One" of Ahasuerus in *Hellas*. She lets the most insistent (or "fiercest") ingredients flowing into her form from the past dissipate and fade as they should, yet she joins the remnants of these elements to other forms (the tree and the stream) toward which she now pours her outward drive. She does not insist on maintaining a single form so much as on being a loving passage through and among different, albeit adjacent, objects of perception, "Partly to tread the waves with feet which kist / The dancing foam, partly to glide along / The airs that roughened the moist amethyst [part of the rainbow], / Or the slant morning beams [new versions of her old ingredients] that fell among / The trees" (ll. 370–75).[90] It is not that she imposes this interplay, this cause of the weaving into oneness, upon the setting; in the manner of the eternal "cup," she is the quiet, almost imperceptible, urging of this operation at a subliminal level of the imaginative process that generates the scene. She prods "with palms so tender [that] / Their tread br[eaks] not the mirror of [the stream's] billow" as it reflects her motion (ll. 361–62).

This turning away from one difference toward others can be as destructive and divisive as it is synaesthetic and unifying. The "tread" of the shape, even when it seems joined to the harmonizing music it helps to arouse among "leaves and winds and waves and birds and bees" (ll. 375–76), also appears "to blot / The thoughts of him who gazed on [her feet]," and it is for that reason that "All that was seemed as if it had been not, / As if the gazer's mind was strewn beneath / Her feet like embers, and she, thought by thought, / Trampled its fires into the dust of death" (ll. 383–88). Her connective movement between moments and elements and even between the words that help create thought, as Paul de Man has observed,[91] is both made possible and countered by a violent and disjunctive tramping between positions, one that does force itself on and break the surface of the flow in the scene. This sheer crossing from figure to figure reannounces the differentiating spaces between words and thus between thoughts. Each rising thought now seems a murderous distancing of the "fading coal" that its predecessor has become, and the meter (or stepping of "feet") in the poetic and musical movement of the shape appears to encourage a regular, rhythmic disfigurement of each thought by the one that follows it only to kill it. Somewhat in the fashion Hillis Miller describes,[92] the quest of one thought or figure for a different one that repeats and confirms it leads to the smothering of the fire that tries to extend its spark from one position to another, because the second term is so different that it cannot be similar enough for a complete rekindling and any achieved similarity must finally be denied by the opposition between the figures. Refiguration, even from thought to thought, as it does when a poet speaks or writes his or her reflections, distorts the fading coals in a medium that leaves them largely behind and so partially "blots," or forgets with a drink of Nepenthe, the very thinking that it would render.

Still, this threat to the shade's memory is only one necessary feature in a larger movement. It is but a momentary result of how much the shape is repeating the "plastic stress" in *Adonais* that is also and always a reimaging of death. For genuine and continual transposition to occur, hence for the drive of the shape to extend its passage across differences, there must be a partial forgetting and blotting of past configurations and obsessions of thought in a series of burials that disfigure each past form so as to resurrect it in some very different transformation. The shade of Rousseau itself cannot be carried to this level of greater awareness if it does not, even before seeing the shape, leave the physical body buried and so "forget / All pleasure and pain, all hate and love" as the man has lived them through (ll. 318–19). Nepenthe, we must remember, is a redemptive drug in the way it makes Telemachos forget his personal sorrow enough to understand, from Helen and Menelaos, the exploits and causes unknown to the boy that underlie his father's distance from home.[93] The process given some figural integrity, then, by the shape and its cup has left the corporeal and emotional Rousseau very much for dead, even in the eyes of his shade. Consequently, unhampered by excessive nostalgia on his past, transference has been able to relocate the image of his death into a thorough recasting of his longings, memories, and writings, one that configures the action that has really made them possible (though it has never appeared too visibly in them). If such a break from the past does not stamp out most of the fading coals in Rousseau's mind, these trailings of light will call him back to a Dantean or Wordsworthian Absolute—or to the sort of heavenly essence sought either by Saint-Preux or by Rousseau himself in *Emile* or the *Confessions*[94]—and he will certainly fail to see the shape's motion as free and decentered from such "imperial" causalities. Granted, as Shelley admits in echoing the "Immortality" ode, the interplay producing the light-figure does trail back toward receding formations, some of which are connected to the historical Rousseau. But the "unbreakable" link allowing past actions or ideologies to predetermine or restrain present modifications while suppressing the actual basis of outdated systems: this inscription on the brain is effaced by an *un*-godly focusing of relations that dimly recalls, yet refuses to become, any monolithic figure from the cultural or personal past.

This kind of figural killing and the revisions, indeed the new *writing*, which it allows therefore guide the shade of Rousseau toward a solution to the "trampling" threat empowered by the trampling itself. He finally sees the idea of the shape as "Day" treading out "lamps of night" (or former images of death, as in the stars of old elegies) only as a prelude to the moment when a renewed "breath / Of darkness [or 'plastic stress'] reillumines even the least / Of heaven's living eyes" (ll. 390–91). Now reconstructive (and written) images of death, fanned by transposition as they are in *Adonais,* can be viewed as drawing out the truly imaginative flights buried in past forms or interpretations and inflaming them again to be starlike examples that call present thinkers into an iconoclastic future. At this point and with this understanding, the shade, the speaker, and perhaps their attentive readers have begun to grasp the great extent to which four notions of oneness have come together in a revolutionary "splendour."

This "shape all light" certainly should be able to combine so many versions of primordial transference. After all, it is transference embodied, almost more than any previous figure that Shelley has employed.[95] It comes into focus after the shade has already perceived "a gentle trace / Of light" being made "diviner than . . . common" sunbeams because of its interplay with the "woods and waters" and "many sounds woven into one," all in a continual, dreamlike blend "confusing sense" with a blurring and yet an assertion of observable differences (ll. 336–41). The shape, in other words, as David Quint and Edward Duffy have noted,[96] is a product and reincarnation of that state which Shelley names "reverie," that regressive condition repeating infant perception where transference is so continual and widely employed that "we are con-scious of no [strict] distinction" between forms of whose difference we are vaguely aware. The figure is thus a mobile embodiment of and emergence from the most unre-stricted and primal interaction of differences, the "motion that produces mind," inso-far as Rousseau's shade can remember the time it first entered consciousness to any degree. Then, too, this composite of memory-traces, certainly including the initial attraction to a mother-figure that is one early result of infant reverie, goes on in the shade's vision to replicate the young Poet's production of his dream-maiden in the vale of Kashmir during *Alastor's* tale within a tale. That self-veiling fabrication, also woven out of transfers, we should recall, is itself a recasting of Rousseau's own process of constructing a feminine *beau idéal* in the youthful or recollective reveries he describes in his writings.[97] But the shape as it alters itself repeatedly in the shade's view of it—until what is left of Rousseau speaks to it, at any rate—reduces the dream-maiden from its eventual status in *Alastor,* that of being a personal ego-ideal combin-ing aspects of the projector alone, back into its foundation in and development out of "the woven sounds of streams and breezes" in the Poet's initial and "inmost sense" of her (*Alastor,* ll. 155–56). This lady-figure, we can even say, presses back through the self-mirroring veils that the *Alastor* Poet and the living Rousseau once cast over her to recover from repression the pre-imaginative *and* imaginative motion that brings all such projected formations about and denies them any permanently restrictive power over their projectors.

As a result, the shape resembles the "little soul" and the central disfiguring figure in *Epipsychidion* and "The Witch of Atlas,"[98] even to the point of intensifying both their liberating and their self-repressing levels. She repeats the *psychidion* mainly to the extent that she first recalls its *Alastor*-like genesis as an "intermixture, made / By love, of light and motion" and then replays that "Diffusion's" return from its suppres-sion behind substitute objects, at which point a "flash[ing]" and "Dissolving . . . res-piration" reasserts its drive to leap outside the limits of conventional man-woman relationships. Therefore, so long as the shade of Rousseau is in touch with this level of the figure, he is recontacting not simply the projective dream-process that transfer-ence can begin but the "woman" in himself (the Asia of Shelley's Prometheus), the becoming-other in his movement from thought to thought that has long been gendered as feminine in mythographic renderings of it. To the extent that the shade sees that dimension, moreover, he is looking at a new reveiling of the Witch of Atlas. The shape is not only born from an *aura seminalis* like hers that produces a figure in a cave from the interplay of light with water; despite beginning in what seems one enclosure, it also drifts among natural and literary locations with her playfulness, disruptiveness, and constant self-veiling in new forms and colors. The womb-cave in the mountain, like the Witch's cavern, we must admit, is a crossing between different texts, even some by Shelley, and really should generate this perpetually intertextual motion that recalls the multi-relational cave of Prometheus/Asia and then emerges from it more and more as free transference becoming "witch Poesy." Yet, even as this vision returns the shade and its listeners to the rootless "root" of the true poetic impulse, the mobile shape, again like the "little soul" and the Witch, can also manifest the ways its process often works to mask its actual nature. The figure's tendency to efface even its own previous formations, aided by the explicit forgetfulness that it holds out to any of its viewers, permits it be seen, as Shelley's Emilia sometimes is, only as a sort of Beatrice veiling "the Sun's image," hence as but a two-leveled figure with its other levels forgotten, giving a "sweet command" grounded on the authority of the deeper level (*Triumph*, l. 403). By imitating the hidden strategies of the Witch as she starts moving subliminally through Egyptian dreams, in fact,[99] the shape covers its underlying power so completely that the visible outpourings of its "obscure tenour" can make it seem "forever lost" (ll. 431–32). Viewing primordial transference again, as the dream-within-a-dream clearly does, can mean confronting both the continuous energy of transfiguration and the self-concealment in it that has kept it from consciousness.

This "dream" of humanity's and one person's beginnings viewed long afterward from the shade's perspective of death, we must conclude, is a thoroughgoing rereading of Western civilization's, Christianity's, Rousseau's, and even Shelley's texts, particularly as those texts are their renderings of the courses their "lives" have taken. To the Dantean and Petrarchan sense of death as a person's reduction to the once-hidden "primal drive" of his or her earthly existence, Shelley has added the eventual leap of those dead who "waged contention with time's decay" in *Adonais*—a group that includes Rousseau at his best (when he was "essentially a poet" by the standards of the *Defence*, p. 502n.)—to a level where their being read by others (as the shade is "read" by Shelley's narrator) brings out in their visions the transference at the root of their texts and thus behind their conceptions of life, self, and human nature.[100] Consequently, the shade of Rousseau in *The Triumph of Life*, urged by the speaker to explain Life's parade and how he first came to view Life both as and better than its victims do, is able to answer by seeing through the appearances of existence-as-perceived to his own earliest sense of how those appearances are generated in thought and, behind that sense, to the reverie-state of fluid intertransference from which those thought-patterns must originally have emerged. In exposing this last and most basic level, at least as it can be figured in an erotically attractive, self-veiling "shape" reminiscent of Rousseau's and Shelley's own reveries, the shade reveals how the different aspects of Shelley's metamorphic and trans-individual One are or can be related to each other. Simultaneously, though, it shows how all these aspects produce covers that conceal their basic process, partly in an effort to keep forgetting their past creations so that former ways of seeing can be transcended in newer relations of thoughts. That almost opaque veiling, we must realize, can bring on the sense of a lost Dantean Eden or a Wordsworthian "home" in heaven as what lies behind the moment (or stream) of forgetfulness, despite this poem's exposure of the movement that really underlies such forms of nostalgia. When the shade puts his lips to the cup of Nepenthe, then, and so brings on his earlier (yet for us later) version of the narrator's dream of Life, we, like the speaker, are poised between the possibilities of, on the one hand, observing the "shape's" constant and loving self-renewal (one way of forgetting past conceptions of life) and, on the other hand, confronting a concealment of that activity (the forgetting of itself that it permits but does not demand) which can lead to absolutist myths with unified centers.

This undersanding of *The Triumph*'s apparent "core," however, raises a great many quandaries for the reader and speaker about the visions of Life (the narrator's, then Rousseau's) that surround that "center" on both sides and even the structure of a poem that shows aspects of that "base" permeating the hellish existence that seems to forget it. We must confess that the shape's capacity for self-projection, along with its continuous, rapid outreach toward distant elements as though they were objects of its desire, is the very sort of process that psychologically drives the captives in the vanguard or the train of Life's triumphal chariot. Whether they "wheel" under the influence of "ghastly shadows [that] interpose / Round them and round each other" (ll. 171–72 in the narrator's own vision) or whether they are seen as constantly drawing "New figures [the sources of the commanding shadows] on [the] false and fragile glass" of a "world" supposedly outside them (ll. 246–47 in the shade's account), these "wretched" people are, as much as "Mitres [and] helms," "Signs of thought's empire over thought" (ll. 210–11). They reveal that their projections or objects are but thoughts sent forth or observed by other thoughts in acts of transference that, to keep the "empire" alive, are continually repeating their activity, the motion of the "shape all light." The forgetting of the shape, or at least its "waning" as an evening or early-morning star (or Venus) behind the glare of existence as usually perceived (ll. 412–19 and 429–31), is really not so much the loss on earth of one unified beauty or imagined perfection, the Platonic descent into everyday appearances that many have regarded as the theme of this poem.[101] It is more a "fall" in awareness from one consciousness of "bright" transference to another where that motion is still quite operative but is increasingly unacknowledged (or "dimmed" by a repression of it). Why does the poem emphasize the similar mobility in these different levels? How is it that the fall occurs as an extension of transference's ability to obscure itself? And what exact decision has Rousseau made, when he touches his lips to the cup, that brings on the vision of Life that *is* "fallen" awareness?

Even the car and the "form" of domineering "Life" itself, we should note, enact a self-concealing mobility while obscuring that "Mother" and claiming to leave her for dead (ll. 84–87). Driven by an appropriately "Janus-visaged Shadow" with four faces that (like transference) look ahead, outward, and backward, the chariot and the Life-figure "bear" a "dim" recollection of a faded light that they "deform" even further over time in a mantle of forgetfulness that resembles a "double cape" and thereby conceals the extent of the deformation (ll. 83–94). As a matter of fact, they do so not strictly under their own power nor that of the Shadow, but upon the "silent storm" of a "rushing splendour," a transpositional drive keeping itself out of sight, wherein "The shapes which [draw the car] in thick lightnings [are] lost" but where, as with the lady-shape's rain turning itself into faint sounds, there remains some poetic "music of . . . ever moving wings" audible on "the air's soft stream" (ll. 86–87 and 95–98). The chariot's motion is empowered, really, as Harold Bloom has shown,[102] by the self-overcoming, ever-aspiring, and mostly invisible "transumption" that has usually underwritten and permeated the very figure of the *Merkabah* or Divine Chariot, especially when it has appeared in the visions of Ezekial, Book VI of *Paradise Lost,* Shelley's own *Prometheus Unbound,* and the chariot of Holy Mother Church that Matilda ushers in on her side of Lethe in the *Purgatorio.* Yes, like Shelley's tyrannizing Moon in *Prometheus,* Life and its car may try to "temper" that light-producing energy into a "dun and faint etherial gloom" more fixed, impenetrable, and supposedly supreme (ll. 92–93), a version of the repression that occurs to different extents in the ultimately centered chariots of Ezekial, Dante, and Milton. But what permits the overall figure to produce that obfuscating palimpsest of veils is the transformative overcoming of previous figures, wheel surrounding wheel even in Ezekial, that the figure tries to dissociate from itself, despite that drive's being the one in the *Merkabah* that generates the refigurations in each version and the later embodiments of it. This figural movement can be denied by a form that so depends upon it only if the parts of the form, using the movement's self-veiling, simply blind themselves to the multi-directional process incarnated by them, much in the way the Janus-faced charioteer chooses to keep his eyes "banded" (l. 100). Moreover, that suppression can remain undetected only if it is supported, and even produced, by the determination of Life's worshippers to interpret an "eclipse" as more powerful and primal than "the true Sun it [has] quenched" (ll. 290–92). Why would "commanding" or "conquering" figurations and those who set them up, thereby losing all hope of any real "apprehension of life" ("On Life," p. 475), employ the self-concealment of transference so much against the transpositional motion within themselves? What makes them lose power over themselves, in the hope of gaining it, by forgetting the power of self-transcendence that is the freedom from dominance (the "transumption") they seek? Why is this loss of power focused on a *Merkabah* chariot and an amorphously "deform[ed]" central figure within it, all of which usually indicates power attained and ruthlessly celebrated?

Meanwhile, surrounding and subsuming these self-confining images, there is also the structure of Shelley's poem, a sequence of episodes that both employs and complicates the *Merkabah* pattern of wheel within wheel or appearance veiling appearance. We do not simply confront a vision of the narrator's, half-obscuring a waking dream-scene in the mountains, which is itself overlaid by Rousseau's explanatory tale, one that also contains a vision of Life's parade veiling a dream-scene centered on a mountain. The similarities, mixed with differences, between these visions and their veiling procedures are presented in a more intertangled and reversible succesion. The second vision (Rousseau's) is earlier and yet serves as a later interpretation of the first vision (the narrator's), even as the latter looks back to an earlier—or is it earlier?—rising of the Sun not unlike, but not the same as, the coming-forth of the "shape of light" described at a later point in the poem. "Each of these scenes," as Miller writes, "reverses the one before, exists inside it, and surrounds it as its explanatory enfolding container," so much so that any "next scene is adjacent to the one before, prior to it as its source, and later than it as its consequence, all at once."[103] The simultaneous recollection, present interplay, and turn toward future relations in the "shape all light" seem to filter, as a sort of provenance behind the visible narratives, into the episodes of the poem and the many different temporal connections between them. It is as if, although preconscious, the lady-figure's process kept an "obscure tenour" (l. 432) in every line or segment and behind every image, even of "fallen" Life. That is certainly what Rousseau's shade feels, even though his vision of Life's triumph has begun, when he senses the figure's process moving behind and "Through the sick day in which we wake to weep" as though she were still haunting him as "the ghost of a forgotten form of sleep" (ll. 430 and 428). Is Miller right, then, in viewing this poem as the piece where Shelley finally confronts the different levels of awareness as all inhabited by the self-destroying movement of language, so much so that there is no real difference between the levels?[104] Is there a genuine distinction between the speaker's view of the triumphal parade and the shade's interpretation of the same sight, considering that the latter is assisted by a glance in flashback at the "forgotten form"? Is the fall from level to level in fact impossible to prevent, given that the basis of all the levels appears the same and includes a forgetful process of self-erasure?

The Triumph of Life, I think, offers at least partial solutions to nearly all these mysteries. Indeed, Shelley's descriptions of Life's victims, once we link such moments to parallels in his earlier works, provide very direct responses to the first set of questions I have asked. The poem emphasizes a movement of transference existing in both the "shape" and the victims because Shelley wants to reveal, even more than he did during the pieces I discussed in Chapter 3, the multiple oppressions of the self by itself that occur when the motion that projects rain and a rainbow in front of an interplay of water with light is skewed into a domination of thought by its own projections regarded as existing "out there." All the different forms taken by tyrannical perversions of transference, usually highlighted one or two at a time in Shelley's other writings, reappear now together in intermingled frenzies of abjection where one such perversion quickly shades off into performing the actions of another, continuing yet further distorting the transference that brings each one about. The "Swift, fierce, and obscene" love-dancers in the chariot's vanguard (l. 137)—so reminiscent of the sinners driven by Lust in the *Inferno* and the "vain folk [who make love] their lord and god" in Petrarch's "Triumph of Love" (p. 8)—strain toward each other without any satisfaction because they have all enthroned a supposedly more perfect self, or ego-ideal, "her who dims the Sun" (l. 148), which now resides strictly outside and beyond them and to which no other figure is completely adequate, no matter how attractive a particular figure seems. Hence, like the lover in *Epipsychidion,* they fly toward and away from substitutes for the ultimate object "like moths by light attracted and [then] repelled" (l. 153). They even seek and turn away from the figures closest to the supposed Ideal because the brightness that appears to underlie those shapes also stands in front of the Sun without providing immediate access to it. Moreover, the lovers do all this in imitation of the others around them, "Kindl[ing] invisibly" with fires of longing only as they "Bend . . . within each other's atmosphere" (ll. 151–52). They are all infected by mimetic desire because they accept the belief that nearby people are more able than themselves to reach the projected objects of their wishes.

Other desirous figures around the chariot, too, whether or not they chase after love-objects per se, are revealed to be equally imprisoned by their self-enforced obedience to belief systems that are just as truly projections at bottom.[105] Seeking self-understanding and self-transcendence in some other construct that appears to grant such states to the projecting self, these victims attach themselves to a "lore" (l. 211), although it is but a reflection of their desires, that apparently offers ideological resolutions to the contradictory state of the human condition that forces each person to seek a "self" in and through some "other." The accepted ideology seems to gain even more defining power once it takes on the exalted symbolic force of "Mitres and helms" or philosophical "wreaths of light" (l. 210), whereupon the believing self is forced to worship such absolutes to attain "identity," however much the actual person realizes his or her loss of power in doing so. In addition, if the Absolute seems incarnated by an exalted person, institution, or position of rule, in spite of the fact that most ruling figures are self-oppressed in similar ways, then all those dependent on him or it must "tame / their spirits to the Conqueror" in the manner of ancient Roman citizens abasing themselves before the car of a triumphant general (ll. 128–29). Life as we know it is for Shelley, in part, a draining of self-images, or potentials for self-recreation, from their projectors toward the scrutiny of a "power" also projected beyond the control of the personal "will" (ll. 228–29). The will feels it must accept this "other" raised to the status of Other even as the same will resists the usurpation of its own prerogatives. Now the very willfulness that once attempted a projection finds itself cut off from and tyrannized by a fabrication of authority that it has produced, albeit with help from other wills, one that it half-resists and might recast if only it saw itself as retaining any powers of transformation. Consequently, for most people there is not just a "God" but a division between a commanding Outside and a devalued inside that has "made irreconcilable / Good [in the abstract] and the [personal] means" for attaining it (ll. 230–31). Worse yet, abasement under that ideology, that ejection of the power of transference by and from the self, leaves the abject person only with the option of a silent "mutiny within" that he keeps trying and failing to "repress" as he links his hope of power to a "morn of truth" removed from himself (ll. 213–14). Even if such a person appears to have authority and self-knowledge in the eyes of others, this tortuous effort makes him seek his identity in a way that half-blinds him, first to what he actually feels and then to what he should really know about the basis of any created and projected "selfhood."

This logic based on and yet denying primal transference is of course permitted by the motion's own tendency to efface its decentered activity. As thought carries through this drive, consciousness is encouraged by that concealment to forget how much thought-projections are transfer-based relocations of the thoughts about them. But there needs to have been an act of will that once intensified and misconstrued that effacement if Life is to be consistently perceived, as it is now, through the lenses of such constructs divorcing the will from power. The shade of Rousseau, in looking back on his and humankind's most persistent tendencies and errors, isolates that act when he remembers the brief moment in which he spoke to the "shape" of reverie and put his lips to her cup. He recalls that, like the *Alastor* Poet facing his dream-maiden, he asked the "shape" to "Shew whence I came, and where I am, and why," even to the point of trying to halt her movement "upon the passing stream" (ll. 398–99). His touching of the cup has therefore taken place only in the context of the lady-figure's urging him to "Arise and quench thy thirst" (l. 400), which he has interpreted as license to regard—and so to try penetrating—her as a figure externally harboring knowledge of his personal origins and reasons for being. Rousseau as this poem perceives him, the more he has sensed the various Ones of transference while supposedly "maturing" beyond the stage of reverie, has decided to construe the "shape all light" on the basis of a "thirsty" will to knowledge and a belief in objectification,[106] the stances used, then rejected, by Shelley's Prometheus and grimly maintained by Julian, Maddalo, the Maniac, Count Cenci, Orsino, and even Beatrice. This decision has naturally precluded all but a subliminal awareness, during Rousseau's life, of the process that both makes such stances possible and denies knowable objective centers outside transfer-relations between thoughts.

Rousseau has taken the self-veiling and self-displacing otherness of the reverie-process and chosen to see a shaping of it, first as a figure for himself possibly more grounded, complete, and all-knowing than its projector (since it *is* other than his desirous inadequacy) and then, consequently, as a palimpsest hiding knowledge of his foundations in "signifieds" behind all the veils and entirely outside the thoughts of the observer. The lady-figure's transfer-process has prompted him to seek and find his selfhood in this Other, but his desire for what seems a lost wholeness and thus for a reflected "identity" has led him to contort her motion, almost to stop it, so that it can serve as the representation of (or phallic Mother betokening) a repository of full knowledge and an objective truth. Rousseau has therefore accepted the figure's offer to drink the forgetfulness of the most established and absolutist beliefs, an offer that, on her side, may be no more than a promise to satisfy his "thirst" for self-transcendence by granting him the redefinition of multiple transfigurations. Yet he has not drunk thoroughly of the kind of forgetting she offers; he has only touched his lips to the self-forgetting in transference,[107] refusing to taste its full potential. He has then continued and covered that effacement with his longing for signs of knowable origins, the desire that traps the living Rousseau within Enlightenment objectivity throughout his quests for truth in the *Confessions* and Saint-Preux's search for the ideal essence in Julie and various Alpine settings.[108]

The result has been both a forgetting of the reverie-state and a transformation of his mind into a blank, sandy expanse covered with erasable tracks (ll. 405–7), which Duffy has aptly read as a Lockean *tabula rasa* that receives forgettable but insistent signs of supposed objects.[109] True, the first traces that can be remembered as crossing this space of inscriptions are those of a gentle and darting "deer" leaping playfully from point to point in the manner of the "shape all light" (l. 407). Nevertheless, this level of perception—and feminine process of sheer transference—is now washed away and quickly replaced by the still-visible "stamp" of the "fierce [masculine] wolf" (ll. 408–9) that has chased the deer off by ravenously seeking to grasp and consume her process as a singular entity or form of an essence, not a primordial "writing." It is this second attitude trampling out what is already obscured by its own trampling process that starts to make Rousseau, hence virtually everyone who does, envision and accept the triumph of Life, the victory of objective and knowing "signs" (the Outside) over a consciousness (or inside) that once knew the signs as but shapes of thought interpreted by other, backward-looking thoughts. That choice, though still driven by transference, is what has set up the external positions of power oppressing all Life's worshippers, whether these victims fill those positions with objectified ego-ideals, other people as standards for desire, ideological constructs, texts of truth, or targets of rebellion that seem only reenforced by all emotional "mutinies" against them.

For Shelley it requires no rapacious lust for power or totally overweening egotism to fall into or exploit this error, even though some of Life's followers are that fiercely wolfish. It is enough for one to be, as the shade of Rousseau now sees himself to have been, "overcome / By [one's] own heart alone" to the point of being unable to "temper [that heart] to its [actual] object" (ll. 240–43). The distance, admittedly, is sometimes small between the attitudes of those who are not "mid the mighty captives seen" (l. 135) and the stances of others remarkably close to them who are revealed to be abject victims. Socrates (he "of Athens" at l. 134) is not among Life's minions because, like Jesus Christ (of "Jerusalem" in the same line), he accepted a state-ordered death rather than view perceptions or words as signs of objects. He would not regard such figures as more than appearances deferring to counterparts in dialectical relations that announce a radical otherness in them all. Plato, his student and faithful scribe, on the other hand, despite avoiding obsessions with such "signs of thought's empire" as "gold . . . or sloth or slavery" (ll. 258–59), now follows the chariot because he took "fair" young men, reportedly including the boy Aster, to be "star[s] that ruled his doom" (l. 254). He behaved as if they were objective incarnations of absolutes that defined his existence instead of viewing them more skeptically as what they really were: figural substitutes for a Beauty projected by thought as much more distant and desirable than any one young man. The living Rousseau, meanwhile, turns out to have been equally poised between the self-liberating and self-confining impulses generated by transference. In Shelley's eyes by this time, Rousseau has died after regaining some contact with the process of reverie, occasionally even going so far in his last book (called *Reveries*) as to forget himself among vales with streams in "waves of desire" that reveal the "continual flux" of perceived existence.[110] He has also been able to contrast that state enough with the usual modern ways of living and perceiving to expose the "calamitous and diseased aspect which, overgrown as it is by the vices of sensuality and selfishness, is exhibited by civilized society" (Rousseau as paraphrased in the "Essay on Christianity," *CW*, VI, 248). Such a vision of Life makes him the perfect Virgil explaining existence from the margins, even as he is linked to some aspects, of what Shelley regards as Hell. At the same time, however, failing to recall the transferential motion in what they approach and so refusing to "temper" their responses to that never-completed process, these insights have led the "heart's" longings in Rousseau to propose a God behind the flux, to pursue the scientific knowledge of physical forms, to seek the complete self in a beautiful mother-figure or ego-ideal, and so to turn the reverie-process into the pursuit of a personal union with "objects" that have "often eluded my senses."[111]

Even so, what motivates this slip from a better to a "fallen" awareness, hence what answers my second set of questions about this poem, is not simply the gift of defining power to an objective Other. That status is granted to observable figures because of the projector's supposed need, the one felt by Prometheus when he enthroned Jupiter, to be *read* by external and "knowing" orders as organized in a particular way so that the "self" can seem cohesive, predictable, comprehensible, and thus able to feel itself the "master" of its multi-leveled situation. In *The Triumph* every captivated figure, including Rousseau at one time by his own account, emits many "phantoms" or self-images frantically desirous of contextualization and definition (l. 482), "dim forms" (l. 483) as hopeful of receptions by receivers as the filmy Lucretian *simulacra* that send images of the self toward observers from the bodies of material persons in *De rerum natura*.[112] As in Lucretius, where these almost invisible "resemblances" cannot be granted existence unless they are reflected back by some particular mirroring (or reading) surface (*De rerum*, IV. 98–109), the "diffused" figures of Shelley's vision are too multiple and indistinct to be precise definitions of the self, too much inclined to "fling" additional and different "shadows" beyond or behind already projected ones at the behest of transference (*Triumph*, ll. 487–88), unless they become "Wrought" by a completely external "ray" of light into pointed knowings of the self, as when the "Sun" appears to "shape the clouds" from above and beyond them (ll. 534–35). Consequently, the vast majority of people, who feel they cannot do without this "reading" that forces their self-images into a restricted identity, grant the power of the all-knowing "ray" to a Life objectified outside them as the provider of their rationales and foundations. They take their composite of perceived (and often power-seeking) personal qualities, which they are already inclined to project as an ego-ideal or more complete and knowing self, and transplant that construct into the chariot of seemingly dominant Life, or at least of the ideology that conceives of Life as more self-sufficient and knowledgeable than the subject perceiving it. She "who dims the sun" in this further conception becomes the very figure of Life itself (l. 148), and everyone caught in this belief system looks to her "car" to cast the "creative ray" on the "stuff" of perceived existence (l. 533), to transform the rapidity of imaginative transfer-projections (the "ray" of true Shelleyan creativity) into more fixed "Signs of thought's empire over thought" positioned as such by a "morn of truth" supposedly radiating down to them from on high.

The *Merkabah* is the perfect figure for incarnating this destructive projection so that we readers, all of us inclined to make such projections, can see that process for the killing of process that it really is. Because it is a "transumptive" action driven by metamorphosis and displacement in each version and from version to version, such a figure already mirrors the self-extending energy flowing through the psyche that looks to this sort of apparently self-sufficient form to be a reflecting Other defining the self. The same form, as early as Ezekial, also embodies the forgetting of transference, permitted by transumption's self-veiling, which allows a motion of shifts between positions and features to be viewed as an object hiding a permanent depth, the very status Rousseau has given to the "shape." The projector's mistaken and objectifying desire for an Other that supposedly harbors that "knowledge," another forgetting of the transference that motivates the desire, therefore seeks itself in something that resembles it—the only way anything can behold itself, for Shelley—by making the chariot the "knowing" source of the external "ray" that defines all projected self-images. What eventuates, not surprisingly, is the death of the self's expansion into myriad possibilities for fluid self-definition, and this strangulation, often of the self by itself, is carried out under the accepted dictates of a "knower" that is also a deadening of transference, Life as Death-in-Life in a very specific sense.

The traditionally invisible or heavily veiled "center" of the *Merkabah*, after all, is turned by Shelley into yet another reworking of Milton's amorphous Death.[113] Light-dimming Life, moreover, is not, like Demogorgon or Adonais, a dissolution truly inviting rebirth in a viewer's reading, but one firmly and restrictively "Crouching within the shadow of a tomb," refusing to proffer an interpretable image of itself, in its "double" covering of its mostly forgotten Mother, the "shape all light" (*Triumph*, ll. 89–90). To take this external and supposedly all-knowing locus to be an essence of existence, and thus a Foucauldian "grid of intelligibility" fixedly defining the place of the self in that existence, is to entomb the pursuer of identity in several death-drives at once. It is, first, to lock him into an established and presumably unchangeable reading, a "text" that makes him a dead letter (so he thinks) unable to expand the references and relationships of the elements in his figure. It is also to make death the projector's only and even predestined objective (as it was for the *Alastor* Poet and the Maniac), either as a point before reverie to which he regressively seeks to return or as an ultimate end to his Life, with no transfiguration after it, which arouses an existential despair. Life regarded as the sign of the essence can appear to hide a reabsorbing origin completely outside difference and change, an origin that must be death in order for it to be the "other side" of temporal existence; or it can seem to restrict future avenues of self-transformation so completely that the only self-transcendence available appears to be the Death that brings Life to a close. To see Life as controlling personal transfiguration, moreover, is to allow a sort of emperor over one's thoughts to drain the energy of transference from the desires of projecting human beings, leaving "The action and the shape" of such longings "without the grace / Of life" (which includes the power of transference), the grace they are, ironically, seeking to attain in their will to knowledge (ll. 522–23). This series of revelations counters, even as it uses, the eventual placement of God's grace in the ruling position of Petrarch's *Triumphs* (esp. pp. 107–8). Shelley's version points up how such a goal of desire initially promises a "One whose judgment will be sure" ("The Triumph of Eternity," p. 110) and then claims this One can be reached only through a Death that already sequesters the ego-ideal (as in "Happy the stone that covers her fair face" at the end of "Eternity" on p. 113). The attainment of absolute self-definition, if that is the objective linked with and used to suppress a more continual transference, becomes synonymous with the pursuit and worship of death, particularly the death of the motion that underwrites this entire effort. Clearly, as Petrarch has already shown without admitting the fact, the triumphal Chariot-figure and its really mobile "center" expose how easily a trans-fer-process (Shelley's oneness) can slip into and behind—and so be buried beneath—the veil of an absolutist sign (thus seeming to offer a traditional One), especially if a reader of such figures wants to cede his or her lust for knowledge to that sign enthroned as *the* reader of the self.

The ease of shifting from a fuller awareness of transference to this latter abasement under an Other's gaze, we should remember, has been underscored for Shelley in the months leading up to the writing of *The Triumph* by his immersion in part 1 of Goethe's *Faust*. The specific debts of *The Triumph* to *Faust* have been noted most extensively, though only briefly, by Duffy and F. Melian Stawell, the latter of whom points aptly at how much "the drowning of the fair Shape in the world's welter" reflects the early speeches of Goethe's title character in which Faust laments "our soul['s] surrender" to "a petty scope" that keeps us from striving after "the spirit's splendour" and its "fire-winged" motion across the spaces of "hope" (to quote Sta-well's translation of part 1, ll. 634–45).[114] But no one has seen how much Faust himself is tossed between impulses that veer both toward and away from the surrender he decries. Though his striving is in touch with the continual metamorphosis that gov-erns all existence, as Goethe's un-Christian Lord emphasizes in the "Prologue" (ll. 323–29, translated by Shelley in *PW*, p. 751), Faust chases after self-completion much of the time by "craving [a] truth" behind the "seals" of a "Nature, in veils, [who] will not let us perceive her" fully (ll. 666–74 as translated by Walter Kaufmann). He is held to a limited "heavy dawn" of objects visible only when the "light of day" is cast upon them (ll. 666 and 673) precisely because he will not work initially to transfigure what he sees, as metamorphosis actually bids him to do, but insists on locating the process and knowledge he would attain in singular, external forms that apparently harbor them behind opaque surfaces. Seeking transposition by that route means being driven, as *Epipsychidion* has revealed, from surface to surface (or self-image to self-image) until "What's better seems [no more than] an idle dream," to quote Faust again, and "the noblest urges" that "gave us our life . . . Are petrified in the earth's vulgar surges," making the questor feel perpetually "dwarfed in impotence" like the victims of Shelleyan Life (*Faust* 1, ll. 638–39 and 613, tr. Kaufmann).

It is because Doctor Faust is inclined toward the right awareness by way of these misguided and repressive methods that Mephisto can even think of tempting him toward the Goethean damnation of a resigned imprisonment within "sensuality's abysmal land" (l. 1750 of part 1). It is this latter inclination, in fact, that permits Mephisto to draw his "master" toward Margarete as a bodily form of the "paragon of womanhood" (l. 2601), even though she cannot finally sustain the unfair pressure on her to symbolize an ego-ideal. The same attraction finally directs Faust to seek the *Walpurgisnacht* revels in which ultimate objects of desire seems to lie behind the "numbing" figures of "enchanted phantom[s]" that are projected as such by their enslaved observers and that doom those projectors to be turned to stone (or fixed postures) if they gaze too long at such Medusas (ll. 4176–4209, tr. by Shelley in *PW*, esp. pp. 761–62).[115] All the while, though, Faust is aware that this will to objective knowledge is but a limited aspect of a larger movement of desire that should not stop there. "Loath[ing] the knowledge [he has too frequently] sought," he also wants to grasp in his forays the self-transcending "restless activity" of dissatisfaction with any single Other or personal posture (ll. 1749 and 1759, tr. Kaufmann). The consequent hovering in his thoughts and speeches, left unresolved in part 1, between living and killing forms of transference (or true and false senses of the One) leads to Shelley feeling caught as he reads this *Tragödie* between the despairing "gloom" and the hopeful and striving "rapidity" of thought that we have seen him mention in one of his letters of 1822. As a further result, all the major figures and symbols in *The Triumph*—Rousseau, the speaker, the chariot, the "etherial gloom" of Life itself, and even the most benign projectors of self-images seeking knowledge of themselves—are presented as similarly oscillating between both inclinations at key points. The ease of shifting from a "bright" to a "dun" awareness manifestly comes from being positioned at this fulcrum of choice by the movement of displacement and substitution that permits each figure to consider both possibilities.

Indeed, I now want to argue, it is the purpose of this poem's structure—and even of Shelley's "obscure" linking of that structure with the movement of the "shape all light"—to situate both the narrator and the reader at that Goethean fulcrum. The answers to my third set of questions about *The Triumph,* in other words, lie in this deft employment of closely related but different episodes, for Shelley has taken the posing of moral choices in the *terza rima* dream-visions of Dante and Petrarch and reworked their designs to give his narrator and reader the option of choosing between repressed and accepted transference, between the all-centering One of Dante, Petrarch, Calderón, and Rousseau himself or the revisionary, self-decentering One of Goethe and Shelley. The reading and recasting of the narrator's vision by the shade's is made similar enough to and yet distinct enough from what immediately precedes it that one can choose how to read the relationship. One can opt for a monological reading that suggests no real options posed by this doubling, or one can see the shade's interpretation as forcing all its readers to confront alternatives that the narrator (and perhaps the reader) does not sufficiently consider during the first sixty stanzas of the poem.

On the one hand, Miller does have some license from the text for his sense that all the levels of awareness in the piece finally uncover the same production and destruction of signifier-relations. There are in fact such similarities as the one between the "seeing and blinded vision" in the chariot and its worshippers (as the narrator perceives them at ll. 44–106) and the "remembering and forgetting" in the dream of the "shape" (as these are recalled by Rousseau's shade at ll. 335–94).[116] The paradoxes in both places, too, which seem unsought (though perhaps accepted) by the particular figures involved, appear generated, as Miller says, by an "impersonal energy of troping" that operates "both inside and outside the encompassing and encompassed consciousness of the poet." On the other hand, however, the second of these visions, partly by being the earlier of the two and more clearly prior (though leading up) to a "wolfish" reading based on objectification, can be interpreted both as exposing the tropic activity that underlies the blinded sight of Life and as being an enactment of the recreative "trampling" in that "energy" which allows its own process to shift beyond any single enslavement under one projection. The vision of the shape, in short, deconstructs, even as it rereads and explains, the forgetful vision of the narrator.[117] Rousseau's shade reveals a free, playful, and ever-shifting action of transposition as basic to yet more mobile and self-surpassing than the centered projections of Life, all of which are therefore exposed as blind to their "grounding" in a decentering activity and sadly oppressed by the fixed absolutes they have set up in its place. That radical re-vision defines the initial sighting of Life's triumph as the result of one choice that may, but does not have to, be made in the face of transference's self-veiling procession. It takes the shade's analysis of what the narrator has seen, we can say, to expose the oft-forgotten existence of options, the very ones that the entire poem also presents to the reader in the way its episodes are made both repetitious and juxta-posed. This progression from one state of awareness to at least the possibility of a deeper one repeats, to a degree, the widening of perspective in Dante's *Comedy* and Petrarch's *Triumphs,* where each advance in level (particularly from *Purgatory* to *Paradise* and "The Triumph of Time" to "The Triumph of Eternity") asks the "I" and the reader to reinterpret the figures they have just beheld to see a hidden "law" in them that reverses the observer's initial reactions ("Triumph of Eternity," p. 95). In the rereading of Shelley's *Triumph,* however, there is less of a thorough transcendence in the shift from vision to vision—the shade of Rousseau being another Virgil who has lived *within* the Hell he now describes from its margins—and more of a probe into the decision that has prevented the transfiguration of people and into the eternal but decentered potentials behind this "fall" that have helped bring it on, remain resistant to it, and still govern some of its motions from a place of exile. Consequently, *The Triumph of Life* highlights a moment of choice, hints at the better choice, and laments the effects of the wrong choice so often made throughout Western history, even as the poem's organization allows the reader either to see or to ignore the fact that there is a choice.

Miller errs, it seems to me, albeit in a way half-encouraged by the poem, when he regards the shade as caught in exactly the same bind as the narrator. The narrator is encountering without knowing it the consequences of a wrong decision already made by most people—and perhaps at times by the speaker himself, considering his view of the Sun as a dominant patriarch (l. 18) who has rightfully "imposed" tasks on "mortal . . . things" (ll. 20 and 16–17) that proceed to worship this Father from "smokeless altars" (l. 5). To be sure, the narrator's "waking dream" (l. 42), in the tradition of revealing and psychomachic dream-visions, at least partially exposes the common, daylight sense of both existence and the "morn of truth" as the "energy of troping" turned into a tyranny of thought's constructs over the thoughts producing them. The narrator is even dimly aware of a repressive process in the figures he beholds, particularly when he confronts Life's chariot as half-recalling/half-forgetting a "ghost" it has "deformed" and when he interprets the car's movement as what is left when the wave of an "Ocean's wrath" has effaced the markings that were previously there on what now seems a "desert shore" (ll. 163–64). But he does not know what is repressed or what empowers the repression. Indeed, he is in danger of being sucked even more into the triumph of Life than he already is, since he is inclined to read this *Inferno* parade in an excessively Platonic manner, the way so many people have, as though the covered "Sun" were an all-commanding light at one with itself while Life's victims were not. The shade's explanatory revision is necessary to rescue the narrator from a quest foredoomed to error, and rescue is possible only because the shade has faced the key choice (as he never quite did in his lifetime) and so has escaped from the very bind into which the narrator is about to be thoroughly drawn. Although the living Rousseau allowed himself to be "swept" into the way of thinking that keeps enthroning Life (ll. 460–68), there was enough questioning of such assumptions in his work that his ghost's relocation after his death in the poetry of a later and even more revisionist writer permits the shade to recast each repetition of the narrator's vision with a telling difference, a re-troping of troping, which makes what has been repressed return to consciousness. The narrator and the most alert readers of this second vision are consequently given the opportunity to see that one can decide between the masculine, "dimming" objectivity that a person is empowered (now sorely tempted) to accept and the electric extension of light-refactions that one can learn to think with in loving, "feminine" dispersals of the changeable self. The shade of Rousseau, as the narrator cannot, shows explicitly how that is the quandary with which primal transference confronts human thought. In the face of the reverie-figure, he now recalls, one is "Suspended," Faustlike, between "desire and shame" (ll. 394–95), the desire to penetrate what seem to be veils hiding a deeper origin and shame at the prospect of thereby violating—and forgetting—an outward-tending process of love.

The movement of the "shape all light," it turns out, has been allowed to disseminate its contradictory tendencies throughout the structure of this poem and then to be seen from different levels of awareness as one vision displaces another in that structure, so that the main speaker and, after him, the reader can themselves be placed in suspension between the different ways of reading and thinking made possible by transference. The shape as the shade of Rousseau views her upon speaking to her, we must remember, is suspended herself between the repression and expansion of her motion and so can prompt denials or realizations of her actual process. Given that fact, many different attitudes are potentially instigated, even validated, by the poem built around her, stances as varied as the many recent but conflicting interpretations of *The Triumph* (certainly the most debated work that Shelley ever wrote). Facing some difference between the visions of the shade and the narrator but still pursuing the absolute center sought—and even connected with the Sun—in the first of the poem's episodes, a reader, once encouraged to forget transference, can see either both visions together or the first one alone as signs of a failure to leap past the world of appearances to a monolithic One Light attainable beyond everyday perception. Such a view, or versions of it, can even regard Shelley, identified with the narrator, as falling back on beliefs close to those of Dante and Petrarch, possibly to the point of using *terza rima* to intimate the oneness of a repeated triad-pattern or to imply a symmetry always turning in on its center so as to reveal a continuing, though hidden, essence. It is equally possible, as it happens, to accept the reverse (and Gnostic) side of this position, wherein the attempt to penetrate appearances or to embody ego-ideals within physical forms must be viewed as fruitless and frustrating, as a sentence to a psychological death or Hell of worshipped icons that are flatly unable to carry their worshippers to the beauties really sought by desire. Within this belief a person should either accept desire as being confined to what the senses perceive[118] or despair at the distance between perceptions and the light of truth—or regard any level immediately beyond the one we see as likely to be just as filled with change, decay, and incompleteness as the one we now behold. The poststructuralist variation on this stance, meanwhile, should see the desire to surpass language as created and confined by the movement of language itself, a movement which therefore reasserts itself any time that the world of signs seems to have been penetrated or overcome by its users. Perhaps, to avoid such impasses, the reader should see confinement within projections as a personal failure of the imagination in many people, even Rousseau and the narrator. Then the "shape" can be regarded as an ideal the imagination can create on its own from the mind's ingredients at any time, compared to which the remnants of such ideals pursued as entirely outside the self are objects of thought sadly disconnected from the ability of the mind to remake or transcend them. The poem can suggest to at least some readers, in other words, that the worship of old constructs or supposed objects of science should be replaced by a devotion to what produced both them and the scientific sense of them: the power of the individual psyche.

Yet the poem also offers moments, as we have seen, which can be read as showing that these interpretations, whether they are finally affirmative or despairing, actually continue and reinforce the triumph of externalized "Life" over thought. Even the temptation to replace the worship of objectified projections with a valuing of the personal imagination can be the pursuit of yet another exalted image of the self. This stance ignores the transpositional and socially oriented drive behind projections of the self's own features outside the self, failing to acknowledge the impersonal transfer that causes a person to speak of the imagination as an entity "over there" subject to the mind's "objective" scrutiny. Granted, the narrator—hence the reader—is enabled by the poem's self-obscuring series of veils over transference to take any one of the foregoing positions, if he (or she) chooses, and so submit to Life even more than he has. "If [an objectivist] thirst for knowledge doth not ... abate" as a result of the second vision in the poem, the shade tells the narrator (ll. 195–96), "Follow [the parade of Life] even to the night" of death, since that is what "you" (the narrator) will really be doing in any case. At the same time the second vision and the early stanzas of the poem as we look back on them from that new perspective can prompt the narrator and us readers to refuse all those stances for the sake of more fluid, relational, unselfish, and transfer-based understandings. The "shape all light" seen as a form of the One can then be read as an eternal motion both entering into and reconfigured by the imagination, as in fact a motion interrelating and altering several eternal drives that helps generate but finally shifts beyond the Ones of Dante and Petrarch. Shelley's opening-out of *terza rima* in the poem—his more frequent use of enjambment, verbs, disruptive rhythms, and sentence-patterns that cross from stanza to stanza, breaking the attempted self-containment of each in Dante and Petrarch[119]—can now be noticed more and revealed as an insistence on the deferral of figure to figure in defiance of older attempts to make verbal triads betoken centered trinities. That deferral, moreover, can be understood both as keeping any sign or projection from uniting with any referent sought by the visible figure and as urging every figure to expand its possibilities, as the "shape" surely does, in a transfer toward others that revive what they recast. The incompleteness in signs can be seen and then used as a renewal and extension of hope rather than its limit, denial, or death. The imagination, too, can happily come to see its function not as the worship of its own objectified power but as the release, realization, and extension of such renewals in "vitally metaphorical" reveilings of existence as currently perceived.

Even so, these potentials, forcefully implied as they are (especially by the "shape"), are stated indirectly in the poem, for the most part, so much so that they can easily be avoided by anyone choosing not to read them there. The suspension between suppressing and announcing transference in the "shape," particularly as it is replayed by the entire structure in which she appears, finally leads to the problem of whether the narrator and the reader will perceive the suspension, the choice it offers, the desirability of one choice over the other, or the difference between life-constricting and liberating readings. The poem becomes, in a sense, the posing of a question not finally answered in a discourse left blatantly incomplete.[120] Therefore, near the end of the long verse-fragment that we have, the narrator asks a form of that question by wondering, "Then, what is Life?" (l. 544). This query is the very one that Shelley posed himself in the essay "On Life" over two years earlier, and in this poem, as in that short excursus, the quandary of the speaker stems from the distancing of the answer in the very asking of the question. The confusion of the narrator must be stated in words so explicitly announcing the otherness of their referent from themselves because, as in the shade's dream of an antenatal state, "our birth is unremembered and our infancy remembered but in fragments"; because we "live on" as observers of signs now divorced from definite origins, "we lose the apprehension of life" in living it out and probing its signifiers ("On Life," p. 475, right after "What is life?"), certainly far more than we lose our beginnings in Wordsworth's "Immortality" ode. To keep seeking to "penetrate the mystery of our being" with words pointing to signs of the inaccessible, as Wordsworth did not see, is to increase our distance from the goal by adding signs to signs (p. 475). Worse yet, it is to load too much significance into the signs taken as the objects of thoughts and words, to contort them into "things" that "remain unchanged" by interpretation and so confine us in our efforts to reach beyond them (p. 478). The utterance "what is Life?" could then reflect "an education of error" (p. 477) if "Life" is finally taken by the questioner or reader to be a knowable object or essence.

If, however, the question assumes or leads to an acceptance of its own divorce from absolute knowledge, if it regards "Life," like "cause," as "only a word expressing a certain state of the human mind" as it relates thoughts to each other (p. 478), this utterance can see itself as little more than an extension of desirous "Thoughts and feelings" aware of "our ignorance to [and of] ourselves" (pp. 475–76). These feelings and thoughts, in turn, can now more clearly sense an oft-forgotten movement within themselves, "looking before and after," which turns toward both "the future and the past," leaving a man "not what he is, but what he has been, and shall be" (p. 476). In this view of the question, which celebrates (rather than laments) the passing of the past, Life as a state of subjection to objective "impressions" is replaced by a reveling in transference without a longing for final knowledge, the true "freedom in which [the mind] would have acted, but for the misuse of words and signs" (p. 477). Just as both options are possible—although the second is more difficult for people to choose—in "On Life," so they both remain potential contexts for the question and the anticipated answers in *The Triumph*. There the use of "what is" in the narrator's query still threatens to but has not yet decided (since "is" is not followed by the objective case) to make a hard-and-fast object out of perceptible Life. If anything, now that the narrator has had a chance to observe all the ways of reading empowered by the poem, he is more hesitant than ever regarding—hence his asking about—what interpretations should be chosen for his question and any proposed rejoinders.

The beginning of the shade's response, too, broken off in mid-sentence as well as mid-line, leaves us just as uncertain as the narrator seems, almost as though the poem had to be left a fragment to be "true" to itself.[121] The shade appears to be turning toward a positive and clearly transfer-based alternative to what the speaker has beheld when Rousseau's ghost prefaces his answer by casting "His eye upon the car . . . as if that look must be the last" (ll. 545–46). But then the shade says, "Happy those for whom the fold / Of" (ll. 547–48) before Shelley stops writing for what may have been the last time. Donald Reiman and Kenneth Neill Cameron maintain that these lines, in a recollection of the "folding" or evening star under which shepherds lead their sheep to the "fold" in Milton's *Comus* (l. 93), echo the chorus in *Hellas* when it calls on future Greeks to "follow Love's folding-star / To the Evening land!" (ll. 1029–30).[122] If that is the case, the "fold" is no longer "a sunnier strand" in the sense of

America's shore (as in *Hellas,* l. 1028) but is the evening star into whose position the "shape all light" seems to have withdrawn when it is obscured by the parade of Life's objectified signs. "Those" folded into that withdrawal, meanwhile, are most likely to be the "sacred few," including but not limited to Socrates and Jesus, "who could not tame / Their spirits to the Conqueror [Life], but as soon / As they had touched the world with living flame / Fled back like eagles to their native noon" (*Triumph,* ll. 128– 31). There have been certain highly imaginative beings, those in the class of an Adon- ais/Keats, in other words, who have died before their natural time (hence into an "Evening land") and who, like the most visionary Greeks, have refused the objectifi- cation made possible by the self-concealment of transference. They can be viewed as having stayed (in their "living flame") with a full attachment to genuine transference, even to the point of having retreated with it from Life into an oft-forgotten eternity of transfers (their "native noon"), where they now survive in memory, with the "shape," as distant "winds of light."[123]

The trouble is that this answer does not really apply to the situations of the nar- rator or the likely reader. Both are oscillating—as the "sacred few" have rarely done— between a forgetting of transference in a desire for objectified identities or ultimate answers and a longing (increased as the poem proceeds) for the reverie-state that hov- ers dimly behind or within the world of objects with a promise of continual and real self-transcendence. The narrator's hesitation even appears in the way he views the nearly forgotten "shape all light" as a star that now seems either an absolute on high or the dim memory of a dream (another realm of evening) that fades with the coming of Life's blinding day. The shade at this point has responded to "what is Life?" by starting a portrait of those who do not really have to ask such a question, possibly because he is now placing himself in that exalted company by refusing to gaze on the parade of Life again. Perhaps this fact, its failure to answer the question, and the impasse that clearly results are what caused Shelley to break off at this point, maybe with the intension of returning to the problem. At the same time, though, the structure and progression of the poem have so effectively placed the narrator and reader at a point of deciding between continued "fall" and "reverie restored" (a new sort of par- adise lost or regained) that there really is very little left for the poem to do but to pose the problem it reveals, suggest alternative attitudes toward the problem, raise the resulting question of what life is or should be in our eyes, and leave all resolutions of this quandary to beings and times outside those in the poem.

Clearly, Shelley's replacement of a fixed and centered One with a self-decentering motion that uses the same name cannot finally achieve on its own, just as *Prometheus Unbound* and the *Philosophical View* cannot, the revolutions in understanding at which the poet has always aimed. Because his questioning of Western belief systems must use the very "words and signs" it often resists—since transference conceals its operation behind the signifiers of its older refigurations—the success of Shelley's cri- tique may result in its failure, in an erasure of its revelations by any reading of its signs. Then, too, the writer and/or the reader of an iconoclastic work may frequently submit, even in the work, to the temptations that transference holds out at the risk of its own suppression: to quests in self-projections for resolutions or fixed identities, to attachments to particular systems of discourse (the supposed reflectors of the self) that work to constrict those who seek definition in them, or to longings, as transfers look toward a past, for causes or origins outside any interplay of thought-relations. Indeed, if the narrator is a persona of Shelley, as his "I's" almost always are, *The Triumph of Life* points even to its author as drawn by these temptations (still) in his own will to knowledge all the while that he is appalled by visible renderings of such tendencies in himself. At the very least, Shelley—hence each of his verbalized projections and sympathetic readers—hesitates between stances at the end of his career,[124] even though the revisionary Ones of the "Essay on Christianity," the *Defence of Poetry, Epipsychidion,* "The Sensitive-Plant," *Hellas, Adonais,* and *The Triumph* itself have offered a conscious submission to their mobility as the key to the free and genuine expansion of human possibilities, personal and cultural. Given the choice of responses offered by the very transference of which he has become increasingly conscious, this poet so thoroughly in touch with the many possible turns in the "train of thoughts" must finally expose the possibilities for himself and for us rather than too simply or myopically (and thus tyrannically) impose a definite choice, especially since he is unclear, even in his own thinking, about which act of will is needed to release transference from repression. As "On Life" puts the matter, thought can be restored to the freedom now denied to it by misused words and signs only if the "political and ethical questions" raised by poetic discourse first expose the "roots of error," then present the remaining quandaries, and finally defer to an unpredetermined "vacancy" in which a decision has yet to be made (*NCE,* p. 477).

It is quite fitting, we might even say, that the questions left for us by *The Triumph of Life* come down to the choice between stances that is allowed by transference, the "root" both of error and of its reversal. This choice is the one being intimated in various ways, though never quite so blatantly, during most of Shelley's earlier writings. Once the young Shelley has half-consciously confronted the problem by noting both the appeal and the disruptive motions in the absolutes he embraced early in his career, the hesitation (or, in rhetorical terms, aporia[125]) between views of existence as it might be perceived appears again and again, despite the very different orientations of the different works. It is there in the *Alastor* Narrator's sense (really anticipating the shade of Rousseau's) of a mobile "Mother" of Nature who can also seem an originating essence; in the continual self-displacements of "Intellectual Beauty" that can make even revolutionary thinkers use Godlike names for its "Power"; in the "coming down in likeness" of "Mont Blanc" that can look back up to a level different enough from the present motion to seem removed from all process; in the "upthrowing" of an anthropomorphic God that comes from the same projection by which the self can behold its greater possibilities in the eyes of a sibling-lover; in the "knowing" of the self in a mythic mirror that may turn round on the self to bind it, as the enthroning of Jupiter binds Shelley's Prometheus; in the placement of "true identity" in another figure who can become an imitated rival threatening violence against the self (until a scapegoat is found in a Maniac or a Beatrice); in the synaesthetic reference of one sense-perception or one sort of perceived object to another that can make Nature seem the interlaced emanation of one mind; in the delegation of labor-management to one or two classes that can then refuse, as in the *Philosophical View,* to return the proceeds of labor's products to the actual laborers; in the attempt of desire—and the words it often uses—to defer the completion of reference beyond the interplay of still-separate differences, particularly in *Epipsychidion,* only to discover more differentiations and to try deferring beyond them until difference seems transcended (although it can never be); in the repetition of perceived historical events with some differences that can be recast, the way Mahmud recasts it in *Hellas,* as the exact repetition of age-old patterns;

in the elegiac image of death, exposed in *Adonais,* that can seem either a reference to an irrecoverable loss or a redirection of the dead being's supposed significance; and in the simultaneous forgetting and recalling of the reverie-state, as thought grows away from it, which allows it to be seen as either the sign of a singular origin or a primal activity that denies any singularity separate from the interplays of perception and reflection. In each case a process of transference inviting interpretation can be read as devolving back on a commanding center at one with itself or as transfiguring its own past motions in revolutionary extensions of the thought-connections it has already formed. The key figural relations are poised in every text between licensing assumptions that imprison thinking under hegemonic strictures or prompting "vital metaphors," unforeseen analogies, that shift beyond yet from within the limits of previous strictures. Transference, after all, is similarly poised itself whenever it has broken out of and past existing constructions and looks back, nevertheless, to particular points of departure that seem to "ground" the newest regroundings of awareness.

As I suggested in my introduction, Shelley is usually confident that truly metaphorical writing has the chance of at least prompting readers to see this basic aporia and then feel the attraction of the as yet "unapprehended relations" being formed in such texts. Yet the resurgence of iconoclastic "electricity" in a truly poetic work for him, as we saw in the passage from the *Defence* with which I began this study, still depends on "conductors" deciding to draw out the reformative current from within the "veils" in which it lies partially hidden. Because the verbal constructs with which a disruption begins are suppressions of transference initially understood by most readers as dissociated from that motion, the reformist writer or speaker, to avoid just talking to himself or herself, must couch his or her disruptions in the symbolic orders they disrupt. Witness Shelley's presentation of "thought's eternal flight" as the "One." Such was the tactic employed, we have seen this poet claim already, even by Jesus Christ at his most revolutionary when he "accommodated his doctrines to the prepossessions of those whom he addressed," virtually "compelled" as he was "to practice this misrepresentation of [his] own feelings and opinions" ("Essay on Christianity," *CW,* VI, 242–43). Modern readers can, as indeed they often do, choose to continue Shelley's partial "misrepresentation" of himself to the point of accepting him as a thinker and poet tied, at least somewhat, to the metaphysics of self-sufficient Centers that underwrote the social hierarchies he challenged. But we can also—as I have been arguing we should—decide to focus more than we have on his skillful process of deconstructing and transposing the Western hegemonies he uses. We can look as we read his works henceforth for his probe into the patterns he employs, his recovery of the transfer-action making those patterns possible (at least in the past), his drawing of that action into the revisionary wording that must be based upon it in order to be disruptive, and his suggestions that we can perform a similar critique and reconstitution in our mental or actively reformist approaches to all the ideological constructs that now confine us. His writing can be the catalyst in its recovery of transference from within the thinking that still keeps it obscured, yet it is up to us to transfer this motion into our own thought, discourse, and social actions. We must deliberately face the quandaries posed in the writing and understand that transference has both posed them and can resolve them if we accept its most radical drives in a true "going out of ourselves."

Shelley's final question, in a sense, of course, is "will we?" We, in turn, can begin to show that we will by asking questions of ourselves, energized by his poetry, questions similar to those he asks at the end of his career of himself and of nearly every figure in (or reader of) his writing. Will we choose to be more conscious than we usually are of transference's pre-conscious provenance in our thinking and in the language that creates patterns of thought? Or will we forget its generation of Western thought's most hegemonic concepts (such as the "One") to the point of losing a sense of the "eternal" impulse (or "flight") that can best undermine those repressions of it? Will we regard the association of remembered perceptions as enlargements of thought's "circumference" forming additional "intervals and interstices" to be filled by later associations, or will we see such interactions as attempts to recover a pre-relational unity to which we must subject ourselves? Will we see the onslaught of perceptions of existence as thrust upon us by a deeper, absolute "Power" or as simply shifting from one mental level toward the revisions fashioned at another? Will we take our transfer-based need to "know ourselves" by way of others' responses or self-projections as an urge to abase ourselves under the standards of "all-knowing" Others? Will we keep granting the power of definition to one side (such as the *male* side) of a relationship that really offers "identity" to the figures within it only as they keep looking to each other in an interplay without a primary term? Will we regard love, transference as felt and extended emotionally, as limited to or coming forth from a single figure, or can we redefine it as a "going out" from anyone who can transport his or her thinking into someone else's situation, a going out to the situations of as many others as time and life permit? Are the discourse-patterns in which we usually fashion and extend ourselves to be regarded as powerfully entrenched or constantly open to revision? In a similar vein, are social class structures to be regarded as firmly established or as increasingly blurred, as inclined to channel the results of production in one class-direction or as turning toward a wide redistribution of once-hoarded resources (another "going out of ourselves")? Can human beings, to be even more precise, avoid the polarization of classes or races or sexes or nationalities that makes each one think itself an identity unto itself and thereby licensed to maintain that identity by doing violence to outsiders? In the late work that most explicitly tries to redefine the Western "One" as an "eternal flight" of relational and not bipolar thought, Shelley leaves us with this last question and all the others that funnel into it, asking his Greek chorus and us to hope against hope for a revision of thought that will leave our worst moral choices behind us:

> O cease! must death and hate return?
>   Cease! must men kill and die?
> Cease! drain not to its dregs the urn
>   Of bitter prophecy.
> The world is weary of [this] past,
> O might it die or rest at last! (*Hellas*, ll. 1096–1101)

Notes

INTRODUCTION: THE LOGIC OF TRANSPOSITION

1. Many scholars have noted this fact, yet none has finally pursued it to the point of confronting its non-Platonic and nonempirical foundations. Examples of such assessments range from Frederick A. Pottle, "The Case of Shelley," *PMLA,* 67 (1952) 589–608, to William Keach, *Shelley's Style* (New York: Methuen, 1984), pp. 118–53.

2. Here, except in parts of his sense of tradition, Shelley anticipates the valuing of "temporal distance" in Hans-Georg Gadamer, to whom I am indebted whenever this distance reappears in my argument. See Gadamer's *Truth and Method,* ed. and trans. Garret Barden and John Cumming (New York: Seabury Press, 1975), esp. pp. 258–74. For more on Shelley thinking this way in one of his best-known but least-interpreted lyrics, see William Freedman, "Postponement and Perspectives in Shelley's 'Ozymandius'," *Studies in Romanticism,* 25 (1986), 63–73.

3. In *Paradiso,* XXVII. 13–21 and 40–45.

4. See Stuart Curran, *Shelley's Annus Mirabilis: The Maturing of an Epic Vision* (San Marino, CA: Huntington Library, 1975), pp. 156–72.

5. The most thorough discussion of this interaction of stanza forms in "the West Wind" is François Jost, "Anatomy of an Ode: Shelley and the Sonnet Tradition," *Comparative Literature,* 34 (1982), 223–46.

6. The best sense of how these "causes" interact during the poet's early years is still the one in Kenneth Neill Cameron, *The Young Shelley: Genesis of a Radical* (1950; rpt. New York: Collier, 1962), esp. pp. 52–147. See also A. M. D. Hughes, *The Nascent Mind of Shelley* (Oxford: Clarendon, 1947), esp. pp. 38–73.

7. The words I quote here are from Pottle, "The Case of Shelley," p. 590, an account more Plotinian than most. But the argument for Shelley as a consistent Neoplatonist (and Plotinian) has persisted for many years and continues to be made. The strongest mid-twentieth-century statements are in Carl Grabo, *The Magic Plant: The Growth of Shelley's Thought* (Chapel Hill: Univ. of North Carolina Press, 1936), pp. 170–84, 226–48, and 350–70; *PS,* pp. 14–371; Richard Harter Fogle, *The Imagery of Keats and Shelley* (Chapel Hill: Univ. of North Carolina Press, 1949), pp. 215–40; and Neville Rogers, *Shelley At Work,* 2nd ed. (Oxford: Clarendon, 1967), esp. pp. 14–194. Rogers even repeats these views in his more recent notes for the *CPW.* Mean-

while, the more strictly Plotinian line has been presented most clearly by Peter Butter, *Shelley's Idols of the Cave* (1954; rpt. New York: Haskell House, 1969), pp. 90–134, and by Ross Grieg Woodman, *The Apocalyptic Vision in the Poetry of Shelley* (Toronto: Univ. of Toronto Press, 1964), pp. 3–72. The argument for Shelley as Platonic has also been revived quite recently in Tracy Ware, "Shelley's Platonism in *A Defence of Poetry*," *SEL*, 23 (1983), 549–66; Carlos Baker, *The Echoing Green: Romanticism, Modernism, and the Phenomenon of Transference in Poetry* (Princeton, NJ: Princeton Univ. Press, 1984), p. 27; and Patricia Hodgart, *A Preface to Shelley* (London: Longman, 1985), pp. 78–92.

8. Here I refer mainly to James Rieger, *The Mutiny Within: The Heresies of Percy Bysshe Shelley* (New York: Braziller, 1967), esp. pp. 207–21. Harold Bloom's early sense of Shelley, however, also turns more and more in this direction, especially after it dispenses with the terms of Martin Buber. See Bloom, *The Visionary Company: A Reading of English Romantic Poetry,* revised from the 1961 edition (Ithaca, NY: Cornell Univ. Press, 1971), pp. 342–50. For a very recent—and essentially Christian—version of this reading, see Andrew J. Welburn, *Power and Self-Consciousness in the Poetry of Shelley* (London: Macmillan, 1986), esp. pp. 1–7, 144–66, and 186–97.

9. This argument is proffered most blatantly in Lloyd Abbey, *Destroyer and Preserver: Shelley's Poetic Skepticism* (Lincoln: Univ. of Nebraska Press, 1979). Yet it is partly echoed, too, throughout Tilottama Rajan's Sartrean reading of Shelley in *Dark Interpreter: The Discourse of Romanticism* (Ithaca, NY: Cornell Univ. Press, 1980), pp. 58–96, and Angela Leighton's supposedly "deconstructive" view in *Shelley and the Sublime: An Interpretation of the Major Poems* (Cambridge: Cambridge Univ. Press, 1984), pp. 25–72. Such redactions have been influenced, moreover, by earlier ones claiming a shift from empiricism toward Platonism in Shelley's thought. See Grabo, *The Magic Plant,* p. 124; Woodman, *The Apocalyptic Vision,* pp. 4–14; Baker, *Shelley's Major Poetry: The Fabric of a Vision* (Princeton, NJ: Princeton Univ. Press, 1948), pp. 215–54; and Milton Wilson, *Shelley's Later Poetry: A Study of His Prophetic Imagination* (New York: Columbia Univ. Press, 1959), pp. 169–255. Finally, for influential studies on how Shelley's style intimates a nonempirical "numinosity" by way of some semi-empirical referents, see Daniel J. Hughes, "Coherence and Collapse in Shelley, with Particular Reference to *Epipsychidion*," *ELH*, 28 (1961), 260–83, and Jerome McGann, "Shelley's Veils: A Thousand Images of Loveliness," in *Romantic and Victorian: Essays for William Marshall,* ed. W. Paul Elledge and Richard L. Hoffman (Cranbury, NJ: Fairleigh Dickinson Univ. Press, 1971), pp. 198–218.

10. The quoted words in this case are Earl R. Wasserman's in *Shelley: A Critical Reading* (Baltimore: The Johns Hopkins Univ. Press, 1971), pp. 131–53. Even so, despite some differences, the case for this poet's skeptical idealism is powerfully made in similar ways by Donald H. Reiman, *Shelley's "The Triumph of Life": A Critical Study,* Illinois Studies in Language and Literature No. 55 (Urbana: Univ. of Illinois Press, 1965), pp. 3–18; Cameron, *Shelley: The Golden Years* (Cambridge, MA: Harvard Univ. Press, 1974), pp. 150–77; and Curran, *Shelley's Annus Mirabilis,* pp. 95–118 and 199–205. For this view carried so far that empirical skepticism becomes the basis of a "monist" and "reductionist" view of causality in Shelley's work, see Curt Zaminsky, "Cause and Effect: A Symbolism for Shelley's Poetry," *JEGP*, 78 (1979), 209–26. These analyses all find their point of departure, in any case, even though they avoid its reclaiming of Shelley for Platonism, in C. E. Pulos, *The Deep Truth: A Study of Shelley's Scepticism* (Lincoln: Univ. of Nebraska Press, 1954).

11. Wasserman, *A Critical Reading,* p. 149.

12. See Leslie Brisman, "Mysterious Tongue: Shelley and the Language of Christianity," *Texas Studies in Literature and Language,* 23 (1981), 389–417.

13. In this and the previous sentence, I am quoting Judith Chernaik, *The Lyrics of Shelley* (Cleveland, OH: Press of Case Western Reserve Univ., 1972), pp. 32–58. See also Michael G. Cooke's placement of Shelley within the governing subjective projections of the best Romantic

poetry in *The Romantic Will* (New Haven, CT: Yale Univ. Press, 1976), pp. 1–51, 76–83, and 216–22.

14. Timothy Webb, *Shelley: A Voice Not Understood* (Manchester: Manchester Univ. Press, 1977), pp. 161, 182, and 257.

15. Richard Cronin, *Shelley's Poetic Thoughts* (New York: St. Martin's Press, 1981), pp. 57 and 195. A less organic, more ironic, but still similar set of "new critical" assumptions also underlies Keach's arguments in *Shelley's Style*, esp. on pp. 40–78 and 184–200. See my reviews of Cronin and Keach in the *Keats-Shelley Journal*, 31 (1982), 212–14, and 35 (1986), 183–88.

16. John W. Wright, *Shelley's Myth of Metaphor* (Athens: Univ. of Georgia Press, 1970), p. 12.

17. Earl J. Schulze, *Shelley's Theory of Poetry: A Reappraisal* (The Hague: Mouton, 1966), p. 110.

18. John Robert Leo, "Criticism of Consciousness in Shelley's *A Defence of Poetry*," *Philosophy and Literature*, 2 (1978), 47.

19. McGann, *"Shelley's Veils,"* pp. 198–99.

20. Wright, *Shelley's Myth*, pp. 29 and 45. See also the arguments for an imaginative coalescence in Shelley using but transcending metaphor in Glenn O'Malley, *Shelley and Synaesthesia* (Evanston, IL: Northwestern Univ. Press, 1964), and Jean Hall, *The Transforming Image: A Study of Shelley's Major Poems* (Urbana: Univ. of Illinois Press, 1980), pp. 9–24.

21. For a useful view of the truly alien and self-alienating Yahweh of the Old Testament, see Herbert Schneidau, *Sacred Discontent: The Bible and Western Tradition* (1976; rpt. Berkeley: Univ. of California Press, 1977), pp. 15–28.

22. Here I reveal my debts to Jacques Derrida, especially to *Of Grammatology,* trans. Gayatri Spivak (Baltimore, MD: The Johns Hopkins Univ. Press, 1976), pp. 30–65. I am particularly beholden to his "arche-writing," the transpositional supplementation that we must be thinking already before we can even conceive of a "thought about a thought" or an "expression" of thought. Yet I do not claim that my study always performs the "deconstructive" process of reading defined by Derrida on pp. 157–64. Instead I propose to reveal Shelley's engagement in that process with the older texts that he recasts. He teases out inorganic transposition (which we usually behold in visible writing) as what really underlies existing concepts claiming to be prior to both writing and transposition. Shelley even performs this Derridean "task," I now want to show, with the already written theories of language pressing in upon him.

23. See Condillac's *Essay,* trans. Thomas Nugent, intr. Robert Weyant (1756; rpt. Gainesville, FL: Scholars' Facsimiles, 1971), pp. 51–58, 169–74, and 283–300; Smith's "Of the Origin and Progress of Language" (1762), *Lectures on Rhetoric and Belles Lettres*, ed. J. C. Bryce (Oxford: Clarendon, 1983), pp. 9–13; Tooke's ΕΠΕΑ ΠΤΕΡΟΕΝΤΑ. *or, the Diversions of Purley* (1786–1805), ed. Richard Taylor (London: Tegg, 1840), pp. 9–22; Godwin's *Enquiry Concerning Political Justice,* 3rd ed. (1797), ed. Isaac Kramnick (Harmondsworth, Eng.: Penguin, 1976), pp. 156–63; Coleridge's sense of the symbol as partly constituting and partaking of its own range of reference in *The Statesman's Manual* (1816) in *The Collected Works*, VI, ed. R. J. White (Princeton, NJ: Princeton Univ. Press, 1972), 28–31 and 78–80, which confirms the longstanding Coleridgean view that the "I AM" comes fully into being only in its concrete "other"; and Bentham's sense of language as so determining the order of thought that "discourse" is often power's means to social dominance in the "Essay on Language" (1816–1831) in *The Works*, ed. John Bowring (1838–1843; rpt. New York: Russell and Russell, 1962), VIII, esp. 329–32. Note also the following discussions of this theoretical line as it feeds into Shelley and his immediate era: Hans Aarsleff, *The Study of Language in England, 1780–1860* (Princeton, NJ: Princeton Univ. Press, 1967), pp. 13–114; Cronin, *Shelley's Poetic Thoughts,* pp. 1–25; and Paul H. Fry on Shelley's *Defence* in *The Reach of Criticism: Method and Perception in Literary Theory* (New Haven, CT: Yale Univ. Press, 1983), pp. 137–43. At the same time we must realize that what Shelley does to modify this counter-tradition is encouraged by all its practitioners when they

devolve, despite the moments I have cited from them, toward words as primarily "the communication of thought" (Bentham, VII, 320). For proof that Shelley read all these thinkers save Condillac, see "Appendix VIII: Shelley's Reading," *L*, II, 467–88, where such authors (with the poet's or Mary Shelley's references to them) are listed alphabetically. The reading of Condillac in the Shelley household is established by Burton R. Pollin, "Philosophical and Literary Sources of *Frankenstein,*" *Comparative Literature*, 17 (1965), 97–108.

24. Locke in *An Essay Concerning Human Understanding* (1690), ed. Peter H. Nidditch (Oxford: Clarendon, 1975), pp. 402–524; Berkeley in *The Principles of Human Knowledge and Three Dialogues Between Hylas and Philonous* (1710–1713), intr. G. J. Warnock (Cleveland, OH: World, 1962), pp. 57–63; Hobbes in *Leviathan* (1651), ed. Michael Oakeshott (New York: Collier, 1962), pp. 33–40; Rousseau in the *Discourse on the Origin of Inequality* (1754) in *The Social Contract and Discourses*, trans. G. D. H. Cole (New York: Dutton, 1950), pp. 213–21; and Monboddo in *Of the Origin and Progress of Language*, 2nd ed. (1774; rpt. New York: Garland, 1970), I, 5–174. All these texts except for Rousseau's *Discourse* are noted in "Shelley's Reading," and the *Discourse* is cited by Shelley himself in his notes to *Queen Mab, PW*, p. 805n. The possible (though not always indisputable) consequences of Shelley's admitted (though I would say partial) use of this tradition are discussed in Stuart Peterfreund, "Shelley, Monboddo, Vico, and the Language of Poetry," *Style*, 15 (1981), 382–400; Keach, *Shelley's Style*, pp. 1–50; and Terence Allan Hoagwood, *Prophecy and the Philosophy of Mind: Traditions of Blake and Shelley* (University: Univ. of Alabama Press, 1985), pp. 11–58. Still, some of the "idea"-based theorists sometimes anticipate Shelley's tilting of their notions toward language's "creation" of thought. See Hobbes, p. 39; Berkeley, p. 60; Rousseau, pp. 217–18; and even Monboddo, I, 482–98, where we cannot have clear auditory ideas imitating nature without "the power of articulation" to reproduce natural sounds.

25. This sense of self-composition by language as the automatic socialization, even alienation, of the constructed "self" into social interchange with other such "figures" is anticipated especially well by Condillac's *Essay*, trans. Nugent, pp. 171–79. Shelley's version, in turn, anticipates Jacques Lacan's sense of the subject constructed as an "other" for others by way of the symbolic order (the Other). See "The Function of Language in Psychoanalysis" in Lacan's *The Language of the Self*, ed. and trans. Anthony Wilden (New York: Dell, 1968), pp. 11–27.

26. See Edward Aveling and Eleanor Marx Aveling, *Shelley's Socialism: Two Lectures* (London: privately printed, 1888); Stefan Morakowski, "Introduction," Karl Marx and Friedrich Engels, *On Literature and Art*, ed. Lee Baxandall and Morakowski (New York: International General, 1973), p. 44; Cameron, *The Golden Years*, pp. 127–49, plus "Shelley and Marx," *The Wordsworth Circle*, 10 (1974), 234–39; and Paul Foot, *Red Shelley* (London: Sidgwick and Jackson, 1980), pp. 81–98 and 227–73.

27. See *The German Ideology*, trans. W. Lough et al., in Karl Marx and Friedrich Engels, *Collected Works*, V, ed. Lev Churbanov (New York: International Publishers, 1976), 41–57, and Hayden White, *Metahistory: The Historical Imagination in Nineteenth-Century Europe* (Baltimore: The John Hopkins Univ. Press, 1973), pp. 297–309.

28. Here I quote or paraphrase *The Interpretation of Dreams* (1900) and "On Narcissicism: An Introduction" (1914) as they appear in *The Standard Edition of the Complete Psychological Works of Sigmund Freud*, ed. and trans. James Strachey et al. (London: Hogarth, 1953–1966), V, 533–609, and XIV, 73–102. The best-known "transference" of Freud (from analysand to analyst) appears in "The Dynamics of Transference" (1912), *Standard Edition*, XII, 99–108. I, meanwhile, am also influenced by Derrida, "Freud and the Scene of Writing," *Writing and Difference*, trans. Alan Bass (Chicago: Univ. of Chicago Press, 1978), pp. 196–231.

29. See Cameron, *The Young Shelley*, pp. 87–88.

30. Here I adopt, because Shelley prefigures them, the "heteroglossia" and the process of self-composition suggested by Mikhail Bakhtin. See "Discourse in the Novel" in Bakhtin's *The Dialogic Imagination: Four Essays*, ed. Michael Holquist, trans. Holquist and Caryl Emerson (Aus-

tin: Univ. of Texas Press, 1981), pp. 259–331. What Shelley does in poetry, however, denies what Bakhtin says here about "poetic style" being strictly monological.

31. This movement is traced through the twentieth century by Meredith Anne Skura, *The Literary Use of the Psychoanalytic Process* (New Haven, CT: Yale Univ. Press, 1981), pp. 1–28.

32. See Hélène Cixous, "The Laugh of the Medusa," trans. Keith and Paula Cohen, *Signs,* 3 (1976), 875–93, and Alice Jardine, *Gynesis: Configurations of Woman and Modernity* (Ithaca, NY: Cornell Univ. Press, 1985), pp. 31–49, 65–87, and 118–44. Jardine's notion of *gynesis* striving toward *gynema* is very close to what I mean by Shelleyan transference. This poet, after all, has already been established as the most protofeminist among the major male Romantic poets in Nathaniel Brown, *Sexuality and Feminism in Shelley* (Cambridge, MA: Harvard Univ. Press, 1979), though there are some telling limitations in the poet's personal attitudes and actions, some of which are noted by Foot in *Red Shelley,* pp. 124–50, and by William Veeder, *Mary Shelley and* Frankenstein: *The Fate of Androgyny* (Chicago: Univ. of Chicago Press, 1986), pp. 47–80.

33. David Simpson, *Irony and Authority in Romantic Poetry* (New York: Macmillan, 1979), pp. 160–65.

34. "Birth and recurrence" *is* the subject of "has no necessary connexion" in the text of *Defence,* p. 506. There is no "birth" of poetry for Shelley without there being a "recurrence" of some "fading" symbolic efforts undergoing transformation. The two movements are so intertwined for him as to be named in his prose by a singular noun-phrase.

35. I quote Bloom's terms and paraphrase his argument from his very specific theoretical essay "Poetic Crossing: Rhetoric and Psychology," *Georgia Review,* 30 (1976), 495–524.

36. In this way Shelley saves "voice" and its "transumption" (or self-salvation) from the death of memory in the merely written text. See Bloom's reading of *The Triumph of Life* in *Poetry and Repression: Revisionism from Blake to Stevens* (New Haven, CT: Yale Univ. Press, 1976), pp. 83–111; Susan Hawk Brisman's "'Unsaying His High Language': The Problem of Voice in *Prometheus Unbound,*" *Studies in Romanticism,* 16 (1977), 51–86; and Leslie Brisman's survey of Shelley's major poems in *Romantic Origins* (Ithaca, NY: Cornell Univ. Press, 1978), pp. 137–82.

37. I refer to Paul Fry writing on Shelley the poet rather than on Shelley the theorist in *The Poet's Calling in the English Ode* (New Haven, CT: Yale Univ. Press, 1980), pp. 186–217. What I say about Fry's "will to die" also applies to the reading of Shelley's "West Wind" as primarily a death drive in Barbara Johnson, "Apostrophe, Animation, and Abortion," *Diacritics,* 16, No. 1 (Spring 1986), esp. 31–32.

38. See "The Subversion of the Subject and the Dialectic of Desire in the Freudian Unconscious" in Lacan's *Écrits: A Selection,* trans. Alan Sheridan (London: Tavistock, 1977), pp. 292–325.

39. See Jean-Paul Sartre's view of rhetorical "freedom" as the state where "the human being *is* his own past . . . in the form of nihilation" when he refers to that past (*Being and Nothingness: An Essay on Phenomenal Ontology,* trans. Hazel Barnes [New York: Philosphical Library, 1956], p. 29). The clearest presentation of Freud's *thanatos* is in his *Beyond the Pleasure Principle* (1920), *Standard Edition,* XVII, 7–64.

40. Julia Kristeva identifies this "activity," which she connects with the multiple shiftings of identity and sensation in the emergence from the mother, as "the instinctual and maternal, *semiotic* processes prepar[ing] the future speaker for entrance into meaning and signification" (my emphasis) in "From One Identity to an Other" (1975), rpt. in Kristeva's *Desire in Language: A Semiotic Approach to Literature and Art,* ed. Leon S. Roudiez, trans. Roudiez, Jardine, and Thomas Gora (New York: Columbia Univ. Press, 1980), pp. 124–47 (I quote p. 136). Cixous uses the word "forelanguage" to indicate the same "economy of drives," the "unconscious" in both sexes, as it is retained especially by the bodies of women in "The Laugh of the Medusa," p. 886. As I am beholden to these two writers, so they are indebted to Lacan's *lalangue* and

"*jouissance* of the body" in his 1972–1973 *Seminar XX,* rpt. in *Feminine Sexuality: Jacques Lacan and the* école freudienne, ed. Juliet Mitchell and Jacqueline Rose, trans. Rose (New York: Pantheon and Norton, 1982), pp. 138–61. Fry completely ignores this level in Lacanian psychoanalysis.

41. The divorce from the mother into sexed and symbolic being is most clearly rendered as announcing "the blow of individual death" in Lacan, *The Four Fundamental Concepts of Psycho-analysis,* ed. Jacques-Alain Miller, trans. Alan Sheridan (London: Hogarth, 1977), p. 205.

42. De Man's words (on pp. 44–45) from his "Shelley Disfigured" in Harold Bloom et al., *Deconstruction and Criticism* (New York: Seabury Press, 1979), pp. 39–73. The Miller essay from which I quote at this point, "The Critic as Host," appears in the same volume on pp. 217–53. For an intriguing sense of why Shelley has attracted such deconstructive readings, see Jonathan Arac, "Shelley, Deconstruction, History," in *Critical Genealogies: Historical Situations for Postmodern Literary Studies* (New York: Columbia Univ. Press, 1987), pp. 97–113.

43. This phrase is not primarily a reference to Viktor Frankl's *The Will to Meaning* (New York: World, 1969), even though my use of it resembles some of what appears on his pp. 51–62. Instead my usage reworks the "will-to-signification" that Eugenio Donato uses to translate Derrida's *vouloir-dire* in "'Here, Now'/'Always, Already': Incidental Remarks on Some Recent Characterizations of the Text," *Diacritics,* 6, No. 3 (Fall 1976), esp. 26–27.

44. See the critique of American (or "Yale School") deconstruction in Michael Ryan, *Marxism and Deconstruction: A Critical Articulation* (Baltimore: The Johns Hopkins Univ. Press, 1982), p. xiii, and Michael Fischer, *Does Deconstruction Make Any Difference?: Poststructuralism and the Defense of Poetry in Modern Criticism* (Bloomington: Indiana Univ. Press, 1985), esp. pp. 60–82 and 97–109, even though I do not agree with everything that both critics say.

1. EARLY ATTACHMENTS: FROM THE "GOTHIC SENSIBILITY" TO "NATURAL PIETY" AND *ALASTOR*

1. See Reiman's "Wordsworth, Shelley, and the Romantic Inheritance," *Romanticism Past and Present,* 5 (1981), 1–22.

2. For evidence that Shelley read all these authors and works by 1810, see Cameron, *The Young Shelley,* pp. 43–51; Richard Holmes, *Shelley: The Pursuit* (London: Weidenfeld and Nicholson, 1974), pp. 13–32; the young poet's own quotations in his early Gothic novels (*CW,* V, 3–193); and *L,* I, 70 and 81.

3. These possible (though partial) foundations of the Fall myth—noted by Freud in *The Future of an Illusion* (1927), *Standard Edition,* XXI, esp. 15–20—are likely motivators for Shelley's "Gothic sensibility," judging by what Holmes describes in *The Pursuit,* pp. 17–36.

4. See the "being thrown" into "being-towards-death" in Martin Heidegger, *Being and Time,* trans. John Macquarrie and Edward Robinson (New York: Harper & Row, 1962), pp. 299–311, and Locke on remembered perceptions as the "tombs" of past sensations in the *Essay,* pp. 151–52. Note also Donato's approach to this section of *Human Understanding,* which he briefly relates to Shelley's poetry, in "The Ruins of Memory: Archeological Fragments and Textual Artifacts," *MLN,* 93 (1978), 575–96.

5. See the sometimes helpful account of the early Shelley's apparent denial of "divine order and human purpose" in Frederick S. Frank's "Introduction" to Shelley's *Zastrozzi and St. Irvyne* (New York: Arno Press, 1977), pp. ix–xxii. For a different view and a placement of these novels in Shelley's career beyond what space permits me here, see my "Shelley's Fiction: The 'Stream of Fate'," *Keats-Shelley Journal,* 30 (1981), 78–99.

6. Fry's words in *The Poet's Calling,* p. 198. Strangely, though, Fry is discussing the 1816 poem "Mont Blanc," a piece that both recalls Shelley's earlier gaze into the Dionysian abyss and resists that Gothic stance with a sense that "vacancy" is already shot through with transference

(see my second chapter). Fry has applied his Nietzschean-Heideggerian configuration to the wrong stage of Shelley's development.

7. See *Spinoza: Selections,* ed. John Wild (New York: Scribner's, 1930), p. 457. There is no firm evidence that Shelley had read Spinoza thoroughly by the start of 1811 (see Cameron, *The Young Shelley,* pp. 381 and 443). But the adolescent poet clearly knows enough about Spinoza's arguments and specific works from lectures, articles, or partial readings to order the *Opera* by name in early 1813 (*L,* I, 347–48).

8. For the timing of and reasons behind Shelley's first attraction to Lucretius, see Cameron, *The Young Shelley,* pp. 88–89, and for a sign of the importance Lucretius comes to assume for Shelley, see the preface to *Laon and Cythna, CPW,* II, 105. See also Paul Turner, "Shelley and Lucretius," *Review of English Studies,* new series, 10 (1959), 269–82.

9. *De rerum,* II. 688–94. This analogy has been granted its telling implications only by Michel Serres in *La naissance de la physique dans le texte de Lucrèce: Fleuves et turbulences* (Paris: Grasset, 1975), a portion of which is translated by Marilyn Sides in Serres's *Hermes: Literature, Science, Philosophy,* ed. Josué V. Harari and David F. Bell (Baltimore: The Johns Hopkins Univ. Press, 1982), pp. 98–124. My sense of what feeds into Shelleyan process from Lucretius is continually indebted to Serres's suggestions.

10. See "On the Improvement of the Understanding" from the *Opera Posthuma, Spinoza,* pp. 13–14.

11. "God, Man, and His Well-being" from the *Opera, Spinoza,* pp. 62–63.

12. Here I quote Hume from his *Dialogues Concerning Natural Religion* (1776), ed. Richard H. Popkin (Indianapolis, IN: Hackett, 1980), pp. 31 and 88.

13. In *Political Justice,* pp. 116–46.

14. I cite Drummond in this paragraph from the original edition of *Academical Questions* (London: Bulmer, 1805), I, 15, 80, 12, 26, 176, 178, and 180.

15. By taking the argument this far, in fact, Shelley has employed Drummond to leap beyond what is permitted in the *Academical Questions* itself. Drummond never precisely connects the self-obscuring of thought by thought, the continual need for thought to reappear in "figurative language" that obscures it (Drummond, I, 28), and the "occult operation" assumed by thought to "ground" all these necessities. But Shelley sees all three levels as versions of the same trans-figurative process, aided by Drummond's Lucretian "train of ideas" and the "displacement" of each part in the train by another part (a figural occulting).

16. See Frank B. Evans, III, "Shelley, Godwin, Hume, and the Doctrine of Necessity," *Studies in Philology,* 37 (1940), 632–40.

17. I quote Holbach's *Système* from the anonymous translation of Shelley's own day entitled *Nature; and Her Laws* (London: Hodgson, 1816), I, 36.

18. There is no record of Shelley ever having read Leibniz, but the poet probably read the accounts of him in Monboddo's *Antient Metaphysics; or, the Science of Universals* (1779; rpt. New York: Garland, 1977), I, 83–85, and Drummond's *Questions,* I, 321–50, where the "monad" theory is compared with Epicurean-Lucretian atomic "declination" so as to reveal the attractions and philosophical problems inherent in all the different versions of "necessarianism." Some of Drummond's judgments in this section obviously carry little weight with Shelley in 1812 and 1813 but much more by 1819 (the year of their meeting and of the very Drummondesque "On Life").

19. Quoted from *The Poems of Alexander Pope,* Twickenham Text reduced, ed. John Butt (New Haven, CT: Yale Univ. Press, 1963).

20. See the "Additional Notes" to Darwin's *The Temple of Nature; or, The Origin of Society* (London: Johnson, 1803), p. 38. The extensive influence of Darwin on Shelley is best recounted by Grabo in *A Newton Among Poets: Shelley's Use of Science in* Prometheus Unbound (Chapel Hill: Univ. of North Carlina Press, 1930), pp. 30–79, and by Desmond King-Hele, *Erasmus Darwin and the Romantic Poets* (London: Macmillan, 1986), pp. 187–226.

21. *Political Justice,* p. 376.

22. Peacock, who was close to Shelley at this time, confirms this devotion to Wordsworth and Coleridge and their almost equal "influence on [Shelley's] style" in *Memoirs of Shelley and Other Essays and Reviews,* ed. Howard Mills (New York: New York Univ. Press, 1970), p. 43.

23. For a helpful Heideggerian sense of how Wordsworth intimates divinity in the way his comings-forth also withdraw back into self-concealment, see Charles Sherry, *Wordsworth's Poetry of the Imagination* (Oxford: Clarendon, 1980), pp. 14–31 and 50–56.

24. See "Lines," ll. 19–90; "France," ll. 1–21, 66–80, and 99–105; and "Hymn," ll. 13–23. The young Shelley probably saw most of these pieces as they appeared in such papers as *The Morning Post* (publishers of "France" in 1798 and the "Hymn" in 1802). We know that Shelley read Coleridge in the *Post* from *L,* I, 235n.

25. *Mary Shelley's Journal,* ed. Frederick L. Jones (Norman: Univ. of Oklahoma Press, 1947), p. 15 (Sept. 14, 1814).

26. The account of the "Intimations" ode (1807) dictated by Wordsworth to Isabella Fenwick. The only accurate printed version of this statement is the one in Wordsworth's *Poems, in Two Volumes, and Other Poems, 1800–1807,* ed. Jared Curtis for *The Cornell Wordsworth* (Ithaca, NY: Cornell Univ. Press, 1983), p. 428.

27. Coleridge articulates this philosophy most fully, of course, in chapters IX–XIII of the *Biographia Literaria,* rev. ed., ed. George Watson (London: Dent, 1965), pp. 79–167 (read by Shelley in 1817). But Shelley probably saw "intimations" of these conclusions prior to the *Biographia* in the 1809–1810 and 1812 editions of *The Friend,* Nos. 9 and 21 especially, now available in *The Collected Works,* IV, pt. 2, ed. Barbara Rooke (Princeton, NJ: Princeton Univ. Press, 1969), 122–33 and 294–96.

28. My emphasis. Bloom establishes "their words" as referring mainly to Wordsworth and Coleridge in *Poetry and Repression,* pp. 109–11.

29. This realization of a radical entropy anticipates the 1931 "Incompleteness Theorem" of Kurt Gödel in which the rules of combination in an expandable system generate systematic combinations that violate and surpass the rules themselves. See the varying discussions of this (or this kind of) paradox of Gödel, *On Formally Undecideable Propositions,* trans. B. Meltzer (London: Oliver and Boyd, 1962), pp. 37–72; Douglas R. Hofstadter, *Gödel, Escher, Bach: An Eternal Golden Braid* (New York: Random House, 1980), esp. pp. 3–28 and 684–719; and Serres, "The Origin of Language: Biology, Information Theory, and Thermodynamics," trans. Mark Anderson, *Hermes,* pp. 71–83.

30. See *The Works* of Peacock, Halliford Edition, ed. H. F. B. Brett-Smith and C. E. Jones (London: Constable, 1927), VI, 183–246.

31. Note Shelley's critiques of Hogg's amorous nature as early as 1811 (in *L,* I, 171–72, for example) and the poet's 1814 review of *Alexy Heimatoff, CW,* VI, esp. 177–81.

32. See Luther L. Scales, "The Poet as Miltonic Adam in *Alastor,*" *Keats-Shelley Journal,* 21–22 (1972–73), 126–44.

33. Compare the *Alastor* Poet's conception of his dream-maiden in an Indian vale (ll. 145–91) with the hero Helarian's first sight of Luxima in *The Missionary: An Indian Tale* (London: Stockdale, 1811), I, 153.

34. See Donald L. Maddox, "Shelley's *Alastor* and the Legacy of Rousseau," *Studies in Romanticism,* 9 (1970), 82–98, plus Rousseau himself in *Confessions* (1770), trans. John Grant (London: Dent, 1931), I, 12–13, 96, 136–37, II, 75–77, and in *The Reveries of the Solitary Walker* (1778), ed. and trans. Charles Butterworth (New York: New York Univ. Press, 1979), esp. pp. 68–71.

35. See *The Excursion,* IX. 614–48. Many critics have enumerated *Alastor's* continuous and revisionist echoings of Wordsworth, starting with Paul Mueschke and Earl L. Griggs, "Wordsworth as the Prototype of the Poet in Shelley's *Alastor,*" *PMLA,* 49 (1934), 229–45. The two recent discussions of this relationship that have been especially helpful to me are Keach, "Obstinate Questionings: The Immortality Ode and *Alastor,*" *The Wordsworth Circle,* 12, No. 1 (Win-

ter 1981), 36–44, and Yvonne M. Carothers, "*Alastor:* Shelley Corrects Wordsworth," *MLQ,* 42 (1981), 21–47. Coleridgean echoes of the same sort are given equal time by Edward Strickland in "Transfigured Night: The Visionary Inversions of *Alastor,*" *Keats-Shelley Journal,* 33 (1984), esp. 149–51.

36. The Comte de Volney's words in *The Ruins, or, Meditation on the Revolutions of Empires,* trans. anon. (New York: Eckler, 1926), p. 148 (a book we know Shelley to have read quite early). Shelley also drew this sense of Dendera from Peacock's knowledge of that temple's zodiac as it had been described already by John Frank Newton and Charles Dupuis, the first of whom Shelley met and the second of whom he probably read. See Peacock's *Memoirs,* pp. 38–39, and Curran, *Shelley's Annus Mirabilis,* pp. 227–28, n. 81. Then, too, Diodorus of Sicily (ordered by Shelley in 1812, according to *L,* I, 344), describes the ancient Nile valley as the "place where all the gods were born" in *The Library of History,* trans. C. H. Oldfather, Loeb Edition, I, 43.

37. Shelley could have found this conflation of myths already complete in several places, as Curran notes in *Annus Mirabilis* on pp. 63–64 and 218–19, n. 41. My readings of the sources Curran cites confirm his claims for them.

38. Curran has firmly established the southern Georgian Caucasus as the final destination of the *Alastor* Poet in *Annus Mirabilis,* p. 64. For the Eden-Caucasus association, see Reiman, *NCE,* p. 76, n. 8, and Scales, "The Poet as Miltonic Adam," pp. 137–38.

39. Wordsworth's definite anticipation of the loss of the Mother in Freud is most accurately explained by Geoffrey Hartman, "A Touching Compulsion: Wordsworth and the Problem of Literary Representation," *Georgia Review,* 31 (1977), 345–61. Meanwhile, Freudian critics who read *Alastor* in the same way miss the fact that Shelley is trying to critique this sense of desire's foundations. The latest example of such an approach and its dangers is the Shelley chapter in Barbara A. Schapiro, *The Romantic Mother: Narcissistic Patterns in Romantic Poetry* (Baltimore: The Johns Hopkins Univ. Press, 1983), pp. 1–32.

40. Here I refer to Derrida's notion of supplementarity in *Of Grammatology,* pp. 144–57. I also recall de Man's sense, in "Shelley Disfigured" (pp. 50–63), of the "shape all light" in *The Triumph of Life* as enacting "the figurality of all signification." Yet de Man mistakenly regards her "stepping" positional movement (on p. 44) as the first thematization of such a process in Shelley's career. So many aspects of the "shape" are anticipated at this point in *Alastor.* This sequence, too, points up the problem in the poem of language being forced to refer to its own metaphoricity as its "object." That paradox is articulated especially well by Neil Fraistat in "Poetic Quests and Questioning in the *Alastor* Collection," *Keats-Shelley Journal,* 33 (1984), esp. 163–164.

41. In *A Critical Reading,* pp. 11–21. Wasserman's famous distinctions, even so, have already been drawn somewhat toward my argument in Keach, *Shelley's Style,* pp. 81–87, where the "wandering Poet may be seen as the narrator's deeper self projected as spectral other" (p. 87). Keach even specifies "transference" as the motive force behind this projection (p. 83), though all the while failing to see how pervasive the process is throughout the poem and how much it determines the reflexivities that Keach attributes mainly to the will of the author.

42. This is the best-known Freudian transference, the one where a subject's hidden obsessions are transported into another subject so that preconscious impulses can both remain hidden and be revealed. But Shelley here anticipates the Lacanian variation on this theory, wherein the subject, starting in the "mirror-stage," projects itself outward as a fabricated, reflective image in order to be constituted as a subject in a symbolic order (which *then* exposes unconscious transfers). See "The Mirror Stage as Formative of the Function of the I" in Lacan's *Écrits,* trans. Sheridan, pp. 1–10.

43. See *Mary Shelley's Journal,* p. 11 (Aug. 24, 1814).

44. Here Shelley anticipates the way an ancient temple's array of symbolic features brings forth a meaningful "world" from a heretofore senseless "earth" in Heidegger's "The Origin of the Work of Art," trans. Albert Hofstadter, in *Philosophies of Art and Beauty: Selected Readings*

in Aesthetics from Plato to Heidegger, ed. Hofstadter and Richard Kuhns (Chicago: Univ. of Chicago Press, 1964), pp. 670–83.

45. Despite claims to the contrary by Carlos Baker and Wasserman (in *Shelley's Major Poetry,* p. 45, and *A Critical Reading,* p. 11n.), it is clear that Peacock remembers at least half-correctly when he recalls proposing *Alastor* as a title to Shelley because of the "evil demon" connotations in the Greek ʾΑλάστωρ. See the *Memoirs of Shelley,* p. 60. For a Greek text that Shelley knew in which *alastor* refers to an avenging power, see the *Agamemnon* of Aeschylus, Loeb Edition, l. 1501.

46. Aeschylus extends the word so that it has this meaning in the *Eumenedes,* l. 236, as does Sophocles in the *Ajax,* l. 374. If one ancient writer could take this double stance on the word, surely Shelley felt he could do the same after Peacock's suggestion, even though the latter's *Memoirs* claim that "many have [wrongly] supposed *Alastor* to be the name of the hero of the poem"—and indeed it is more an analogue for him than it is his name.

47. See Steinman in "Shelley's Skepticism: Allegory in 'Alastor'," *ELH,* 45 (1978), 255–69.

48. See the "Seventh Walk" in Rousseau's *Reveries,* pp. 89–103, where the sin Shelley castigates in *Alastor* is blatantly exemplified by the speaker: "I have become solitary, or, as they say, unsociable and misanthropic" because "I can no longer, as before, throw myself headfirst into this vast ocean of nature" (p. 95).

2. THE POLES OF BEING AND THE SURPASSING OF PRECURSORS: THE "HYMN TO INTELLECTUAL BEAUTY" AND "MONT BLANC"

1. See Holmes, *Shelley: The Pursuit,* pp. 159–60.

2. The quoted words are from the response of the *Eclectic Review* in October 1816, reprinted in Newman Ivey White, *The Unextinguished Hearth: Shelley and His Contemporary Critics* (1938; rpt. New York: Octagon, 1966), p. 107. For Shelley's "sensitive" reaction (his word) to the various reviews of *Alastor and Other Poems,* see *L,* I, 440 (a letter to Godwin of December 1816).

3. Byron was completing the Third Canto at the time of the 1816 boat trip, so there must have been considerable discussion of it between the two travellers and some Byronic commentary on Rousseau (resembling the words in the canto) while Shelley was reading *Julie* in Byron's company. Shelley was entrusted with the manuscript of the canto when he returned to England later that summer (see *L,* I, 504: Sept. 8, 1816).

4. *The History of Agathon,* trans. anon. (London: T. Cadell, 1773), IV, 48–49. See also *PS,* pp. 197–98.

5. *La nouvelle Héloïse* (1762), ed. and trans. Judith H. McDowell (University Park: Pennsylvania State Univ. Press, 1968), p. 35 (pt. I, letter 5). All subsequent references to this novel will be to this edition.

6. The first critic to call sustained attention to these particular poem/precursor-poem relationships was, of course, the early Harold Bloom in *Shelley's Mythmaking* (1959; rpt. Ithaca, NY: Cornell Univ. Press, 1969), pp. 11–43.

7. See Charles E. Robinson, *Shelley and Byron: The Snake and Eagle Wreathed in Flight* (Baltimore: The Johns Hopkins Univ. Press, 1976), pp. 21–22. I cannot agree with this book, however, that the reading of all of Shelley's poetry before the summer of 1816 converted Byron to a "transcendental vision of nature"—though he did have one—that was Shelley's own view at the time (p. 18). Robinson's claim is valid only insofar as Byron felt the influence of *Queen Mab* and Wordsworth as the latter was transmitted by Shelley. *Alastor* puts transcendentalism into question, and the Shelley poems written near Byron in 1816 intensify that effort in reaction to Byron's acceptance of some of the *Alastor* Poet's worst attitudes.

8. Here and later Shelley anticipates the shift in recent senses of the lyric away from a focus on the ahistorical identity or governing attitude of a clearly "situated speaker" and toward an understanding of how such a "character is engendered in the first place through colliding modes

of signification" (the words of Herbert F. Tucker). For the older, standard view of the lyric as it still persists—a view that has often been used to downgrade Shelley—see Cleanth Brooks, *The Well-Wrought Urn: Studies in the Structure of Poetry* (New York: Harcourt, 1947), pp. 192–214; William K. Wimsatt, "Organic Form: Some Questions about a Metaphor," in *Romanticism: Vistas, Instances, Continuities,* ed. David Thorburn and Geoffrey Hartman (Ithaca, NY: Cornell Univ. Press, 1973), pp. 13–37; Barbara Herrnstein Smith, *On the Margins of Discourse: The Relation of Literature to Language* (Chicago: Univ. of Chicago Press, 1978), pp. 8–40; M. H. Abrams, "Lyric," *A Glossary of Literary Terms,* 4th ed. (New York: Norton, 1981), p. 99; and Sharon Cameron, *Lyric Time: Dickinson and the Limits of Genre* (Baltimore: The Johns Hopkins Univ. Press, 1979), pp. 1–25 and 201–60. This last book, to be sure, helps to begin a shift of focus, yet not enough to keep itself from misreading Shelley's lyric objective as a "self-transcendence" in a "conflation of subject and object" where the difference disappears altogether (p. 216). For alternative views more attuned (sometimes directly) to Shelley, see the essays by Jonathan Culler, Paul de Man, John Brenkman, Tilottama Rajan, Cynthia Chase, and Herbert Tucker in *Lyric Poetry: Beyond New Criticism,* ed. Chaviva Hašek and Patricia Parker (Ithaca, NY: Cornell Univ. Press, 1985). I quote Tucker from "Dramatic Monologue and the Overhearing of Lyric" in this volume, p. 243.

9. See Fry, *The Poet's Calling,* pp. 1–14; *Pindar's Odes,* ed. and trans. Roy Arthur Swanson (Indianapolis, IN: Bobbs-Merrill, 1974), pp. xlv–xlviii and 106–110 (Pindar's "Pythian 8"); and Stuart Curran, *Poetic Form and British Romanticism* (New York: Oxford Univ. Press, 1986), pp. 56–84.

10. Note Rousseau's paean to the "general will" as "sovereign" in *The Social Contract and Discourses,* pp. 13–15 and 85–86, and Byron's call to the "Sons of Spain" to reinvoke forgotten "Chivalry" in Canto the First of *Childe Harold,* stanza xxxvii.

11. On these displays and their influence on the 1816 lyrics, see Gerald McNiece's definitive account in *Shelley and the Revolutionary Idea* (Cambridge, MA: Harvard Univ. Press, 1969), pp. 117–25.

12. On the recollection of Delphic, Vedic, and biblical patterns in Shelley's hymns and odes, see Curran, *Shelley's Annus Mirabilis,* pp. 156–80, and Webb, *A Voice Not Understood,* pp. 176–80.

13. Chernaik makes this point quite helpfully in *The Lyrics of Shelley,* pp. 36–39, except that she goes so far as to see Shelley reacting to the threat of meaningless death in the "Hymn" by "substituting images of divine and external authority for his own mind and conscience" (p. 37). To Shelley such a projection would be an enslavement of the self by projected dieties, and the "Hymn" is written against poems or prose works that uphold and enforce that process.

14. This dimension in the "Hymn" is explored most thoroughly in Spencer Hall, "Power and the Poet: Religious Mythmaking in Shelley's 'Hymn to Intellectual Beauty'," *Keats-Shelley Journal,* 32 (1983), 123–49. I agree with Hall's conclusions, yet he fails to account for the process, though it *is* rendered in the poem, that demands a skeptical hypothesis about the unknowable while insisting that what is hypothesized remain unknown.

15. Even some advocates of Shelley as a skeptical empiricist give into this originally Neoplatonic view. See Wasserman in *A Critical Reading,* p. 192, and Cameron in *The Golden Years,* pp. 239–43.

16. *A Voice Not Understood,* pp. 33–38.

17. Here Shelley represses, more than he does in *Alastor,* the connection he senses between transference and the nature of the "feminine." The pressure he puts on himself to compete with masculine or neutered absolutes in Wordsworth and Coleridge may have contributed to this brief denial of what he knows already. But even in the "Hymn" (aided by *Julie*) he starts recalling, near the end of the poem (l. 71), the feminine "LOVELINESS" that underlies his "spirit," anticipating what he will do in later works.

18. Cronin's view of the "Hymn" in *Shelley's Poetic Thoughts,* pp. 224–30.

19. See the early draft of the "Hymn" in Chernaik, *The Lyrics of Shelley,* pp. 285–87.

20. See *The Social Contract and Discourses,* pp. 182–85 (esp. 182, n. 2).

21. In *Adultery in the Novel: Contract and Transgression* (Baltimore: The Johns Hopkins Univ. Press, 1974), pp. 113–78, Tony Tanner argues that this self-abnegating choice of Julie's carries through the bourgeois repression of "the dissolving liquifications of passion" by confining them within "the binding structurations of marriage" (p. 172), a course that Shelley would hardly ever endorse. It is odd that the poet never mentions reading *Julie* this way, since Tanner's view points out some of Shelley's favorite targets of scorn. But then, too, Shelley's interest, as the "Hymn" develops from aspects of *Julie,* is in the capacity of Beauty's process to extend its "passion" beyond its own repressions of it while the repressions continue.

22. The many debts of this poem to *De rerum* have already been enumerated to a great extent in Jane E. Phillips, "Lucretian Echoes in Shelley's 'Mont Blanc','" *Classical and Modern Literature,* 2 (1982), 71–93. Even so, this article astonishingly maintains (as others have) a distance between Lucretian metaphysics and Shelleyan metaphysics much greater than the one that actually appears in "Mont Blanc" itself.

23. Here Shelley participates in the transition from particle physics to wave theory, which was developing, under some impetus from Lucretius, from the nineteenth into the twentieth century. See Serres, *La naissance,* pp. 9–15, and O. E. Lowenstein, "The Pre-Socratics, Lucretius, and Modern Science," *Lucretius,* ed. D. R. Dudley (New York: Basic Books, 1965), pp. 1–17.

24. At such points in Shelley's writing, we can see the merits in the early Bloom's now discredited use of an "I-thou" vocabulary in *Shelley's Mythmaking,* esp. pp. 11–35. Though that study does retain enough of Martin Buber to see the "thou" in the mountain as already spiritualized when the human spirit confronts it, Bloom admits that this self-other relationship depends on earlier "symbolic linking" in which differences work to become reflections of and relations to each other (p. 35). A more recent essay has also underlined what Bloom suggests at this point by rightly emphasizing the sheer compulsion to form relations in this poem. See Frances Ferguson, "Shelley's *Mont Blanc:* What the Mountain Said," in *Romanticism and Language,* ed. Arden Reed (Ithaca, NY: Cornell Univ. Press, 1984), pp. 202–14. I cannot accept this important analysis, though, when it claims that such a drive toward interplay is interpretation's and language's inevitable response to a meaningless "materiality." The "physicality" of the mountain perceived in the poem is already a relational concatenation, even before consciousness reacts by asserting additional interactions.

25. Herman Rapaport does suggest them in "Staging *Mont Blanc*" in *Displacement: Derrida and After,* ed. Marc Krupnik (Bloomington: Indiana Univ. Press, 1983), pp. 59–73. Indeed, this essay is quite revealing in the way it presents the Shelleyan image or "stage" as a "frame, set, or screen upon and through which another image is viewed," as a "staging of desire" on which the "earlier" image really depends for its re-cognition (pp. 61–62). But I cannot agree entirely with Rapaport that the preconscious impetus for nearly all Shelley's work (exemplified in "Mont Blanc") is always and only a "forestalling" of "death" in a way that also "build[s] a monument to mother" (p. 72).

26. Wordsworth uses the phrase "secret Power that reigns" as early as line 346 of his 1793 "Descriptive Sketches taken during a Pedestrian Tour among the Alps" (*Wordsworth: Poetical Works,* p. 13).

27. Both Webb (*A Voice Not Understood,* pp. 138–39) and Phillips ("Lucretian Echoes," pp. 80–81) connect these lines with Lucretius's *templa serena,* where the gods are inaccessibly beyond and serenely unresponsible for the processes of nature (see *De rerum,* I. 44–49; II. 646–51 and 1093–94; and V. 146–49). Shelley is surely making this allusion to counteract the usual presence of Divinity *in* natural process, but that does not mean he is pointing to a platonically immovable level, as Webb hints and Phillips maintains. Indeed, by placing the "breast" at that level (as Lucretius does not), Shelley may again be recalling, as he did in *Alastor,* the metamorphic process of procreation and withdrawal that is the Lucretian Venus.

28. One of the best views of this double attitude in the poem, though I cannot always agree

with this article's sense of what prompts the attitude, is John Rieder, "Shelley's 'Mont Blanc': Landscape and the Ideology of the Sacred Text," *ELH,* 48 (1981), 778–98. See also, in a similar vein, McNiece's provocative "The Poet as Ironist in 'Mont Blanc' and 'Hymn to Intellectual Beauty'," *Studies in Romanticism,* 15 (1975), 311–27.

29. Indeed, this poem picks up on several of the classical *and* radical features of this special mode of address, including its knowledge of its own fictionality and its decentered temporality, enumerated by Jonathan Culler in "Apostrophe," *Diacritics,* 7, No. 4 (Winter 1977), 59–69.

30. For how a poem can style (or restyle) its reader as well as its speaking "voice," see Walter Ong, S. J., "The Writer's Audience is Always a Fiction," *PLMA,* 90 (1975), 9–21.

31. The shift between the poem's last two sentences, in fact, is more than just a passage between attitudes. It is a turning, as Paul de Man would say, *from* a "semiotic" attachment of a signified (the "strength") to certain signifiers *toward* a "rhetorical" performance—in fact a rhetorical question, to which there is no answer (or an answer of "nothing")—which does not cohere with the previous sentence's claim to provide the answer. The second sentence asks for and denies that it is asking for an answer. It shows that the "silence and solitude" (l. 144) in which the "strength" might be located are adjacent to this latter "signified" only in a rhetorical positioning—an initially senseless placement in the march of language—and not primarily in a simple act of reference, unless the reader wants to wrench this sequence toward that sort of one-way logic. The hesitation between attitudes here is underwritten by an *aporia* between linguistic modes that is always potential in the operation of language. See de Man's "Semiology and Rhetoric," *Diacritics,* 3, No. 1 (Fall 1973), rpt. in *Textual Strategies: Perspectives in Post-Structuralist Criticism,* ed. Josué Harari (Ithaca, NY: Cornell Univ. Press, 1979), pp. 121–40.

32. Keach's brilliant description of this lyric's verse-pattern in *Shelley's Style,* pp. 195–97.

33. Keach, p. 196, my emphasis.

34. See the discussions of this theory by Werner Heisenberg, Gordon Reece, Jerzy Rayski, Jaček M. Rayaski, and David Bohm in *The Uncertainty Principle and the Foundations of Quantum Mechanics: A Fifty-Years' Survey,* ed. William S. Price and Seymour S. Chissick (New York: Wiley, 1977), pp. 3–20 and 559–63.

35. See the Comte de Buffon's *Natural History of Animals, Vegetables, and Minerals, with the Theory of the Earth in General,* trans. William Kenrick and J. Murdoch (London: Bell, 1775–76), V, 328–30, and Peacock's incomplete *Ahrimanes* (ca. 1812–15) in the Halliford *Works,* VII, 422–32.

36. Drummond's skeptical syncretism crosses Hebrew legends with sun-worship among the Egyptians, the Persians, and the Indians, thereby giving all these systems a common root that questions "the literal sense of the scriptures" in a way the antinomian Peacock and Shelley must have relished. See *The Oedipus Judaicus,* rev. ed. (London: Reeves and Turner, 1866), esp. pp. 111–40.

37. Compare Shelley's "Mutability" (*NCE,* p. 88) and Peacock's "Palmyra" (1806) in the Halliford *Works,* VI, 7–22.

38. See the excellent account of this rebellious brotherhood and its purposes in Marilyn Butler, "Myth and Mythmaking in the Shelley Circle," *ELH,* 49 (1982), 50–72, a shortened version of which appears in *Shelley Revalued: Essays from the Gregynog Conference,* ed. Kelvin Everest (New York: Barnes and Noble, 1983), 1–19.

39. In addition to Wordsworth's "Immortality" ode, see Milton's *Paradise Lost,* III. 1–55; Shakespeare's *Hamlet Prince of Denmark,* ed. Willard Farnham, in *The Complete Works,* Pelican Text Revised (New York: Viking, 1969), III. i. 64–68; and Ovid's *Metamorphoses,* Loeb Edition, XI. 610–15 (trans. Frank Justus Miller).

40. See the *Works and Days,* 42–50, in the Loeb *Hesiod: The Homeric Hymns and Homerica.*

41. Note the *Odyssey,* XI. 35–41; the *Aeneid,* VI. 893, where Aeneas leaves the world of shades through the Portal of Sleep; and *Timaeus,* 36c-d.

42. *Timaeus,* 45e–46a (trans. Benjamin Jowett), speaks of sleep as allowing the "greater motions" to be reflected in "dreams" in the manner of "images in mirrors." But the awakened,

disciplined reason comes closer to seeing the innermost circles of Being *without* refraction or reversal as that faculty makes the "circle of the diverse" reveal clear "intimations" of the circle of "the same" (*Timaeus,* 37b).

43. See Buffon's *Natural History,* V, 321–31, and Parkinson's *Organic Remains of a Former World,* 2nd ed. (London: Nattali, 1833), I, 456–57.

44. Peacock encourages this sense as an undermining of absolute divinities in "The Spirit of Fire" (1812) in the Halliford *Works,* VI, 247–60. There is no evidence that Shelley ever read Heraclitus directly.

45. For examples, see Bloom, *The Visionary Company,* p. 296; Reiman, *Percy Bysshe Shelley* (New York: Twayne, 1969), p. 44; Wasserman, *A Critical Reading,* pp. 237–38; Chernaik, *The Lyrics,* p. 49; Webb, *A Voice Not Understood,* pp. 138–39; Leighton, *Shelley and the Sublime,* pp. 70–72; and Ferguson, "Shelley's *Mont Blanc,*" pp. 210–14.

3. THE KEY TO ALL TYRANNIES: FROM *LAON AND CYTHNA* TO *THE CENCI*

1. Shelley is firm in this awareness well before 1816 and 1817, as when he tells Elizabeth Hitchener that hegemonic "Art" has "distinguished degrees" in society by fostering the illusion that "Nature" has done so first (*L,* I, 135–36). For a helpful recent Marxist sense of ideological representations as history's principal method for explaining and concealing its inequities, see Fredric Jameson, *The Political Unconscious: Narrative as a Socially Symbolic Act* (Ithaca, NY: Cornell Univ. Press, 1981), pp. 74–102, and William C. Dowling, *Jameson, Althusser, Marx: An Introduction to* The Political Unconscious (Ithaca, NY: Cornell Univ. Press, 1984), pp. 76–93.

2. Bacon first uses this notion in the *Novum Organum* (1620), Book I, aphorism 44. See *The New Organon and Related Writings,* trans. James Spedding et al., ed. Fulton Anderson (New York: Liberal Arts Press, 1960), pp. 49–50. For Shelley's reading of this treatise, see *L,* II, 468, and the "Essay on Christianity" (1817), *CW,* VI, 245.

3. I quote Hume throughout this paragraph from the original edition of *Four Dissertations* (1757; rpt. New York: Garland, 1970), pp. 14–17.

4. Here I am citing Godwin's *Enquiry,* ed. Kramnick, from pp. 156–63 and 410–11.

5. References to Wollstonecraft at this point are to the Norton Critical Edition of *A Vindication* (which uses the second version of 1792), ed. Carol H. Poston (New York: Norton, 1975), pp. 8, 36, and 11.

6. Compare Wollstonecraft on physical "inferiority" as a "law of nature" in the first edition of the *Vindication* (Norton Critical Edition, p. 8, n. 3) to Shelley's use of his strong soldier-heroine in *Laon and Cythna,* esp. ll. 2497–2523 (*CPW,* II, 188–89).

7. "Gender," after all, is not identical to "sex" but is rather a linguistic-rhetorical-ideological shaping or construct ("man" or "woman") attached by social convention *with the aid* of sex to any person being born into any society. This "socially divided portraiture," though "no more natural and inevitable than [an] occupational role," operates as a given "anchoring of activity," a grounding of a person's potentials in a limited set of prescribed qualities and acts, in the words of Erving Goffman, *Frame Analysis: An Essay on the Organization of Experience* (Cambridge, MA.: Harvard Univ. Press, 1974), p. 285. See also Joan Scott, "Gender: A Useful Category of Historical Analysis," *American Historical Review,* 91 (1986), 1053–75. Though Wollstonecraft sees more biological destiny behind such constructs than these views imply, she and others help awaken Shelley to this kind of understanding. To "wear the shape of woman," he writes, is to bear a "curse" used by male discourse to make woman a "slave" (*Laon and Cythna,* ll. 1036–53; *CPW,* II, 141–42).

8. "No. 9. Thursday, October 12, 1809," to be exact, now in the *Collected Works,* IV, pt. 2, ed. Rooke, 123–33.

9. Most vividly in *Violence and the Sacred,* trans. Patrick Gregory (Baltimore: The Johns Hopkins Univ. Press, 1977), pp. 143–49.

10. Quoted here from *The Social Contract and Discourses,* pp. 193–205.

11. References to Freud in this paragraph are exclusively to "On Narcissism," esp. to *Standard Edition,* XIV, 76–81 and 87–102. For the best Freudian reading of this poem thus far, though I cannot agree with its sense of a primal unity of the sexes in Shelley's vision, see Stuart Sperry, "The Sexual Theme in Shelley's *The Revolt of Islam,*" *JEGP,* 82 (1983), 32–49.

12. Sartre is cited during this section, as before, from *Being and Nothingness,* trans. Barnes, this time from pp. 252–91.

13. See stanzas vii and x in Canto the Second of *Ahrimanes* in the Halliford *Works* of Peacock, VII, 279–81.

14. Note the parallel to this aspect of the master/slave relationship in G. W. F. Hegel, *The Phenomenology of Mind,* trans. J. B. Baillie, intr. George Lichthcim (New York: Harper & Row, 1967), pp. 218–40, and in Alexandre Kojéve, *Introduction to the Reading of Hegel: Lectures on the* Phenomenology of Spirit, ed. Raymond Queneau and Allan Bloom, trans. James H. Nichols, Jr. (1969; rpt. Ithaca, NY: Cornell Univ. Press, 1980), esp. pp. 3–9. I do not agree, though, with Wasserman's effort (in line with the "history of ideas" assumptions once pervasive at Johns Hopkins) to see numerous parallels between Shelley and Hegel in *A Critical Reading,* pp. 374–75. As I have noted in chapter 1, Shelley was opposed to Germanic notions of an absolute spirit working itself out through time (or in master/slave relations), and he very likely never read the *Phenomenology* in any case. The only "spirit" struggling to emerge through its "others" for this poet is the human impulse toward free and reciprocal transference, which never attains an *Aufhebung* beyond relations between "others." Shelley is closer to Kojéve than to Hegel, in that the former is more existential when he focuses on the drive of "Desire directed towards another Desire" (Introduction, p. 7). I am therefore indebted to Kojéve's reworking of Hegel at various points throughout this chapter.

15. *Mary Shelley's Journal* (on p. 90) cites a rereading of *Political Justice* as one of Shelley's tasks in 1817, thereby placing that reacquaintance during and/or just after the completion of *Laon and Cythna.* The "Plays of Aeschylus" are on the same list.

16. The Titan's own words in Aeschylus, *Prometheus Bound,* ll. 201–20.

17. See Wilson, *Shelley's Later Poetry,* 70–72; Bloom, *The Visionary Company,* pp. 307–9; Rieger, *The Mutiny Within,* pp. 104–5; Reiman, *Percy Bysshe Shelley,* p. 79; Wasserman, *A Critical Reading,* pp. 257–61; M. H. Abrams, *Natural Supernaturalism: Tradition and Revolution in Romantic Literature* (New York: Norton, 1971), pp. 300–303; Leon Woldoff, "The Father-Son Conflict in *Prometheus Unbound,*" *The Psychoanalytic Review,* 62 (1975), 79–96; Curran, *Shelley's Annus Mirabilis,* p. 74; Hall, *The Transforming Image,* pp. 73–76; Melanie Bandy, *Mind Forg'd Manacles: Evil in the Poetry of Blake and Shelley* (University: Univ. of Alabama Press, 1981), pp. 96–125; Cronin, *Shelley's Poetic Thoughts,* pp. 137–40; and Leighton, *Shelley and the Sublime,* pp. 85–86. The words not from Shelley quoted in the current sentence are Reiman's from his p. 79.

18. The quotations, other than those from Shelley, in this and the next sentence are from Geoffry Ward, "Transforming Presence: Poetic Idealism in *Prometheus Unbound* and *Epipsychidion,*" in *Essays on Shelley,* ed. Miriam Allott (Liverpool: Univ. of Liverpool Press, 1982), pp. 195–97.

19. Lloyd Abbey, more than any other Shelley scholar, at least begins to see this fact in *Destroyer and Preserver* when he says that the "fall of Prometheus occurred when he came to *ascribe* autonomous existence to the objects of his thought" (p. 56, my italics).

20. "Thou art omnipotent," Prometheus asserts in recalling how he set up the Jupiter-image, because "O'er all things but thyself I gave thee power, / And my own will" (I. 272–74). There is a syntactic ambiguity here—"my own will" follows "but" at a distance—and that allows rebellious Prometheus to keep his will independent (as Jupiter is) of Olympian domination. But the immediate sense of these lines—"I gave thee . . . my own will"—suggests that omnipotence is permitted only when the will of the projector is handed over to the projection.

21. I quote *Beyond Good and Evil* in this and the next paragraph from the Helen Zimmern translation in *The Complete Works of Friedrich Nietzsche,* ed. Oscar Levy (1909–11; rpt. New York: Russell and Russell, 1964), XII, 25–28.

22. Trans. Maximillian A. Mügge, *Complete Works,* II, 173–92.

23. As Stuart Curran aptly writes, "this universe is firmly, if quietly, without [one] point of origin" (*Shelley's Annus Mirabilis,* p. 39).

24. See Hesiod's *Theogony* (where the source of all is Chaos at ll. 116–25); Ovid's *Metamorphoses* (where "God or Nature calmed the elements of chaos" at I. 21); Genesis 1:1–27, of course; and *Ahrimanes* (I. xvii–xx) in the Halliford *Works,* VII, 271–73.

25. See *Theogony,* II. 139–210, wherein Earth even "bore starry Heaven" to be "equal to herself" and to "cover her" sexually (ll. 126–30).

26. In his "Essay on Christianity," Shelley sees the myth of a Golden Age during the reign of Saturn as but a "child . . . of [the] airy hope" that projects a "happier state" in to the past from a state of "despondency" (*CW,* VI, 250). Asia's speech here intensifies this irony by seeing that projection as being attempted in the Golden Age itself.

27. In *The Will to Power,* trans. Anthony M. Ludovici, *Complete Works,* XV, 11–12 (no. 480).

28. Seeing this link, which is made by Asia's very words, helps us refute the most sustained analysis of her rationale for Jupiter's reign: the reading of her "creation" speech in Michael Scrivener, *Radical Shelley: The Philosophical Anarchism and Utopian Thought of Percy Bysshe Shelley* (Princeton, NJ: Princeton Univ. Press, 1982), pp. 158–61. I am indebted, though, to portions of Scrivener's commentary, as when he suggests that "Jupiter [may be created to] take the blame for the sufferings actually caused by Prometheus' commitment to *conquer* nature and ignorance" (p. 159, my emphasis).

29. For Foucault's relationship to Nietzsche, see the former's "Nietzsche, Genealogy, History," trans. Donald F. Bouchard and Sherry Simon, in Foucault's *Language, Counter-Memory, Practice,* ed. Bouchard (Ithaca, NY: Cornell Univ. Press, 1977), pp. 139–64. The best rendering of the "will to knowledge" at work, meanwhile, is in Foucault's *The History of Sexuality: Volume I* (originally titled *La volonté de savoir*), trans. Robert Hurley (New York: Pantheon, 1978), esp. pp. 77–131, to which I am repeatedly indebted in this chapter.

30. In "Of Truth and Falsity," *Complete Works,* II, 187–92.

31. On this longstanding rhetorical method for making man the Standard and woman the "Other," see Simone de Beauvoir, *The Second Sex,* trans. H. M. Parshley (New York: Knopf, 1952), pp. xvi–xxix.

32. See Sherry B. Ortner, "Is Female to Male as Nature Is to Culture?" in *Woman, Culture, and Society,* ed. Michelle Zimbalist Rosaldo and Louisa Lamphere (Stanford, CA: Stanford Univ. Press, 1974), pp. 67–87.

33. That double-voicedness of woman articulating herself in a male-dominated language is what many present-day feminists see as both necessary now and revolutionary in the end. See Adrienne Rich, "When We Dead Awaken: Writing as Re-vision," *College English,* 34 (1972), rpt. in Rich's *On Lies, Secrets, and Silence: Selected Prose, 1966–1978* (New York: Norton, 1979), pp. 63–84; Mary Jacobus, "The Difference of View," in *Women's Writing and Writing About Women,* ed. Jacobus (New York: Barnes and Noble, 1979), pp. 10–28; Elaine Showalter, "Feminist Criticism in the Wilderness," *Critical Inquiry,* 8 (1981), rpt. in *The New Feminist Criticism,* ed. Showalter (New York: Pantheon, 1985), where "double-voiced discourse" is actually used on p. 266; and especially Luce Irigaray in the title essay of *This Sex Which Is Not One,* trans. Catherine Porter (Ithaca, NY: Cornell Univ. Press, 1985), esp. pp. 28–33.

34. See my introduction, n. 32 and 40, above. Note, too, that feminine Asia as the forgotten "origin" of strictly masculine Prometheus is implied by Shelley's selection of her (encouraged only by Herodotus) as the Titan's primal self-projection and object of desire (analogous to the mother for Freudians and the "mother's breast" for Shelley). In some ancient accounts, Asia *is* Prometheus's mother. See Curran, *Shelley's Annus Mirabilis,* p. 45. Note also Ross Woodman's

statement that the "directing Promethean mind of the poet [at its best] is the willing servant of an unconscious feminine process" in "The Androgyne in *Prometheus Unbound*," *Studies in Romanticism*, 20 (1981), 228.

35. Here and in the next sentence I quote Foucault from *The Order of Things: An Archeology of the Human Sciences,* trans. anon. (New York: Random House, 1970), pp. 251 and 267.

36. See Donald Reiman regarding "On Life's" composition in *S&C,* VI, 971, note to line 423. He makes it clear, though he does not say so, that "On Life" is a long footnote to the *Philosophical View* which examines the virtues and errors of the Enlightenment empiricism summarized during the *View*'s history of the West.

37. See Ronald V. Sampson, *The Psychology of Power* (New York: Pantheon, 1965), esp. pp. 150–62.

38. In an 1820 letter to the publisher of *Prometheus Unbound,* Shelley refers to *Julian and Maddalo* as "a *sermo pedestris* way of treating human nature quite opposed to the idealism of the [lyrical] drama" (*L*, II, 196). He thus alludes to the established name given to certain Horation satires in dialogue form (noted for their formalized conversational quality) *and* to Horace's own use of *sermone pedestri* in the *Ars Poetica* (ll. 95–97) to describe "the language of prose" in tragedy as opposed to the hero's usually elevated "bombast" (*Horace: Satires, Epistles, and Ars Poetica,* Loeb Edition, trans. H. Rushton Fairclough). Cronin has seen this and the Pope connection better than anyone in *Shelley's Poetic Thoughts,* pp. 109–10, but he limits the extent to which these sources are used as well as altered in *Julian and Maddalo* by concentrating too much (albeit helpfully) on Shelley's rejoining of sympathetic *pathos* to Pope's judgmental *ethos.* Although there are a few resemblances between the debate in Shelley's piece and the one, say, in Pope's "The First Satire of the Second Book of Horace Imitated" (*The Poems,* ed. Butt, pp. 613–18), the design of *Julian and Maddalo* recalls Horace more directly, as I now proceed to show.

39. *Horace: Satires, Epistles, and Ars Poetica,* pp. 152–81.

40. See Wasserman, *A Critical Reading,* pp. 57–83; Holmes, *Shelley: The Pursuit,* pp. 451–57; Curran, *Annus Mirabilis,* p. 137; Bernard A. Hirsch, "'A Want of That True Theory': *Julian and Maddalo* as Dramatic Monologue," *Studies in Romanticism,* 17 (1978), 13–34; Cronin, *Poetic Thoughts,* pp. 108–30; Vincent Newey, "The Shelleyan Psycho-drama: 'Julian and Maddalo'," *Essays on Shelley,* ed. Allott, pp. 71–104; Scrivener, *Radical Shelley,* pp. 180–87; and Kelvin Everest, "Shelley's Doubles: An Approach to 'Julian and Maddalo'," *Shelley Revalued,* ed. Everest, pp. 63–88.

41. These sources for the characters in the poem are best assessed and summarized in Robinson, *Shelley and Byron,* pp. 81–96.

42. In a letter to Byron penned shortly after the one to Charles Ollier on *Julian and Maddalo,* Shelley writes in reaction to a scene in *Don Juan:* "Where did you learn all these secrets? I should like to go to school there" (*L*, II, 198).

43. "Shelley's Doubles," pp. 74, 79, and 87. For another view of what such an ideological struggle produces in this piece, see Marjorie Levinson, *The Romantic Fragment Poem: A Critique of a Form* (Chapel Hill: Univ. of North Carolina Press, 1986), pp. 151–66.

44. In *Radical Shelley,* p. 187.

45. See the struggle of the "work" (the projection of desire) between the turning out of the "earth" toward a "world"-order and the pull of earth back into itself in Heidegger's "Origin of the Work of Art," *Philosophies of Art and Beauty,* ed. Hofstadter and Kuhns, esp. pp. 669–700.

46. Shelley was an enthusiastic admirer of high to late Renaissance painters, including such Venetians as Titian (mentioned by the poet in a letter of February 1819 [*L*, II, 81]). See Frederic S. Colwell, "Shelley and Italian Painting," *Keats-Shelley Journal,* 29 (1980), 43–66. Moreover, the 1818–1819 correspondence of Shelley includes detailed descriptions of landscapes receding in layers to a vanishing distance. See, for example, *L*, II, 50 (on "Samson Drinking Water" by Guido Reni) and *L*, II, 42–43 (Shelley's own verbal painting of Venice itself "framed" alongside his description of the view from the house he rented at Este). Further proof that Shelley is con-

cerned with the forcing of this sort of perspective near the beginning of *Julian and Maddalo* even appears in one of the notebooks that he was using in 1819. I refer specifically to p. 65 in what is now Bodleian MS. Shelley adds. e. 11, a page reprinted on p. 221 of Nancy Moore Goslee, "Shelley at Play: A Study of Sketch and Text in his *Prometheus* Notebooks," *Huntington Library Quarterly,* 48 (1985), 210–55. That page offers handwritten jottings of lines 30 and 65–87 of *Julian and Maddalo*—portions of the segment I am now discussing—plus (at the bottom) a drawn landscape with a pyramid placed in the upper middle section of the scene and a pair of disembodied eyes positioned over the pyramid and slightly to the right of center. Although, as Goslee suggests on her p. 222, Shelley may be recalling an Egyptian symbol that places an eye at the top of a pyramid (a figure still pictured on American one-dollar bills), the poet, in using *two* eyes and letting the pyramid stand alone as a drawing imposed on distant treetops, is very likely visualizing the way all the radii in a scene can be drawn back to a center point and draw the eyes of the perceiver to that point as well. Moreover, the placement and largeness of the bodiless eyes indicate how much this centering of human awareness has been connected (in Western mythology and *Julian and Maddalo*) with the projection of "human seeing" out to and above that center, a projection that carries this seeing to a point where insight is enlarged to an anthropomorphic level of greater (almost divine) perception. This reading of the drawing and its connection with the poem finally differs from Goslee's proposal on her p. 226, but I agree with her general sense (also on 226) that the sketch "may somehow represent the problems of relating art and consciousness to natural process."

47. See this process as a "Romantic" tendency persisting from the time of Rousseau well into the nineteenth century in Georges Poulet, *The Metamorphoses of the Circle,* trans. Carley Dawson and Elliott Coleman (Baltimore, MD: The Johns Hopkins Univ. Press, 1966), pp. 91–118.

48. In *A Critical Reading,* p. 62, where this phrase is offered as reflecting one of Shelley's longest-lasting beliefs (one I think the poet attacks in this poem).

49. What I note in this last sentence makes it very likely that, as a few have suggested (such as Cameron in *The Golden Years,* p. 257), Shelley drew the name "Julian" *and* some character qualities from Julian the Apostate in Chapters X and XI of Edward Gibbon's *Decline and Fall of the Roman Empire* (read by Shelley with strong agreement many times, as one can see just from *L,* II, 474–75). In his devotion to the "kings of old philosophy" over Christianity (l. 188) and yet in his projection of a "spirit" into an objective center, Shelley's Julian sounds very like these sentences on the Apostate in Gibbon: "Julian recollected with terror the observation of his master Plato that the government of our flocks and herds is always committed to beings of a superior species and that the conduct of nations requires and deserves the celestial powers of the Gods or of the Genii. From this principle he justly concluded that the man who presumes to reign should aspire to the perfection of divine nature" (*Decline and Fall,* ed. Dero A. Saunders [1952; rpt. New York: Penguin, 1981], p. 460). This description surely prompted Shelley to consider his own aristocratic status and how he sometimes drew on it to support a "ruling stature" even when he was "terrified" of and opposed to it. Moreover, if these sentences in Gibbon are a source for Shelley's Julian, the critique in the poet's rendering of this character cannot be denied any longer.

50. Wasserman, *A Critical Reading,* p. 72.

51. This latter ideology has toyed and struggled with an egalitarian (mainly bourgeois) counterpart for over a century prior to *Julian and Maddalo.* Pope, one of the source-authors for this piece, forecasts Julian's attempt in the *Essay on Criticism* (1711) when he allows that "most have the *seeds* of Judgment in their Mind" as traces of *"Light"* from Heaven but insists that different degrees of light are granted different classes of people, some of whom "Nature meant but *Fools*" (ll. 20–21 and 26; *The Poems,* ed. Butt, pp. 144–45). This essentialist—indeed, most often, aristocratic—rhetoric persists even in those Enlightenment egalitarians who try to overthrow hierarchical differences. The heaven-granted essence that has been the supposed basis of higher-class (or lower-class) potentials is used after 1770 to say that all men, and sometimes women and men, are "created equal" by God. See Wollstonecraft, *A Vindication,* pp. 11–38,

and Marilyn Butler, *Romantics, Rebels, and Reactionaries: English Literature and Its Background, 1760–1830* (New York: Oxford Univ. Press, 1981), pp. 16–38. Shelley, as an egalitarian aristocrat, was in an especially good position to see, even in himself, the irony of this rhetoric, especially considering its use by such contemporaries as the Duke of Norfolk, Lord Grey, and Sir Francis Burdett. See also Cameron, *The Young Shelley*, pp. 55–69, and P. M. S. Dawson, *The Unacknowledged Legislator: Shelley and Politics* (Oxford: Clarendon, 1980), pp. 17–25.

52. The name "Maddalo" comes from Count Maddalo Fucci of Venice, about whom Shelley read in his research on Tasso, just as Carlos Baker tells us in *Shelley's Major Poetry*, p. 129. Shelley even uses the name in part of what survives from his drama about Tasso (*PW*, pp. 558–59). But, as we know, his letters also refer to Byron as "mad," especially after *Manfred* and *Childe Harold* IV.

53. *The Visionary Company*, rev. ed., p. 245.

54. See J. Paul Hunter, *The Reluctant Pilgrim: Defoe's Emblematic Method and Quest for Form in* Robinson Crusoe (Baltimore, MD: The Johns Hopkins Univ. Press, 1966), pp. 93–122; Boyd M. Berry, *Process of Speech: Puritan Religious Writing and* Paradise Lost (Baltimore, MD: The Johns Hopkins Univ. Press, 1976), pp. 124–35; and Herman Rapaport, *Milton and the Postmodern* (Lincoln: Univ. of Nebraska Press, 1983), pp. 15–21, 30–33, and 209–39.

55. See Hans Jonas, *The Gnostic Religion: The Message of the Alien God and the Beginnings of Christianity,* 2nd ed. (Boston, MA: Beacon Press, 1963), pp. 42–97, and Jacques Lecarrière, *The Gnostics,* trans. Nina Rootes (New York: Dutton, 1977), pp. 15–39. What James Rieger says about Shelley's attraction to Gnosticism in *The Mutiny Within*, pp. 133–62, may refer to the poet's stance in his Byronic moments. But such views are not the attitudes that Shelley usually thought best. Certainly *Julian and Maddalo* does not imply for me what Reiger seems to find in *Prometheus Unbound:* that Shelley would unite Gnostic Light with Eternal Love as ultimate goals and so approach "the more nearly orthodox solution of Milton" (p. 162). Shelley sees dangerous objectifications in nearly all transcendent and monolithic absolutes, despite his attraction to some less orthodox types as counters to the most established ones.

56. See Robert F. Gleckner, *Byron and the Ruins of Paradise* (Baltimore: The Johns Hopkins Univ. Press, 1967), pp. xviii–xxiv, 57–90, and 225–97, and Leslie Brisman, *Milton's Poetry of Choice and Its Romantic Heirs* (Ithaca, NY: Cornell Univ. Press, 1973), pp. 133–50, where the "moment of choice" in Shelley at his most Miltonic (hence Byronic) "becomes a choice of moments" that seek an impossible "arrest of time."

57. William Veeder in *Mary Shelley and* Frankenstein (pp. 47–80) aptly notes how the erotic worship of a projected male self feminizes the projector in just this way throughout Shelley's poetry. Veeder, though, seems to agree with what he admits is principally Mary's view: that "Percy never accepted her idea of complementarity," an ideal interchange of qualities between relative equals who are both somewhat androgynous (p. 101). I find that Shelley values that prospect often in his writing. In *Julian and Maddalo,* he castigates only those self/other constructs bent on exalting the male self *in* the female counterpart and so draining the projector of the maleness he projects. Shelley may have been guilty—indeed he admits it—of what Mary critiques in *Frankenstein* (1818), but he is also capable of a self-criticism very like her analysis of him and perhaps of even learning from *Frankenstein* itself prior to the writing of *Julian and Maddalo.*

58. See Rapaport, *Milton and the Postmodern,* pp. 23–49. This critic would rightly point out here, I think, that the Maniac is a "melancholic" in Freud's sense of the term, a person who takes the absence of love-object as the definer of the ego's options despite the object's withdrawal. See "Mourning and Melancholy" in the *Standard Edition* of Freud, XVII, 245.

59. Stertinius, for example, anatomizes Ajax, who killed his own sheep because he believed that such an act would free impounded ships, as simply the type "who conceives ideas that are other than true" and so commits the "perverse folly" that "is the height of madness" (*Horace: Satires,* ll. 208–10 in the third satire of the Second Book).

60. For more ways in which the Maniac reworks or generalizes Byron and his self-projec-

tions, see Robinson, *Shelley and Byron,* pp. 91–104, though I do not agree with this study when it argues that the Maniac is almost exclusively Byronic in nature.

61. See Everest, "Shelley's Doubles," pp. 83–84.

62. See Newman Ivey White, *Shelley* (New York: Knopf, 1947), II, 46–50, and Cameron, *The Golden Years,* pp. 261–66.

63. Here I try to refine the case for the poem as a generalizing dramatization (not sheer autobiography), a case begun in G. M. Matthews, "'Julian and Maddalo': The Draft and Meaning," *Studia Neophilologica,* 35 (1963), esp. 74–83, and advanced eloquently in Levinson, *The Romantic Fragment Poem,* esp. pp. 158–66.

64. See, among the early Renaissance lyrics most admired by Shelley, numbers XIII, XIX, XXIX, XXXI, and LXIII in *Petrarch: Sonnets and Songs,* trans. Anna Maria Arms (New York: Pantheon, 1946). Note also the abasement of the Christian warriors under the "double charm" of the deceptive Armida in Tasso's own *Jerusalem Delivered,* trans. Edward Fairfax, intr. John Charles Nelson (New York: Capricorn, 1963), IV, lxvi–xcvi (pp. 76–83).

65. The most precise enumeration of what Shelley knew and read relative to Tasso is still the one in Baker, *Shelley's Major Poetry,* pp. 128–35.

66. Cf. Girard, *Violence and the Sacred,* p. 146.

67. See n. 42 above and *L,* II, 323, where "I despair of rivalling Lord Byron, as well I may, [though] there is no other with whom it is worth contending." For more on Shelley's inclinations to both worship Lord Byron and pull back from his influence, see Holmes, *Shelley: The Pursuit,* pp. 336–38 and 448–49. Even some of the later sentences in the present paragraph are influenced by these perceptive pages.

68. The Maniac really embodies mimetic desire in a host of different ways, even though the "other" he imitates (the Lady) seems to be more the object and less the model of his desire. Actually, she is his "spirit's mate" because she seems to desire and even *define* the more fulfilled state of manhood that becomes his objective because of and by way of her. Since she is his means to that end, she can come to seem the possessor of and rival for his manhood and so appear to have the right to call for his self-castration. Then, too, he incarnates the ways Byron and Shelley try to articulate and so achieve their poetic natures by imitating models. If the Maniac's soliloquy is an extension of Byron's and Shelley's earlier efforts to voice their situations through Tasso's—through a Renaissance model for their imprisoned positions as "insane" poets for many—then his madness is theirs without seeming theirs at all. Shelley is using this creation to reflect, again self-critically, on what he and Byron have actually been doing in writing laments by Tasso. In any event, the Maniac meets all the requirements for a ritual scapegoat laid out by Girard in *Violence and the Sacred* (pp. 269–73), in no small measure by being a poet and thus an easily maligned "outsider" on the inside of a society whose tendencies he verbalizes.

69. *Violence and the Sacred,* pp. 160–68.

70. *Violence and the Sacred,* p. 148.

71. *Violence and the Sacred,* p. 148 (without italics).

72. The best account of the "occasion" for *The Mask* is Robert Walmsley, *Peterloo: The Case Reopened* (New York: Augustus Kelley, 1969), but only as its conservative bias is modified by Cameron, *The Golden Years,* pp. 343–47, and Scrivener, *Radical Shelley,* pp. 196–210.

73. Any would-be opposite, in fact, is prone to this paradox, all the more so when a total opposition is being claimed. By its very nature an opposite is dependent on the figure it opposes in order to declare itself an opposite in the first place. See Michael Ryan's discussion of this point in *Marxism and Deconstruction,* pp. 25–32.

74. For the clearest explanation of the delay between composition and publication, see Baker, *Shelley's Major Poetry,* p. 164.

75. *Shelley's Annus Mirabilis,* pp. 190 and 188. Cameron in *The Golden Years* is right, however, to maintain (on his p. 346) that the connection of "power" to "Mask" for Shelley was first made in *The Examiner* editorials on Peterloo that the poet must have read, especially at the point where the Tories are called "Men in Brazen Masks" (*The Examiner,* No. 608 [Aug. 22,

1819], 530). Shelley simply extended "mask" in this context to the courtly "masquerade" in which the powerful have traditionally justified their power plays and hidden their roots in violence using costumes and masks as cover.

76. *Shelley's Annus Mirabilis*, p. 191.

77. This point is made even more directly in the opening scene of Shelley's aborted tragedy *Charles the First* (left fragmentary in 1821). There a masque proceeding through the Inns of Court celebrates the power of the Stuart monarchy by including an antimasque of "lean outcasts" amid chariots of "painted pomp." An aging onlooker sees the masque/antimasque relationship here as "the sign and the thing signified," both in the sense that royalty is built on the violent degradation of victim-scapegoats and in the sense that class conflict is the actual meaning of the ruling "order" that the masque claims to represent. See *PW*, p. 492, ll. 154–73 of sc. I, and Cronin's relation of this scene to *The Mask* in *Shelley's Poetic Thoughts*, pp. 51–53, even though Cronin has too little evidence for claiming that the poet "began work [on *Charles*] in 1819 just after completing *The Mask of Anarchy*."

78. For the most likely sources of the Liberty figure, see Richard Hendrix on this piece in "The Necessity of Response: How Shelley's Radical Poetry Works," *Keats-Shelley Journal*, 27 (1978), esp. 58–59.

79. That these are what the "old laws" refer to for the sort of liberal Shelley was is proven by *The Examiner*'s lead editorial on August 15, 1819, the day before the Manchester Massacre. There Leigh Hunt claims that "as long as the constitution is usurped, and some of the most essential provisions of Magna Charta and the Bill of Rights set at nought . . . so long will it be impossible for an honest observer not to regard [the] dispute [over reform] as one between might and right" ("Increasing Dispute Between Reformers and Their Opponents," *The Examiner*, No. 607, 513).

80. I agree with these interpretations by Curran in *Shelley's Annus Mirabilis*, p. 146, and Cameron in *The Golden Years*, p. 352, even though I want to be more precise about the basis and nature of those "formulations."

81. The most basic sense is the one established by the fact that Shelley's poem is the third *Peter Bell* in English verse published within the space of a year. The "first" one is John Hamilton Reynolds's parody of Wordsworth's affected "rural" style issued under the title *Peter Bell*, and the "second" is Wordsworth's own narrative poem focused on a character so called, which was advertized enough in advance for Reynolds to beat it into print with his veiled attack on the "country manner" of a now Tory writer who may not really support the interests of the common man. Shelley's explicit acknowledgment of this succession in his title, I might add, is itself evidence that his poem is a probe into a pattern of mimetic desire at the "root" of what he parodies. The "primal ancestor" in this series of poems (the Reynolds piece), as Shelley would surely have seen, is obsessed with both admiration for a model and an effort to differentiate the writer from that model. As Keats said at the time in his review of the Reynolds *Peter Bell*, the work reveals a certain "love," however "splenetic," for the conservative poet being burlesqued even as the burlesque places its author at a satirist's distance from a supposedly hypocritical style. Shelley therefore has a definite license from the start for seeing mimetic desire as the "father of the line" in the "ancestry" that he now takes to task. That is what he implies in his prologue when he calls "The First Peter" a "shadow," like John the Baptist, who looks to and makes way for the larger "glass" (itself a reflector) that is Wordsworth's attempt at a more "substantial" assertion (*Peter Bell the Third*, ll. 13–16). For the Keats review, see *The Examiner*, No. 591 (Apr. 25, 1818), 270. See also Reynolds's *Peter Bell. Lyrical Ballad* (London: Taylor and Hessey, 1819), rpt. in *John Hamilton Reynolds: Peter Bell, Benjamin the Waggoner, and The Fancy*, intr. Donald H. Reiman (New York: Garland, 1977). Granted, there is still debate over whether Shelley read the Reynolds piece itself or just Keats's account of it. Even so, Carlos Baker makes a persuasive case that Shelley read both, citing the poet's use of a Reynolds character not noted in the review, in *Shelley's Major Poetry*, p. 166, n. 16.

82. See *Peter Bell: A Tale*, ll. 499–530 and 916–1135, in *Wordsworth: Poetical Works*, pp.

192–93 and 196–98. For the now widely accepted claim that Shelley read Wordsworth's *Peter Bell* and not just the review in *The Examiner,* see Jack Benoit Gohn, "Did Shelley Know Wordsworth's *Peter Bell?*" *Keats-Shelley Journal,* 28 (1979), 20–24, and Cameron, *The Golden Years,* pp. 626–27, n. 21.

83. *"Peter Bell, a Lyrical Ballad, by Wm. Wordsworth,"* *The Examiner,* No. 592 (May 2, 1819), 282–83. All citations from this review will refer to these two pages.

84. According to Ziva Ben-Porat, such "parodic representations expose the model's conventions and lay bare its devices through the coexistence of [at least] two codes [the model's and the parodist's] in the same message." See Ben-Porat's "Method in Madness: Notes on the Structure of Parody," *Poetics Today,* 1 (1979), 247, and Linda Hutcheson, *A Theory of Parody* (New York: Methuen, 1985), pp. 30–49. The *Peter Bell* of Wordsworth, we can even say, is the perfect point of departure for such a "laying bare" of its author. It claims to encompass most of the older poet's entire career, admitting that it was written in 1798 (the year of the *Lyrical Ballads*) and then revised to gain a "favorable reception," presumably from the monarchical and Anglican conservatives who once attacked the *Ballads* (Preface to *Peter Bell, Wordsworth: Poetical Works,* p. 188). That very alteration encapsulates the course of Wordsworth's submission to absolutist thinking. His poem, then, especially when parodied, shows him to be inclined toward such thinking at an earlier stage and then drawn into it further by that need to imitate powerful systems with which he seems to have started.

85. See Max Byrd, *London Transformed: Images of the City in the Eighteenth Century* (New Haven, CT: Yale Univ. Press, 1978).

86. Quoted in the Hunt review, p. 283, even though this stanza was quickly cut from the poem and did not appear in any subsequent edition or Wordsworth collection (until recently, of course).

87. Shelley must have seen this notion repeatedly connected with Wesleyans and Calvinists in Hunt's *Attempt to Shew the Folly and Dangers of Methodism,* which was published in parts in *The Examiner* from May to December 1808, and issued in book form in 1809. See especially Essay IV of the *Attempt,* "On Methodistical Inspiration," in *The Examiner,* No. 24 (June 12, 1808), 380–82. Hunt's series of essays even shows increasingly how Methodism is actually based on mimetic thinking and a resulting penchant for transferring all sins to non-Methodist victims. Calvin is presented as aping a rival by enacting the very religious persecution he once fought against in Essay V, "On Methodists," *The Examiner,* No. 28 (July 10, 1808), 444–46. Then Methodists are depicted as trying "to please God by rejoicing in the suffering which they imagine he has destined for others" in the conclusion of Essay V, *The Examiner,* No. 29 (July 17, 1808), 461.

88. I am not proposing that Shelley simply thought of Coleridge as being introduced to Wordsworth by Southey. The "Devil" in this poem is not just a Southey-figure but also an embodiment of how much relationships in a mimetic world are brought about from the start by imitative interaction, the kind of connection that occurs here between the Wordsworth and Coleridge figures. Shelley finds Wordsworth, in (say) "Tintern Abbey" or the "Immortality" ode, to be more imitative of Coleridge's German-Christian idealism than scholars are inclined to find him today. For how much Germanic Romanticism was targeted by Shelley (and other skeptics near him) as self-absorbed, God-centered, and fundamentally hierarchical, see Marilyn Butler in *Peacock Displayed: A Satirist in His Context* (London: Routledge, 1979), pp. 102–39. Parts of Peacock's *Nightmare Abbey* (1818), I would even argue, must have been pretexts for at least "Part Fifth" in *Peter Bell the Third.* Certainly in "Part Third" a possible consequence of an English-German connection is alluded to when London is envisioned as a place where "German soldiers" might yet appear to reinforce Tory "despotism" (ll. 173–74).

89. For a clear and concise account of why this reaction to Wordsworth occurred in the British reviews, see Butler, *Romantics, Rebels, and Reactionaries,* pp. 58–68.

90. Pope's *Poems,* ed. Butt, pp. 146, 722, and 740.

91. On the blatant conflict of styles in Shelley's *Mask,* see Thomas T. Edwards, *Imagination*

and Power: A Study of Poetry on Public Themes (London: Oxford Univ. Press, 1971), pp. 159–68; Hendrix, "The Necessity of Response," pp. 49–65; and Cronin, *Shelley's Poetic Thoughts,* pp. 39–55.

92. The use of satirical poems in popular styles to advance royalist, Tory, or pro-government positions has a long history, as Shelley was aware, one best revealed today in *Poems on Affairs of State,* ed. Elias F. Mengel, Jr., Frank H. Ellis, et al., 7 vols. (New Haven, CT: Yale Univ. Press, 1963–1975). See, for examples, such pieces in these volumes as "The Wiltshire Ballad," "The Essex Ballad," and "The Cabal" (*Poems on Affairs,* II, 312–38) or "The Procession" (*Poems on Affairs,* VII, 514–19). Examples during Shelley's day abound, especially in what was published by *The Anti-Jacobin, or Weekly Examiner* set up to support Pitt's Tory government. Tory poems remarkably similar in style to *The Mask of Anarchy* appear in *Poetry of the Anti-Jacobin,* ed. L. Rice-Exley (Oxford: Basil Blackwell, 1924), on pp. 10–11, 12–14, 22–24, 33–36, 83–85, 100–106, and 166–68. There was, however, an even larger circulation of anti-government broadsides.

93. See Ann Thompson, "Shelley and 'Satire's Scourge'," in *Literature of the Romantic Period, 1750–1850,* ed. R. T. Davies and B. G. Beatty (Liverpool: Liverpool Univ. Press, 1976), pp. 135–50.

94. The allusions to possible attacks on Southey in this fragment indicate that it may be a response to—and a critique of—Byron's swipe at Southey in the 1819 "Dedication" to *Don Juan.* Surely, too, Shelley is thinking of Byron's liking for satire in general and how that liking is imitated in *Peter Bell the Third* (where Southey is at least one ingredient of the Devil). Robinson comes close to making this connection when he refers to the "Satire on Satire" in *Shelley and Byron,* pp. 142–43, but he surprisingly backs away from this conclusion despite having provided much of the evidence for it.

95. The tone for those readings that argue for a balance among the factors (even to the point of paradox) has been set by Baker, *Shelley's Major Poetry,* pp. 149–50; intensified by Joseph W. Donohue, Jr., "Shelley's Beatrice and the Romantic Conception of Tragic Character," *Keats-Shelley Journal,* 17 (1968), 53–73, a piece expanded in Donohue's *Dramatic Character in the English Romantic Age* (Princeton, NJ: Princeton Univ. Press, 1970), pp. 157–86; and refined by Stuart Sperry, "The Ethical Politics of Shelley's *The Cenci,*" *Studies in Romanticism,* 25 (1986), 411–27. For those who emphasize Beatrice as culpable despite provocation, the most-often-used rationale is the one offered by Wilson, *Shelley's Later Poetry,* pp. 78–101, and developed most fully in Wasserman, *A Critical Reading,* pp. 84–128. The most thorough case for Beatrice as forced to succumb to an oppressive universe is the one in Stuart Curran, *Shelley's* Cenci: *Scorpions Ringed with Fire* (Princeton, NJ: Princeton Univ. Press., 1970), esp. pp. 129–54, as modified (but not recanted) by Curran in *Shelley's Annus Mirabilis,* pp. 120–36. I write not simply to dispute any of these arguments but to show that what they all reveal comes out of several kinds of regressive transference permeating the play, kinds that are both individually chosen and culturally imposed.

96. I cannot agree with Curran in *Shelley's* Cenci (p. 139) that Shelley here refers only to "the Beatrice of history." The poet is pointing out what makes the "character" he now offers a "dramatic" and "tragic" one (his words at this point in the Preface, p. 240).

97. See E. S. Bates, *A Study of Shelley's Drama,* The Cenci (New York: Columbia Univ. Press, 1908), pp. 54–55; David Lee Clark, "Shelley and Shakespeare," *PMLA,* 54 (1939), 261–87; Frederick L. Jones, "Shelley and Shakespeare: A Supplement," *PMLA,* 59 (1944), 591–96; Beach Langston, "Shelley's Use of Shakespeare," *Huntington Library Quarterly,* 12 (1949), 163–90; Curran, *Shelley's* Cenci, pp. 37–39 (which wisely warns against pressing the Shakespeare influence too far); Paul Cantor, "A Distorting Mirror: Shelley's *The Cenci* and Shakespeare's Tragedy," *Shakespeare: Aspects of Influence,* Harvard English Studies No. 7, ed. G. Blakemore Evans (Cambridge, MA: Harvard Univ. Press, 1976), pp. 91–108 (which shows how Shelley can pit Shakespeare's words against the latter's assumptions); D. Harrington-Lueker, "Imagination versus Introspection: *The Cenci* and *Macbeth,*" *Keats-Shelley Journal,* 32 (1983), 172–89; and

Jonathan Bate, *Shakespeare and the Romantic Imagination* (Oxford: Clarendon, 1986), pp. 202–21.

98. See, for examples, *Hamlet Prince of Denmark,* II. ii. 556–91; *Othello the Moor of Venice,* I. iii. 128–68; *King Lear,* III. iv. 28–36; and *Macbeth,* I. iii. 130–42, as all these appear in *The Complete Works,* Pelican Text Revised. On why such patterns are necessary and how some of them work in this period, see Stephen Greenblatt, *Renaissance Self-Fashioning: From More to Shakespeare* (Chicago: Univ. of Chicago Press, 1980), pp. 1–9 and 222–54. On how the launching of the subject into a world of signs—including personal body-language—generates the quest for a "reader" in the stagings of the self, see Lacan, "The Function of Language in Psychoanalysis," *The Language of the Self,* ed. and trans. Wilden, p. 31.

99. All this, of course, is partly because Shelly is extending—and critquing—the stock figure of the raging or vengeful aristocrat on the tragic stage of his own day, designed as that Gothic type was for an Edmund Kean and for the "thrill of terror" it supposedly aroused, usually in the women of a Covent Garden audience. See Curran, *Shelley's* Cenci, pp. 160–71, plus Alan S. Downer, "Players and the Painted Stage: Nineteenth-Century Acting," *PMLA,* 61 (1946), 522–76; Bertrand Evans, *Gothic Drama from Walpole to Shelley,* Univ. of California Publications in English, Vol. 18 (Berkeley: Univ. of California Press, 1947), pp. 86–89 and 228–32; Richard M. Fletcher, *English Romantic Drama, 1795–1843* (New York: Exposition Press, 1966), pp. 70–121 (the chapter in which *The Cenci* is discussed); and Donohue, *Theater in the Age of Kean* (Oxford: Basil Blackwell, 1975), pp. 84–142. Sartre, moreover, has revealed how dependent on an Other's reception this very kind of actor-character is in *Kean, or Disorder and Genius: Based on the Play by Alexandre Dumas,* trans. Kitty Black (London: Hamish Hamilton, 1954), esp. acts II, IV, and V.

100. *Being and Nothingness,* p. 372. See also Murray L. Cohen et al., "The Psychology of Rapists," in *Forcible Rape: The Crime, the Victim, and the Offender,* ed. Duncan Chappell, Robley Geis, and Gilbert Geis (New York: Columbia Univ. Press, 1977), pp. 291–314; A. Nicholas Groth, *Men Who Rape: The Psychology of the Offender* (New York: Plenum, 1979), pp. 12–61; and Donna Iven Qureshi, *Rape: Social Facts from England and America* (Champaign, IL: Stipes, 1979), pp. 15–26.

101. I cite *Hamlet* in this paragraph, using Willard Farnham's edition in the Pelican *Complete Works,* from I. ii. 146; II. ii. 533–54; II. ii. 584–89; and V. ii. 10–11 and 204–11. For helpful recent feminist readings of this play moving more and more in the direction I argue here, see David Leverenz, "The Woman in Hamlet: an Interpersonal View," *Signs,* 4 (1978), 291–308; parts of the essays by Murray Schwartz, Madelon Gohlke, Joel Fineman, Richard Wheeler, and David Willbern in *Representing Shakespeare: New Psychoanalytic Essays,* ed. Schwartz and Coppelia Kahn (Baltimore: The Johns Hopkins Univ. Press, 1980); Marilyn French, *Shakespeare's Division of Experience* (New York: Summit, 1981), pp. 5–28 and 145–58; Kahn, *Man's Estate: Masculine Identity in Shakespeare* (Berkeley: Univ. of California Press, 1981), pp. 21–46 and 132–40; Peter Erickson, *Patriarchal Structures in Shakespeare's Drama* (Berkeley: Univ. of California Press, 1985), pp. 66–80; and my "Teaching the Politics of Gender in Literature: Two Proposals for Reform, with a Reading of *Hamlet,*" in *Changing Our Minds: Feminist Transformations of Knowledge,* ed. Susan Hardy Aiken et al. (Albany: State University of New York Press, 1988), pp. 98–133.

102. By employing this repetition of the sophist's "soul upthrown," Shelley's Cenci departs in very significant ways from the Count as he is rendered in the "Relation of the Death of the Family of the Cenci" (the already mentioned chief source for the play). The Francesco Cenci of the "Relation" remains a thoroughgoing "atheist," though he does build a "small chapel . . . in the court of his palace" for burying—and thus concealing his crimes against—his children (*CW,* II, 159). He therefore does not answer Beatrice's appeals to Catholicism and God (noted in the "Relation," *CW,* II, 160) with similar forms of justification for his insistance on patriarchal power. Indeed he approaches Beatrice sexually in the "Relation" (without ever quite completing the act) not to match her assertions of supremacy with a reverse-reflection of them but because

she really appeals to his senses, as do concubines in his palace whom Shelley does not mention, *and* because he wants to prevent a costly marriage like the one that her elder sister (not in Shelley's play) has made against his will. Shelley's version makes a point of mirroring-reactions and imitative performances that the "Relation" does not emphasize nearly as much. There could hardly be clearer evidence that Shelley is deliberately skewing the basic story he receives to depict mirrored power plays as the basis of action in *The Cenci*. A similar point can be made about what Shelley does with the few elements he borrowed from Vincenzio Pieracci's *Beatrice Cenci*, a tragedy published in 1816 and circulated in Italy while Shelley was there. See a translation of that play and some comparisons between it and *The Cenci* in George Yost, *Pieracci and Shelley: An Italian* Ur-Cenci (Potomac, MD: Scripta Humanistica, 1986).

103. This problem throughout the play is thoroughly assessed by Michael Worton, "Speech and Silence in *The Cenci,*" in *Essays on Shelley,* ed. Allott, pp. 105–24. I write here to further what Worton suggests by revealing the larger causes in cultural discourse for the fear of language he notes.

104. It is mainly this dimension of Shelley's play that Antonin Artaud intensifies in his 1935 version of *The Cenci,* first staged with himself as both the director and Count Cenci (as well as the rewriter—or should one say *de*writer?—of the script). The words adapted from Shelley by way of Stendhal's translation, Artaud admits, are pared down almost to mere gestures that carry through the sheer, amoral, impersonal will to power that hurls each character toward the others. What text there is becomes the violence of the father/Count/director (costumed as a skeletal, death-dealing Anarchy) provoking imitated violence from the object of his staged attack. In the last line of Artaud's *Cenci,* as a result, Beatrice fears "that death may teach me that I have ended by resembling . . . my father." This modern transposition thus brings out the mirroring theatricality of reciprocal violence in Shelley's version, making that element easier to see. Shelley might argue, though, that Artaud's assumptions about the will to power result from perversions of transference that the "original" play reveals and the later version represses for the sake of the director's Cenci-like attempt to subject the interplay of characters to his master text. See Artaud's two defenses of his production and an English text of the play itself in his *Playscript 12: "The Cenci,"* trans. Simon Watson-Taylor (London: Calder and Boyers, 1969).

105. Jean Hall quite rightly points out this failure in Beatrice to "achieve poetic distancing" from hegemonic modes of thought in "The Socialized Imagination: Shelley's *The Cenci* and *Prometheus Unbound,*" *Studies in Romanticism,* 23 (1984), 339–50.

106. Robinson in *Shelley and Byron* (pp. 143–60) outdistances most other analysts—and concurs with Curran's sense of inescapable cultural orientations—in focusing on the total domination of Catholic thinking over Beatrice's decisions. Though often helpful, such a view ignores how much she chooses that domination for the sake of rhetorical power over some others who have gained sanction from the same source. For more on Beatrice's decision to appeal to God's will the way her father does, see Wasserman, *A Critical Reading,* p. 93, and Terry Otten, *The Deserted Stage: The Search for Dramatic Form in Nineteenth-Century England* (Athens: Ohio Univ. Press, 1972), pp. 20–24.

107. It is her attempt to set up this Beginning and End for her father that leads Beatrice to describe the "deep ravine" into which she wants him hurled (III. i. 245–65), using images from the description of Hell's entrance in Calderón's *Purgatorio de San Patricio* (admitted as a source by Shelley in his Preface, *NCE,* p. 241n.). This allusion returns the features of Beatrice's vision quite literally to their Catholic, late Renaissance, and rhetorical sources. Calderón's images in Shelley's eyes, after all, like Beatrice's thinking, are filled with "rigidly-defined and ever-repeated idealisms of distorted superstition" (*Defence,* p. 490).

108. Especially Wasserman in *A Critical Reading,* pp. 101–15.

109. See "The Plague in Literature and Myth," *Texas Studies in Literature and Language,* 15 (1974), rpt. in Girard's *"To Double Business Bound": Essays on Literature, Myth, and Anthropology* (Baltimore, MD: The Johns Hopkins Univ. Press, 1978), pp. 136–54, plus such later Girard essays on specific plays as "'To entrap the wisest': A Reading of *The Merchant of*

Venice," in *Literature and Society,* ed. Edward Said (Baltimore, MD: The Johns Hopkins Univ. Press, 1979), pp. 100–19; "Myth and Ritual in Shakespeare: *A Midsummer Night's Dream"* in *Textual Strategies,* ed. Harari, pp. 189–212; and "Hamlet's Dull Revenge," *Stanford Literature Review,* 1 (1984), rpt. in *Literary Theory/Renaissance Texts,* ed. Patricia Parker and David Quint (Baltimore, MD: The Johns Hopkins Univ. Press, 1986), pp. 280–302.

110. This vision of creation as therefore divided into hierarchical levels of true and false gods is what James Rieger discusses as "Paterin" about Beatrice in *The Mutiny Within,* pp. 111–28. I am here suggesting what impels Beatrice to construct the universe in the fashion Rieger describes.

111. On these various senses of "abjection," I am indebted to Julia Kristeva, *Powers of Horror: An Essay on Abjection,* trans. Leon S. Roudiez (New York: Columbia Univ. Press, 1982). I am also influenced in what now follows by Kristeva's sense of the primal "throwing away." For her it is mainly the casting-off of the multi-dimensional birth state, a suppression demanded by the human search for an identity that such a state (if continued) would disallow. See my use and explanation of Kristeva's notion in "The Struggle for a Dichotomy: Abjection in Jekyll and His Interpreters" in *Dr Jekyll and Mr Hyde After One Hundred Years,* ed. William Veeder and Gordon Hirsch (Chicago: Univ. of Chicago Press, 1988), esp. pp. 171–76.

112. Freud's death wish, in other words, as presented in *Beyond the Pleasure Principle* and later pieces (see my introduction, n. 39), is for Shelley one consequence of a misconstruction turning the birth stage into an emergence from an absolute origin (the Beginning and the End).

4. UNCHAINING MYTHOGRAPHY: *PROMETHEUS UNBOUND* AND ITS AFTERMATH

1. See *Shelley's Mythmaking,* pp. 6–8 and 91–97. Note also the similar views of *Prometheus Unbound* in Abrams, *Natural Supernaturalism,* pp. 299–307; Hall, *The Transforming Image,* pp. 79–98; and Richard Harter Fogle, "Image and Imagelessness: A Limited Reading of *Prometheus Unbound,"* *Keats-Shelley Journal,* 1 (1952), rpt. in Fogle's *The Permanent Pleasure: Essays on Classics of Romanticism* (Athens: Univ. of Georgia Press, 1974), pp. 69–86.

2. I quote Frye here from *A Study of English Romanticism* (New York: Random House, 1968), pp. 104 and 121, and *Anatomy of Criticism: Four Essays* (Princeton, NJ: Princeton Univ. Press, 1957), p. 117.

3. *A Critical Reading,* p. 275.

4. *Shelley's Annus Mirabilis,* pp. 102–3, 106, and 96–97.

5. This sense of separation and distance redeclaring themselves in attempts at the interrelation of differences is what leads the early Bloom, though he does not say so, to point out Shelley's realization that the unifying effort of "mythopoesis" must always remain incomplete and deferred. See *Shelley's Mythmaking,* p. 145.

6. As thoroughly demonstrated by Albert J. Kuhn in "English Deism and the Development of Romantic Mythological Syncretism," *PMLA,* 71 (1956), 1094–1116.

7. In *A Critical Reading,* p. 271, and *Shelley's Annus Mirabilis,* p. 44. Indeed, more recently, Curran distances Shelley even farther from the assumptions of most eighteenth- and nineteenth-century syncretists while still maintaining the poet's syncretic methods in "The Political Prometheus," *Studies in Romanticism,* 25 (1986), 430–32.

8. Quoted from the anonymous translation of *The Ruins* noted earlier, pp. 174–75.

9. See Volney, *The Ruins,* pp. 130 and 175, and Shelley's exposure, during the very letter wherein he speaks of the "harmonizing" treatise, of a power play disguised as an assertion of God's truth in Book V, Canto ii, of Spenser's *Fairie Queene.* Shelley refers, right after refusing to attempt a syncretic work, to "cast[ing] what weight I can [instead] into the right scale of that balance which the Giant (of Athegall) holds" (*L,* II, 71). The poet's refusal of syncretism, as Peacock says in annotating this letter, stems from a desire to avoid the imposition of a unifying

order on an equalizing of differences. That very imposition is what occurs, Peacock remembers Shelley saying, when "Arthegall's iron man knocks [the giant] over into the sea" after said giant has weighed different attempts to "rectify the physical and moral evils which result from inequality of condition" (*L*, II, 71, n. 5). Shelley sees himself as "of the Giant's faction," so he wants no part of a single-minded philosophy that tries tyrannically to subsume (and thereby drown) every particular method for overcoming hegemonies.

10. *The Destiny of the Warrior*, trans. Alf Hiltebeitel (Chicago: Univ. of Chicago Press, 1969), p. 3.

11. The clearest rendering by Marx himself of this struggle between emergent "modes" and existing "methods" appears in *A Contribution to the Critique of Political Economy*, trans. S. W. Ryazanskaya, ed. Maurice Dobb (New York: International Publishers, 1970), pp. 20–22 and 205–14. By exacerbating and thus pointing to this conflict in the very writing of his lyrical drama, Shelley in fact anticipates Marx's personal sense that suppressed modes of labor can be embodied by Prometheus. Consequently, Shelley helps to establish, without knowing he is doing so, the many comparisons that can be made between the Marxist sense of history and the Prometheus story. Both Marx's allusions to the Titan and many of those parallels are detailed by Leonard P. Wessell, Jr., in *Prometheus Bound: The Mythic Structure of Karl Marx's Scientific Thinking* (Baton Rouge: Louisiana State Univ. Press, 1984), pp. 64–103 and 144–284. Curiously, though, Wessell never mentions Shelley's *Prometheus Unbound*, despite Marx's admiration for Shelley and the way nineteenth-century Marxists embraced the poet as one of their own (as noted by Marx's daughter in the *Shelley's Socialism* lectures mentioned above in n. 26 of my introduction). Wessell also fails to see that Marx's debts to the Prometheus tale may be connected, as Shelley's were, with a deconstruction rather than a simple use of reigning myths. For Wessell, Marx seems to embrace an older mythic structure as it stands in order to give shape to a new social vision. In Shelley's eyes, and surely Marx's, such a decision could result in an excessive submission to hegemonic constructs.

12. Though only the *Prometheus Bound* of Aeschylus survived the ancient world, Shelley's preface to his lyrical drama assumes other "lost" Prometheus plays—hence a sequence of them that includes a Greek *Prometheus Unbound* in which the Titan "unsay[s] his [rebellious] high language [of the available play] and quail[s] before his successful and perfidious adversary," the "Oppressor of mankind" whose supremacy he never doubts (*NCE*, p. 133). Shelley is plainly determined to reverse this "binding" in what he knew of the Aeschylean *Prometheus Unbound* by intensifying, even unleashing, potentials intimated but not entirely licensed in *Prometheus Bound*. Such a defiant aim is one of the overtones suggested, somewhat as Bloom says in *Shelley's Mythmaking* (pp. 46–48) and Wasserman argues in *A Critical Reading* (pp. 282–84), by the epigraph Shelley chooses for his play (*NCE*, p. 132): "Audisne haec, Amphiarae, sub terram abdite?" ("Do you hear this, Amphiares, under the earth?"). This line is a fragment surviving from Aeschylus's *Epigoni*, quoted by Cicero (and found by Shelley) in the *Tusculan Disputations*, and yet ironically addressed by Shelley in one of his notebooks—and surely here as well— "To the Ghost of Aeschylus" and, as Bloom rightly says, to other "halfhearted rebels become [conservative] oracular gods." Amphiarus the seer, after all, was a rebel against the attack of the seven against Thebes but was so devoted to the will of Zeus that the latter pulled him into the earth when the attack threatened the seer's dismemberment. Additional implications in this choice of an epigraph not noticed by Bloom and Wasserman are discussed below in n. 36 of this chapter.

13. That is one of the points Shelley is making in his preface when he says that his imagery, like Dante's and Shakespeare's, renders "the operations of the human mind" to themselves (*NCE*, p. 133). The resulting poetic "analogy with those sources of emotion and thought" reveals (and, of course, helps create) both the "external" restrictions upon and the "internal" potentials within the "contemporary condition of" the mind (pp. 134–35). On this positive function for ideological constructs, though admittedly one that can be skewed into hegemonic grids of intel-

ligibility, see Ernst Cassirer, *Language and Myth,* trans. Suzanne K. Langer (1946; rpt. New York: Dover, 1953), pp. 62–99, and Raymond Williams, *Marxism and Literature* (New York: Oxford Univ. Press, 1977), pp. 66–71.

14. See Curran, "The Political Prometheus," pp. 436–55, and Raymond Trousson, *Le thème de Promethée dans la littérature européene* (Geneva: Librarie Droz, 1964), II, 281–386.

15. In 1810, Charles Bloomfield published a new Greek text of *Prometheus Vinctus,* usually referred to thereafter as the "Cambridge Aeschylus," which aroused wide acclaim and controversy in educated circles for several years following its appearance. See again Curran, "The Political Prometheus," pp. 434–35, where this fact reveals an "unusual intensity of popular interest" in the Prometheus plays of Aeschylus, one which clearly reached a sort of climax in the eighteen-teens.

16. The words of Herbert Schneidau in *Sacred Discontent,* p. 58. For a wider survey of the various sentiments and of texts by Byron with which Shelley's drama disagrees, see Robinson, *Shelley and Byron,* pp. 133–37, and Neil Fraistat, *The Poem and the Book: Interpreting Collections of Romantic Poetry* (Chapel Hill: Univ. of North Carolina Press, 1985), pp. 147–49.

17. According to *Mary Shelley's Journal,* p. 93.

18. Here and in the next four sentences I quote Schlegel's *Lectures* from the translation of John Black, 2nd ed., rev. A. J. W. Morrison (London: G. Bell, 1902), pp. 93 and 26–27. There were, of course, some areas of agreement between Shelley's and Schlegel's senses of Prometheus, a few of which are noted by Curran in *Shelley's Annus Mirabilis,* pp. 33–35, and by Angela Leighton in *Shelly and the Sublime,* pp. 76–77 and 88–89. But we miss part of the poet's aim if we fail to note the great differences and how much the orthodox and hierarchical assumptions in Schlegel's view must have prompted Shelley to fashion an anti-mythic alternative.

19. Aeschylus revises some earlier senses of Prometheus even as he upholds the right of Zeus to an Olympian rule subject only to the laws of Necessity. Hesiod's *Theogony* (ll. 520–64) offers Prometheus only as the Titan who often tricked the king of the Olympian order that conquered that demi-god's own race. Aeschylus (esp. at ll. 105–6 and 199–223 of *Prometheus Bound*) emphasizes how much the Titan, with his foresight, aided in the victory of the Olympians and knew the dictates of Necessity as prior to and overarching the reign of the Olympians and his own relationship to them. The Aeschylus version thus makes Prometheus more of an ironic and legitimate threat to the power of Zeus than he frequently was in previous accounts. Certainly there were Shelley contemporaries who saw Aeschylus as determined to offer such a vision in the name of Athenian liberty from Persian domination. See Thomas Northmore's preface to his *Washington, or Liberty Restored* (London: Longman's, 1809), p. iii. Milton, too, regards the epic forms he recalls as subject to quite radical revisions according to his own Puritan sense of what true "epic heroism" should be. See T. J. B. Spencer, "*Paradise Lost:* The Anti-epic," *Approaches to* Paradise Lost, ed. C. A. Patrides (Toronto: Univ. of Toronto Press, 1968), 81–98; Ralph Waterbury Condee, "Milton's Dialogue with the Epic: *Paradise Regained* and the Tradition," *Yale Review,* 59 (1969–70), 357–75; Joseph Anthony Wittreich, *Angel of Apocalypse: Blake's Idea of Milton* (Madison: Univ. of Wisconsin Press, 1975), pp. 151–71; Curran, "*Paradise Regained:* Implications of Epic," *Milton Studies,* 17 (1983), 209–24; and Barbara Kiefer Lewalski, Paradise Lost *and the Rhetoric of Literary Forms* (Princeton, NJ: Princeton Univ. Press, 1985), pp. 3–24 and 254–79.

20. Schneidau's *Sacred Discontent* is cited in this and the next two sentences from pp. 50, 31, and 44. For Shelley's extensive reading of the Old Testament, see the list of his and Mary's references to it in *L,* II, 469.

21. See Hesiod's *Theogony,* ll. 561–69 and 453–91; Aeschylus's *Prometheus Bound,* ll. 108–14 and 209–20; and Carl Kerényi, *Prometheus: Archetypal Image of Human Existence,* trans. Ralph Manheim (New York: Pantheon, 1963), which, on p. 52, places the Titan explicitly in "the position of the mediator, with the hovering in the middle typical of the messenger" Hermes, another longstanding figure of transference and one to whom the Titan is therefore connected in both Aeschylus and Shelley.

22. Cf. Aeschylus, *Prometheus Bound*, ll. 484–97 and 910–17, and Kerényi, *Prometheus*, pp. 96–99 and 105–6.

23. These are brought together in their most influential form in the Prometheus *plasticator* sequence of Ovid's *Metamorphoses*, I. 76–90. This segment in Ovid, as Shelley would surely have noticed, ends with a portrait of man as "godlike" but not a god and therefore as gazing, more than animals do, toward the sky (toward the place from which parts of human nature have been transferred by Prometheus). That portrait then becomes the cue for Ovid to assert a self-transformative principle retained in the human form, a principle that can potentially lead to "unknown species of mankind" if it is fully unleashed.

24. See Plato, *Gorgias*, 523e.

25. See Jacob Bryant, *A New System, or, An Analysis of Ancient Mythology* (London: Payne, Elmsly, White, and Walter, 1774), II, 202–03; George Stanley Faber, *The Origin of Pagan Idolatry* (London: Rivington, 1816), I, 172; and Thomas Taylor, *The Six Books of Proclus the Platonic Successor* (London: privately printed for the translator, 1816), II, 230–31. I should add that I have been directed to these sources and those mentioned in n. 26 and 27 of this chapter by Curran, *Shelley's Annus Mirabilis*, pp. 43–94 and 213–30.

26. As in Natalis Comes, *Mythologie, ou Explication des fables* (Paris: Chevalier, 1627), pp. 296–307.

27. For the sense of the Titan as Providence incarnate, see Francis Bacon, *The Wisedome of the Ancients* (1619; rpt. New York: Da Capo, 1968), p. 124. For Prometheus as a form of Noah, see Bryant, *A New System*, II, 206–7 and 274–75, and Faber, *Pagan Idolatry*, II, 193–94. For several such incarnations—and especially for the analogies between Prometheus and Christ—listed all at once in a sequence of fourteen mythic uses of the figure, see the entry under "Prometheus" in Alexander Ross's encyclopedia/dictionary of mythological beings, the *Mystagogus Poeticus, or the Muses Interpreter*, 2nd ed. (London: Whitaker, 1648), pp. 366–68. On the Titan as Christ, see also Kerényi, p. 3, and Wasserman, *A Critical Reading*, pp. 293–97.

28. See Baker, *Shelley's Major Poetry*, pp. 96–101; Butter, *Shelley's Idols*, pp. 169–77; Wilson, *Shelley's Later Poetry*, pp. 54–62; Bloom, *Shelley's Mythmaking*, pp. 92–93 and 100–102; and Wasserman, *A Critical Reading*, pp. 257–61.

29. Shelley's own preface discusses the resemblance of Prometheus to Satan and the poet's effort to divorce the Titan from that connection after a definite limit of similarity has been reached (*NCE*, p. 133). For a look at the most significant allusions to Milton's Satan in act 1, see Wasserman, *A Critical Reading*, pp. 294–95. For the first extensive list of the many echoes of Milton in *Prometheus Unbound*, see Frederick L. Jones, "Shelley and Milton," *Studies in Philology*, 49 (1952), esp. 499–504.

30. See the assessment of Milton's Jesus in Curran, *"Paradise Regained,"* pp. 210–17. Note, too, how Milton anticipates some of Shelley's concerns by using the name of Jesus (the revolutionary) rather than the word "Christ," the symbol of a dictatorial institution. For a history of all the older critical readings that link Shelley's Prometheus with Christ—but without specifying the Jesus of *Paradise Regained*—see Lawrence John Zillman's *Variorum Edition* (hereafter the "Zillman *Variorum*") of *Prometheus Unbound* (Seattle: Univ. of Washington Press, 1959), pp. 45 and 311.

31. Paine's clearest sense of Jesus as anti-hierarchical appears during *The Age of Reason* in *The Complete Writings of Thomas Paine*, ed. Philip S. Foner (New York: Citadel, 1945), I, 469 and 480, and this characterization is accompanied by an attack (pp. 469–70) on the ways in which orthodox Christian mythology has legitimized itself by deceptively reworking the myth of the war between Jupiter and the Titans. *The Age of Reason*, in other words, is an additional influence on the entire anti-mythological stance of *Prometheus Unbound*. Spinoza's view can be found in the *Tractatus Theologico-Politicus*, which Shelley began translating in 1817. There Christ is contrasted with the Old Testament prophets, who slavishly followed "the command of God" when they spoke His patriarchal will. Jesus is depicted as more of a participant in and continuation of the thought-process of universal law that *is* God for Spinoza; the apostles of

Christ are therefore more inclined than a Moses or Elijah to argue for an ethical living-out of God's love in mind and action and to do so in statements worked out "by the light of natural reason" instead of the glow of inspiration from above (*A Theologico-Political Treatise and A Politcal Treatise,* trans. R. H. M. Elwes [1883; rpt. New York: Dover 1951], pp. 157, 18–19, and 161). See also Scrivener, *Radical Shelley,* pp. 93–95 and 101.

32. See the definitive account of this connection in Curran, *Shelley's Annus Mirabilis,* pp. 67–71.

33. Curran's words in *Shelley's Annus Mirabilis,* p. 73. See also n. 58 on p. 223 of that book. Shelley probably drew this Zoroastrian vision from Abraham Anquetil du Perron's French translation of the *Zend-Avesta* (Paris: Tilliard, 1771), II, 254–76, and from Bryant's *A New System,* II, 108–25.

34. *A Theory of Literary Production,* trans. Geoffrey Wall (London: Routledge, 1978), p. 237.

35. In "The Philosophy of Shelley's Poetry" (1903) in *Essays and Introductions* (New York: Macmillan, 1961), p. 79. For a survey of the few readings since Yeats that even partially apply this idea to the realm of shades, see the Zillman *Variorum,* pp. 360–61. Norman Thurston makes one of the most erroneous, yet in the end one of the most helpful, uses of this concept in "The Second Language of *Prometheus Unbound,*" *PQ,* 55 (1976), 126–33. He wrongly argues that Shelley's world of the dead contains the "true" language of the self that all earthly figures should try to approach in metaphors. Yet he rightly notes that the "language of the *uncommunicating* dead" in this play (my emphasis), which I find to be the language of the forgotten Spirits suppressed by the ruling figures in the Great Memory, draws conscious language toward an openness to new verbal relations that can "endlessly" expand human self-knowledge.

36. There is a strong resemblance, after all, between this resplendent underworld and the vast labyrinth adjacent to Lake Moeris in ancient Egypt where, according to Herodotus's *History* (Loeb Edition, Book II, section 148), the most wealthy kings placed memorials of the dictatorial power they held when they were alive. As Michael Grant briefly suggests, moreover (in *Myths of the Greeks and Romans* [New York: New American Library, 1962], p. 187), Shelley's drama may be alluding, particularly at this point, to Robert Blair's poem *The Grave* (1808) and especially to some illustrations appended to it by William Blake, perhaps the only work by Blake that Shelley may ever have perused. See Robert N. Essick and Morton D. Paley, *Robert Blair's The Grave, Illustrated by William Blake: A Study and Facsimile* (London: Scholar Press, 1982), esp. the page facing p. 11 of the poem. Shelley, however, prompted somewhat by Blair's lines at their least orthodox moments (as on p. 30 of the poem), clearly views the death of such older figures, mythographic or otherwise, the way James Parkinson regards dead bodies in the *Organic Remains of a Former World:* as shapes undergoing a chemical change in their decay that encourages the generation of "new combinations" from the decaying materials (*Remains,* 2nd ed., I, 80). In the words of Richard Cronin's reading of *Prometheus Unbound,* the "past is confronted [mainly] in order to remove the obstacles erected in the past against change" (*Shelley's Poetic Thoughts,* p. 136). Now we can grasp the additional dimensions in the epigraph to Shelley's work addressed to Aeschylus's ghost and other reactionaries with Aeschylus's words (and already mentioned in n. 12 of the current chapter). The placement of the addressee "under the earth," we can see by this realm of shades, clearly locates this lyrical drama's principal literary ancestor in the Great Memory along with a host of influential mythographs (including the oracular Amphiarus himself). That fact reveals the living writer and his text as pulled, the way Shelley's Prometheus is pulled, in two directions at once. On the one hand, the dead letters of Aeschylus and other relevant precursors can be used, as they are by Cicero when he tells of one Stoic using the call to Amphiarus as a way of keeping another Stoic true to the ideals of the dead Zeno, to tie down the new variant to a past set of standards that has provided the basic figural patterns. Amphiarus, we should remember, was preserved by Zeus below ground because of his unswerving obedience to absolutist Olympian decrees. (See the *Tusculan Disputations,* Loeb Edition, II. 60–66, and the accounts of Bloom and Wasserman on the pages cited in n. 12 above.) On the other hand, the death of old authors or prophets and their ideologies in and behind the old

figures—aided by the fact that these particular words from Aeschylus are parts of a fragment sundered from an unrecovered whole—hollows out all those entities enough so that they can be attached to different contexts and thereby turned against the tyrannical values they once inscribed. That possibility is present just in the way Cicero and Shelley can recontextualize the *Epigoni* fragment to make Amphiarus refer to Zeno in one case and Aeschylus himself in the other. The situation of Shelley's epigraph is thus quite similar to that of the title *Prometheus Unbound*. Both look to a specific (albeit fragmented) previous and hegemonic use of all their words by a remembered author, but those words are repeated with such radical differences connected to them that they are largely unbound—though they can never be completely— from what defined them in the past. See, despite its excessive emphasis on sheer re-voicing as what permits the unbinding, Susan Hawk Brisman, "'Unsaying His High Language'," esp. pp. 55–73, and, for how Shelley's epigraph may be a reference to and defiance of Byron (among others), Robinson, *Shelley and Byron*, p. 126, and Fraistat, *The Poem and the Book*, pp. 146–48.

37. Wasserman is thus wrong to suggest, in *A Critical Reading*, p. 274, that "Lear's [attempted] relation to his daughters" becomes conceptually "inoperative" in this skewed repetition of it. Shelley, as he so often does, is ironically retaining that context of the words in order to announce the projective basis of the tyranny in them.

38. See Grant's *Myths*, pp. 170–71; Homer's *Odyssey*, XI. 271–82; and Aeschylus's *Eumenides*, ll. 299–388.

39. At ll. 734–41 of the *Eumenides*, where Athena, despite her own femininity, intones the law of male dominance by terming man "the master of the house" and noting her own birth from the mind of a male god without a "mother" as intermediary (in the translation of Aeschylus by Herbert Weir Smyth).

40. Here I quote Berkeley from *Siris: A Chain of Philosophical Reflexions and Inquires* (1744) in *The Works of George Berkeley*, ed. A. A. Luce and T. E. Jessup (London: Thomas Nelson, 1953), V. 82. But I could make the same point using some of the other authors, especially Dyer, quoted on "ether" by Curran in *Shelley's Annus Mirabilis*, pp. 106–9.

41. See Stuart Sperry, "Necessity and the Role of the Hero in Shelley's *Prometheus Unbound*," *PMLA*, 96 (1981), 242–54. Sperry's essay, however, does raise the problem of whether Shelley is concerned primarily in this work with the potentials of the personal imagination, the submission of individual thought to a more interpersonal/historical drive, or the search for a harmony between the former and the latter. This problem has been raised again recently by John Reider in "The 'One' in *Prometheus Unbound*," *SEL*, 25 (1985), 775–800, which argues that the play can only struggle to resolve an antagonism in Shelley's assumptions between "individualist" and "necessitarian" ideologies. Still, though Shelley is torn by ideological conflict, as my chapters 3 and 5 try to point out, I find this problem elided in *Prometheus Unbound* by the fact that transference is opened up there as an interplay moving (1) through, beyond, and back toward individual perceptions at subliminal levels and (2) among the mythographs into which people have long projected their desires for more extensive transfigurations of the self. To focus on an increasing interplay of myth-figures across remembered and possible history, as this play does, is to face the mind with its own basic process in what resembles the process from outside it *and* to urge the process upon minds from outside their awareness because they are now too divorced from a sense of that motion's history, nature, and potential.

42. As in Cameron, *The Golden Years*, pp. 495–502; Leighton, *Shelley and the Sublime*, pp. 80–82; and Daniel Hughes, "Prometheus Made Capable Poet in Act One of *Prometheus Unbound*," *Studies in Romanticism*, 17 (1978), 3–11.

43. See the Loeb *Herodotus*, Book IV, section 45, and Curran, *Shelley's Annus Mirabilis*, p. 45.

44. *Prometheus Bound*, ll 700–72.

45. See ll. 111–59 of the poem and Frances Ferguson, *Wordsworth: Language as Counter-Spirit* (New Haven, CT: Yale Univ. Press, 1977), pp. 144–54.

46. Examples in Dante include sections III, V, VI, IX, XXIII, XXV, XXX, and XXXV of the *Vita Nuova* plus the *Inferno,* I. 112–35 and II. 52–126.

47. For the multiple sources of these names and figures, see Curran, *Shelley's Annus Mirabilis,* pp. 47–49. For one of the only senses prior to mine, though, of how both figures carry "the sleeping potentiality of relationship" into "some kinetic manifestation," see Fraistat, *The Poem and the Book.* pp. 152–53.

48. The most influential statements of this position are Baker's in *Shelley's Major Poetry,* esp. pp. 109–14; Frederick A. Pottle's in "The Role of Asia in the Dramatic Action of *Prometheus Unbound,*" in *Shelley: A Collection of Critical Essays,* ed. George M. Ridenour (Englewood Cliffs, NJ: Prentice-Hall, 1965), esp. pp. 141–43; Wasserman's in *A Critical Reading,* esp. pp. 225–56; and Curran's in *Shelley's Annus Mirabilis,* where the play is "at its most abstract level wholly a psychodrama" on p. 114. This view has been somewhat common, however, at least since William Rossetti, "*Prometheus Unbound:* A Study of Its Meanings and Personages" (1886), in *The Shelley Society's Papers,* series 1, no. 1, pt. 1 (London: Reeves and Turner, 1888), 50–72, and is articulated especially well in Melvin Solve, *Shelley: His Theory of Poetry* (1927; rpt. New York: Russell and Russell, 1964), pp. 90–91. One of the best refutations of this conception is Tilottama Rajan's in "Romanticism and the Death of Lyric Consciousness," *Lyric Poetry: Beyond New Criticism,* ed. Hašek and Parker, esp. pp. 202–207. Here the centripetal drive of any attempts at lyrical subjectivity in *Prometheus Unbound* is shown to be countered by a centrifugal, dramatic pulling of consciousness into the "dialogic nature of language," whereupon any supposed "lyrical voice is now situated among other voices that are not at one with it."

49. As in the accounts listed in the Zillman *Variorum,* pp. 329–30, plus Pottle, "The Role of Asia," p. 141; Wasserman, *A Critical Reading,* pp. 276–77 and 299; Abrams, *Natural Supernaturalism,* p. 307; Cameron, *The Golden Years,* pp. 509–10; and Nathaniel Brown, *Sexuality and Feminism in Shelley,* where Asia is "nature's life principle" on p. 61.

50. See Curran, *Shelley's Annus Mirabilis,* p. 46, and the poet's likely source for this connection: Francis Wilford, "On Mount Caucasus," *Asiatic Researches,* 6 (1801), 504.

51. See the *Theory,* ed. D. D. Raphael and A. L. MacFie, in the *Glasgow Edition of the Works and Correspondence* of Smith (Oxford: Clarendon, 1976), I, i.1.4–i.5.5, plus Roy R. Male, "Shelley and the Doctrine of Sympathy," *Studies in English,* 29 (1950), 183–203, and Brown, *Sexuality and Feminism,* pp. 29–34.

52. See again Curran, *Shelley's Annus Mirabilis,* p. 46, and Wilford, *Asiatic Researches,* 6, 495, and 8 (1805), 279. In this use of Eastern analogues, we see another example of what I mention in n. 34 of chapter 3: Shelley's combination in Asia of *projections* from Prometheus with the *origins* of his very possibility and the possibility of a projective transference allowing the self to be remade in different figures. Shelley's Asia is in danger, modern femininists may (understandably) feel, of being a sheer vessel for Prometheus's self-extension and self-expansion. There is some truth in the statement of B. Rajan that Asia is primarily the figurative agent who "universalizes the mental reorganization of Prometheus" ("The Motivation of Shelley's *Prometheus,*" *Review of English Studies,* 19 [1943], 299). Yet the fact that Shelley uses a goddess-figure who can, on many levels, "give birth" to Prometheus's nature as well as fulfill it shows some attempt on his part to counter that potentially "secondary" positioning of her. Indeed, the more Asia discovers that her informed dissemination of transference is what makes possible her lover's "unbinding," the more she emerges (I will soon show) as the primordial "feminine" transference, noted briefly in chapter 3, that "mothers" all free interplays of perceptions and all mythographs constructed from such interplays.

53. See *NCE,* p. 178, n. 2, and the Loeb *Da natura derum,* III. xxiii, where this multiplicity of possibly "origins" is used in a skeptical argument to refute the certain and permanent existence of such figures.

54. In *Aeneid,* VI. 42–101. Compare this sequence to the portrait of the Maenads in

Euripedes' *Bacchae*, ll. 64–168. This use of Virgil in act 2, moreover, significantly alters Wasserman's conclusions (in *A Critical Reading*, pp. 310–16) about how Shelley employs that poet in Asia's quest for deeper understanding.

55. I want to add this reading, then, to what is already suggested by G. M. Matthews in "A Volcano's Voice in Shelley," *ELH*, 27 (1957), the most important parts of which are reprinted in *Shelley*, ed. Ridenour, pp. 111–31.

56. See the discussion of such meteorology in Wasserman, *A Critical Reading*, pp. 328–29.

57. See Boccaccio, *Genealogiae* (1494; rpt. New York: Garland, 1976), libr. I, cap. iii–ix. Note also, on this idea of the figure, Wasserman, *A Critical Reading*, p. 332; Curran, *Shelley's Annus Mirabilis*, pp. 51–53; and Leighton, *Shelley and the Sublime*, pp. 89–98. I find Wasserman and Curran, in fact, coming as close to my sense of Shelley's Demogorgon as any critics do, since most of them (as in the survey of them in the Zillman *Variorum*, pp. 317–19) are mired in seeing the shapeless figure simply as an embodiment of material Necessity's hidden laws. Wasserman specifies him/it as a "center of [sheer] potentiality" (p. 341), and Curran defines him as "the principle of attraction" between differences whose "'mighty law' is desire, a quickening force within" (pp. 110 and 106).

58. From the note to p. 68, l. 3, of *Rhododaphne* in the Halliford *Works*, VII, 94—a statement made after an extensive survey of Demogorgon's many earlier incarnations (clear evidence of the figure's being, like Prometheus, an impulse toward self-transfiguration).

59. See Hesiod's *Theogony*, ll. 116–38; *Prometheus Unbound*, I. 152–62; and Heidegger's sense of Being's primordial process as the sheer coming-forth of an action that both unconceals and conceals in "The Origin of the Work of Art," *Philosophies of Art and Beauty*, ed. Hofstadter and Kuhns, pp. 674–77.

60. In addition to the male culture/female nature opposition discussed by the article cited in n. 32 of chapter 3, consider the longstanding British feminization of the colonized or "barbaric" East. This gendering is present even in the syncretic English accounts (already cited) of the feminine principles of life *(Haysa, Isi)* in the Hindu religion, the faith of the India so often referred to as "her." Most British syncretism, in fact, as Shelley must have seen, aims at subsuming—and thus "mastering"—the mythologies of the great She-continent into the purview of a patriarchal religious system.

61. For the world as perceived to be returned to this sort of primal fluidity in Shelley's eyes, after all, is for human awareness to recover the cascade of ever-changing intersubjective crossings (the basic flow) in "Mont Blanc" and the reverie-state blurring, though never dissolving, all absolute distinctions between thoughts and minds in the essay "On Life." These potentials for infinite metamorphosis can now encourage in each mind a multiplicity of future interplays among perceived social roles.

62. See Bryant, *A New System*, II, 269–71.

63. Theresa M. Kelley argues, quite helpfully, that this unbinding is the aim of several English Romantic works (including *Prometheus Unbound*) that use Proteus to empower and embody their newly "dynamic" and "tentative" form of allegory. See her "Proteus and Romantic Allegory," *ELH*, 49 (1982), 623–52.

64. As in the rapid darting between types of stanzas and different meters, the breaking away from previous limits on style to open more dialogue among styles, in *Prometheus Unbound*, IV. 1–178. Particularly in this increased dialogism, the progression of the play becomes both an attempt to prompt and "an expression of a progressive going out of our own nature" (to use more words from Cronin, *Shelley's Poetic Thoughts*, p. 163).

65. Compare acts 3 and 4 with Holbach's *Nature: and Her Laws*, I, 597–623; the Marquis de Condorcet's "Sketch for a Historical Picture of the Progress of the Human Mind" (1793), trans. June Barraclough, in *Condorcet: Selected Writings*, ed. Keith Michael Baker (Indianapolis, IN: Bobbs-Merrill, 1976), pp. 258–81; Erasmus Darwin's *Temple of Nature*, III. 117–495; and *Queen Mab*, VIII–IX (*PW*, pp. 792–800, plus the notes to these sections on pp. 825–34).

66. See the discussion of the "oscillating wave-like" progress in the word-clusters of the last two acts in V. A. De Luca, "The Style of Millennial Announcement in *Prometheus Unbound*," *Keats-Shelley Journal,* 18 (1979), 78–101.

67. Several Shelley scholars have mentioned this device, but the most thorough explorations of it to date are Timothy Webb's in "The Unascended Heaven: Negatives in *Prometheus Unbound*," *Shelley Revalued,* ed. Everest, pp. 37–62, and P. M. S. Dawson's in *The Unacknowledged Legislator,* pp. 120–133.

68. This point has already been made to some extent by Scrivener, *Radical Shelley,* p. 179; by Tilottama Rajan's third foray into Shelley's lyrical drama, "Deconstruction or Reconstruction: Reading Shelley's *Prometheus Unbound*," *Studies in Romanticism,* 23 (1984), 317–38; and by Marlon B. Ross, "Shelley's Wayward Dream-Poem: The Apprehending Reader in *Prometheus Unbound*," *Keats-Shelley Journal,* 36 (1987), 110–33.

69. See Erich Auerbach, "'Figura'," trans. Ralph Manheim, in Auerbach's *Scenes from the Drama of European Literature* (New York: Meridian, 1959), esp. pp. 28–76; A. C. Charity, *Events and Their Afterlife: The Dialectics of Christian Typology in the Bible and Dante* (Cambridge: Cambridge Univ. Press, 1966), pp. 1–9, 67–80, and 148–64; Paul Korshin, "The Development of Abstracted Typology in England, 1650–1820," in *Literary Uses of Typology from the Late Middle Ages to the Present,* ed. Earl Miner (Princeton, NJ: Princeton Univ. Press, 1977), pp. 147–204 (where Shelley is mentioned on pp. 196–202 in ways I try to be more specific about); and Leslie Tannenbaum, *Biblical Tradition in Blake's Early Prophecies: The Great Code of Art* (Princeton, NJ: Princeton Univ. Press, 1982), pp. 88–117.

70. The attack on typology appears in Paine's *Complete Writings,* ed. Foner, I, 552–55. What I quote from Tannenbaum in the next sentence comes from *Biblical Tradition,* p. 103.

71. See Van Ghent in *The English Novel: Form and Function* (New York: Rinehart, 1953), p. 11. Isaiah, incidentally, one of the prophets most used by both Christian typologists and Shelley, reveals how typology can be turned in such a parodic direction. Note his reference (in 43:16–19) to "making a way" through the sea in Exodus and his sudden attempt to dismiss the recollection while it is still being invoked: "Remember ye not the former things, neither consider the things of old. Behold, I will do a new thing; now it shall spring forth; shall ye not know it? I will even make a way in the wilderness, and rivers in the desert." Such evidence, moreover, counters Bloom's sense, on pp. 93–96 in *Poetry and Repression,* of Shelley "weakly" trying to answer one use of *figura* with another in acts 3 and 4.

72. Such interplays of separate sense perceptions are examples of the many noted in Shelley's poetry by such studies as Fogle's *Imagery of Keats and Shelley* (pp. 101–38) and O'Malley's *Shelley and Synesthesia* (which treats *Prometheus Unbound* on pp. 144–73). But this use of synaesthetic transference refutes the conclusions in such books that Shelley is simply revealing the actual but unseen union of all phenomena that imagination struggles to know as the "deep truth" of existence. Here we see instead an iconoclastic effort to break down distances and hierarchies keeping figures from potential—and future (not Platonically pre-existent)—relationships.

73. On this last allusion and how far it extends into this sequence in act 4, see Ants Oras, "The Multitudinous Orb: Some Miltonic Elements in Shelley," *MLQ,* 16 (1955), 247–57, and Bloom, *Shelley's Mythmaking,* p. 144.

74. This parodic turn refutes Bloom's further assertion in *Poetry and Repression,* pp. 96–98, that *Prometheus Unbound* cannot overcome the force of Milton's influence to the same extent as *The Triumph of Life* succeeds in doing with *its* ironic use of the Divine Chariot. Bloom misses the point he half-makes that the Chariot-figure contains self-altering elements in its "transumption" that virtually insist on each use of the figure being parodic of earlier ones. See my reading of *The Triumph* and my references to *Poetry and Repression* in the final section of my chapter 6.

75. See Thomas A. Reisner, "Some Scientific Models for Shelley's Multitudinous Orb,"

Keats-Shelley Journal, 23 (1974), esp. 57, which cites Euler from his *Recherches sur le mouvement de rotation des corps célestes.*

76. See Cameron's account of the Orb, with extensive quotations from Dalton, Walter, and Davy, in *The Golden Years,* pp. 548–51, plus Grabo, *A Newton Among Poets,* pp. 139–58. As Fraistat points out (*The Poem and the Book.* pp. 165–66), Shelley would also have known the medieval-Renaissance Ptolemaic conception of the known world as a series of spheres containing spheres. But this notion is linked for the poet with the Leibnizian vision of concentric monads and so is being turned, along with that view, toward the far more mobile conception in these dynamic (almost thermodynamic) theories.

77. Quoted from the 1812 *Elements of Chemical Philosophy* in *The Collected Works of Sir Humphry Davy,* ed. John Davy (1840; rpt. New York: Johnson Reprint, 1972), IV, 66–67.

78. Though Cameron is right that these shapes can and should "flow invisibly through one another," Shelley's use of "shapes" not yet fully imaginable denies the claim in *The Golden Years* (p. 550) that they simply represent the "constituents . . . of electricity, magnetism," and other "fluids" moving between atoms. Even more to my point, these figures able to be produced by an ever-mobile interplay among orbs refute the many readings of this portrait of transfigured Earth that see its movement as a rising toward a numenal stasis that it has always desired. These readings are offered in such famous discussions as Grabo, *A Newton,* pp. 195–200; G. Wilson Knight, *The Starlit Dome: Studies in the Poetry of Vision* (1941; rpt. New York: Oxford Univ. Press, 1971), pp. 203–24; Bloom, *Shelley's Mythmaking,* p. 145; Wilson, *Shelley's Later Poetry,* pp. 207–17; Daniel Hughes, "Potentiality in *Prometheus Unbound,*" *Studies in Romanticism,* 2 (1963), rpt. in *NCE,* pp. 603–20; Wasserman, *A Critical Reading,* pp. 359–73; and James B. Twitchell, "Shelley's Metapsychological System in Act IV of *Prometheus Unbound,*" *Keats-Shelley Journal,* 24 (1975), 29–48. A quite recent extension of this view appears in Andrew Welburn's *Power and Self-Consciousness in the Poetry of Shelley,* pp. 170–77. Coming progressively closer to my view of the "multitudinous orb," meanwhile, are Curren, *Shelley's Annus Mirabilis,* pp. 117–18; Webb, *Shelley: A Voice Not Understood,* pp. 253–58; and Scrivener, *Radical Shelley,* pp. 243–46.

79. See Buffon's *Natural History,* trans. Kenrick and Murdoch, V, 313–55; Cuvier, *Essay on the Theory of the Earth,* trans. Robert Kerr (London: Murray and Baldwin, 1815), pp. 6–17; and Parkinson, *Organic Remains,* 2nd ed. I, 217, and 456–57. The latter work especially shows how basic the "catastrophe" theory is to Shelley's sense of history as a series of radical transfigurations when the first volume concludes with this: "If it be apparent that, from the breaking up of a preceding world, the present has derived a higher degree of utility and beauty; may not this [present world] also be preparing to undergo, at some distant era, a new recomposition, by which it may be made to exceed this . . . ?" (p. 457).

80. For a list of sources known to Shelley in which portrayals of that cave were available, see Curran, *Shelley's Annus Mirabilis,* pp. 75 and 224, n. 62.

81. From the portrait of Zoroaster in the translation of Porphyry's *De antro nympharum* in *Thomas Taylor the Platonist: Selected Writings,* ed. Kathleen Raine and George Mills Harper (Princeton, NJ: Princeton Univ. Press, 1968), esp. p. 301.

82. As in Butter, *Shelley's Idols of the Cave,* pp. 197–98, or Oscar W. Firkins, *Power and Elusiveness in Shelley* (London: Oxford Univ. Press, 1937), pp. 183–84.

83. Noted as androgynous by Ross Woodman in "The Androgyne in *Prometheus Unbound,*" esp. pp. 237–40, though I think act 3 resists Woodman's sense that this state in the cave is a divine Platonic oneness from which humankind has fallen and to which it can ultimately return. By "androgynous" I mean not a dissolution of separate sexes or gendered mythographs into one but a free crossing of traditionally *gendered* thoughts and qualities back and forth between different but interacting figures. Here I think Shelley's conception approaches both the vision of Carolyn Heilbrun in *Towards a Recognition of Androgyny* (New York: Knopf, 1973) and the prospect held out by the principal speaker in "Women in the Beehive: A Seminar with Jacques

Derrida," trans. James Ardner, *Subjects/Objects,* 4 (1984), 5–19. I think, then, that Shelley's best writing resists, to some degree (though not entirely), the sense of the androgynous ideal advanced by Brown in *Sexuality and Feminism,* pp. 212–28.

84. See the discussion of the imagination's process as it is rendered by Shelley's *Defence of Poetry* in the third section of my Chapter 6. That process in the thinking of poets, Shelley believes, is the focused culmination of this activity in the cultural unconscious, provided a poetic attitude chooses to release the latter movement from suppression.

85. See esp. Rossetti, *"Prometheus Unbound,"* p. 62; Baker, *Shelley's Major Poetry,* pp. 113–14; Butter, *Shelley's Idols,* p. 197; Curran, *Shelley's Annus Mirabilis,* pp. 75–77; Woodman, "The Androgyne," p. 228; and Fraistat, *The Poem and the Book,* pp. 159–62.

86. For Shelley's attempt at such a society in his own domestic surroundings, see the "Letter to Maria Gisborne" (1820, the year *Prometheus Unbound* was published), ll. 303–323.

87. For how such ruins can, in this poet's eyes, immediately suggest the now-uprooted survival of the "abstractions of the mind" once connected to them, see the Shelley letter from Naples of December 1818, where "Rome is a city as it were of the dead, or rather of those who [now] cannot die, & who survive the puny generations which inhabit & pass over the spot" (*L,* II, 59). See also Donald Reiman's "Roman Scenes in *Prometheus Unbound* III. iv." *PQ,* 45 (1967), esp. 73–78.

88. See Shelley's 1819 "Notes on Sculptues in Rome and Florence" (*CW,* VI, 309–32), where he frequently intones this sense of a classical or Hellenistic Greek statue catching motions of deferral in instants of process. One case in point is a Venus Anadyomene where "fine limbs flow into each other" to carry through "desire and enjoyment and the pleasure arising from both" (VI, 320–21).

89. The quoted phrase in this sentence comes from Shelley's notes on a Niobe, *CW,* VI, 330.

90. See Curran's reading of this poem in *Shelley's Annus Mirabilis,* pp. 156–72. This account begins a refutation of all the readings that present the speaker as longing to join the force of a singular, albeit non-Christian, deity, a view that has gained considerable impetus from Fogle's "The Imaginal Design in Shelley's *Ode to the West Wind,*" *ELH,* 15 (1949), rpt. in *The Permanent Pleasure,* pp. 60–68, and culminated powerfully in Chernaik's *The Lyrics of Shelley,* pp. 90–97.

91. Note Shelley's description, as Reiman suggests (*NCE,* p. 222, n. 1), of Maenads sculpted in relief on an altar devoted to Minerva in "Notes on Sculptures" (*CW,* VI, 323).

92. See esp. ll. 103–20 of Coleridge's "Ode to the Departing Year," even though Shelley's ode is surely written in part to counter that lyric's final stanza, where "I recentre my immortal mind / In the deep sabbath of meek self-content" (ll. 158–59). For more on how the "Ode to the West Wind" culminates a Shelleyan repetition and rejection of the Coleridgean ode, see Paul Fry in *The Poet's Calling,* pp. 186–90.

93. A collection of poems later incorporated into *The Poetical Works of Leigh Hunt,* ed. H. S. Milford (London: Oxford Univ. Press, 1923). See especially "The Nymphs" from that collection, pt. II, ll. 26–206 (pp. 326–30).

94. Particularly in "West Wind" and "The Cloud," as Grabo points out in *A Newton Among Poets,* pp. 119–21, and Desmond King-Hele notes in *Shelley: His Thought and Work,* 3rd ed. (London: Macmillan, 1984), pp. 213–27.

95. Here the speaker's frustration resembles that of Shakespeare's Hamlet (again), particularly the way the Dane finds his jibe at Horatio ("There are more things in heaven and earth . . . Than are dreamt of in your philosophy" [I. v. 165–66]) redounding upon himself in his famous "To be or not to be" speech, where each image we have of death suggests another until we face an eternal sleep in which innumerable "dreams may come" that we cannot yet imagine (III. i. 66). Shelley, however, finally asks his readers to accept the pull toward that uncertainty because submission to such a movement will open us to future transfigurations of our present situations and longings.

96. Addison refers to "Reason's Ear" at l. 21 of this widely circulated poem first published in *The Spectator* on Aug. 23, 1712. The text to which I refer is the one in *A Collection of English Poems, 1660–1800,* ed. Ronald S. Crane (New York: Harper & Row, 1932), p. 291.

97. He uses an established mythological figure of Liberty, of course, in *The Mask of Anarchy,* as we saw in the previous chapter, because that broadside-ballad is directed at an unspeculative, sometimes barely educated readership to whom he wants to appeal with points of departure already familiar in political iconography and poetry (see the article cited in n. 78 of Chapter 3). Even in that device, however, he wants to unsettle the mythograph, as I have discussed in my section on the *Mask of Anarchy,* and now I can detail purposes in that disruption beyond the ones I have already presented.

98. Most of these figures concatenating into the movement among them that is the Witch have been related to her by other critics already, though not all the allusions have been noted in any one account. See A. M. D. Hughes, "Shelley's 'Witch of Atlas'," *Modern Language Review,* 7 (1912), 508–16; Carl Grabo, *The Meaning of "The Witch of Atlas"* (Chapel Hill: Univ. of Noth Carolina Press, 1935), pp. 3–20; Douglas Bush, *Mythology and the Romantic Tradition in English Poetry* (1937; rpt. New York: Norton, 1963), pp. 138–43; Baker, *Shelley's Major Poetry,* p. 208; and Newman Ivey White, *Shelley,* II, 219–21, whose linking of "The Witch" to Shelley's perusal of Forteguerri is confirmed by a look at the *Ricciardetto di Niccolo Carteromaco* (Milan: Bernardoni, 1813), I, 10–22 and II, 271–77 (key passages focused on the *maga* Stella and the *maga* Lirina in Ethiopia). I have noticed even more analogues not mentioned in these source studies by comparing ll. 121–54 of "The Witch" with Homer's *Odyssey,* V. 61–74 (Calypso in her cave and its surroundings); Shelley's *maga* as a mobile knowledge above "recreant mortality" with the more judgmental Witch of the Alps who uses those words in Byron's *Manfred* (II. ii. 126); Shelley's Witch as coming into or forth from her cave as an innocent figure of "soft smiles" (l. 86) with the stranded young Haidee in *Don Juan* (II. cxli–cxliv), utterly different from the Witch of the Alps; and Shelley's "lovely lady garmented in light / From her own beauty" (ll. 81–82) with Dante's Beatrice in the *Purgatorio,* XXX. 61–81, or with Petrarch's Laura in *Sonnets and Songs,* CCXVIII, CCXIX, CCXXVII, CCLI, and CCLXXIX.

99. See, despite my disagreements with his conclusions, Frederic Colwell's very informative "Shelley's 'Witch of Atlas' and the Mythic Geography of the Nile," *ELH,* 45 (1978), 69–92.

100. Stated by Hunt in *Lord Byron and Some of his Contemporaries* (1828) and excerpted from there by Theodore Redpath in *The Young Romantics and Critical Opinion, 1807–1824* (New York: St. Martin's Press, 1973), p. 406. Repetitions of this statement, despite their different emphases, include Bush, *Mythology and the Romantic Tradition,* p. 140; Knight, *The Starlit Dome,* pp. 224–34; Bloom, *Shelley's Mythmaking,* pp. 165–204; Cameron, *The Golden Years,* pp. 273–75; Scrivener, *Radical Shelley,* pp. 260–61; David Rubin, "A Study of Antinomies in Shelley's *The Witch of Atlas,*" *Studies in Romanticism,* 8 (1969), 216–28; and Andelys Wood, "Shelley's Ironic Vision: *The Witch of Atlas,*" *Keats-Shelley Journal,* 29 (1980), 67–82. More accurate in some ways are statements that see a failure of integration in the poem as it "flits from one myth to another." These readings range from a paragraph in William Hazlitt's *Edinburgh Review* essay on Shelley's *Posthumous Poems* (1824), rpt. in Redpath, p. 393, to King-Hele's reaction (which provides the words I quote in the previous sentence) in *Shelley: His Thought and Work,* 3rd ed., pp. 258–62.

101. "Shelley's Witch: The Naked Conception," *Concerning Poetry,* 10 (1977), 33–43.

102. Compare ll. 62–65 and 78–80 of "The Witch" with the *aura seminalis* generating Belphoebe and Amoret in *The Fairie Queene,* III. vi. 5–10; the Witch's cave with the "study" of Archimago in *Fairie Queene,* I. i. 36–38; and the fact that the scrolls both recall the "Saturnian" Golden Age and reveal the "inmost lore of Love" (l. 199) with the knowledge of that age and the awareness of love's role in its "guilelessness" in the speech of the Samian prophet (*Metamorphoses,* XV. 96–103). My citations from Spenser's writing in this and my sixth chapters all

come from *Spenser: Poetical Works,* ed. J. C. Smith and E. de Selincourt (London: Oxford Univ. Press, 1912). For a sense of how Spenser's figures have the potential to shift into Ovidian motions, see Angus Fletcher, *The Prophetic Moment: An Essay on Spenser* (Chicago: Univ. of Chicago Press, 1971), pp. 90–106.

103. *Mary Shelley's Journal* (pp. 136–37) records her husband's journey to San Peligrino on Aug. 12, 1820, two days before she notes the commencement of "The Witch of Atlas." For the fact that Shelley hiked to a chapel near the top of the mountain, see Richard Holmes, *Shelley: The Pursuit,* p. 604.

104. The way this source was mistakenly proposed, partly by Herodotus and then by others in his wake, is detailed by Colwell in "Shelley's 'Witch of Atlas'," pp. 71–72. For more on how this and other origins are exposed by Shelley as the retrospective products of transference, see my "Metaphor and Metamorphosis in Shelley's 'The Witch of Atlas'," *Studies in Romanticism,* 19 (1980), esp. 332–34 and 342–43. Some of my observations in that article (though still useful, I hope) are not repeated here, partly because I want to devote most of the space I now have to discoveries I have made about this poem since my essay was published.

105. See how Herodotus reveals the supposed origin of the Nile as determined by a transference between its apparent course and that of the Danube (or "Ister") in the Loeb Edition, Book I, section 34.

106. Mary's *Journal* (pp. 135–36) records how Shelley and she "read Lucretius" together from June 28 to July 11, 1820, slightly more than a month before "The Witch of Atlas" was written.

107. Here Shelley is drawing allegory toward the continual reopening in words of an otherness-as-such (a deferral of every figure, usually to other figures, across gaps in space and time) that is really the basis of and constant irony in symbolic performances. See that sense of allegory as both underlying the work of and resisted by most "Romantic" writers in Paul de Man, "The Rhetoric of Temporality," *Interpretation: Theory and Practice,* ed. Charles Singleton (1969), rpt. in de Man's *Blindness and Insight: Essays on the Rhetoric of Contemporary Criticism,* 2nd ed., intr. Wlad Godzich, Theory and History of Literature, Vol. 7 (Minneapolis: Univ. of Minnesota Press, 1983), esp. pp. 187–208. For more on Shelley's radical use of allegory in the later poetry, see the concluding paragraphs of the seventh section in my Chapter 6.

108. In most medieval Catholic theories of allegory, the word "allegory" itself refers to the second level of "reference elsewhere," the stratum just above the "literal" one, where the present text alludes to a piece of holy scripture or where a portion of the scriptures refers to another portion. See Thomas Aquinas, "The Nature and Domain of Sacred Doctrine" from the *Summa Theologicae,* in *Critical Theory Since Plato,* ed. Hazard Adams (New York: Harcourt, 1971), p. 119.

109. The most observant look at the bathos in this poem is Cronin's in "Shelley's Witch of Atlas," *Keats-Shelley Journal,* 26 (1977), rpt. and expanded in *Shelley's Poetic Thoughts,* pp. 55–75.

110. Both Ariostos's *Orlando Furioso* and Tasso's *Gerusalemme Liberata* were written in Italian and translated into English (by Sir John Harington and Edward Fairfax, respectively) in *ottava rima.* The interplays of comic, epic, and tragic elements in these works, plus their multiplicity of interpolated epyllions, aroused well-known controversies in Italy and England about their generic purity and formal unity. See such written contributions to the debate as *Giraldi Cinthio on Romance* (1554), trans. and ed. Henry L. Snuggs (Lexington: Univ. of Kentucky Press, 1968), esp. pp. 11–29, 35–40, and 82–85; Antonio Minturno, selections from *L'arte poetica* (1564), trans. Allan H. Gilbert, *Literary Criticism: Plato to Dryden,* ed. Gilbert (New York: American Book Co., 1940), esp. pp. 275–89; and Tasso's own *Discourses on the Heroic Poem* (1594), trans. Mariella Cavalchini and Irene Samuel (Oxford: Clarendon, 1971), esp. pp. 64–79. We know Shelley to have read at least this last work because of his quotation from it in *L,* II, 30.

111. On Shelley's "Witch" as partly a reaction to *Don Juan,* see Cronin, *Shelley's Poetic Thoughts,* pp. 55–58 and 63–64. For more on the "spectacle of incongruities" in *Don Juan* that this poem both extends and critiques, see Jerome McGann, *Don Juan in Context* (Chicago: Univ. of Chicago Press, 1976), which uses the words I have just quoted on p. 95, and Jean Hall, "The Evolution of the Surface Self: Byron's Poetic Career," *Keats-Shelley Journal,* 36 (1987), esp. 145–57.

112. See the "Morall" and "Allegorical" conclusions to each "Booke" and the closing "Briefe and Summarie Allegorie" (pp. 558–68) provided by the translator—with some encouragement from Ariosto in stanzas such as XIV. lxxv and XVII. i—in Harington's version of *Orlando Furioso,* ed. Robert McNulty (Oxford: Clarendon, 1972); *Jerusalem Delivered,* trans. Fairfax, I. vii–xviii; and, of course, the "Cantos of Mutabilitie" (vi–viii) in *The Fairie Queene (Spenser: Poetical Works,* pp. 394–406). For how often the interlaced structure of medieval and Renaissance romance is designed to manifest divine order amid confusion, see Eugene Vinaver, *The Rise of Romance* (Oxford: Clarendon, 1971), pp. 68–122. For a brief look at Shelley—and "The Witch of Atlas"—in relation to the romance tradition, see Curran, *Poetic Form and British Romanticism,* pp. 146–49.

113. Such moments occur particularly in the *Orlando Furioso,* trans. Harington, Books VIII, XI, XV, XXX, XXXIII, and in *The Fairie Queene,* esp. Cantos i–viii in Books III and IV. Recent criticism has focused on these very texts, consequently, as examples of a deferral across different signifiers by which language carries human desire outside a strictly linear succession or an organic development of episodes. See Eugenio Donato, "'*Per selve e boscherecci labirinti*': Desire and Narrative Structure in Ariosto's *Orlando Furioso,*" *Barocco,* 4 (1972), rpt. in *Literary Theory/Renaissance Texts,* ed. Parker and Quint, pp. 33–62, and Jonathan Goldberg, *Endlesse Werke: Spenser and the Structures of Discourse* (Baltimore, MD: The Johns Hopkins Univ. Press, 1981).

114. See Holmes, *Shelley: The Pursuit,* p. 605.

115. On the avoidance of sexual intercourse and the normal birth-process in the creation of the Creature, see Ellen Moers, *Literary Women* (Garden City, NY: Doubleday, 1976), pp. 90–98; Sandra M. Gilbert and Susan Gubar, *The Madwoman in the Attic: The Woman Writer and the Nineteenth-Century Literary Imagination* (New Haven, CT: Yale Univ. Press, 1979), esp. pp. 230–34; and Veeder, *Mary Shelley and* Frankenstein, pp. 81–123. On the characters in *Frankenstein* (1818) as patchings-together of incompatible texts, see my "Otherness in *Frankenstein:* The Confinement/Autonomy of Fabrication," *Structuralist Review,* 2 (1980), 20–40. Though Mary may well have seen, as some of these accounts suggest, Victor Frankenstein's avoidance of women and the womb as something of an attack on the aloof Shelleyan imagination, Shelley appears to have considered that suggestion enough to make the initial workings of imagination female and the womb from which they emerge the cultural intertext from which both men and women draw in order to write.

116. Timothy Webb connects "The Witch of Atlas" with this ancient Greek (as well as Lucretian and post-Christian) understanding in "Shelley and the Religion of Joy," *Studies in Romanticism,* 15 (1976), esp. on 377–78 and 381.

117. It is in playing out this very subliminal and sheer turning from figure to figure that Shelley's Witch becomes—more than any other projection in Shelley's writing except the "shape" in *The Triumph of Life*—the embodiment of what Alice Jardine has called *gynesis.* In the words of Jardine's essay with this title (which has since led to the book of the same name mentioned earlier), the Witch is an affirmative "putting into [male-authored] discourse of 'woman' as [the interrelational] process beyond the Cartesian Subject, the Dialectic of Representation, or Man's Truth," the process usually gendered as "irrationally" female (when it is confronted at all). See "Gynesis," *Diacritics,* 12, No. 2 (Summer 1982), rpt. in *Critical Theory Since 1965,* ed. Hazard Adams and Leroy Searle (Tallahassee: Florida State Univ. Press, 1986), p. 564.

5. THE DISTRIBUTION OF TRANSFERENCE: *A PHILOSOPHICAL VIEW OF REFORM AND ITS SATELLITES*

1. Marilyn Butler shows how and why it was that Shelley and his circle felt themselves moving in this direction around 1819–1820 in "Myth and Mythmaking," *ELH* version, pp. 67–71.

2. "Relative Means and Ends in Shelley's Social-Political Thought," *SEL*, 22 (1982), 622.

3. Here I add an impetus in Shelley's logic that underlies, without denying, the other reasons for his gradualism noted by P. M. S. Dawson in *The Unacknowledged Legislator*, esp. pp. 185–95.

4. The fact of and reasons for Shelley's connections with—or at least readings of—all these people have aleady been established by Cameron in *The Young Shelley*, pp. 52–100, 180–203, 302–16, and in *The Golden Years*, pp. 115–49; by Dawson in *The Unacknowledged Legislator*, pp. 11–109 and 167–71; and by Scrivener in *Radical Shelley*, pp. 3–34, 45–67, 108–18, 133–39, and 211–18.

5. See Cameron, *The Golden Years*, pp. 121–27; Paul Foot, *Red Shelley*, pp. 19–45; Scrivener, *Radical Shelley*, pp. 108–19, Sir Llewellyn Woodward, *The Age of Reform, 1815–1870* (Oxford: Clarendon, 1962), pp. 1–30; and E. P. Thompson, *The Making of the English Working Class* (New York: Pantheon, 1963), pp. 189–268.

6. See Paine on *The Rights of Man* in the *Complete Works*, ed Foner, I, 340, and Rousseau, "On the Origin of Inequality," in *The Social Contract and Discourses*, pp. 201–03.

7. On November 2 in Vol. 31 (1816), 546–48.

8. In her *Vindication of the Rights of Woman*, pp. 60–69, 83–85, 145–50, and 166–72.

9. I accept the last two words in this phrase as part of what Shelley wanted his readers to see, even though these words are partially crossed out in the manuscript of the *Philosophical View*. The crossing-through is incomplete, arguably hesitant, and the rest of the sentence is ungrammatical unless the words remain.

10. To see this pattern in Shelley's account is to revise significantly, without invalidating, the important perspectives on the poet's sense of history in Cameron, *The Golden Years*, pp. 131–37; Scrivener, *Radical Shelley*, pp. 212–15; and William Royce Campbell, "Shelley's Philosophy of History: A Reconsideration," *Keats-Shelley Journal*, 21–22 (1972–1973), 43–63.

11. *Complete Works*, ed. Foner, I, 251.

12. According to the general criteria laid down in his *Metahistory* (pp. 1–42), Hayden White would see this turning of data into modes of plot, argument, and ideological assertion as governed by an interplay of metonymic and ironic rhetorical patterns (or "tropological protocols"). Shelley's spiral of historical "progress" is metonymic in the sense that each part leads almost mechanistically to a later part in a manner whereby the latter repeats its predecessor with only a few differences, all in a tragic development where usurpations continue to be destructive forms of one another. Yet this method for constructing a history is both reinforced and countered by an ironic sense that the repetitions are often borrowings from a side now being overturned by its own devices. Shelley thus allows for willed, rhetorical (or more blatant) reversals of the past by resistant classes of people or members of those classes while presenting all such beings as engulfed by longstanding transpersonal inclinations toward transfigurative repetitions. In any case, Shelley as an historian should not be viewed the way most see him: as "Romantic," "anarchistic," and mainly "metaphorical" in his vision, by White's standards—though the poet does posit ultimate aims characterized by such qualities. As an interpretation of past events, Shelley's *View* is more a cross between the "liberal" and "radical" visions that White associates with the ironic and metonymic modes.

13. We know that Shelley was trying for this increased interplay because he digressed into the essay "On Life," a major statement on epistemology and metaphysics, right in the midst of (indeed, as an addendum to) the history of Enlightenment philosophy in the *View*. See n. 36 of my Chapter 3. There is also the fact that the later sections of the *Speculations* (the ones probably

written as late as 1821, judging by the notebooks in which they appear) are synoptic attempts (on the entire "Science of Morals" in one case) to connect social progress with the basic tendencies of personal thought. See the helpful dating of Shelley's prose works—put together from conclusions reached mainly by Cameron, Reiman, and Webb—in Dawson, *The Unacknowledged Legislator,* pp. 282–84.

14. See Paine's *Complete Works,* ed. Foner, I, 325, and Cameron, *The Golden Years,* pp. 116–17.

15. Specifically in the Glasgow Edition, I. i.1.

16. In the *Enquiry Concerning Political Justice,* ed. Kramnick, pp. 169 and 175.

17. Particularly in the "Remarks on the Systems of Hartley and Helvetius" published with *An Essay on the Principles of Human Action,* intr. John R. Nabholtz (1805; rpt. Gainesville, FL: Scholars' Facsimiles and Reprints, 1969), pp. 215–27. For the wider influence of Hazlitt on Shelley's sense of the mind's ethical possibilities, see Dawson, *The Unacknowledged Legislator,* pp. 230–36.

18. See his *Introduction to the Principles of Morals and Legislation* (1789), ed. J. H. Burns and H. L. A. Hart (London: Athlone, 1970), pp. 125–57.

19. I quote Hunt here from "Christmas and Other Old Natural Merry-makings Considered," *The Examiner,* No. 507 (Dec. 21, 1817), rpt. in *Leigh Hunt's Political and Occasional Essays,* ed. Lawrence and Carolyn Houtchens (New York: Columbia Univ. Press, 1962), pp. 162–64.

20. See Cameron, *The Young Shelley,* pp. 52–54.

21. See "Of Public Credit" in Hume's *Essays and Treatises on Several Subjects* (London: Millar, 1764), I, 383–400, a piece clearly influential on much of the *Philosophical View.*

22. Cobbett briefly flirts with the notion of seizing "the estates of the landholders" so that much of that property can be "given to the freeholders" in his "Address to the Men of Bristol," *Political Register,* 32 (1811), 57. Cameron discusses Cobbett's continual influence on this area of Shelley's thinking in "Shelley, Cobbett, and the National Debt," *JEGP,* 42 (1943), 197–209. Curiously, however (on p. 207 especially), Cameron fails to see how much Cobbett anticipates Shelley on this particular point.

23. Foot is especially firm in presenting Shelley as more a "leveller" than a communist in *Red Shelley,* pp. 81–98.

24. Compare Shelley's *View,* for example, to "Supply without Burthen, or Escheat Vice Taxation" (1795) in *Jeremy Bentham's Economic Writings,* ed. W. Stark (London: Allen and Unwin, 1952), I, 291–97. Godwin also suggests something like this sort of calculus in *Political Justice,* ed. Kramnick, pp. 709–24.

25. For instance, in the *Political Register,* 31 (1816), 546.

26. Smith is the one quoted throughout the present paragraph, and I cite him, naturally, from *An Inquiry into the Nature and Causes of the Wealth of Nations,* 3rd. ed. (1784), ed. R. H. Campbell, A. S. Skinner, and W. B. Todd for the Glasgow Edition of the *Works* (Oxford: Clarendon, 1976), II, pt. 1, I.iv.13–I.v.21 and I.vi.1–I.vii.21. See also Hume's "Of Money" in *Essays and Treatises,* p. 315. My uses of "exchange-value" and "use-value," by the way, refer directly to Smith's (*Wealth,* pt. 1, I.iv.13) and only indirectly to Marx's, even though the latter has made the most famous distinction between these terms. It is with knowledge of Smith's definitions, after all, that Shelley writes the *Philosophical View.*

27. See *On the Principles of Political Economy and Taxation* (1817) in *The Works and Correspondence of David Ricardo,* ed. Piero Sraffa and M. H. Dobb (London: Cambridge Univ. Press, 1962), I, 11–25 and 52–66. My quotation is from I, 64. On products and wages as representations of concealed labor and the differences between Smith and Ricardo on that point, see also Michel Foucault, *The Order of Things,* pp. 221–26 and 253–63.

28. *Wealth of Nations,* pt. 1, I.v.7.

29. Shelley probably has his facts wrong when he makes this claim, if we believe Thompson, *The Making of the Working Class,* pp. 216–33.

30. *Wealth of Nations,* pt. 1, I.vii.31.

31. See Ricardo's "The Price of Gold" (1809) in *Works and Corrrespondence,* III, 15–21, and Cameron, "Shelley, Cobbett, and the National Debt," pp. 197–99.

32. "The High Price of Bullion" (1811) in *Works and Correspondence,* III, 94.

33. *On the Principles of Political Economy* in *Works and Correspondence,* I, 45.

34. *Capital,* 3rd ed. (1883), ed. Friedrich Engels, trans. Samuel Moore and Edward Aveling (London: Glaisher, 1912), p. 62. The quotation in the next sentence is from the same source, this time from p. 54.

35. Mainly in the fifth chapter of *An Essay Concerning the True Original, Extent, and End of Civil Government,* published in 1689–1690 as the second of Locke's *Two Treatises of Government,* 2nd ed., ed. Peter Laslett (Cambridge: Cambridge Univ. Press, 1967), pp. 303–20.

36. In *Reflections on the French Revolution* (1970), intr. A. J. Grieve (London: Dent, 1910), pp. 48–49.

37. See Owen's *A New View of Society,* 3rd ed. (1817; rpt. Glencoe, IL: Free Press, n.d.), esp. pp. 161–84, and Cameron, *The Golden Years,* pp. 118–19. I cannot entirely agree, however, with the reasons for Shelley's avoidance of a really Marxist solution offered by Cameron in this latter book (pp. 136–37) and in his "Shelley and Marx" article (cited in n. 26 of my introduction).

38. As noted by Cameron in *The Young Shelley,* pp. 15–16.

39. Discussed as such by Dawson in *The Unacknowledged Legislator,* pp. 14–24.

40. In addition to moments from these authors which have been cited already in the notes for this chapter, see Volney, *The Ruins,* pp. 172–76; Hume, *A Treatise of Human Nature* (1739–1740), 2nd ed., ed. L. A. Selby-Bigge, rev. P. H. Nidditch (Oxford: Clarendon, 1978), pp. 329–47; Smith, *Wealth of Nations,* pt. 1, II.iii.1–33; Ricardo, *On the Principles of Political Economy,* in *Works and Correspondence,* I, 278–81; Rousseau, *Confessions,* trans. Grant, II, 277–84; and Godwin, *Political Justice,* ed. Kramnick, p. 703.

41. See Jameson's "Magical Narratives: Romance as Genre," *New Literary History,* 7 (1975), reworked in *The Political Unconscious,* pp. 103–50.

42. What Shelley is referring to at this point in the *Speculations* is "that species of influence" which has to affect every "social" being in a nation to some degree, "imperfect as [that influence] is from a variety of causes." Yet this "power" over people is usually known, the poet goes on to say, by the form it assumes over time "in [the] government [and] religion" (same page of the *Speculations*). As soon as Shelley makes this latter qualification, he is employing and critiquing an already well-established view of what the unwritten British Constitution is. For a widely known rendering of that view, see again Burke, *Reflections on the Revolution,* pp. 29–32.

43. *Political Justice,* ed. Kramnick, pp. 687–88 and 692.

44. After surveying a good deal of Western history, Carol Gilligan has more recently presented this opposition in the handling of ethical problems as a difference between what is usually a male approach (strictly legalistic) and what generally seems a female approach (more situational and relational). Shelley can thus be seen again, though differently now, as partially "feminizing" the reworked basis of excessively "masculine" systems in an act of "gynesis." See Gilligan's *In a Different Voice: Psychological Theory and Women's Development* (Cambridge, MA: Harvard Univ. Press, 1982), pp. 24–105.

45. See Godwin's ideal for an underlying standard of right in *Political Justice,* ed. Kramnick, pp. 540–45, and his disapproval of the existing kinds of "Constitutions" in the same volume, pp. 603–9. Note also Shelley's attraction to the *polis* tradition of small city-states as that preference is discussed by Scrivener in *Radical Shelley,* p. 213.

46. As shown in such overviews as the one by Peter Jupp, which includes long accounts written by actual voters or candidates of the era, in *British and Irish Elections, 1784–1831* (New York: Barnes and Noble, 1973), esp. pp. 13–77.

47. See the *Plan of Parliamentary Reform, in the Form of a Catechism* in *The Works of Jeremy Bentham,* ed. John Bowring (Edinburgh: Tait, 1839), V, 487–89.

48. Ed. Kramnick, p. 611.

49. In the chapter on "the Dissolution of Government" in the Kramnick edition, p. 552.

50. See *Political Justice,* ed. Kramnick, pp. 553–54.

51. See *Political Justice,* ed. Kramnick, pp. 282–92.

52. Noted by Dawson, *The Unacknowledged Legislator,* p. 174.

53. Kramnick edition, p. 291.

54. Also discussed by Dawson in *The Unacknowledged Legislator,* this time on p. 163.

55. Here I quote a book that Shelley read by two fromer United Irishmen, William James MacNeven and Thomas Addis Emmet: *Pieces of Irish History, Illustrative of the Conditions of the Catholics in Ireland* (New York: Dornin, 1807), p. 16. For evidence that Shelley read this work and his interest in the United Irishmen, see *L,* I, 264–65 and 304, and Dawson, *The Unacknowledged Legislator,* pp. 154–65.

56. See Dawson, *The Unacknowledged Legislator,* p. 176, and Thompson, *The Making of the Working Class,* pp. 649–69.

57. *Political Register,* 31 (1816), 488. To make matters worse, the basis of those principles for Cobbett should be the "true" British Constitution.

58. *The Unacknowledged Legislator,* p. 158. Later parts of the present paragraph are indebted to pp. 159–62 of this book, though often to the point of disagreeing with some of Dawson's conclusions. See also Gerald McNiece, *Shelley and the Revolutionary Idea,* pp. 95–112.

59. All my quotations from Barruel in this paragraph are from the *Memoirs* as translated by Robert Clifford (London: privately published, 1797–1798), III, 408 and 115.

60. See Cameron, *The Young Shelley,* pp. 160–61; Dawson, *The Unacknowledged Legislator,* pp. 136–38 and 151–57; and Scrivener, *Radical Shelley,* pp. 62–63.

61. Dawson, *The Unacknowledged Legislator,* p. 174.

62. See Keith Michael Baker's introduction to *Condorcet: Selected Writings,* pp. xxix–xxxvii.

63. See G. M. Matthews, "A Volcano's Voice," pp. 124–26, and especially Foot, *Red Shelley,* pp. 196–201.

64. My sense of the main proponents for each of these demands is indebted to Cameron's very accurate list—and to his citations of the documentary evidence (all of which I have corroborated)—in *The Golden Years,* pp. 141 and 597, n. 71–76.

65. See Dawson, *The Unacknowledged Legislator,* p. 176.

66. See Donald Reiman on the probable dates of and reasons for composition and abandonment in *S&C,* VI, 953–54, plus Woodward, *The Age of Reform,* pp. 64–69, and Thompson, *The Rise of the Working Class,* pp. 724–30.

6. THE "ONE" IN THE LATER WORKS: "THOUGHT'S ETERNAL FLIGHT"

1. See the contemporary reviews of *Prometheus Unbound, with Other Poems* reprinted in the Zillman *Variorum,* pp. 690–97 and 701–15.

2. Butler, "Myth and Mythmaking," *ELH* version, pp. 69–70. See also Shelley's preface to *Epipsychidion,* esp. p. 373, and *L,* 262–63.

3. See the *Four Ages* in the Halliford *Works,* VIII, esp. 10–25. I must, however, agree in general with Butler's argument in *Peacock Displayed,* pp. 290–313, that the *Defence* responds to the *Four Ages* using skeptical assumptions that Peacock frequently accepts. The transfiguration of verbalized thought by later thoughts about it in Peacock—his explanation for primitive poetry's loss of ideological force—becomes the poetic process for Shelley, as we shall see, in both the primal "chaotic" poem and in later imaginative revisions of that chaos. Part of Shelley's brilliance in the *Defence* lies in his ways of countering his friendly opponent with the basis of opponent's logic.

4. Compare the shade of Rousseu's dream with the conclusion of Plato's *Republic,* 6

5. Quoted from l. 4 of Calderón's *The Great Stage of the World,* trans. Walter Brar chester: Manchester Univ. Press, 1976).

6. At ll. 3438–3445 of pt. 1. All my citations (including this one) from *Faust* in

other than those from Shelley's translations of it, come from the bilingual Anchor edition with trans. by Walter Kaufmann (Garden City, NY: Doubleday, 1963).

7. *The Violet in the Crucible: Shelley and Translation* (Oxford: Clarendon, 1976), p. 217.

8. See *PS*, p. 462, and Notopoulos, "New Texts of Shelley's Plato," *Keats-Shelley Journal*, 15 (1966), 104–5.

9. This sense of Socrates' rhetorical position anticipates the ones in Søren Kierkegaard, *The Concept of Irony, with Constant Reference to Socrates*, trans. Lee M. Capel (New York: Harper & Row, 1965), esp. pp. 259–88, and Jacques Derrida, "Plato's Pharmacy," in *Dissemination*, trans. Barbara Johnson (Chicago: Univ. of Chicago Press, 1981), pp. 61–171. I am indebted to both these theorists at this point. Also, for suggestive discussions of how the ironies of Socrates undercut attempts to rest on comprehensible absolutes in Plato's texts, see Jay Farness, "Text and Tradition in Plato's *Ion*," *PQ*, 64 (1985), 155–74, and "Missing Socrates: Socratic Rhetoric in a Platonic Text," *Philosophy and Rhetoric*, 20 (1987), 41–59.

10. See *PS*, pp. 64–65.

11. Shelley here addresses—and ends up on both sides of—the debate presented best by the various essays in *Plato: Democrat or Totalitarian?*, ed. Thomas Landon Thorson (Englewood Cliffs, NJ: Prentice-Hall, 1963).

12. Webb's words in "Shelley's Religion of Joy," pp. 372–73.

13. Shelley's words in "A Discourse on the Manners of the Ancient Greeks Relative to the Subject of Love," *PS*, pp. 407 and 410. See also Webb, "Shelley's Religion of Joy," p. 353.

14. Here I quote ll. 3446–49 from pt. 1 in the Kaufmann translation.

15. From Shelley's translation of the prologue as it appears in Webb, *The Violet in the Crucible*, pp. 189–90.

16. *Academical Questions*, I, 244. Note also Cameron, *The Golden Years*, p. 156.

17. The *Academical Questions* even sees its One as a "boundary to the utmost *excursions* of the imagination" (I, 244). The failure of critics to note this factor in Shelley's "one mind" argument has distorted the debate about that passage for some time. The results are especially apparent in Wasserman, *A Critical Reading*, pp. 144–53, and Robinson's retort to Wasserman, *Shelley and Byron*, pp. 245–48.

18. Echoes of or variations on these particular theorists are easy to find (and have often been found already) in Shelley's *Defence*. Melvin Solve looks quite thoroughly at Shelley's echoes of Plato, though he does miss many of the ironies in them, in *His Theory of Poetry*, pp. 159–76. I have commented on an echo of Horace's "teach and delight" in the first section of my introduction, above. Particular stress is laid upon Sidney as well as Horace in Lucas Verkoren, *A Study of Shelley's "Defence of Poetry": Its Origin, Textual History, Sources, and Significance* (1937; rpt. Folcroft, PA: Folcroft Press, 1969), pp. 68–77 and 82–83. See Cameron's emphasis on Johnson in "A New Source for Shelley's *A Defence of Poetry*," *Studies in Philology*, 38 (1941), 629–44. The links to Wordsworth have been made especially clear by B. R. McElderry, Jr., "Common Elements in Wordsworth's Preface and Shelley's Defence of Poetry," *MLQ*, 5 (1944), 175–81. The Coleridge connection is helpfully discussed by Earl J. Schulze in *Shelley's Theory of Poetry: A Reappraisal*, pp. 223–32. And one of these influences has been treated almost exhaustively in John S. Flagg, "Shelley and Aristotle: Elements of the *Poetics* in Shelley's Theory of Poetry," *Studies in Romanticism*, 9 (1970), 44–67. For the most thorough presentation of the source-echoes in each paragraph of the *Defence*, see Fanny Delisle, *A Study of Shelley's A Defence of Poetry: A Textual and Critical Evaluation*, 2 vols., Salzburg Studies in English Literature: Romantic Reassessment, No. 27 (Salzburg: Institut für Englische Sprache und Literatur, 1974).

19. Such transcendentals appear prominently in the major theoretical statements of all the I have mentioned in the previous sentence and n. 18. I have already discussed Shelley's response to Plato. But Aristotle's *Poetics* refers, as Shelley knew, despite disagreements to, to the revelation (by "imitation") of a universal, unchangeable, and unified *entelechy* 've principle). This latter notion is discussed in the *Metaphysics*, as in the selection

from it translated by W. D. Ross in the *Introduction to Aristotle*, ed. Richard McKeon (New York: Modern Library, 1947), pp. 243–96. Coleridge's sense of imagination, moreover, as I have briefly noted earlier, is based on a Kantian knowledge of ultimate unities in the pure reason and of the God whose creation is repeated by poetic achievements, particularly in the *Biographia Literaria*, ed. Watson, pp. 91–167 (where a clear political conservatism intermixes with a belief in a divine "I AM"). Similar absolutes even surface in the major documents of the other noted theorists as these statements appear in *Critical Theory Since Plato*, ed. Hazard Adams, the source of the page numbers I now proceed to cite. Horace's "teachable" universals are the unalterable characteristics of types and ranks, human or animal, in the "Art of Poetry," trans. E. C. Wickham, pp. 70–71; Sidney's flights of poetic fancy try to raise us back toward the understanding of "the heavenly Maker" in *An Apology for Poetry*, p. 158; Johnson's poet, to be the "legislator of mankind," must "rise to general and transcendental truths, which will always be the same" in chapter X of *Rasselas*, p. 328; and Wordsworth's "immortal" poetic "knowledge" is of how much "the mind of man [is] naturally the [at least half-passive] mirror of the fairest and most interesting properties of [a basically changeless] nature" in the "Preface to the Second Edition of *Lyrical Ballads*," p. 439.

20. *The Collected Works of Sir Humphry Davy*, IV, 163. For more on the use of this passage and on other moments in the *Defence* that I do not treat adequately here, see my "Shelley's Poetics: The Power as Metaphor," *Keats-Shelley Journal*, 31 (1982), 159–97.

21. This temporal and ever-deferred movement of desire in the *Commedia* is best interpreted by Giuseppe Mazzatta, *Dante, Poet of the Desert: History and Allegory in The Divine Comedy* (Princeton, NJ: Princeton Univ. Press, 1979).

22. "Poetic Crossing: Rhetoric and Psychology," p. 513.

23. This reading, like some of my others, is heavily indebted to Derrida, especially to the "iterability" in his "Signature Event Context," trans. Samuel Weber and Jeffrey Mehlman, *Glyph 1: Johns Hopkins Textual Studies* (Baltimore, MD: The Johns Hopkins Univ. Press, 1977), pp. 172–97.

24. Section II of the *Vita* as translated by Musa. The best studies up to now on what Shelley uses and reworks from that poet in this poem are Frank McConnell, "Shelleyan 'Allegory': *Epipsychidion*," *Keats-Shelley Journal*, 20 (1971), 100–12, and Schulze, "The Dantean Quest of *Epipsychidion*," *Studies in Romanticism*, 21 (1982), 191–216, to both of which I am indebted despite my disagreement with some of their assumptions.

25. According to Notopoulos in *PS*, p. 338.

26. As Reiman points out (*NCE*, p. 372), *epi* is the Greek preposition meaning "on" or "regarding" (plus, I would add, "in the direction of"), and *psychidion* is a Greek noun meaning "soul" *(psyche)* with the diminutive added *(dion,* "little"). Astonishingly, Reiman pulls away from the obvious conclusion suggested by these facts to claim that the title means "On the Subject of the Soul." He is heavily influenced, quite clearly, by Wasserman, who makes the same error in *A Critical Reading*, p. 418–19. At least we are not still mired, however, as readings of Shelley were for many years, in positing an "epipsyche" as the individual mind's ultimate, albeit projected, complement or emanation. The most influential statements of this view appear in Baker, *Shelley's Major Poetry*, pp. 49–55 and 215–30, and Bloom, *Shelley's Mythmaking*, pp. 205–19.

27. Here Shelley, as if to continue the very interchange he now describes, is accepting *and* extending the meaning of certain words already written in Italian by Teresa Viviani (the living model for "Emilia") in some lines of prose that the poet uses as an epigraph to the poem. The lines can be translated thus: "The loving soul launches beyond creation, and creates for itself in the infinite a world all its own, far different from this dark and terrifying gulf" (*NCE*, p. 373n.). Shelley has made the projected world a release into infinite and greater differences of the self from itself. He has also established his pursuit of this process in the poem as an effort to transmogrify—and thereby liberate the self (and himself) from—the ties that bind the figures in the work too strictly to actual personalities and situations known to the author in early 1821. See

John F. Slater, "Self-concealment and Self-revelation in Shelley's 'Epipsychidion'," *PLL,* 11 (1975), 279–92.

28. The best biographical reading of the poem, which makes this point as well as others (though it takes insufficient account of what is mentioned in n. 27 of this chapter), remains Cameron's "The Planet-Tempest Passage in *Epipsychidion,*" *PMLA,* 63 (1948), rpt. in *NCE,* pp. 637–58, and reworked in *The Golden Years,* pp. 275–88.

29. Cameron draws parallels between the moon-figure, the Maniac's lady, and the poet's sense of Mary Shelley in *The Golden Years,* pp. 255–66 and 281–83. But Shelley is perhaps a little fairer to Mary in *Julian and Maddalo,* where the emphasis is more on (though *Epipsychidion* does address) the *misuse* of a woman as the projected definer of a male self.

30. The epics of Homer are still thought to have been written in an ancient "Ionian" dialect used particularly by those speakers of Greek living on the western coast of Asia Minor and on many islands to the east of mainland Greece. See Andrew Robert Burn on the Ionians in *The Oxford Classical Dictionary,* 2nd ed. (1970). Moreover, insofar as the later Greek romance— particularly by such authors as Longus (mentioned by Shelley in *L,* II, 213)—is regarded as one of the narrative forms derived from Homer and Ionic poetry, it too can be viewed as a product of the Ionian area, particularly since its mixture of languages, even of Greek with Latin, makes it an ancient interplay of nearly cacophonous differences. See R. L. Hunter, *A Study of* Daphnis and Chloe (Cambridge: Cambridge Univ. Press, 1983), pp. 2–15, and Mikhail Bakhtin, "Forms of Time and of the Chronotope in the Novel: Notes Towards a Historical Poetics," *The Dialogic Imagination,* p. 89, where the polyglot Greek romance is seen as having "utilized and fused together in its structure almost all genres of ancient literature."

31. On Shelley's opposition to homosexual relations (where there may be insufficient difference for a thorough transfer of the self's possibilities into an other), see Brown, *Sexuality and Feminism in Shelley,* pp. 117–49.

32. Robert N. Essick addresses this problem better than anyone ever has, and so I am indebted to what he says, in "'A shadow of some golden dream': Shelley's Language in *Epipsychidion,*" *PLL,* 22 (1986), 165–75. See also J. Hillis Miller, "The Critic as Host," pp. 236–47.

33. Quoted by Webb in *The Violet in the Crucible,* p. 221.

34. For the plant as poets in general and a version of Shelley in 1820, see White, *Shelley,* II, 439, and Cameron, *The Golden Years,* pp. 288–90.

35. Shelley need not have reached far in his thinking to see an analogy between the essential self on a higher plane pictured in images of the *Fravashi*—as in the example reprinted from Jacob Bryant's *New System* by Curran in *Shelley's Annus Mirabilis,* p. 72—and Plato's location of ideas at the level of "the soul's ascension to the intelligible region" (*Republic,* 517b, trans. Shorey). *Shelley's Annus Mirabilis* stops short of making this connection, however, in its one reference to "The Sensitive-Plant" (pp. 134–35), since that poem lies outside the time-frame of this book's discussion. Here, then, I try to complete a suggestion that Curran only begins to offer.

36. See Wasserman's survey of the ladies and gardens of previous poetry that are brought together here in *A Critical Reading,* pp. 155–57.

37. Nearly all those who have written on this "One" in *Hellas* have made it too Platonic— if not Hegelian, as Wasserman makes it in *A Critical Reading,* pp. 374–413. There is a belief in a timeless "Necessity" working through "eternal Thought" even in the otherwise commendable account of *Hellas* in Carl Woodring, *Politics in English Romantic Poetry* (Cambridge, MA: Harvard Univ. Press, 1970), pp. 313–18. Nonetheless, there is a perceptive discussion of this work that has helped lead me to my own analysis: Constance Walker, "The Urn of Bitter Prophecy: Antithetical Patterns in *Hellas,*" *Keats-Shelley Memorial Bulletin,* 33 (1982), 36–48.

38. As we see in Dero Saunders's Penguin edition of the *Decline and Fall,* pp. 676–685, the sequence from which I quote in the next paragraph. Shelley cites Gibbon explicitly in a footnote to ll. 814–15 of this work ("Notes to *Hellas,*" *PW,* p. 479).

39. This same type of superstition, Shelley must have noticed, was what drove the cowering Christians to the church of St. Sophia in Gibbon's account of the fall of Istanbul: "Their confi-

dence was founded on the prophecy of an enthisiast or imposter that one day the Turks would enter Constantinople and pursue the Romans [only] as far as the column of Constantine in the square before St. Sophia" (*Decline and Fall*, ed. Saunders, p. 679). The translation of *The Persians* from which I quote here, by the way, is the especially fine one in the Penguin *Prometheus Unbound and Other Plays* (Baltimore, MD: Penguin Books, 1961).

40. See the *View* in *S&C*, VI, 974–78.

41. The most accepted redactions of *Adonais* regard the visions of cyclical resurrection in the first third of the poem as being revised later by increasingly abstract beliefs, ones that finally propose a unity outside process as the true origin and destination of the fallen poet. The most often cited versions of this interpretation, notwithstanding their disagreements, are Ross Woodman's in *The Apocalyptic Vision*, pp. 158–79, and Wasserman's in *A Critical Reading*, pp. 462–502. Significant precursors and followers of these readings include Benjamin Kurtz, *The Pursuit of Death: A Study of Shelley's Poetry* (New York: Oxford Univ. Press, 1933), pp. 264–323; Baker, *Shelley's Major Poetry*, pp. 239–54; *PS*, pp. 291–301; Wilson, *Shelley's Later Poetry*, pp. 236–55; Reiman, *Percy Bysshe Shelley*, pp. 133–41; Abbey, *Destroyer and Preserver*, pp. 105–19; Hodgart, *Preface to Shelley*, pp. 86–88; Richard Harter Fogle, "Dante and Shelley's *Adonais*," *Bucknell Review*, 15 (1967), rpt. in Fogle's *The Permanent Pleasure*, pp. 87–99; and Stephen Rogers, *Classical Greece and the Poetry of Chenier, Shelley, and Leopardi* (Notre Dame, IN: Univ. of Notre Dame Press, 1974), pp. 116–29. I agree that *Adonais* engages in continual recastings of death and its resurrection, but I find the reasons and goals to be different from the ones offered in these interpretations.

42. This hopeful projection, as Woodman reveals better than most do (in *The Apocalyptic Vision*, p. 173), resembles the ego-ideal in *Alastor*, "On Love," *Prometheus Unbound*, and *Epipsychidion*. Keats transformed into the influential, widely read visionary is a version of Shelley's constructed figure of his own more "complete" and perfected "self." This "ideal prototype" finds its "antitype" in the dead poet thought of as sympathetically read throughout future ages, and that projection makes this version of Keats a kind of "superego" calling the speaker to seek self-completion in a movement toward such an exalted "reader." Peter Sacks uses this maneuver in Shelley's elegy to empower his ingenious psychoanalytic view of the poem in "Last Clouds: A Reading of *Adonais*," *Studies in Romanticism*, 23 (1984), rpt. and more fully contextualized in Sacks's *The English Elegy: Studies in the Genre from Spenser to Yeats* (Baltimore, MD: The Johns Hopkins Univ. Press, 1985), pp. 145–65. I am occasionally indebted to this essay in what follows even though it finally duplicates, by newly justifying, the standard readings of the poem.

43. In *Acts of Inclusion: Studies Bearing on an Elementary Theory of Romanticism* (New Haven, CT: Yale Univ. Press, 1979), pp. 30–48, Michael Cooke shows with considerable accuracy how *Adonais* shifts from the conventions of elegy to those of satire and prophecy. To be sure, he is trying to establish a general, and even Kantian, Romantic drive (one that we have already seen Shelley resist) wherein the all-unifying imagination strives for an "incorporation" of myriad and different kinds of experience. But Cooke also shows (esp. on pp. 35–36) that elegy at its base includes the *potential* for satire and prophecy. I now want to explore what in the poem encourages this last suggestion.

44. In *Shelley's* Adonais: *A Critical Edition* (New York: Columbia Univ. Press, 1984), p. 94, though Knerr notes the allusion in the interest of supporting a firmly Platonic reading of the poem. At this point he is, after all, developing observations made by Notopoulos in *PS* on p. 297.

45. *Biographia Literaria*, ed. Watson, pp. 91 and 167. Coleridge admits the extent of his debt to, though not his plagiarisms from, Schelling's "Dynamic System" on pp. 87–88 of this edition.

46. Nearly all the quoted words in these phrases come from Shelley's own translation of the "Elegy on the Death of Bion" (*PW*, p. 722). "Legend" is translated more literally as "letter," though, in the "Lament for Bion" in *The Greek Bucolic Poets*, trans. and ed. A. S. F. Gow (Cambridge: Cambridge Univ. Press, 1953), p. 133. The more complete translation in this latter volume also shows how the elegist goes on to make himself the "heir" of Bion's "Dorian Muse"

on p. 136. "The springs their waters change to tears," meanwhile, in l. 31 of Shelley's version of Bion's "Elegy on the Death of Adonis" (*PW*, pp. 721–22), and the full translation of this poem in the Dow collection goes on to emphasize the peace that comes from a precise burial ceremony and from the verbal repetitions of it in the Spring "dirges" of "another year" (*Bucolic Poets*, p. 147).

47. See *The Greek Bucolic Poets*, pp. 147 and 135–37.

48. See Theocritus in *The Greek Bucolic Poets*, esp. on pp. 3–8 ("Thyrsis or the Song" on the death of Daphnis) and 56–62 (the dialogue between two Egyptian women visiting an indoor ceremony in memory of Adonis).

49. Shelley's allusion to this aspect of Virgil's *Eclogues* (which I quote from *Virgil's Works*, trans. J. W. Mackail [New York: Modern Library, 1934]) tempts several intelligent modern critics into a hazardous, though attractive, half-reading of *Adonais*. Such renderings view Shelley's translation of the dead Adonis-flower into an eternal star as an announcement of the creative mind's power to turn dissolutions into resurrections by its own capacity to imagine desire fulfilled in metaphoric constructs. See John Wright, *Shelley's Myth of Metaphor*, pp. 59–73; Jean Hall, *The Transforming Image*, pp. 125–42; and Richard Cronin, *Shelley's Poetic Thoughts*, pp. 169–201. These views, as I read them, avoid the other half of what the debt to Virgil reveals: concentration on a transformative procedure *prior* (albeit basic) to every imaginative response to death. Still, I am indebted to Cronin in particular for pointing out the importance of the fifth eclogue for scholarly readings of *Adonais*.

50. See "Critical Observations on the Design of the Sixth Book of the Aeneid" (1770) in Gibbon's *Miscellaneous Works*, ed. John, Lord Sheffield (London: J. Murray, 1814), IV, 487–89, and Wasserman, *A Critical Reading*, pp. 310–13.

51. See "John Milton" in Johnson's *Lives of the English Poets*, intr. L. Archer-Hind (London: Dent, 1925), I, 95–96.

52. Herman Rapaport does much the same thing in the *Lycidas* chapter of *Milton and the Postmodern*, pp. 103–28, to which the present paragraph is indebted.

53. The cave of the Witch, in fact, alludes to several Spenserian retreats where metamorphoses (evil and good) can and do take place in what is deposited there. Note the "study" of Archimago (in *Fairie Queene*, I.i. stanzas 36–45), the woodland retreat surrounding the birth of Belphoebe and Amoret (III.iv.6–10), and especially the cave of Mammon (II.vii.20–63), all of which the Shelley of *Adonais* should remember in harking back to Spenser as often as he does.

54. Compare *Astrophel*, ll. 55–186, and *Metamophoses*, X. 519–59 and 708–39. For the extent of Shelley's borrowings from the Venus and Adonis myth as it is rendered especially in Ovid and Spenser, see Edward B. Hungerford, *Shores of Darkness* (New York: Columbia Univ. Press, 1941), pp. 218–23.

55. The connection between *Astrophel*, the Garden of Adonis, and *Adonais* is one of the most helpful revelations (on pp. 33–34) in Edwin B. Silverman, *Poetic Synthesis in Shelley's* Adonais (The Hague: Mouton, 1972), a thorough examination of this elegy's allusions to Spenser. Anxious to use Spenser in support of a Platonic reading of Shelley's poem, however, Silverman has little to say about the "mutabilitie" and "successions" that Shelley's "eternal stress" clearly draws from Spenser's *Astrophel* and Garden.

56. See Derrida on death as an image—and on the consequences of that fact—in *Of Grammatology*, pp. 183–92, and "Fors, " trans. Barbara Johnson, *Georgia Review*, 31 (1977), 64–122. I am beholden to these pieces throughout the rest of my sections on *Adonais*. Then, too, for death presented as this kind of "re-sign" (for purposes both similar to and different from Shelley's) in one of the precursor-authors most influential on *Adonais*, see R. A. Shoaf, *Milton, Poet of Duality: A Study of Semiosis in the Poetry and Prose* (New Haven, CT: Yale Univ. Press, 1985), pp. 40–51.

57. Kenneth Niell Cameron notes better than anyone the importance of *Adonai* and *Adonia* to Shelley's title (*The Golden Years*, p. 432). By doing so, in fact, Cameron helps to counter Wasserman's influential claim (in *A Critical Reading*, pp. 464–65) that *Adonai* for Shelley is

primarily a Hebrew word for "master" or "lord," a word that allows *Adonais* to raise Keats from the state of an oppressed Greek shepherd to the level of a sun-god. Shelley may well have known the Hebrew *Adonai* from the syncretizing mythologists he read, but for him the *ai* and the *ias* in association with *Adonis* are first elements in the language and ceremonial patterns celebrating that slain Greek hero. As I have already suggested, Shelley knew the fifteenth idyll of Theocritus, where *Adonai* is used as another name for Adonis and *Adonia* indicates the formal ritual memorializing the story of Adonis's death (*The Greek Bucolic Poets,* trans. Dow, pp. 60–62). Shelley had also read, of course, the "Lamia" of Keats himself, where the title figure first sees the mortal object of her desire on the "night before / The Adonian feast" ll. 319–20). If *Adonais* does connect Adonis/Adonai/Adonias with a Hebrew variant, it does so only as one consequence of "Adonis's" initial displacement into such additional terms. There are also no direct indications in Shelley's elegy of a pre-Christian Hebrew mythology being brought in as a result of these other forms of the name.

58. One reason, to be sure, is to prevent the spread of disease and additional death by covering and then burying bodies. But the main reason, the one emphasized by pastoral elegies, is indeed to *position* the dead figure in a setting or context that allows all signs of death to be interpreted in ways that release people from grief. See the helpful observations of Ellen Zetzel Lambert in *Placing Sorrow: A Study of the Pastoral Elegy Convention from Theocritus to Milton* (Chapel Hill: Univ. of North Carolina Press, 1976), esp. pp. xi–xxxiv. What Lambert points out becomes possible, however, only *after* death is already an image or figure.

59. The most recent and thorough assessment of this license as the poem carries it through is James A. W. Heffernan, "*Adonais:* Shelley's Consumption of Keats," *Studies in Romanticism,* 23 (1984), 295–315, even though this article fails to note the permission that Shelley gains from the elegy tradition and does so in order to sustain a reading in which "a Platonic oneness [finally] consumes identity" just as Shelley supposedly "consumed" Keats (p. 314).

60. See Wasserman, *A Critical Reading,* pp. 469–75, and Lambert, *Placing Sorrow,* pp. xxiv–xxxiv, despite the fact that both finally interpret this analogy differently than I do.

61. Shelley makes this point partly in the way he disruptively reworks the old Spenserian stanza-form in *Adonais.* Spenser's own *Fairie Queene* and Keats's "Eve of St. Agnes" use the alexandrine that closes every nine-line sequence to finalize the image framed off by each individual stanza. The alexandrine in these cases either states a succession's concluding event or employs the opposed phrases on the two sides of the line's caesura to bring separate elements into a firm equipoise, the momentary closure that makes every stanza seem a little world unto itself. See, for example, *The Fairie Queene,* II.i.1–61, and "The Eve of St. Agnes," stanzas 2–12. The alexandrines in *Adonais,* by contrast, consistently employ the length and the two parts of the line to question attempted closures whenever death or one of its resurrections seem about to reach an apparent finality. Stanza 42, to take one instance, ends by suggesting how the "Spreading . . . Power" of the "plastic stress," which seems to incorporate everything into its "love," divides that very conflation into its past and present impetus on the one hand (the "sustaining from beneath") and its present-to-future potential on the other (the "kindling above"). In addition, the projection here is "completed" only by another projection, itself deferring beyond itself, in stanza 43, since 43 is the one that ends with the "bursting" of the "stress" that carries all "kindling" toward the new "successions" that transference keeps anticipating. Sacks, in fact, has already noted (albeit briefly) this "progressive crossing of thresholds" in Shelley's alexandrines in *The English Elegy,* p. 151, although this study restricts its observations excessively to just one sequence in the poem and mistakenly sees the device as an attempt to further Spenser's Neoplatonism (p. 347, n. 14).

62. The speaker of Keats's "Ode to a Nightingale" longs to "fade far away" specifically from "The weariness [and] fever . . . where youth grows pale, and spectre-thin, and dies" (ll. 21–26). Shelley's "unlamented urn," of course, alludes to the "Ode on a Grecian Urn," which focuses on the "legends" covering a burial vase that allow a "cold pastoral" to "tease us out of thought" (ll. 44–45). Few poets, in point of fact, have ever written more than Keats did about the image

of death as Shelley uses it in *Adonais*. For studies that see how often—though not always the extent to which—Keats is quoted or paraphrased in *Adonais*, see M. de G. Verrall, "Allusions in *Adonais* to the Poems of Keats," *Modern Language Review*, 6 (1911), 354–59; Reiman, "Keats and Shelley: Personal and Literary Relations," in *S&C*, V, 426; Abbey, *Destroyer and Preserver*, p. 108; and Stuart Curran, "*Adonais* in Context," in *Shelley Revalued*, ed. Kelvin Everest, esp. pp. 170–79.

63. See "The Mourning That Is Language," chapter IV of Sharon Cameron's *Lyric Time* (pp. 136–99), even though this piece is not quite as sensitive as *Adonais* to how the image of death makes "language . . . the picture that replaces not presence but its image, different from the original and with space intervening" (*Lyric Time*, p. 198).

64. For Shelley's sense of this volume, which he had with him when he drowned, see *L*, II, 239, 244, 252, 262, 290, and 297 (where *Adonais* is announced).

65. See Freud's *Beyond the Pleasure Principle* in *Standard Edition*, XVII, 34–43, and Sacks, *The English Elegy*, pp. 15–16 and 148–50.

66. See the second section of my fourth chapter, above. Note also that Adonais is made to resemble Shelley's Prometheus in being called toward hopelessness and down to the Great Memory by a version of Mother Earth. The dead poet is drawn, after all, toward a graveyard in Rome that is clearly a form of the Great Memory's mausoleum "where kingly Death / Keeps his pale court in beauty and decay" (*Adonais*, ll. 55–56).

67. These indications that Urania is an influential but obsolete (and thus merely temporal) anachronism refute the most accepted interpretations of her role in the poem: Baker's in *Shelley's Major Poetry*, pp. 240–47; Notopoulos's in *PS*, pp. 293–94; Wasserman's in *A Critical Reading*, pp. 495–99; and especially Woodman's in *The Apocalyptic Vision*, pp. 168–70, revised and extended in "Shelley's Urania," *Studies in Romanticism*, 17 (1978), 61–75.

68. For a poet to be so fixated, in fact, would be for him to fall into a melancholic psychosis like that of the Maniac in *Julian and Maddalo*. That is what Freud would say, as we have seen in noting his "Mourning and Melancholy" essay, and what Sacks nearly says in *The English Elegy* on pp. 155–58. Yet Sacks fails to note that Urania is not just a mother-figure but the pull of authoritative poetic conventions as well. That omission begins what I find to be the wrong turn in Sacks's interpretation, whereby Shelley's speaker escapes the death wish attached psychologically to the Muse-mother by a submission to authorized (father-dominated) verbal forms that draw him toward an "enskied" ego-ideal. The elegy, as we shall see, has long been a resistance to reigning authority, at some levels at least, and that potential is brought out by Shelley—and even Keats—far more than Sacks allows.

69. As Reiman points out (*NCE*, p. 403, n. 69), Sidney not only died in the Netherlands of wounds sustained against the forces of power-hungry Spain but reputedly did so after sending water intended for him to a common soldier. He also wrote in the *Apology for Poetry* that the poet, "disdaining to be tied to any . . . subjection" to established visions of nature, "doth grow in effect another nature" so as to "draw us to as high a perfection as our degenerate souls . . . can be capable of" (*Critical Theory Since Plato*, pp. 157 and 159). Shelley may well have felt that some implications of these words could be freed, and are nearly freed by Sidney himself, from their attachment in the *Apology* to aristocratic privilege and references to the Christian Fall.

70. See Heffernan, "*Adonais:* Shelley's Consumption," pp. 296–300.

71. See Heffernan, pp. 302–4, and then note Reiman on the efforts of Keats to keep distancing himself from Shelley (despite the latter's influence on the former) in "Keats and Shelley," pp. 403–08.

72. See Renato Poggioli, *The Oaten Flute: Essays on Pastoral Poetry and the Pastoral Ideal* (Cambridge, MA: Harvard Univ. Press, 1975), pp. 1–31, and Andrew V. Ettin, *Literature and the Pastoral* (New Haven, CT: Yale Univ. Press. 1984), pp. 8–53.

73. Cf. *L*, II, 262 and 290, and Reiman, "Shelley and Keats," pp. 411–18.

74. Here I am respectfully disagreeing with Curran's "*Adonais* in Context," even though this

piece sees, more than any other, multiple echoes of *Hyperion* in *Adonais.* Curran is determined to read Shelley as answering the quandaries about death in Keat's poems with an assertion like those mentioned in n. 49 of this chapter: a vision of the *mind's* individual power to "destroy [fading] worlds so as to make them anew" (*Shelley Revalued,* p. 178). To me *Adonais's* clear reversion to the Hesiodic metaphysics of *Hyperion*—the one allusion Curran misses—shows both Shelley and Keats looking to a dynamism prior to the personal imagination and basic to the many revisions of tradition in the history of poetry and mythography. Curran and others should note the best study of Keats that views him as sensing an impersonal transfiguration into which his poetry steps—and so as altering the traditions he employs: Geoffrey Hartman, "Poem and Ideology: A Study of Keats' 'To Autumn',." in *The Fate of Reading and Other Essays* (Chicago: Univ. of Chicago Press, 1975), pp. 124–146. Portions of the current and my previous paragraph are indebted to this piece. For recent discussions of Keats's revisionist postures that build on Hartman's essay and show how right Shelley was about his fellow poet's flirtations with radicalism, see the essays published under the general title "Keats and Politics: A Forum," *Studies in Romanticism,* 25 (1986), 171–209.

75. In addition to Fogle, "Dante and Shelley's *Adonais,*" and Woodman, *The Apocalyptic Vision,* pp. 158–61 and 176–79, see Baker, *Shelley's Major Poetry,* pp. 248–51; O'Malley, *Shelley and Synesthesia,* pp. 137–38; Webb, *The Violet in the Crucible,* pp. 222 and 233 (on the Calderón influence); and Knerr, *Shelley's* Adonais, pp. 8 and 96–104.

76. Chatterton is placed in this iconoclastic group not just because Keats read him extensively and dedicated *Endymion* to his memory *and* not just because of the "agony" that lead to his suicide at age 17; there is also the "contention" with ruling figures and their hierarchical ideas in his poetry. See the moral contrast between the "greate" nobleman of the title and the war-mongering King Edward he opposes in "Bristowe Tragedie or the Dethe of Syr Charles Bawdin" (1768) and the difference between the snobbish high-class priest and the charitable lower-class one in "An Excelente Balade of Charitie" (1770). These appear in *The Complete Works of Thomas Chatterton: A Bicentenary Edition,* ed. Donald S. Taylor (Oxford: Clarendon, 1971), I, 6–20 and 644–48.

77. This juxtaposition, in addition to the way the grassy plot duplicates the ironic stance of pastoral poetry toward grand imperial forms, contradicts Wasserman's influential reading of the pyramidal tomb as a fixed symbol of the Shelleyan "pure spirit flow[ing] back to its origin, the 'burning fountain'" (*A Critical Reading,* p. 495). Wasserman points out that Cestius was known as a "defender of the common people against the patricians" in his role as a "tribune of the plebians" (p. 493). But *Adonais* refers to the tomb only as "Pavilioning the dust of him who planned / This refuge for his memory" as did many a military officer of the Roman Empire (ll. 445–46). That emphasis recalls the even more ancient Egyptian pyramids that turned the fire of fading aristocrats into permanent flames of stone that seemed to preserve the memories of absolute dictators and god-figures—all in products of extensive slave labor. In any case, Shelley associates the tomb of Cestius far more with "time's decay" than with "contention" against death, since it is built into one of the "gray walls [that] moulder round" the scene (l. 442).

78. The omission of this role for words in Angela Leighton's apparently Derridean analysis of *Adonais* limits both her intriguing response to the poem and the actual range of Derrida's insights. She rightly sees in this elegy, from part of what Derrida suggests, that words must keep confronting their distance from their own aims even as they strive to surpass the language of the moment. But a facing of this fact need not lead to a "celebration of despair," as she says it does, either in *Adonais* or in Derrida's sense of deferral. It can be a victory in that it opens awareness to a decentered movement of continual revisions almost unconfined by tyrannizing restrictions. Derrida emphasizes the liberation in this extension toward the always distant other-as-such, particulary in *The Ear of the Other: Otobiography, Transference, Translation,* trans. Avital Ronell and Peggy Kamuf, ed. Christie V. McDonald (New York: Schocken, 1985), esp. pp. 9–12, 26–28, 43–47, and 55–59. For Leighton's argument, see "*Adonais:* The Voice and the Text," *Keats-Shelley Memorial Bulletin,* 31 (1980), extended in her "Deconstruction Criticism

and Shelley's *Adonais*" in *Shelley Revalued,* ed. Everest, and developed further in her *Shelley and the Sublime,* pp. 125–49.

79. The definitive statement of this position is surely Woodman's in *The Apocalyptic Vision,* pp. 158–77. I think however, as Woodman does not, that Shelley is tempted into both echoing Dante and resisting his Roman Catholicism by the fact that the older poet was buried, as something of an exile and a questioner of authority, outside the gates of his native city-state. Byron reminds Shelley of that fact in 1819 by having the old poet himself ruminate over it in "The Prophecy of Dante," I. 34–44 and 60–84. Certainly Dante's apparent status as an outsider near the inside of Catholicism is analogous to the placement of Keats in the un-Catholic cemetary of a Catholic city. This analogy, consequently, sets up Shelley's anti-Catholic use of Catholic allegory.

80. This allusion has been noticed and examined most thoroughly by A. C. Bradley in "Notes on Shelley's 'Triumph of Life'," *Modern Language Review,* 9 (1914), 442–43, and Bloom in *Shelley's Mythmaking,* pp. 239–40.

81. See F. Melian Stawell, "Shelley's 'Triumph of Life'," *Essays and Studies by Members of the English Association,* V, ed. Oliver Elton (Oxford: Clarendon, 1914), 124; Baker, *Shelley's Major Poetry,* p. 265; Kenneth Allott, "Bloom on 'The Triumph of Life'," *Essays in Criticism,* 10 (1960), 223–24; G. M. Matthews, "On Shelley's 'The Triumph of Life'," *Studia Neophilologica,* 34 (1962), 107; Peter Butter, "Sun and Shape in Shelley's *The Triumph of Life,*" *Review of English Studies,* new series, 13 (1962), 44–45; Reiman, *Shelley's "The Triumph of Life": A Critical Study,* p. 61; and Cameron, *The Golden Years,* p. 465.

82. Bloom, in fact, makes so much of the *Triumph's* recollection of the "Ode" (though some of those mentioned in n. 81 announce the connection earlier) that he proposes, in *Shelley's Mythmaking* (pp. 263–65) and subsequent readings, that no birth-memories arise in Rousseau's dream. For Bloom the dream is concerned, as is the "Ode," only with a growing child's submission to Nature's masking of the primal light (or the "clouds of glory" we "trail"), and he is right to suggest that those childhood-to-adolescent years of forgetting are among those recalled by the shade. Yet Bloom more and more wants to set up the "Intimations" ode too much as *the* poem that Shelley remembers, represses, and revises in *The Triumph,* so he fails to see how transference in the piece can join recollections of the very distant past (even of birth) to the loss of what is recalled as the transfer-motion proceeds.

83. This skeptical revision of Dante and Wordsworth is well explained by Reiman, *Shelley's "The Triumph,"* pp. 61–62, and then related helpfully to the very language of skepticism in Lisa Steinman, "From 'Alastor' to 'The Triumph of Life': Shelley on the Nature and Source of Linguistic Pleasure," *Romanticism Past and Present,* 7 (1983), 23–36.

84. Matthews, one of the fathers of the standard "moral" reading, argues that the narrator feels a déjà vu in his own vision because he is "obscurely recollecting," among other things, "Rousseau's birth and [young] manhood," an earlier source for what the narrator now confronts ("On Shelley's 'The Triumph'," p. 108). Paul de Man, in his deconstructive approach, hones in on this sequence with an equal sense of how underlying it is. For him it is only "a reading of [this] scene" that exposes a "figure for the figurality of all signification" (according to the section of "Shelley Disfigured" that I have mentioned in n. 40 of Chapter 1). Meanwhile, Leslie Brisman (in *Romantic Origins,* pp. 170–81) sees the "antecedent dream" as answering the "the spectre of repetition" in the narrator's vision with a "reimagined place of origin" from which poetry can seem to spring as something prior to repetition.

85. John Hodgson has focused on this fact more than anyone else in "The World's Mysterious Doom: Shelley's *The Triumph of Life,*" *ELH,* 42 (1975), esp. 598–610, and he has been abetted most fervently by Robinson, *Shelley and Byron,* pp. 221–30. Both critics remind us of what too many readers have tended to forget, but I cannot agree with their sense that Rousseau's death-state reveals Shelley's fear that the triumph of Death-in-Life may be eternal and irreversible. Such a view fails to consider that Shelley is using Rousseau's shade initially just as Dante uses any dead figure in the *Inferno:* to offer a warning about decisions and a visualization of

their consequences. For discussions of just how close Shelley had gotten to the *Commedia* by 1822, see Webb, *The Violet in the Crucible,* pp. 310–36, and T. S. Eliot, "A Talk on Dante," *Kenyon Review,* 15 (1952), 183–84.

86. I cite Petrarch throughout this section from *The Triumphs,* trans. Ernest Hatch Wilkins (Chicago: Univ. of Chicago Press, 1962), in which no line numbers are given.

87. That is not to say, as the later Freud would and as Matthews does, that "the pre-natal and the posthumous sleep are one and (in the present context) interchangeable" ("On Shelley's 'The Triumph'," p. 108). As he did in *Adonais,* Shelley is placing the dead in the reflective stance—as we read them—of reading themselves and their immediate survivors from a position of later, greater, and more disruptive knowledge. Just in the way Rousseau is the speaker's revealing double as the *Alastor* Poet was to his narrator, the dead are projected reflectors of personal and communal desire reading back to their projectors the foundations and the results of such longing.

88. Reiman has paid the most attention of anyone to the combining of Aristotelean elements in this poem (as early, in fact, as his introduction to *Shelley's "The Triumph,"* pp. 12–17). But he also wants to regard the combination, with the Sun's fire representing the dominant unifier (hence the imagination), as achieving an organic unity that is always available to be sought again after it has been obscured by daily life's appearances. There is no such organic unity for Shelley, as I read him, even in the "weaving into one" of Rousseau's vision, unless it can be said to include its own re-dispersion and self-forgetting.

89. *Odyssey,* IV. 219–32. This sequence from Homer is even recalled in *The Triumph* when the shade of Rousseau describes the curative forgetfulness of his death sleep (ll. 318–26). It is also echoed earlier by Shelley in *Prometheus Unbound* when the Spirit of the Hour views trans-figured humankind and finds that no "treasured gall," such as "jealousy" or "envy," henceforth spoils "the sweet taste of the nepenthe, love," which now helps people forget such former incli-nations (III. iv. 161–63).

90. It is not just that the figure is produced by imaginative synaesthesia, as Glenn O'Malley emphasizes (*Shelley and Synesthesia,* pp. 81–84); the figure is also an enactment of the process prompting such combinations of different sense perceptions. In performing that activity, more-over, the "shape" becomes a form of the relation-oriented "nepenthe, love."

91. Especially in "Shelley Disfigured," pp. 53–65. Steinman's "From 'Alastor' to 'The Triumph'," by the way, justifies this very reading—up to a point—on the basis of Shelley's own skeptical epistemology.

92. During the "Shelley" chapter, focused entirely on *The Triumph of Life,* in *The Linguistic Moment: From Wordsworth to Stevens* (Princeton, NJ: Princeton Univ. Press, 1985), pp. 114–79.

93. Helen and then Menelaos recount for Telemachos both the most exemplary deeds of Odysseus at Troy and an explanation of his wandering. The latter story they even tell with the aid of statements from ever-changing Proteus (once that god has been captured by Menelaos)—but only after Telemachos has taken enough Nepenthe that his once-dominant emotions do not prevent him from observing the knowledge and process that Proteus keeps reembodying. See *Odyssey,* IV. 235–592.

94. See, in addition to *La nouvelle Héloïse,* pt. I, letter xxiii (already noted), the *Confessions,* trans. Grant, II, 43–44, and *Emile, or On Education,* trans. Allan Bloom (New York: Basic Books, 1979), pp. 272–78.

95. The reading that comes closest to adopting this view is Jean Hall's in *The Transforming Image,* pp. 151–64, where the "shape" is the supreme incarnation of the redemptive mental construct in Hall's title. But this view stops short of committing itself to a mobile transubstan-tiation in the figure. Hall prefers to posit a contrast between an "*unmoving* center that could change the world" (p. 155, my emphasis) and a rapid movement of "desire" that (granted) drives all those enslaved by Life's hellish way of seeing into frantically "speeding up their life pro-cesses" at every moment (p. 154).

96. Quint in "Representation and Ideology in *The Triumph of Life*," *SEL,* 18 (1978), esp. 646–54, and Duffy in *Rousseau in England: The Context for Shelley's Critique of the Enlightenment* (Berkeley: Univ. of California Press, 1979), pp. 109–14 and 141–48.

97. *The Triumph's* reworkings of this and other moments in *Alastor*—and the ways these look back to Rousseau (as *Alastor* did)—have been noted most thoroughly by Reiman, *Shelley's "The Triumph,"* pp. 62–63; Hodgson, "The World's Doom," pp. 614–15; Duffy, *Rousseau in England,* pp. 93–95; and Abbey, *Destroyer and Preserver,* pp. 128 and 147–49, though I do not agree with their conclusions about this repetition. For Rousseau's dreams of this sort, and in an Edenic garden setting, see *Confessions,* trans. Grant, I, 176–78.

98. The figure's allusion to *Epipsychidion* has been most pointedly noticed by Baker, *Shelley's Major Poetry,* p. 266n; Cameron, *The Golden Years,* pp. 465–67; and Miriam Allott, "The Reworking of a Literary Genre: Shelley's 'The Triumph of Life'," in *Essays on Shelley,* ed. Allott, p. 259. The similarity of the shape to the Witch, though firmly denied by Bloom in *Shelley's Mythmaking* (p. 267), has been argued best, from far different premises than mine, by Bradley, "Notes," p. 444; Notopoulos, *PS,* p. 312; Butter, "Sun and Shape," pp. 48–49; and Reiman, *Shelley's "The Triumph,"* pp. 63–64.

99. The Witch, we should recall, urges those dreams toward greater transference among their elements, even when the dreamers awaken, by offering those she visits at subliminal levels of thought "Strange panacea in a chrystal bowl" (a kind of Nepenthe), a release from previous controls on thought that acts like a "sweet wave" and so effaces former inscriptions—including a sense of her operation—on the sands of the mind ("Witch," ll. 594–95).

100. In the "Essay on Christianity," after all, death for Shelley should be a "time when the human mind [feels] visited exclusively by the influence of the benignant power" that the essay describes as a loving transference (*CW,* VI, 235). See Stawell on this point in "Shelley's 'Triumph'," p. 117.

101. See Bradley, "Notes," p. 456; Stawell, "Shelley's 'Triumph'," pp. 116–26; Kurtz, *The Pursuit of Death,* pp. 323–37; Baker, *Shelley's Major Poetry,* pp. 255–75; *PS,* pp. 312–20; Wilson, *Shelley's Later Poetry,* pp. 293–98; Bloom, *Shelley's Mythmaking,* p. 231; Allott, "Bloom on 'The Triumph'," p. 106; Butter, "Sun and Shape," pp. 48–51; Matthews, "On Shelley's 'The Triumph'," p. 106; O'Malley, *Shelley and Synesthesia,* pp. 77–87; Reiman, *Shelley's "The Triumph,"* pp. 62–73; James Rieger, *The Mutiny Within,* pp. 207–21; Cameron, *The Golden Years,* pp. 466–70; Hodgson, "The World's Doom," pp. 610–14; and King-Hele, *Shelley,* 3rd ed., p. 359.

102. First in *Shelley's Mythmaking,* pp. 232–37, and even more so later in *Poetry and Repression,* pp. 83–111. Curiously, Bloom's powerful sense of the *Merkabah's* figural energy in the latter book impedes his own thesis there. *Poetry and Repression* tries to assert Shelley's recovery of an originating voice in his attachment to the Chariot's "transumptive" ability to remake past forms of itself. If the voice needs an already existing transumption to seem a new origin, however, then the power is revealed as coming more from the Chariot's figural process than from the poet's will.

103. *The Linguistic Moment,* pp. 147–48.

104. *The Linguistic Moment,* pp. 164–67.

105. See Quint, "Representation and Ideology," pp. 639–46.

106. Such an understanding of this key mistake has been approached helpfully, albeit only partially, by Reiman, *Shelley's "The Triumph,"* pp. 67–73; Dawson, *The Unacknowledged Legislator,* pp. 273–80; Quint, "Representation and Ideology," pp. 648–50; and Duffy, *Rousseau in England,* pp. 128–32.

107. Carlos Baker began a long controversy by pointing out this mere touch in *Shelley's Major Poetry,* p. 267, and virtually no one since has really supported him by seeing a precise significance in this failure to drink deeply. I am trying here to justify Baker's observation, even as I resist his final interpretation. In any case, we should note that it is only at and after *this* point in the poem that the Nepenthe shifts from its connections to the *Odyssey* and recalls, as

Reiman notes, the evil use of the same drug in Milton's *Comus,* where "Whoever tasted, lost his upright shape" (l. 52). See Reiman, notwithstanding his slight imprecision on this point, in *Shelley's "The Triumph,"* pp. 64–65.

108. Rousseau is very flatly an objectivist in the *Confessions,* where he writes as follows: "While examining myself, and endeavoring to find, in the case of others, upon what [all our] different conditions of being depend, I discovered that they depended in great part upon the impression that external objects had previously made upon us. [Such] observations [even] furnish an external rule of conduct" (trans. Grant, II, 259). The same *Confessions* also reveal him as finding significance in woman-figures only insofar as they render him back to himself from outside himself. "I would have confined my whole existence in [the Thérèse he finally married]," Rousseau writes, "if I had been able to confine hers to me" (II, 65). For Shelley's critique of Saint-Preux, see my discussion of the "Hymn to Intellectual Beauty" in Chapter 2, above.

109. *Rousseau in England,* pp. 129–30.

110. *Reveries of a Solitary,* trans. Butterworth, pp. 67–68.

111. *Reveries,* p. 71.

112. This echo in *The Triumph* was first noticed by Paul Turner in "Shelley and Lucretius," pp. 281–82. The theory of these "resemblances" in *De rerum* itself dominates Book IV from lines 26 to 323.

113. This allusion was first discovered in this century by I. A. Richards in *Principles of Literary Criticism* (1925; rpt. New York: Harcourt, n.d.), p. 217.

114. "Shelley's 'Triumph'," p. 125.

115. Stawell points out parallels between Shelley's *Triumph* and Goethe's *Walpurgisnacht* in "Shelley's 'Triumph'" on p. 115.

116. The quotations from *The Linguistic Moment* in this and the next sentence come from pp. 155 and 157.

117. Indeed, Shelley's use of a rereading Virgil-figure in this poem parallels Derrida's procedure in his "deconstructive" rereadings more than it anticipates Miller's "Derridean" sense of *The Triumph* (really quite a repetitively *centered* reading in the end). See, for example, Derrida's approach to Rousseau in *Of Grammatology,* pp. 141–268. Miller, I find, refuses to see that the leap of figures from the death of their pasts—and from killing restrictions—toward regenerative reworkings by additional "readers" in *The Triumph* anticipates what Derrida calls the "Eternal Feminine," a movement very like that of the "shape all light," in *The Ear of the Other,* pp. 14–16, 53, 79, and 88–89.

118. This reading, one of the few that I have not yet connected with an existing study of Shelley, is best articulated by Jerome McGann in "The Secrets of an Elder Day: Shelley After *Hellas,*" *Keats-Shelley Journal,* 15 (1966), esp. 34–41.

119. Well documented in Reiman, *Shelley's "The Triumph,"* pp. 87–100. See also William Keach, *Shelley's Style,* pp. 187–94, on how this poem's use of rhyme both repeats and counteracts sheer forgetfulness and erasure.

120. Susan Wolfson is therefore right to see this poem as one culmination of a growing tendency toward skeptical questioning—and requestioning—in English Romantic writing, even though she fails to see how much Shelley's version of this inclination revises and radicalizes the asking of questions in the poets she treats more extensively. See Wolfson's *The Questioning Presence: Wordsworth, Keats, and the Interrogative Mode in Romantic Poetry* (Ithaca, NY: Cornell Univ. Press, 1986), pp. 23–25.

121. Though I now want to offer some different reasons for it, this statement has been made in some convincing ways already by Matthews in "On Shelley's 'The Triumph'," pp. 105, 110–11, 128–34; Tilottama Rajan in *Dark Interpreter,* pp. 61–71; and especially Balachandra Rajan in *The Form of the Unfinished: English Poetics from Spenser to Pound* (Princeton, NJ: Princeton Univ. Press, 1985), pp. 184–210, to which I am occasionally indebted at this point.

122. See Reiman in *Shelley's "The Triumph,"* pp. 82–83, and Cameron in *The Golden Years,* p. 473.

123. In part, such figures in such a desired situation, of course, reflect Shelley's increasingly sought projection of a limited circle of enlightened and loving people who might withdraw into an island of sympathetic and nonhierarchical interplay. See, in addition to the "Letter to Maria Gisborne" and the *Epipsychidion* mentioned in such connections already, "To Jane. The Invitation" and "To Jane. The Recollection," two of the poems to Jane Williams written around the time of *The Triumph,* where "peace" is sought in a "magic circle" of isolated lovers and loved ones are raised to a reverie-state that seems to contain the "harmonies and hues" of "Heaven" ("The Recollection," ll. 44, 47, 52, and 26–27). All this while, though, Shelley realizes, especially in *Epipsychidion, Adonais, Hellas,* and "The Serpent Is Shut Out from Paradise" (another poem to Jane), that such a supposed place is most likely to exist, always deferred to the future or the past, outside civilized life and earthly existence as these are almost always perceived—and then perhaps only in the minds of sympathetic readers looking back on the written hopes of those who have "gone before."

124. Matthews has already made one persuasive case about such a hesitation at the time of this poem in the biographical section of "On Shelley's 'The Triumph'," pp. 128–33. More can even be made, I think, of Matthews's vision of Shelley as torn between a Rousseauean desire for Jane Williams and a determination to continue his troubled alliance with Mary (and all those related to her), between the longing for what sometimes seemed an ideal release from myriad cares (as a possible affair with "Emilia" Viviani once seemed) and an acquiescence to uneasy, often painful sets of relationships to which he had long been committed and for which he saw no single resolution of the conflicts. Yet for Shelley to choose Jane unequivocally, even just mentally, might have been for him to pursue the sort of timeless *beau idéal* that shuts down transference. He writes in a letter of June 1822 that just being with Jane and her guitar could lift him into a "present [which] would content me so well that I could say with Faust to the passing moment 'Remain, thou art so beautiful'" (*L,* II, 436)—a result that might well have trapped Shelley in a Goethean damnation. Perhaps it was better, Shelley may have felt at this time, to maintain the unresolved complexity and incompleteness of his current relations, even with Jane and Edward Williams, in a course of action that was more a going out of himself toward the needs of many others in circumstances perpetually subject to mutability. That outreach in several directions, even to the point of helping Mary through a miscarriage while he takes walks with Jane, is the larger subject of the same June letter, which even includes an attack on himself for having pursued "Emilia" and there sought "in a mortal image the likeness of what is perhaps [as a reverie-interplay] eternal" (*L,* II, 434). Still, there remains the pull of projected ego-ideals. Hence the wavering in the 1822 lyrics to Jane, which I do not have the space to treat in detail here, between seeing her guitar (or the lady herself) as opening in shape and sound toward all the changes in the seasons ("With a Guitar. To Jane," ll. 43–90) and regarding her as the prompter of a desire for a distant transcendence ("One Word Is Too Often Profaned," ll. 9–16). After all, Shelley now oscillates just as much in his stance toward the social injustices that he has assaulted so directly in the *Philosophical View of Reform.* He rails in a letter of July 1822, one of his last epistles before the fatal voyage, about the need for "every man plainly to utter his sentiments on the inefficacy of the existing religions no less than the political system for restraining . . . mankind," yet he nearly despairs of that prospect because "all, more or less, subdue themselves to the element that surrounds them" in what is very clearly the current triumph of Life (*L,* II, 441–42). Shelley, in fact, is not sure, any more than his poem's narrator, whether he is among the "more" or the "less" subdued. "I once thought to study these affairs & write or act in them," he says, as if about to utter his sentiments in a direct way once again, but the sense that "all" are now subdued before he speaks makes him "glad that my good genius said *refrain*" (*L,* II, 442). Is he resigned to the triumph of Life and thus one of its victims? Or will he still stand against its dominance in some effective way? *The Triumph of Life,* one could argue, is evidence that he was still asking such questions of himself and others when he and Edward Williams set off into the Gulf of Spezia.

125. This oscillation between rhetorical modes or stances in Shelley's writing, however, is

not simply the "aporia" defined by de Man (in, say, "Shelley Disfigured," pp. 61–69) or the "undecideability" proposed by Hillis Miller (more pointedly in "The Critic as Host," pp. 224–38, than in the Shelley chapter of *The Linguistic Moment*). Shelley does repeatedly confront the oscillation, interplay, and occasional contradiction between the sheer positioning of differentiated figures and the desire for meaning in the reader's (or each figure's) movement across the words in a discourse. See, for example, my chapter 3, n. 31, above. But since Shelley connects the differentiation of figures and their will to meaning more than de Man and Miller do in reading him, his greater concern becomes the difference *between* those rhetorical and conceptual systems which are aware of the relational and disruptive transfer-process that make systems possible *and* those bent on disguising that fact behind a veneer of centered and hierarchical logic. Since transference is the basic impetus behind both possibilities, depending on how the human will chooses to carry it out, people for Shelley are always at a juncture of choice (a rhetorical hesitation) between these different patterns of thought and discourse. To that extent, as Shelley sees it, the rhetorical hesitation is always a moral one as well.

Index

Due to space limitations, names and titles cited only in the notes, or just once in the text or notes, a normally not listed here. The only works listed separately from their author's name, meanwhile, are the on written by Shelley himself.